A Compendium Of Orthodox Services
Volume 2

To the glory of God.

Version 1v8

Changelog: Version 1v6   Minor spelling corrections.

Version 1v7   Changed "will" to "shall", this is more accurate for "thee/thou".

Version 1v8   Inserted two missing prayers for Great Week.

Index

Index Of Volume 1	**Page**

"The Compendium is a magnificent undertaking that will help all those who wish to know about our Orthodox Church, the structure and order of its worship, and its rich spiritual treasures.

I am happy to give this work my formal commendation for use for consultative purposes, since a deeper understanding and appreciation of the Orthodox Ethos is essential not only for our Faithful and for Academia but also for those who are responsible for the worship of our Church being carried out in an orderly, dignified and spiritual fashion."

His Eminence Gregorios, Archbishop of Thyateira and Great Britain.
12th April 2018.

"Concerning the two volume compendium of church services. I am sure that this publication will prove of very great value to all Orthodox - parishes, monasteries and individual Christians - who use the English language in their worship. I shall certainly wish to buy a copy, and I will gladly make it known to others."

+ Metropolitan Kallistos of Diokleia
27th June 2018.

Orthros & First Hour For Great and Holy Monday

[For Sunday Evening]

The Trisagion Prayers

Priest: Blessed is our God, always, now and ever, and unto the ages of ages.

People: *Amen.*

Priest: Glory to Thee, our God, glory to Thee.

O Heavenly King, Comforter, Spirit of Truth, Who art everywhere present and fillest all things, Treasury of blessings and Giver of life: Come and abide in us and cleanse us from every impurity and save our souls, O Good One.

Reader: Holy God, Holy Mighty, Holy Immortal, have mercy on us. **(x3)**

Glory be to the Father, and to the Son, and to the Holy Spirit;

Both now and forever, and unto the ages of ages. Amen.

O Most Holy Trinity, have mercy on us.

O Lord, cleanse us from our sins.

O Master, pardon our iniquities.

O Holy One, visit and heal our infirmities, for Thy names sake.

Lord have mercy. **(x3)**

Glory be be to the Father and to the Son and to the Holy Spirit;

Both now and forever, and unto the ages of ages. Amen.

People: *Our Father, Who art in Heaven, hallowed be Thy Name. Thy Kingdom come, Thy will be done, on earth as it is in Heaven. Give us this day our daily bread, and forgive us our trespasses, as we forgive those who trespass against us; and lead us not into temptation, but deliver us from the evil one.*

Priest: For Thine is the kingdom and the power and the glory of the Father and of the Son and of the Holy Spirit; both now and forever and unto the ages of ages

People: *Amen.*

Lord, have mercy. **(x12)**

Glory be be to the Father and to the Son and to the Holy Spirit;

Both now and forever and unto the ages of ages. Amen.

Come, let us worship God, our King.

Come, let us worship and fall down before Christ, our King and our God.

Come, let us worship and fall down before Christ Himself, our King and our God.

Psalm 19

The Lord hear thee in the day of affliction; the name of the God of Jacob defend thee. Let Him send forth unto thee help from His sanctuary, and out of Zion let Him help thee. Let Him remember every sacrifice of thine, and thy whole burnt offering let Him fatten. The Lord grant thee according to thy heart, and fulfil all thy purposes. We will rejoice in Thy salvation, and in the name of the Lord our God shall we be magnified. The Lord fulfil all thy requests. Now have I known that the Lord hath saved His anointed one; He will hearken unto him out of His holy heaven; in mighty deeds is the salvation of His right hand. Some trust in chariots, and some in horses, but we will call upon the name of the Lord our God. They have been fettered and have fallen, but we are risen and are set upright. O Lord, save the king, and hearken unto us in the day when we call upon Thee.

Psalm 20

O Lord, in Thy strength the king shall be glad, and in Thy salvation shall he exceedingly rejoice. The desire of his heart hast Thou granted unto him, and hast not denied him the requests of his lips. Thou wentest before him with the blessings of goodness, Thou hast set upon his head a crown of precious stone. He asked life of Thee, and Thou gavest him length of days unto ages of ages. Great is his glory in Thy salvation; glory and majesty shalt Thou lay upon him. For Thou shalt give him blessing for ever and ever, Thou shalt gladden him in joy with Thy countenance. For the king hopeth in the Lord, and through the mercy of the Most High shall he not be shaken. Let Thy hand be found on all Thine enemies; let Thy right hand find all that hate Thee. For Thou wilt make them as an oven of fire in the time of Thy presence; the Lord in His wrath will trouble them sorely and fire shall devour them. Their fruit wilt Thou destroy from the earth, and their seed from the sons of men. For they have intended evil against Thee, they have devised counsels which they shall not be able to establish. For Thou shalt make them turn their backs; amongst those that are Thy remnant, Thou shalt make ready their countenance. Be Thou exalted, O Lord, in Thy strength; we will sing and chant of Thy mighty acts.

Holy God, Holy Mighty, Holy Immortal, have mercy on us. **(x3)**

Glory be to the Father and to the Son and to the Holy Spirit,

Both now and forever and unto the ages of ages. Amen.

O Most Holy Trinity, have mercy on us.

O Lord, cleanse us from our sins.

O Master, pardon our iniquities.

O Holy One, visit and heal our infirmities, for Thy names sake.

Lord have mercy. **(x3)**

People: Our Father, Who art in Heaven, hallowed be Thy Name. Thy Kingdom come, Thy will be done, on earth as it is in Heaven. Give us this day our daily bread, and forgive us our trespasses, as we forgive those who trespass against us; and lead us not into temptation, but deliver us from the evil one.

Priest: For Thine is the kingdom and the power, and the glory: of the Father and of the Son, and of the Holy Spirit, now and ever, and unto the ages of ages.

People: Amen.

Troparia

O Lord, save Thy people and bless Thine inheritance. Grant victory unto Orthodox Christians over their enemies, and by the power of Thy Cross do Thou preserve Thy commonwealth.

Glory be to the Father and to the Son and to the Holy Spirit,

O Thou Who wast lifted up willingly upon the Cross, bestow Thy mercies upon the new community named after Thee, O Christ God; gladden with Thy power the Orthodox Christians, granting them victory over enemies; may they have as Thy help the weapon of peace, the invincible trophy.

Both now and forever and unto the ages of ages. Amen.

O Awesome intercession that cannot be put to shame, O good one, disdain not our prayer; O all hymned Theotokos, establish the commonwealth of the Orthodox, save the Orthodox Christians, and grant unto them victory from heaven, for thou didst bring forth God, O thou only blessed one.

Priest: Have mercy on us, O God, according to Thy great mercy, we pray Thee, hearken and have mercy.

People: *Lord, have mercy.* **(x3)**

Priest: Again we pray for our His Holiness Patriarch Bartholomew; and for our Archbishop Nikitas.

People: *Lord, have mercy.* **(x3)**

Priest: Again we pray for all the brethren and for all Christians.

People: *Lord, have mercy.* **(x3)**

Priest: For a merciful God art Thou, and the Lover of mankind; and unto Thee do we send up glory: to the Father, and to the Son, and to the Holy Spirit, both now and forever, and unto the ages of ages.

People: *Amen. Holy Father bless.*

Priest: Glory to the holy, and consubstantial, and life creating, and indivisible Trinity, always, now and ever, and unto the ages of ages.

People: *Amen.*

The Six Psalms

Reader: Glory to God in the highest, and on earth peace, good will amongst men. *(cross and bow)* **(x3)**

Chorus: *O Lord, Thou shalt open my lips, and my mouth shall declare Thy praise.* **(x2)**

Psalm 3

O Lord, why are they multiplied that afflict me? Many rise up against me. Many say unto my soul: There is no salvation for him in his God. But Thou, O Lord, art my helper, my glory, and the lifter up of my head. I cried unto the Lord with my voice, and He heard me out of His holy mountain. I laid me down and slept; I awoke, for the Lord will help me. I will not be afraid of ten thousands of people that set themselves against me round about. Arise, O Lord, save me, O my God, for Thou hast smitten all who without cause are mine enemies; the teeth of sinners hast Thou broken. Salvation is of the Lord, and Thy blessing is upon Thy people. I laid me down and slept; I awoke, for the Lord will help me.

Psalm 37

O Lord, rebuke me not in Thine anger, nor chasten me in Thy wrath. For Thine arrows are fastened in me, and Thou hast laid Thy hand heavily upon me. There is no healing in my flesh in the face of Thy wrath; and there is no peace in my bones in the face of my sins. For mine iniquities are risen higher than my head; as a heavy burden have they pressed heavily upon me. My bruises are become noisome and corrupt in the face of my folly. I have been wretched and utterly bowed down until the end; all the day long I went with downcast face. For my loins are filled with mockings, and there is no healing in my flesh. I am afflicted and exceedingly humbled, I have roared from the groaning of my heart. O Lord, before Thee is all my desire, and my groaning is not hid from Thee. My heart is troubled, my strength hath failed me; and the light of mine eyes, even this is not with me. My friends and my neighbours drew nigh over against me and stood, and my nearest of kin stood afar off. And they that sought after my soul used violence; and they that sought evils for me spake vain things, and craftinesses all the day long did they meditate. But as for me, like a deaf man I heard them not, and was as a speechless man that openeth not his mouth. And I became as a man that heareth not, and that hath in his mouth no reproofs. For in Thee have I hoped, O Lord; Thou wilt hearken unto me, O Lord my God. For I said: Let never mine enemies rejoice over me; yea, when my feet were shaken, those men spake boastful words against me. For I am ready for scourges, and my sorrow is continually before me. For I will declare mine iniquity, and I will take heed concerning my sin. But mine enemies live and are made stronger than I, and they that hated me unjustly are multiplied. They that render me evil for good slandered me, because I pursued goodness. Forsake me not, O Lord my God, depart not from me. Be attentive unto my help, O Lord of my salvation.

Psalm 62

O God, my God, unto Thee I rise early at dawn. My soul hath thirsted for Thee; how often hath my flesh longed after Thee in a land barren and untrodden and unwatered. So in the sanctuary have I appeared before Thee to see Thy power and Thy glory. For Thy mercy is better than lives; my lips shall praise Thee. So shall I bless Thee in my life, and in Thy name will I lift up my hands. As with marrow and fatness let my soul be filled, and with lips of rejoicing shall my mouth praise Thee. If I remembered Thee on my bed, at the dawn I meditated on Thee. For Thou art become my helper; in the shelter of Thy wings will I rejoice. My soul hath cleaved after Thee, Thy right hand hath been quick to help me. But as for these, in vain have they sought after my soul; they shall go into the nethermost parts of the earth, they shall be surrendered unto the edge of the sword; portions for foxes shall they be. But the king shall be glad in God, everyone shall be praised that sweareth by Him; for the mouth of them is stopped that speak unjust things.

At the dawn I meditated on Thee. For Thou art become my helper; in the shelter of Thy wings will I rejoice. My soul hath cleaved after Thee, Thy right hand hath been quick to help me.

After The Psalm

Glory be to the Father and to the Son and to the Holy Spirit,
Both now and forever and unto the ages of ages. Amen.

Halleluiah, Halleluiah, Halleluiah. Glory to Thee, O God. **(x3)**
Lord. have mercy. **(x3)**

Glory be to the Father and to the Son and to the Holy Spirit,
Both now and forever and unto the ages of ages. Amen.

Psalm 87

O Lord God of my salvation, by day have I cried and by night before Thee. Let my prayer come before Thee, bow down Thine ear unto my supplication. For filled with evils is my soul, and my life unto hades hath drawn nigh. I am counted with them that go down into the pit; I am become as a man without help, free amongst the dead. Like the bodies of the slain that sleep in the grave, whom Thou rememberest no more, and they are cut off from Thy hand. They laid me in the lowest pit, in darkness and in the shadow of death. Against me is Thine anger made strong, and all Thy billows hast Thou brought upon me. Thou hast removed my friends afar from me; they have made me an abomination unto themselves. I have been delivered up, and have not come forth; mine eyes are grown weak from poverty. I have cried unto Thee, O Lord, the whole day long; I have stretched out my hands unto Thee. Nay, for the dead wilt Thou work wonders? Or shall physicians raise them up that they may give thanks unto Thee? Nay, shall any in the grave tell of Thy mercy, and of Thy truth in that destruction? Nay, shall Thy wonders be known in that darkness, and Thy righteousness in that land that is forgotten? But as for me, unto Thee, O Lord, have I cried; and in the morning shall my prayer come before Thee. Wherefore, O Lord, dost Thou cast off my soul and turnest Thy face away from me? A poor man am I, and in troubles from my youth; yea, having been exalted, I was humbled and brought to distress. Thy furies have passed upon me, and Thy terrors have sorely troubled me. They came round about me like water, all the day long they compassed me about together. Thou hast removed afar from me friend and neighbour, and mine acquaintances because of my misery. O Lord God of my salvation, by day have I cried and by night before Thee. Let my prayer come before Thee, bow down Thine ear unto my supplication.

Psalm 102

Bless the Lord, O my soul, and all that is within me bless His holy name. Bless the Lord, O my soul, and forget not all that He hath done for thee, Who is gracious unto all thine iniquities, Who healeth all thine infirmities, Who redeemeth thy life from corruption, Who crowneth thee with mercy and compassion, Who fulfilleth thy desire with good things; thy youth shall be renewed as the eagles. The Lord performeth deeds of mercy, and executeth judgement for all them that are wronged. He hath made His ways known unto Moses, unto the sons of Israel the things that He hath willed. Compassionate and merciful is the Lord, long suffering and plenteous in mercy; not unto the end will He be angered, neither unto eternity will He be wroth. Not according to our iniquities hath He dealt with us, neither according to our sins hath He rewarded us. For according to the height of heaven from the earth, the Lord hath made His mercy to prevail over them that fear Him. As far as the east is from the west, so far hath He removed our iniquities from us. Like as a father hath compassion upon his sons, so hath the Lord had compassion upon them that fear Him; for He knoweth whereof we are made, He hath remembered that we are dust. As for man, his days are as the grass; as a flower of the field, so shall he blossom forth. For when the wind is passed over it, then it shall be gone, and no longer will it know the place thereof. But the mercy of the Lord is from eternity, even unto eternity, upon them that fear Him. And His righteousness is upon sons of sons, upon them that keep His testament and remember His commandments to do them. The Lord in heaven hath prepared His throne, and His kingdom ruleth over all. Bless the Lord, all you His angels, mighty in strength, that perform His word, to hear the voice of His words. Bless the Lord, all you His hosts, His ministers that do His will. Bless the Lord, all you His works, in every place of His dominion. Bless the Lord, O my soul. In every place of His dominion, bless the Lord, O my soul.

Psalm 142

O Lord, hear my prayer, give ear unto my supplication in Thy truth; hearken unto me in Thy righteousness. And enter not into judgement with Thy servant, for in Thy sight shall no man living be justified. For the enemy hath persecuted my soul; he hath humbled my life down to the earth. He hath seated me in darkness as those that have been long dead, and my spirit within me is become despondent; within me my heart is troubled. I remembered days of old, I meditated on all Thy works, I pondered on the creations of Thy hands. I stretched forth my hands unto Thee; my soul thirsteth after thee like a waterless land. Quickly hear me, O Lord; my spirit hath fainted away. Turn not Thy face away from me, lest I be like unto them that go down into the pit. Cause me to hear Thy mercy in the morning; for in Thee have I put my hope. Cause me to know, O Lord, the way wherein I should walk; for unto Thee have I lifted up my soul. Rescue me from mine enemies, O Lord; unto Thee have I fled for refuge. Teach me to do Thy will, for Thou art my God. Thy good Spirit shall lead me in the land of uprightness; for Thy names sake, O Lord, shalt Thou quicken me. In Thy righteousness shalt Thou bring my soul out of affliction, and in Thy mercy shalt Thou utterly destroy mine enemies. And Thou shalt cut off all them that afflict my soul, for I am Thy servant.

Hearken unto me, O Lord, in Thy righteousness, and enter not into judgement with Thy servant. **(x2)**
Thy good Spirit shall lead me in the land of uprightness.

After The Psalm

Glory be to the Father and to the Son and to the Holy Spirit,
Both now and forever and unto the ages of ages. Amen.

Halleluiah, Halleluiah, Halleluiah. Glory to Thee, O God. *(cross and bow)* **(x3)**
O Lord our hope, glory to Thee.

Great Litany

Deacon: In peace let us pray to the Lord.

People: *Lord, have mercy.*

Deacon: For the peace from above, and the salvation of our souls; let us pray to the Lord.

People: *Lord, have mercy.*

Deacon: For the peace of the whole world, the good estate of the holy churches of God, and the union of all, let us pray to the Lord.

People: *Lord, have mercy.*

Deacon: For this holy temple, and for them that with faith, reverence, and the fear of God enter herein, let us pray to the Lord

People: *Lord, have mercy.*

Deacon: Again we pray for our His Holiness Patriarch Bartholomew; for our Archbishop Nikitas, for the venerable priesthood, the diaconate in Christ, for all the clergy and people, let us pray to the Lord.

People: *Lord, have mercy.*

Deacon: For this *[city / town / village / monastery]*, for every city and country, and the faithful that dwell therein, let us pray to the Lord.

People: *Lord, have mercy.*

Deacon: For seasonable weather, an abundance of the fruits of the earth, and peaceful times, let us pray to the Lord.

People: *Lord, have mercy.*

Deacon: For travellers by sea, land and air; for the sick, the suffering, the imprisoned, and for their salvation, let us pray to the Lord.

People: *Lord, have mercy.*

Deacon: That we may be delivered from all tribulation, wrath, and necessity, let us pray to the Lord.

People: *Lord, have mercy.*

Deacon: Help us, save us, have mercy on us, and keep us, O God, by Thy grace.

People: *Lord, have mercy.*

Deacon: Calling to remembrance our most holy, most pure, most blessed, glorious Lady Theotokos and Ever Virgin Mary with all the saints, let us commit ourselves and one another and all our life unto Christ our God.

People: *To Thee O Lord.*

Deacon: For unto Thee is due all glory, honour and worship; to the Father, and to the Son, and to the Holy Spirit, now and ever, and unto the ages of ages.

People: *Amen.*

Halleluiarion

Reader: Out of the night my spirit waketh at dawn unto Thee, O God;

   For Thy commandments are light upon the earth.

People: *Halleluiah, Halleluiah, Halleluiah.*

Reader: Learn righteousness, you that dwell upon the earth.

People: *Halleluiah, Halleluiah, Halleluiah.*

Reader: Zeal shall lay hold upon an uninstructed people.

People: *Halleluiah, Halleluiah, Halleluiah.*

Reader: Add more evils upon them, O Lord. Add more evils upon them that are glorious upon the earth.

People: *Halleluiah, Halleluiah, Halleluiah.*

Troparion

Tone 8   Humility, tranquillity, repose, suffering, pleading.   *C, D, Eb, F, G, A, Bb, C.*

Behold, the Bridegroom cometh at midnight, and blessed is that servant whom He shall find watching; but unworthy is he whom He shall find heedless. Beware, therefore, O my soul, lest thou be weighed down with sleep; lest thou be given up to death, and be shut out from the kingdom. But rouse thyself and cry: Holy, Holy, Holy art Thou, O God, through the prayers of all the saints have mercy on us.

Glory be to the Father and to the Son and to the Holy Spirit,

Behold, the Bridegroom cometh at midnight, and blessed is that servant whom He shall find watching; but unworthy is he whom He shall find heedless. Beware, therefore, O my soul, lest thou be weighed down with sleep; lest thou be given up to death, and be shut out from the kingdom. But rouse thyself and cry: Holy, Holy, Holy art Thou, O God, through the prayers of *[Saint of the parish]* have mercy on us.

Both now and forever and unto the ages of ages. Amen.

Behold, the Bridegroom cometh at midnight, and blessed is that servant whom He shall find watching; but unworthy is he whom He shall find heedless. Beware, therefore, O my soul, lest thou be weighed down with sleep; lest thou be given up to death, and be shut out from the kingdom. But rouse thyself and cry: Holy, Holy, Holy art Thou, O God, through the prayers of the Theotokos have mercy on us.

Chorus: Lord, have mercy. **(x3)**

Glory be to the Father and to the Son and to the Holy Spirit,
Both now and forever and unto the ages of ages. Amen.

Kathismata – Stasis 1

Tone 1   Magnificent, happy and earthy.   *C, D, Eb, F, G, A, Bb, C.*

Today the Holy Passion shines forth upon the world with the light of salvation; for Christ in His love hastens to His sufferings, He Who holds all things in the hollow of His hand consents to be hung upon the Tree, that He may save mankind.

Chorus: *Glory be to the Father and to the Son and to the Holy Spirit,*

Kathismata – Stasis 2

O Judge invisible, how art Thou made visible in the flesh? How dost Thou now draw near to be slain by lawless men, condemning by Thy Passion our own condemnation? Therefore with one accord, O Word, we ascribe praise, majesty, and glory to Thy power.

Chorus: *Both now and forever and unto the ages of ages. Amen.*

Kathismata – Stasis 3

Tone 8   Humility, tranquillity, repose, suffering, pleading.   *C, D, Eb, F, G, A, Bb, C.*

The first fruits of the Lord's Passion fill this day with light. Come then, all who love to keep the feast, and let us welcome it with songs. For the Creator draws near to undergo the Cross: He is questioned, beaten, and brought to Pilate for judgement; a servant strikes Him on the face, and all this He endures that He may save mankind. Therefore let us cry aloud to Him: O Christ our God who lovest man, grant remission of sins to those who venerate in faith Thy Holy Passion.

Deacon: And that He will vouchsafe unto us the hearing of the Holy Gospel, let us pray unto the Lord God.
People: *Lord, have mercy.* **(x3)**
Deacon: Wisdom. Stand up. Let us hear the Holy Gospel.
Priest: Peace be unto all.

People: *And with thy spirit.*

Priest: The Reading is from the Holy Gospel according to Matthew.

People: *Glory to Thee, O Lord, glory to Thee.*

Deacon: Let us attend.

The Gospel According To Matthew, § 84 To The First Verse Of § 88 [21:18-43].

Now in the morning as he returned into the city, he hungered. And when he saw a fig tree in the way, he came to it, and found nothing thereon, but leaves only, and said unto it, "Let no fruit grow on thee henceforward for ever." And presently the fig tree withered away. And when the disciples saw it, they marvelled, saying, "How soon is the fig tree withered away." Jesus answered and said unto them, "Verily I say unto you, If you have faith, and doubt not, you shall not only do this which is done to the fig tree, but also if you shall say unto this mountain, Be thou removed, and be thou cast into the sea; it shall be done. And all things, whatsoever you shall ask in prayer, believing, you shall receive."

And when he was come into the temple, the chief priests and the elders of the people came unto him as he was teaching, and said, "By what authority doest thou these things? And who gave thee this authority?" And Jesus answered and said unto them, "I also will ask you one thing, which if you tell me, I in like wise will tell you by what authority I do these things. The baptism of John, whence was it; from heaven, or of men?" And they reasoned with themselves, saying, "If we shall say, 'From heaven'; he will say unto us, 'Why did you not then believe him?' But if we shall say, 'Of men'; we fear the people; for all hold John as a prophet." And they answered Jesus, and said, "We cannot tell." And he said unto them, "Neither tell I you by what authority I do these things. But what think ye? A certain man had two sons; and he came to the first, and said, 'Son, go work to day in my vineyard.' He answered and said, 'I will not.' But afterwards he repented, and went. And he came to the second, and said likewise. And he answered and said, 'I go, sir.' And went not. Whether of them twain did the will of his father?" They said unto him, "The first." Jesus saith unto them, "Verily I say unto you, That the publicans and the harlots go into the kingdom of God before you. For John came unto you in the way of righteousness, and you believed him not: but the publicans and the harlots believed him: and ye, when you had seen it, repented not afterwards, that you might believe him.

"Hear another parable: There was a certain householder, who planted a vineyard, and hedged it round about, and dug a wine press in it, and built a tower, and let it out to husbandmen, and went into a far country. And when the time of the fruit drew near, he sent his servants to the husbandmen, that they might receive the fruits of it. And the husbandmen took his servants, and beat one, and killed another, and stoned another. Again, he sent other servants more than the first: and they did unto them likewise. But last of all he sent unto them his son, saying, They will reverence my son. But when the husbandmen saw the son, they said amongst themselves, This is the heir; come, let us kill him, and let us seize on his inheritance. And they caught him, and cast him out of the vineyard, and slew him. When the lord therefore of the vineyard cometh, what will he do unto those husbandmen?" They said unto him, "He will miserably destroy those wicked men, and will let out his vineyard unto other husbandmen, who shall render him the fruits in their seasons." Jesus saith unto them, "Did you never read in the scriptures, The stone which the builders rejected, the same is become the head of the corner: this is the Lords doing, and it is marvellous in our eyes? Therefore say I unto you, The kingdom of God shall be taken from you, and given to a nation bringing forth the fruits thereof."

People: *Glory to Thee, O Lord, glory to Thee.*

Psalm 50

Have mercy on me, O God, according to Thy great mercy; and according to the multitude of Thy compassions blot out my transgression. Wash me thoroughly from mine iniquity, and cleanse me from my sin. For I acknowledge mine iniquity, and my sin is ever before me. Against Thee, Thee only have I sinned, and done evil in Thy sight, that Thou mayest be found just when Thou speakest, and victorious when Thou art judged. For behold, I was conceived in iniquity, and in sin my mother bore me. For behold, Thou hast loved truth; Thou hast made known to me the hidden and secret things of Thy wisdom. Thou shalt sprinkle me with hyssop, and I shall be made clean; Thou shalt wash me, and I shall be whiter than snow. Make me to hear joy and gladness; that the humbled bones may rejoice. Turn Thy face away from my sins, and blot out all mine iniquities.

Create in me a clean heart, O God, and renew a steadfast spirit within me. Cast me not away from Thy presence, and take not Thy Holy Spirit from me. Restore to me the joy of Thy salvation, and establish me with Thy governing Spirit. I shall teach transgressors Thy ways, and the ungodly shall turn back to Thee. Deliver me from blood guiltiness, O God, the God of my salvation; my tongue shall joyfully declare Thy righteousness. Lord, open my lips, and my mouth shall declare Thy praise. For if Thou hadst desired sacrifice, I would give it; Thou dost not delight in burnt offerings. A sacrifice to God is a broken spirit; God will not despise a broken and a humbled heart. Do good, O Lord, in Thy good pleasure to Zion, and let the walls of Jerusalem be builded. Then Thou shalt be pleased with a sacrifice of righteousness, with oblation and whole burned offerings. Then shall they offer bulls on Thine altar.

Katavasia
Ode I

Eirmos

Tone 2   Majesty, gentleness, hope, repentance and sadness.   *E, F, G, Ab, B, C.*

Let us sing to the Lord who by His divine command dried up the billowing sea where none might walk, and through it led the people of Israel on foot: for He has been greatly glorified.

Chorus: *Glory be to the Father and to the Son and to the Holy Spirit;*

Ineffable is the condescension of the Word of God. Christ is Himself both God and man; yet He counted not His Godhead a thing to be seized and held fast, and this He showed to His disciples by taking the form of a servant: for He has been greatly glorified.

Chorus: *Both now and forever, and unto the ages of ages. Amen.*

Reader: "I who am rich in Godhead have come to minister to Adam who is grown poor. I who fashioned him have of Mine own will put on his form. I who am impassable in my divinity have come to lay down my life as a ransom for him."

Chorus: *Let us sing to the Lord who by His divine command dried up the billowing sea where none might walk, and through it led the people of Israel on foot: for He has been greatly glorified.*

Little Litany

Deacon: Again and again, in peace let us pray to the Lord.

People: Lord, have mercy.

Deacon: Help us, save us, have mercy on us, and keep us, O God, by Thy grace.

People: Lord, have mercy.

Deacon: Calling to remembrance our most holy, most pure, most blessed, glorious Lady Theotokos and Ever Virgin Mary with all the saints, let us commit ourselves and one another and all our life unto Christ our God.

People: To Thee, O Lord.

Deacon: For Thou art the King of Peace and the Saviour of our souls, and unto Thee do we send up glory, to the Father, and to the Son, and to the Holy Spirit, now and ever, and unto the ages of ages.

People: Amen.

Kontakion

Tone 8   Humility, tranquillity, repose, suffering, pleading.   *C, D, Eb, F, G, A, Bb, C.*

Jacob lamented the loss of Joseph, but his righteous son was seated in a chariot and honoured as a king. For he was not enslaved to the pleasures of Egypt, but he was glorified by God who sees the hearts of men and bestows on them a crown incorruptible.

Ikos

Let us now add our lamentation to the lamentation of Jacob, and let us weep with him for Joseph, his wise and glorious son who was enslaved in body but kept his soul free from bondage, and became lord over all Egypt. For God grants unto his servants a crown incorruptible.

Synaxarion

On this day begins the anniversary of the holy Passion of the Saviour, He of whom Joseph of exceeding beauty is taken as the earliest symbol; for this Joseph was the eleventh of the sons of Jacob, and because his father exceedingly loved him, his brothers envied him and threw him into a pit. Then they took him out and sold him to strangers, who sold him in Egypt. He was slandered for his chastity, and was thrown into prison. But finally he was taken out of prison, and he attained a high rank, and received honours worthy of kings, becoming governor of the whole of Egypt, whose people he supported. Then he symbolised in himself the Passion of our Lord Jesus Christ and His consequent great glory.

[Genesis 40; 41.]

To the remembrance of Joseph is added the story of the fig tree which the Lord cursed on this day (corresponding at that time to the nineteenth of the month of March) because of its barrenness, so that it dried up. The fig tree was a symbol of the Council of the Jews which did not show the necessary fruits of virtue and righteousness, so that Christ stripped it of every spiritual grace.

[Matthew 21:18-20.]

Wherefore, by the intercessions of the all comely Joseph, O Christ, have mercy upon us. Amen.

Katavasia (Continued)
Ode VIII

Eirmos

Tone 2   Majesty, gentleness, hope, repentance and sadness.   *E, F, G, Ab, B, C.*

The unwearied fire, fed with endless fuel, drew back in fear before the pure bodies and pure souls of the holy Children; and as the undying flame decreased in strength, they sang an everlasting song: O all you works, praise you the Lord and exalt Him above all forever.

Chorus: *Glory be to the Father and to the Son and to the Holy Spirit;*

"Then shall all men know that you are my disciples, if you keep my commandments", said the Saviour to His friends, as He went to His Passion. "Be at peace with one another and with all men; think humbly of yourselves and you shall be exalted; acknowledge me as Lord, and praise and exalt Me above all forever."

Chorus: *Both now and forever, and unto the ages of ages. Amen.*

"Let your power over your fellow men be altogether different from the dominion of the Gentiles: their self willed pride is not the order that I have appointed, but a tyranny. He therefore who would be the first amongst you, let him be the last of all. Acknowledge Me as Lord, and praise and exalt Me above all forever."

Chorus: *We praise, we bless, we worship the Lord.*

The unwearied fire, fed with endless fuel, drew back in fear before the pure bodies and pure souls of the holy Children; and as the undying flame decreased in strength, they sang an everlasting song: O all you works, praise you the Lord and exalt Him above all forever.

Deacon: The Theotokos and Mother of the Light, let us honour and magnify in song.

Ode IX

Eirmos

Tone 2   *Majesty, gentleness, hope, repentance and sadness.*   *E, F, G, Ab, B, C.*

Thou hast magnified, O Christ, the Theotokos who bore Thee. From her, O our Creator, hast Thou taken a body of like passions to our own, and so hast set us free from all our ignorance. Therefore with all generations we call her blessed and we magnify Thee.

Chorus: *Glory be to the Father and to the Son and to the Holy Spirit;*

"Cast away all impurity of the passions and obtain a wise understanding, worthy of God's Kingdom", Thou hast said, O Wisdom of all, to Thine apostles; "and you shall be glorified, and shine forth brighter than the sun."

Chorus: *Both now and forever, and unto the ages of ages. Amen.*

"Taking Me as your example," Thou hast said, O Lord, to Thy disciples, "think not proud thoughts but be content with what is humble. You shall drink out of the cup from which I drink, and so you shall be glorified with me in the Kingdom of the Father."

Thou hast magnified, O Christ, the Theotokos who bore Thee. From her, O our Creator, hast Thou taken a body of like passions to our own, and so hast set us free from all our ignorance. Therefore with all generations we call her blessed and we magnify Thee.

Little Litany

Deacon: Again and again, in peace let us pray to the Lord.

People: *Lord, have mercy.*

Deacon: Help us, save us, have mercy on us, and keep us, O God, by Thy grace.

People: *Lord, have mercy.*

Deacon: Calling to remembrance our most holy, most pure, most blessed, glorious Lady Theotokos and Ever Virgin Mary with all the saints, let us commit ourselves and one another and all our life unto Christ our God.

People: *To Thee, O Lord.*

Priest: For all the Hosts of Heaven praise Thee, and unto Thee do we send up glory, to the Father, and to the Son, and to the Holy Spirit, now and ever and unto the ages of ages.

People: *Amen.*

Exapostilarion

Tone 3   *Arrogant, brave, and mature atmosphere.*   *F, G, A, A#, C, D, E, F.*

I see Thy bridal chamber adorned, O my Saviour, and I have no wedding garment that I may enter there. Make the robe of my soul to shine, O Giver of Light, and save me.

Chorus: *Glory be to the Father and to the Son and to the Holy Spirit;*

I see Thy bridal chamber adorned, O my Saviour, and I have no wedding garment that I may enter there. Make the robe of my soul to shine, O Giver of Light, and save me.

Chorus: *Both now and forever, and unto the ages of ages. Amen.*

I see Thy bridal chamber adorned, O my Saviour, and I have no wedding garment that I may enter there. Make the robe of my soul to shine, O Giver of Light, and save me.

Lauds (Praises)

Tone 1   *Magnificent, happy and earthy.*   *C, D, Eb, F, G, A, Bb, C.*

Let everything that has breath praise the Lord. Praise you the Lord from the heavens: praise Him in the heights. To Thee, O God, is due our song. Praise Him all His angels: praise you Him, all His hosts. To Thee, O God, is due our song.

Psalm 150 - Pt 1

Tone 1   *Magnificent, happy and earthy.*   *C, D, Eb, F, G, A, Bb, C.*

Chorus: *Praise the Lord. Praise God in His sanctuary; praise Him in His mighty firmament. Praise Him for His mighty acts; praise Him according to His excellent greatness.*

Reader: As the Lord went to His voluntary Passion, He said to His apostles on the way: "Behold, we go up to Jerusalem, and the Son of man shall be betrayed, as it is written of Him." Come, then, and let us also journey with Him, purified in mind; let us be crucified with Him and die for His sake to the pleasures of this life, that we may also live with Him and hear Him say: "No longer do I ascend to the earthly Jerusalem to suffer, but I ascend to My Father and your Father, and to My God and your God; and I shall raise you up to the Jerusalem on High in the Kingdom of heaven."

Psalm 150 - Pt 2

Tone 5   *Stimulating, dancing, and rhythmical.*   *C, D, Eb, F, G, A, Bb, C.*

Chorus: *Praise Him with the timbrel and dance; praise Him with stringed instruments and flutes.*

Reader: We have come, O faithful, to the saving Passion of Christ our God: let us glorify His ineffable forbearance, that in His tender mercy He may also raise us up who have been slain by sin, for He is good and loves mankind.

Chorus: *Glory be to the Father, and to the Son, and to the Holy Spirit;*
        Both now and forever, and unto the ages of ages. Amen.

Reader: O Lord, as Thou camest to Thy Passion, Thou hast strengthened the faith of Thy disciples, taking them aside and saying to them: "How have you forgotten what I told you before? According to the Scriptures, it cannot be that a prophet should be killed save in Jerusalem. Now is the time at hand, of which I spake to you: for see, I am betrayed into the hands of sinners; they shall mock Me and nail Me to the Cross and deliver Me up for burial, with loathing looking on Me as a corpse. Yet be of good courage: for on the third day I shall rise, bringing joy and life eternal to the faithful."

Thine is the glory, O Lord our God, and unto Thee we ascribe glory; to the Father, and to the Son, and to the Holy Spirit; both now and forever, and unto the ages of ages. Amen.

Lesser Doxology

Glory to God, Who has shown us the Light. Glory to God in the highest, and on earth, peace, good will toward men. We praise Thee. We bless Thee. We worship Thee. We glorify Thee and give thanks to Thee for Thy great glory. O Lord God, Heavenly King, God the Father Almighty. O Lord, the Only Begotten Son, Jesus Christ, and the Holy Spirit. \

O Lord God, Lamb of God, Son of the Father, Who takes away the sins of the world, have mercy on us. Thou, Who takes away the sins of the world, receive our prayer. Thou, Who sittest at the right hand of God the Father, have mercy on us. /

For Thou alone art holy, and Thou alone art Lord. Thou alone, O Lord Jesus Christ, are most high in the glory of God the Father. Amen. I will give thanks to Thee every day and praise Thy Name forever and ever. Lord, Thou hast been our refuge from generation to generation. I said, *"Lord, have mercy on me. Heal my soul, for I have sinned against Thee."* \

Lord, I flee to Thee. Teach me to do Thy will, for Thou art my God. For with Thee is the fountain of Life, and in Thy light we shall see light. Continue Thy loving kindness to those who know Thee. Vouchsafe, O Lord, to keep us this day without sin. Blessed art Thou, O Lord, the God of our fathers, and praised and glorified is Thy Name forever. Amen. Let Thy mercy be upon us, O Lord, even as we have set our hope on Thee.

Blessed art Thou, O Master; teach me Thy statutes.

Blessed art Thou, O Lord; enlighten me with Thy commandments.

Blessed art Thou, O Holy One; make me to understand Thy precepts.

Thy mercy endures forever, O Lord. Do not despise the works of Thy hands. To Thee belongs worship, to Thee belongs praise, to Thee belongs glory: to the Father and to the Son and to the Holy Spirit, both now and forever and unto the ages of ages. Amen. \

Priest:	Let us complete our morning prayer unto the Lord.
People:	*Lord, have mercy.*
Priest:	Help us, save us, have mercy on us, and keep us, O God, by Thy grace.
People:	*Lord, have mercy.*
Priest:	That the whole day may be perfect, holy, peaceful and sinless, let us ask of the Lord.
People:	*Grant this, O Lord.*
Priest:	An angel of peace, a faithful guide, a guardian of our souls and bodies, let us ask of the Lord.
People:	*Grant this, O Lord.*
Priest:	Pardon and remission of our sins and offences, let us ask of the Lord.

People: *Grant this, O Lord.*

Priest: Things good and profitable for our souls, and peace for the world, let us ask of the Lord.

People: *Grant this, O Lord.*

Priest: That we may complete the remaining time of our life in peace and repentance, let us ask of the Lord.

People: *Grant this, O Lord.*

Priest: A Christian ending to our life, painless, blameless, peaceful, and a good defence before the dread judgement seat of Christ, let us ask.

People: *Grant this, O Lord.*

Priest: Calling to remembrance our most holy, most pure, most blessed, glorious Lady Theotokos and Ever Virgin Mary with all the saints, let us commit ourselves and one another and all our life unto Christ our God.

People: *To Thee, O Lord.*

Priest: For Thou art a God of mercy, compassion, and love for mankind, and unto Thee do we send up glory: to the Father, and to the Son, and to the Holy Spirit, now and ever, and unto the ages of ages.

People: *Amen.*

Priest: Peace be with you all.

People: *And with thy spirit.*

Priest: Let us bow down our heads unto the Lord.

People: *To Thee, O Lord.*

Priest *[soto voce]*: O Holy Lord, who dwelleth on high and regardest the humble of heart, and with thine all seeing eye dost behold all creation, unto Thee have we bowed the neck of our soul and body, and we entreat Thee: O Holy of holies, stretch forth Thine invisible hand from Thy holy dwelling place, and bless us all. And if in aught we have sinned, whether voluntarily or involuntarily, forgive, inasmuch as Thou art a good God, and lovest mankind, vouchsafing unto us Thy earthly and heavenly good things.

Priest *[aloud]*: For Thine it is to show mercy and to save us, O our God, and unto Thee do we send up glory: to the Father, and to the Son, and to the Holy Spirit, now and ever, and unto the ages of ages.

People: *Amen.*

Aposticha

Tone 5   Stimulating, dancing, and rhythmical.   *C, D, Eb, F, G, A, Bb, C.*

O Lord, the mother of the sons of Zebedee, not understanding the hidden mystery of Thy dispensation, asked Thee to give the honours of a temporal kingdom to her sons. But instead of this Thou hast promised to Thy friends that they should drink the cup of death; and Thou hast said that Thou wouldst drink this cup before them, to cleanse men from their sins. Therefore we cry aloud to Thee: O salvation of our souls, glory to Thee.

Stichos

We were filled in the morning with Thy mercy, O Lord and we rejoiced and were glad. In all our days, let us be glad for the days wherein Thou didst humble us, for the years wherein we saw evils. And look upon Thy servants, and upon Thy works, and do Thou guide their sons.

O Lord, teaching Thy disciples to think perfect thoughts, Thou hast said to them: "Be not like the Gentiles, who exercise dominion over those who are less strong. But it shall not be so amongst you, My disciples, for I of mine own will am poor. Let him, then, who is first amongst you be the minister of all. Let the ruler be as the ruled, and let the first be as the last. For I Myself have come to minister to Adam in his poverty, and to give my life as a ransom for the many who cry aloud to Me: Glory to Thee."

Stichos

Tone 8   Humility, tranquillity, repose, suffering, pleading.   *C, D, Eb, F, G, A, Bb, C.*

Reader: And let the brightness of the Lord our God be upon us, and the works of our hand do Thou guide aright upon us, yea, the work of our hands do Thou guide aright.

O brethren, let us fear the punishment of the fig tree, withered because it was unfruitful; and let us bring worthy fruits of repentance unto Christ, who grants us His great mercy.

Chorus: *Glory be to the Father, and to the Son, and to the Holy Spirit;*

Reader: Both now and forever and unto the ages of ages. Amen.

Chorus: The serpent found a second Eve in the Egyptian woman, and with words of flattery he sought to make Joseph fall. But, leaving his garments behind him, Joseph fled from sin; and like the first man before his disobedience, though naked he was not ashamed. At his prayers, O Christ, have mercy upon us.

Reader: It is good to give praise unto the Lord, and to chant unto Thy name, O Most High, to proclaim in the morning Thy mercy, and Thy truth by night.

Holy God, Holy Mighty, Holy Immortal, have mercy on us. **(x3)**

Glory be to the Father, and to the Son, and to the Holy Spirit;
Both now and forever and unto the ages of ages. Amen.

O Most Holy Trinity, have mercy on us.

O Lord, cleanse us from our sins.

O Master, pardon our iniquities.

O Holy One, visit and heal our infirmities, for Thy names sake.

Lord have mercy. **(x3)**

Glory be to the Father, and to the Son, and to the Holy Spirit;
Both now and forever and unto the ages of ages. Amen.

People: *Our Father, Who art in Heaven, hallowed be Thy Name. Thy Kingdom come, Thy will be done, on earth as it is in Heaven. Give us this day our daily bread, and forgive us our trespasses, as we forgive those who trespass against us; and lead us not into temptation, but deliver us from the evil one.*

Priest: For Thine is the Kingdom, and the power, and the glory; of the Father, and of the Son, and of the Holy Spirit, now and ever, and unto the ages of ages.

People: *Amen.*

Kontakion

Jacob wailed the loss of Joseph while that brave youth was sitting in a chariot like an honoured king; for at that time, not having enslaved himself to the pleasures of Egypt, he was glorified instead by God, who looketh into the hearts of men, and who granteth them incorruptible crowns.

Lord have mercy. **(x40)**

Glory be to the Father, and to the Son, and to the Holy Spirit;
Both now and forever and unto the ages of ages. Amen.

Greater in honour than the Cherubim and beyond compare more glorious than the Seraphim; without corruption thou gavest birth to God the Word, truly the Theotokos, we magnify thee.

Holy Father, bless.

Priest: He that is is blessed, Christ our God, always, now and ever, and unto the ages of ages.

People: *Amen.*

Reader: O Heavenly King, strengthen Orthodox Christians, establish the Faith, subdue the nations, give peace to the world, keep well this *[city / town / village]*; settle our departed fathers and brethren in the tabernacles of the righteous, and receive us in penitence and confession, for Thou art good and the Lover of mankind.

Prayer Of St Ephraim The Syrian

Priest: O Lord and Master of my life, a spirit of idleness, despondency, ambition, and idle talking give me not. *prostration*

Priest: But rather a spirit of chastity, humble mindedness, patience, and love bestow upon me Thy servant. *prostration*

Priest: Yea, O Lord King, grant me to see mine own failings and not condemn my brother; for blessed art Thou unto the ages of ages. Amen. *prostration*

O God, cleanse me a sinner. **(x12)**

O Lord and Master of my life, a spirit of idleness, despondency, ambition, and idle talking give me not. But rather a spirit of chastity, humble mindedness, patience, and love bestow upon me Thy servant. Yea, O Lord King, grant me to see mine own failings and not condemn my brother; for blessed art Thou unto the ages of ages.

People: *Amen.*   ****prostration****

Priest: Glory to Thee, O Christ and our God and our Hope, glory to Thee.

Reader: *Glory be to the Father, and to the Son, and to the Holy Spirit;*

Both now and forever and unto the ages of ages. Amen.

Lord, have mercy. **(x3)**

Holy Father, bless.

Little Dismissal

Priest: May He who is going to His voluntary passion for our salvation, Christ our true God, through the intercessions of His all immaculate and all blameless holy Mother; by the protection of the honourable bodiless powers of heaven; of *[Saint of the parish]*; of the holy and righteous ancestors of God Joachim and Anna; and of all the Saints: have mercy on us and save us forasmuch as He is good and loveth mankind.

Through the prayers of our Holy Fathers, O Lord Jesus Christ our God, have mercy upon us and save us.

People: *Amen.*

[Then the reader immediately begins the first hour.]

Reader:

Come, let us worship God, our King.

Come, let us worship and fall down before Christ, our King and our God.

Come, let us worship and fall down before Christ Himself, our King and our God.

Psalm 5

Unto my words give ear, O Lord, hear my cry. Attend unto the voice of my supplication, O my King and my God; for unto Thee will I pray, O Lord. In the morning shalt Thou hear my voice. In the morning shall I stand before Thee, and Thou shalt look upon me; for not a God that willest iniquity art Thou. He that worketh evil shall not dwell near Thee nor shall transgressors abide before Thine eyes. Thou hast hated all them that work iniquity; Thou shalt destroy all them that speak a lie. A man that is bloody and deceitful shall the Lord abhor. But as for me, in the multitude of Thy mercy shall I go into Thy house; I shall worship toward Thy holy temple in fear of Thee. O Lord, guide me in the way of Thy righteousness; because of mine enemies, make straight my way before Thee, For in their mouth there is no truth; their heart is vain. Their throat is an open sepulchre, with their tongues have they spoken deceitfully; judge them, O God. Let them fall down on account of their own devisings; according to the multitude of their ungodliness, cast them out, for they have embittered Thee, O Lord. And let all them be glad that hope in Thee; they shall rejoice, and Thou shalt dwell amongst them. And all shall glory in Thee that love Thy name, for Thou shalt bless the righteous. O Lord, as with a shield of Thy good pleasure hast Thou crowned us.

Psalm 89

Lord, Thou hast been our refuge in generation and generation. Before the mountains came to be and the earth was formed and the world, even from everlasting to everlasting art Thou. Turn not man away unto lowliness; yea, Thou hast said: Turn back you sons of men. For a thousand years in Thine eyes, O Lord, are but as yesterday that is past, and as a watch in the night. Things of no account shall their years be; in the morning like grass shall man pass away. In the morning shall he bloom and pass away. In the evening shall he fall and grow withered and dry. For we have fainted away in Thy wrath, and in Thine anger have we been troubled. Thou hast set our iniquities before us; our lifespan is in the light of Thy countenance. For all our days are faded away, and in Thy wrath are we fainted away; our years have, like a spider, spun out their tale. As for the days of our years, in their span, they be threescore years and ten. And if we be in strength, mayhap fourscore years; and what is more than these is toil and travail. For mildness is come upon us, and we shall be chastened. Who knoweth the might of Thy wrath? And out of fear of Thee, who can recount Thine anger? So make Thy right hand known to me, and to them that in their heart are instructed in wisdom. Return, O Lord; how long? And be Thou entreated concerning Thy servants. We were filled in the morning with Thy mercy, O Lord, and we rejoiced and were glad. In all our days, let us be glad for the days wherein Thou didst humble us, for the years wherein we saw evils. And look upon Thy servants, and upon Thy works, and do Thou guide their sons. And let the brightness of the Lord our God be upon us, and the works of our hands do Thou guide aright upon us, yea, the works of our hands do Thou guide aright.

Psalm 100

Of mercy and judgement will I sing to Thee, O Lord; I will chant and have understanding in a blameless path. When wilt Thou come unto me? I have walked in the innocence of my heart in the midst of my house. I have no unlawful thing before mine eyes; the workers of transgressions I have hated. A crooked heart hath not cleaved unto me; as for the wicked man who turned from me, I knew him not. Him that privily talked against his neighbour did I drive away from me. With him whose eye was proud and his heart insatiate, I did not eat. Mine eyes were upon the faithful of the land, that they might sit with me; the man that walked in the blameless path, he ministered unto me. The proud doer dwelt not in the midst of my house; the speaker of unjust things prospered not before mine eyes. In the morning I slew all the sinners of the land, utterly to destroy out of the city of the Lord all them that work iniquity.

After The Psalm

Glory be to the Father, and to the Son, and to the Holy Spirit;
Both now and forever, and unto the ages of ages. Amen.

Halleluiah, Halleluiah, Halleluiah. Glory to Thee, O God. **(x3)**

Lord, have mercy. **(x3)**

Priest: Unto my words give ear, O Lord, hear my cry.
Reader: In the morning, hearken unto my voice, O my king and God.
            prostration

Priest: For unto Thee will I pray, O Lord.
Reader: In the morning, hearken unto my voice, O my king and God.
            prostration

Priest: Glory to the Father and to the Son and to the Holy Spirit.
Reader: Both now and ever, and unto the ages of ages. Amen.

Theotokion

What shall we call thee, O thou who art full of grace? Heaven, for from thee hast dawned forth the Sun of Righteousness. Paradise, for from thee hath blossomed forth the flower of immortality. Virgin, for thou hast remained incorrupt. Pure Mother, for thou hast held in thy holy embrace the Son, the God of all. Do thou entreat Him to save our souls.

Tone 6   Rich texture, funereal character, sorrowful tone.   *D, Eb, F##, G, A, Bb, C##, D.*

- My steps do Thou direct according to Thy saying, and let no iniquity have dominion over me.   **(x2)**
- Deliver me from the false accusations of men, and I will keep Thy commandments.   **(x2)**
- Make Thy face to shine upon Thy servant, and teach me Thy statutes.   **(x2)**
- Let my mouth be filled with Thy praise, O Lord, that I may hymn Thy glory and Thy majesty all the day long.

    (x3)

- Holy God, Holy Mighty, Holy Immortal, have mercy on us.   **(x3)**

Glory be to the Father and to the Son and to the Holy Spirit;

Both now and forever and unto the ages of ages. Amen.

O Most Holy Trinity, have mercy on us.

O Lord, cleanse us from our sins.

O Master, pardon our iniquities.

O Holy One, visit and heal our infirmities, for Thy names sake.

Lord have mercy. **(x3)**

Glory be to the Father and to the Son and to the Holy Spirit,

Both now and forever and unto the ages of ages. Amen.

People: *Our Father, Who art in Heaven, hallowed be Thy Name. Thy Kingdom come, Thy will be done, on earth as it is in Heaven. Give us this day our daily bread, and forgive us our trespasses, as we forgive those who trespass against us; and lead us not into temptation, but deliver us from the evil one.*

Priest: For Thine is the Kingdom, and the power, and the glory; of the Father, and of the Son, and of the Holy Spirit, now and ever, and unto the ages of ages.

People: *Amen.*

Reader: Jacob lamented the loss of Joseph, but his righteous son was seated in a chariot and honoured as a king. For he was not enslaved to the pleasures of Egypt, but he was glorified by God who sees the hearts of men and bestows on them a crown incorruptible.

Lord, have mercy. **(x40)**

The Prayer Of The Hours

At all times and in every hour, Thou art worshipped and glorified in heaven and on earth, Christ our God. Long in patience, great in mercy and compassion, Thou lovest the righteous and showest mercy to sinners. Thou callest all to salvation through the promise of good things to come. Lord, receive our prayers at the present time. Direct our lives according to Thy commandments. Sanctify our souls. Purify our bodies. Set our minds aright. Cleanse our thoughts, and deliver us from all sorrow, evil and distress. Surround us with Thy holy angels, that, guarded and guided by their host, we may arrive at the unity of the faith and the understanding of Thine ineffable glory. For Thou art blessed to the ages of ages. Amen.

Lord, have mercy. **(x3)**

Glory be to the Father and to the Son and to the Holy Spirit,
Both now and forever and unto the ages of ages. Amen.

Greater in honour than the Cherubim and beyond compare more glorious than the Seraphim; without corruption thou gavest birth to God the Word, truly the Theotokos, we magnify thee.

Holy Father, bless.

Priest: God be gracious unto us and bless us, and cause Thy face to shine upon us and have mercy on us.
People: *Amen.*
Priest: O Lord and Master of my life, a spirit of idleness, despondency, ambition, and idle talking give me not.   ***prostration**

But rather a spirit of chastity, humble mindedness, patience, and love bestow upon me Thy servant.
                                    prostration

Yea, O Lord King, grant me to see mine own failings and not condemn my brother; for blessed art Thou unto the ages of ages. Amen.   ***prostration***

O God, cleanse me a sinner. *[cross and bow]* **(x12)**

O Lord and Master of my life, a spirit of idleness, despondency, ambition, and idle talking give me not. But rather a spirit of chastity, humble mindedness, patience, and love bestow upon me Thy servant. Yea, O Lord King, grant me to see mine own failings and not condemn my brother; for blessed art Thou unto the ages of ages. Amen.   ***prostration***

Reader: Holy God, Holy Mighty, Holy Immortal, have mercy on us. **(x3)**

Glory be to the Father and to the Son and to the Holy Spirit,
Both now and forever and unto the ages of ages. Amen.

O Most Holy Trinity, have mercy on us.
O Lord, cleanse us from our sins.
O Master, pardon our iniquities.
O Holy One, visit and heal our infirmities, for Thy names sake.

Lord have mercy. **(x3)**

Glory be to the Father and to the Son and to the Holy Spirit,
Both now and forever and unto the ages of ages. Amen.

People: *Our Father, Who art in Heaven, hallowed be Thy Name. Thy Kingdom come, Thy will be done, on earth as it is in Heaven. Give us this day our daily bread, and forgive us our trespasses, as we forgive those who trespass against us; and lead us not into temptation, but deliver us from the evil one.*

Priest: For Thine is the Kingdom, and the power, and the glory; of the Father, and of the Son, and of the Holy Spirit, now and ever, and unto the ages of ages.

People: *Amen.*

   Lord, have mercy. **(x12)**

The Prayer Of The First Hour

Priest: O Christ, the True Light, Who enlightenest and sanctifiest every man that cometh into the world: Let the Light of Thy countenance be signed upon us, that in it we may see the Unapproachable Light, and guide our steps in the doing of Thy commandments, through the intercessions of Thy most pure Mother, and of all Thy saints.

People: *Amen.*

Theotokion

   Tone 8   *Humility, tranquillity, repose, suffering, pleading.*   C, D, Eb, F, G, A, Bb, C.

To Thee, the Champion Leader, we Thy servants dedicate a feast of victory and of thanksgiving as ones rescued out of sufferings, O Theotokos: but as Thou art one with might which is invincible, from all dangers that can be do Thou deliver us, that we may cry to Thee: Rejoice, Thou Bride Unwedded.

Priest: Glory to Thee, O Christ our God and our hope, glory to Thee.

   Glory be to the Father and to the Son and to the Holy Spirit,
   Both now and forever and unto the ages of ages. Amen.

Lord, have mercy. **(x3)**
Holy Father, bless.

Priest: May Christ our true God, the Lord who for our salvation went to His voluntary Passion, through the intercessions of His most pure Mother; of the holy and glorious apostles; of the holy and righteous ancestors of God, Joachim and Anna; and of all the saints: have mercy on us and save us, for He is good and lovest mankind.

People: *Amen.*

[For Monday Evening]

The Trisagion Prayers

Priest: Blessed is our God, always, now and ever, and unto the ages of ages.

People: *Amen.*

Priest: Glory to Thee, our God, glory to Thee.

O Heavenly King, Comforter, Spirit of Truth, Who art everywhere present and fillest all things, Treasury of blessings and Giver of life: Come and abide in us and cleanse us from every impurity and save our souls, O Good One.

Reader: Holy God, Holy Mighty, Holy Immortal, have mercy on us. **(x3)**

Glory be to the Father, and to the Son, and to the Holy Spirit;

Both now and forever, and unto the ages of ages. Amen.

O Most Holy Trinity, have mercy on us.

O Lord, cleanse us from our sins.

O Master, pardon our iniquities.

O Holy One, visit and heal our infirmities, for Thy names sake.

Lord have mercy. **(x3)**

Glory be be to the Father and to the Son and to the Holy Spirit;

Both now and forever, and unto the ages of ages. Amen.

People: *Our Father, Who art in Heaven, hallowed be Thy Name. Thy Kingdom come, Thy will be done, on earth as it is in Heaven. Give us this day our daily bread, and forgive us our trespasses, as we forgive those who trespass against us; and lead us not into temptation, but deliver us from the evil one.*

Priest: For Thine is the kingdom and the power and the glory of the Father and of the Son and of the Holy Spirit; both now and forever and unto the ages of ages.

People: *Amen.*

Lord, have mercy. **(x3)**

Glory be be to the Father and to the Son and to the Holy Spirit;

Both now and forever and unto the ages of ages. Amen.

Come, let us worship God, our King.

Come, let us worship and fall down before Christ, our King and our God.

Come, let us worship and fall down before Christ Himself, our King and our God.

Psalm 19

The Lord hear thee in the day of affliction; the name of the God of Jacob defend thee. Let Him send forth unto thee help from His sanctuary, and out of Zion let Him help thee. Let Him remember every sacrifice of thine, and thy whole burnt offering let Him fatten. The Lord grant thee according to thy heart, and fulfil all thy purposes. We will rejoice in Thy salvation, and in the name of the Lord our God shall we be magnified. The Lord fulfil all thy requests. Now have I known that the Lord hath saved His anointed one; He will hearken unto him out of His holy heaven; in mighty deeds is the salvation of His right hand. Some trust in chariots, and some in horses, but we will call upon the name of the Lord our God. They have been fettered and have fallen, but we are risen and are set upright. O Lord, save the king, and hearken unto us in the day when we call upon Thee.

Psalm 20

O Lord, in Thy strength the king shall be glad, and in Thy salvation shall he exceedingly rejoice. The desire of his heart hast Thou granted unto him, and hast not denied him the requests of his lips. Thou wentest before him with the blessings of goodness, Thou hast set upon his head a crown of precious stone. He asked life of Thee, and Thou gavest him length of days unto ages of ages. Great is his glory in Thy salvation; glory and majesty shalt Thou lay upon him. For Thou shalt give him blessing for ever and ever, Thou shalt gladden him in joy with Thy countenance. For the king hopeth in the Lord, and through the mercy of the Most High shall he not be shaken. Let Thy hand be found on all Thine enemies; let Thy right hand find all that hate Thee. For Thou wilt make them as an oven of fire in the time of Thy presence; the Lord in His wrath will trouble them sorely and fire shall devour them. Their fruit wilt Thou destroy from the earth, and their seed from the sons of men. For they have intended evil against Thee, they have devised counsels which they shall not be able to establish. For Thou shalt make them turn their backs; amongst those that are Thy remnant, Thou shalt make ready their countenance. Be Thou exalted, O Lord, in Thy strength; we will sing and chant of Thy mighty acts.

Holy God, Holy Mighty, Holy Immortal, have mercy on us. **(x3)**

Glory be to the Father and to the Son and to the Holy Spirit,
Both now and forever and unto the ages of ages. Amen.

O Most Holy Trinity, have mercy on us.

O Lord, cleanse us from our sins.

O Master, pardon our iniquities.

O Holy One, visit and heal our infirmities, for Thy names sake.

Lord have mercy. **(x3)**

Glory be to the Father and to the Son and to the Holy Spirit,
Both now and forever and unto the ages of ages. Amen.

People: *Our Father, Who art in Heaven, hallowed be Thy Name. Thy Kingdom come, Thy will be done, on earth as it is in Heaven. Give us this day our daily bread, and forgive us our trespasses, as we forgive those who trespass against us; and lead us not into temptation, but deliver us from the evil one.*

Priest: For Thine is the kingdom and the power, and the glory: of the Father and of the Son, and of the Holy Spirit, now and ever, and unto the ages of ages.

People: *Amen.*

Troparia

O Lord, save Thy people and bless Thine inheritance. Grant victory unto Orthodox Christians over their enemies, and by the power of Thy Cross do Thou preserve Thy commonwealth.

Glory be to the Father and to the Son and to the Holy Spirit,

O Thou Who wast lifted up willingly upon the Cross, bestow Thy mercies upon the new community named after Thee, O Christ God; gladden with Thy power the Orthodox Christians, granting them victory over enemies; may they have as Thy help the weapon of peace, the invincible trophy.

Both now and forever and unto the ages of ages. Amen.

O Awesome intercession that cannot be put to shame, O good one, disdain not our prayer; O all hymned Theotokos, establish the commonwealth of the Orthodox, save the Orthodox Christians, and grant unto them victory from heaven, for thou didst bring forth God, O thou only blessed one.

Ektenia

Priest: Have mercy on us, O God, according to Thy great mercy, we pray Thee, hearken and have mercy.

People: *Lord, have mercy.* **(x3)**

Deacon: Again we pray for His Holiness Patriarch Bartholomew; and for our Most Reverend Archbishop Nikitas, whose diocese this is.

People: *Lord, have mercy.* **(x3)**

Deacon: Again we pray for all the brethren and for all Christians.

People: *Lord, have mercy.* **(x3)**

Deacon: For a merciful God art Thou, and the Lover of mankind, and unto Thee do we send up glory: to the Father, and to the Son, and to the Holy Spirit, both now and forever, and unto the ages of ages.

People: *Amen. Holy Father bless.*

Priest: Glory to the holy, and consubstantial, and life creating, and indivisible Trinity, always, now and ever, and unto the ages of ages.

People: *Amen.*

Reader: Glory to God in the highest, and on earth peace, good will amongst men. *(cross and bow)* **(x3)**
O Lord, Thou shalt open my lips, and my mouth shall declare Thy praise. **(x2)**

The Six Psalms
Psalm 3

O Lord, why are they multiplied that afflict me? Many rise up against me. Many say unto my soul: There is no salvation for him in his God. But Thou, O Lord, art my helper, my glory, and the lifter up of my head. I cried unto the Lord with my voice, and He heard me out of His holy mountain. I laid me down and slept; I awoke, for the Lord will help me. I will not be afraid of ten thousands of people that set themselves against me round about. Arise, O Lord, save me, O my God, for Thou hast smitten all who without cause are mine enemies; the teeth of sinners hast Thou broken. Salvation is of the Lord, and Thy blessing is upon Thy people. I laid me down and slept; I awoke, for the Lord will help me.

Psalm 37

O Lord, rebuke me not in Thine anger, nor chasten me in Thy wrath. For Thine arrows are fastened in me, and Thou hast laid Thy hand heavily upon me. There is no healing in my flesh in the face of Thy wrath; and there is no peace in my bones in the face of my sins. For mine iniquities are risen higher than my head; as a heavy burden have they pressed heavily upon me. My bruises are become noisome and corrupt in the face of my folly. I have been wretched and utterly bowed down until the end; all the day long I went with downcast face. For my loins are filled with mockings, and there is no healing in my flesh. I am afflicted and exceedingly humbled, I have roared from the groaning of my heart. O Lord, before Thee is all my desire, and my groaning is not hid from Thee. My heart is troubled, my strength hath failed me; and the light of mine eyes, even this is not with me. My friends and my neighbours drew nigh over against me and stood, and my nearest of kin stood afar off. And they that sought after my soul used violence; and they that sought evils for me spake vain things, and craftinesses all the day long did they meditate. But as for me, like a deaf man I heard them not, and was as a speechless man that openeth not his mouth. And I became as a man that heareth not, and that hath in his mouth no reproofs. For in Thee have I hoped, O Lord; Thou wilt hearken unto me, O Lord my God. For I said: Let never mine enemies rejoice over me; yea, when my feet were shaken, those men spake boastful words against me. For I am ready for scourges, and my sorrow is continually before me. For I will declare mine iniquity, and I will take heed concerning my sin. But mine enemies live and are made stronger than I, and they that hated me unjustly are multiplied. They that render me evil for good slandered me, because I pursued goodness. Forsake me not, O Lord my God, depart not from me. Be attentive unto my help, O Lord of my salvation.

Psalm 62

O God, my God, unto Thee I rise early at dawn. My soul hath thirsted for Thee; how often hath my flesh longed after Thee in a land barren and untrodden and unwatered. So in the sanctuary have I appeared before Thee to see Thy power and Thy glory. For Thy mercy is better than lives; my lips shall praise Thee. So shall I bless Thee in my life, and in Thy name will I lift up my hands. As with marrow and fatness let my soul be filled, and with lips of rejoicing shall my mouth praise Thee. If I remembered Thee on my bed, at the dawn I meditated on Thee. For Thou art become my helper; in the shelter of Thy wings will I rejoice. My soul hath cleaved after Thee, Thy right hand hath been quick to help me. But as for these, in vain have they sought after my soul; they shall go into the nethermost parts of the earth, they shall be surrendered unto the edge of the sword; portions for foxes shall they be. But the king shall be glad in God, everyone shall be praised that sweareth by Him; for the mouth of them is stopped that speak unjust things. At the dawn I meditated on Thee. For Thou art become my helper; in the shelter of Thy wings will I rejoice. My soul hath cleaved after Thee, Thy right hand hath been quick to help me.

After The Psalm

Glory be to the Father and to the Son and to the Holy Spirit,
Both now and forever and unto the ages of ages. Amen.

Halleluiah, Halleluiah, Halleluiah. Glory to Thee, O God. **(x3)**
Lord. have mercy. **(x3)**

Glory be to the Father and to the Son and to the Holy Spirit,
Both now and forever and unto the ages of ages. Amen.

Psalm 87

O Lord God of my salvation, by day have I cried and by night before Thee. Let my prayer come before Thee, bow down Thine ear unto my supplication. For filled with evils is my soul, and my life unto hades hath drawn nigh. I am counted with them that go down into the pit; I am become as a man without help, free amongst the dead. Like the bodies of the slain that sleep in the grave, whom Thou rememberest no more, and they are cut off from Thy hand. They laid me in the lowest pit, in darkness and in the shadow of death. Against me is Thine anger made strong, and all Thy billows hast Thou brought upon me. Thou hast removed my friends afar from me; they have made me an abomination unto themselves. I have been delivered up, and have not come forth; mine eyes are grown weak from poverty. I have cried unto Thee, O Lord, the whole day long; I have stretched out my hands unto Thee. Nay, for the dead wilt Thou work wonders? Or shall physicians raise them up that they may give thanks unto Thee? Nay, shall any in the grave tell of Thy mercy, and of Thy truth in that destruction? Nay, shall Thy wonders be known in that darkness, and Thy righteousness in that land that is forgotten? But as for me, unto Thee, O Lord, have I cried; and in the morning shall my prayer come before Thee. Wherefore, O Lord, dost Thou cast off my soul and turnest Thy face away from me? A poor man am I, and in troubles from my youth; yea, having been exalted, I was humbled and brought to distress. Thy furies have passed upon me, and Thy terrors have sorely troubled me. They came round about me like water, all the day long they compassed me about together. Thou hast removed afar from me friend and neighbour, and mine acquaintances because of my misery. O Lord God of my salvation, by day have I cried and by night before Thee. Let my prayer come before Thee, bow down Thine ear unto my supplication.

Psalm 102

Bless the Lord, O my soul, and all that is within me bless His holy name. Bless the Lord, O my soul, and forget not all that He hath done for thee, Who is gracious unto all thine iniquities, Who healeth all thine infirmities, Who redeemeth thy life from corruption, Who crowneth thee with mercy and compassion, Who fulfilleth thy desire with good things; thy youth shall be renewed as the eagles. The Lord performeth deeds of mercy, and executeth judgement for all them that are wronged. He hath made His ways known unto Moses, unto the sons of Israel the things that He hath willed. Compassionate and merciful is the Lord, long suffering and plenteous in mercy; not unto the end will He be angered, neither unto eternity will He be wroth. Not according to our iniquities hath He dealt with us, neither according to our sins hath He rewarded us. For according to the height of heaven from the earth, the Lord hath made His mercy to prevail over them that fear Him. As far as the east is from the west, so far hath He removed our iniquities from us. Like as a father hath compassion upon his sons, so hath the Lord had compassion upon them that fear Him; for He knoweth whereof we are made, He hath remembered that we are dust. As for man, his days are as the grass; as a flower of the field, so shall he blossom forth. For when the wind is passed over it, then it shall be gone, and no longer will it know the place thereof. But the mercy of the Lord is from eternity, even unto eternity, upon them that fear Him. And His righteousness is upon sons of sons, upon them that keep His testament and remember His commandments to do them. The Lord in heaven hath prepared His throne, and His kingdom ruleth over all. Bless the Lord, all you His angels, mighty in strength, that perform His word, to hear the voice of His words. Bless the Lord, all you His hosts, His ministers that do His will. Bless the Lord, all you His works, in every place of His dominion. Bless the Lord, O my soul. In every place of His dominion, bless the Lord, O my soul.

Psalm 142

O Lord, hear my prayer, give ear unto my supplication in Thy truth; hearken unto me in Thy righteousness. And enter not into judgement with Thy servant, for in Thy sight shall no man living be justified. For the enemy hath persecuted my soul; he hath humbled my life down to the earth. He hath seated me in darkness as those that have been long dead, and my spirit within me is become despondent; within me my heart is troubled. I remembered days of old, I meditated on all Thy works, I pondered on the creations of Thy hands. I stretched forth my hands unto Thee; my soul thirsteth after thee like a waterless land. Quickly hear me, O Lord; my spirit hath fainted away. Turn not Thy face away from me, lest I be like unto them that go down into the pit. Cause me to hear Thy mercy in the morning; for in Thee have I put my hope. Cause me to know, O Lord, the way wherein I should walk; for unto Thee have I lifted up my soul. Rescue me from mine enemies, O Lord; unto Thee have I fled for refuge. Teach me to do Thy will, for Thou art my God. Thy good Spirit shall lead me in the land of uprightness; for Thy names sake, O Lord, shalt Thou quicken me. In Thy righteousness shalt Thou bring my soul out of affliction, and in Thy mercy shalt Thou utterly destroy mine enemies. And Thou shalt cut off all them that afflict my soul, for I am Thy servant.

Hearken unto me, O Lord, in Thy righteousness, and enter not into judgement with Thy servant. **(x2)**
Thy good Spirit shall lead me in the land of uprightness.

After The Psalm

Glory be to the Father and to the Son and to the Holy Spirit,
Both now and forever and unto the ages of ages. Amen.

Halleluiah, Halleluiah, Halleluiah. Glory to Thee, O God. *(cross and bow)* **(x3)**

O Lord our Hope, glory to Thee.

Great Litany

Deacon: In peace let us pray to the Lord.

People: *Lord, have mercy.*

Deacon: For the peace from above, and the salvation of our souls; let us pray to the Lord.

People: *Lord, have mercy.*

Deacon: For the peace of the whole world, the good estate of the holy churches of God, and the union of all, let us pray to the Lord.

People: *Lord, have mercy.*

Deacon: For this holy temple, and for them that with faith, reverence; and the fear of God enter herein, let us pray to the Lord.

People: *Lord, have mercy.*

Deacon: Again we pray for our His Holiness Patriarch Bartholomew; for our Archbishop Nikitas, whose diocese this is; for the venerable priesthood, the diaconate in Christ, for all the clergy and people, let us pray to the Lord.

People: *Lord, have mercy.*

Deacon: For this land, its authorities and armed forces, let us pray to the Lord.

People: *Lord, have mercy.*

Deacon: For the people of the Holy Orthodox Church, and for their salvation; let us pray to the Lord.

People: *Lord, have mercy.*

Deacon: That He may deliver His people from enemies both visible and invisible, and confirm in us oneness of mind, brotherly love and piety, let us pray to the Lord.

People: *Lord, have mercy.*

Deacon: For this *[city / town / village / monastery]*, for every city and country, and the faithful that dwell therein, let us pray to the Lord.

People: *Lord, have mercy.*

Deacon: For seasonable weather, an abundance of the fruits of the earth, and peaceful times, let us pray to the Lord.

People: *Lord, have mercy.*

Deacon: For travellers by sea, land and air; for the sick, the suffering, the imprisoned, and for their salvation, let us pray to the Lord.

People: *Lord, have mercy.*

Deacon: That we may be delivered from all tribulation, wrath, and necessity, let us pray to the Lord.

People: *Lord, have mercy.*

Deacon: Help us, save us, have mercy on us, and keep us, O God, by Thy grace.

People: *Lord, have mercy.*

Deacon: Calling to remembrance our most holy, most pure, most blessed, glorious Lady Theotokos and Ever Virgin Mary with all the saints, let us commit ourselves and one another and all our life unto Christ our God.

People: *To Thee O Lord.*

Deacon: For unto Thee is due all glory, honour and worship; to the Father, and to the Son, and to the Holy Spirit, now and ever, and unto the ages of ages.

People: *Amen.*

Deacon: Out of the night my spirit waketh at dawn unto Thee, O God;

For Thy commandments are light upon the earth.

Halleluiarion

People: *Halleluiah, Halleluiah, Halleluiah.*

Reader: Learn righteousness, you that dwell upon the earth.

People: *Halleluiah, Halleluiah, Halleluiah.*

Reader: Zeal shall lay hold upon an uninstructed people.

People: *Halleluiah, Halleluiah, Halleluiah.*

Reader: Add more evils upon them, O Lord; add more evils upon them that are glorious upon the earth.

People: *Halleluiah, Halleluiah, Halleluiah.*

Troparion

Tone 8   Humility, tranquillity, repose, suffering, pleading.   *C, D, Eb, F, G, A, Bb, C.*

Behold, the Bridegroom cometh at midnight, and blessed is that servant whom He shall find watching; but unworthy is he whom He shall find heedless. Beware, therefore, O my soul, lest thou be weighed down with sleep; lest thou be given up to death, and be shut out from the kingdom. But rouse thyself and cry: Holy, Holy, Holy art Thou, O God, through the intercessions of the Forerunner, have mercy on us.

Glory be to the Father and to the Son and to the Holy Spirit,

Behold, the Bridegroom cometh at midnight, and blessed is that servant whom He shall find watching; but unworthy is he whom He shall find heedless. Beware, therefore, O my soul, lest thou be weighed down with sleep; lest thou be given up to death, and be shut out from the kingdom. But rouse thyself and cry: Holy, Holy, Holy art Thou, O God, through the intercessions of *[Saint of the parish]* have mercy on us.

Both now and forever and unto the ages of ages. Amen.

Behold, the Bridegroom cometh at midnight, and blessed is that servant whom He shall find watching; but unworthy is he whom He shall find heedless. Beware, therefore, O my soul, lest thou be weighed down with sleep; lest thou be given up to death, and be shut out from the kingdom. But rouse thyself and cry: Holy, Holy, Holy art Thou, O God, through the intercessions of the Theotokos have mercy on us.

Little Litany

Deacon: Again and again, in peace let us pray to the Lord.

People: Lord, have mercy.

Deacon: Help us, save us, have mercy on us, and keep us, O God, by Thy grace.

People: Lord, have mercy.

Deacon: Calling to remembrance our most holy, most pure, most blessed, glorious Lady Theotokos and Ever Virgin Mary with all the saints, let us commit ourselves and one another and all our life unto Christ our God.

People: To Thee, O Lord.

Priest: For Thine is the Kingdom, and the power, and the glory; of the Father, and of the Son, and of the Holy Spirit, now and ever, and unto the ages of ages.

People: Amen.

First Kathisma

Tone 4   Festive, joyous and expressing deep piety.   *C, D, Eb, F, G, A, Bb, C.*

Brethren, let us love the Bridegroom and prepare our lamps with care, shining with the virtues and right faith; that, like the wise virgins of the Lord, we may be ready to enter with Him into the wedding feast. For God the Bridegroom grants to all the crowns incorruptible.

Tone 4   Festive, joyous and expressing deep piety.   *C, D, Eb, F, G, A, Bb, C.*

The priests and scribes with wicked envy gathered a lawless council against Thee, and persuaded Judas to betray Thee. Shamelessly he went and spoke against Thee to the transgressing people: "What will you give me, and I will betray Him into your hands?" Deliver our souls, O Lord, from the condemnation that was his.

Glory be to the Father and to the Son and to the Holy Spirit,
Both now and forever and unto the ages of ages. Amen.

Tone 8   Humility, tranquillity, repose, suffering, pleading.   *C, D, Eb, F, G, A, Bb, C.*

Impious Judas with avaricious thoughts plots against the Master, and ponders how he will betray Him. He falls away from the light and accepts the darkness; he agrees upon the payment and sells Him that is above all price; and as the reward for his actions, in his misery he receives a hangmans noose and death in agony. O Christ our God, deliver us from such a fate as his, and grant remission of sins to those who celebrate with love Thy most pure Passion.

The Orthros Gospel

Deacon: And that He will vouchsafe unto us the hearing of the Holy Gospel, let us pray unto the Lord.

People: *Lord, have mercy.* **(x3)**

Deacon: Wisdom, Aright. Let us hear the Holy Gospel.

Priest: Peace be with you all.

People: *And with thy spirit.*

Priest: The Reading is from the Holy Gospel according to Matthew.

People: *Glory to Thee, O Lord, glory to Thee.*

Deacon: Let us attend.

The Gospel According To Matthew, § 90 To § 96 [Matthew 22:15 -23:39].

Then went the Pharisees, and took counsel how they might entangle him in his talk. And they sent out unto him their disciples with the Herodians, saying: "Master, we know that thou art true, and teachest the way of God in truth, neither carest thou for any for thou regardest not the person of men. Tell us therefore, What thinkest thou? Is it lawful to give tribute unto Caesar, or not?" But Jesus perceived their wickedness, and said, "Why tempt you me, you hypocrites? Shew me the tribute money." And they brought unto him a penny. And he saith unto them; "Whose this image and superscription?" They said unto him; "Caesars." Then saith he unto them; "Render therefore unto Caesar the things which are Caesars; and unto God the things that are God's." When they had heard these words, they marvelled, and left him, and went their way.

The same day came to him the Sadducees, who say that there is no resurrection, and asked him, saying; "Master, Moses said, If a man die, having no children, his brother shall marry his wife, and raise up seed unto his brother. Now there were with us seven brethren: and the first, when he had married a wife, deceased, and, having no issue, left his wife unto his brother. Likewise the second also, and the third, unto the seventh. And last of all the woman died also. Therefore in the resurrection whose wife shall she be of the seven? For they all had her." Jesus answered and said unto them; "You do err, not knowing the scriptures, nor the power of God. For in the resurrection they neither marry, nor are given in marriage, but are as the angels of God in heaven. But as touching the resurrection of the dead, have you not read that which was spoken unto you by God, saying, 'I am the God of Abraham, and the God of Isaac, and the God of Jacob?' God is not the God of the dead, but of the living." And when the multitude heard this, they were astonished at his doctrine.

But when the Pharisees had heard that he had put the Sadducees to silence, they were gathered together. Then one of them, who was a lawyer, asked him a question, tempting him, and saying; "Master, which is the great commandment in the law?" Jesus said unto him; "Thou shalt love the Lord thy God with all thy heart, and with all thy soul, and with all thy mind. This is the first and great commandment. And the second is like unto it, Thou shalt love thy neighbour as thyself. On these two commandments hang all the law and the prophets."

While the Pharisees were gathered together, Jesus asked them, saying; "What think you of Christ? Whose son is he?" They said unto him; "The Son of David." He said unto them, "How then doth David in spirit call him Lord, saying; "The LORD said unto my Lord, Sit thou on my right hand, till I make thine enemies thy footstool? If David then call him Lord, how is he his son?" And no man was able to answer him a word, neither durst any man from that day forth ask him any more questions.

Then spake Jesus to the multitude, and to his disciples, saying; "The scribes and the Pharisees sit in Moses' seat. All therefore whatsoever they bid you observe, observe and do; but do not you after their works: for they say, and do not. For they bind heavy burdens and grievous to be borne, and lay them on men's shoulders; but they themselves will not move them with one of their fingers. But all their works they do for to be seen of men: they make broad their phylacteries, and enlarge the borders of their garments, and love the uppermost rooms at feasts, and the chief seats in the synagogues, and greetings in the markets, and to be called of men, Rabbi, Rabbi. But be not you called Rabbi: for one is your Master, even Christ; and all you are brethren. And call no man your father upon the earth: for one is your Father, which is in heaven. Neither be you called masters: for one is your Master, even Christ. But he that is greatest amongst you shall be your servant. And whosoever shall exalt himself shall be abased; and he that shall humble himself shall be exalted. But woe unto you, scribes and Pharisees, hypocrites. for you shut up the kingdom of heaven against men: for you neither go in yourselves, neither suffer you them that are entering to go in. Woe unto you, scribes and Pharisees, hypocrites. for you devour widows' houses, and for a pretence make long prayer: therefore you shall receive the greater damnation. Woe unto you, scribes and Pharisees, hypocrites. for you compass sea and land to make one proselyte, and when he is made, you make him twofold more the child of hell than yourselves. Woe unto you, you blind guides, which say, Whosoever shall swear by the temple, it is nothing; but whosoever shall swear by the gold of the temple, he is a debtor. You fools and blind: for whether is greater, the gold, or the temple that sanctifieth the gold? And, Whosoever shall swear by the altar, it is nothing; but whosoever sweareth by the gift that is upon it, he is guilty. You fools and blind: for whether is greater, the gift, or the altar that sanctifieth the gift? Whoso therefore shall swear by the altar, sweareth by it, and by all things thereon. And whoso shall swear by the temple, sweareth by it, and by him that dwelleth therein. And he that shall swear by heaven, sweareth by the throne of God, and by him that sitteth thereon. "Woe unto you, scribes and Pharisees, hypocrites. for you pay tithe of mint and anise and cummin, and have omitted the weightier matters of the law, judgement, mercy, and faith: these ought you to have done, and not to leave the other undone. You blind guides, which strain at a gnat, and swallow a camel. Woe unto you, scribes and Pharisees, hypocrites. For you make clean the outside of the cup and of the platter, but within they are full of extortion and excess. Thou blind Pharisee, cleanse first that which is within the cup and platter, that the outside of them may be clean also. Woe unto you, scribes and Pharisees, hypocrites. for you are like unto whited sepulchres, which indeed appear beautiful outward, but are within full of dead men's bones, and of all uncleanness. Even so you also outwardly appear righteous unto men, but within you are full of hypocrisy and iniquity. Woe unto you, scribes and Pharisees, hypocrites. Because you build the tombs of the prophets, and garnish the sepulchres of the righteous, and say, 'If we had been in the days of our fathers, we would not have been partakers with them in the blood of the prophets.' Wherefore you be witnesses unto yourselves, that you are the children of them who killed the prophets. Fill you up then the measure of your fathers. You serpents, you generation of vipers, how can you escape the damnation of hell?

"Wherefore, behold, I send unto you prophets, and wise men, and scribes: and some of them you shall kill and crucify; and some of them shall you scourge in your synagogues, and persecute them from city to city: That upon you may come all the righteous blood shed upon the earth, from the blood of righteous Abel unto the blood of Zacharias son of Barachias, whom you slew between the temple and the altar. Verily I say unto you, All these things shall come upon this generation. O Jerusalem, Jerusalem, thou that killest the prophets, and stonest them which are sent unto thee, how often would I have gathered thy children together, even as a hen gathereth her chickens under her wings, and you would not. Behold, your house is left unto you desolate. For I say unto you, You shall not see me henceforth, till you shall say, 'Blessed is he that cometh in the name of the Lord.'"

People: *Glory to Thee, O Lord, glory to Thee.*

Psalm 50

Have mercy on me, O God, according to Thy great mercy; and according to the multitude of Thy compassions blot out my transgression. Wash me thoroughly from mine iniquity, and cleanse me from my sin. For I acknowledge mine iniquity, and my sin is ever before me. Against Thee, Thee only have I sinned, and done evil in Thy sight, that Thou mayest be found just when Thou speakest, and victorious when Thou art judged. For behold, I was conceived in iniquity, and in sin my mother bore me. For behold, Thou hast loved truth; Thou hast made known to me the hidden and secret things of Thy wisdom. Thou shalt sprinkle me with hyssop, and I shall be made clean; Thou shalt wash me, and I shall be whiter than snow. Make me to hear joy and gladness; that the humbled bones may rejoice. Turn Thy face away from my sins, and blot out all mine iniquities.

Create in me a clean heart, O God, and renew a steadfast spirit within me. Cast me not away from Thy presence, and take not Thy Holy Spirit from me. Restore to me the joy of Thy salvation, and establish me with Thy governing Spirit. I shall teach transgressors Thy ways, and the ungodly shall turn back to Thee. Deliver me from blood guiltiness, O God, the God of my salvation; my tongue shall joyfully declare Thy righteousness. Lord, open my lips, and my mouth shall declare Thy praise. For if Thou hadst desired sacrifice,

I would give it; Thou dost not delight in burnt offerings. A sacrifice to God is a broken spirit; God will not despise a broken and a humbled heart. Do good, O Lord, in Thy good pleasure to Zion, and let the walls of Jerusalem be builded. Then Thou shalt be pleased with a sacrifice of righteousness, with oblation and whole burned offerings. Then shall they offer bulls on Thine altar.

Little Litany

Deacon: Again and again, in peace let us pray to the Lord.

People: *Lord, have mercy.*

Deacon: Help us, save us, have mercy on us, and keep us, O God, by Thy grace.

People: *Lord, have mercy.*

Deacon: Calling to remembrance our most holy, most pure, most blessed, glorious Lady Theotokos and Ever Virgin Mary with all the saints, let us commit ourselves and one another and all our life unto Christ our God.

People: *To Thee, O Lord.*

Priest: For a merciful God art Thou, and the Lover of mankind, and unto Thee do we send up glory: to the Father, and to the Son, and to the Holy Spirit, both now and forever, and unto the ages of ages.

People: *Amen.*

The Kontakion

Tone 2   *Majesty, gentleness, hope, repentance and sadness.*   *E, F, G, Ab, B, C.*

Think, wretched soul, upon the hour of the end; recall with fear how the fig tree was cut down. Work diligently with the talent that is given to thee; be vigilant and cry aloud: May we not be left outside the bridal chamber of Christ.

Ikos

Chorus: Why art thou slothful, O my wretched soul? Why dost thou waste thy days in thinking of unprofitable cares? Why art thou busy with the things that pass away? The last hour is at hand and we shall soon be parted from all that is here. While there is still time, return to soberness and cry: I have sinned against Thee, O my Saviour, do not cut me down like the unfruitful fig tree; but, O Christ, in Thy compassion take pity on me as I call on Thee in fear: May we not be left outside the bridal chamber of Christ.

Reader: On this day we make remembrance of the Parable of the Ten Virgins which Jesus spoke along with others as he was coming to the Passion. It teaches us not to rest as though safe in virginity, but to guard it whenever possible, and not to desist from any virtues and good deeds, especially deeds of mercy, which make the lamp of virginity brilliantly shine. It teaches us also to be ready for our end, not knowing when our hour is coming, as the wise virgins were ready to meet the bride, lest death overtake us and close the door to the heavenly chamber in our face, and we hear the terrible judgement which the foolish virgins heard, "Verily, verily, I know you not."

[Matthew 25:1-13].

Katavasia

Ode VIII

Eirmos

Tone 2   Majesty, gentleness, hope, repentance and sadness.   *E, F, G, Ab, B, C.*

The three holy Children were not obedient to the decree of the tyrant; but when cast into the furnace they confessed God, singing: O all you works of the Lord, bless the Lord.

Let us cast aside slothfulness and go to meet Christ, the immortal Bridegroom, with brightly shining lamps and with hymns crying: O all you works of the Lord, bless you the Lord.

Glory be to the Father and to the Son and to the Holy Spirit;

May there be sufficient oil of fellowship in the vessels of our soul, and then we shall not lose our reward because we have gone to buy oil; and let us sing: O all you works of the Lord, bless you the Lord.

Both now and forever and unto the ages of ages. Amen.

You have all received equal grace from God; cause your talent to increase, with the help of Christ who gave it you, and sing: O all you works of the Lord, bless you the Lord.

Ode IX

Deacon: The Theotokos and Mother of the Light, let us honour and magnify in song.

Eirmos

Tone 2   Majesty, gentleness, hope, repentance and sadness.   *E, F, G, Ab, B, C.*

Thou hast enclosed within thy womb the God whom nothing can enclose, and thou hast brought joy into the world. We sing thy praises, O most holy Virgin.

Glory be to the Father and to the Son and to the Holy Spirit,

"Watch". Thou hast said to Thy disciples, O loving Saviour. "For you know not in what hour the Lord shall come to reward every man."

Both now and forever and unto the ages of ages. Amen.

At Thy fearful second coming, O Master, number me with the sheep at Thy right hand, overlooking the multitude of my sins. Thou hast enclosed within thy womb the God whom nothing can enclose, and thou hast brought joy into the world. We sing thy praises, O most holy Virgin.

Little Litany

Deacon: Again and again, in peace let us pray to the Lord.

People: *Lord, have mercy.*

Deacon: Help us, save us, have mercy on us, and keep us, O God, by Thy grace.

People: *Lord, have mercy.*

Deacon: Calling to remembrance our most holy, most pure, most blessed, glorious Lady Theotokos and Ever Virgin Mary with all the saints, let us commit ourselves and one another and all our life unto Christ our God.

People: *To Thee, O Lord.*

Priest: For all the Hosts of Heaven praise Thee, and unto Thee do we send up glory, to the Father, and to the Son, and to the Holy Spirit, now and ever and unto the ages of ages.

People: *Amen.*

Exapostilarion

Tone 3 *Arrogant, brave, and mature atmosphere.* *F, G, A, A#, C, D, E, F.*

I see Thy bridal chamber adorned, O my Saviour, and I have no wedding garment that I may enter there. Make the robe of my soul to shine, O Giver of Light, and save me. **(x3)**

The Lauds (Praises)
Psalm 148

Tone 1 *Magnificent, happy and earthy.* *C, D, Eb, F, G, A, Bb, C.*

Chorus: *Praise the Lord. Praise the Lord from the heavens; praise Him in the heights. To Thee, O God, is due our song.*

Reader: Praise Him, all His angels; praise Him, all His hosts. To Thee, O God, is due our song.

Psalm 150 - Pt 1

Chorus: *Praise the Lord. Praise God in His sanctuary; praise Him in His mighty firmament. Praise Him for His mighty acts; praise Him according to His excellent greatness.*

Reader: Into the splendour of Thy saints how shall I enter? For I am unworthy, and if I dare to come into the bridal chamber, my clothing will accuse me, since it is not a wedding garment; and I shall be cast out by the Angels, bound hand and foot. Cleanse, O Lord, the filth from my soul and save me in Thy love for mankind.

Psalm 150 - Pt 2

Chorus: *Praise Him with the sound of the trumpet; praise Him with the lute and harp.*

Reader: Into the splendour of Thy saints how shall I enter? For I am unworthy, and if I dare to come into the bridal chamber, my clothing will accuse me, since it is not a wedding garment; and I shall be cast out by the Angels, bound hand and foot. Cleanse, O Lord, the filth from my soul and save me in Thy love for mankind.

Psalm 150 - Pt 3

Chorus: *Praise Him with the timbrel and dance; praise Him with stringed instruments and flutes.*

Reader: I slumber in slothfulness of soul, O Christ the Bridegroom; I have no lamp that burns with virtue, and like the foolish virgins I go wandering when it is time to act. Close not Thy compassionate heart against me, Master, but dispel dark sleep from me and rouse me up; and lead me with the wise virgins into the bridal chamber, where those who feast sing with pure voice unceasingly: O Lord, glory to Thee.

Psalm 150 - Pt 4

Tone 2   *Majesty, gentleness, hope, repentance and sadness.*   *E, F, G, Ab, B, C.*

Chorus: *Praise Him with loud cymbals; praise Him with high sounding cymbals. Let everything that has breath praise the Lord.*

Reader: I slumber in slothfulness of soul, O Christ the Bridegroom; I have no lamp that burns with virtue, and like the foolish virgins I go wandering when it is time to act. Close not Thy compassionate heart against me, Master, but dispel dark sleep from me and rouse me up; and lead me with the wise virgins into the bridal chamber, where those who feast sing with pure voice unceasingly: O Lord, glory to Thee.

Chorus: *Glory be to the Father and to the Son and to the Holy Spirit,*
         Both now and forever and unto the ages of ages. Amen.

Tone 4   *Festive, joyous and expressing deep piety.*   *C, D, Eb, F, G, A, Bb, C.*

Reader: O my soul, thou hast heard the condemnation of him who hid his talent: hide not the word of God. Proclaim His wonders, increase the gifts of grace entrusted to thee, and thou shall enter into the joy of thy Lord.

Lesser Doxology

Glory to God, Who has shown us the Light. Glory to God in the highest, and on earth, peace, good will toward men. We praise Thee. We bless Thee. We worship Thee. We glorify Thee and give thanks to Thee for Thy great glory. O Lord God, Heavenly King, God the Father Almighty. O Lord, the Only Begotten Son, Jesus Christ, and the Holy Spirit. \

O Lord God, Lamb of God, Son of the Father, Who takes away the sins of the world, have mercy on us. Thou, Who takes away the sins of the world, receive our prayer. Thou, Who sittest at the right hand of God the Father, have mercy on us. /

For Thou alone art holy, and Thou alone art Lord. Thou alone, O Lord Jesus Christ, are most high in the glory of God the Father. Amen. I will give thanks to Thee every day and praise Thy Name forever and ever. Lord, Thou hast been our refuge from generation to generation. I said, *"Lord, have mercy on me. Heal my soul, for I have sinned against Thee."* \

Lord, I flee to Thee. Teach me to do Thy will, for Thou art my God. For with Thee is the fountain of Life, and in Thy light we shall see light. Continue Thy loving kindness to those who know Thee. Vouchsafe, O Lord, to keep us this day without sin. Blessed art Thou, O Lord, the God of our fathers, and praised and glorified is Thy Name forever. Amen. Let Thy mercy be upon us, O Lord, even as we have set our hope on Thee.

Blessed art Thou, O Master; teach me Thy statutes.

Blessed art Thou, O Lord; enlighten me with Thy commandments.

Blessed art Thou, O Holy One; make me to understand Thy precepts.

Thy mercy endures forever, O Lord. Do not despise the works of Thy hands. To Thee belongs worship, to Thee belongs praise, to Thee belongs glory: to the Father and to the Son and to the Holy Spirit, both now and forever and unto the ages of ages. Amen. \

Litany Of Supplication

Priest: Let us complete our morning prayer unto the Lord.

People: *Lord, have mercy.*

Priest: Help us, save us, have mercy on us, and keep us, O God, by Thy grace.

People: *Lord, have mercy.*

Priest: That the whole day may be perfect, holy, peaceful and sinless, let us ask of the Lord.

People: *Grant this, O Lord.*

Priest: An angel of peace, a faithful guide, a guardian of our souls and bodies, let us ask of the Lord.

People: *Grant this, O Lord.*

Priest: Pardon and remission of our sins and offences, let us ask of the Lord.

People: *Grant this, O Lord.*

Priest: Things good and profitable for our souls, and peace for the world, let us ask of the Lord.

People: *Grant this, O Lord.*

Priest: That we may complete the remaining time of our life in peace and repentance, let us ask of the Lord.

People: *Grant this, O Lord.*

Priest: A Christian ending to our life, painless, blameless, peaceful, and a good defence before the dread judgement seat of Christ, let us ask.

People: *Grant this, O Lord.*

Priest: Calling to remembrance our most holy, most pure, most blessed, glorious Lady Theotokos and Ever Virgin Mary with all the saints, let us commit ourselves and one another and all our life unto Christ our God.

People: *To Thee, O Lord.*

Priest: For Thou art a God of mercy, compassion, and love for mankind, and unto Thee do we send up glory: to the Father, and to the Son, and to the Holy Spirit, now and ever, and unto the ages of ages.

People: *Amen.*

Priest: Peace be unto all.

People: *And to thy spirit.*

Priest: Let us bow down our heads unto the Lord.

People: *To Thee, O Lord.*

Priest *[soto voce]*: O Holy Lord, who dwelleth on high and regardest the humble of heart, and with thine all seeing eye dost behold all creation, unto Thee have we bowed the neck of our soul and body, and we entreat Thee: O Holy of holies, stretch forth Thine invisible hand from Thy holy dwelling place, and bless us all. And if in aught we have sinned, whether voluntarily or involuntarily, forgive, inasmuch as Thou art a good God, and lovest mankind, vouchsafing unto us Thy earthly and heavenly good things.

Priest *[aloud]*: For Thine it is to show mercy and to save us, O our God, and unto Thee do we send up glory: to the Father, and to the Son, and to the Holy Spirit, now and ever, and unto the ages of ages.

People: *Amen.*

The Aposticha

Tone 6   Rich texture, funereal character, sorrowful tone.   *D, Eb, F##, G, A, Bb, C##, D.*

Come, you faithful, and let us serve the Master eagerly, for He gives riches to His servants. Each of us according to the measure that we have received, let us increase the talent of grace. Let one gain wisdom through good deeds; let another celebrate the Liturgy with beauty; let another share his faith by preaching to the uninstructed; let another give his wealth to the poor. So shall we increase what is entrusted to us, and as faithful stewards of His grace we shall be counted worthy of the Master's joy. Bestow this joy upon us, Christ our God, in Thy love for mankind.

Stichos

We were filled in the morning with Thy mercy, O Lord and we rejoiced and were glad. In all our days, let us be glad for the days wherein Thou didst humble us, for the years wherein we saw evils. And look upon Thy servants, and upon Thy works, and do Thou guide their sons.

When Thou shalt come, O Jesus, in glory with the angelic hosts and shalt sit upon the throne of judgement, do not send me from Thy presence, O good Shepherd. Thou dost accept those who stand upon the right, but those upon the left have turned away from Thee. Destroy me not with the goats, though I am hardened in sin, but number me with the sheep on Thy right hand, and save me in Thy love for mankind.

Stichos

Tone 8   Humility, tranquillity, repose, suffering, pleading.   *C, D, Eb, F, G, A, Bb, C.*

And let the brightness of the Lord our God be upon us, and the works of our hand do Thou guide aright upon us, yea, the work of our hands do Thou guide aright.

O Bridegroom, surpassing all in beauty, Thou hast called us to the spiritual feast of Thy bridal chamber. Strip from me the disfigurement of sin, through participation in Thy sufferings; clothe me in the glorious robe of Thy beauty, and in Thy compassion make me feast with joy at Thy Kingdom.

Glory be to the Father and to the Son and to the Holy Spirit,
Both now and forever and unto the ages of ages. Amen.

Tone 7   Manly character and strong melody.   *F, G, A, A#, C, D, E, F.*

Behold my soul, the Master entrusts thee with a talent. Receive His gift with fear; make it gain interest for Him; distribute to the needy, and make the Lord thy friend. So shalt thou stand on the right hand when He comes in glory, and thou shalt hear His blessed words: "Enter, servant, into the joy of thy Lord." I have gone astray, O Saviour, but in Thy great mercy count me worthy of this joy.

Priest: It is good to give praise unto the Lord, and to chant unto Thy name, O Most High, to proclaim in the morning Thy mercy, and Thy truth by night.

Trisagion

Holy God, Holy Mighty, Holy Immortal, have mercy on us. **(x3)**

Glory be to the Father and to the Son and to the Holy Spirit,
Both now and forever and unto the ages of ages. Amen.

O Most Holy Trinity, have mercy on us.
O Lord, cleanse us from our sins.
O Master, pardon our iniquities.
O Holy One, visit and heal our infirmities, for Thy names sake.

Lord have mercy. **(x3)**

Glory be to the Father and to the Son and to the Holy Spirit,
Both now and forever and unto the ages of ages. Amen.

People: *Our Father, Who art in Heaven, hallowed be Thy Name. Thy Kingdom come, Thy will be done, on earth as it is in Heaven. Give us this day our daily bread, and forgive us our trespasses, as we forgive those who trespass against us; and lead us not into temptation, but deliver us from the evil one.*
Priest: For Thine is the Kingdom, and the power, and the glory; of the Father, and of the Son, and of the Holy Spirit, now and ever, and unto the ages of ages.
People: *Amen.*

Kontakion

Reader: Think, wretched soul, upon the hour of the end; recall with fear how the fig tree was cut down. Work diligently with the talent that is given to thee; be vigilant and cry aloud: May we not be left outside the bridal chamber of Christ.

Lord have mercy. **(x40)**

Glory be to the Father and to the Son and to the Holy Spirit,
Both now and forever and unto the ages of ages. Amen.

Greater in honour than the Cherubim and beyond compare more glorious than the Seraphim; without corruption thou gavest birth to God the Word, truly the Theotokos, we magnify thee.

People: *Holy Father bless.*

Priest: He that is is blessed, Christ our God, always, now and ever; and unto the ages of ages.

People: *Amen.*

Reader: O Heavenly King, strengthen Orthodox Christians, establish the Faith, subdue the nations, give peace to the world, keep well this *[city / town / village / monastery]*; settle our departed fathers and brethren in the tabernacles of the righteous, and receive us in penitence and confession, for Thou art good and the Lover of mankind.

Prayer Of St Ephraim The Syrian

Priest: O Lord and Master of my life, a spirit of idleness, despondency, ambition, and idle talking give me not. *prostration*

Priest: But rather a spirit of chastity, humble mindedness, patience, and love bestow upon me Thy servant. *prostration*

Priest: Yea, O Lord King, grant me to see mine own failings and not condemn my brother; for blessed art Thou unto the ages of ages. Amen. *prostration*

Priest: O Lord and Master of my life, a spirit of idleness, despondency, ambition, and idle talking give me not. But rather a spirit of chastity, humble mindedness, patience, and love bestow upon me Thy servant. Yea, O Lord King, grant me to see mine own failings and not condemn my brother; for blessed art Thou unto the ages of ages. Amen. *prostration*

Dismissal

[Now or after the first hour]

Priest: Glory to Thee, O Christ our God and our hope, glory to Thee.

Reader: *Glory be to the Father and to the Son and to the Holy Spirit,*

Both now and forever and unto the ages of ages. Amen.

Lord, have mercy. **(x3)**

Holy Father, bless.

Priest: May Christ our true God, the Lord who for our salvation went to His voluntary Passion, through the intercessions of His most pure Mother; of the holy and glorious apostles; of the holy and righteous ancestors of God, Joachim and Anna; and of all the saints: have mercy on us and save us, for He is good and lovest mankind.

People: *Amen.*

[Then the reader immediately begins the first hour.]

Reader:

Come, let us worship God, our King.

Come, let us worship and fall down before Christ, our King and our God.

Come, let us worship and fall down before Christ Himself, our King and our God.

Psalm 5

Unto my words give ear, O Lord, hear my cry. Attend unto the voice of my supplication, O my King and my God; for unto Thee will I pray, O Lord. In the morning shalt Thou hear my voice. In the morning shall I stand before Thee, and Thou shalt look upon me; for not a God that willest iniquity art Thou. He that worketh evil shall not dwell near Thee nor shall transgressors abide before Thine eyes. Thou hast hated all them that work iniquity; Thou shalt destroy all them that speak a lie. A man that is bloody and deceitful shall the Lord abhor. But as for me, in the multitude of Thy mercy shall I go into Thy house; I shall worship toward Thy holy temple in fear of Thee. O Lord, guide me in the way of Thy righteousness; because of mine enemies, make straight my way before Thee, For in their mouth there is no truth; their heart is vain. Their throat is an open sepulchre, with their tongues have they spoken deceitfully; judge them, O God. Let them fall down on account of their own devisings; according to the multitude of their ungodliness, cast them out, for they have embittered Thee, O Lord. And let all them be glad that hope in Thee; they shall rejoice, and Thou shalt dwell amongst them. And all shall glory in Thee that love Thy name, for Thou shalt bless the righteous. O Lord, as with a shield of Thy good pleasure hast Thou crowned us.

Psalm 89

Lord, Thou hast been our refuge in generation and generation. Before the mountains came to be and the earth was formed and the world, even from everlasting to everlasting art Thou. Turn not man away unto lowliness; yea, Thou hast said: Turn back you sons of men. For a thousand years in Thine eyes, O Lord, are but as yesterday that is past, and as a watch in the night. Things of no account shall their years be; in the morning like grass shall man pass away. In the morning shall he bloom and pass away. In the evening shall he fall and grow withered and dry. For we have fainted away in Thy wrath, and in Thine anger have we been troubled. Thou hast set our iniquities before us; our lifespan is in the light of Thy countenance. For all our days are faded away, and in Thy wrath are we fainted away; our years have, like a spider, spun out their tale. As for the days of our years, in their span, they be threescore years and ten. And if we be in strength, mayhap fourscore years; and what is more than these is toil and travail. For mildness is come upon us, and we shall be chastened. Who knoweth the might of Thy wrath? And out of fear of Thee, who can recount Thine anger? So make Thy right hand known to me, and to them that in their heart are instructed in wisdom. Return, O Lord; how long? And be Thou entreated concerning Thy servants. We were filled in the morning with Thy mercy, O Lord, and we rejoiced and were glad. In all our days, let us be glad for the days wherein Thou didst humble us, for the years wherein we saw evils. And look upon Thy servants, and upon Thy works, and do Thou guide their sons. And let the brightness of the Lord our God be upon us, and the works of our hands do Thou guide aright upon us, yea, the works of our hands do Thou guide aright.

Psalm 100

Of mercy and judgement will I sing to Thee, O Lord; I will chant and have understanding in a blameless path. When wilt Thou come unto me? I have walked in the innocence of my heart in the midst of my house. I have no unlawful thing before mine eyes; the workers of transgressions I have hated. A crooked heart hath not cleaved unto me; as for the wicked man who turned from me, I knew him not. Him that privily talked against his neighbour did I drive away from me. With him whose eye was proud and his heart insatiate, I did not eat. Mine eyes were upon the faithful of the land, that they might sit with me; the man that walked in the blameless path, he ministered unto me. The proud doer dwelt not in the midst of my house; the speaker of unjust things prospered not before mine eyes. In the morning I slew all the sinners of the land, utterly to destroy out of the city of the Lord all them that work iniquity.

After The Psalm

Glory be to the Father, and to the Son, and to the Holy Spirit;
Both now and forever, and unto the ages of ages. Amen.

Halleluiah, Halleluiah, Halleluiah. Glory to Thee, O God. **(x3)**

Lord, have mercy. **(x3)**

Tone 6 *Rich texture, funereal character, sorrowful tone.*		*D, Eb, F##, G, A, Bb, C##, D.*
Priest:	In the morning, hearken unto my voice, O my king and God.	
Chorus:	*In the morning, hearken unto my voice, O my king and God.*	*prostration*
Priest:	Unto my words give ear, O Lord, hear my cry.	
Chorus:	*In the morning, hearken unto my voice, O my king and God.*	*prostration*
Priest:	For unto Thee will I pray, O Lord.	
Chorus:	*In the morning, hearken unto my voice, O my king and God.*	*prostration*
Priest:	Glory be to the Father and to the Son and to the Holy Spirit,	
Reader:	Both now and forever and unto the ages of ages. Amen.	

Theotokion

What shall we call thee, O thou who art full of grace? Heaven, for from thee hast dawned forth the Sun of Righteousness. Paradise, for from thee hath blossomed forth the flower of immortality. Virgin, for thou hast remained incorrupt. Pure Mother, for thou hast held in thy holy embrace the Son, the God of all. Do thou entreat Him to save our souls.

Tone 6 *Rich texture, funereal character, sorrowful tone.*	*D, Eb, F##, G, A, Bb, C##, D.*
My steps do Thou direct according to thy saying, and let no iniquity have dominion over me.	**(x2)**
Deliver me from the false accusations of men, and I will keep Thy commandments.	**(x2)**
Make Thy face to shine upon Thy servant, and teach me Thy statutes.	**(x2)**
Let my mouth be filled with Thy praise, O Lord, that I may hymn Thy glory and majesty all the day long.	**(x3)**

Holy God, Holy Mighty, Holy Immortal, have mercy on us. **(x3)**

Glory be to the Father and to the Son and to the Holy Spirit,
Both now and forever and unto the ages of ages. Amen.

O Most Holy Trinity, have mercy on us.

O Lord, cleanse us from our sins.

O Master, pardon our iniquities.

O Holy One, visit and heal our infirmities, for Thy names sake.

Lord have mercy. **(x3)**

Glory be to the Father and to the Son and to the Holy Spirit,
Both now and forever and unto the ages of ages. Amen.

People: *Our Father, Who art in Heaven, hallowed be Thy Name. Thy Kingdom come, Thy will be done, on earth as it is in Heaven. Give us this day our daily bread, and forgive us our trespasses, as we forgive those who trespass against us; and lead us not into temptation, but deliver us from the evil one.*

Priest: For Thine is the Kingdom, and the power, and the glory; of the Father, and of the Son, and of the Holy Spirit, now and ever, and unto the ages of ages.

People: *Amen.*

Lord, have mercy. **(x40)**

The Prayer Of The Hours

At all times and in every hour, Thou art worshipped and glorified in heaven and on earth, Christ our God. Long in patience, great in mercy and compassion, Thou lovest the righteous and showest mercy to sinners. Thou callest all to salvation through the promise of good things to come. Lord, receive our prayers at the present time. Direct our lives according to Thy commandments. Sanctify our souls. Purify our bodies. Set our minds aright. Cleanse our thoughts, and deliver us from all sorrow, evil and distress. Surround us with Thy holy angels, that, guarded and guided by their host, we may arrive at the unity of the faith and the understanding of Thine ineffable glory. For Thou art blessed to the ages of ages. Amen.

Lord, have mercy. **(x3)**

Glory be to the Father and to the Son and to the Holy Spirit,
Both now and forever and unto the ages of ages. Amen.

Greater in honour than the Cherubim and beyond compare more glorious than the Seraphim; without corruption thou gavest birth to God the Word, truly the Theotokos, we magnify thee.

Holy Father bless.

Priest: God be gracious unto us and bless us, and cause Thy face to shine upon us and have mercy on us.
People: Amen.

Priest: O Lord and Master of my life, a spirit of idleness, despondency, ambition, and idle talking give me not.   ***prostration***

But rather a spirit of chastity, humble mindedness, patience, and love bestow upon me Thy servant.
                    prostration

Yea, O Lord King, grant me to see mine own failings and not condemn my brother; for blessed art Thou unto the ages of ages. Amen.   ***prostration***

O God, cleanse me a sinner. *[cross and bow]* **(x12)**

O Lord and Master of my life, a spirit of idleness, despondency, ambition, and idle talking give me not. But rather a spirit of chastity, humble mindedness, patience, and love bestow upon me Thy servant. Yea, O Lord King, grant me to see mine own failings and not condemn my brother; for blessed art Thou unto the ages of ages.
People: Amen.   ***prostration***

Reader: Holy God, Holy Mighty, Holy Immortal, have mercy on us. **(x3)**

Glory be to the Father and to the Son and to the Holy Spirit,
Both now and forever and unto the ages of ages. Amen.

O Most Holy Trinity, have mercy on us.
O Lord, cleanse us from our sins.
O Master, pardon our iniquities.
O Holy One, visit and heal our infirmities, for Thy names sake.

Lord have mercy. **(x3)**

Glory be to the Father and to the Son and to the Holy Spirit,
Both now and forever and unto the ages of ages. Amen.

People: *Our Father, Who art in Heaven, hallowed be Thy Name. Thy Kingdom come, Thy will be done, on earth as it is in Heaven. Give us this day our daily bread, and forgive us our trespasses, as we forgive those who trespass against us; and lead us not into temptation, but deliver us from the evil one.*

Priest: For Thine is the Kingdom, and the power, and the glory; of the Father, and of the Son, and of the Holy Spirit, now and ever, and unto the ages of ages.

People: *Amen.*

Lord, have mercy. **(x12)**

The Prayer Of The First Hour

Priest: O Christ, the True Light, Who enlightenest and sanctifiest every man that cometh into the world: Let the Light of Thy countenance be signed upon us, that in it we may see the Unapproachable Light, and guide our steps in the doing of Thy commandments, through the intercessions of Thy most pure Mother, and of all Thy saints. Amen.

Kontakion For The Annunciation

Tone 8   Humility, tranquillity, repose, suffering, pleading.   *C, D, Eb, F, G, A, Bb, C.*

To Thee, the Champion Leader, we Thy servants dedicate a feast of victory and of thanksgiving as ones rescued out of sufferings, O Theotokos: but as Thou art one with might, which is invincible, from all dangers that can be, do Thou deliver us, that we may cry to Thee: Rejoice, Thou Bride Unwedded.

Dismissal

Priest: Glory to Thee, O Christ our God and our hope, glory to Thee.

Reader: *Glory be to the Father and to the Son and to the Holy Spirit,*

Both now and forever and unto the ages of ages. Amen.

Lord, have mercy. **(x3)**

Holy Father, bless.

Priest: May Christ our true God, the Lord who for our salvation went to His voluntary Passion, through the intercessions of His most pure Mother; of the holy and glorious apostles; of the holy and righteous ancestors of God, Joachim and Anna; and of all the saints: have mercy on us and save us, for He is good and lovest mankind.

People: *Amen.*

[For Tuesday Evening]

The Trisagion Prayers

Priest: Blessed is our God, always, now and ever, and unto the ages of ages.

People: *Amen.*

Priest: Glory to Thee, our God, glory to Thee.

O Heavenly King, Comforter, Spirit of Truth, Who art everywhere present and fillest all things, Treasury of blessings and Giver of life: Come and abide in us and cleanse us from every impurity and save our souls, O Good One.

Reader: Holy God, Holy Mighty, Holy Immortal, have mercy on us. **(x3)**

Glory be to the Father, and to the Son, and to the Holy Spirit;

Both now and forever, and unto the ages of ages. Amen.

O Most Holy Trinity, have mercy on us.

O Lord, cleanse us from our sins.

O Master, pardon our iniquities.

O Holy One, visit and heal our infirmities, for Thy names sake.

Lord have mercy. **(x3)**

Glory be to the Father, and to the Son, and to the Holy Spirit;

Both now and forever, and unto the ages of ages. Amen.

People: *Our Father, Who art in Heaven, hallowed be Thy Name. Thy Kingdom come, Thy will be done, on earth as it is in Heaven. Give us this day our daily bread, and forgive us our trespasses, as we forgive those who trespass against us; and lead us not into temptation, but deliver us from the evil one.*

Priest: For Thine is the kingdom and the power and the glory of the Father and of the Son and of the Holy Spirit; both now and forever and unto the ages of ages.

People: *Amen.*

Lord, have mercy. **(x12)**

Glory be to the Father, and to the Son, and to the Holy Spirit;

Both now and forever, and unto the ages of ages. Amen.

Come, let us worship God, our King.

Come, let us worship and fall down before Christ, our King and our God.

Come, let us worship and fall down before Christ Himself, our King and our God.

Psalm 19

The Lord hear thee in the day of affliction; the name of the God of Jacob defend thee. Let Him send forth unto thee help from His sanctuary, and out of Zion let Him help thee. Let Him remember every sacrifice of thine, and thy whole burnt offering let Him fatten. The Lord grant thee according to thy heart, and fulfil all thy purposes. We will rejoice in Thy salvation, and in the name of the Lord our God shall we be magnified. The Lord fulfil all thy requests. Now have I known that the Lord hath saved His anointed one; He will hearken unto him out of His holy heaven; in mighty deeds is the salvation of His right hand. Some trust in chariots, and some in horses, but we will call upon the name of the Lord our God. They have been fettered and have fallen, but we are risen and are set upright. O Lord, save the king, and hearken unto us in the day when we call upon Thee.

Psalm 20

O Lord, in Thy strength the king shall be glad, and in Thy salvation shall he exceedingly rejoice. The desire of his heart hast Thou granted unto him, and hast not denied him the requests of his lips. Thou wentest before him with the blessings of goodness, Thou hast set upon his head a crown of precious stone. He asked life of Thee, and Thou gavest him length of days unto ages of ages. Great is his glory in Thy salvation; glory and majesty shalt Thou lay upon him. For Thou shalt give him blessing for ever and ever, Thou shalt gladden him in joy with Thy countenance. For the king hopeth in the Lord, and through the mercy of the Most High shall he not be shaken. Let Thy hand be found on all Thine enemies; let Thy right hand find all that hate Thee. For Thou wilt make them as an oven of fire in the time of Thy presence; the Lord in His wrath will trouble them sorely and fire shall devour them. Their fruit wilt Thou destroy from the earth, and their seed from the sons of men. For they have intended evil against Thee, they have devised counsels which they shall not be able to establish. For Thou shalt make them turn their backs; amongst those that are Thy remnant, Thou shalt make ready their countenance. Be Thou exalted, O Lord, in Thy strength; we will sing and chant of Thy mighty acts.

Holy God, Holy Mighty, Holy Immortal, have mercy on us. **(x3)**

Glory be to the Father, and to the Son, and to the Holy Spirit;

Both now and forever, and unto the ages of ages. Amen.

O Most Holy Trinity, have mercy on us.

O Lord, cleanse us from our sins.

O Master, pardon our iniquities.

O Holy One, visit and heal our infirmities, for Thy names sake.

Lord have mercy. **(x3)**

People: *Our Father, Who art in Heaven, hallowed be Thy Name. Thy Kingdom come, Thy will be done, on earth as it is in Heaven. Give us this day our daily bread, and forgive us our trespasses, as we forgive those who trespass against us; and lead us not into temptation, but deliver us from the evil one.*

Priest: For Thine is the kingdom and the power, and the glory: of the Father and of the Son, and of the Holy Spirit, now and ever, and unto the ages of ages.

People: *Amen.*

Troparia

O Lord, save Thy people and bless Thine inheritance. Grant victory unto Orthodox Christians over their enemies, and by the power of Thy Cross do Thou preserve Thy commonwealth.

Glory be to the Father and to the Son and to the Holy Spirit,

O Thou Who wast lifted up willingly upon the Cross, bestow Thy mercies upon the new community named after Thee, O Christ God; gladden with Thy power the Orthodox Christians, granting them victory over enemies; may they have as Thy help the weapon of peace, the invincible trophy.

Both now and forever and unto the ages of ages. Amen.

O Awesome intercession that cannot be put to shame, O good one, disdain not our prayer; O all hymned Theotokos, establish the commonwealth of the Orthodox, save the Orthodox Christians, and grant unto them victory from heaven, for thou didst bring forth God, O thou only blessed one.

Augmented Ektenia

Priest: Have mercy on us, O God, according to Thy great mercy, we pray Thee, hearken and have mercy.

People: *Lord, have mercy.* **(x3)**

Priest: Again we pray for all the brethren and for all Orthodox Christians.

People: *Lord, have mercy.* **(x3)**

Priest: Again we pray for His Holiness Patriarch Bartholomew and for our Archbishop Nikitas.

People: *Lord, have mercy.* **(x3)**

Priest: For a merciful God art Thou, and the Lover of mankind, and unto Thee do we send up glory: to the Father, and to the Son, and to the Holy Spirit, both now and forever, and unto the ages of ages.

People: *Amen. Holy Father bless.*

Priest: Glory to the holy, and consubstantial, and life creating, and indivisible Trinity, always, both now and forever, and unto the ages of ages.

People: *Amen.*

The Six Psalms

Reader: Glory to God in the highest, and on earth peace, good will amongst men. *(cross and bow)* **(x3)**

Chorus: *O Lord, Thou shalt open my lips, and my mouth shall declare Thy praise.* **(x2)**

Psalm 3

Lord, how they have increased who trouble me. Many are they who rise up against me. Many are they who say of me, "There is no help for him in God." But Thou, O Lord, art a shield for me, my glory and the One Who lifts up my head. I cried to the Lord with my voice, and He heard me from His holy hill. I lay down and slept; I awoke, for the Lord sustained me. I will not be afraid of ten thousands of people who have set themselves against me all around. Arise, O Lord; save me, O my God. For Thou hast struck all mine enemies on the cheekbone; Thou hast broken the teeth of the ungodly. Salvation belongs to the Lord. Thy blessing is upon Thy people.

Psalm 37

O Lord, do not rebuke me in Thy wrath, nor chasten me in Thy hot displeasure. For Thine arrows deeply pierce me, and Thine hand presses me down. There is no soundness in my flesh because of Thine anger, Nor is there any health in my bones because of my sin. For mine iniquities have gone over my head; like a heavy burden they are too heavy for me. My wounds are foul and festering because of my foolishness. I am troubled, I am bowed down greatly; I go mourning all the day long. For my loins are full of inflammation, and there is no soundness in my flesh. I am feeble and severely broken; I groan because of the turmoil of my heart. Lord, all my desire is before Thee; and my sighing is not hidden from Thee. My heart pants, my strength fails me; as for the light of mine eyes, it also has gone from me. My loved ones and my friends stand aloof from my plague, and my kinsmen stand afar off. Those also who seek my life lay snares for me; those who seek my hurt speak of destruction, and plan deception all the day long. But I, like a deaf man, do not hear; and I am like a mute who does not open his mouth. Thus I am like a man who does not hear, and in whose mouth is no response. For in Thee, O Lord, I hope; Thou wilt hear, O Lord my God. For I said, *"Hear me, lest they rejoice over me, lest, when my foot slips, they magnify themselves against me."* For I am ready to fall, and my sorrow is continually before me. For I will declare mine iniquity; I will be in anguish over my sin. But mine enemies are vigorous, and they are strong; and those who wrongfully hate me have multiplied. Those also who render evil for good, they are mine adversaries, because I follow what is good. Do not forsake me, O Lord; O my God, be not far from me. Make haste to help me, O Lord, my salvation.

Psalm 62

O God, Thou art my God; early will I seek Thee; my soul thirsts for Thee; My flesh longs for Thee in a dry and thirsty land where there is no water. So I have looked for Thee in the sanctuary, to see Thy power and Thy glory. Because Thy loving kindness is better than life, my lips shall praise Thee. Thus I will bless Thee while I live; I will lift up my hands in Thy name. My soul shall be satisfied as with marrow and fatness, and my mouth shall praise Thee with joyful lips. When I remember Thee on my bed, I meditate on Thee in the night watches. Because Thou hast been my help, therefore in the shadow of Thy wings I will rejoice. My soul follows close behind Thee; Thy right hand upholds me. But those who seek my life, to destroy it, shall go into the lower parts of the earth. They shall fall by the sword; they shall be a portion for jackals. But the king shall rejoice in God; everyone who swears by Him shall glory; but the mouth of those who speak lies shall be stopped.

After The Psalm

Glory be to the Father and to the Son and to the Holy Spirit,
Both now and forever and unto the ages of ages. Amen.

Halleluiah, Halleluiah, Halleluiah. Glory to Thee, O God. **(x3)**
Lord. have mercy. **(x3)**

Glory be to the Father and to the Son and to the Holy Spirit,
Both now and forever and unto the ages of ages. Amen.

Psalm 87

O Lord, God of my salvation, I have cried out day and night before Thee. Let my prayer come before Thee; incline Thine ear to my cry. For my soul is full of troubles, and my life draws near to the grave. I am counted with those who go down to the pit; I am like a man who has no strength, Adrift among the dead, like the slain who lie in the grave, whom Thou rememberest no more, and who are cut off from Thine hand. Thou hast laid me in the lowest pit, in darkness, in the depths. Thy wrath lies heavy upon me, and Thou hast afflicted me with all Thy waves. Thou hast put away mine acquaintances far from me; Thou hast made me an abomination to them; I am shut up, and I cannot get out; Mine eye wastes away because of affliction. Lord, I have called daily upon Thee; I have stretched out my hands to Thee. Willest Thou work wonders for the dead? Shall the dead arise and praise Thee? Shall Thy loving kindness be declared in the grave? Or Thy faithfulness in the place of destruction? Shall Thy wonders be known in the dark? And Thy righteousness in the land of forgetfulness? But to Thee I have cried out, O Lord, and in the morning my prayer comes before Thee. Lord, why dost Thou cast off my soul? Why dost Thou hide Thy face from me? I have been afflicted and ready to die from my youth up; I suffer Thy terrors; I am distraught. Thy fierce wrath has gone over me; Thy terrors have cut me off. They came around me all day long like water; they engulfed me altogether. Loved one and friend Thou hast put far from me, and mine acquaintances into darkness.

Psalm 102

Bless the Lord O my soul; and all that is within me, bless His holy name. Bless the Lord O my soul, and forget not all His benefits: Who forgives all thine iniquities, Who heals all thy diseases, Who redeems thy life from destruction, Who crowns thee with loving kindness and tender mercies, Who satisfies thy mouth with good things, so that thine youth is renewed like the eagles. The Lord executes righteousness and justice for all who are oppressed. He made known His ways to Moses, His acts to the children of Israel. The Lord is merciful and gracious, slow to anger, and abounding in mercy. He will not always strive with us, nor will He keep His anger forever. He has not dealt with us according to our sins, nor punished us according to our iniquities. For as the heavens are high above the earth, so great is His mercy toward those who fear Him; As far as the east is from the west, so far has He removed our transgressions from us. As a father pities his children, so the Lord pities those who fear Him. For He knows our frame; He remembers that we are dust. As for man, his days are like grass; as a flower of the field, so he flourishes. For the wind passes over it, and it is gone, and its place remembers it no more. But the mercy of the Lord is from everlasting to everlasting on those who fear Him, and His righteousness to childrens children, To such as keep His covenant, and to those who remember His commandments to do them. The Lord has established His throne in heaven, and His kingdom rules overall. Bless the Lord you His angels, who excel in strength, who do His word, heeding the voice of His word. Bless the Lord all you His hosts, you ministers of His, who do His pleasure. Bless the Lord all His works, in all places of His dominion. Bless the Lord O my soul.

Psalm 142

Lord, hear my prayer; in Thy truth give ear to my supplications; in Thy righteousness hear me. Enter not into judgement with Thy servant, for no one living is justified in Thy sight. For the enemy has pursued my soul; he has crushed my life to the ground. He has made me to dwell in darkness, like those that have long been dead, and my spirit within me is overwhelmed; my heart within me is distressed. I remembered the days of old, I meditated on all Thy works, I pondered on the creations of Thine hands. I stretched forth my hands to Thee; my soul longs for Thee like a thirsty land. Lord, hear me quickly; my spirit fails. Turn not Thy face away from me, lest I be like those who go down into the pit. Let me hear Thy mercy in the morning; for in Thee have I put my trust. Lord, teach me to know the way wherein I should walk; for I lift up my soul to Thee. Rescue me, Lord, from mine enemies, to Thee have I fled for refuge. Teach me to do Thy will, for Thou art my God. Thy good Spirit shall lead me on a level path. Lord, for Thy names sake Thou shalt preserve my life. In Thy righteousness Thou shalt bring my soul out of trouble, and in Thy mercy Thou shalt utterly destroy my enemies. And Thou shalt destroy all those who afflict my soul, for I am Thy servant.

Hearken unto me, O Lord, in Thy righteousness, and enter not into judgement with Thy servant. **(x2)**
Thy good Spirit shall lead me in the land of uprightness.

After The Psalm

Glory be to the Father and to the Son and to the Holy Spirit,
Both now and forever and unto the ages of ages. Amen.

Halleluiah, Halleluiah, Halleluiah. Glory to Thee, O God. *(cross and bow)* **(x3)**

O Lord our Hope, glory to Thee.

Great Litany

Deacon: In peace let us pray to the Lord.

People: *Lord, have mercy.*

Deacon: For the peace from above, and the salvation of our souls; let us pray to the Lord.

People: *Lord, have mercy.*

Deacon: For the peace of the whole world, the good estate of the holy churches of God, and the union of all, let us pray to the Lord.

People: *Lord, have mercy.*

Deacon: For this holy temple, and for them that with faith, reverence; and the fear of God enter herein, let us pray to the Lord

People: *Lord, have mercy.*

Deacon: Again we pray for our His Holiness Patriarch Bartholomew; for our Archbishop Nikitas, whose diocese this is; for the venerable priesthood, the diaconate in Christ, for all the clergy and people, let us pray to the Lord.

People: *Lord, have mercy.*

Deacon: For this land, its authorities and armed forces, let us pray to the Lord.

People: *Lord, have mercy.*

Deacon: For this *[city / town / village / monastery]*, for every city and country, and the faithful that dwell therein, let us pray to the Lord.

People: *Lord, have mercy.*

Deacon: For seasonable weather, an abundance of the fruits of the earth, and peaceful times, let us pray to the Lord.

People: *Lord, have mercy.*

Deacon: For travellers by sea, land and air; for the sick, the suffering, the imprisoned, and for their salvation, let us pray to the Lord.

People: *Lord, have mercy.*

Deacon: That we may be delivered from all tribulation, wrath, and necessity, let us pray to the Lord.

People: *Lord, have mercy.*

Deacon: Help us, save us, have mercy on us, and keep us, O God, by Thy grace.

People: *Lord, have mercy.*

Deacon: Calling to remembrance our most holy, most pure, most blessed, glorious Lady Theotokos and Ever Virgin Mary with all the saints, let us commit ourselves and one another and all our life unto Christ our God.

People: *To Thee O Lord.*

Priest: For unto Thee is due all glory, honour and worship; to the Father, and to the Son, and to the Holy Spirit, now and ever, and unto the ages of ages.

People: *Amen.*

Halleluiarion

Reader: Out of the night my spirit waketh at dawn unto Thee, O God;

For Thy commandments are light upon the earth.

People: *Halleluiah, Halleluiah, Halleluiah.*

Reader: Learn righteousness, you that dwell upon the earth.

People: *Halleluiah, Halleluiah, Halleluiah.*

Reader: Zeal shall lay hold upon an uninstructed people.

People: *Halleluiah, Halleluiah, Halleluiah.*

Reader: Add more evils upon them O Lord. Add more evils upon them that are glorious upon the earth.

People: *Halleluiah, Halleluiah, Halleluiah.*

Troparion

Tone 8   Humility, tranquillity, repose, suffering, pleading.   C, D, Eb, F, G, A, Bb, C.

Behold, the Bridegroom cometh at midnight, and blessed is that servant whom He shall find watching; but unworthy is he whom He shall find heedless. Beware, therefore, O my soul, lest thou be weighed down with sleep; lest thou be given up to death, and be shut out from the kingdom. But rouse thyself and cry: Holy, Holy, Holy art Thou, O God, by the power of Thy Cross, have mercy on us.

Glory be to the Father and to the Son and to the Holy Spirit,

Behold, the Bridegroom cometh at midnight, and blessed is that servant whom He shall find watching; but unworthy is he whom He shall find heedless. Beware, therefore, O my soul, lest thou be weighed down with sleep; lest thou be given up to death, and be shut out from the kingdom. But rouse thyself and cry: Holy, Holy, Holy art Thou, O God, through the intercessions of *[the saint of the parish]* have mercy on us.

Both now and forever and unto the ages of ages. Amen.

Behold, the Bridegroom cometh at midnight, and blessed is that servant whom He shall find watching; but unworthy is he whom He shall find heedless. Beware, therefore, O my soul, lest thou be weighed down with sleep; lest thou be given up to death, and be shut out from the kingdom. But rouse thyself and cry: Holy, Holy, Holy art Thou, O God, through the intercessions of the Theotokos have mercy on us.

Little Litany

Deacon: Again and again, in peace let us pray to the Lord.

People: *Lord, have mercy.*

Deacon: Help us, save us, have mercy on us, and keep us, O God, by Thy grace.

People: *Lord, have mercy.*

Deacon: Calling to remembrance our most holy, most pure, most blessed, glorious Lady Theotokos and Ever Virgin Mary with all the saints, let us commit ourselves and one another and all our life unto Christ our God.

People: *To Thee, O Lord.*

Priest: For Thine is the majesty and Thine is the kingdom and the power and the glory of the Father and of the Son and of the Holy Spirit; both now and forever and unto the ages of ages.

People: *Amen.*

Kathisma

Troparia

Tone 3   Arrogant, brave, and mature atmosphere.   *F, G, A, A#, C, D, E, F.*

The harlot drew near Thee, O Thou who lovest mankind, and poured out on Thy feet the oil of myrrh with her tears; and at Thy command she was delivered from the foul smell of her evil deeds. But the ungrateful disciple, though he breathed Thy grace, rejected it and defiled himself in filth, selling Thee from love of money. Glory be to Thy compassion, O Christ.

Glory be to the Father and to the Son and to the Holy Spirit,

Tone 4   Festive, joyous and expressing deep piety.   *C, D, Eb, F, G, A, Bb, C.*

Deceitful Judas, in his love for money, pondered cunningly how he might betray Thee, O Lord, the Treasure of Life. Therefore in drunken folly he hastened to the Jews and said to the transgressors: "What will you give me, and I will deliver Him unto you to be crucified?"

Both now and forever and unto the ages of ages. Amen.

Tone 1   Magnificent, happy and earthy.   *C, D, Eb, F, G, A, Bb, C.*

To Thee the harlot cried lamenting, O merciful Lord; ardently she wiped Thy pure feet with the hair of her head, and from the depth of her heart she groaned: "Cast me not from Thee, neither abhor me, O my God, but receive me in repentance and save me, for Thou alone lovest mankind."

The Orthros Gospel

Deacon: That He will vouchsafe unto us the hearing of the Holy Gospel, let us pray to the Lord God.

People: *Lord, have mercy.* **(x3)**

Deacon: Wisdom, Attend. Let us hear the Holy Gospel.

Priest: Peace be with you all.

People: *And with thy spirit.*

Priest: The Reading is from the Holy Gospel according to John.

People: *Glory to Thee, O Lord, glory to Thee.*

Deacon: Let us attend.

The Gospel According To John, § 41 Half Through § 44 [John 12:17-50].

Priest: The people therefore who were with him when he called Lazarus out of his grave, and raised him from the dead, bore record. For this cause the people also met him, for that they heard that he had done this miracle. The Pharisees therefore said amongst themselves, "Perceive you how you prevail nothing? Behold, the world is gone after him." And there were certain Greeks amongst them that came up to worship at the feast: The same came therefore to Philip, which was of Bethsaida of Galilee, and desired him, saying, "Sir, we would see Jesus." Philip cometh and telleth Andrew: and again Andrew and Philip tell Jesus. And Jesus answered them, saying, "The hour is come, that the Son of man should be glorified. Verily, verily, I say unto you, Except a corn of wheat fall into the ground and die, it abideth alone: but if it die, it bringeth forth much fruit. He that loveth his life shall lose it; and he that hateth his life in this world shall keep it unto life eternal. If any man serve me, let him follow me; and where I am, there shall also my servant be: if any man serve me, him will my Father honour. Now is my soul troubled; and what shall I say? Father, save me from this hour: but for this cause came I unto this hour. Father, glorify thy name." Then came there a voice from heaven, saying, "I have both glorified it, and will glorify it again."

The people therefore, that stood by, and heard it, said that it thundered: others said, "An angel spoke to him." Jesus answered and said, "This voice came not because of me, but for your sakes. Now is the judgement of this world: now shall the prince of this world be cast out. And I, if I be lifted up from the earth, will draw all men unto me." This he said, signifying what death he should die. The people answered him, "We have heard out of the law that Christ abideth for ever: and how sayest thou, The Son of man must be lifted up? Who is this Son of man?"

Then Jesus said unto them, "Yet a little while is the light with you. Walk while you have the light, lest darkness come upon you: for he that walketh in darkness knoweth not whither he goeth. While you have light, believe in the light, that you may be the children of light." These things spoke Jesus, and departed, and did hide himself from them.

But though he had done so many miracles before them, yet they believed not on him: That the saying of Isaiah the prophet might be fulfilled, which he spoke, "Lord, who hath believed our report? And to whom hath the arm of the Lord been revealed?" Therefore they could not believe, because that Isaiah said again, "He hath blinded their eyes, and hardened their heart; that they should not see with their eyes, nor understand with their heart, and be converted, and I should heal them." These things said Isaiah, when he saw his glory, and spoke of him.

Nevertheless amongst the chief rulers also many believed on him; but because of the Pharisees they did not confess Him, lest they should be put out of the synagogue: For they loved the praise of men more than the praise of God. Jesus cried and said, "He that believeth on me, believeth not on me, but on him that sent me. And he that seeth me seeth him that sent me. I am come a light into the world, that whosoever believeth on me should not abide in darkness. And if any man hear my words, and believe not, I judge him not: for I came not to judge the world, but to save the world. He that rejecteth me, and receiveth not my words, hath one that judgeth him: the word that I have spoken, the same shall judge him in the last day. For I have not spoken of myself; but the Father which sent me, he gave me a commandment, what I should say, and what I should speak. And I know that his commandment is life everlasting: whatsoever I speak therefore, even as the Father said unto me, so I speak."

People: *Glory to Thee, O Lord, glory to Thee.*

Psalm 50

Reader: Have mercy on me, O God, according to Thy great mercy; and according to the multitude of Thy compassions blot out my transgression. Wash me thoroughly from mine iniquity, and cleanse me from my sin. For I acknowledge mine iniquity, and my sin is ever before me. Against Thee, Thee only have I sinned, and done evil in Thy sight, that Thou mayest be found just when Thou speakest, and victorious when Thou art judged. For behold, I was conceived in iniquity, and in sin my mother bore me. For behold, Thou hast loved truth; Thou hast made known to me the hidden and secret things of Thy wisdom. Thou shalt sprinkle me with hyssop, and I shall be made clean; Thou shalt wash me, and I shall be whiter than snow. Make me to hear joy and gladness; that the humbled bones may rejoice. Turn Thy face away from my sins, and blot out all mine iniquities.

Create in me a clean heart, O God, and renew a steadfast spirit within me. Cast me not away from Thy presence, and take not Thy Holy Spirit from me. Restore to me the joy of Thy salvation, and establish me with Thy governing Spirit. I shall teach transgressors Thy ways, and the ungodly shall turn back to Thee. Deliver me from blood guiltiness, O God, the God of my salvation; my tongue shall joyfully declare Thy righteousness. Lord, open my lips, and my mouth shall declare Thy praise. For if Thou hadst desired sacrifice, I would give it; Thou dost not delight in burnt offerings. A sacrifice to God is a broken spirit; God will not despise a broken and a humbled heart. Do good, O Lord, in Thy good pleasure to Zion, and let the walls of Jerusalem be builded. Then Thou shalt be pleased with a sacrifice of righteousness, with oblation and whole burned offerings. Then shall they offer bulls on Thine altar.

Little Litany

Deacon: Again and again, in peace let us pray to the Lord.

People: *Lord, have mercy.*

Deacon: Help us, save us, have mercy on us, and keep us, O God, by Thy grace.

People: *Lord, have mercy.*

Deacon: Calling to remembrance our most holy, most pure, most blessed, glorious Lady Theotokos and Ever Virgin Mary with all the saints, let us commit ourselves and one another and all our life unto Christ our God.

People: *To Thee, O Lord.*

Priest: For Thou art a merciful God and lovest mankind, and to Thee we ascribe glory to the Father and to the Son and to the Holy Spirit; both now and forever and unto the ages of ages.

People: *Amen.*

Katavasia - The Canon

Ode III

Eirmos

Tone 2   Majesty, gentleness, hope, repentance and sadness.   *E, F, G, Ab, B, C.*

By establishing me on the rock of faith, Thou hast enlarged my mouth over mine enemies, and my spirit rejoiceth when I sing: There is none holy as our God, and none righteous beside Thee, O Lord.

Glory be to the Father and to the Son and to the Holy Spirit;

In vain the Sanhedrin of the transgressors gathers together with an evil purpose, to pronounce sentence of condemnation upon Thee, O Christ our Deliverer, to whom we sing: Thou art our God and none is holy save Thee, O Lord.

Both now and forever, and unto the ages of ages. Amen.

The wicked assembly of the transgressors, with souls full of hatred for God, considers how to kill as a malefactor the righteous Christ, to whom we sing: Thou art our God and there is none holy save Thee, O Lord. By establishing me on the rock of faith, Thou hast enlarged my mouth over mine enemies, and my spirit rejoiceth when I sing: There is none holy as our God, and none righteous beside Thee, O Lord.

Little Litany

Deacon: Again and again, in peace let us pray to the Lord.

People: *Lord, have mercy.*

Deacon: Help us, save us, have mercy on us, and keep us, O God, by Thy grace.

People: *Lord, have mercy.*

Deacon: Calling to remembrance our most holy, most pure, most blessed, glorious Lady Theotokos and Ever Virgin Mary with all the saints, let us commit ourselves and one another and all our life unto Christ our God.

People: *To Thee, O Lord.*

Priest: For Thou art a merciful God and lovest mankind, and to Thee we ascribe glory to the Father and to the Son and to the Holy Spirit; both now and forever and unto the ages of ages.

People: *Amen.*

Kontakion

Tone 4   Festive, joyous and expressing deep piety.   *C, D, Eb, F, G, A, Bb, C.*

I have transgressed more than the harlot, O loving Lord, yet never have I offered Thee my flowing tears. But in silence I fall down before Thee and with love I kiss Thy most pure feet, beseeching Thee as Master to grant me remission of sins; and I cry to Thee, O Saviour: Deliver me from the filth of my works.

Ikos

The woman who was once a prodigal suddenly became chaste, and hating the works of shameful sin and the pleasures of the body, she thought upon her deep disgrace and the torment to which harlots and prodigals shall be condemned. Of them I am the first and I am afraid, yet senselessly I continue in my evil ways. But the woman who was a harlot, filled with fear, made haste and came crying to the Deliverer: "O merciful Lord who lovest mankind, deliver me from the filth of my works."

Synaxarion Of Great And Holy Wednesday

[Plain reading] The more accurate and exacting of the commentators on the four Gospels say that two women anointed the Lord, one long before his Passion, and one a few days before. One of these was a harlot, whilst the other was a chaste, virtuous woman. On this day the Church commemorates this act of piety and righteousness which proceeded from the harlot, contrasting it with the treachery of Judas and his Betrayal of Christ. Both of these acts fell on Wednesday, corresponding to the twenty first of March, two days before the Mosaic Passover, as it appears from the course of the account of Saint Matthew the Evangelist.

The above mentioned harlot anointed the head and feet of Jesus with spikenard, and wiped them with the hair of her head. The precious ointment was worth three thousand dinars, or about fifteen pieces of Venetian gold. When the disciples saw this they stumbled, especially Judas, the money lover, and were angry because of the wasting of such an amount of ointment. Jesus rebuked them, lest the woman be embarrassed. Judas was wroth, and went to the high priests, where they were gathered in the house of Caiaphas, taking counsel against Jesus, and agreed with them to deliver the Master for thirty pieces of silver. From that time Judas sought an opportunity to deliver Him (Matthew 26:2-16). Because of this the fast of Wednesday was instituted from the days of the apostolic age itself.

[Chant] Wherefore, O Christ God, anointed with the super sensuous ointment, deliver us from suffering, and have mercy upon us.

Katavasia Continued
Ode VIII

Eirmos

Tone 2   Majesty, gentleness, hope, repentance and sadness.   *E, F, G, Ab, B, C.*

The command of the tyrant prevailed, and the furnace was heated sevenfold. Yet the flames did not burn the Children, who had trampled underfoot the decree of the king, but they cried aloud: "O all you works of the Lord, praise you the Lord and exalt Him above all forever."

The woman poured precious oil of myrrh upon Thine awesome and royal head, O Christ our God, and she laid hold of Thy pure feet with her polluted hands and cried aloud: "O all you works of the Lord, praise you the Lord and exalt Him above all forever."

Glory be to the Father and to the Son and to the Holy Spirit;

Guilty of sin, she washed with tears the feet of her Creator and wiped them with her hair; and so she received forgiveness for all that she had done in life, and she cried aloud: "O all you works of the Lord, praise you the Lord and exalt Him above all forever."

Both now and forever, and unto the ages of ages. Amen.

Through the saving love for God and the fountain of her tears, the grateful woman was ransomed from her sins; washed clean by her confession, she was not ashamed but cried aloud: "O all you works of the Lord, praise you the Lord and exalt Him above all forever."

We praise, we bless, and we worship the Lord.

The command of the tyrant prevailed, and the furnace was heated sevenfold. Yet the flames did not burn the Children, who had trampled underfoot the decree of the king, but they cried aloud: "O all you works of the Lord, praise you the Lord and exalt Him above all forever."

Ode IX

Deacon: The Theotokos and Mother of the Light, let us honour and magnify in song.

Eirmos

Tone 2   Majesty, gentleness, hope, repentance and sadness.   *E, F, G, Ab, B, C.*

With pure souls and unpolluted lips, come and let us magnify the undefiled and most holy Mother of Emmanuel, and through her let us bring our prayer to the Child she bore: Spare our souls, O Christ our God, and save us.

Ungrateful and envious in his wickedness, wretched Judas calculates the value of the gift worthy of God, whereby the woman gained release from the debt of her sins, and he traffics in the grace of divine love. Spare our souls, O Christ our God, and save us.

Glory be to the Father and to the Son and to the Holy Spirit;

Judas goes to the lawless rulers and says: "What will you give me, if I deliver to you Christ whom you seek?" And so in exchange for money he rejects fellowship with Christ. Spare our souls, O Christ our God and save us.

Both now and forever, and unto the ages of ages. Amen.

Unrelenting in blind avarice, how hast thou forgotten what Christ taught thee, that thy soul is more in value than the whole world. For in despair, O traitor, thou hast hanged thyself. Spare our souls, O Christ our God, and save us.

With pure souls and unpolluted lips, come and let us magnify the undefiled and most holy Mother of Emmanuel, and through her let us bring our prayer to the Child she bore: Spare our souls, O Christ our God, and save us.

Little Litany

Deacon: Again and again, in peace let us pray to the Lord.

People: *Lord, have mercy.*

Deacon: Help us, save us, have mercy on us, and keep us, O God, by Thy grace.

People: *Lord, have mercy.*

Deacon: Calling to remembrance our most holy, most pure, most blessed, glorious Lady Theotokos and Ever Virgin Mary with all the saints, let us commit ourselves and one another and all our life unto Christ our God.

People: *To Thee, O Lord.*

Priest: For all the Hosts of Heaven praise Thee, and unto Thee do we send up glory, to the Father, and to the Son, and to the Holy Spirit, now and ever and unto the ages of ages.

People: *Amen.*

Exapostilarion

Tone 3 *Arrogant, brave, and mature atmosphere.* *F, G, A, A#, C, D, E, F.*

I see Thy bridal chamber adorned, O my Saviour, and I have no wedding garment that I may enter there. Make the robe of my soul to shine, O Giver of Light, and save me.

Glory be to the Father and to the Son and to the Holy Spirit,

I see Thy bridal chamber adorned, O my Saviour, and I have no wedding garment that I may enter there. Make the robe of my soul to shine, O Giver of Light, and save me.

Both now and forever and unto the ages of ages. Amen.

I see Thy bridal chamber adorned, O my Saviour, and I have no wedding garment that I may enter there. Make the robe of my soul to shine, O Giver of Light, and save me.

Lauds (The Praises)
Psalm 148 – extract.

Tone 1 *Magnificent, happy and earthy.* *C, D, Eb, F, G, A, Bb, C.*

Chorus: *Let everything that has breath praise the Lord. Praise the Lord from the heavens;*
Praise Him in the heights.

Reader: To Thee, O God, is due our song.

Chorus: *Praise Him, all His angels; praise Him, all His hosts.*

Reader: To Thee, O God, is due our song.

Psalm 150 - Pt 1

Chorus: *Praise the Lord. Praise God in His sanctuary; praise Him in His mighty firmament. Praise Him for His mighty acts; praise Him according to His excellent greatness.*

Reader: O Son of the Virgin, the harlot knew Thee to be God and she prayed to Thee lamenting, for she had committed sins worthy of tears. "Loose me from my debt", she cried, "as I unloose my hair. Show love to her who loves Thee, though rightly she deserves Thy hatred, and with the publicans I shall proclaim Thee, O Benefactor who lovest mankind."

Psalm 150 - Pt 2

Chorus: *Praise Him with the sound of the trumpet; praise Him with the lute and harp.*

Reader: The harlot mingled precious oil of myrrh with her tears and poured it on Thy most pure feet, as she kissed them; and straightway Thou hast proclaimed her justified. To us also grant forgiveness, O Lord who hast suffered for our sake, and save us.

Psalm 150 - Pt 3

Chorus: *Praise Him with the timbrel and dance; praise Him with stringed instruments and flutes.*

Reader: While the sinful woman brought oil of myrrh, the disciple came to an agreement with the transgressors. She rejoiced to pour out what was very precious, he made haste to sell the One who is above all price. She acknowledged Christ as Lord, he severed himself from the Master. She was set free, but Judas became the slave of the enemy. Grievous was his lack of love. Great was her repentance. Grant such repentance also unto me, O Saviour who hast suffered for our sake, and save us.

Psalm 150 - Pt 4

Chorus: *Praise Him with loud cymbals; praise Him with high sounding cymbals. Let everything that has breath praise the Lord.*

Reader: O misery of Judas. He saw the harlot kiss Thy feet, and deceitfully he plotted to betray Thee with a kiss. She loosed her hair and he was bound a prisoner by fury, bearing in place of myrrh the stink of evil: for envy knows not how to choose its own advantage. O misery of Judas. From this deliver our souls, O God.

Glory be to the Father, and to the Son, and to the Holy Spirit;

Tone 2   Majesty, gentleness, hope, repentance and sadness.   E, F, G, Ab, B, C.

The sinful woman hastened to buy precious oil of myrrh, with which to anoint the Benefactor, and she cried aloud to the merchant: "Give me oil of myrrh that I may anoint Him who has cleansed me from all my sins."

Both now and forever, and unto the ages of ages. Amen.

Tone 6   Rich texture, funereal character, sorrowful tone.   *D, Eb, F##, G, A, Bb, C##, D.*

Drowning in sin, she found in Thee a haven of salvation, and pouring out the oil of myrrh with her tears, she cried to Thee: "Lo, Thou art He who accepts the repentance of the sinful. O Master, save me from the waves of sin in Thy great mercy."

Lesser Doxology

Glory to God, Who has shown us the Light. Glory to God in the highest, and on earth, peace, good will toward men. We praise Thee. We bless Thee. We worship Thee. We glorify Thee and give thanks to Thee for Thy great glory. O Lord God, Heavenly King, God the Father Almighty. O Lord, the Only Begotten Son, Jesus Christ, and the Holy Spirit. \

O Lord God, Lamb of God, Son of the Father, Who takes away the sins of the world, have mercy on us. Thou, Who takes away the sins of the world, receive our prayer. Thou, Who sittest at the right hand of God the Father, have mercy on us. /

For Thou alone art holy, and Thou alone art Lord. Thou alone, O Lord Jesus Christ, are most high in the glory of God the Father. Amen. I will give thanks to Thee every day and praise Thy Name forever and ever. Lord, Thou hast been our refuge from generation to generation. I said, *"Lord, have mercy on me. Heal my soul, for I have sinned against Thee."* \

Lord, I flee to Thee. Teach me to do Thy will, for Thou art my God. For with Thee is the fountain of Life, and in Thy light we shall see light. Continue Thy loving kindness to those who know Thee. Vouchsafe, O Lord, to keep us this day without sin. Blessed art Thou, O Lord, the God of our fathers, and praised and glorified is Thy Name forever. Amen. Let Thy mercy be upon us, O Lord, even as we have set our hope on Thee.

Blessed art Thou, O Master; teach me Thy statutes.

Blessed art Thou, O Lord; enlighten me with Thy commandments.

Blessed art Thou, O Holy One; make me to understand Thy precepts.

Thy mercy endures forever, O Lord. Do not despise the works of Thy hands. To Thee belongs worship, to Thee belongs praise, to Thee belongs glory: to the Father and to the Son and to the Holy Spirit, both now and forever and unto the ages of ages. Amen. \

Litany Of Supplication

Priest: Let us complete our morning prayer unto the Lord.

People: Lord, have mercy.

Priest: Help us, save us, have mercy on us, and keep us, O God, by Thy grace.

People: Lord, have mercy.

Priest: That the whole day may be perfect, holy, peaceful and sinless, let us ask of the Lord.

People: Grant this, O Lord.

Priest: An angel of peace, a faithful guide, a guardian of our souls and bodies, let us ask of the Lord.

People: Grant this, O Lord.

Priest: Pardon and remission of our sins and offences, let us ask of the Lord.

People: Grant this, O Lord.

Priest: Things good and profitable for our souls, and peace for the world, let us ask of the Lord.

People: Grant this, O Lord.

Priest: That we may complete the remaining time of our life in peace and repentance, let us ask of the Lord.

People: Grant this, O Lord.

Priest: A Christian ending to our life, painless, blameless, peaceful, and a good defence before the dread judgement seat of Christ, let us ask.

People: Grant this, O Lord.

Priest: Calling to remembrance our most holy, most pure, most blessed, glorious Lady Theotokos and Ever Virgin Mary with all the saints, let us commit ourselves and one another and all our life unto Christ our God.

People: To Thee, O Lord.

Priest: For Thou art a God of mercy, compassion, and love for mankind, and unto Thee do we send up glory: to the Father, and to the Son, and to the Holy Spirit, now and ever, and unto the ages of ages.

People: Amen.

Priest: Peace be with you all.

People: And with thy spirit.

Priest: Let us bow down our heads unto the Lord.

People: To Thee, O Lord.

Priest *[soto voce]*: O Holy Lord, who dwelleth on high and regardest the humble of heart, and with thine all seeing eye dost behold all creation, unto Thee have we bowed the neck of our soul and body, and we entreat Thee: O Holy of holies, stretch forth Thine invisible hand from Thy holy dwelling place, and bless us all. And if in aught we have sinned, whether voluntarily or involuntarily, forgive, inasmuch as Thou art a good God, and lovest mankind, vouchsafing unto us Thy earthly and heavenly good things.

Priest *[aloud]*: For Thine it is to show mercy and to save us, O our God, and unto Thee do we send up glory: to the Father, and to the Son, and to the Holy Spirit, now and ever, and unto the ages of ages.

People: Amen.

The Aposticha

Tone 6   Rich texture, funereal character, sorrowful tone.   *D, Eb, F##, G, A, Bb, C##, D.*

Reader: Today Christ comes to the house of the Pharisee, and the sinful woman draws near and falls down at His feet, crying: "Behold me sunk in sin, filled with despair by reason of my deeds, yet not rejected by Thy love. Grant me, Lord, remission of my sins, and save me."

Chorus: We were filled in the morning with Thy mercy, O Lord and we rejoiced and were glad.

Reader: The harlot spread out her hair before Thee, O Master, while Judas stretched out his hands to the transgressors: she, to receive forgiveness; and he, to receive money. Therefore we cry aloud to Thee who wast sold and hast set us free: O Lord, glory to Thee.

Chorus: In all our days, let us be glad for the days wherein Thou didst humble us, for the years wherein we saw evils. And look upon Thy servants, and upon Thy works, and do Thou guide their sons.

Reader: Evil smelling and defiled, the woman drew near to Thee, shedding tears upon Thy feet, O Saviour, and proclaiming Thy Passion. "How can I look upon Thee, O Master? Yet Thou hast come to save the harlot. I am dead: raise me from the depths, as Thou has raised Lazarus on the fourth day from the tomb. Accept me in my wretchedness, O Lord, and save me."

Chorus: *And let the brightness of the Lord our God be upon us, and the works of our hand do Thou guide aright upon us, yea, the work of our hands do Thou guide aright.*

Reader: Full of despair on account of her life, her evil ways well known, she came to Thee, bearing oil of myrrh, and cried aloud: "Harlot though I am, cast me not out, O Son of the Virgin; despise not my tears, O Joy of the angels; but receive me in repentance, O Lord, and in Thy great mercy reject me not, a sinner."

Chorus: *Glory be to the Father, and to the Son, and to the Holy Spirit;*
Both now and forever and unto the ages of ages. Amen.

The Hymn Of Kassiani

Tone 8   Humility, tranquillity, repose, suffering, pleading.   *C, D, Eb, F, G, A, Bb, C.*

Reader: The woman who had fallen into many sins, perceiving Thy divinity, O Lord, fulfilled the part of a myrrh bearer; and with lamentations she brought sweet smelling oil of myrrh to Thee before Thy burial. "Woe is me", she said, "for night surrounds me, dark and moonless, and stings my lustful passion with the love of sin. Accept the fountain of my tears, O Thou who drawest down from the clouds the waters of the sea. Incline to the groanings of my heart, O Thou who in Thine ineffable self emptying hast bowed down the heavens. I shall kiss Thy most pure feet and wipe them with the hairs of my head, those feet whose sound Eve heard at dusk in Paradise, and hid herself for fear. Who can search out the multitude of my sins and the abyss of Thy judgements, O Saviour of my soul? Despise me not, Thine handmaiden, for Thou hast mercy without measure."

Priest: It is good to give praise unto the Lord, and to chant unto Thy name, O Most High, to proclaim in the morning Thy mercy, and Thy truth by night.

The Trisagion Prayers

Holy God, Holy Mighty, Holy Immortal, have mercy on us. **(x3)**

Glory be to the Father and to the Son and to the Holy Spirit,
Both now and forever and unto the ages of ages. Amen.

O Most Holy Trinity, have mercy on us.
O Lord, cleanse us from our sins.
O Master, pardon our iniquities.
O Holy One, visit and heal our infirmities, for Thy names sake.

Lord have mercy. **(x3)**

Glory be to the Father and to the Son and to the Holy Spirit,
Both now and forever and unto the ages of ages. Amen.

People: *Our Father, Who art in Heaven, hallowed be Thy Name. Thy Kingdom come, Thy will be done, on earth as it is in Heaven. Give us this day our daily bread, and forgive us our trespasses, as we forgive those who trespass against us; and lead us not into temptation, but deliver us from the evil one.*

Priest: For Thine is the Kingdom, and the power, and the glory; of the Father, and of the Son, and of the Holy Spirit, now and ever, and unto the ages of ages.

People: *Amen.*

Kontakion

Reader: I have sinned against Thee, O Good One, more than the adulterous woman, and have not even offered Thee a flood of tears. But silently and calmly I kneel asking, kissing Thy pure feet with longing, that Thou mayest grant me O Saviour, since Thou art the Master, remission of my sins, I who cry: Deliver me from the mire of my deeds.

Lord have mercy. **(x40)**

Chorus: *Glory be to the Father and to the Son and to the Holy Spirit,*
Both now and forever and unto the ages of ages. Amen.

Reader: Greater in honour than the Cherubim and beyond compare more glorious than the Seraphim; without corruption thou gavest birth to God the Word, truly the Theotokos, we magnify thee.

People: *Holy Father bless.*

Priest: He that is is blessed, Christ our God, always, now and forever; and unto the ages of ages.

People: *Amen.*

Priest: O Heavenly King, strengthen Orthodox Christians, establish the Faith, subdue the nations, give peace to the world, keep well this *[city / town / village / monastery]*; settle our departed fathers and brethren in the tabernacles of the righteous, and receive us in penitence and confession, for Thou art good and the Lover of mankind.

Prayer Of St Ephraim The Syrian

Priest: O Lord and Master of my life, a spirit of idleness, despondency, ambition, and idle talking give me not.   *prostration*

Priest: But rather a spirit of chastity, humble mindedness, patience, and love bestow upon me Thy servant.

prostration

Priest: Yea, O Lord King, grant me to see mine own failings and not condemn my brother; for blessed art Thou unto the ages of ages. Amen.   *prostration*

Priest: O God, cleanse me a sinner. *(cross and bow)* **(x12)**

Priest: O Lord and Master of my life, a spirit of idleness, despondency, ambition, and idle talking give me not. But rather a spirit of chastity, humble mindedness, patience, and love bestow upon me Thy servant. Yea, O Lord King, grant me to see mine own failings and not condemn my brother; for blessed art Thou unto the ages of ages. Amen.   *prostration*

Prayers Before The Holy Doors

Priest: Glory to Thee, O Christ our God and our Hope, glory to Thee.

Chorus: *Glory be to the Father and to the Son and to the Holy Spirit,*

Both now and forever and unto the ages of ages. Amen.

Lord Have mercy. **(x3)**

Holy Father, bless.

Priest: May He who is going to His voluntary passion for our salvation, Christ our true God, through the intercessions of his all immaculate and all blameless holy Mother, by the might of the precious and life giving Cross, of *[saint of the parish]*, of the holy and righteous ancestors of God Joachim and Anna, and of all the Saints, have mercy on us and save us, forasmuch as He is good and the lover of mankind.

Through the prayers of our Holy Fathers, O Lord Jesus Christ our God, have mercy on us and save us.

People: Amen.

[Then the reader immediately begins the first hour.]

Reader:

Come, let us worship God, our King.

Come, let us worship and fall down before Christ, our King and our God.

Come, let us worship and fall down before Christ Himself, our King and our God.

Psalm 5

Unto my words give ear, O Lord, hear my cry. Attend unto the voice of my supplication, O my King and my God; for unto Thee will I pray, O Lord. In the morning shalt Thou hear my voice. In the morning shall I stand before Thee, and Thou shalt look upon me; for not a God that willest iniquity art Thou. He that worketh evil shall not dwell near Thee nor shall transgressors abide before Thine eyes. Thou hast hated all them that work iniquity; Thou shalt destroy all them that speak a lie. A man that is bloody and deceitful shall the Lord abhor. But as for me, in the multitude of Thy mercy shall I go into Thy house; I shall worship toward Thy holy temple in fear of Thee. O Lord, guide me in the way of Thy righteousness; because of mine enemies, make straight my way before Thee, For in their mouth there is no truth; their heart is vain. Their throat is an open sepulchre, with their tongues have they spoken deceitfully; judge them, O God. Let them fall down on account of their own devisings; according to the multitude of their ungodliness, cast them out, for they have embittered Thee, O Lord. And let all them be glad that hope in Thee; they shall rejoice, and Thou shalt dwell among them. And all shall glory in Thee that love Thy name, for Thou shalt bless the righteous. O Lord, as with a shield of Thy good pleasure hast Thou crowned us.

Psalm 89

Lord, Thou hast been our refuge in generation and generation. Before the mountains came to be and the earth was formed and the world, even from everlasting to everlasting art Thou. Turn not man away unto lowliness; yea, Thou hast said: Turn back you sons of men. For a thousand years in Thine eyes, O Lord, are but as yesterday that is past, and as a watch in the night. Things of no account shall their years be; in the morning like grass shall man pass away. In the morning shall he bloom and pass away. In the evening shall he fall and grow withered and dry. For we have fainted away in Thy wrath, and in Thine anger have we been troubled. Thou hast set our iniquities before us; our lifespan is in the light of Thy countenance. For all our days are faded away, and in Thy wrath are we fainted away; our years have, like a spider, spun out their tale. As for the days of our years, in their span, they be threescore years and ten. And if we be in strength, mayhap fourscore years; and what is more than these is toil and travail. For mildness is come upon us, and we shall be chastened. Who knoweth the might of Thy wrath? And out of fear of Thee, who can recount Thine anger? So make Thy right hand known to me, and to them that in their heart are instructed in wisdom. Return, O Lord; how long? And be Thou entreated concerning Thy servants. We were filled in the morning with Thy mercy, O Lord, and we rejoiced and were glad. In all our days, let us be glad for the days wherein Thou didst humble us, for the years wherein we saw evils. And look upon Thy servants, and upon Thy works, and do Thou guide their sons. And let the brightness of the Lord our God be upon us, and the works of our hands do Thou guide aright upon us, yea, the works of our hands do Thou guide aright.

Psalm 100

Of mercy and judgement will I sing to Thee, O Lord; I will chant and have understanding in a blameless path. When wilt Thou come unto me? I have walked in the innocence of my heart in the midst of my house. I have no unlawful thing before mine eyes; the workers of transgressions I have hated. A crooked heart hath not cleaved unto me; as for the wicked man who turned from me, I knew him not. Him that privily talked against his neighbour did I drive away from me. With him whose eye was proud and his heart insatiate, I did not eat. Mine eyes were upon the faithful of the land, that they might sit with me; the man that walked in the blameless path, he ministered unto me. The proud doer dwelt not in the midst of my house; the speaker of unjust things prospered not before mine eyes. In the morning I slew all the sinners of the land, utterly to destroy out of the city of the Lord all them that work iniquity.

After The Psalm

Glory be to the Father, and to the Son, and to the Holy Spirit;
Both now and forever, and unto the ages of ages. Amen.

Halleluiah, Halleluiah, Halleluiah. Glory to Thee, O God. **(x3)**

Lord, have mercy. **(x3)**

Tone 6 *Rich texture, funereal character, sorrowful tone.*		*D, Eb, F##, G, A, Bb, C##, D.*
Priest: In the morning, hearken unto my voice, O my king and God.		
Chorus: *In the morning, hearken unto my voice, O my king and God.*		***prostration***
Priest: Unto my words give ear, O Lord, hear my cry.		
Chorus: *In the morning, hearken unto my voice, O my king and God.*		***prostration***
Priest: For unto Thee will I pray, O Lord.		
Chorus: *In the morning, hearken unto my voice, O my king and God.*		***prostration***
Priest: Glory be to the Father and to the Son and to the Holy Spirit,		
Reader: Both now and forever and unto the ages of ages. Amen.		

Theotokion

What shall we call thee, O thou who art full of grace? Heaven, for from thee hast dawned forth the Sun of Righteousness. Paradise, for from thee hath blossomed forth the flower of immortality. Virgin, for thou hast remained incorrupt. Pure Mother, for thou hast held in thy holy embrace the Son, the God of all. Do thou entreat Him to save our souls.

Tone 6   Rich texture, funereal character, sorrowful tone.   *D, Eb, F##, G, A, Bb, C##, D.*

Chorus: *My steps do Thou direct according to thy saying, and let no iniquity have dominion over me.* **(x2)**

Reader: Deliver me from the false accusations of men; and I will keep Thy commandments.   **(x2)**

Make Thy face to shine upon Thy servant, and teach me Thy statutes.   **(x2)**

Let my mouth be filled with Thy praise, O Lord, that I may hymn Thy glory and majesty all the day long. **(x3)**

Holy God, Holy Mighty, Holy Immortal, have mercy on us. **(x3)**

Glory be to the Father and to the Son and to the Holy Spirit,
Both now and forever and unto the ages of ages. Amen.

O Most Holy Trinity, have mercy on us.

O Lord, cleanse us from our sins.

O Master, pardon our iniquities.

O Holy One, visit and heal our infirmities, for Thy names sake.

Lord have mercy. **(x3)**

Glory be to the Father and to the Son and to the Holy Spirit,
Both now and forever and unto the ages of ages. Amen.

People: *Our Father, Who art in Heaven, hallowed be Thy Name. Thy Kingdom come, Thy will be done, on earth as it is in Heaven. Give us this day our daily bread, and forgive us our trespasses, as we forgive those who trespass against us; and lead us not into temptation, but deliver us from the evil one.*

Priest: For Thine is the Kingdom, and the power, and the glory; of the Father, and of the Son, and of the Holy Spirit, now and ever, and unto the ages of ages.

People: *Amen.*

Reader: Think, wretched soul, upon the hour of the end; recall with fear how the fig tree was cut down. Work diligently with the talent that is given to thee; be vigilant and cry aloud: May we not be left outside the bridal chamber of Christ.

Lord, have mercy. **(x40)**

The Prayer Of The Hours

At all times and in every hour, Thou art worshipped and glorified in heaven and on earth, Christ our God. Long in patience, great in mercy and compassion, Thou lovest the righteous and showest mercy to sinners. Thou callest all to salvation through the promise of good things to come. Lord, receive our prayers at the present time. Direct our lives according to Thy commandments. Sanctify our souls. Purify our bodies. Set our minds aright. Cleanse our thoughts, and deliver us from all sorrow, evil and distress. Surround us with Thy holy angels, that, guarded and guided by their host, we may arrive at the unity of the faith and the understanding of Thine ineffable glory. For Thou art blessed to the ages of ages. Amen.

Lord, have mercy. **(x3)**

Glory be to the Father and to the Son and to the Holy Spirit,
Both now and forever and unto the ages of ages. Amen.

Greater in honour than the Cherubim and beyond compare more glorious than the Seraphim; without corruption thou gavest birth to God the Word, truly the Theotokos, we magnify thee.

Holy Father bless.

Priest: God be gracious unto us and bless us, and cause Thy face to shine upon us and have mercy on us.
People: Amen.
Priest: O Lord and Master of my life, a spirit of idleness, despondency, ambition, and idle talking give me not. *prostration*
Priest: But rather a spirit of chastity, humble mindedness, patience, and love bestow upon me Thy servant. *prostration*
Priest: Yea, O Lord King, grant me to see mine own failings and not condemn my brother; for blessed art Thou unto the ages of ages. Amen. *prostration*

O God, cleanse me a sinner. *(cross and bow)* **(x12)**

O Lord and Master of my life, a spirit of idleness, despondency, ambition, and idle talking give me not. But rather a spirit of chastity, humble mindedness, patience, and love bestow upon me Thy servant. Yea, O Lord King, grant me to see mine own failings and not condemn my brother; for blessed art Thou unto the ages of ages. Amen. *prostration*

Reader: Holy God, Holy Mighty, Holy Immortal, have mercy on us. **(x3)**

Glory be to the Father and to the Son and to the Holy Spirit,
Both now and forever and unto the ages of ages. Amen.

O Most Holy Trinity, have mercy on us.
O Lord, cleanse us from our sins.
O Master, pardon our iniquities
O Holy One, visit and heal our infirmities, for Thy names sake.

Lord have mercy. **(x3)**

Glory be to the Father and to the Son and to the Holy Spirit,
Both now and forever and unto the ages of ages. Amen.

People: *Our Father, Who art in Heaven, hallowed be Thy Name. Thy Kingdom come, Thy will be done, on earth as it is in Heaven. Give us this day our daily bread, and forgive us our trespasses, as we forgive those who trespass against us; and lead us not into temptation, but deliver us from the evil one.*

Priest: For Thine is the Kingdom, and the power, and the glory; of the Father, and of the Son, and of the Holy Spirit, now and ever, and unto the ages of ages.

People: *Amen.*

Lord, have mercy. **(x12)**

The Prayer Of The First Hour

Priest: O Christ, the True Light, Who enlightenest and sanctifiest every man that cometh into the world: Let the Light of Thy countenance be signed upon us, that in it we may see the Unapproachable Light, and guide our steps in the doing of Thy commandments, through the intercessions of Thy most pure Mother, and of all Thy saints. Amen.

Kontakion For The Annunciation

Tone 8   Humility, tranquillity, repose, suffering, pleading.   *C, D, Eb, F, G, A, Bb, C.*

To Thee, the Champion Leader, we Thy servants dedicate a feast of victory and of thanksgiving as ones rescued out of sufferings, O Theotokos: but as Thou art one with might, which is invincible, from all dangers that can be, do Thou deliver us, that we may cry to Thee: Rejoice, Thou Bride Unwedded.

Priest: Glory to Thee, O Christ our God and our hope, glory to Thee.

Reader: *Glory be to the Father and to the Son and to the Holy Spirit,*
Both now and forever and unto the ages of ages. Amen.

Lord, have mercy. **(x3)**

Holy Father, bless.

Priest: May Christ our true God, the Lord who for our salvation went to His voluntary Passion, through the intercessions of His most pure Mother; of the holy and glorious apostles; of the holy and righteous ancestors of God, Joachim and Anna; and of all the saints: have mercy on us and save us, for He is good and lovest mankind.

People: *Amen.*

[For Wednesday Evening]

- *This service is held in the Nave of the Church, before the Holy Doors. Priest in Phelonion.*
- *A small table upon which is set the Holy Gospel, a Cross, Candles, and a vessel in the middle, containing wheat; and on the wheat is placed an Oil Lamp filled with oil and a little wine.*
- *Seven wands with cotton tips are thrust into the wheat around the lamp. These are used to anoint those who are repenting from their sins.*
- *Also, seven lit candles are thrust into the wheat around the lamp. At the completion of the service, the faithful come forward and are anointed with the Holy Oil by the Priest.*

The Trisagion Prayers

Priest: Blessed is our God, always, now and ever, and unto the ages of ages.

People: *Amen.*

Priest: Glory to Thee, our God, glory to Thee.

O Heavenly King, Comforter, Spirit of Truth, Who art everywhere present and fillest all things, Treasury of blessings and Giver of life: Come and abide in us and cleanse us from every impurity and save our souls, O Good One.

Reader: Holy God, Holy Mighty, Holy Immortal, have mercy on us. **(x3)**

Glory be to the Father, and to the Son, and to the Holy Spirit;
Both now and forever, and unto the ages of ages. Amen.

O Most Holy Trinity, have mercy on us.

O Lord, cleanse us from our sins.

O Master, pardon our iniquities.

O Holy One, visit and heal our infirmities, for Thy names sake.

Lord have mercy. **(x3)**

Glory be be to the Father and to the Son and to the Holy Spirit;
Both now and forever, and unto the ages of ages. Amen.

People: Our Father, Who art in Heaven, hallowed be Thy Name. Thy Kingdom come, Thy will be done, on earth as it is in Heaven. Give us this day our daily bread, and forgive us our trespasses, as we forgive those who trespass against us; and lead us not into temptation, but deliver us from the evil one.

Priest: For Thine is the kingdom and the power and the glory of the Father and of the Son and of the Holy Spirit; both now and forever and unto the ages of ages.

People: *Amen.*

Lord, have mercy. **(x12)**

> *Glory be be to the Father and to the Son and to the Holy Spirit;*
> *Both now and forever and unto the ages of ages. Amen.*

Come, let us worship God, our King.

Come, let us worship and fall down before Christ, our King and our God.

Come, let us worship and fall down before Christ Himself, our King and our God.

Psalm 142

Hear my prayer, O Lord, give ear to my supplications. In Thy faithfulness answer me, and in Thy righteousness. Do not enter into judgement with Thy servant, for in Thy sight no one living is righteous. For the enemy has persecuted my soul; he has crushed my life to the ground; he has made me dwell in darkness, like those who have long been dead. Therefore my spirit is overwhelmed within me; my heart within me is distressed. I remember the days of old; I meditate on all Thy works; I muse on the work of Thine hands. I spread out my hands to Thee; my soul longs for Thee like a thirsty land. Answer me speedily, O Lord; my spirit fails. Do not hide Thy face from me, lest I be like those who go down into the pit. Cause me to hear Thy loving kindness in the morning, for in Thee do I trust; cause me to know the way in which I should walk, for I lift up my soul to Thee. Deliver me, O Lord, from mine enemies; in Thee I take shelter. Teach me to do Thy will, for Thou art my God; Thy Spirit is good. Lead me in the land of uprightness. Revive me, O Lord, for Thy names sake. For Thy righteousness' sake bring my soul out of trouble. In Thy mercy cut off mine enemies, and destroy all those who afflict my soul; for I am Thy servant.

After The Psalm

> *Glory be to the Father and to the Son and to the Holy Spirit,*
> *Both now and forever and unto the ages of ages. Amen.*

Halleluiah, Halleluiah, Halleluiah. Glory to Thee, O God. **(x3)**

O our God and our hope, glory to Thee.

Great Litany

Priest: Again and again, in peace let us pray to the Lord.

People: *Lord have mercy.*

Priest: Help us, save us, have mercy upon us, and keep us O God, by Thy grace.

People: *Lord have mercy.*

Priest: Calling to remembrance our All Holy Immaculate, Most Blessed and Glorious Lady Theotokos and ever Virgin Mary, with all the saints, let us commend ourselves and each other, and all our life unto Christ our God.

People: To Thee, O Lord.

Priest: For unto Thee are due all glory, honour and worship, to the Father, and to the Son, and to the Holy Spirit, both now and forever and unto the ages of ages.

People: Amen.

Halleluiarion

People: *Halleluiah. Halleluiah. Halleluiah.*

Reader: O Lord, rebuke me not in Thine indignation, neither chasten me in Thy displeasure.

People: *Halleluiah. Halleluiah. Halleluiah.*

Reader: Have mercy upon us, O Lord, have mercy upon us.

People: *Halleluiah. Halleluiah. Halleluiah.*

The Penitential Troparia

   Tone 6   Rich texture, funeral, sorrowful.   *D, Eb, F##, G, A, Bb, C##, D.*

Reader: O Lord, have mercy upon us, for in Thee have we put our trust; be not exceedingly wroth with us, neither remember our iniquities, but look down upon us even now as Thou art compassionate, and deliver us from our enemies. For Thou art our God, and we are Thy people; we are all the work of Thy hands, and we call upon Thy name.

Chorus: *Glory be to the Father and to the Son and to the Holy Spirit,*

Reader: Lord, have mercy upon us, for in Thee have we put our trust; be not very wroth against us, neither remember our iniquities; but look down upon us even now; since Thou art compassionate, and deliver us from our enemies. For Thou art our God, and we are Thy people; we are all the work of Thy hands, and we call upon Thy Name.

Chorus: *Both now and forever and unto the ages of ages. Amen.*

Reader: Open unto us the door of Thy tender compassion, O Blessed Theotokos. Hoping that we shall not fail, in putting our trust in Thee. That, through Your intercessions, we may be saved from all tribulations. For Thou art the salvation of all Christians.

Psalm 50

Reader: Have mercy on me, O God, according to Thy great mercy; and according to the multitude of Thy compassions blot out my transgression. Wash me thoroughly from mine iniquity, and cleanse me from my sin. For I acknowledge mine iniquity, and my sin is ever before me. Against Thee, Thee only have I sinned, and done evil in Thy sight, that Thou mayest be found just when Thou speakest, and victorious when Thou art judged. For behold, I was conceived in iniquity, and in sin my mother bore me. For behold, Thou hast loved truth; Thou hast made known to me the hidden and secret things of Thy wisdom. Thou shalt sprinkle me with hyssop, and I shall be made clean; Thou shalt wash me, and I shall be whiter than snow. Make me to hear joy and gladness; that the humbled bones may rejoice. Turn Thy face away from my sins, and blot out all mine iniquities.

Create in me a clean heart, O God, and renew a steadfast spirit within me. Cast me not away from Thy presence, and take not Thy Holy Spirit from me. Restore to me the joy of Thy salvation, and establish me with Thy governing Spirit. I shall teach transgressors Thy ways, and the ungodly shall turn back to Thee. Deliver me from blood guiltiness, O God, the God of my salvation; my tongue shall joyfully declare Thy righteousness. Lord, open my lips, and my mouth shall declare Thy praise. For if Thou hadst desired sacrifice, I would give it; Thou dost not delight in burnt offerings. A sacrifice to God is a broken spirit; God will not despise a broken and a humbled heart. Do good, O Lord, in Thy good pleasure to Zion, and let the walls of Jerusalem be builded. Then Thou shalt be pleased with a sacrifice of righteousness, with oblation and whole burned offerings. Then shall they offer bulls on Thine altar.

The Canon
Ode 1

Eirmos

Tone 4   Festive, joyous and expressing deep piety.   *C, D, Eb, F, G, A, Bb, C.*

Reader: When Israel of old had passed through the Abyss of the Red Sea, with unwet feet, he overcame the power of Amalek in the wilderness, when the hands of Moses were stretched forth in the shape of a cross.

Stichos

Chorus: *O merciful Lord, hearken to the prayer of Thy servants supplicating Thee.*

Troparion

Reader: O Master, who with the oil of compassion dost ever cheer both the souls and bodies of mortals, and dost guard the faithful with oil; be Thou clement now to those who approach Thee by means of oil.

Stichos

Chorus: *O merciful Lord, hearken to the prayer of Thy servants supplicating Thee.*

Reader: The whole earth is full of Thy mercy, O Master; wherefore, we who today are mystically anointed with Thine oil divine, ask in faith that Thine inestimable mercy may be granted us.

Chorus: *Glory be to the Father and to the Son and to the Holy Spirit,*

Reader: O Lover of mankind, who in pity for Thine ailing servants, didst command Thine Apostles to perform Thy saved unction, do Thou, through their entreaties, have mercy on all by Thy seal.

Chorus: *Both now and forever and unto the ages of ages. Amen.*

Theotokion

O, thou only chaste one, who didst bear the bountiful sea of Peace; by thy constant intercession with God deliver thy servants from infirmities and griefs, that they may ceaselessly magnify thee.

Ode 3

Eirmos

Tone 3   Arrogant, brave, and mature atmosphere.   *F, G, A, A#, C, D, E, F.*

In Thee Thy Church is glad, O Christ, crying: Thou art my fortress, O Lord, both refuge and support.

Stichos

Chorus: *O merciful Lord, hearken to the prayer of Thy servants supplicating Thee.*

Thou Who alone art marvellous and merciful to faithful men; grant Thy grace from above, O Christ, to those who are grievously afflicted.

Chorus: *O merciful Lord, hearken to the prayer of Thy servants supplicating Thee.*

O Lord, Who of yore for Thy divine token that the flood had ceased, didst show forth an olive branch, by Thy mercy save those who suffer.

Chorus: *Glory be to the Father and to the Son and to the Holy Spirit,*

With a lamp of light divine, in Thy mercy, O Christ, illumine with anointing those who now with faith hasten to Thy mercy.

Chorus: *Both now and forever and unto the ages of ages. Amen.*

Theotokion

Graciously look down from above, O Mother of the Creator of all, and through thine intercessions loose the bitter pangs of those who are ill.

Kathisma

Tone 8   Humility, tranquillity, repose, suffering, pleading.   *C, D, Eb, F, G, A, Bb, C.*

Since Thou art a divine river of mercy, like unto a fathomless gulf of plentiful sympathy, O Bountiful One; manifest the divine streams of Thy mercy, and heal all men. Abundantly pour forth fountains of wonders and cleanse all; for resorting ever unto Thee, we fervently implore Thy grace.

Kathisma

Tone 4   Festive, joyous and expressing deep piety.   *C, D, Eb, F, G, A, Bb, C.*

Physician and help of those in sickness, Redeemer and Saviour of the infirm, do Thou, the Master and Lord of all, grant healing to Thine infirm servants. Be clement, show mercy to those who have sinned much, and deliver them, O Christ, from their iniquities, that they may glorify Thy might divine.

Ode 4

Eirmos

Tone 4   Festive, joyous and expressing deep piety.   *C, D, Eb, F, G, A, Bb, C.*

The Church, beholding Thee uplifted upon the Cross, O sun of righteousness, remained steadfast in its praises and worthily cried unto Thee, glory to Thy might, O Lord.

Stichos

Chorus: *O merciful Lord, hearken to the prayer of Thy servants supplicating Thee.*

Troparion

Thou, O Saviour, art as incorruptible myrrh, emptied of Thy grace and cleansing the world: divinely show pity and mercy to those who with faith anoint their bodily wounds.

Chorus: *O merciful Lord, hearken to the prayer of Thy servants supplicating Thee.*

Now that the senses of Thy servants are signed with the seal of the joy of Thy mercy, O Master, make inaccessible and impenetrable the entry of all adverse powers.

Chorus: *Glory be to the Father and to the Son and to the Holy Spirit,*

Thou Who lovest man didst bid the ailing to summon Thy godly priests, and by their prayers and anointing with Thine oil to be saved; of Thy mercy, save whose who suffer.

Chorus: *Both now and forever and unto the ages of ages. Amen.*

Theotokion

O all holy Theotokos, ever virgin, strong shelter and defence, thou haven and wall, both ladder and partition, have mercy and pity on the sick; for they have fled to thee alone.

Ode 5

Eirmos

Thou art come, O My Lord, as a light to the world, a holy light, turning from the darkness of ignorance those who with faith sing praises unto Thee.

Stichos

Chorus: *O merciful Lord, hearken to the prayer of Thy servants supplicating Thee.*

Troparion

Thou Who are good, an abyss of mercy; of Thy compassion, O merciful One, show mercy through Thy mercy divine, on those who suffer.

Chorus: *O merciful Lord, hearken to the prayer of Thy servants supplicating Thee.*

Reader: O Christ, who hast ineffably sanctified our souls and bodies by Thy divine impress of sealing from above, with Thine own hand heal us all.

Chorus: *Glory be to the Father and to the Son and to the Holy Spirit,*

Reader: O Lord exceeding good, who through Thine inexpressible tenderness didst accept myrrh anointing from the harlot, have pity on Thy servants.

Chorus: *Both now and forever and unto the ages of ages. Amen.*

Theotokion

All lauded, pure, most gracious Sovereign Lady, have mercy on those anointed with the oil divine, and save Thy servants.

Ode 6

Eirmos

The Church crieth unto Thee, O Lord, I will sacrifice unto Thee, with a voice of praise and thanksgiving, purified from the evil of demons, with the blood which flowed from Thy side, with the abundance of Thy mercy.

Stichos

Chorus: *O merciful Lord, hearken to the prayer of Thy servants supplicating Thee.*

Troparion

O Lover of mankind, who by Thy word didst show anointing is for kings, and the same through High Priests didst perform: save also those who suffer, by the seal of Thy compassion.

Chorus: *O merciful Lord, hearken to the prayer of Thy servants supplicating Thee.*

Let no interposition of malignant demons, O Saviour, touch the senses of those signed with divine anointing; but hedge them about with the shelter of Thy glory.

Chorus: *Glory be to the Father and to the Son and to the Holy Spirit,*

Stretch forth from on high Thy hand, O Thou who lovest man, and having sanctified Thine oil, O Saviour, impart it to Thy servants unto healing and deliverance from all ills.

Chorus: *Both now and forever and unto the ages of ages. Amen.*

Theotokion

O Mother of the Creator, in thy divine temple thou hast revealed thyself a fruitful olive tree, whereby the world is found filled with mercy. Therefore by the touching of thine intercessions save those who suffer.

Kontakion

Tone 2   Majesty, gentleness, hope, repentance and sadness.   *E, F, G, Ab, B, C.*

Thou art the source of mercy, O exceeding Good One, do Thou deliver from every calamity those who with fervent faith bow down before Thine unspeakable mercy; and, Compassionate One, taking away their maladies, grant them Thy divine grace from on high.

Ode 7

Eirmos

Tone 4   Festive, joyous and expressing deep piety.   *C, D, Eb, F, G, A, Bb, C.*

The Abrahamic children in the Persian furnace, fired rather by love of godliness than by the flame, cried aloud: Blessed art Thou, O Lord, in the Tabernacle of Thy glory.

Stichos

Chorus: *O merciful Lord, hearken to the prayer of Thy servants supplicating Thee.*

Troparion

Thou who in Thy mercies and bounties, O Saviour only God, dost heal the passions of soul and contritions of body of all men, be Thou physician for those who suffer from infirmities, and restore them.

Chorus: *O merciful Lord, hearken to the prayer of Thy servants supplicating Thee.*

When the heads of all are anointed with the oil of unction, grant those who seek the mercy of Thy deliverance, O Christ, the delight of joy, bestowing upon them Thy rich mercies, O Lord.

Chorus: *Glory be to the Father and to the Son and to the Holy Spirit,*

Thy seal, O Saviour, against the demons is a sword; the entreaties of priests are a fire consuming the passions of the soul; wherefore, we who receive healing, with faith praise Thee.

Chorus: Both now and forever and unto the ages of ages. Amen.

Theotokion

O Mother of God, who within thy womb in god-like manner didst hold, and ineffably didst incarnate, Him who holdeth all things in His grasp; entreat Him for those who suffer, we beseeth thee.

Ode 8

Eirmos

Tone 4   *Festive, joyous and expressing deep piety.*   C, D, Eb, F, G, A, Bb, C.

Daniel stretched forth his hand, and stopped the gaping mouths of the lions in the pit. And the Holy children, zealous in piety, girding themselves with virtue, quenched the raging fire, as they cried: "O all you works of the Lord, bless you the Lord."

Stichos

Chorus: O merciful Lord, hearken to the prayer of Thy servants supplicating Thee.

Reader: Thou showest mercy on all men, O Saviour, according to mercy mighty and divine: for which cause we all are gathered here, O Master, mystically representing the condescension of Thy mercies, and have brought in faith the unction with oil unto the servants, whom also do Thou visit.

Chorus: O merciful Lord, hearken to the prayer of Thy servants supplicating Thee.

Reader: By the streams of Thy mercy, O Christ, and through anointing by Thy priests, wash away, in that Thou art compassionate, O Lord, the ills and afflictions, and the assault of maladies of those tormented by the stress of sufferings, that saved, they may glorify Thee with thanksgiving.

Chorus: Glory be to the Father and to the Son and to the Holy Spirit,

Reader: Forasmuch as Thy mercy divine hath been decreed to us from above, O Master, as a symbol of condescension and of joy; withdraw not Thy mercy, neither despise those who ever cry faithfully: "Bless the Lord, all you works of the Lord."

Chorus: Both now and forever and unto the ages of ages. Amen.

Theotokion

Nature received thy divine child bearing, O Pure One, as a crown most glorious which crushed the hosts of foes, and vanquished their dominion. Wherefore, crowned with the festal brightness of Thy grace, we extol thee, O most lauded Sovereign Lady.

Ode 9

Eirmos

Tone 4   Festive, joyous and expressing deep piety.   *C, D, Eb, F, G, A, Bb, C.*

O Virgin, the stone which is unhewn by hand, was the cornerstone hewn from thy unquarried mount; for it is Christ who has bound together the divided nature, therefore, with gladness, we magnify Thee O Theotokos.

Stichos

Chorus: *O merciful Lord, hearken to the prayer of Thy servants supplicating Thee.*

Troparion

Look down from heaven, O Bountiful One, and show Thy mercy unto all. Thine assistance and Thy strength bestow on those who draw near to Thee, through the divine unction of Thy priests, O Thou who lovest man.

Chorus: *O merciful Lord, hearken to the prayer of Thy servants supplicating Thee.*

Reader: O Saviour most good, rejoicing have we seen the oil divine, which through Thy godlike condescension Thou hast received, and, above the merits of the recipients, hast symbolically imparted to those who have shared in the laver divine.

Chorus: *Glory be to the Father and to the Son and to the Holy Spirit,*

Reader: Be clement, have mercy, O Saviour, deliver from terrors and pains, deliver from the darts of the evil one the souls and bodies of Thy servants; since Thou art a merciful Lord, who healest by grace divine.

Chorus: *Both now and forever and unto the ages of ages. Amen.*

Theotokion

As thou receivest the hymns and supplications of thy servants, O Virgin, so do thou also deliver through thine intercessions, from harsh suffering and pain those who, through us, O all immaculate one, flee to thy sacred shelter.

Chorus: *[Archangel Gabriel: It is truly right to call thee blessed, who gavest birth to God, ever-blessed and God-obedient the Mother of our God.] Greater in honour than the Cherubim and beyond compare more glorious than the Seraphim; without corruption thou gavest birth to God the Word, truly the Mother of God, we magnify thee.*

The Little Litany

Deacon: Again and again, in peace let us pray to the Lord.

People: *Lord have mercy.*

Deacon: Help us, save us, have mercy upon us, and keep us O God, by Thy grace.

People: *Lord have mercy.*

Deacon: Calling to remembrance our All Holy Immaculate, Most Blessed and Glorious Lady Theotokos and ever Virgin Mary, with all the saints, let us commend ourselves and each other, and all our life unto Christ our God.

People: *To Thee, O Lord.*

Priest: For all the powers of heaven praise Thee, and unto Thee do we ascribe glory; to the Father, and to the Son, and to the Holy Spirit, both now and forever and unto the ages of ages.

People: *Amen.*

Exapostilarion

Tone 3   Arrogant, brave, and mature atmosphere.   *F, G, A, A#, C, D, E, F.*

O Gracious One, cast Thine merciful sight upon the petitions of us, who today are gathered in Thy Holy Temple, and anoint with Thine Divine Oil, Thy penitent servants. with love they may glorify Thee, magnifying Thy majestic power.

Chorus: *Glory be to the Father, and to the Son, and to the Holy Spirit;*

O Gracious One, cast Thine merciful sight upon the petitions of us, who today are gathered in Thy Holy Temple, and anoint with Thine Divine Oil, Thy penitent servants. with love they may glorify Thee, magnifying Thy majestic power.

Chorus: *Both now and forever, and unto the ages of ages. Amen.*

O Gracious One, cast Thine merciful sight upon the petitions of us, who today are gathered in Thy Holy Temple, and anoint with Thine Divine Oil, Thy penitent servants. with love they may glorify Thee, magnifying Thy majestic power.

Einos / Lauds

Tone 4   Festive, joyous and expressing deep piety.   *C, D, Eb, F, G, A, Bb, C.*

Chorus: *Praise Him with the sound of the trumpet. Praise Him with the psaltery and harp.*

Reader: Thou hast given Thy grace through Thine Apostles, O Good Physician, Lover of mankind, to heal the wounds and infirmities of all men through Thy holy oil. Therefore, inasmuch as Thou art compassionate, sanctify, be merciful, and cleanse from every ailment, and make worthy of Thy food incorruptible, those who now with faith approach Thine oil.

Chorus: *Praise Him with the timbrels and the dance. Praise Him with stringed instruments and organs.*

Reader: O incomprehensible One, look down from heaven, for Thou art compassionate; and seal, O lover of mankind, with Thy invisible hand, our senses, with Thy Divine Oil. Grant unto those who come to Thee with faith; beseeching forgiveness of transgressions, and healing of their souls and bodies alike, that with love they may glorify Thee, magnifying Thy majestic power.

Chorus: *Praise Him with high sounding cymbals. Praise Him with cymbals of joy. Let everything which hath breath, praise the Lord.*

Reader: Through anointing with Thine oil, and the touch of Thy priests, O Lover of mankind, sanctify Thy servants from on high. Free from infirmities. Cleanse their spiritual defilements. Wash them, O Saviour, and deliver from scandals manifold. Assuage their maladies. Banish their hindrances and destroy their afflictions; forasmuch as Thou art Bountiful and Compassionate.

Chorus: *Glory be to the Father, and to the Son, and to the Holy Spirit;*
Both now and forever, and unto the ages of ages. Amen.

Reader: O most pure palace of the King, O greatly extolled One, I implore Thee, to purify my mind which is stained with all manners of sin. Make me the fair abided of the exceedingly divine Trinity; that, being saved, I, Thy meek servant, may magnify Thy power, and Thy boundless mercy. Praise you Him, all His angels; praise you Him, all His hosts; for to Thee praise is due, O God. Praise you the Lord in His sanctuary. Praise you Him in the firmament of His power. Praise you Him according to the multitude of His greatness. Praise Him with the sound of the trumpet. Praise Him with psalms and the harp.

Theotokion

Tone 4   Festive, joyous and expressing deep piety.   C, D, Eb, F, G, A, Bb, C.

O most pure palace of the King, O greatly extolled One, I implore Thee, to purify my mind which is stained with all manners of sin. Make me the fair abided of the exceedingly divine Trinity; that, being saved, I, Thy meek servant, may magnify Thy power, and Thy boundless mercy.

The Trisagion Prayers

Reader: Holy God, Holy Mighty, Holy Immortal, have mercy on us. **(x3)**

O Most Holy Trinity, have mercy on us.

O Lord, cleanse us from our sins.

O Master, pardon our iniquities.

O Holy One, visit and heal our infirmities, for Thy names sake.

Lord have mercy. **(x3)**

Glory be be to the Father and to the Son and to the Holy Spirit;

Both now and forever, and unto the ages of ages. Amen.

People: *Our Father, Who art in Heaven, hallowed be Thy Name. Thy Kingdom come, Thy will be done, on earth as it is in Heaven. Give us this day our daily bread, and forgive us our trespasses, as we forgive those who trespass against us; and lead us not into temptation, but deliver us from the evil one.*

Priest: For Thine is the kingdom and the power and the glory of the Father and of the Son and of the Holy Spirit; both now and forever and unto the ages of ages.

People: *Amen.*

Troparion

Tone 4   Festive, joyous and expressing deep piety.   *C, D, Eb, F, G, A, Bb, C.*

O Christ, in Thee alone we have a speedy succour, manifest Thy speedy visitation from on high upon Thy servants, who are in pain; deliver them from their infirmities, and cruel pain; and raise them up again to sing praises unto Thee ceaselessly; through the intercessions of the Holy Theotokos, O Thou who alone is the lover of mankind.

The Great Ektenia

Priest: In peace let us pray to the Lord.

People: *Lord have mercy.*

Priest: For the peace of the whole world; for the good estate of the Holy Churches of God; and for the union of all men; let us pray to the Lord.

People: *Lord have mercy.*

Priest: For this Holy Temple, and for those who with faith, reverence, and fear of God, enter therein; let us pray to the Lord.

People: *Lord have mercy.*

Priest: That this oil will be blessed with the power, operation, and descent of the Holy Spirit; let us pray to the Lord.

People: *Lord have mercy.*

Priest: For the servants of God who are repenting from their sins, that they may deserve the visitation of God; and that the grace of the Holy Spirit may descend upon them; let us pray to the Lord.

People: *Lord have mercy.*

Priest: For their deliverance and our deliverance, from all tribulation, wrath, danger and necessity; let us pray to the Lord.

People: *Lord have mercy.*

Priest: Help us, save us, have mercy upon us, and keep us O God by Thy grace.

People: *Lord have mercy.*

Priest: Calling to remembrance our all Holy, Immaculate Most Blessed, and Glorious, Lady Theotokos, and ever Virgin Mary, with all the saints; let us commend ourselves and each other, and all our life unto Christ our God.

People: *To Thee, O Lord.*

Priest: For unto Thee are due all glory, honour, and worship: To the Father, and to the Son, and to the Holy Spirit: Now and ever and unto ages of ages.

People: *Amen.*

The Prayer Over The Oil

Priest: O Lord, who in Thy mercies and bounties, healest the disorders of our souls and bodies: Do Thou, O Master, sanctify this oil, that it may be effectual for those who shall be anointed therewith, unto healing, and unto redemption from every passion, every malady of the flesh and of the Spirit, and all evil, and that therein may be glorified Thy most Holy Name, of the Father, and of the Son, and of the Holy Spirit, both now and forever and unto the ages of ages.

People: *Amen.*

Troparia At The Blessing Of The Oil

To Jesus Christ

Tone 4   Festive, joyous and expressing deep piety.   *C, D, Eb, F, G, A, Bb, C.*

Do Thou, O Christ, who alone dost speed to help, manifest Thy speedy visitation from on high upon Thy suffering servants; deliver them from their infirmities, and bitter pain; and raise them up again to praise and glorify Thee unceasingly; through the intercessions of the Theotokos, O Thou who alone lovest mankind.

To Jesus Christ, The Shining Light

Tone 4   Festive, joyous and expressing deep piety.   *C, D, Eb, F, G, A, Bb, C.*

Blind of my spiritual eyes, I come to Thee, O Christ, as did the man blind from his birth, and I cry to Thee in penitence: Thou art the shining light of those in darkness.

To Jesus Christ, The Compassionate God

Tone 3   Arrogant, brave, and mature atmosphere.   *F, G, A, A#, C, D, E, F.*

By Thy divine intervention, O Lord, raise Thou up my soul, which by every kind of sin and unbecoming deeds so grievously is paralysed, as Thou of old didst upraise the paralytic; that, being saved, I may cry to Thee: Grant healing unto me, O Christ Compassionate.

To Saint James

Tone 4   Festive, joyous and expressing deep piety.   *C, D, Eb, F, G, A, Bb, C.*

As the Lord's disciple, thou, O righteous One, didst receive the Gospel; as a martyr thou dost possess that which unwritten is; thou hast boldness, as the brother of God; as hierarch, thou hast power in prayer. Intercede with Christ our God that our souls may be saved.

Another To Saint James

Tone 4   Festive, joyous and expressing deep piety.   *C, D, Eb, F, G, A, Bb, C.*

The only begotten Word of God the Father, who in latter days hath come to us, declared thee, O divine James, the first pastor and teacher of those in Jerusalem, and a faithful steward of spiritual mysteries; wherefore, O Apostle, we all honour thee.

Kontakion Of Saint Nicholas

Tone 3   Arrogant, brave, and mature atmosphere.   *F, G, A, A#, C, D, E, F.*

Thou wast a faithful minister of God in Myra, O Saint Nicholas. For having fulfilled the Gospel Of Christ, thou didst die for the people and save the innocent. Therefore thou wast sanctified as a great initiate of the grace of God.

To Saint Demetrios

Tone 3   Arrogant, brave, and mature atmosphere.   *F, G, A, A#, C, D, E, F.*

The world hath found in thee a mighty champion in dangers, O endurer of pain, who overcame the heathen. For like as thou didst humble Lyaeus' pride, and in the strife make Nestor brave, so Saint Demetrius, entreat Christ our God to bestow on us great mercy.

To Saint Panteleimon, The Unmercenary Healer

Tone 3   Arrogant, brave, and mature atmosphere.   *F, G, A, A#, C, D, E, F.*

O holy endurer of pain and physician Panteleimon, intercede with the merciful God that He may grant our souls remission of iniquities.

To The Unmercenary Healers

Tone 8   Humility, tranquillity, repose, suffering, pleading.   *C, D, Eb, F, G, A, Bb, C.*

O holy Unmercenaries and Wonder Workers, visit you our weaknesses; freely you have received, freely give to us.

To Saint John The Theologian

Tone 2   Majesty, gentleness, hope, repentance and sadness.   *E, F, G, Ab, B, C.*

Thy grandeur, O virgin saint, who shall declare? For thou dost overflow with wonders, and pourest forth healing; and as theologian and friend of Christ, thou intercedest for our souls.

Theotokion

Tone 2   Majesty, gentleness, hope, repentance and sadness.   *E, F, G, Ab, B, C.*

O fervent supplicant and wall impregnable, source of mercy, refuge of the world; to thee we earnestly do cry: "Theotokos, Sovereign Lady, aforehand come to us and deliver us from danger, thou who alone art quick to intercede."

Prokeimenon

Deacon: The Prokeimenon.

Reader: Let Thy mercy be upon us, O Lord, as we have put our trust in Thee.

People: *Let Thy mercy be upon us, O Lord, as we have put our trust in Thee.*

Reader: Rejoice in the Lord, O you righteous: praise becometh the righteous.

People: *Let Thy mercy be upon us, O Lord, as we have put our trust in Thee.*

Reader: Let Thy mercy be upon us, O Lord | as we have put our trust in Thee.

The First Epistle

Deacon: Wisdom.

Reader: The lesson is from the General Epistle of James (5:10-17).

Deacon: Let us attend.

Reader: Brethren: take the prophets, who have spoken in the name of the Lord, for an example of suffering affliction, and of patience. Behold, we count them happy which endure. You have heard of the patience of Job, and have seen the end of the Lord; that the Lord is very pitiful, and of tender mercy. But above all things, my brethren, swear not, neither by heaven, neither by the earth, neither by any other oath: but let your yea, be yea; and your nay, be nay; lest you fall into condemnation. Is any among you afflicted? let him pray. Is any merry? let him sing psalms. Is any sick among you? let him call for the elders of the church; and let them pray over him, anointing him with oil in the Name of the Lord: and the prayer of faith shall save the sick, and the Lord shall raise him up; and if he have committed sins, they shall be forgiven him. Confess your faults one to another, and pray one for another, that you may be healed. The effectual fervent prayer of a righteous man availeth much.

Priest: Peace be with you who read.

Reader: And with thy spirit.

Chorus: *Halleluiah. Halleluiah. Halleluiah.*

Reader: Of mercy and judgement, will I sing unto Thee, O Lord.

Chorus: *Halleluiah. Halleluiah. Halleluiah.*

The First Gospel

Deacon: Wisdom. Attend. Let us hear the Holy Gospel.

Priest: Peace be with you all.

People: *And with thy spirit.*

Priest: The lesson is from the Holy Gospel according to Luke (10:25-37).

People: *Glory to Thee, O Lord, glory to Thee.*

Deacon: Let us attend.

Priest: In that time, a certain lawyer stood up, and tempted Him, saying, "Master, what shall I do to inherit eternal life?" He said unto him, "What is written in the law? how readest thou?" And he answering said, "Thou shalt love the Lord thy God with all thy heart, and with all thy soul and with all thy strength, and with all thy mind; and thy neighbour as thyself." And He said unto him, "Thou hast answered right: This do, and thou shalt live." But he, willing to justify himself, said unto Jesus, "And who is my neighbour?" And Jesus answering, said, "A certain man went down from Jerusalem to Jericho, and fell among thieves, which stripped him of his raiment, and wounded him, and departed, leaving him half dead. And by chance there came down a certain priest that way; and when he saw him, he passed by on the other side. And likewise a Levite, and when he was at the place, came and looked on him, and passed by on the other side. But a certain Samaritan, as he journeyed, came where he was: and when he saw him, he had compassion on him, and went to him, and bound up his wounds, pouring in oil and wine, and set him on his beast, and brought him to an inn, and took care of him. And on the morrow, when he departed, he took out two pence, and gave them to the host, and said unto him, Take care of him: and whatsoever thou spendest more, when I come again, I will repay thee. Which now of these three, thinkest thou, was neighbour unto him that fell among the thieves?" And he said, "He that showed mercy on him." Then said Jesus unto him, "Go, and do thou likewise."

People: *Glory to Thee, O Lord, glory to Thee.*

The Ektenia Of Fervent Supplication

Priest: Have mercy upon us, O God, according to Thy great goodness, we pray Thee, hearken and have mercy.

People: *Lord have mercy.* (**x3**)

Priest: Again, we pray for mercy, life, peace, health, salvation, and visitation, for the servants of God, and for the remission of their sins.

People: *Lord have mercy.* (**x3**)

Priest: Again, we pray for the pardon of their every transgression, whether voluntary or involuntary.

People: *Lord have mercy.* (**x3**)

Priest: For Thou art a merciful God, and lovest mankind, and unto Thee we ascribe glory, to the Father, and to the Son, and to the Holy Spirit, both now and forever and unto the ages of ages.

People: *Amen.*

Priest: Let us pray to the Lord.

People: *Lord have mercy.*

The First Prayer Over The Holy Oil

Priest: O Thou art eternal, and without beginning, the Holy of Holies; who didst send forth Thine only begotten son to heal every infirmity and every weakness, in both our souls and bodies: Send down Thy Holy Spirit, and sanctify this Oil; and cause it to be the complete salvation of the sins, of Thy servants, who are about to be anointed with it; and for their inheritance of the heavenly kingdom. For thou art God, great and wonderful, who keepest Thy covenant and Thy mercy unto those who love Thee; who givest deliverance and from sins through Thy holy Child, Jesus Christ; who regeneratest us from sin; who enlightenest the blind, raisest up those who art cast down; who lovest the the blind, raisest up those who art cast down; who lovest the righteous and showest mercy unto sinners; who leadest us forth again out of darkness and the shadow of death, saying to those in bonds, "Come forth;" and to those in darkness. "Be you unveiled." For the light of the knowledge of Thine Only begotten Son shone in our hearts, since for our sakes he appeared on earth, and dwelt among men; and to those who accepted Him, he gave power to become the children of God; granting to us sonship through the laver of regeneration, and made us to have no participation in the tyranny of the Devil.

And inasmuch as it hath not pleased Him that we should be purified by blood, but by holy oil, He gave us the image of His Cross, that we may be a flock of Christ, a royal priesthood, a holy nation; and didst purify us by water, and sanctify us by Thy Holy Spirit. Do Thou Thyself, O Master Lord, give us grace in this ministration, as Thou gavest it to Moses, Thine accepted, and to Samuel, Thy beloved, and to John, Thine elect, and to all those who, from generation to generation, have been well pleasing unto Thee. And so make us also to be ministers of the new Covenant of Thy Son upon this oil, which Thou has made Thine own through the precious Blood of Thy Christ; that putting away worldly lusts, we may die unto sin and live unto righteousness, being clothed upon with our Lord Jesus Christ through the anointing of sanctification of this oil which we desire to use. Let this oil, O Lord, be an oil of gladness, an oil of sanctification, a royal raiment, an armour of might, an averting of every diabolical operation, an inviolable seal, a rejoicing of the heart, an everlasting gladness; that those also who are anointed with this oil of regeneration may be terrible to adversaries, and may shine in the radiance of Thy Saints, having neither spot nor wrinkle; and that they may be received into Thine eternal rest, and gain the prize of the calling from on high.

For Thine is is to show mercy, and salvation, O our God, and unto Thee we ascribe glory, to the Father, and to the Son, and to the Holy Spirit, both now and forever and unto the ages of ages.

People: Amen.

Prokeimenon

Priest: Let us attend. The Prokeimenon.

Reader: The Lord is my strength and my song, and is become my salvation.

People: The Lord is my strength and my song, and is become my salvation.

Reader: In chastising, the Lord has chastised me, and he has not surrendered me unto death.

People: The Lord is my strength and my song, and is become my salvation.

Reader: The Lord is my strength and my song | and is become my salvation.

The Second Epistle

Deacon: Wisdom.

Reader: The lesson is from the Epistle of the Holy Apostle Paul to the Romans (15:1-8).

Deacon: Let us attend.

Reader: Brethren, we then that are strong ought to bear the infirmities of the weak, and not to please ourselves. Let every one of us please his neighbour for his good to edification. For even Christ pleased not himself; but, as it is written, the reproaches of them that reproached thee fell on me. For whatsoever things were written aforetime, were written for our learning, that we, through patience and comfort of the scriptures, might have hope. Now the God of patience and consolation grant you to be like minded one toward another according to Christ Jesus: That you may with one mind and one mouth glorify God, even the Father of our

Lord, Jesus Christ. Wherefore receive you one another, as Christ also received us, to the glory of God. Welcome one another, therefore, as Christ has welcomed you, for the glory of God.

Priest: Peace be with you who read.

Reader: And with thy spirit.

Chorus: *Halleluiah. Halleluiah. Halleluiah.*

Reader: Of Thy mercy, will I sing forever, O Lord.

Chorus: *Halleluiah. Halleluiah. Halleluiah.*

The Second Gospel

Deacon: Wisdom. Attend. Let us hear the Holy Gospel.

Priest: Peace be with you all.

People: *And with thy spirit.*

Priest: The lesson is from the Holy Gospel according to Luke (19:1-10).

People: *Glory to Thee, O Lord, glory to Thee.*

Deacon: Let us attend.

Priest: At that time Jesus entered and passed through Jericho. And behold, there was a man named Zaccheus, which was the chief among the Publicans, and he was rich. And he sought to see Jesus who He was; and could not for the press, because he was little of stature. And he ran before, and climbed up into a sycamore tree to see Him; for He was to pass that way. And when Jesus came to the place, He looked up, and saw him, and said unto him, "Zaccheus, make haste, and come down: For today I must abide at thy house." And he made haste, and came down, and received Him joyfully. And when they saw it, they all murmured, saying, that: "He was gone to be guest with a man that is a sinner." And Zaccheus stood, and said unto the Lord; "Behold, Lord, the half of my goods I give to the poor; and if I have taken anything from any man by false accusation, I restore him fourfold." And Jesus said unto him, "This day is salvation come to this house, forasmuch as he also is a son of Abraham. For the Son of man is come to seek and to save that which was lost."

People: *Glory to Thee, O Lord, glory to Thee.*

The Ektenia Of Fervent Supplication

Priest: Have mercy upon us O God, according to Thy great goodness, we pray Thee, hearken and have mercy.

People: *Lord have mercy.* **(x3)**

Priest: Again, we pray for mercy, life, peace, health, salvation and visitation, for the servants of God, and for the remission of their sins.

People: *Lord have mercy.* **(x3)**

Priest: Again, we pray for the pardon of their every transgression, whether voluntary or involuntary.

People: *Lord have mercy.* **(x3)**

Priest: For Thou art a merciful God, and lovest mankind, and unto Thee, we ascribe glory to the Father, and to the Son, and to the Holy Spirit, both now and forever and unto the ages of ages.

People: *Amen.*

Priest: Let us pray to the Lord.

People: *Lord have mercy.*

The Second Prayer Over The Holy Oil

Priest: O God, great and supreme, who art adored by all creatures, O fountain of wisdom and goodness and the unlimited sea of mercy; do Thou, Master, God of wonders and all things eternal, at whom no one can look; look down and hear us, Thine unworthy servants, and in Thy great name, we present this oil; send down the gift of Thy healing, and remission of sins; and heal Thy servants in the multitude of Thy mercies, yea, O Lord, who art easy to be entreated, who repentest Thee of our evil deeds, who knowest that man is inclined unto wickedness, from the beginning of his youth; who desirest not the death of a sinner, but rather that he should return and live again, who, while He was still God, became incarnate, for the salvation of the sinners; Thou hast said, "I am not come to call the righteous, but the sinners to repentance;" and there will be joy in heaven over one sinner, who repents. Thou art He who sought the lost sheep; Thou art He who diligently sought the lost drachma, and found it; Thou didst say, "He that cometh unto Me I will in no wise case out"; Thou didst not abhor the sinful woman, when she washed Thy precious feet with her tears; Thou didst say, "As often as thou fallest, arise, and thou shalt be saved"; Thou art He who saith: "There is joy in heaven over one sinner who repenteth". Do Thou, O Master, look down from the height of Thy sanctuary, overshadowing us at this hour, with the grace of the Holy Spirit. Take up Thy abode, in these Thy servants, who repent of their iniquities, and accept them, because of Thy love towards mankind; forgiving them, whatsoever wrong they have committed, whether by word or deed, or thought; purify them from every sin; preserve the remainder of their lives; abiding in Thy statutes; and in them, may Thy most Holy Name be glorified; for Thy property it is to show mercy and to save us, O Christ our God; and unto Thee do we ascribe glory, together with Thy Father who is from everlasting, and Thine all Holy, and good, and life creating Spirit, both now and forever and unto the ages of ages.

People: *Amen.*

Prokeimenon

Priest: Let us attend. The Prokeimenon.

Reader: The Lord is my light, and my salvation; whom shall I fear?

People: *The Lord is my light, and my salvation; whom shall I fear?*

Reader: The Lord is the defender of my life; of whom shall I be afraid?

People: *The Lord is my light, and my salvation; whom shall I fear?*

Reader: The Lord is my light, and my salvation | whom shall I fear?

The Third Epistle

Deacon: Wisdom.

Reader: The lesson is from the First Epistle of the Apostle Paul to the Corinthians (12:27-13:8).

Deacon: Let us attend.

Reader: Brethren, now you are the body of Christ, and members in particular. And God hath set some in the Church, first apostles, secondarily prophets, thirdly, teachers, after that, miracles, then gifts of healings, helps, governments, diversities of tongues. Are all Apostles? Are all prophets? Are all teachers? Are all workers of miracles? Have all the gifts of healing? Do all speak with tongues? Do all interpret? But covet earnestly the best gifts. And yet shew I unto you a more excellent way. Though I speak with the tongues of men and of angels, and have not love, I am become as sounding brass, or a tinkling cymbal. And though I have the gift of prophecy, and understand all mysteries, and all knowledge; and though I have all faith, so that I could remove mountains, and have not love, I am nothing. And though I bestow all my goods to feed the poor, and though I give my body to be burned, and not have love, it profiteth me nothing. Love suffereth long, and is kind; love envieth not; love vaunteth not itself, is not puffed up, doth not behave itself unseemly, seeketh not her own, is not easily provoked, thinketh no evil. Rejoiceth not in iniquity, but rejoiceth in the truth; beareth all things, believeth all things, hopeth all things, endureth all things. Love never faileth.

Priest: Peace be with you who read.

Reader: And with thy spirit.

Chorus: *Halleluiah. Halleluiah. Halleluiah.*

Reader: O Lord, in Thee have I trusted; let me never be confounded.

Chorus: *Halleluiah. Halleluiah. Halleluiah.*

The Third Gospel

Deacon: Wisdom. Attend. Let us hear the Holy Gospel.

Priest: Peace be with you all.

People: *And with thy spirit.*

Priest: The lesson is from the Holy Gospel according to Matthew (10:1, 5-9).

People: *Glory to Thee, O Lord, glory to Thee.*

Deacon: Let us attend.

Priest: At that time, when Jesus had called unto Him His twelve disciples, He gave them power against unclean spirits, to cast them out, and to heal all manner of sickness, and all manner of disease. These twelve Jesus sent forth, and commanded them, saying, "Go not into the way of the Gentiles, and into any city of the Samaritans enter you not. But go rather to the lost sheep of the House of Israel. And as you go, preach saying, 'The Kingdom of Heaven is at hand.' Heal the sick. Cleanse the lepers, raise the dead, cast out devils: Freely you have received, freely give."

People: *Glory to Thee, O Lord, glory to Thee.*

The Ektenia Of Fervent Supplication

Priest: Have mercy upon us O God, according to Thy great goodness, we pray Thee, hearken and have mercy.

People: *Lord have mercy.* **(x3)**

Priest: Again, we pray for mercy, life, peace, health, salvation and visitation, for the servants of God, and for the remission of their sins.

People: *Lord have mercy.* **(x3)**

Priest: Again, we pray for the pardon of their every transgression, whether voluntary or involuntary.

People: *Lord have mercy.* **(x3)**

Priest: For Thou art a merciful God, and lovest mankind, and unto Thee, we ascribe glory to the Father, and to the Son, and to the Holy Spirit, both now and forever and unto the ages of ages.

People: *Amen.*

Priest: Let us pray to the Lord.

People: *Lord have mercy.*

The Third Prayer Over The Holy Oil

Priest: O Almighty Master, O Holy King, who chastenest and yet slayest not; who raisest up them that fall, and restorest them that are cast down; who relievest the bodily afflictions of men; Thee do we beseech, O our God, to direct Thy mercy upon this oil, and upon all who shall be anointed, therewith in Thy name; that it may be effectual unto the healing of their souls and bodies, and unto the putting away of every infirmity, and disease, and malady, and every defilement, both of body and spirit. And send down, O Lord, from heaven, Thy healing might; touch the body, quench the fever, soothe the suffering, and banish every hidden ailment. Be Thou the physician of these Thy servants; raise them up from the bed of sickness, and from their couch of vexation whole and perfectly restored, granting unto them, through Thy Church, complete restoration of health; that they shall do and act in accordance with Thy will, and what is pleasing to Thy Holy Majesty. For it is Thine property, to show mercy and to save us, O our God, and unto Thee, do we ascribe glory to the Father, and to the Son, and to the Holy Spirit, both now and ever and unto ages of ages.

People: *Amen.*

Prokeimenon

Priest: Let us attend. The Prokeimenon.

Reader: In the day when I shall call upon Thee, speedily hear me.

People: *In the day when I shall call upon Thee, speedily hear me.*

Reader: O Lord, hear my prayer and my cry.

People: *In the day when I shall call upon Thee, speedily hear me.*

Reader: In the day when I shall call upon Thee | speedily hear me.

The Fourth Epistle

Deacon: Wisdom.

Reader: The lesson is from the Second Epistle of the Apostle Paul to the Corinthians (6:16-7:1).

Deacon: Let us attend.

Reader: Brethren, you are the temple of the living God; as God hath said, I will dwell in them and walk in them; and I will be their God, and they shall be my people. Wherefore come out from among them, and be you separate, saith the Lord, and touch not the unclean thing; and I will receive you; and will be a Father unto you, and you shall be My sons and daughters, said the Lord Almighty. Having therefore these promises, dearly beloved, let us cleanse ourselves from all filthiness of the flesh and spirit, perfecting holiness in the fear of God.

Priest: Peace be with you who read.

Reader: And with thy spirit.

Chorus: *Halleluiah. Halleluiah. Halleluiah.*

Reader: I waited patiently for the Lord, and he heard me.

Chorus: *Halleluiah. Halleluiah. Halleluiah.*

The Fourth Gospel

Deacon: Wisdom. Attend. Let us hear the Holy Gospel.

Priest: Peace be with you all.

People: *And with thy spirit.*

Priest: The lesson is from the Holy Gospel according to Matthew (8:14-23).

People: *Glory to Thee, O Lord, glory to Thee.*

Deacon: Let us attend.

Priest: At that time, when Jesus was come into Peters house, he saw his wifes mother laid, and sick of a fever. And He touched her hand, and the fever left her: And she arose, and ministered unto them. When the evening was come, they brought unto Him many that were possessed with devils: And He cast out the spirits with His word, and healed all that were sick; that it might be fulfilled which was spoken by Isaiah the prophet, saying, "Himself took our infirmities and bare our sickness." Now, when Jesus saw great multitudes about Him, He gave commandment to depart unto the other side. And a certain scribe came, and said unto Him, "Master, I will follow Thee whithersoever Thou goest." And Jesus saith unto him, "The foxes have caves, and the birds of the air have nests; but the Son of man hath not where to lay His head." And another of His disciples said unto Him, "Lord, suffer me first to go and bury my father." But Jesus said unto him, "Follow Me; and let the dead bury their dead." And when He was entered into a ship, His disciples followed Him.

People: *Glory to Thee, O Lord, glory to Thee.*

The Ektenia Of Fervent Supplication

Priest: Have mercy upon us O God, according to Thy great goodness, we pray Thee, hearken and have mercy.

People: Lord have mercy. **(x3)**

Priest: Again, we pray for mercy, life, peace, health, salvation and visitation, for the servants of God, and for the remission of their sins.

People: Lord have mercy. **(x3)**

Priest: Again, we pray for the pardon of their every transgression, whether voluntary or involuntary.

People: Lord have mercy. **(x3)**

Priest: For Thou art a merciful God, and lovest mankind, and unto Thee, we ascribe glory to the Father, and to the Son, and to the Holy Spirit, both now and forever and unto the ages of ages.

People: Amen.

Priest: Let us pray to the Lord.

People: Lord have mercy.

The Fourth Prayer Over The Holy Oil

Priest: O good Lord who lovest mankind, exceedingly merciful, God of all comfort; who through Thy Holy Apostles, has granted us, the power to heal the infirmities of Thy people, with oil and prayer: Do Thou confirm this oil, unto the healing of those who shall be anointed with it, unto relief from every ailment and from every malady: Unto deliverance from every evil. Yea, O Lord, our God, Thee do we beseech, O Almighty One, to save us, and to sanctify us all. Heal Thy servants, and protect them, with the mercies of Thy goodness, visit them with Thy mercies. And if we are favoured with Thine inexpressible love towards mankind, we may praise and glorify Thee who performest glorious deeds both great and miraculous. For unto Thee is to show mercy and to save us, O our God, and unto Thee we ascribe glory, both now and forever and unto the ages of ages.

People: Amen.

Prokeimenon

Priest: Let us attend. The Prokeimenon.

Reader: Thou, O Lord, shalt keep us and protect us, from this generation, forevermore.

People: Thou, O Lord, shalt keep us and protect us, from this generation, forevermore.

Reader: Save me, O Lord, for the righteous are become few.

People: Thou, O Lord, shalt keep us and protect us, from this generation, forevermore.

Reader: Thou, O Lord, shalt keep us and protect us, from this generation | forevermore.

The Fifth Epistle

Deacon: Wisdom.

Reader: The lesson is from the Second Epistle of the Apostle Paul to the Corinthians (1:8-11).

Deacon: Let us attend.

Reader: Brethren, for we would not have you ignorant of our trouble which came to us in Asia, that we were pressed out of measure, above strength, insomuch that we despaired even of life; but we had the sentence of death in ourselves, that we should not trust in ourselves, but in God which raiseth the dead: Who delivered us from so great a death, and doth deliver: in whom we trust that He will deliver us; you also helping together by prayer for us, that for the gift bestowed upon us by the means of many persons, thanks may be given by many on our behalf.

Priest: Peace be with you who read.

Reader: And with thy spirit.

Chorus: *Halleluiah. Halleluiah. Halleluiah.*

Reader: I will sing praises unto thy mercy, O Lord, forever.

Chorus: *Halleluiah. Halleluiah. Halleluiah.*

The Fifth Gospel

Deacon: Wisdom. Attend. Let us hear the Holy Gospel.

Priest: Peace be with you all.

People: *And with thy spirit.*

Priest: The lesson is from the Holy Gospel according to Matthew (25:1-13).

People: *Glory to Thee, O Lord, glory to Thee.*

Deacon: Let us attend.

Priest: The Lord spake this parable; "Then shall the kingdom of heaven be likened unto ten virgins, which took their lamps and went forth to meet the bridegroom, and five of them were wise, and five were foolish. They that were foolish took their lamps. And took no oil with them: But the wise took oil in their vessels with their lamps. While the bridegroom tarried, they all slumbered and slept. And at midnight there was a cry made; behold, the bridegroom cometh; 'go you out to meet him'. Then all those virgins arose, and trimmed their lamps. And the foolish said unto the wise, 'give us of your oil: For our lamps are gone out'. But the wise answered, saying, 'not so, lest there be not enough for us and you: But go you rather to them that sell, and buy for yourselves'. And while they went to buy, the bridegroom came; and they that were ready, went in with him to the marriage: And the door was shut. Afterward came also the other virgins, saying, 'Lord, Lord, open unto us'. But he answered and said, 'verily, I say unto you, I know you not.'" Watch therefore, for you know neither the day nor the hour wherein the Son of Man cometh.

People: *Glory to Thee, O Lord, glory to Thee.*

The Ektenia Of Fervent Supplication

Priest: Have mercy upon us O God, according to Thy great goodness, we pray Thee, hearken and have mercy.

People: *Lord have mercy.* **(x3)**

Priest: Again, we pray for mercy, life, peace, health, salvation and visitation, for the servants of God, and for the remission of their sins.

People: *Lord have mercy.* **(x3)**

Priest: Again, we pray for the pardon of their every transgression, whether voluntary or involuntary.

People: *Lord have mercy.* **(x3)**

Priest: For Thou art a merciful God, and lovest mankind, and unto Thee, we ascribe glory to the Father, and to the Son, and to the Holy Spirit, both now and forever and unto the ages of ages.

People: *Amen.*

Priest: Let us pray to the Lord.

People: *Lord have mercy.*

The Fifth Prayer Over The Holy Oil

Priest: O Lord our God, who chastenest and healest, who raisest up the poor from the earth, and lifts the miserable man from the dunghill; O Father of orphans, and the physician of the ailing, the haven of the tempest tossed, who painlessly didst bear our diseases and our infirmities, who showest mercy and forgiveness, who art quick to help, and slow in wrath; who didst breathe upon Thy disciples, and said to them, "Receive you the Holy Spirit, whosoever sins you shall remit, they are emitted unto them;" who hast called me, Thy humble and sinful, and unworthy servant, entangled in many sins, and wallowing in the lusts of pleasures, to the Holy and high degree of the Priesthood, and to enter into the Holy of Holies, where, also the angels long to penetrate, to hear and to behold, the glad tidings, from the voice of the Lord God; and to take delight in the Divine Liturgy; Thou who enabled me to administer Thy heavenly mysteries, and to offer unto Thee gifts and sacrifices for our sins, and for the ignorances of Thy people. Listen to my prayers, and hear the voice of my supplications, and grant healing unto Thy servants, pardoning their transgressions, both voluntary and involuntary; O Thou, who didst touch the mother-in-law of Peter, whereupon the fever left her, and she arose and ministered unto Thee. Do Thou, O Master, call to mind Thy rich mercies, and how perpetual the mind of man inclineth unto evil, even from his youth; for Thou art alone without sin, who didst come down and saved the human race, and freed us from the bondage of the enemy. For no one is pure of stain; and every mouth shall fail to answer, or to give excuse. Wherefore, O Lord, remember Thou not the sins of our youth; for Thou art the hope of the hopeless, and the rest of those who labour, and are heavy laden with iniquity, and unto Thee do we ascribe glory, together with Thy Father who is from everlasting, and thine all holy and life creating Spirit; both now and forever and unto the ages of ages.

People: *Amen.*

Prokeimenon

Priest: Let us attend. The Prokeimenon.

Reader: Have mercy upon me, O God according to Thy great mercy.

People: *Have mercy upon me, O God according to Thy great mercy.*

Reader: *Create in me a pure heart, O God; and renew a right spirit within me.*

People: *Have mercy upon me, O God according to Thy great mercy.*

Reader: Have mercy upon me, O God | according to Thy great mercy.

The Sixth Epistle

Deacon: Wisdom.

Reader: The lesson is from the Epistle of the Apostle Paul to the Galatians (5:22 - 6:2).

Deacon: Let us attend.

Reader: Brethren, the fruit of the spirit is love, joy, peace, long suffering, gentleness, goodness, faith, meekness, temperance; against such there is no law. And they that are Christs' have crucified the flesh, with the affections and lusts. If we live in the Spirit, let us also walk in the Spirit. Let us not be desirous of vain glory. Provoking one another, envying one another. Brethren, if a man be overtaken in a fault, you which are spiritual, restore such a one in the spirit of meekness; considering thyself, let thou also be tempted. Bear you one anothers burdens, and so fulfil the law of Christ.

Priest: Peace be with you who read.

Reader: And with thy spirit.

Chorus: *Halleluiah. Halleluiah. Halleluiah.*

Reader: Blessed is the man that feareth the Lord. In His commandments he rejoiceth exceedingly.

Chorus: *Halleluiah. Halleluiah. Halleluiah.*

The Sixth Gospel

Deacon: Wisdom. Attend. Let us hear the Holy Gospel.

Priest: Peace be with you all.

People: *And with thy spirit.*

Priest: The lesson is from the Holy Gospel according to Matthew (15:21-28).

People: *Glory to Thee, O Lord, glory to Thee.*

Deacon: Let us attend.

Priest: At that time Jesus went thence, and departed into the coasts of Tyre and Sidon. And behold, a woman of Canaan came out of the same coasts, and cried unto Him, saying, "Have mercy on me, O Lord, Thou Son of David; my daughter is grievously vexed with a devil." But He answered her not a word. And His disciples came and besought Him, saying send her away; "for she crieth after us." But He answered and said, "I am not sent but unto the lost sheep of the house of Israel." Then came she and worshipped Him, saying, "Lord, help me." But He answered and said, "It is not meet to take the childrens bread and to cast it to dogs." And she said, "Truth, Lord, yet the dogs eat of the crumbs which fall from their masters table." Then Jesus answered and said unto her, "O woman, great is thy faith: Be it unto thee even as thou wilt." And her daughter was made whole from that very hour.

People: *Glory to Thee, O Lord, glory to Thee.*

The Ektenia Of Fervent Supplication

Priest: Have mercy upon us O God, according to Thy great goodness, we pray Thee, hearken and have mercy.

People: *Lord have mercy.* (x3)

Priest: Again, we pray for mercy, life, peace, health, salvation and visitation, for the servants of God, and for the remission of their sins.

People: *Lord have mercy.* **(x3)**

Priest: Again, we pray for the pardon of their every transgression, whether voluntary or involuntary.

People: *Lord have mercy.* **(x3)**

Priest: For Thou art a merciful God, and lovest mankind, and unto Thee, we ascribe glory to the Father, and to the Son, and to the Holy Spirit, both now and forever and unto the ages of ages.

People: *Amen.*

Priest: Let us pray to the Lord.

People: *Lord have mercy.*

The Sixth Prayer Over The Holy Oil

Priest: We thank Thee, O Lord our God, who art good and lovest mankind, the physician of our souls and bodies; who hast borne our infirmities painlessly; by whose wounds, we have all been healed, O Thou good shepherd, who didst come to seek the wandering sheep, who givest consolation to the faint hearted, and life unto those who are broken hearted; who didst heal the woman who had an issue of blood; who didst free the daughter of the woman of Canaan from the demon; who forgave the two debtors, their debts; who healed the paralytic and forgave his sins; who justified the publican; and didst accept the

confession of the thief; who lifted the sins of the world; and nailed it to the cross. Thee do we beseech, O God, in Thy goodness, forgive the sins of these Thy servants, and all their iniquities, whether voluntary or involuntary; whether of knowledge or of ignorance. Forgive them and us, for Thou art a good God. Fill their mouths with Thy praises; open their lips, to glorify Thy Name; stretch forth their hands in the performance of Thy statutes. Guide their feet, in the way of Thy Gospel. For Thou art our God, who hast commanded us, through Thy Holy Apostles saying: "whatsoever you bind on earth shall be bound in heaven, and whatsoever you loose on earth shall be loosed in heaven." And as Thou didst hearken unto Ezekiel in the sorrow of his soul, at the hour of his death, and didst not refuse his supplications, in like manner, hearken unto me, Thy sinful and unworthy servant. For Thou, O Lord, didst command to forgive the erring, even unto seven times seventy; who repentest Thee of our wickedness, and rejoicest over the return of those who have gone astray. Unto Thee do we ascribe glory, together with Thy Father who is from everlasting, and Thine all Holy, and good and life creating Spirit, now and ever and unto the ages of ages.

People: *Amen.*

Prokeimenon

Priest: Let us attend. The Prokeimenon.

Reader: O Lord, rebuke me not in Thine wrath; neither chasten me in Thine anger.

People: *O Lord, rebuke me not in Thine wrath; neither chasten me in Thine anger.*

Reader: Have mercy upon me, O Lord, for I am weak.

People: *O Lord, rebuke me not in Thine wrath; neither chasten me in Thine anger.*

Reader: O Lord, rebuke me not in Thine wrath | neither chasten me in Thine anger.

The Seventh Epistle

Deacon: Wisdom.

Reader: The lesson is from the First Epistle of the Apostle Paul to the Thessalonians (5:14-23).

Deacon: Let us attend.

Reader: Brethren, now we exhort you, to warn them that are unruly, comfort the feeble minded, support the weak, be patient toward all men, see that none render evil for evil unto any man; but ever follow that which is good. Both among yourselves, and to all men. Rejoice evermore. Pray without ceasing. In everything give thanks: for this is the will of God in Christ Jesus concerning you. Quench not the Spirit. Despise not prophesyings. Prove all things; hold fast that which is good. Abstain from all appearance of evil. And the very God of peace sanctify you wholly; and I pray God your whole spirit and soul and body be preserved blameless unto the coming of our Lord Jesus Christ.

Priest: Peace be with you who read.

Reader: And with thy spirit.

Chorus: *Halleluiah. Halleluiah. Halleluiah.*

Reader: The Lord hear thee in the day of trouble. The Name of the God of Jacob defend thee.

Chorus: *Halleluiah. Halleluiah. Halleluiah.*

The Seventh Gospel

Deacon: Wisdom. Attend. Let us hear the Holy Gospel.

Priest: Peace be with you all.

People: *And with thy spirit.*

Priest: The lesson is from the Holy Gospel according to Matthew (9:9-13).

People: *Glory to Thee, O Lord, glory to Thee.*

Deacon: Let us attend.

Priest: At that time, as Jesus passed forth from thence, he saw a man, named Matthew, sitting at the receipt of custom: and He saith unto him, "Follow Me." And he arose, and followed Him. And it came to pass, as Jesus sat at meat in the house, behold many Publicans and sinners came and sat down with Him and His Disciples. And when the Pharisees saw it, they said unto His Disciples, "Why eateth your Master with Publicans and sinners?" But when Jesus heard that, He said unto them, "they that be whole need not a physician, but they that are sick. But go you and learn what that meaneth, I will have mercy, and not sacrifice: for I am not come to call the righteous, but sinners to repentance."

People: *Glory to Thee, O Lord, glory to Thee.*

The Ektenia Of Fervent Supplication

Priest: Have mercy upon us O God, according to Thy great goodness, we pray Thee, hearken and have mercy.

People: *Lord have mercy.* **(x3)**

Priest: Again, we pray for mercy, life, peace, health, salvation and visitation, for the servants of God, and for the remission of their sins.

People: *Lord have mercy.* **(x3)**

Priest: Again, we pray for the pardon of their every transgression, whether voluntary or involuntary.

People: *Lord have mercy.* **(x3)**

Priest: For Thou art a merciful God, and lovest mankind, and unto Thee, we ascribe glory to the Father, and to the Son, and to the Holy Spirit, both now and forever and unto the ages of ages.

People: *Amen.*

Priest: Let us pray to the Lord.

People: *Lord have mercy.*

The Seventh Prayer Over The Holy Oil

Priest: O Lord, our God, the physician of souls and bodies; the healer of all infirmities and all lingering diseases; who desirest that all men should be saved, and should come to the knowledge of Thy truth; who didst ordain repentance unto sinners, in the ancient covenant, unto David and Ninevites, and others; who didst come on earth, and didst become incarnate; Thou callest not the righteous, but sinners, as the Publican, the sinful woman, and the thief; and didst accept the Great Paul, who blasphemed against Thee. Thou didst accept Thy Apostle, Peter, after he had denied Thee thrice, promising him, saying, "Thou art Peter and upon this rock will I build my church, and the gates of hell shall not prevail against it, and I shall give thee the keys of the kingdom of heaven." For which cause, we are confident of Thy promises; Thee do we beseech, and Thee do we ask, at this hour, to hear and accept our supplications, as an incense offered unto Thee; visit these Thy servants; pardon and forgive them, O God; overlook their sins, that they hath committed, in word, deed, or thought, whether in knowledge or without knowledge; for there is no man who liveth and sinneth not, for Thou only art without sin, and Thy righteousness is right, and Thy word is truth. For Thou hast not created man for destruction, but for the keeping of Thy commandments, and for the inheritance of everlasting life; unto Thee we ascribe glory, with Thy Father, who is without beginning, and Thine all Holy Spirit, both now and forever and unto the ages of ages.

People: *Amen.*

[People kneel. Priest opens the Gospel face down, raised above the heads of those attending. Whilst:]

Priest: Let us pray to the Lord:

People: *Lord have mercy.*

Priest: O Holy King, compassionate and all merciful, Lord Jesus Christ, Son and Word of the living God, who desirest not the death of a sinner, but that he shall return and live; I lay not my sinful hand upon the heads of these, who come unto Thee in their iniquities, and asketh of Thee, through us, the pardon of their sins; but Thy mighty hand, which is in this, Thy Holy Gospels. I also beseech Thy compassion, and Thy love of mankind, O Saviour, who did give to David, through the prophet Nathan, remission of his sins, when he repented of them; and as Thou didst accept the contrite prayers of Mannases. Receive now, also according to Thy love of mankind, these Thy servants, who are repenting from their sins, regarding not all their trespasses.

For Thou art our God, who hast commanded, that those who fall into sin be forgiven, even unto seven times seventy. For as is Thy majesty, so also is Thy mercy; and unto Thee are due all glory, honour, and worship, O Father, Son, and Holy Spirit; both now and forever and unto the ages of ages.

People: Amen.

[People stand.]

The Anointing Of The Faithful

Priest raises the Gospel, and (because it is a Sacrament) the Orthodox only come forward to kiss it, and to be anointed with the Holy Oil, on their foreheads and their palms. Whilst:]

Chorus: *Glory be to the Father, and to the Son, and to the Holy Spirit;*

Troparion To The Unmercenary Healers

Tone 4   *Festive, joyous and expressing deep piety.*   *C, D, Eb, F, G, A, Bb, C.*

O Holy and unmercenary ones, forasmuch you have acquired a fountain of healing; you shall bestow healing unto those who beseech Thee; for you have earned the great gifts from the ever flowing fountain, our Saviour. For He said unto you, you are equal in zeal to the apostles: Behold, I have given you power over the unclean spirits; to cast them out, and to heal every malady and infirmity. Wherefore, as you have walked nobly in His commandments, you have received freely; so freely give us, healing the sufferings of our souls and bodies.

Chorus: *Both now and forever, and unto the ages of ages. Amen.*

Theotokion

O Gracious and Immaculate Lady, be favourable unto the prayers of those who entreat Thee, and stop the fierce attacks upon us, and deliver us from all sorrows. For Thou alone, we have as our safe pier and our firm protection. We have taken Thee as our helper, and we shall not be ashamed to call upon Thee. Make haste in answering the call of those who call unto Thee in faith. Rejoice, O Gracious Lady, O help of all, their shield and joy, and the salvation of our souls.

The Dismissal

Priest: Glory to Thee, O Christ, our God and our hope, glory to Thee.

Reader: *Glory be to the Father, and to the Son, and to the Holy Spirit;*
           Both now and forever, and unto the ages of ages. Amen.

Lord, have mercy. **(x3)**

Holy Father, bless.

Priest: O Christ our true God, who voluntarily didst suffer for our salvation; through the intercessions of His most pure and blameless Holy Mother; and of our righteous and Godmantled Fathers; of the Holy Apostle James; of the righteous saints, grandparents of Christ, Joachim and Anna; and of Ss *N*, patron saints of this church; and of all the saints, have mercy upon us and save us, for Thou art the lover of mankind. Through the prayers of our Holy Fathers, Lord Jesus Christ our God, have mercy upon us and save us.

People: Amen.

Priest: Through the prayers of our holy fathers, Lord Jesus Christ, our God, have mercy on us and save us.

People: Amen.

[For Wednesday Evening]

The Trisagion Prayers

Priest: Blessed is our God, always, now and ever, and unto the ages of ages.

People: *Amen.*

Priest: Glory to Thee, our God, glory to Thee.

O Heavenly King, Comforter, Spirit of Truth, Who art everywhere present and fillest all things, Treasury of blessings and Giver of life: Come and abide in us and cleanse us from every impurity and save our souls, O Good One.

Reader: Holy God, Holy Mighty, Holy Immortal, have mercy on us. **(x3)**

Glory be to the Father, and to the Son, and to the Holy Spirit;

Both now and forever, and unto the ages of ages. Amen.

O Most Holy Trinity, have mercy on us.

O Lord, cleanse us from our sins.

O Master, pardon our iniquities.

O Holy One, visit and heal our infirmities, for Thy names sake.

Lord have mercy. **(x3)**

Glory be be to the Father and to the Son and to the Holy Spirit;

Both now and forever, and unto the ages of ages. Amen.

People: *Our Father, Who art in Heaven, hallowed be Thy Name. Thy Kingdom come, Thy will be done, on earth as it is in Heaven. Give us this day our daily bread, and forgive us our trespasses, as we forgive those who trespass against us; and lead us not into temptation, but deliver us from the evil one.*

Priest: For Thine is the kingdom and the power and the glory of the Father and of the Son and of the Holy Spirit; both now and forever and unto the ages of ages.

People: *Amen.*

Lord, have mercy. **(x3)**

Glory be be to the Father and to the Son and to the Holy Spirit;

Both now and forever and unto the ages of ages. Amen.

Come, let us worship God, our King.

Come, let us worship and fall down before Christ, our King and our God.

Come, let us worship and fall down before Christ Himself, our King and our God.

Psalm 142

Hear my prayer, O Lord, give ear to my supplications. In Thy faithfulness answer me, and in Thy righteousness. Do not enter into judgement with Thy servant, for in Thy sight no one living is righteous. For the enemy has persecuted my soul; he has crushed my life to the ground; he has made me dwell in darkness, like those who have long been dead. Therefore my spirit is overwhelmed within me; my heart within me is distressed. I remember the days of old; I meditate on all Thy works; I muse on the work of Thine hands. I spread out my hands to Thee; my soul longs for Thee like a thirsty land. Answer me speedily, O Lord; my spirit fails. Do not hide Thy face from me, lest I be like those who go down into the pit. Cause me to hear Thy loving kindness in the morning, for in Thee do I trust; cause me to know the way in which I should walk, for I lift up my soul to Thee. Deliver me, O Lord, from mine enemies; in Thee I take shelter. Teach me to do Thy will, for Thou art my God; Thy Spirit is good. Lead me in the land of uprightness. Revive me, O Lord, for Thy names sake. For Thy righteousness' sake bring my soul out of trouble. In Thy mercy cut off mine enemies, and destroy all those who afflict my soul; for I am Thy servant.

After The Psalm

Glory be to the Father and to the Son and to the Holy Spirit,
Both now and forever and unto the ages of ages. Amen.
Holy God, Holy Mighty, Holy Immortal, have mercy on us. **(x3)**
O our God and our Hope, glory to Thee.

Little Litany

Deacon: Again and again, in peace let us pray to the Lord.

People: Lord, have mercy.

Deacon: Help us, save us, have mercy on us, and keep us, O God, by Thy grace.

People: Lord, have mercy.

Deacon: Calling to remembrance our most holy, most pure, most blessed, glorious Lady Theotokos and Ever Virgin Mary with all the saints, let us commit ourselves and one another and all our life unto Christ our God.

People: To Thee, O Lord.

Priest: For Thou art our God, and unto Thee do we send up glory, to the Father, and to the Son, and to the Holy Spirit, now and ever, and unto the ages of ages.

People: Amen.

Halleluiarion

People: *Halleluiah, Halleluiah, Halleluiah.*

Reader: O Lord, rebuke me not in Thine indignation, neither chasten me in Thy displeasure.

People: *Halleluiah, Halleluiah, Halleluiah.*

Reader: Have mercy on me, O Lord, for I am weak.

People: *Halleluiah, Halleluiah, Halleluiah.*

The Penitential Troparia

Tone 6   *Rich texture, funereal character, sorrowful tone.*   *D, Eb, F##, G, A, Bb, C##, D.*

Have mercy on us, O Lord, have mercy on us; for we sinners, void of all defence, offer unto Thee as Master, this supplication: have mercy on us.

Glory be to the Father and to the Son and to the Holy Spirit.

Lord, have mercy on us, for in Thee have we put our trust; be not very wroth against us, neither remember our iniquities; but look down upon us even now, since Thou art compassionate, and deliver us from our enemies. For Thou art our God, and we are Thy people; we are all the work of Thy hands, and we call upon Thy Name.

Both now and forever and unto the ages of ages. Amen.

Open the doors of mercy unto us, O Blessed Theotokos; in that we have set our hope in thee, may we not perish, but through thee he delivered from peril, for thou art the salvation of the Christian race.

Psalm 50

Have mercy on me, O God, according to Thy great mercy; and according to the multitude of Thy compassions blot out my transgression. Wash me thoroughly from mine iniquity, and cleanse me from my sin. For I acknowledge mine iniquity, and my sin is ever before me. Against Thee, Thee only have I sinned, and done evil in Thy sight, that Thou mayest be found just when Thou speakest, and victorious when Thou art judged. For behold, I was conceived in iniquity, and in sin my mother bore me. For behold, Thou hast loved truth; Thou hast made known to me the hidden and secret things of Thy wisdom. Thou shalt sprinkle me with hyssop, and I shall be made clean; Thou shalt wash me, and I shalt be whiter than snow. Make me to hear joy and gladness; that the humbled bones may rejoice. Turn Thy face away from my sins, and blot out all mine iniquities.

Create in me a clean heart, O God, and renew a steadfast spirit within me. Cast me not away from Thy presence, and take not Thy Holy Spirit from me. Restore to me the joy of Thy salvation, and establish me with Thy governing Spirit. I shall teach transgressors Thy ways, and the ungodly shall turn back to Thee. Deliver me from blood guiltiness, O God, the God of my salvation; my tongue shall joyfully declare Thy righteousness.

Lord, open my lips, and my mouth shall declare Thy praise. For if Thou hadst desired sacrifice, I would give it; Thou dost not delight in burned offerings. A sacrifice to God is a broken spirit; God will not despise a broken and a humbled heart. Do good, O Lord, in Thy good pleasure to Zion, and let the walls of Jerusalem be builded. Then Thou shalt be pleased with a sacrifice of righteousness, with oblation and whole burned offerings. Then shall they offer bulls on Thine altar.

Psalm 19

The Lord hear thee in the day of affliction; the name of the God of Jacob defend thee. Let Him send forth unto thee help from His sanctuary, and out of Zion let Him help thee. Let Him remember every sacrifice of thine, and thy whole burnt offering let Him fatten. The Lord grant thee according to thy heart, and fulfil all thy purposes. We will rejoice in Thy salvation, and in the name of the Lord our God shall we be magnified. The Lord fulfil all thy requests. Now have I known that the Lord hath saved His anointed one; He will hearken unto him out of His holy heaven; in mighty deeds is the salvation of His right hand. Some trust in chariots, and some in horses, but we will call upon the name of the Lord our God. They have been fettered and have fallen, but we are risen and are set upright. O Lord, save the king, and hearken unto us in the day when we call upon Thee.

Psalm 20

O Lord, in Thy strength the king shall be glad, and in Thy salvation shall he exceedingly rejoice. The desire of his heart hast Thou granted unto him, and hast not denied him the requests of his lips. Thou wentest before him with the blessings of goodness, Thou hast set upon his head a crown of precious stone. He asked life of Thee, and Thou gavest him length of days unto ages of ages. Great is his glory in Thy salvation; glory and majesty shalt Thou lay upon him. For Thou shalt give him blessing for ever and ever, Thou shalt gladden him in joy with Thy countenance. For the king hopeth in the Lord, and through the mercy of the Most High shall he not be shaken. Let Thy hand be found on all Thine enemies; let Thy right hand find all that hate Thee. For Thou wilt make them as an oven of fire in the time of Thy presence; the Lord in His wrath will trouble them sorely and fire shall devour them. Their fruit wilt Thou destroy from the earth, and their seed from the sons of men. For they have intended evil against Thee, they have devised counsels which they shall not be able to establish. For Thou shalt make them turn their backs; amongst those that are Thy remnant, Thou shalt make ready their countenance. Be Thou exalted, O Lord, in Thy strength; we will sing and chant of Thy mighty acts.

Glory be to the Father and to the Son and to the Holy Spirit,
Both now and forever and unto the ages of ages. Amen.

O Most Holy Trinity, have mercy on us.

O Lord, cleanse us from our sins.

O Master, pardon our iniquities.

O Holy One, visit and heal our infirmities, for Thy names sake.

Lord have mercy. **(x3)**

People: *Our Father, Who art in Heaven, hallowed be Thy Name. Thy Kingdom come, Thy will be done, on earth as it is in Heaven. Give us this day our daily bread, and forgive us our trespasses, as we forgive those who trespass against us; and lead us not into temptation, but deliver us from the evil one.*

Priest: For Thine is the kingdom and the power, and the glory: of the Father and of the Son, and of the Holy Spirit, now and ever, and unto the ages of ages.

People: *Amen.*

Troparia

O Lord, save Thy people and bless Thine inheritance. Grant victory unto Orthodox Christians over their enemies, and by the power of Thy Cross do Thou preserve Thy commonwealth.

Glory be to the Father and to the Son and to the Holy Spirit,

O Thou Who wast lifted up willingly upon the Cross, bestow Thy mercies upon the new community named after Thee, O Christ God; gladden with Thy power the Orthodox Christians, granting them victory over enemies; may they have as Thy help the weapon of peace, the invincible trophy.

Both now and forever and unto the ages of ages. Amen.

O Awesome intercession that cannot be put to shame, O good one, disdain not our prayer; O all hymned Theotokos, establish the commonwealth of the Orthodox, save the Orthodox Christians, and grant unto them victory from heaven, for thou didst bring forth God, O thou only blessed one.

Little Litany

Priest: Have mercy on us O God, according to Thy great mercy we pray Thee, hearken and have mercy.

People: *Lord, have mercy.* **(x3)**

Priest: Again we pray for His Holiness Patriarch Bartholomew; and for our Archbishop Nikitas.

People: *Lord, have mercy.* **(x3)**

Priest: Again we pray for all the brethren and for all Christians.

People: *Lord, have mercy.* **(x3)**

Priest: For a merciful God art Thou, and the Lover of mankind, and unto Thee do we send up glory: to the Father, and to the Son, and to the Holy Spirit, both now and forever, and unto the ages of ages.

People: *Amen. Holy Father bless.*

Priest: Glory to the holy, and consubstantial, and life creating, and indivisible Trinity, always, now and ever, and unto the ages of ages.

People: *Amen.*

Doxology Glory to God in the highest and on earth peace good will toward men. *(cross and bow)* **(x3)**

Psalm 50 O Lord, open my lips, and my mouth shall proclaim Thy praise. **(x2)**

The Six Psalms
Psalm 3

Lord, how they have increased who trouble me. Many are they who rise up against me. Many are they who say of me, "There is no help for him in God." But Thou, O Lord, art a shield for me, my glory and the One Who lifts up my head. I cried to the Lord with my voice, and He heard me from His holy hill. I lay down and slept; I awoke, for the Lord sustained me. I will not be afraid of ten thousands of people who have set themselves against me all around. Arise, O Lord; save me, O my God. For Thou hast struck all mine enemies on the cheekbone; Thou hast broken the teeth of the ungodly. Salvation belongs to the Lord. Thy blessing is upon Thy people.

Psalm 37

O Lord, do not rebuke me in Thy wrath, nor chasten me in Thy hot displeasure. For Thine arrows deeply pierce me, and Thine hand presses me down. There is no soundness in my flesh because of Thine anger, Nor is there any health in my bones because of my sin. For mine iniquities have gone over my head; like a heavy burden they are too heavy for me. My wounds are foul and festering because of my foolishness. I am troubled, I am bowed down greatly; I go mourning all the day long. For my loins are full of inflammation, and there is no soundness in my flesh. I am feeble and severely broken; I groan because of the turmoil of my heart. Lord, all my desire is before Thee; and my sighing is not hidden from Thee. My heart pants, my strength fails me; as for the light of mine eyes, it also has gone from me. My loved ones and my friends stand aloof from my plague, and my kinsmen stand afar off. Those also who seek my life lay snares for me; those who seek my hurt speak of destruction, and plan deception all the day long. But I, like a deaf man, do not hear; and I am like a mute who does not open his mouth. Thus I am like a man who does not hear, and in whose mouth is no response. For in Thee, O Lord, I hope; Thou wilt hear, O Lord my God. For I said, "Hear me, lest they rejoice over me, lest, when my foot slips, they magnify themselves against me." For I am ready to fall, and my sorrow is continually before me. For I will declare mine iniquity; I will be in anguish over my sin. But mine enemies are vigorous, and they are strong; and those who wrongfully hate me have multiplied. Those also who render evil for good, they are mine adversaries, because I follow what is good. Do not forsake me, O Lord; O my God, be not far from me. Make haste to help me, O Lord, my salvation.

Psalm 62

O God, Thou art my God; early will I seek Thee; my soul thirsts for Thee; My flesh longs for Thee in a dry and thirsty land where there is no water. So I have looked for Thee in the sanctuary, to see Thy power and Thy glory. Because Thy loving kindness is better than life, my lips shall praise Thee. Thus I will bless Thee while I live; I will lift up my hands in Thy name. My soul shall be satisfied as with marrow and fatness, and my mouth shall praise Thee with joyful lips. When I remember Thee on my bed, I meditate on Thee in the night watches. Because Thou hast been my help, therefore in the shadow of Thy wings I will rejoice. My soul follows close behind Thee; Thy right hand upholds me. But those who seek my life, to destroy it, shall go into the lower parts of the earth. They shall fall by the sword; they shall be a portion for jackals. But the king shall rejoice in God; everyone who swears by Him shall glory; but the mouth of those who speak lies shall be stopped.

After The Psalm

Glory be to the Father and to the Son and to the Holy Spirit,

Both now and forever and unto the ages of ages. Amen.

Halleluiah, Halleluiah, Halleluiah. Glory to Thee, O God. **(x3)**

Lord. have mercy. **(x3)**

Glory be to the Father and to the Son and to the Holy Spirit,

Both now and forever and unto the ages of ages. Amen.

Psalm 87

O Lord, God of my salvation, I have cried out day and night before Thee. Let my prayer come before Thee; incline Thine ear to my cry. For my soul is full of troubles, and my life draws near to the grave. I am counted with those who go down to the pit; I am like a man who has no strength, Adrift amongst the dead, like the slain who lie in the grave, whom Thou rememberest no more, and who are cut off from Thine hand. Thou hast laid me in the lowest pit, in darkness, in the depths. Thy wrath lies heavy upon me, and Thou hast afflicted me with all Thy waves. Thou hast put away mine acquaintances far from me; Thou hast made me an abomination to them; I am shut up, and I cannot get out; Mine eye wastes away because of affliction. Lord, I have called daily upon Thee; I have stretched out my hands to Thee. Willest Thou work wonders for the dead? Shall the dead arise and praise Thee? Shall Thy loving kindness be declared in the grave? Or Thy faithfulness in the place of destruction? Shall Thy wonders be known in the dark? And Thy righteousness in the land of forgetfulness? But to Thee I have cried out, O Lord, and in the morning my prayer comes before Thee. Lord, why dost Thou cast off my soul? Why dost Thou hide Thy face from me? I have been afflicted and ready to die from my youth up; I suffer Thy terrors; I am distraught. Thy fierce wrath has gone over me; Thy terrors have cut me off. They came around me all day long like water; they engulfed me altogether. Loved one and friend Thou hast put far from me, and mine acquaintances into darkness.

Psalm 102

Bless the Lord O my soul; and all that is within me, bless His holy name. Bless the Lord O my soul, and forget not all His benefits: Who forgives all thine iniquities, Who heals all thy diseases, Who redeems thy life from destruction, Who crowns thee with loving kindness and tender mercies, Who satisfies thy mouth with good things, so that thine youth is renewed like the eagles. The Lord executes righteousness and justice for all who are oppressed. He made known His ways to Moses, His acts to the children of Israel. The Lord is merciful and gracious, slow to anger, and abounding in mercy. He will not always strive with us, nor will He keep His anger forever. He has not dealt with us according to our sins, nor punished us according to our iniquities. For as the heavens are high above the earth, so great is His mercy toward those who fear Him; As far as the east is from the west, so far has He removed our transgressions from us. As a father pities his children, so the Lord pities those who fear Him. For He knows our frame; He remembers that we are dust. As for man, his days are like grass; as a flower of the field, so he flourishes. For the wind passes over it, and it is gone, and its place remembers it no more. But the mercy of the Lord is from everlasting to everlasting on those who fear Him, and His righteousness to childrens children, To such as keep His covenant, and to those who remember His commandments to do them. The Lord has established His throne in heaven, and His kingdom rules overall. Bless the Lord you His angels, who excel in strength, who do His word, heeding the voice of His word. Bless the Lord all you His hosts, you ministers of His, who do His pleasure. Bless the Lord all His works, in all places of His dominion. Bless the Lord O my soul.

Hearken unto me, O Lord, in Thy righteousness, and enter not into judgement with Thy servant. **(x2)**

Thy good Spirit shall lead me in the land of uprightness.

After The Psalm

Glory be to the Father and to the Son and to the Holy Spirit,

Both now and forever and unto the ages of ages. Amen.

Halleluiah, Halleluiah, Halleluiah. Glory to Thee, O God. *(cross and bow)* **(x3)**

Great Litany

Deacon: In peace let us pray to the Lord.

People: *Lord, have mercy.*

Deacon: For the peace from above, and the salvation of our souls; let us pray to the Lord.

People: *Lord, have mercy.*

Deacon: For the peace of the whole world, the good estate of the holy churches of God, and the union of all, let us pray to the Lord.

People: *Lord, have mercy.*

Deacon: For this holy temple, and for them that with faith, reverence; and the fear of God enter herein, let us pray to the Lord

People: *Lord, have mercy.*

Deacon: Again we pray for our His Holiness Patriarch Bartholomew; for our Archbishop Nikitas; for the venerable priesthood, the diaconate in Christ, for all the clergy and people, let us pray to the Lord.

People: *Lord, have mercy.*

Deacon: For this land, its authorities and armed forces, let us pray to the Lord.

People: *Lord, have mercy.*

Deacon: For the people of the Holy Orthodox Church, and for their salvation; let us pray to the Lord.

People: *Lord, have mercy.*

Deacon: That He may deliver His people from enemies both visible and invisible, and confirm in us oneness of mind, brotherly love and piety, let us pray to the Lord.

People: *Lord, have mercy.*

Deacon: For this *[city / town / village / monastery]*, for every city and country, and the faithful that dwell therein, let us pray to the Lord.

People: *Lord, have mercy.*

Deacon: For seasonable weather, an abundance of the fruits of the earth, and peaceful times, let us pray to the Lord.

People: *Lord, have mercy.*

Deacon: For travellers by sea, land and air; for the sick, the suffering, the imprisoned, and for their salvation, let us pray to the Lord.

People: *Lord, have mercy.*

Deacon: That we may be delivered from all tribulation, wrath, and necessity, let us pray to the Lord.

People: *Lord, have mercy.*

Deacon: Help us, save us, have mercy on us, and keep us, O God, by Thy grace.

People: *Lord, have mercy.*

Deacon: Calling to remembrance our most holy, most pure, most blessed, glorious Lady Theotokos and Ever Virgin Mary with all the saints, let us commit ourselves and one another and all our life unto Christ our God.

People: *To Thee O Lord.*

Deacon: For unto Thee is due all glory, honour and worship; to the Father, and to the Son, and to the Holy Spirit, now and ever, and unto the ages of ages.

People: *Amen.*

Halleluiarion

Reader: Out of the night my spirit waketh at dawn unto Thee, O God;

For Thy commandments are light upon the earth.

People: *Halleluiah, Halleluiah, Halleluiah.*

Reader: Learn righteousness, you that dwell upon the earth.

People: *Halleluiah, Halleluiah, Halleluiah.*

Reader: Zeal shall lay hold upon an uninstructed people.

People: *Halleluiah, Halleluiah, Halleluiah.*

Reader: Add more evils upon them, O Lord. Add more evils upon them that are glorious upon the earth.

People: *Halleluiah, Halleluiah, Halleluiah.*

Tone 8   Humility, tranquillity, repose, suffering, pleading.   *C, D, Eb, F, G, A, Bb, C.*

When the glorious disciples were enlightened at the washing of the feet, then Judas the ungodly one was stricken and darkened with the love of silver. And unto the lawless judges did he deliver Thee, the righteous

Judge. Behold, O lover of money, him that for the sake thereof did hang himself; flee from that insatiable soul that dared such things against the Master. O Thou Who art good unto all, Lord, glory be to Thee.

Glory be to the Father and to the Son and to the Holy Spirit,

When the glorious disciples were enlightened at the washing of the feet, then Judas the ungodly one was stricken and darkened with the love of silver. And unto the lawless judges did he deliver Thee, the righteous Judge. Behold, O lover of money, him that for the sake thereof did hang himself; flee from that insatiable soul that dared such things against the Master. O Thou Who art good unto all, Lord, glory be to Thee.

Both now and forever and unto the ages of ages. Amen.

When the glorious disciples were enlightened at the washing of the feet, then Judas the ungodly one was stricken and darkened with the love of silver. And unto the lawless judges did he deliver Thee, the righteous Judge. Behold, O lover of money, him that for the sake thereof did hang himself; flee from that insatiable soul that dared such things against the Master. O Thou Who art good unto all, Lord, glory be to Thee.

Deacon: And that He will vouchsafe unto us the hearing of the Holy Gospel, let us pray unto the Lord God.
People: *Lord, have mercy.* **(x3)**
Deacon: Wisdom, Aright. Let us hear the Holy Gospel.
Priest: Peace be with you all.
People: *And with thy spirit.*
Priest: The Reading is from the Holy Gospel according to Luke.
People: *Glory to Thee, O Lord, glory to Thee.*
Deacon: Let us attend.

The Gospel According To Luke, § 108 (from half) to § 109 [Luke 22:1-39].

At that time, the Feast of Unleavened Bread drew near, which is called Passover. And the chief priests and the scribes sought how they might kill Jesus, for they feared the people. Then Satan entered Judas, surnamed Iscariot, who was numbered amongst the twelve. So he went his way and conferred with the chief priests and captains, how he might betray Him to them. And they were glad, and agreed to give him money. So he promised and sought opportunity to betray Him to them in the absence of the multitude. Then came the Day of Unleavened Bread, when the Passover must be killed. And He sent Peter and John, saying, "Go and prepare the Passover for us, that we may eat." So they said to Him, "Where will Thou that we prepare?" And He said to them, "Behold, when you have entered the city, a man will meet you carrying a pitcher of water; follow him into the house which he enters. Then you shall say to the master of the house, 'The Teacher says to you, "Where is the guest room where I may eat the Passover with My disciples?" Then he will show you a large, furnished upper room; there make ready." So they went and found it just as He had said to them, and they prepared the Passover.

When the hour had come, He sat down, and the twelve apostles with Him. Then He said to them, "With fervent desire I have desired to eat this Passover with you before I suffer; for I say to you, I will no longer eat of it until it is fulfilled in the kingdom of God." Then He took the cup, and gave thanks, and said, "Take this and divide it amongst yourselves; for I say to you, I will not drink of the fruit of the vine until the kingdom of God comes." And He took bread, gave thanks and broke it, and gave it to them, saying, "This is My body which is given for you; do this in remembrance of Me." Likewise He also took the cup after supper, saying, "This cup is the new covenant in My blood, which is shed for you. But behold, the hand of My betrayer is with Me on the table. And truly the Son of Man goes as it has been determined, but woe to that man by whom He is betrayed." Then they began to question amongst themselves, which of them it was who would do this thing.

Now there was also a dispute amongst them, as to which of them should be considered the greatest. And He said to them, "The kings of the Gentiles exercise lord ship over them, and those who exercise authority over them are called 'benefactors.' But not so amongst you; on the contrary, he who is greatest amongst you, let him be as the younger, and he who governs as he who serves. For who is greater, he who sits at the table, or he who serves? Is it not he who sits at the table? Yet I am amongst you as the One Who serves. But you are those who have continued with Me in My trials. And I bestow upon you a kingdom, just as My Father bestowed one upon Me, that you may eat and drink at My table in My kingdom, and sit on thrones judging the twelve tribes of Israel."

And the Lord said, "Simon, Simon. Indeed, Satan has asked for you, that he may sift you as wheat. But I have prayed for you, that your faith should not fail; and when you have returned to Me, strengthen your brethren." But he said to Him, "Lord, I am ready to go with Thee, both to prison and to death." Then He said, "I tell you, Peter, the rooster shall not crow this day before you will deny three times that you know Me." And He said to them, "When I sent you without money bag, knapsack, and sandals, did you lack anything?" So they said, "Nothing." Then He said to them, "But now, he who has a money bag, let him take it, and likewise a knapsack; and he who has no sword, let him sell his garment and buy one. For I say to you that this which is written must still be accomplished in Me: 'And He was numbered with the transgressors.' For the things concerning Me have an end." So they said, "Lord, look, here are two swords." And He said to them, "It is enough." Coming out, He went to the Mount of Olives, as He was accustomed, and His disciples also followed Him.

People: *Glory to Thee, O Lord, glory to Thee.*

The Canon

Ode I

Eirmos

Tone 6   *Rich texture, funereal character, sorrowful tone.*   *D, Eb, F##, G, A, Bb, C##, D.*

The Red Sea was parted by a blow from Moses' staff, and the deep with its waves grew dry. It served as a path to the unarmed people of Israel, but to the Egyptians in full armour it proved a grave. A hymn of praise was sung, well pleasing to God: Christ our God is greatly glorified.

People: *Glory to Thee, O Lord, glory to Thee.*

Cause of all and Bestower of life, the infinite Wisdom of God has built His house, from a pure Mother who has not known man. For, clothing Himself in a bodily temple, Christ our God is greatly glorified.

People: *Glory to Thee, O Lord, glory to Thee.*

Instructing His friends in the Mysteries, the true Wisdom of God prepares a table that gives food to the soul, and He mingles for the faithful the cup of the wine of life eternal. Let us approach with reverence and cry aloud: Christ our God is greatly glorified.

Glory be to the Father and to the Son and to the Holy Spirit,
Both now and forever and unto the ages of ages. Amen.

You faithful, let us all give ear to the exalted preaching of the uncreated and consubstantial Wisdom of God, for He cries aloud: "O taste and see that I am good." O sing: Christ our God is greatly glorified.

Katavasia

Tone 6   Rich texture, funereal character, sorrowful tone.   *D, Eb, F##, G, A, Bb, C##, D.*

The Red Sea was parted by a blow from Moses' staff, and the deep with its waves grew dry. It served as a path to the unarmed people of Israel, but to the Egyptians in full armour it proved a grave. A hymn of praise was sung, well pleasing to God: Christ our God is greatly glorified.

Ode III

Eirmos

Tone 6   Rich texture, funereal character, sorrowful tone.   *D, Eb, F##, G, A, Bb, C##, D.*

O God the Lord and Creator of all, Thou art become poor, uniting a created nature to Thyself, while remaining free from passion. Since Thou art the Passover, Thou hast offered Thyself to those for whose sake Thou wast soon to die; and Thou hast cried: "Eat My Body, and you shall be firmly established in the faith."

People: *Glory to Thee, O Lord, glory to Thee.*

Filling Thy cup of salvation with joy, O loving Lord, Thou hast made Thy disciples drink from it. For Thou offerest Thyself in sacrifice, crying: "Drink My Blood, and you shall be firmly established in the faith."

Glory be to the Father and to the Son and to the Holy Spirit,
Both now and forever and unto the ages of ages. Amen.

"How foolish is the traitor in your midst." In Thy forbearance Thou hast said to Thy disciples. "He will not know or understand these things. But abide in Me, and you shall be firmly established in the faith."

Katavasia

Tone 6   Rich texture, funereal character, sorrowful tone.   *D, Eb, F##, G, A, Bb, C##, D.*

O God the Lord and Creator of all, Thou art become poor, uniting a created nature to Thyself, while remaining free from passion. Since Thou art the Passover, Thou hast offered Thyself to those for whose sake Thou wast soon to die; and Thou hast cried: "Eat My Body, and you shall be firmly established in the faith."

Deacon: Again and again, in peace let us pray to the Lord.

People: *Lord, have mercy.*

Deacon: Help us, save us, have mercy on us, and keep us, O God, by Thy grace.

People: *Lord, have mercy.*

Deacon: Calling to remembrance our most holy, most pure, most blessed, glorious Lady Theotokos and Ever Virgin Mary with all the saints, let us commit ourselves and one another and all our life unto Christ our God.

People: *To Thee, O Lord.*

Priest: For Thou art our God, and unto Thee do we send up glory, to the Father, and to the Son, and to the Holy Spirit, now and ever, and unto the ages of ages.

People: *Amen.*

The Sessional Hymns

Tone 1   Magnificent, happy and earthy.   *C, D, Eb, F, G, A, Bb, C.*

He who made the lakes and springs and seas, wishing to teach us the surpassing value of humility, girded Himself with a towel and washed the feet of the disciples, humbling Himself in the abundance of His great compassion and raising us from the depths of wickedness, for He alone loves mankind.

Glory be to the Father and to the Son and to the Holy Spirit,

Tone 3   Arrogant, brave, and mature atmosphere.   *F, G, A, A#, C, D, E, F.*

Humbling Thyself in Thy compassion, Thou hast washed the feet of Thy disciples, teaching them to take the path which as God Thou hast followed. And Peter, who at first refused to be washed, yielded then to the divine command, and earnestly entreated Thee that we may be granted Thy great mercy.

Both now and forever and unto the ages of ages. Amen.

Tone 4   Festive, joyous and expressing deep piety.   *C, D, Eb, F, G, A, Bb, C.*

Eating, O Master, with Thy disciples, Thou hast mystically revealed Thy holy death, which delivers us from corruption, who honour Thy sacred Passion.

Ode IV

Eirmos

Tone 6   Rich texture, funereal character, sorrowful tone.   *D, Eb, F##, G, A, Bb, C##, D*

Foreseeing Thy secret mystery, O Christ, the Prophet cried: "Thou hast manifested the mighty power of Thy love, O merciful Father, for in Thy goodness Thou has sent Thine only begotten Son to the world as atonement."

Glory to Thee, O our God, glory to Thee.

Going to Thy Passion that frees from passion all the posterity of Adam, Thou hast said, O Christ, to Thy friends: "I have desired to eat this Passover with you; for the Father has sent Me, His only begotten Son, to the world as atonement."

Glory to Thee, O our God, glory to Thee.

Partaking from the cup, O Lord Immortal, Thou hast cried to the disciples: "In this present life I will no more drink with you from the fruit of the vine. For the Father has sent Me, His only begotten Son, to the world as atonement."

Glory be to the Father and to the Son and to the Holy Spirit,
Both now and forever and unto the ages of ages. Amen.

"In My Kingdom", Thou hast said, O Christ, to Thy friends, "I shall drink a new drink beyond your understanding; I shall be with you as God amongst gods. For the Father has sent Me, His only begotten Son, to the world as atonement."

Katavasia

Tone 6   Rich texture, funereal character, sorrowful tone.   *D, Eb, F##, G, A, Bb, C##, D*

Foreseeing Thy secret mystery, O Christ, the Prophet cried: "Thou hast manifested the mighty power of Thy love, O merciful Father, for in Thy goodness Thou has sent Thine only begotten Son to the world as atonement."

Ode V

Eirmos

Tone 6   Rich texture, funereal character, sorrowful tone.   *D, Eb, F##, G, A, Bb, C##, D*

United by the bond of love, and offering themselves to Christ the Lord, the apostles were washed clean; and with feet made beautiful, they preached to all the Gospel of peace.

Glory to Thee, O our God, glory to Thee.

The Wisdom of God that restrains the untamed fury of the waters that are above the firmament, that sets a bridle on the deep and keeps back the seas, now pours water into a basin; and the Master washes the feet of His servants.

Glory be to the Father and to the Son and to the Holy Spirit,
Both now and forever and unto the ages of ages. Amen.

The Master shows to His disciples an example of humility; he who wraps the heaven in clouds girds Himself with a towel; and He in whose hand is the life of all things kneels down to wash the feet of His servants.

Katavasia

Tone 6   Rich texture, funereal character, sorrowful tone.   *D, Eb, F##, G, A, Bb, C##, D*

United by the bond of love, and offering themselves to Christ the Lord, the apostles were washed clean; and with feet made beautiful, they preached to all the Gospel of peace.

Ode VI

Eirmos

Tone 6   Rich texture, funereal character, sorrowful tone.   *D, Eb, F##, G, A, Bb, C##, D*

The uttermost depths of sin have compassed me about; and no longer able to endure its stormy waves, as Jonah I cry out to Thee, O Master: Lead me up from corruption.

Glory to Thee, O our God, glory to Thee.

"O disciples, you call Me Lord and Master, and so I am", Thou hast cried, O Saviour. "Follow then the example that you have seen in Me."

Glory be to the Father and to the Son and to the Holy Spirit,
Both now and forever and unto the ages of ages. Amen.

"He who is free from defilement needs no washing of the feet. Now you are clean, My disciples, but not all of you. For one of you inclines to wild folly in his heart."

Katavasia

Tone 6   Rich texture, funereal character, sorrowful tone.   *D, Eb, F##, G, A, Bb, C##, D*

The uttermost depths of sin have compassed me about; and no longer able to endure its stormy waves, as Jonah I cry out to Thee, O Master: Lead me up from corruption.

Deacon: Again and again, in peace let us pray to the Lord.
People: *Lord, have mercy.*
Deacon: Help us, save us, have mercy on us, and keep us, O God, by Thy grace.
People: *Lord, have mercy.*

Deacon: Calling to remembrance our most holy, most pure, most blessed, glorious Lady Theotokos and Ever Virgin Mary with all the saints, let us commit ourselves and one another and all our life unto Christ our God.

People: *To Thee, O Lord.*

Deacon: For Thou art the King of Peace and the Saviour of our souls, and unto Thee do we send up glory, to the Father, and to the Son, and to the Holy Spirit, now and ever, and unto the ages of ages.

People: *Amen.*

Kontakion

Tone 2   Majesty, gentleness, hope, repentance and sadness.   E, F, G, Ab, B, C.

Taking the bread into his hands, the betrayer stretched them forth secretly and receiveth the price of Him that, with His Own hands, fashioned man. And Judas, the servant and deceiver, remained incorrigible.

Ikos

Let us all draw near in fear to the mystical table, and with pure souls let us receive the Bread; let us remain at the Master's side, that we may see how He washes the feet of the disciples and wipes them with a towel; and let us do as we have seen, subjecting ourselves to each other and washing one another's feet. For such is the commandment that Christ Himself gave to His disciples; but Judas servant and deceiver, paid no heed.

Ode VII

Eirmos

Tone 6   Rich texture, funereal character, sorrowful tone.   D, Eb, F##, G, A, Bb, C##, D

In Babylon the Children did not fear the fiery furnace; but cast into the midst of the flames they were refreshed with dew and sang: "O God of our fathers, blessed art Thou."

Glory to Thee, O our God, glory to Thee.

With head bowed, Judas plotted evil, seeking opportunity to deliver for condemnation the Judge who is Lord of all and God of our fathers.

Glory to Thee, O our God, glory to Thee.

"Amongst you there is one that shall betray Me", Christ cried to His friends; and they forgetting their gladness, were seized with grief and anguish, saying: "Who shall this be? Tell us, O God of our fathers."

Glory be to the Father and to the Son and to the Holy Spirit,
Both now and forever and unto the ages of ages. Amen.

"He that dares to dip his hand with Me in the dish; and it had been good for that man if he had never passed through the gates of life." So did Christ, the God of our fathers, speak of the one who should betray Him.

Katavasia

Tone 6 Rich texture, funereal character, sorrowful tone.   *D, Eb, F##, G, A, Bb, C##, D*

In Babylon the Children did not fear the fiery furnace; but cast into the midst of the flames they were refreshed with dew and sang: "O God of our fathers, blessed art Thou."

Ode VIII

Tone 6 Rich texture, funereal character, sorrowful tone.   *D, Eb, F##, G, A, Bb, C##, D*

Accepting danger for the sake of their fathers' laws, the blessed Children in Babylon scorned the foolish order of the King. Standing together in the fire which burnt them not, they sang a song fitting for God almighty: "O you works of the Lord, praise you the Lord and exalt Him above all forever."

Glory to Thee, O our God, glory to Thee.

Blessed guests in Zion, faithful companions of the Word, the apostles followed the Shepherd like sheep. Firmly united to Christ and feeding upon the divine Word, they cried in thanksgiving: "O you works of the Lord, praise you the Lord and exalt Him above all forever."

We bless Father, Son and Holy Spirit, the Lord.

Iniquitous Iscariot, forgetful of the law of friendship, hastened to the betrayal on the feet which Thou hadst washed. Eating Thy Bread, the divine Body, he lifted up his heel against Thee; for he knew not how to cry: "O you works of the Lord, praise you the Lord and exalt Him above all forever."

Both now and ever, and unto the ages of ages. Amen.

Lacking all conscience, he received the Body that delivers men from sin and the divine Blood that was shed for the world. He was not ashamed to drink what he had sold for money; he felt no anger against sin; for he knew not how to cry: "O you works of the Lord, praise you the Lord and exalt Him above all forever."

People: *We praise, we bless, we worship the Lord. Praising and supremely exalting Him unto all ages.*

Katavasia

Tone 6 Rich texture, funereal character, sorrowful tone.   *D, Eb, F##, G, A, Bb, C##, D*

Accepting danger for the sake of their fathers' laws, the blessed Children in Babylon scorned the foolish order of the King. Standing together in the fire which burnt them not, they sang a song fitting for God almighty: "O you works of the Lord, praise you the Lord and exalt Him above all forever."

Ode IX

Eirmos

Tone 6   Rich texture, funereal character, sorrowful tone.   *D, Eb, F##, G, A, Bb, C##, D*

Come, you faithful, let us raise our minds on high and enjoy the Master's hospitality and the table of immortal life in the upper room; and let us hear the exalted teaching of the Word whom we magnify.

Glory to Thee, O our God, glory to Thee.

"Go", said the Word to the disciples, "and prepare the Passover for those whom I call to share in the Mystery: with the unleavened bread of the word of truth prepare the Passover in the upper room where the mind is established, and magnify the strength of grace."

Glory to Thee, O our God, glory to Thee.

Before the ages the Father begat Me, who am Wisdom and Creator, and He established Me as the beginning of His ways. He appointed Me to perform the works which now are mystically accomplished. For though I am by nature the uncreated Word, I make Mine own the speech and qualities of the manhood that I have assumed.

Glory be to the Father and to the Son and to the Holy Spirit,
Both now and forever and unto the ages of ages. Amen.

Since I am man not merely in appearance but in reality, the human nature united to Me is made godlike through the exchange of attributes. Know Me, then, as one single Christ, who saves those amongst whom I have been born and whose nature I have taken.

Katavasia

Tone 6   Rich texture, funereal character, sorrowful tone.   *D, Eb, F##, G, A, Bb, C##, D*

Come, you faithful, let us raise our minds on high and enjoy the Master's hospitality and the table of immortal life in the upper room; and let us hear the exalted teaching of the Word whom we magnify.

Little Litany

Deacon: Again and again, in peace let us pray to the Lord.

People: *Lord, have mercy.*

Deacon: Help us, save us, have mercy on us, and keep us, O God, by Thy grace.

People: *Lord, have mercy.*

Deacon: Calling to remembrance our most holy, most pure, most blessed, glorious Lady Theotokos and Ever Virgin Mary with all the saints, let us commit ourselves and one another and all our life unto Christ our God.

People: *To Thee, O Lord.*

Priest: For all the Hosts of Heaven praise Thee, and unto Thee do we send up glory, to the Father, and to the Son, and to the Holy Spirit, now and ever and unto the ages of ages.

People: *Amen.*

Exapostilarion

Tone 3   Arrogant, brave, and mature atmosphere.   *F, G, A, A#, C, D, E, F.*

I see Thy bridal chamber adorned, O my Saviour, and I have no wedding garment that I may enter there. Make the robe of my soul to shine, O Giver of Light, and save me.

Glory be to the Father and to the Son and to the Holy Spirit,

Tone 3   Arrogant, brave, and mature atmosphere.   *F, G, A, A#, C, D, E, F.*

I see Thy bridal chamber adorned, O my Saviour, and I have no wedding garment that I may enter there. Make the robe of my soul to shine, O Giver of Light, and save me.

Both now and forever and unto the ages of ages. Amen.

Tone 3   Arrogant, brave, and mature atmosphere.   *F, G, A, A#, C, D, E, F.*

I see Thy bridal chamber adorned, O my Saviour, and I have no wedding garment that I may enter there. Make the robe of my soul to shine, O Giver of Light, and save me.

The Lauds (Praises)
Psalm 148

Reader: Praise the Lord. Praise the Lord from the heavens; praise Him in the heights. Praise Him, all His angels; praise Him, all His hosts. Praise Him, sun and moon; praise Him, all you stars of light. Praise Him, you heavens of heavens, and you waters above the heavens. Let them praise the name of the Lord, for He commanded and they were created. He has also established them forever and ever; He has made a decree which shall not pass away. Praise the Lord from the earth, you great sea creatures and all the depths; Fire and hail, snow and clouds; stormy wind, fulfilling His word; Mountains and all hills; fruitful trees and all cedars; Beasts and all cattle; creeping things and flying fowl; Kings of the earth and all peoples; princes and all judges of the earth; Both young men and maidens; old men and children. Let them praise the name of the Lord, for His name alone is exalted; His glory is above the earth and heaven. And He has exalted the horn of His people, the praise of all His saints - of the children of Israel, a people near to Him. Praise the Lord.

Psalm 149

Praise the Lord. Sing to the Lord a new song, and His praise in the congregation of saints. Let Israel rejoice in their Maker; let the children of Zion be joyful in their King. Let them praise His name with the dance; let them sing praises to Him with the timbrel and harp. For the Lord takes pleasure in His people; He will beautify the humble with salvation. Let the saints be joyful in glory; let them sing aloud on their beds. Let the high praises of God be in their mouth, and a two edged sword in their hand, To execute vengeance on the nations, and punishments on the peoples; To bind their kings with chains, and their nobles with fetters of iron; To execute on them the written judgement; this honour have all His saints. Praise the Lord.

Psalm 150 - Pt 1

Tone 2   Majesty, gentleness, hope, repentance and sadness.   *E, F, G, Ab, B, C.*

Chorus: *Praise the Lord. Praise God in His sanctuary; praise Him in His mighty firmament. Praise Him for His mighty acts; praise Him according to His excellent greatness.*

Reader: In haste the council of the Jews assembles, to deliver the Fashioner and Creator of all to Pilate. O transgressors, O unbelievers. For they make ready to surrender unto judgement Him who comes to judge the living and the dead; they prepare the Passion of Him who heals the passions. Great is Thy mercy, O long suffering Lord: glory to Thee.

Psalm 150 - Pt 2

Chorus: *Praise Him with the sound of the trumpet; praise Him with the lute and harp.*

Reader: Judas the transgressor at the supper dipped his hand into the dish with Thee, O Lord, yet sinfully he reached out his hands to receive the money. He reckoned up the value of the oil of myrrh, and yet was not afraid to sell Thee who art above all price. He stretched out his feet to be washed, yet deceitfully he kissed the Master and betrayed Him to the breakers of the Law. Cast out of the company of the apostles, he threw away the thirty pieces of silver, and did not see Thy Resurrection on the third day. Through this Thy Resurrection have mercy on us.

Psalm 150 - Pt 3

Chorus: *Praise Him with the timbrel and dance; praise Him with stringed instruments and flutes.*

Reader: Judas, the deceitful traitor, with a deceitful kiss betrayed the Lord and Saviour; he sold the Master of all as a slave to the transgressors; the Lamb of God, the Son of the Father, went as a sheep to the slaughter: for He alone is rich in mercy.

Psalm 150 - Pt 4

Chorus: *Praise Him with loud cymbals; praise Him with high sounding cymbals. Let everything that has breath praise the Lord.*

Reader: Judas, servant and deceiver, disciple and traitor, friend and false accuser, was revealed by his deeds. For he followed the Master, yet inwardly he plotted to betray Him. He said in himself: "I shall deliver Him up and gain the money that is promised." He desired the oil of myrrh to be sold and Jesus to be taken by deceit. He gave a kiss and handed over Christ; and the Lord went as a sheep to the slaughter, for He alone is compassionate and loves mankind.

Chorus: *Glory be to the Father and to the Son and to the Holy Spirit,*
            Both now and forever and unto the ages of ages. Amen.

Tone 2   Majesty, gentleness, hope, repentance and sadness.   *E, F, G, Ab, B, C.*

Reader: The Lamb whom Isaiah proclaimed goes of His own will to the slaughter. He gives His back to scourging, and His cheeks to blows, and turns not away His face from the shame of their spitting; He is condemned to a disgraceful death. Though sinless, He accepts all these things willingly, that He may grant to all men resurrection from the dead.

Priest: Glory to Thee Who hast shown forth the light.

Lesser Doxology

Glory to God, Who has shown us the Light. Glory to God in the highest, and on earth, peace, good will toward men. We praise Thee. We bless Thee. We worship Thee. We glorify Thee and give thanks to Thee for Thy great glory. O Lord God, Heavenly King, God the Father Almighty. O Lord, the Only Begotten Son, Jesus Christ, and the Holy Spirit. \

O Lord God, Lamb of God, Son of the Father, Who takes away the sins of the world, have mercy on us. Thou, Who takes away the sins of the world, receive our prayer. Thou, Who sittest at the right hand of God the Father, have mercy on us. /

For Thou alone art holy, and Thou alone art Lord. Thou alone, O Lord Jesus Christ, are most high in the glory of God the Father. Amen. I will give thanks to Thee every day and praise Thy Name forever and ever. Lord, Thou hast been our refuge from generation to generation. I said, *"Lord, have mercy on me. Heal my soul, for I have sinned against Thee."* \

Lord, I flee to Thee. Teach me to do Thy will, for Thou art my God. For with Thee is the fountain of Life, and in Thy light we shall see light. Continue Thy loving kindness to those who know Thee. Vouchsafe, O Lord, to keep us this day without sin. Blessed art Thou, O Lord, the God of our fathers, and praised and glorified is Thy Name forever. Amen. Let Thy mercy be upon us, O Lord, even as we have set our hope on Thee.

Blessed art Thou, O Master; teach me Thy statutes.

Blessed art Thou, O Lord; enlighten me with Thy commandments.

Blessed art Thou, O Holy One; make me to understand Thy precepts.

Thy mercy endures forever, O Lord. Do not despise the works of Thy hands. To Thee belongs worship, to Thee belongs praise, to Thee belongs glory: to the Father and to the Son and to the Holy Spirit, both now and forever and unto the ages of ages. Amen. \

Priest: Let us complete our morning prayer unto the Lord.

People: Lord, have mercy.

Priest: Help us, save us, have mercy on us, and keep us, O God, by Thy grace.

People: Lord, have mercy.

Priest: That the whole day may be perfect, holy, peaceful and sinless, let us ask of the Lord.

People: Grant this, O Lord.

Priest: An angel of peace, a faithful guide, a guardian of our souls and bodies, let us ask of the Lord.

People: Grant this, O Lord.

Priest: Pardon and remission of our sins and offences, let us ask of the Lord.

People: *Grant this, O Lord.*

Priest: Things good and profitable for our souls, and peace for the world, let us ask of the Lord.

People: *Grant this, O Lord.*

Priest: That we may complete the remaining time of our life in peace and repentance, let us ask of the Lord.

People: *Grant this, O Lord.*

Priest: A Christian ending to our life, painless, blameless, peaceful, and a good defence before the dread judgement seat of Christ, let us ask.

People: *Grant this, O Lord.*

Priest: Calling to remembrance our most holy, most pure, most blessed, glorious Lady Theotokos and Ever Virgin Mary with all the saints, let us commit ourselves and one another and all our life unto Christ our God.

People: *To Thee, O Lord.*

Priest: For Thou art a God of mercy, compassion, and love for mankind, and unto Thee do we send up glory: to the Father, and to the Son, and to the Holy Spirit, now and ever, and unto the ages of ages.

People: *Amen.*

Priest: Peace be unto all.

People: *And with thy spirit.*

Priest: Let us bow down our heads unto the Lord.

People: *To Thee, O Lord.*

Priest *[soto voce]*: O Holy Lord, who dwelleth on high and regardest the humble of heart, and with thine all seeing eye dost behold all creation, unto Thee have we bowed the neck of our soul and body, and we entreat Thee: O Holy of holies, stretch forth Thine invisible hand from Thy holy dwelling place, and bless us all. And if in aught we have sinned, whether voluntarily or involuntarily, forgive, inasmuch as Thou art a good God, and lovest mankind, vouchsafing unto us Thy earthly and heavenly good things.

Priest *[aloud]*: For Thine it is to show mercy and to save us, O our God, and unto Thee do we send up glory: to the Father, and to the Son, and to the Holy Spirit, now and ever, and unto the ages of ages.

People: *Amen.*

The Aposticha

Tone 8   Humility, tranquillity, repose, suffering, pleading.   *C, D, Eb, F, G, A, Bb, C.*

Reader: Today the evil Sanhedrin has assembled against Christ and devised vain things against Him, plotting to deliver Him, though innocent, to Pilate to be put to death. Today Judas places round his neck the noose of money, and deprives himself of life both temporal and divine. Today Caiaphas prophesies against his will, saying: "It is expedient that one man should perish for the people." He came to suffer for our sins, that He might set us free from the bondage of the enemy: for He is good and loves mankind.

Chorus: *He who ate My bread hath lifted up his heel against Me.*

Reader: Today Judas lays aside his outward pretence of love for the poor, and openly displays his greed for money. No longer does he take thought for the needy. He offers now for sale, not the oil of myrrh brought by the sinful woman, but the Myrrh from heaven, and he takes the pieces of silver. He runs to the Jews and says to the transgressors: "What will you give me if I deliver Him up to you?" O avarice of the traitor. He reckons the sale profitable, and, agreeing with the wishes of the purchasers, he concludes the transaction. He does not dispute about the price but sells the Lord like a runaway slave; for it is the custom of thieves to throw away what is precious. So the disciple cast that which is holy to the dogs, and the madness of avarice fills him with fury against his own Master. Let us flee from such folly, and cry: O long suffering Lord, glory to Thee.

Chorus: *He gathered iniquity unto himself; He went forth and spake in a like manner.*

Reader: Deceitful are thy ways, lawless Judas. Sick with the love of money, thou hast come to hate mankind. If thou lovest riches, why become disciple of Him who teaches poverty? But if thy love is for Him, why sell the Lord that is above all price and hand Him over to be murdered? Tremble, O sun; groan, earth, and quaking cry aloud: O long suffering Lord, glory to Thee.

Chorus: *They spoke lawless words against Me.*

Reader: O you faithful, let none who is uninstructed in the Mystery draw near to the table of the Lord's Supper; let none approach deceitfully as Judas. For he received his portion, yet he betrayed the Bread. In outward appearance he was a disciple, yet in reality he was present as a murderer. He rejoiced with the Jews, though he sat at supper with the apostles. He kissed in hatred, and with his kiss he sold the God and Saviour of our souls, who has redeemed us from the curse.

Chorus: *Glory be to the Father, and to the Son, and to the Holy Spirit.*

Reader: Deceitful are thy ways, lawless Judas. Sick with the love of money, thou hast come to hate mankind. If thou lovest riches, why become disciple of Him who teaches poverty? But if thy love is for Him, why sell the Lord that is above all price and hand Him over to be murdered? Tremble, O sun; groan, earth, and quaking cry aloud: O long suffering Lord, glory to Thee.

Chorus: *Both now and forever and unto the ages of ages. Amen.*

Tone 5   *Stimulating, dancing, and rhythmical.*   C, D, Eb, F, G, A, Bb, C.

Reader: Instructing Thy disciples in the Mystery, O Lord, Thou hast taught them saying: "My friends, take care that fear does not separate you from Me. For though I suffer, yet it is for the sake of the world. Do not be scandalized because of me; for I have come not to be ministered unto, but to minister, and to give My life as a ransom for the world. If then you are My friends, you will do as I do. He who will be first, let him be the last; let the master be as the servant. Abide in Me, that you may bear fruit: for I am the Vine of Life." It is good to give praise unto the Lord, and to chant unto Thy name, O Most High, to proclaim in the morning Thy mercy, and Thy truth by night. **(x2)**

Chorus: *Holy God, Holy Mighty, Holy Immortal, have mercy on us.* **(x3)**

Glory be to the Father and to the Son and to the Holy Spirit;
Both now and forever and unto the ages of ages. Amen.

O Most Holy Trinity, have mercy on us.

O Lord, cleanse us from our sins.

O Master, pardon our iniquities.

O Holy One, visit and heal our infirmities, for Thy names sake.

Lord have mercy. **(x3)**

Glory be to the Father and to the Son and to the Holy Spirit,
Both now and forever and unto the ages of ages. Amen.

People: *Our Father, Who art in Heaven, hallowed be Thy Name. Thy Kingdom come, Thy will be done, on earth as it is in Heaven. Give us this day our daily bread, and forgive us our trespasses, as we forgive those who trespass against us; and lead us not into temptation, but deliver us from the evil one.*

Priest: For Thine is the Kingdom, and the power, and the glory; of the Father, and of the Son, and of the Holy Spirit, now and ever, and unto the ages of ages.

People: *Amen.*

Tone 8   Humility, tranquillity, repose, suffering, pleading.   *C, D, Eb, F, G, A, Bb, C.*

Chorus: When the glorious disciples were enlightened at the washing of the feet, then Judas the ungodly one was stricken and darkened with the love of silver. And unto the lawless judges did he deliver Thee, the righteous Judge. Behold, O lover of money, him that for the sake thereof did hang himself; flee from that insatiable soul that dared such things against the Master. O Thou Who art good unto all, Lord, glory be to Thee.

Great Litany

Priest: Have mercy on us, O God, according to Thy great mercy, we pray Thee, hearken and have mercy.

People: *Lord, have mercy.* **(x3)**

Deacon: Again we pray for His Holiness Patriarch Bartholomew; and for our Archbishop Nikitas.

People: *Lord, have mercy.* **(x3)**

Deacon: For this land, its authorities and armed forces, let us pray to the Lord.

People: *Lord, have mercy.* **(x3)**

Deacon: For the people of the Holy Orthodox Church, and for their salvation; let us pray to the Lord.

People: *Lord, have mercy.* **(x3)**

Deacon: That He may deliver His people from enemies both visible and invisible, and confirm in us oneness of mind, brotherly love and piety, let us pray to the Lord.

People: *Lord, have mercy.* **(x3)**

Deacon: Again we pray for the blessed and ever memorable, holy Orthodox patriarchs; for pious kings and right believing queens; and for the founders of this holy *[temple / monastery]*: and for all our fathers and brethren gone to their rest before us, and the Orthodox here and everywhere laid to rest.

People: *Lord, have mercy.* **(x3)**

Deacon: Again we pray for them that bring offerings and do good works in this holy and all venerable temple; for them that minister and them that chant, and for all the people here present, that await of Thee great and abundant mercy.

People: *Lord, have mercy.* **(x3)**

Priest: For a merciful God art Thou, and the Lover of mankind, and unto Thee do we send up glory: to the Father, and to the Son, and to the Holy Spirit, now and ever, and unto the ages of ages.

People: *Amen.*

Priest: Wisdom.

People: *Holy Father bless.*

Priest: He that is is blessed, Christ our God, always, now and ever, and unto the ages of ages.

People: *Amen.*

Reader: Establish, O God, the holy Orthodox Faith of Orthodox Christians unto the ages of ages.

[Then the reader immediately begins the first hour.]

Reader:

Come, let us worship God, our King.

Come, let us worship and fall down before Christ, our King and our God.

Come, let us worship and fall down before Christ Himself, our King and our God.

Psalm 5

Unto my words give ear, O Lord, hear my cry. Attend unto the voice of my supplication, O my King and my God; for unto Thee will I pray, O Lord. In the morning shalt Thou hear my voice. In the morning shall I stand before Thee, and Thou shalt look upon me; for not a God that willest iniquity art Thou. He that worketh evil shall not dwell near Thee nor shall transgressors abide before Thine eyes. Thou hast hated all them that work iniquity; Thou shalt destroy all them that speak a lie. A man that is bloody and deceitful shall the Lord abhor. But as for me, in the multitude of Thy mercy shall I go into Thy house; I shall worship toward Thy holy temple in fear of Thee. O Lord, guide me in the way of Thy righteousness; because of mine enemies, make straight my way before Thee, For in their mouth there is no truth; their heart is vain. Their throat is an open sepulchre, with their tongues have they spoken deceitfully; judge them, O God. Let them fall down on account of their own devisings; according to the multitude of their ungodliness, cast them out, for they have embittered Thee, O Lord. And let all them be glad that hope in Thee; they shall rejoice, and Thou shalt dwell amongst them. And all shall glory in Thee that love Thy name, for Thou shalt bless the righteous. O Lord, as with a shield of Thy good pleasure hast Thou crowned us.

Psalm 89

Lord, Thou hast been our refuge in generation and generation. Before the mountains came to be and the earth was formed and the world, even from everlasting to everlasting art Thou. Turn not man away unto lowliness; yea, Thou hast said: Turn back you sons of men. For a thousand years in Thine eyes, O Lord, are but as yesterday that is past, and as a watch in the night. Things of no account shall their years be; in the morning like grass shall man pass away. In the morning shall he bloom and pass away. In the evening shall he fall and grow withered and dry. For we have fainted away in Thy wrath, and in Thine anger have we been troubled. Thou hast set our iniquities before us; our lifespan is in the light of Thy countenance. For all our days are faded away, and in Thy wrath are we fainted away; our years have, like a spider, spun out their tale. As for the days of our years, in their span, they be threescore years and ten. And if we be in strength, mayhap fourscore years; and what is more than these is toil and travail. For mildness is come upon us, and we shall be chastened. Who knoweth the might of Thy wrath? And out of fear of Thee, who can recount Thine anger? So make Thy right hand known to me, and to them that in their heart are instructed in wisdom. Return, O Lord; how long? And be Thou entreated concerning Thy servants. We were filled in the morning with Thy mercy, O Lord, and we rejoiced and were glad. In all our days, let us be glad for the days wherein Thou didst humble us, for the years wherein we saw evils. And look upon Thy servants, and upon Thy works, and do Thou guide their sons. And let the brightness of the Lord our God be upon us, and the works of our hands do Thou guide aright upon us, yea, the works of our hands do Thou guide aright.

Psalm 100

Of mercy and judgement will I sing to Thee, O Lord; I will chant and have understanding in a blameless path. When wilt Thou come unto me? I have walked in the innocence of my heart in the midst of my house. I have no unlawful thing before mine eyes; the workers of transgressions I have hated. A crooked heart hath not cleaved unto me; as for the wicked man who turned from me, I knew him not. Him that privily talked against his neighbour did I drive away from me. With him whose eye was proud and his heart insatiate, I did not eat. Mine eyes were upon the faithful of the land, that they might sit with me; the man that walked in the blameless path, he ministered unto me. The proud doer dwelt not in the midst of my house; the speaker of unjust things prospered not before mine eyes. In the morning I slew all the sinners of the land, utterly to destroy out of the city of the Lord all them that work iniquity.

After The Psalm

Glory be to the Father, and to the Son, and to the Holy Spirit;
Both now and forever, and unto the ages of ages. Amen.

Halleluiah, Halleluiah, Halleluiah. Glory to Thee, O God. **(x3)**

Lord, have mercy. **(x3)**

Glory be to the Father and to the Son and to the Holy Spirit.

When the glorious disciples were enlightened at the washing of the feet, then Judas the ungodly one was stricken and darkened with the love of silver. And unto the lawless judges did he deliver Thee, the righteous Judge. Behold, O lover of money, him that for the sake thereof did hang himself; flee from that insatiable soul that dared such things against the Master. O Thou Who art good unto all, Lord, glory be to Thee.

Both now and for ever, and unto the ages of ages. Amen.

Theotokion

What shall we call thee, O thou who art full of grace? Heaven, for from thee hast dawned forth the Sun of Righteousness. Paradise, for from thee hath blossomed forth the flower of immortality. Virgin, for thou hast remained incorrupt. Pure Mother, for thou hast held in thy holy embrace the Son, the God of all. Do thou entreat Him to save our souls.

Tone 3   Arrogant, brave, and mature atmosphere.   *F, G, A, A#, C, D, E, F.*

Thou wast struck on the face for the sake of mankind, yet was not moved to anger. Deliver our life from corruption, O Lord and save us.

Glory be to the Father, and to the Son, and to the Holy Spirit;
Both now and forever, and unto the ages of ages. Amen.

Tone 3   Arrogant, brave, and mature atmosphere.   *F, G, A, A#, C, D, E, F.*

Thou wast struck on the face for the sake of mankind, yet was not moved to anger. Deliver our life from corruption, O Lord and save us.

Prokeimenon

Priest: Let us attend. The Prokeimenon.

Reader: Let the nations understand that Thy name is Lord.

People: *Let the nations understand that Thy name is Lord.*

Reader: O God, who shall be likened unto Thee?

People: *Let the nations understand that Thy name is Lord.*

Reader: Let the nations understand | that Thy name is Lord.

Priest: Wisdom.

Reader: The Reading is from the Prophecy of Jeremiah.

Priest: Let us attend.

Reader: O Lord, teach me, and I shall know; then I saw their practices. But I, as an innocent lamb led to the slaughter, knew not; for against me they devised an evil device, saying: Come and let us put wood into his bread, and let us utterly destroy him from off the land of the living, and let his name not be remembered any more. O Lord of hosts, that judgest righteously, trying the reins and hearts, let me see Thy vengeance upon them, for to Thee have I declared my cause. Therefore thus saith the Lord concerning the men of Anathoth that seek my life, that say: Thou shalt not prophesy at all in the name of the Lord, but if thou dost, thou shalt die by our hands. Therefore thus saith the Lord of hosts: Behold, I will visit upon them; their young men shall die by the sword, and their sons and their daughters shall die of famine, and there shall be no remnant left of them; for I will bring evil upon the dwellers in Anathoth, in the year of their visitation. Righteous art Thou, O Lord, that I may make my defence to Thee; yea, I will speak to Thee of judgements. Why is it that the way of the ungodly prospereth? That all that deal very treacherously are flourishing? Thou hast planted them, and they have taken root; they have begotten children, and become fruitful; Thou art near to their mouth, and far from their reins. But Thou, O Lord, knowest me, hast seen me, and hast proved my heart before Thee; pull them out like sheep for the slaughter, and purify them for the day of their slaughter. How long shall the land mourn, and the grass of every field wither for the wickedness of them that dwell in it? The beasts and birds are utterly destroyed, because they said: God shall not see our ways. Thy feet run, and they cause thee to faint. Go ye, gather together all the wild beasts of the field, and let them come to devour her. Many shepherds have destroyed My vineyard, they have defiled My portion, they have made My desirable portion a trackless wilderness, it is made complete ruin. For thus saith the Lord concerning all the evil neighbours that touch Mine inheritance, which I have divided to My people Israel: Behold, I will draw them away from their land, and I will cast out the house of Judah from the midst of them. But it shall come to pass, after I have caste them out, that I will return and have mercy upon them, and will cause them to dwell every one in his inheritance and every one in his land.

Prokeimenon

Priest: Let us attend. Wisdom. The Prokeimenon.

Reader: Make your vows and pay them to the Lord our God.

People: *Make your vows and pay them to the Lord our God.*

Reader: In Judea is God known, His name is great in Israel.

People: *Make your vows and pay them to the Lord our God.*

Reader: Make your vows and pay them | to the Lord our God.

Reader: My steps do Thou direct according to thy saying, and let no iniquity have dominion over me. Deliver me from the false accusations of men, and I will keep Thy commandments. Make Thy face to shine upon Thy servant, and teach me Thy statutes.

Let my mouth be filled with Thy praise, that I may hymn Thy glory and Thy majesty all the day long.

Holy God, Holy Mighty, Holy Immortal, have mercy on us. **(x3)**

> *Glory be to the Father, and to the Son, and to the Holy Spirit;*
> *Both now and forever, and unto the ages of ages. Amen.*

O Most Holy Trinity, have mercy on us.

O Lord, cleanse us from our sins.

O Master, pardon our iniquities.

O Holy One, visit and heal our infirmities, for Thy names sake.

Lord have mercy. **(x3)**

> *Glory be to the Father and to the Son and to the Holy Spirit,*
> *Both now and forever and unto the ages of ages. Amen.*

People: *Our Father, Who art in Heaven, hallowed be Thy Name. Thy Kingdom come, Thy will be done, on earth as it is in Heaven. Give us this day our daily bread, and forgive us our trespasses, as we forgive those who trespass against us; and lead us not into temptation, but deliver us from the evil one.*

Priest: For Thine is the Kingdom, and the power, and the glory; of the Father, and of the Son, and of the Holy Spirit, now and ever, and unto the ages of ages.

People: *Amen.*

Reader: Taking the bread into his hands, the betrayer stretched them forth secretly and receiveth the price of Him that, with His Own hands, fashioned man. And Judas, the servant and deceiver, remained incorrigible.

Lord, have mercy. **(x40)**

The Prayer Of The Hours

At all times and in every hour, Thou art worshipped and glorified in heaven and on earth, Christ our God. Long in patience, great in mercy and compassion, Thou lovest the righteous and showest mercy to sinners. Thou callest all to salvation through the promise of good things to come. Lord, receive our prayers at the present time. Direct our lives according to Thy commandments. Sanctify our souls. Purify our bodies. Set our minds aright. Cleanse our thoughts, and deliver us from all sorrow, evil and distress. Surround us with Thy holy angels, that, guarded and guided by their host, we may arrive at the unity of the faith and the understanding of Thine ineffable glory. For Thou art blessed to the ages of ages. Amen.

Lord, have mercy. **(x3)**

Glory be to the Father and to the Son and to the Holy Spirit,
Both now and forever and unto the ages of ages. Amen.

Greater in honour than the Cherubim and beyond compare more glorious than the Seraphim; without corruption thou gavest birth to God the Word, truly the Theotokos, we magnify thee.

Holy Father bless.

Priest: God be gracious unto us and bless us, and cause Thy face to shine upon us and have mercy on us.
People: *Amen.*

The Prayer Of The First Hour

Priest: O Christ, the True Light, Who enlightenest and sanctifiest every man that cometh into the world: Let the Light of Thy countenance be signed upon us, that in it we may see the Unapproachable Light, and guide our steps in the doing of Thy commandments, through the intercessions of Thy most pure Mother, and of all Thy saints. Amen.

Kontakion For The Annunciation

Tone 8   Humility, tranquillity, repose, suffering, pleading.   *C, D, Eb, F, G, A, Bb, C.*
To Thee, the Champion Leader, we Thy servants dedicate a feast of victory and of thanksgiving as ones rescued out of sufferings, O Theotokos: but as Thou art one with might, which is invincible, from all dangers that can be, do Thou deliver us, that we may cry to Thee: Rejoice, Thou Bride Unwedded.

Priest: Glory to Thee, O Christ our God and our hope, glory to Thee.
Reader: *Glory be to the Father and to the Son and to the Holy Spirit,*

Both now and forever and unto the ages of ages. Amen.

Lord, have mercy. **(x3)**

Holy Father, bless.

Priest: May Christ our true God, the Lord who for our salvation went to His voluntary Passion, through the intercessions of His most pure Mother; of the holy and glorious apostles; of the holy and righteous ancestors of God, Joachim and Anna; and of all the saints: have mercy on us and save us, for He is good and lovest mankind.

People: Amen.

[For Thursday Evening]

The Trisagion Prayers

Priest: Blessed is our God, always, now and ever, and unto the ages of ages.

People: *Amen.*

Priest: Glory to Thee, our God, glory to Thee.

O Heavenly King, Comforter, Spirit of Truth, Who art everywhere present and fillest all things, Treasury of blessings and Giver of life: Come and abide in us and cleanse us from every impurity and save our souls, O Good One.

Reader: Holy God, Holy Mighty, Holy Immortal, have mercy on us. **(x3)**

Glory be to the Father, and to the Son, and to the Holy Spirit;

Both now and forever, and unto the ages of ages. Amen.

O Most Holy Trinity, have mercy on us.

O Lord, cleanse us from our sins.

O Master, pardon our iniquities.

O Holy One, visit and heal our infirmities, for Thy names sake.

Lord have mercy. **(x3)**

Glory be be to the Father and to the Son and to the Holy Spirit;

Both now and forever, and unto the ages of ages. Amen.

People: *Our Father, Who art in Heaven, hallowed be Thy Name. Thy Kingdom come, Thy will be done, on earth as it is in Heaven. Give us this day our daily bread, and forgive us our trespasses, as we forgive those who trespass against us; and lead us not into temptation, but deliver us from the evil one.*

Priest: For Thine is the kingdom and the power and the glory of the Father and of the Son and of the Holy Spirit; both now and forever and unto the ages of ages.

People: *Amen.*

Lord, have mercy. **(x3)**

Glory be be to the Father and to the Son and to the Holy Spirit;

Both now and forever and unto the ages of ages. Amen.

Come, let us worship God, our King.

Come, let us worship and fall down before Christ, our King and our God.

Come, let us worship and fall down before Christ Himself, our King and our God.

[Priest censes with small hand censer whilst:]

Psalm 19

The Lord hear thee in the day of affliction; the name of the God of Jacob defend thee. Let Him send forth unto thee help from His sanctuary, and out of Zion let Him help thee. Let Him remember every sacrifice of thine, and thy whole burnt offering let Him fatten. The Lord grant thee according to thy heart, and fulfil all thy purposes. We will rejoice in Thy salvation, and in the name of the Lord our God shall we be magnified. The Lord fulfil all thy requests. Now have I known that the Lord hath saved His anointed one; He will hearken unto him out of His holy heaven; in mighty deeds is the salvation of His right hand. Some trust in chariots, and some in horses, but we will call upon the name of the Lord our God. They have been fettered and have fallen, but we are risen and are set upright. O Lord, save the king, and hearken unto us in the day when we call upon Thee.

Psalm 20

O Lord, in Thy strength the king shall be glad, and in Thy salvation shall he exceedingly rejoice. The desire of his heart hast Thou granted unto him, and hast not denied him the requests of his lips. Thou wentest before him with the blessings of goodness, Thou hast set upon his head a crown of precious stone. He asked life of Thee, and Thou gavest him length of days unto ages of ages. Great is his glory in Thy salvation; glory and majesty shalt Thou lay upon him. For Thou shalt give him blessing for ever and ever, Thou shalt gladden him in joy with Thy countenance. For the king hopeth in the Lord, and through the mercy of the Most High shall he not be shaken. Let Thy hand be found on all Thine enemies; let Thy right hand find all that hate Thee. For Thou wilt make them as an oven of fire in the time of Thy presence; the Lord in His wrath will trouble them sorely and fire shall devour them. Their fruit wilt Thou destroy from the earth, and their seed from the sons of men. For they have intended evil against Thee, they have devised counsels which they shall not be able to establish. For Thou shalt make them turn their backs; amongst those that are Thy remnant, Thou shalt make ready their countenance. Be Thou exalted, O Lord, in Thy strength; we will sing and chant of Thy mighty acts.

Holy God, Holy Mighty, Holy Immortal, have mercy on us. **(x3)**

Glory be to the Father and to the Son and to the Holy Spirit,

Both now and forever and unto the ages of ages. Amen.

O Most Holy Trinity, have mercy on us.

O Lord, cleanse us from our sins.

O Master, pardon our iniquities.

O Holy One, visit and heal our infirmities, for Thy names sake.

Lord have mercy. **(x3)**

Glory be to the Father and to the Son and to the Holy Spirit,
Both now and forever and unto the ages of ages. Amen.

People: *Our Father, Who art in Heaven, hallowed be Thy Name. Thy Kingdom come, Thy will be done, on earth as it is in Heaven. Give us this day our daily bread, and forgive us our trespasses, as we forgive those who trespass against us; and lead us not into temptation, but deliver us from the evil one.*

Priest: For Thine is the kingdom and the power, and the glory: of the Father and of the Son, and of the Holy Spirit, now and ever, and unto the ages of ages.

People: *Amen.*

Troparia

O Lord, save Thy people and bless Thine inheritance. Grant Thou victory unto Orthodox Christians over their enemies, and by the power of Thy Cross do Thou preserve Thy commonwealth.

Glory be to the Father and to the Son and to the Holy Spirit,

O Thou Who wast lifted up willingly upon the Cross, bestow Thy mercies upon the new community named after Thee, O Christ God; gladden with Thy power the Orthodox Christians, granting them victory over enemies; may they have as Thy help the weapon of peace, the invincible trophy.

Both now and forever and unto the ages of ages. Amen.

O Awesome intercession that cannot be put to shame, O good one, disdain not our prayer; O all hymned Theotokos, establish the commonwealth of the Orthodox, save the Orthodox Christians, and grant unto them victory from heaven, for thou didst bring forth God, O thou only blessed one.

Little Litany

Priest: Have mercy on us, O God, according to Thy great mercy, we pray Thee, hearken and have mercy.

People: *Lord, have mercy.* **(x3)**

Priest: Again we pray for all the pious and all Orthodox Christians.

People: *Lord, have mercy.* **(x3)**

Priest: Again we pray for His Holiness Patriarch Bartholomew; and our Archbishop Nikitas.

People: *Lord, have mercy.* **(x3)**

Priest: For a merciful God art Thou, and the Lover of mankind, and unto Thee do we send up glory: to the Father, and to the Son, and to the Holy Spirit, both now and forever, and unto the ages of ages.

People: *Amen. Holy Father bless.*

Priest: Glory to the holy, and consubstantial, and life creating, and indivisible Trinity, always, now and ever, and unto the ages of ages.

People: *Amen.*

Doxology - excerpt
Reader: Glory to God in the highest and on earth peace good will toward men. *(cross and bow)* **(x3)**

Psalm 50 - excerpt
Chorus: O Lord, open my lips, and my mouth shall proclaim Thy praise. **(x2)**

The Six Psalms
Psalm 3

Lord, how they have increased who trouble me. Many are they who rise up against me. Many are they who say of me, "There is no help for him in God." But Thou, O Lord, art a shield for me, my glory and the One Who lifts up my head. I cried to the Lord with my voice, and He heard me from His holy hill. I lay down and slept; I awoke, for the Lord sustained me. I will not be afraid of ten thousands of people who have set themselves against me all around. Arise, O Lord; save me, O my God. For Thou hast struck all mine enemies on the cheekbone; Thou hast broken the teeth of the ungodly. Salvation belongs to the Lord. Thy blessing is upon Thy people.

Psalm 37

O Lord, do not rebuke me in Thy wrath, nor chasten me in Thy hot displeasure. For Thine arrows deeply pierce me, and Thine hand presses me down. There is no soundness in my flesh because of Thine anger, Nor is there any health in my bones because of my sin. For mine iniquities have gone over my head; like a heavy burden they are too heavy for me. My wounds are foul and festering because of my foolishness. I am troubled, I am bowed down greatly; I go mourning all the day long. For my loins are full of inflammation, and there is no soundness in my flesh. I am feeble and severely broken; I groan because of the turmoil of my heart. Lord, all my desire is before Thee; and my sighing is not hidden from Thee. My heart pants, my strength fails me; as for the light of mine eyes, it also has gone from me. My loved ones and my friends stand aloof from my plague, and my kinsmen stand afar off. Those also who seek my life lay snares for me; those who seek my hurt speak of destruction, and plan deception all the day long. But I, like a deaf man, do not hear; and I am like a mute who does not open his mouth. Thus I am like a man who does not hear, and in whose mouth is no response.

For in Thee, O Lord, I hope; Thou wilt hear, O Lord my God. For I said, "Hear me, lest they rejoice over me, lest, when my foot slips, they magnify themselves against me." For I am ready to fall, and my sorrow is continually before me. For I will declare mine iniquity; I will be in anguish over my sin. But mine enemies are vigorous, and they are strong; and those who wrongfully hate me have multiplied. Those also who render evil for good, they are mine adversaries, because I follow what is good. Do not forsake me, O Lord; O my God, be not far from me. Make haste to help me, O Lord, my salvation.

Psalm 62

O God, Thou art my God; early will I seek Thee; my soul thirsts for Thee; My flesh longs for Thee in a dry and thirsty land where there is no water. So I have looked for Thee in the sanctuary, to see Thy power and Thy glory. Because Thy loving kindness is better than life, my lips shall praise Thee. Thus I will bless Thee while I live; I will lift up my hands in Thy name. My soul shall be satisfied as with marrow and fatness, and my mouth shall praise Thee with joyful lips. When I remember Thee on my bed, I meditate on Thee in the night watches. Because Thou hast been my help, therefore in the shadow of Thy wings I will rejoice. My soul follows close behind Thee; Thy right hand upholds me. But those who seek my life, to destroy it, shall go into the lower parts of the earth. They shall fall by the sword; they shall be a portion for jackals. But the king shall rejoice in God; everyone who swears by Him shall glory; but the mouth of those who speak lies shall be stopped.

After The Psalm

Glory be to the Father and to the Son and to the Holy Spirit,
Both now and forever and unto the ages of ages. Amen.
Halleluiah, Halleluiah, Halleluiah. Glory to Thee, O God. **(x3)**
Lord. have mercy. **(x3)**

Glory be to the Father and to the Son and to the Holy Spirit,
Both now and forever and unto the ages of ages. Amen.

Psalm 87

O Lord, God of my salvation, I have cried out day and night before Thee. Let my prayer come before Thee; incline Thine ear to my cry. For my soul is full of troubles, and my life draws near to the grave. I am counted with those who go down to the pit; I am like a man who has no strength, Adrift amongst the dead, like the slain who lie in the grave, whom Thou rememberest no more, and who are cut off from Thine hand. Thou hast laid me in the lowest pit, in darkness, in the depths. Thy wrath lies heavy upon me, and Thou hast afflicted me with all Thy waves. Thou hast put away mine acquaintances far from me; Thou hast made me an abomination to them; I am shut up, and I cannot get out; Mine eye wastes away because of affliction. Lord, I have called daily upon Thee; I have stretched out my hands to Thee. Willest Thou work wonders for the dead? Shall the dead arise and praise Thee? Shall Thy loving kindness be declared in the grave? Or Thy faithfulness in the place of destruction? Shall Thy wonders be known in the dark? And Thy righteousness in the land of forgetfulness? But to Thee I have cried out, O Lord, and in the morning my prayer comes before Thee. Lord, why dost Thou cast off my soul? Why dost Thou hide Thy face from me? I have been afflicted and ready to die from my youth up; I suffer Thy terrors; I am distraught. Thy fierce wrath has gone over me; Thy terrors have cut me off. They came around me all day long like water; they engulfed me altogether. Loved one and friend Thou hast put far from me, and mine acquaintances into darkness.

Psalm 102

Bless the Lord O my soul; and all that is within me, bless His holy name. Bless the Lord O my soul, and forget not all His benefits: Who forgives all thine iniquities, Who heals all thy diseases, Who redeems thy life from destruction, Who crowns thee with loving kindness and tender mercies, Who satisfies thy mouth with good things, so that thine youth is renewed like the eagles. The Lord executes righteousness and justice for all who are oppressed. He made known His ways to Moses, His acts to the children of Israel. The Lord is merciful and gracious, slow to anger, and abounding in mercy. He will not always strive with us, nor will He keep His anger forever. He has not dealt with us according to our sins, nor punished us according to our iniquities. For as the heavens are high above the earth, so great is His mercy toward those who fear Him; As far as the east is from the west, so far has He removed our transgressions from us. As a father pities his children, so the Lord pities those who fear Him. For He knows our frame; He remembers that we are dust. As for man, his days are like grass; as a flower of the field, so he flourishes. For the wind passes over it, and it is gone, and its place remembers it no more. But the mercy of the Lord is from everlasting to everlasting on those who fear Him, and His righteousness to childrens children, To such as keep His covenant, and to those who remember His commandments to do them. The Lord has established His throne in heaven, and His kingdom rules overall. Bless the Lord you His angels, who excel in strength, who do His word, heeding the voice of His word. Bless the Lord all you His hosts, you ministers of His, who do His pleasure. Bless the Lord all His works, in all places of His dominion. Bless the Lord O my soul.

Psalm 142

Hear my prayer, O Lord, give ear to my supplications. In Thy faithfulness answer me, and in Thy righteousness. Do not enter into judgement with Thy servant, for in Thy sight no one living is righteous. For the enemy has persecuted my soul; he has crushed my life to the ground; he has made me dwell in darkness, like those who have long been dead. Therefore my spirit is overwhelmed within me; my heart within me is distressed. I remember the days of old; I meditate on all Thy works; I muse on the work of Thine hands. I spread out my hands to Thee; my soul longs for Thee like a thirsty land. Answer me speedily, O Lord; my spirit fails. Do not hide Thy face from me, lest I be like those who go down into the pit. Cause me to hear Thy loving kindness in the morning, for in Thee do I trust; cause me to know the way in which I should walk, for I lift up my soul to Thee. Deliver me, O Lord, from mine enemies; in Thee I take shelter. Teach me to do Thy will, for Thou art my God; Thy Spirit is good. Lead me in the land of uprightness. Revive me, O Lord, for Thy names sake. For Thy righteousness' sake bring my soul out of trouble. In Thy mercy cut off mine enemies, and destroy all those who afflict my soul; for I am Thy servant.

Hearken unto me, O Lord, in Thy righteousness, and enter not into judgement with Thy servant. **(x2)**

Thy good Spirit shall lead me in the land of uprightness.

After The Psalm

Glory be to the Father and to the Son and to the Holy Spirit,
Both now and forever and unto the ages of ages. Amen.

Halleluiah, Halleluiah, Halleluiah. Glory to Thee, O God. **(x3)**
O our God and our hope, glory to Thee.

Great Litany

Deacon: In peace let us pray to the Lord.

People: *Lord, have mercy.*

Deacon: For the peace from above, and the salvation of our souls; let us pray to the Lord.

People: *Lord, have mercy.*

Deacon: For the peace of the whole world, the good estate of the holy churches of God, and the union of all, let us pray to the Lord.

People: *Lord, have mercy.*

Deacon: For this holy temple, and for them that with faith, reverence; and the fear of God enter herein, let us pray to the Lord

People: *Lord, have mercy.*

Deacon: Again we pray for our His Holiness Patriarch Bartholomew; for our Archbishop Nikitas; for the venerable priesthood, the diaconate in Christ, for all the clergy and people, let us pray to the Lord.

People: *Lord, have mercy.*

Deacon: For this land, the Royal family, the authorities and armed forces, let us pray to the Lord.

People: *Lord, have mercy.*

Deacon: For this [city / town / village / monastery], for every city and country, and the faithful that dwell therein, let us pray to the Lord.

People: *Lord, have mercy.*

Deacon: For seasonable weather, an abundance of the fruits of the earth, and peaceful times, let us pray to the Lord.

People: *Lord, have mercy.*

Deacon: For travellers by sea, land and air; for the sick, the suffering, the imprisoned, and for their salvation, let us pray to the Lord.

People: *Lord, have mercy.*

Deacon: That we may be delivered from all tribulation, wrath, and necessity, let us pray to the Lord.

People: *Lord, have mercy.*

Deacon: Help us, save us, have mercy on us, and keep us, O God, by Thy grace.

People: *Lord, have mercy.*

Deacon: Calling to remembrance our most holy, most pure, most blessed, glorious Lady Theotokos and Ever Virgin Mary with all the saints, let us commit ourselves and one another and all our life unto Christ our God.

People: *To Thee O Lord.*

Deacon: For unto Thee is due all glory, honour and worship; to the Father, and to the Son, and to the Holy Spirit, now and ever, and unto the ages of ages.

People: *Amen.*

Halleluiarion

Tone 8   Humility, tranquillity, repose, suffering, pleading.   C, D, Eb, F, G, A, Bb, C.

Reader: Out of the night my spirit waketh at dawn unto Thee, O God;

For Thy commandments are a light upon the earth.

People: *Halleluiah, Halleluiah, Halleluiah.*

Reader: Learn righteousness, you that dwell upon the earth.

People: *Halleluiah, Halleluiah, Halleluiah.*

Reader: Zeal shall lay hold upon an uninstructed people.

People: *Halleluiah, Halleluiah, Halleluiah.*

Reader: Add more evils upon them, O Lord; add more evils upon them that are glorious upon the earth.

People: *Halleluiah, Halleluiah, Halleluiah.*

[Priest, in Phelonion, brings out the Gospel to the centre of the Church, censes the altar and the Church. A candle is lit during each of the 12 Gospels.]

Troparion

Tone 8   Humility, tranquillity, repose, suffering, pleading.   C, D, Eb, F, G, A, Bb, C.

When the glorious disciples were enlightened at the washing of the feet, then Judas the ungodly one was stricken and darkened with the love of silver. And unto the lawless judges did he deliver Thee, the righteous Judge. Behold, O lover of money, him that for the sake thereof did hang himself; flee from that insatiable soul that dared such things against the Master. O Thou Who art good unto all, Lord, glory be to Thee.

Glory be be to the Father and to the Son and to the Holy Spirit;

When the glorious disciples were enlightened at the washing of the feet, then Judas the ungodly one was stricken and darkened with the love of silver. And unto the lawless judges did he deliver Thee, the righteous Judge. Behold, O lover of money, him that for the sake thereof did hang himself; flee from that insatiable soul that dared such things against the Master. O Thou Who art good unto all, Lord, glory be to Thee.

Both now and forever and unto the ages of ages. Amen.

When the glorious disciples were enlightened at the washing of the feet, then Judas the ungodly one was stricken and darkened with the love of silver. And unto the lawless judges did he deliver Thee, the righteous Judge. Behold, O lover of money, him that for the sake thereof did hang himself; flee from that insatiable soul that dared such things against the Master. O Thou Who art good unto all, Lord, glory be to Thee.

The First Gospel

Deacon: That He will vouchsafe unto us the hearing of the Holy Gospel, let us pray unto the Lord God.

People: *Lord, have mercy.* **(x3)**

Deacon: Wisdom. Stand up. Let us hear the Holy Gospel.

Priest: Peace be with you all.

People: *And with thy spirit.*

Priest: The Reading is from the Holy Gospel according to John.

People: *Glory to Thy Passion, O Lord, glory to Thee.*

Deacon: Let us attend.

John §46 To §58 [13:31-18:1].

Therefore, when he was gone out, Jesus said; "Now is the Son of man glorified, and God is glorified in him. If God be glorified in him, God shall also glorify him in himself, and shall straightaway glorify him. Little children, yet a little while I am with you. You shall seek me: and as I said unto the Jews, Whither I go, you cannot come; so now I say to you. A new commandment I give unto you, That you love one another; as I have loved you, that you also love one another. By this shall all men know that you are my disciples, if you have love one to another."

Simon Peter said unto him, "Lord, whither goest thou?" Jesus answered him, "Whither I go, thou cannot follow me now; but thou shalt follow me afterwards." Peter said unto him, "Lord, why cannot I follow thee now? I will lay down my life for thy sake." Jesus answered him, "Wilt thou lay down thy life for my sake? Verily, verily, I say unto thee, The cock shall not crow, till thou hast denied me thrice. Let not thy heart be troubled: thou believest in God, believe also in me. In my Fathers house are many mansions: if it were not so, I would have told thee. I go to prepare a place for you. And if I go and prepare a place for you, I will come again, and receive you unto myself; that where I am, there you may be also. And whither I go you know, and the way you know."

Thomas saith unto him, "Lord, we know not whither thou goest; and how can we know the way?" Jesus saith unto him, "I am the way, the truth, and the life: no man cometh unto the Father, but by me. If you had known me, you should have known my Father also: and from henceforth you know him, and have seen him."

Philip saith unto him, "Lord, shew us the Father, and it sufficeth us." Jesus saith unto him, "Have I been so long time with you, and yet hast thou not known me, Philip? He that hath seen me hath seen the Father; and how sayest thou then, Show us the Father? Believest thou not that I am in the Father, and the Father in me? The words that I speak unto you I speak not of myself: but the Father that dwelleth in me, he doeth the works. Believe me that I am in the Father, and the Father in me: or else believe me for the very works' sake. Verily, verily, I say unto you, He that believeth on me, the works that I do shall he do also; and greater works than these shall he do; because I go unto my Father. And whatsoever you shall ask in my name, that will I do, that the Father may be glorified in the Son. If you shall ask any thing in my name, I will do it. If you love me, keep my commandments. And I will pray the Father, and he shall give you another Comforter, that he may abide with you for ever; Even the Spirit of truth; whom the world cannot receive, because it seeth him not, neither knoweth him: but you know him; for he dwelleth with you, and shall be in you. I will not leave you comfortless: I will come to you. Yet a little while, and the world seeth me no more; but you see me: because I live, you shall live also. At that day you shall know that I am in my Father, and you in me, and I in you. He that hath my commandments, and keepeth them, he it is that loveth me: and he that loveth me shall be loved of my Father, and I will love him, and will manifest myself to him."

Judas saith unto him, not Iscariot, "Lord, how is it that thou wilt manifest thyself unto us, and not unto the world?" Jesus answered and said unto him, "If a man love me, he will keep my words: and my Father will love him, and we will come unto him, and make our abided with him. He that loveth me not keepeth not my sayings: and the word which you hear is not mine, but the Fathers which sent me. These things have I spoken unto you, being yet present with you. But the Comforter, which is the Holy Ghost, whom the Father will send in my name, he shall teach you all things, and bring all things to your remembrance, whatsoever I have said unto you. Peace I leave with you, my peace I give unto you: not as the world giveth, give I unto you. Let not your heart be troubled, neither let it be afraid. You have heard how I said unto you, I go away, and come again unto you. If you loved me, you would rejoice, because I said, I go unto the Father: for my Father is greater than I. And now I have told you before it come to pass, that, when it is come to pass, you might believe. Hereafter I will not talk much with you: for the prince of this world cometh, and hath nothing in me. But that the world may know that I love the Father; and as the Father gave me commandment, even so I do. Arise, let us go hence. I am the true vine, and my Father is the husbandman. Every branch in me that beareth not fruit he taketh away: and every branch that beareth fruit, he purgeth it, that it may bring forth more fruit. Now you are clean through the word which I have spoken unto you. Abide in me, and I in you. As the branch cannot bear fruit of itself, except it abide in the vine; no more can ye, except you abide in me. I am the vine, you are the branches: He that abideth in me, and I in him, the same bringeth forth much fruit: for without me you can do nothing. If a man abide not in me, he is cast forth as a branch, and is withered; and men gather them, and cast them into the fire, and they are burned. If you abide in me, and my words abide in you, you shall ask what you will, and it shall be done unto you. Herein is my Father glorified, that you bear much fruit; so shall you be my disciples. As the Father hath loved me, so have I loved you: continue you in my love. If you keep my commandments, you shall abide in my love; even as I have kept my Fathers commandments, and abide in his love. These things have I spoken unto you, that my joy might remain in you, and that your joy might be full. This is my commandment, That you love one another, as I have loved you. Greater love hath no man than this, that a man lay down his life for his friends. You are my friends, if you do whatsoever I command you. Henceforth I call you not servants; for the servant knoweth not what his lord doeth: but I have called you friends; for all things that I have heard of my Father I have made known unto you. You have not chosen me, but I have chosen you, and ordained you, that you should go and bring forth fruit, and that your fruit should remain: that whatsoever you shall ask of the Father in my name, he may give it you. These things I command you, that you love one another. If the world hate you, you know that it hated me before it hated you. If you were of the world, the world would love his own: but because you are not of the world, but I have chosen you out of the world, therefore the world hateth you. Remember the word that I said unto you, The servant is not greater than his lord. If they have persecuted me, they will also persecute you; if they have kept my saying, they will keep yours also. But all these things will they do unto you for my names sake, because they know not him that sent me. If I had not come and spoken unto them, they had not had sin: but now they have no cloak for their sin. He that hateth me hateth my Father also. If I had not done amongst them the works which none other man did, they had not had sin: but now have they both seen and hated both me and my Father. But this cometh to pass, that the word might be fulfilled that is written in their law, They hated me without a cause. But when the Comforter is come, whom I will send unto you from the Father, even the Spirit of truth, which proceedeth from the Father, he shall testify of me: And you also shall bear witness, because you have been with me from the beginning. These things have I spoken unto you, that you should not be offended. They shall put you out of the synagogues: yea, the time cometh, that whosoever killeth you will think that he doeth God service. And these things will they do unto you, because they have not known the Father, nor me. But these things have I told you, that when the time shall come, you may remember that I told you of them. And these things I said not unto you at the beginning, because I was with you. But now I go my way to him that sent me; and none of you asketh me, Whither goest thou? But because I have said these things unto you, sorrow hath filled your heart. Nevertheless I tell you the truth; It is expedient for you that I go away: for if I go not away, the Comforter will not come unto you; but if I depart, I will send him unto you. And when he is come, he will reprove the world of sin, and of righteousness, and of judgement: Of sin, because they believe not on me; Of righteousness, because I go to my Father, and you see me no more; Of judgement, because the prince of this world is judged. I have yet many things to say unto you, but you cannot bear them now. Howbeit when he, the Spirit of truth, is come, he will guide you into all truth: for he shall not speak of himself; but whatsoever he shall hear, that shall he speak: and he will shew you things to come. He shall glorify me: for he shall receive of mine, and shall shew it unto you. All things that the Father hath are mine: therefore said I, that he shall take of mine, and shall shew it unto you. A little while, and you shall not see me: and again, a little while, and you shall see me, because I go to the Father."

Then said some of his disciples amongst themselves, "What is this that he saith unto us, A little while, and you shall not see me: and again, a little while, and you shall see me: and, Because I go to the Father?" They said therefore, "What is this that he saith, A little while? we cannot tell what he saith."

Now Jesus knew that they were desirous to ask him, and said unto them, "Do you enquire amongst yourselves of that I said, 'A little while, and you shall not see me: and again, a little while, and you shall see me?' Verily, verily, I say unto you, That you shall weep and lament, but the world shall rejoice: and you shall be sorrowful, but your sorrow shall be turned into joy. A woman when she is in travail hath sorrow, because her hour is come: but as soon as she is delivered of the child, she remembereth no more the anguish, for joy that a man is born into the world. And you now therefore have sorrow: but I will see you again, and your heart shall rejoice, and your joy no man taketh from you. And in that day you shall ask me nothing. Verily, verily, I say unto you, Whatsoever you shall ask the Father in my name, he will give it you. Hitherto have you asked nothing in my name: ask, and you shall receive, that your joy may be full. These things have I spoken unto you in proverbs: but the time cometh, when I shall no more speak unto you in proverbs, but I shall shew you plainly of the Father. At that day you shall ask in my name: and I say not unto you, that I will pray the Father for you: For the Father himself loveth you, because you have loved me, and have believed that I came out from God. I came forth from the Father, and am come into the world: again, I leave the world, and go to the Father."

His disciples said unto him, "Lo, now speakest thou plainly, and speakest no proverb. Now are we sure that thou knowest all things, and needest not that any man should ask thee: by this we believe that thou camest forth from God." Jesus answered them, "Do you now believe? Behold, the hour cometh, yea, is now come, that you shall be scattered, every man to his own, and shall leave me alone: and yet I am not alone, because the Father is with me. These things I have spoken unto you, that in me you might have peace. In the world you shall have tribulation: but be of good cheer; I have overcome the world."

These words spake Jesus, and lifted up his eyes to heaven, and said, "Father, the hour is come; glorify thy Son, that thy Son also may glorify thee: As thou hast given him power over all flesh, that he should give eternal life to as many as thou hast given him. And this is life eternal, that they might know thee the only true God, and Jesus Christ, whom thou hast sent. I have glorified thee on the earth: I have finished the work which thou gavest me to do. And now, O Father, glorify thou me with thine own self with the glory which I had with thee before the world was. I have manifested thy name unto the men which thou gavest me out of the world: thine they were, and thou gavest them me; and they have kept thy word. Now they have known that all things whatsoever thou hast given me are of thee. For I have given unto them the words which thou gavest me; and they have received them, and have known surely that I came out from thee, and they have believed that thou didst send me. I pray for them: I pray not for the world, but for them which thou hast given me; for they are thine. And all mine are thine, and thine are mine; and I am glorified in them. And now I am no more in the world, but these are in the world, and I come to thee. Holy Father, keep through thine own name those whom thou hast given me, that they may be one, as we are. While I was with them in the world, I kept them in thy name: those that thou gavest me I have kept, and none of them is lost, but the son of perdition; that the scripture might be fulfilled. And now come I to thee; and these things I speak in the world, that they might have my joy fulfilled in themselves. I have given them thy word; and the world hath hated them, because they are not of the world, even as I am not of the world. I pray not that thou shouldest take them out of the world, but that thou shouldest keep them from the evil. They are not of the world, even as I am not of the world. Sanctify them through thy truth: thy word is truth. As thou hast sent me into the world, even so have I also sent them into the world. And for their sakes I sanctify myself, that they also might be sanctified through the truth. Neither pray I for these alone, but for them also which shall believe on me through their word; That they all may be one; as thou, Father, art in me, and I in thee, that they also may be one in us: that the world may believe that thou hast sent me. And the glory which thou gavest me I have given them; that they may be one, even as we are one: I in them, and thou in me, that they may be made perfect in one; and that the world may know that thou hast sent me, and hast loved them, as thou hast loved me. Father, I will that they also, whom thou hast given me, be with me where I am; that they may behold my glory, which thou hast given me: for thou loved me before the foundation of the world. O righteous Father, the world hath not known thee: but I have known thee, and these have known that thou hast sent me. And I have declared unto them thy name, and will declare it: that the love wherewith thou hast loved me may be in them, and I in them."

When Jesus had spoken these words, he went forth with his disciples over the brook Kidron, where was a garden, into the which he entered, and his disciples.

People: *Glory to Thy Long suffering, O Lord, glory to Thee.*

Antiphon I

Tone 8   Humility, tranquillity, repose, suffering, pleading.   *C, D, Eb, F, G, A, Bb, C.*

The rulers of the people took counsel together against the Lord and against His Christ. They laid a lawless accusation against Me. O Lord, Lord, forsake Me not. Let us bring to Christ pure senses and affections, and as His friends let us sacrifice our lives for His sake. Let us not, as Judas, choke ourselves with the cares of this life, but in the inner chambers of our hearts let us cry: "Our Father who art in the heavens, deliver us from the evil one."

Glory be to the Father and to the Son and to the Holy Spirit,
Both now and forever and unto the ages of ages. Amen.

Theotokion

As a virgin inviolate thou hast borne child and hast remained a virgin, O Mother who hast not known wedlock, Theotokos Mary. Pray to Christ our God that we may be saved.

Antiphon II

Tone 6   Rich texture, funereal character, sorrowful tone.   *D, Eb, F##, G, A, Bb, C##, D.*

Judas ran to the lawless scribes and said: "What will you give me, and I shall deliver Him to you?" And while they conspired together, Thou against whom thy were conspiring, wast Thyself standing invisibly in their midst. O Thou who knowest the hearts of men, spare our souls. In loving compassion let us minister to God, as Mary at the supper; and let us not as Judas acquire love of money, that we may ever abide with Christ our God.

Let us serve the Lord with mercy, like Mary at Supper. And let us not be possessed of the love of silver, like Judas, that we may be always with Christ.

Glory be to the Father and to the Son and to the Holy Spirit,
Both now and forever and unto the ages of ages. Amen.

Theotokion

Cease not to pray, O Virgin, unto Him Whom thou hast borne in ways past all interpretation, for He loves mankind: that He may save from danger all who flee to thee for refuge.

Antiphon III

Tone 2   Majesty, gentleness, hope, repentance and sadness.   *E, F, G, Ab, B, C.*

• Because of the raising of Lazarus, the children of the Hebrews cried Hosanna unto Thee, O Lord Who lovest mankind: but Judas the transgressor had no wish to understand.

• At Thy supper, O Christ our God, Thou hast foretold to Thy disciples: "One of you shall betray Me." But Judas the transgressor had no wish to understand.

• When John asked Thee, O Lord, "Who is he that shall betray Thee?" Thou hast shown him through the giving of the bread. But Judas the transgressor had no wish to understand.

- With thirty pieces of silver, O Lord, and with a false kiss, the Jews sought to kill Thee. But Judas the transgressor had no wish to understand.

- During the washing of the feet, O Christ our God, Thou hast commanded Thy disciples, "Do as you have seen Me do." But Judas the transgressor had no wish to understand.

- "Watch and pray, that you enter not into temptation", Thou, our God, hast said to Thy disciples. But Judas the transgressor had no wish to understand.

Glory be to the Father and to the Son and to the Holy Spirit,
Both now and forever and unto the ages of ages. Amen.

- Keep thy servants safe from danger, O Theotokos, for after God we all flee to thee for refuge, as an unconquerable rampart and protection.

Kathisma

Tone 7   Manly character and strong melody.   *F, G, A, A#, C, D, E, F.*

As Thou gavest food to the disciples at the Supper, knowing the plot for Thy betrayal, Thou hast accused Judas of it. Thou hast understood that he would not come to repentance, yet hast Thou desired to show to all that Thou was betrayed of Thine own will, to save the world from the enemy. O long suffering Lord, glory to Thee.

The Second Gospel

Deacon: That He will vouchsafe unto us the hearing of the Holy Gospel, let us pray unto the Lord God.

People: *Lord, have mercy.* **(x3)**

Deacon: Wisdom. Stand up. Let us hear the Holy Gospel.

Priest: Peace be unto all.

People: *And with thy spirit.*

Priest: The Reading is from the Holy Gospel according to John.

People: *Glory to Thy Passion, O Lord, glory to Thee.*

Deacon: Let us attend.

John §58 [18:1-28].

When Jesus had spoken these words, he went forth with his disciples over the brook Kidron, where was a garden, into the which he entered, and his disciples. And Judas also, which betrayed him, knew the place: for Jesus oft times resorted thither with his disciples. Judas then, having received a band of men and officers from the chief priests and Pharisees, cometh thither with lanterns and torches and weapons. Jesus therefore, knowing all things that should come upon him, went forth, and said unto them, "Whom seek ye?" They answered him, "Jesus of Nazareth." Jesus saith unto them, "I am he." And Judas also, which betrayed him, stood with them. As soon then as he had said unto them, "I am he", they went backward, and fell to the ground. Then asked he them again, Whom seek ye? And they said, "Jesus of Nazareth." Jesus answered, "I have told you that I am he: if therefore you seek me, let these go their way: That the saying might be fulfilled, which he spake, 'Of them which thou gavest me have I lost none.'"

Then Simon Peter having a sword drew it, and smote the high priests servant, and cut off his right ear. The servants name was Malchus. Then said Jesus unto Peter, "Put up thy sword into the sheath: the cup which my Father hath given me, shall I not drink it?" Then the band and the captain and officers of the Jews took Jesus, and bound him, And led him away to Annas first; for he was father in law to Caiaphas, which was the high priest that same year. Now Caiaphas was he, which gave counsel to the Jews, that it was expedient that one man should die for the people.

And Simon Peter followed Jesus, and so did another disciple: that disciple was known unto the high priest, and went in with Jesus into the palace of the high priest. But Peter stood at the door without. Then went out that other disciple, which was known unto the high priest, and spake unto her that kept the door, and brought in Peter. Then saith the damsel that kept the door unto Peter, "Art not thou also one of this mans disciples?" He saith, "I am not." And the servants and officers stood there, who had made a fire of coals; for it was cold: and they warmed themselves: and Peter stood with them, and warmed himself.

The high priest then asked Jesus of his disciples, and of his doctrine. Jesus answered him, "I spake openly to the world; I ever taught in the synagogue, and in the temple, whither the Jews always resort; and in secret have I said nothing. Why askest thou me? Ask them which heard me, what I have said unto them: behold, they know what I said." And when he had thus spoken, one of the officers which stood by struck Jesus with the palm of his hand, saying, "Answerest thou the high priest so?" Jesus answered him, "If I have spoken evil, bear witness of the evil: but if well, why smitest thou me?" Now Annas had sent him bound unto Caiaphas the high priest.

And Simon Peter stood and warmed himself. They said therefore unto him, "Art not thou also one of his disciples?" He denied it, and said, "I am not." One of the servants of the high priest, being his kinsman whose ear Peter cut off, saith, "Did not I see thee in the garden with him?" Peter then denied again: and immediately the cock crew.

Then led they Jesus from Caiaphas unto the hall of judgement: and it was early; and they themselves went not into the judgement hall, lest they should be defiled; but that they might eat the passover.

People: *Glory to Thy long suffering, O Lord. Glory to Thee.*

Antiphon IV

Tone 5 *Stimulating, dancing, and rhythmical.* *C, D, Eb, F, G, A, Bb, C.*

Today Judas forsakes the Master and accepts the devil: he is blinded by the passion of avarice and darkened he falls from the Light. For how could he see, who sold the Light for thirty pieces of silver? But He who suffered for the world has shone upon us as the dawn. To Him, let us cry: O Thou who sufferest with men and for their sakes, glory to Thee.

Today Judas makes a pretence of Godliness and become a stranger to the gifts of grace; though a disciple, he turns traitor, and under a guise of friendship he conceals deceit. In his foolishness he prefers thirty pieces of silver to the Master's love, and acts as guide to the lawless Sanhedrin. But we have Christ as our salvation: let us glorify Him.

Tone 1   Magnificent, happy and earthy.   *C, D, Eb, F, G, A, Bb, C.*

As brethren in Christ, let us acquire brotherly love; and let us not be lacking in compassion for our neighbour, lest for money's sake we be condemned like the unmerciful servant, and repent like Judas to no purpose.

Glory be to the Father, and to the Son, and to the Holy Spirit;
Both now and forever, and unto the ages of ages. Amen.

Theotokion

Glorious things are spoken of thee throughout all the world, for thou hast borne in the flesh the Maker of all, O Theotokos Mary unwedded, worthy of all praise.

Antiphon V

Tone 6   Rich texture, funereal character, sorrowful tone.   *D, Eb, F##, G, A, Bb, C##, D.*

The disciple agreed upon the price of the Master, and for thirty pieces of silver he sold the Lord; with a deceitful kiss he betrayed Him to the transgressors to be put to death.

Today the Creator of heaven and earth said to His disciples: "The hour is at hand, and Judas who betrays Me has drawn near. Let none of you deny Me when you see Me on the Cross between two thieves. For as man I suffer, but as Lover of mankind I save those who believe in Me."

Glory be to the Father, and to the Son, and to the Holy Spirit;
Both now and forever, and unto the ages of ages. Amen.

Theotokion

O Virgin who in the last days hast ineffably conceived and borne thine own Creator, save those who magnify thee.

Antiphon VI

Tone 7   Manly character and strong melody.   *F, G, A, A#, C, D, E, F.*

Today Judas watches how he may deliver up the Lord, the pre-eternal Saviour of the world, who with five loaves satisfied the multitude. Today the transgressor denies his Teacher; though a disciple he betrays the Master. He sells for money the Lord who fed His people with manna in the wilderness.

Today the Jews nailed to the Cross the Lord who divided the sea with a rod and led them through the wilderness. Today they pierced with a lance the side of Him Who for their sake smote Egypt with plagues. They gave Him gall to drink, Who rained down manna on them for food.

O Lord, as Thou camest to Thy voluntary Passion, Thou hast cried aloud to Thy disciples: "If you could not even watch with Me one hour, why then did you promise to die for My sake? See you how Judas sleeps not, but makes haste to deliver Me to the transgressors? Awake, rise and pray, and let none deny Me when he sees Me on the Cross." O long suffering Lord, glory to Thee.

Glory be to the Father, and to the Son, and to the Holy Spirit;
Both now and forever, and unto the ages of ages. Amen.

Theotokion

Rejoice, Theotokos, who hast contained within thy womb Him Whom the heavens cannot contain. Rejoice, Virgin whom the prophets preached: through thee Emmanuel has shone forth upon us. Rejoice, Mother of Christ our God.

Kathisma

Tone 7   Manly character and strong melody.   *F, G, A, A#, C, D, E, F.*

What reason led thee, Judas to betray the Saviour? Did He expel thee from the company of the apostles? Did He deprive thee of the gift of healing? When thou wast at supper with the others, did He drive thee from the table? When He washed the other's feet, did He pass thee by? How many are the blessings that thou hast forgotten. Thou art condemned for thine ingratitude, but His measureless long suffering and great mercy are proclaimed to all.

The Third Gospel

Deacon: That He will vouchsafe unto us the hearing of the Holy Gospel, let us pray unto the Lord God.

People: *Lord, have mercy.* **(x3)**

Deacon: Wisdom. Stand up. Let us hear the Holy Gospel.

Priest: Peace be with you all.

People: *And with thy spirit.*

Priest: The Reading is from the Holy Gospel according to Matthew.

People: *Glory to Thy Passion, O Lord, glory to Thee.*

Deacon: Let us attend.

Matthew §109 [26:57-75].

And they that had laid hold on Jesus led him away to Caiaphas the high priest, where the scribes and the elders were assembled. But Peter followed him afar off unto the high priests palace, and went in, and sat with the servants, to see the end.

Now the chief priests, and elders, and all the council, sought false witness against Jesus, to put him to death; But found none: yea, though many false witnesses came, yet found they none. At the last came two false witnesses, And said, "This fellow said, 'I am able to destroy the temple of God, and to build it in three days.'" And the high priest arose, and said unto him, "Answerest thou nothing? What is it which these witness against thee?" But Jesus held his peace, And the high priest answered and said unto him, "I adjure thee by the living God, that thou tell us whether thou be the Christ, the Son of God." Jesus saith unto him, "Thou hast said: nevertheless I say unto you, Hereafter shall you see the Son of man sitting on the right hand of power, and coming in the clouds of heaven."

Then the high priest rent his clothes, saying, "He hath spoken blasphemy; what further need have we of witnesses? behold, now you have heard his blasphemy. What think ye?" They answered and said, "He is guilty of death." Then did they spit in his face, and buffeted him; and others smote him with the palms of their hands, Saying, "Prophesy unto us, thou Christ, Who is he that smote thee?"

Now Peter sat without in the palace: and a damsel came unto him, saying, "Thou also wast with Jesus of Galilee." But he denied before them all, saying, "I know not what thou sayest." And when he was gone out into the porch, another maid saw him, and said unto them that were there, "This fellow was also with Jesus of Nazareth." And again he denied with an oath, "I do not know the man." And after a while came unto him they that stood by, and said to Peter, "Surely thou also art one of them; for thy speech betrayeth thee." Then began he to curse and to swear, saying, "I know not the man." And immediately the cock crew. And Peter remembered the word of Jesus, which said unto him, "Before the cock crow, thou shalt deny me thrice." And he went out, and wept bitterly.

People: *Glory to Thy Long suffering, O Lord, glory to Thee.*

Antiphon VII

Tone 8   Humility, tranquillity, repose, suffering, pleading.   *C, D, Eb, F, G, A, Bb, C.*

Suffering the transgressors to lay hold on Thee, O Lord, Thou hast cried aloud: Although you smite the Shepherd and scatter abroad the twelve sheep, My disciples, yet could I call to Mine aid more than twelve legions of angels. But in My patience I forbear, that the hidden secrets I made known to you through My prophets may be fulfilled." O Lord, glory to Thee.

Peter denied Thee three times, and straightway he understood Thy words; but he offered Thee tears of repentance. O God, be merciful to me and save me.

Glory be be to the Father and to the Son and to the Holy Spirit;
Both now and forever and unto the ages of ages. Amen.

Theotokion

The holy Virgin is a gateway of salvation, a fair Paradise, and a cloud of everlasting light: let us all sing in praise of her and say to her, "Rejoice."

Antiphon VIII

Tone 2   Majesty, gentleness, hope, repentance and sadness.   *E, F, G, Ab, B, C.*

O you transgressors, tell us what you heard from our Saviour? Did He not expound the Law and the teaching of the prophets? How then have you taken counsel to deliver up to Pilate Him Who is God the Word that came from God, and the Deliverer of our souls?

"Let Him be crucified." they cried, though they had always taken pleasure in Thy gifts of grace; and the murderers of the righteous asked for the release of an evildoer in place of their Benefactor. But Thou, O Christ, wast silent and hast endured their impudence, wishing to suffer and to save us in Thy love for mankind.

Glory be be to the Father and to the Son and to the Holy Spirit;
Both now and forever and unto the ages of ages. Amen.

Theotokion

As there is no boldness in us because of the multitude of our sins, do thou, O Virgin Theotokos, intercede with the Son Whom thou hast borne, for the entreaty of His Mother has great power to win the favour of the Master. Despise not, O all honoured Lady, the prayer of sinners, for He who took upon Himself to suffer for our sake is merciful and strong to save.

Antiphon IX

Tone 3   Arrogant, brave, and mature atmosphere.   *F, G, A, A#, C, D, E, F.*

They took the thirty pieces of silver, the price of Him that was valued, on Whom the children of Israel had set a price. Watch and pray, that you enter not into temptation: the spirit indeed is willing but the flesh is weak. Therefore watch.

They gave Me gall to eat, and in My thirst they gave me vinegar to drink. But do Thou raise Me up, O Lord, and I shall grant them their reward.

Glory be be to the Father and to the Son and to the Holy Spirit;
Both now and forever and unto the ages of ages. Amen.

Theotokion

We Gentiles sing of thee, O pure Theotokos, for thou hast borne Christ our God, Who through thee delivered mankind from the curse.

Kathisma

Tone 8   Humility, tranquillity, repose, suffering, pleading.   *C, D, Eb, F, G, A, Bb, C.*

O how could Judas, who was once Thy disciple, plot to betray Thee. In his treachery and wickedness he ate with Thee at the supper, and then he went to the priests and said: "What will you give me, and I will deliver to you Him Who set the Law at naught and defiled the Sabbath?" O long suffering Lord, glory to Thee.

The Fourth Gospel

Deacon: That He will vouchsafe unto us the hearing of the Holy Gospel, let us pray unto the Lord God.

People: *Lord, have mercy.* **(x3)**

Deacon: Wisdom. Stand up. Let us hear the Holy Gospel.

Priest: Peace be unto all.

People: *And with thy spirit.*

Priest: The Reading is from the Holy Gospel according to John.

People: *Glory to Thy Passion, O Lord, glory to Thee.*

Deacon: Let us attend.

John §59 [18:28-19:16].

Then led they Jesus from Caiaphas unto the hall of judgement: and it was early; and they themselves went not into the judgement hall, lest they should be defiled; but that they might eat the passover. Pilate then went out unto them, and said, "What accusation bring you against this man?" They answered and said unto him, "If he were not a malefactor, we would not have delivered him up unto thee." Then said Pilate unto them, "Take you him, and judge him according to your law. "The Jews therefore said unto him, "It is not lawful for us to put any man to death." That the saying of Jesus might be fulfilled, which he spake, signifying what death he should die. Then Pilate entered into the judgement hall again, and called Jesus, and said unto him, "Art thou the King of the Jews?" Jesus answered him, "Sayest thou this thing of thyself, or did others tell it thee of me?" Pilate answered, "Am I a Jew? Thine own nation and the chief priests have delivered thee unto me: what hast thou done?" Jesus answered, "My kingdom is not of this world: if my kingdom were of this world, then would my servants fight, that I should not be delivered to the Jews: but now is my kingdom not from hence."

Pilate therefore said unto him, "Art thou a king then?" Jesus answered, "Thou sayest that I am a king. To this end was I born, and for this cause came I into the world, that I should bear witness unto the truth. Every one that is of the truth heareth my voice."

Pilate saith unto him, "What is truth? And when he had said this, he went out again unto the Jews, and saith unto them, "I find in him no fault at all. But you have a custom, that I should release unto you one at the passover: will you therefore that I release unto you the King of the Jews?" Then cried they all again, saying, "Not this man, but Barabbas." Now Barabbas was a robber. Then Pilate therefore took Jesus, and scourged him. And the soldiers plaited a crown of thorns, and put it on his head, and they put on him a purple robe, And said, "Hail, King of the Jews." and they smote him with their hands. Pilate therefore went forth again, and saith unto them, Behold, I bring him forth to you, that you may know that I find no fault in him. Then came Jesus forth, wearing the crown of thorns, and the purple robe. And Pilate saith unto them, "Behold the man." When the chief priests therefore and officers saw him, they cried out, saying, "Crucify him, crucify him." Pilate saith unto them, "Take you him, and crucify him: for I find no fault in him." The Jews answered him, "We have a law, and by our law he ought to die, because he made himself the Son of God."

When Pilate therefore heard that saying, he was the more afraid; and went again into the judgement hall, and saith unto Jesus, "Whence art thou?" But Jesus gave him no answer. Then saith Pilate unto him, "Speakest thou not unto me? Knowest thou not that I have power to crucify thee, and have power to release thee?" Jesus answered, "Thou couldest have no power at all against me, except it were given thee from above: therefore he that delivered me unto thee hath the greater sin." And from thenceforth Pilate sought to release him: but the Jews cried out, saying, "If thou let this man go, thou art not Caesars friend: whosoever maketh himself a king speaketh against Caesar." When Pilate therefore heard that saying, he brought Jesus forth, and sat down in the judgement seat in a place that is called the Pavement, but in the Hebrew, Gabbatha. And it was the preparation of the passover, and about the sixth hour: and he saith unto the Jews, "Behold your King." But they cried out, "Away with him, away with him, crucify him." Pilate saith unto them, "Shall I crucify your King?" The chief priests answered, "We have no king but Caesar." Then delivered he him therefore unto them to be crucified. And they took Jesus, and led him away.

People: *Glory to Thy Long suffering, O Lord, glory to Thee.*

Antiphon X

Tone 6   Rich texture, funereal character, sorrowful tone.   *D, Eb, F##, G, A, Bb, C##, D.*

He Who clothes Himself in light as in a garment, stood naked at the judgement; on His cheek He received blows from the hands which He had formed. The lawless people nailed to the Cross the Lord of Glory. Then the veil of the temple was rent in twain and the sun was darkened, for it could not bear to see such outrage done to God, before Whom all things tremble. Let us worship Him.

The disciples denied Thee and the thief cried aloud: Remember me, O Lord, in Thy Kingdom.

Glory be be to the Father and to the Son and to the Holy Spirit;
Both now and forever and unto the ages of ages. Amen.

Theotokion

O Lord Who lovest mankind, for the sake of Thy servants Thou wast pleased to take flesh from the Virgin: grant peace to the world, that with one accord we may glorify Thee.

Antiphon XI

Tone 6   Rich texture, funereal character, sorrowful tone.   *D, Eb, F##, G, A, Bb, C##, D.*

In return for the blessings which Thou hast granted, O Christ, to the people of the Hebrews, they condemned Thee to be crucified, giving Thee vinegar and gall to drink. But render unto them, O Lord, according to their works, for they have not understood Thy loving self abasement.

The people of the Hebrews were not satisfied with Thy betrayal, O Christ, but they wagged their heads, and reviled and mocked Thee. But render unto them, O Lord, according to their works, for they have devised vain things against Thee.

Neither the quaking of the earth, nor the splitting of the rocks, nor the rending of the veil of the temple, nor the resurrection of the dead persuaded the Jews. But render unto them, O Lord, according to their works, for they have devised vain things against Thee.

Glory be be to the Father and to the Son and to the Holy Spirit;
Both now and forever and unto the ages of ages. Amen.

Theotokion

O Theotokos Virgin, who alone art pure and alone blessed, through thee we have come to know God, for He took flesh from thee. Therefore without ceasing we sing thy praises and we magnify thee.

Antiphon XII

Tone 8   Humility, tranquillity, repose, suffering, pleading.   *C, D, Eb, F, G, A, Bb, C.*

Thus saith the Lord to the Jews: "O My people, what have I done unto thee? Or wherein have I wearied thee? I gave light to thy blind and cleansed thy lepers, I raised up the man who lay upon his bed. O My people, what have I done unto thee, and how hast thou repaid Me? Instead of manna thou hast given Me gall, instead of water vinegar; instead of loving Me, thou hast nailed Me to the Cross. I can endure no more. I shall call My gentiles and they shall glorify Me with the Father and the Spirit; and I shall bestow on them eternal life."

Today the veil of the temple is rent in twain, as a reproof against the transgressors; and the sun hides it own rays, seeing the Master crucified.

O lawgivers of Israel, you Jews and Pharisees, the company of the apostles cries aloud to you: Behold the Temple that you have destroyed; behold the Lamb that you have crucified. You gave Him over to the tomb, but by His own power He has risen again. Be not deceived, you Jews: for this is He Who saved you in the sea and led you in the wilderness. He is the Life and Light and Peace of the world.

Glory be be to the Father and to the Son and to the Holy Spirit;
Both now and forever and unto the ages of ages. Amen.

Theotokion

Rejoice, gate of the King of Glory, through which the Most High alone has passed; and He left thee sealed, for the salvation of our souls.

Kathisma

Tone 8   Humility, tranquillity, repose, suffering, pleading.   C, D, Eb, F, G, A, Bb, C.

When Thou the Judge, O God, wast standing before Caiaphas and wast delivered unto Pilate, then the powers of heaven quaked with fear. Thou wast raised upon the Cross between two thieves, and though sinless Thou wast numbered with transgressors, for the salvation of mankind. O long suffering Lord, glory to Thee.

The Fifth Gospel

Deacon: That He will vouchsafe unto us the hearing of the Holy Gospel, let us pray unto the Lord God.

People: *Lord, have mercy.* **(x3)**

Deacon: Wisdom. Stand up. Let us hear the Holy Gospel.

Priest: Peace be unto all.

People: *And with thy spirit.*

Priest: The Reading is from the Holy Gospel according to Matthew.

People: *Glory to Thy Passion, O Lord, glory to Thee.*

Deacon: Let us attend.

Matthew §111 [27:3-32].

Then Judas, which had betrayed him, when he saw that he was condemned, repented himself, and brought again the thirty pieces of silver to the chief priests saying, "I have sinned in that I have betrayed the innocent blood." And they said, "What is that to us? See thou to that." And he cast down the pieces of silver in the temple, and departed, and went and hanged himself. And the chief priests took the silver pieces, and said, "It is not lawful for to put them into the treasury, because it is the price of blood." And they took counsel, and bought with them the potters field, to bury strangers in. Wherefore that field was called, The field of blood, unto this day. Then was fulfilled that which was spoken by Jeremiah the prophet, saying, "And they took the thirty pieces of silver, the price of him that was valued, whom they of the children of Israel did value; And gave them for the potters field, as the Lord appointed me."

And Jesus stood before the governor: and the governor asked him, saying, "Art thou the King of the Jews?" And Jesus said unto him, "Thou sayest." And when he was accused of the chief priests and elders, he answered nothing. Then said Pilate unto him, "Hearest thou not how many things they witness against thee?" And he answered him to never a word; insomuch that the governor marvelled greatly. Now at that feast the governor was wont to release unto the people a prisoner, whom they would. And they had then a notable prisoner, called Barabbas. Therefore when they were gathered together, Pilate said unto them, "Whom will you that I release unto you? Barabbas, or Jesus which is called Christ?" For he knew that for envy they had delivered him.

When he was set down on the judgement seat, his wife sent unto him, saying, "Have thou nothing to do with that just man: for I have suffered many things this day in a dream because of him." But the chief priests and elders persuaded the multitude that they should ask Barabbas, and destroy Jesus. The governor answered and said unto them, "Whether of the twain will you that I release unto you?" They said, "Barabbas." Pilate saith unto them, "What shall I do then with Jesus which is called Christ?" They all said unto him, "Let him be crucified." And the governor said, "Why, what evil hath he done?" But they cried out the more, saying, "Let him be crucified."

When Pilate saw that he could prevail nothing, but that rather a tumult was made, he took water, and washed his hands before the multitude, saying, "I am innocent of the blood of this just person: see you to it. Then answered all the people, and said, "His blood be on us, and on our children." Then released he Barabbas unto them: and when he had scourged Jesus, he delivered him to be crucified. Then the soldiers of the governor took Jesus into the common hall, and gathered unto him the whole band of soldiers. And they stripped him, and put on him a scarlet robe. And when they had plaited a crown of thorns, they put it upon his head, and a reed in his right hand: and they bowed the knee before him, and mocked him, saying, "Hail, King of the Jews." And they spit upon him, and took the reed, and smote him on the head. And after that they had mocked him, they took the robe off from him, and put his own raiment on him, and led him away to crucify him. And as they came out, they found a man of Cyrene, Simon by name: him they compelled to bear his cross.

People: *Glory to Thy Long suffering, O Lord, glory to Thee.*

Antiphon XIII

Tone 6   Rich texture, funereal character, sorrowful tone.   *D, Eb, F##, G, A, Bb, C##, D.*

The assembly of the Jews besought Pilate to crucify Thee, O Lord. For though they found no guilt in Thee, they released Barabbas the malefactor and condemned Thee the Righteous; and so they incurred the guilt of murder. But give them, O Lord, their reward, for they devised vain things against Thee.

He before Whom all things quake and tremble, to Whom every tongue gives praise, Christ the Power of God and the Wisdom of God, is struck on the face by the priests, and they give Him gall to drink. Yet He was pleased to suffer all things, wishing to save us from our sins by His own blood, in His love for mankind.

Glory be be to the Father and to the Son and to the Holy Spirit;
Both now and forever and unto the ages of ages. Amen.

Theotokion

O Theotokos, who through a word in ways past speech hast borne thine own Creator, pray unto Him for the salvation of our souls.

Antiphon XIV

Tone 8   Humility, tranquillity, repose, suffering, pleading.   *C, D, Eb, F, G, A, Bb, C.*

O Lord, Thou hast taken as Thy companion the thief who had soiled his hands with blood: in Thy goodness and love for mankind, number us also with him.

Few were the words that the thief uttered upon the Cross, yet great was the faith that he showed. In one moment he was saved: He opened the gates of Paradise and wast the first to enter in. O Lord, Who hast accepted his repentance, glory to Thee.

Glory be be to the Father and to the Son and to the Holy Spirit;
Both now and forever and unto the ages of ages. Amen.

Theotokion

Rejoice, for through the angel thou hast received the joy of the world. Rejoice, for thou hast borne thy Maker and thy Lord. Rejoice, for thou wast counted worthy to become Mother of Christ our God.

[Entry with the Crucifix:

1) All kneel.

2) Priest carries the Cross from the sanctuary and sets it up in the centre of the church.

3) Church is darkened. Whilst:]

Antiphon XV

Tone 6   Rich texture, funereal character, sorrowful tone.   *D, Eb, F##, G, A, Bb, C##, D.*

Priest: Today He Who hung the earth upon the waters is hung upon the Cross. **(x3)**

He Who is King of the angels is arrayed in a crown of thorns. He Who wraps the heaven in clouds is wrapped in the purple of mockery. He Who in Jordan set Adam free receives blows upon His face. The Bridegroom of the Church is transfixed with nails. The Son of the Virgin is pierced with a spear.

We venerate Thy Passion, O Christ. **(x3)**

Show us also Thy glorious Resurrection.

Reader: Let us not keep festival as the Jews: for Christ our God and Passover is sacrificed for us. But let us cleanse ourselves from all defilement, and with sincerity entreat Him. Arise, O Lord, and save us in Thy love for mankind.

Thy Cross, O Lord, is life and resurrection to Thy people; and putting all our trust in it, we sing to Thee, our crucified God: Have mercy upon us.

Glory be be to the Father and to the Son and to the Holy Spirit;
Both now and forever and unto the ages of ages. Amen.

Theotokion

Beholding Thee hanging on the Cross, O Christ, Thy Mother cried aloud: "O my Son, what is this strange mystery that I behold? Nailed in the flesh, O Giver of Life, how dost Thou die upon the Tree?"

Sessional Hymn

Tone 4   Festive, joyous and expressing deep piety.   *C, D, Eb, F, G, A, Bb, C.*

Thou hast redeemed us from the curse of the law by Thy precious Blood. Having been nailed to the Cross and pierced with a spear, Thou hast poured forth immortality upon mankind. O our Saviour, glory to Thee.

The Sixth Gospel

Deacon: That He will vouchsafe unto us the hearing of the Holy Gospel, let us pray unto the Lord God.

People: *Lord, have mercy.* **(x3)**

Deacon: Wisdom. Stand up. Let us hear the Holy Gospel.

Priest: Peace be unto all.

People: *And with thy spirit.*

Priest: The Reading is from the Holy Gospel according to Mark.

People: *Glory to Thy Passion, O Lord, glory to Thee.*

Deacon: Let us attend.

Mark §67 [15:16-32].

And the soldiers led him away into the hall, called Praetorium; and they call together the whole band. And they clothed him with purple, and plaited a crown of thorns, and put it about his head, And began to salute him, "Hail, King of the Jews." And they smote him on the head with a reed, and did spit upon him, and bowing their knees worshipped him. And when they had mocked him, they took off the purple from him, and put his own clothes on him, and led him out to crucify him. And they compelled one Simon a Cyrenian, who passed by, coming out of the country, the father of Alexander and Rufus, to bear his cross. And they brought him unto the place Golgotha, which is, being interpreted, The place of a skull. And they gave him to drink wine mingled with myrrh: but he received it not. And when they had crucified him, they parted his garments, casting lots upon them, what every man should take. And it was the third hour, and they crucified him.

And the superscription of his accusation was written over, "THE KING OF THE JEWS." And with him they crucify two thieves; the one on his right hand, and the other on his left. And the scripture was fulfilled, which saith, "And he was numbered with the transgressors." And they that passed by railed on him, wagging their heads, and saying, "Ah, thou that destroyest the temple, and buildest it in three days, Save thyself, and come down from the cross." Likewise also the chief priests mocking said amongst themselves with the scribes, "He saved others; himself he cannot save. Let Christ the King of Israel descend now from the cross, that we may see and believe." And they that were crucified with him reviled him.

People: *Glory to Thy Long suffering, O Lord, glory to Thee.*

Tone 4   Festive, joyous and expressing deep piety.   *C, D, Eb, F, G, A, Bb, C.*

In Thy Kingdom; Remember us, O Lord, when Thou comest in Thy kingdom.

Blessed are the poor in spirit, for theirs is the kingdom of heaven.

Blessed are they that mourn, for they shall be comforted.

Blessed are the meek, for they shall inherit the earth.

Through a tree Adam lost his home in Paradise, and through the Tree of the Cross the thief made Paradise his home. For the one, by eating, transgressed the commandment of his Maker; but the other, crucified at Thy side, confessed Thee as the hidden God. Remember us also, Saviour, in Thy Kingdom.

Blessed are they that hunger and thirst after righteousness; for they shall be filled.

The lawless people bought the Maker of the Law from His disciple, and they led Him as a transgressor before the judgement seat of Pilate, crying "Crucify Him", though it was He Who gave them manna in the wilderness. But, following the example of the righteous thief, we cry with faith: Remember us also, Saviour, in Thy Kingdom.

Blessed are the merciful, for they shall obtain mercy.

The murderers of God, the lawless nation of the Jews, cried to Pilate in their madness, saying, "Crucify the innocent Christ"; and they asked rather for Barabbas. But with the words of the good thief we cry to Him: Remember us also, Saviour, in Thy Kingdom.

Blessed are the pure in heart, for they shall see God.

Thy life giving side, O Christ, flowing as a fountain from Eden, waters Thy Church as a living Paradise. Then, dividing into the four branches of the Gospels, with its streams it refreshes the world, making glad the creation and teaching the nations to venerate Thy Kingdom with faith.

Blessed are the peacemakers, for they shall be called the children of God.

For my sake Thou wast crucified, to become for me a fountain of forgiveness. Thy side was pierced, that Thou mightest pour upon me streams of life. Thou wast transfixed with nails, that through the depths of Thy sufferings I might know with certainty the height of Thy power, and cry to Thee, O Christ the Giver of Life: O Saviour glory to Thy Cross and Passion.

Blessed are they that are persecuted for righteousness' sake;
For theirs is the kingdom of heaven.

When Thou wast crucified, O Christ, all the creation saw and trembled. The foundations of the earth quaked in fear of Thy power. The lights of heaven hid themselves and the veil of the temple was rent in twain, the mountains trembled and the rocks were split. With the faithful thief we cry: Remember us, O Saviour.

Blessed are you when men shall revile you, and persecute you;
And shall say all manner of evil against you falsely for My sake.

O Lord, on the Cross Thou hast torn up the record of our sins; numbered amongst the departed, Thou hast bound fast the ruler of hell, delivering all men from the chains of death by Thy Resurrection. Through this Thy Resurrection, O Lord Who lovest mankind we have been granted light, and cry to Thee: Remember us also, Saviour, in Thy Kingdom.

Rejoice and be exceeding glad, for great is your reward in heaven.

Thou wast lifted up, O Lord, upon the Cross and hast destroyed the power of death; and as God Thou hast blotted out the record of our sins that was against us. Grant to us also the repentance of the thief, O Christ our God Who alone lovest mankind, for we worship Thee with faith and cry to Thee: Remember us also, Saviour, in Thy Kingdom.

Glory be to the Father, and to the Son, and to the Holy Spirit;

Let us the faithful pray with one accord that we may rightly glorify the Father, Son and Holy Spirit, one Godhead in three Persons, remaining unconfused, simple, undivided; Whom no man can approach, and by Whom we are delivered from the fire of punishment.

Both now and forever, and unto the ages of ages. Amen.

Theotokion

O Christ, we offer Thee as intercessor Thy Mother who without seed bore Thee in the flesh, true Virgin who remained inviolate after childbirth. O Master rich in mercy, ever grant forgiveness of their sins unto those who cry: Remember us also, Saviour, in Thy Kingdom.

Prokeimenon

Deacon: Let us attend. Wisdom. The Prokeimenon.

Reader: They have parted my garments amongst themselves; and for my vesture have they cast lots.

People: *They have parted my garments amongst themselves; and for my vesture have they cast lots.*

Reader: O God, my God, attend to me; why hast Thou forsaken me?

People: *They have parted my garments amongst themselves; and for my vesture have they cast lots.*

Reader: They have parted my garments amongst themselves | *and for my vesture have they cast lots.*

The Seventh Gospel

Deacon: That He will vouchsafe unto us the hearing of the Holy Gospel, let us pray unto the Lord God.

People: *Lord, have mercy.* **(x3)**

Deacon: Wisdom. Stand up. Let us hear the Holy Gospel.

Priest: Peace be unto all.

People: *And with thy spirit.*

Priest: The Reading is from the Holy Gospel according to Matthew.

People: *Glory to Thy Passion, O Lord, glory to Thee.*

Deacon: Let us attend.

Matthew §113 [27:33-54].

And when they were come unto a place called Golgotha, that is to say, a place of a skull, they gave him vinegar to drink mingled with gall: and when he had tasted thereof, he would not drink. And they crucified him, and parted his garments, casting lots: that it might be fulfilled which was spoken by the prophet, They parted my garments amongst them, and upon my vesture did they cast lots. And sitting down they watched him there; and set up over his head his accusation written, "THIS IS JESUS THE KING OF THE JEWS." Then were there two thieves crucified with him, one on the right hand, and another on the left. And they that passed by reviled him, wagging their heads, and saying, "Thou that destroyest the temple, and buildest it in three days, save thyself. If thou be the Son of God, come down from the cross."

Likewise also the chief priests mocking him, with the scribes and elders, said, "He saved others; himself he cannot save. If he be the King of Israel, let him now come down from the cross, and we will believe him. He trusted in God; let him deliver him now, if he will have him: for he said, 'I am the Son of God.'" The thieves also, which were crucified with him, cast the same in his teeth.

Now from the sixth hour there was darkness over all the land unto the ninth hour. And about the ninth hour Jesus cried with a loud voice, saying, "Eli, Eli, lama sabachthani?" That is to say, "My God, my God, why hast thou forsaken me?" Some of them that stood there, when they heard that, said, "This man calleth for Elijah." And straightway one of them ran, and took a sponge, and filled it with vinegar, and put it on a reed, and gave him to drink. The rest said, "Let be, let us see whether Elijah will come to save him."

Jesus, when he had cried again with a loud voice, yielded up the ghost. And, behold, the veil of the temple was rent in twain from the top to the bottom; and the earth did quake, and the rocks rent; and the graves were opened; and many bodies of the saints which slept arose, and came out of the graves after his resurrection, and went into the holy city, and appeared unto many.

Now when the centurion, and they that were with him, watching Jesus, saw the earthquake, and those things that were done, they feared greatly, saying, "Truly this was the Son of God."

People: *Glory to Thy Long suffering, O Lord, glory to Thee.*

Psalm 50

Have mercy on me, O God, according to Thy great mercy; and according to the multitude of Thy compassions blot out my transgression. Wash me thoroughly from mine iniquity, and cleanse me from my sin. For I acknowledge mine iniquity, and my sin is ever before me. Against Thee, Thee only have I sinned, and done evil in Thy sight, that Thou mayest be found just when Thou speakest, and victorious when Thou art judged. For behold, I was conceived in iniquity, and in sin my mother bore me. For behold, Thou hast loved truth; Thou hast made known to me the hidden and secret things of Thy wisdom. Thou shalt sprinkle me with hyssop, and I shall be made clean; Thou shalt wash me, and I shall be whiter than snow. Make me to hear joy and gladness; that the humbled bones may rejoice. Turn Thy face away from my sins, and blot out all mine iniquities.

Create in me a clean heart, O God, and renew a steadfast spirit within me. Cast me not away from Thy presence, and take not Thy Holy Spirit from me. Restore to me the joy of Thy salvation, and establish me with Thy governing Spirit. I shall teach transgressors Thy ways, and the ungodly shall turn back to Thee. Deliver me from blood guiltiness, O God, the God of my salvation; my tongue shall joyfully declare Thy righteousness. Lord, open my lips, and my mouth shall declare Thy praise. For if Thou hadst desired sacrifice, I would give it; Thou dost not delight in burnt offerings. A sacrifice to God is a broken spirit; God will not despise a broken and a humbled heart. Do good, O Lord, in Thy good pleasure to Zion, and let the walls of Jerusalem be builded. Then Thou shalt be pleased with a sacrifice of righteousness, with oblation and whole burned offerings. Then shall they offer bulls on Thine altar.

The Eighth Gospel

Deacon: That He will vouchsafe unto us the hearing of the Holy Gospel, let us pray unto the Lord God.

People: *Lord, have mercy.* **(x3)**

Deacon: Wisdom. Stand up. Let us hear the Holy Gospel.

Priest: Peace be unto all.

People: *And with thy spirit.*

Priest: The Reading is from the Holy Gospel according to Luke.

People: *Glory to Thy Passion, O Lord, glory to Thee.*

Deacon: Let us attend.

Luke § 111 [23:32-49].

And when they were come to the place, which is called Calvary, there they crucified him, and the malefactors, one on the right hand, and the other on the left. Then said Jesus, "Father, forgive them; for they know not what they do." And they parted his raiment, and cast lots. And the people stood beholding. And the rulers also with them derided him, saying, "He saved others; let him save himself, if he be Christ, the chosen of God." And the soldiers also mocked him, coming to him, and offering him vinegar, and saying, "If thou be the king of the

Jews, save thyself." And a superscription also was written over him in letters of Greek, and Latin, and Hebrew, "THIS IS THE KING OF THE JEWS." And one of the malefactors which were hanged railed on him, saying, "If thou be Christ, save thyself and us." But the other answering rebuked him, saying, "Dost not thou fear God, seeing thou art in the same condemnation? And we indeed justly; for we receive the due reward of our deeds: but this man hath done nothing amiss." And he said unto Jesus, "Lord, remember me when thou comest into thy kingdom." And Jesus said unto him, "Verily I say unto thee, To day shalt thou be with me in paradise.

And it was about the sixth hour, and there was a darkness over all the earth until the ninth hour. And the sun was darkened, and the veil of the temple was rent in the midst. And when Jesus had cried with a loud voice, he said, "Father, into thy hands I commend my spirit." Having said this, he gave up the ghost.

Now when the centurion saw what was done, he glorified God, saying, "Certainly this was a righteous man." And all the people that came together to that sight, beholding the things which were done, smote their breasts, and returned. And all his acquaintance, and the women that followed him from Galilee, stood afar off, beholding these things.

People: *Glory to Thy Long suffering, O Lord, glory to Thee.*

The Three Canticled Canon *By St Kosmas*
Ode V

Eirmos

Tone 6   *Rich texture, funereal character, sorrowful tone.*   *D, Eb, F##, G, A, Bb, C##, D.*

I seek Thee early in the morning, Word of God; for in Thy tender mercy towards fallen man, without changing Thou hast emptied Thyself, and impassibly Thou hast submitted to Thy Passion. Grant me Thy peace, O Lord Who lovest mankind.

Glory be to Thee, O our God, glory to Thee.

Their feet were washed, and in preparation they were cleansed by partaking of the divine Mystery; and now, O Christ, Thy servants went up with Thee from Zion to the great Mount of Olives, singing Thy praises, O Lord Who lovest mankind.

Glory be be to the Father and to the Son and to the Holy Spirit;
Both now and forever and unto the ages of ages. Amen.

"See that you be not troubled, O My friends", Thou hast said. "For now the hour is come when I shall be taken and slain by the hands of wicked men; and you shall all be scattered and forsake Me. But I shall gather you together to proclaim Me, in My love for mankind."

Kontakion

Tone 8   Humility, tranquillity, repose, suffering, pleading.   *C, D, Eb, F, G, A, Bb, C.*

Come, and let us all sing the praises of Him Who was crucified for us. For Mary said, when she beheld Him on the Tree: "Though Thou dost endure the Cross, yet Thou art my Son and God."

Ikos

Seeing her own Lamb led to the slaughter, Mary His Mother followed Him with the other woman and in her grief she cried: "Where dost Thou go, my Child? Why dost Thou run so swiftly? Is there another wedding in Cana, and art Thou hastening there, to turn the water into wine? Shall I go with Thee, my Child, or shall I wait for Thee? Speak some word to me, O Word; do not pass me by in silence. Thou hast preserved me in virginity, and Thou art my Son and God."

Synaxarion

[plain reading]

On this great and holy Friday we celebrate the holy, dread and saving Passion of our Lord God and Saviour Jesus Christ, the spittings, blows and scourges; the curses, cheers and the wearing of the purple, the rod, sponge and vinegar; the nails, the spear and especially the Cross and death; that He received willingly for our sakes. We celebrate also the confession of salvation that the grateful thief made on the cross with Him.

Ode VIII

Eirmos

Tone 6   Rich texture, funereal character, sorrowful tone.   *D, Eb, F##, G, A, Bb, C##, D.*

The holy Children brought mockery upon the idol of ungodly wickedness; and the lawless Sanhedrin raged and took vain counsel against Christ, purposing to kill Him Who holds life in the hollow of His hand. The whole creation blesses Him, and glorifies Him to all ages.

"Shake the sleep now from your eyelids," Thou hast said to the disciples, O Christ. "Watch in prayer, that you fall not into temptation. And thou, O Simon, most of all: for the trial is greater to the strong. Know Me, O Peter, for the whole creation blesses me and glorifies Me to all ages."

"No profane word shall ever pass my lips, O Master," Peter cried. "Gladly will I die with Thee, though all men shall deny Thee. Neither flesh nor blood, but Thy Father has revealed Thee to me: and the whole creation blesses Thee and glorifies Thee to all ages."

Glory be to the Father and to the Son and to the Holy Spirit.

"Thou hast not fathomed the full depth of divine wisdom and knowledge," said the Lord. "Thou hast not understood the abyss of My judgements. Therefore do not boast, for thou art flesh, and three times shalt thou deny Me, though the whole creation blesses Me and glorifies Me to all ages."

Both now and ever, and unto the ages of ages. Amen.

"Thou dost protest, O Simon Peter, against the very thing that thou shalt shortly do, even as I have foretold. A maidservant shall suddenly approach and fill thee with fear," said the Lord. "Yet weeping bitterly, thou shalt find Me merciful; for the whole creation blesses Me and glorifies Me to all ages."

We praise, we bless, we worship the Lord.

The divine youths exposed the God-contending pillar of wickedness; and the assembly of the wicked ones, roaring at Christ, conspired falsely, and studied how to kill Him him who holdeth life in His grasp, whom all creation doth bless, glorifying me unto all ages.

Ode IX

Deacon: The Theotokos and the Mother of the Light, let us honour and magnify in song.

Eirmos

Tone 6   Rich texture, funereal character, sorrowful tone.   *D, Eb, F##, G, A, Bb, C##, D.*

Greater in honour than the Cherubim and beyond compare more glorious than the Seraphim; without corruption thou gavest birth to God the Word, truly the Theotokos, we magnify thee.

The destructive band of evil men, hateful to heaven, the synagogue of the murderers of God, drew near to Thee, O Christ, and as a malefactor they led Thee away, Who art the Creator of all. Thee do we magnify.

Ignorant of the Law in their impiety, studying the words of the prophets in vain and to no purpose, unjustly they led Thee, the Master of all, as a lamb to the slaughter. Thee do we magnify.

Glory be to the Father and to the Son and to the Holy Spirit.

Moved by jealous wickedness, the priests and scribes took Him Who is by nature Life and Life giver, and they delivered Him to the Gentiles to be put to death. Him do we magnify.

Both now and forever, and unto the ages of ages. Amen.

Like many dogs they compassed Thee, O King, and struck Thee on the face; they questioned Thee and bore false witness against Thee. And all of these things Thou hast endured to save us all.

Theotokion

Tone 6   Rich texture, funereal character, sorrowful tone.   *D, Eb, F##, G, A, Bb, C##, D.*

Greater in honour than the Cherubim and beyond compare more glorious than the Seraphim; without corruption thou gavest birth to God the Word, truly the Theotokos, we magnify thee.

Little Litany

Deacon: Again and again, in peace let us pray to the Lord.

People: *Lord, have mercy.*

Priest: Help us, save us, have mercy on us, and keep us, O God, by Thy grace.

People: *Lord, have mercy.*

Priest: Calling to remembrance our most holy, most pure, most blessed, glorious Lady Theotokos and Ever Virgin Mary with all the saints, let us commit ourselves and one another and all our life unto Christ our God.

People: *To Thee, O Lord.*

Priest: For all the Hosts of Heaven praise Thee, and unto Thee do we send up glory, to the Father, and to the Son, and to the Holy Spirit, now and ever and unto the ages of ages.

People: *Amen.*

Exapostilarion

Tone 3   Arrogant, brave, and mature atmosphere.   *F, G, A, A#, C, D, E, F.*

O Lord, this very day hast Thou vouchsafed the Good Thief Paradise. By the Wood of the Cross do Thou enlighten me also and save me.

Glory be be to the Father and to the Son and to the Holy Spirit;

O Lord, this very day hast Thou vouchsafed the Good Thief Paradise. By the Wood of the Cross do Thou enlighten me also and save me.

Both now and forever and unto the ages of ages. Amen.

O Lord, this very day hast Thou vouchsafed the Good Thief Paradise. By the Wood of the Cross do Thou enlighten me also and save me.

The Ninth Gospel

Deacon: That He will vouchsafe unto us the hearing of the Holy Gospel, let us pray unto the Lord God.

People: *Lord, have mercy.* **(x3)**

Deacon: Wisdom. Stand up. Let us hear the Holy Gospel.

Priest: Peace be unto all.

People: *And with thy spirit.*

Priest: The Reading is from the Holy Gospel according to John.

People: *Glory to Thy Passion, O Lord, glory to Thee.*

Deacon: Let us attend.

John §61 [19:25-37].

Now there stood by the cross of Jesus his mother, and his mothers sister, Mary the wife of Cleophas, and Mary Magdalene. When Jesus therefore saw his mother, and the disciple standing by, whom he loved, he saith unto his mother, "Woman, behold thy son." Then saith he to the disciple, "Behold thy mother." And from that hour that disciple took her unto his own home. After this, Jesus knowing that all things were now accomplished, that the scripture might be fulfilled, saith, "I thirst." Now there was set a vessel full of vinegar: and they filled a sponge with vinegar, and put it upon hyssop, and put it to his mouth. When Jesus therefore had received the vinegar, he said, "It is finished" And he bowed his head, and gave up the ghost.

The Jews therefore, because it was the preparation, that the bodies should not remain upon the cross on the Sabbath day, (for that Sabbath day was a high day,) besought Pilate that their legs might be broken, and that they might be taken away. Then came the soldiers, and broke the legs of the first, and of the other which was crucified with him. But when they came to Jesus, and saw that he was dead already, they brake not his legs: But one of the soldiers with a spear pierced his side, and forthwith came there out blood and water. And he that saw it bore record, and his record is true: and he knoweth that he saith true, that you might believe. For these things were done, that the scripture should be fulfilled, "A bone of him shall not be broken." And again another scripture saith, "They shall look on him whom they pierced."

People: Glory to Thy Long suffering, O Lord, glory to Thee.

Lauds (The Praises)
Psalm 148

Reader: Let every breath praise the Lord.

Chorus: *Let every breath praise the Lord. Praise the Lord from the heavens, praise Him in the highest. To Thee is due praise, O God. Praise Him, all you His angels; praise Him, all you His hosts. To Thee is due praise, O God.*

Reader: Praise God in His sanctuary, praise Him in the firmament of His power.

Tone 3   Arrogant, brave, and mature atmosphere.   *F, G, A, A#, C, D, E, F.*

Reader: Israel, My first born Son, has committed two evils: he has forsaken Me, the fountain of the water of life, and dug for himself a broken cistern. Upon the Cross has he crucified Me, but asked for Barabbas and let him go. Heaven at this was amazed and the sun hid its rays; yet thou, O Israel, wast not ashamed, but hast delivered Me to death. Forgive them, Holy Father, for they do not know what they have done.

Chorus: *Praise Him for His mighty acts, praise Him according to His excellent greatness.*

Reader: Every member of Thy holy body endured dishonour for our sakes: Thy head, the thorns; Thy face, the spitting; Thy cheeks, the buffeting; Thy mouth, the taste of gall mingled with vinegar; Thine ears, the impious blasphemies; Thy back, the scourging and Thy hand, the reed; Thy whole body, the stretching on the Cross; Thy limbs, the nails; and Thy side, the spear. Thou hast suffered for us and by Thy Passion set us free from passions; in loving self abasement Thou hast stooped down to us and raised us up: O Saviour almighty, have mercy upon us.

Chorus: *Praise Him with the sound of trumpet. Praise Him with the psaltery and harp.*

Reader: Seeing Thee crucified, O Christ, the whole creation trembled. The foundations of the earth shook with fear at Thy power. For when Thou wast raised up today, the people of the Hebrews was destroyed. The veil of the temple was rent in twain, the graves were opened, and the dead rose from the tombs. When the centurion saw the wonder, he was filled with dread. And Thy Mother, standing by Thee, cried with a mother's sorrow: "How shall I not lament and strike my breast, seeing Thee stripped naked and hung upon the wood as one condemned?" Thou wast crucified and buried, and Thou hast risen from the dead: O Lord, glory be to Thee.

Chorus: *Glory be be to the Father and to the Son and to the Holy Spirit;*

Tone 6   Rich texture, funereal character, sorrowful tone.   D, Eb, F##, G, A, Bb, C##, D.

Reader: They stripped Me of My garments and clothed Me in a scarlet robe; they set a crown of thorns upon My head and placed a reed in My right hand, that I may break them in pieces like a potter's vessel.

Chorus: *Both now and forever and unto the ages of ages. Amen.*

Reader: I gave My back to scourging; I did not turn away My face from spitting; I stood before the judgement seat of Pilate, and endured the Cross for the salvation of the world.

The Tenth Gospel

Deacon: That He will vouchsafe unto us the hearing of the Holy Gospel, let us pray unto the Lord God.

People: *Lord, have mercy.* **(x3)**

Deacon: Wisdom. Stand up. Let us hear the Holy Gospel.

Priest: Peace be unto all.

People: *And with thy spirit.*

Priest: The Reading is from the Holy Gospel according to Mark **(§69 [15:43-47])**.

People: *Glory to Thy Passion, O Lord, glory to Thee.*

Deacon: Let us attend.

Priest: Joseph of Arimathaea, an honourable counsellor, which also waited for the kingdom of God, came, and went in boldly unto Pilate, and craved the body of Jesus. And Pilate marvelled if he were already dead: and calling unto him the centurion, he asked him whether he had been any while dead. And when he knew it of the centurion, he gave the body to Joseph. And he bought fine linen, and took him down, and wrapped him in the linen, and laid him in a sepulchre which was hewn out of a rock, and rolled a stone unto the door of the sepulchre. And Mary Magdalene and Mary the mother of Joses beheld where he was laid.

People: *Glory to Thy Long suffering, O Lord, glory to Thee.*

Lesser Doxology

Reader: Glory to God, Who has shown us the Light. Glory to God in the highest, and on earth, peace, good will toward men. We praise Thee. We bless Thee. We worship Thee. We glorify Thee and give thanks to Thee for Thy great glory. O Lord God, Heavenly King, God the Father Almighty. O Lord, the Only Begotten Son, Jesus Christ, and the Holy Spirit. \

O Lord God, Lamb of God, Son of the Father, Who takes away the sins of the world, have mercy on us. Thou, Who takes away the sins of the world, receive our prayer. Thou, Who sittest at the right hand of God the Father, have mercy on us. /

For Thou alone art holy, and Thou alone art Lord. Thou alone, O Lord Jesus Christ, are most high in the glory of God the Father. Amen. I will give thanks to Thee every day and praise Thy Name forever and ever. Lord, Thou hast been our refuge from generation to generation. I said, *"Lord, have mercy on me. Heal my soul, for I have sinned against Thee."* \

Lord, I flee to Thee. Teach me to do Thy will, for Thou art my God. For with Thee is the fountain of Life, and in Thy light we shall see light. Continue Thy loving kindness to those who know Thee. Vouchsafe, O Lord, to keep us this day without sin. Blessed art Thou, O Lord, the God of our fathers, and praised and glorified is Thy Name forever. Amen. Let Thy mercy be upon us, O Lord, even as we have set our hope on Thee.

Blessed art Thou, O Master; teach me Thy statutes.

Blessed art Thou, O Lord; enlighten me with Thy commandments.

Blessed art Thou, O Holy One; make me to understand Thy precepts.

Thy mercy endures forever, O Lord. Do not despise the works of Thy hands. To Thee belongs worship, to Thee belongs praise, to Thee belongs glory: to the Father and to the Son and to the Holy Spirit, both now and forever and unto the ages of ages. Amen. \

Great Litany

Deacon: Let us complete our morning prayer unto the Lord.

People: *Lord, have mercy.*

Deacon: Help us, save us, have mercy on us, and keep us, O God, by Thy grace.

People: *Lord, have mercy.*

Deacon: That the whole day may be perfect, holy, peaceful and sinless, let us ask of the Lord.

People: *Grant this, O Lord.*

Deacon: An angel of peace, a faithful guide, a guardian of our souls and bodies, let us ask of the Lord.

People: *Grant this, O Lord.*

Deacon: Pardon and remission of our sins and offences, let us ask of the Lord.

People: *Grant this, O Lord.*

Deacon: Things good and profitable for our souls, and peace for the world, let us ask of the Lord.

People: *Grant this, O Lord.*

Deacon: That we may complete the remaining time of our life in peace and repentance, let us ask of the Lord.

People: *Grant this, O Lord.*

Deacon: A Christian ending to our life, painless, blameless, peaceful, and a good defence before the dread judgement seat of Christ, let us ask.

People: *Grant this, O Lord.*

Deacon: Calling to remembrance our most holy, most pure, most blessed, glorious Lady Theotokos and Ever Virgin Mary with all the saints, let us commit ourselves and one another and all our life unto Christ our God.

People: *To Thee, O Lord.*

Priest: For Thou art a God of mercy, compassion, and love for mankind, and unto Thee do we send up glory: to the Father, and to the Son, and to the Holy Spirit, now and ever, and unto the ages of ages.

People: *Amen.*

Priest: Peace be unto all.

People: *And with thy spirit.*

Deacon: Let us bow our heads unto the Lord.

People: *To Thee, O Lord.*

Priest: *[soto voce]* O holy Lord, who dwelleth on high and regardest the humble of heart and with Thine all seeing eye dost behold all creation, unto Thee have we bowed the neck of our soul and body, and we entreat Thee: O Holy of holies, stretch forth Thine invisible hand from Thy holy dwelling place and bless us all. And if in aught we have sinned, whether voluntarily or involuntarily, forgive, inasmuch as Thou art a good God, and lovest mankind, vouchsafing unto us Thy earthly and heavenly good things.

[Aloud] For Thine it is to show mercy and to save us, O our God, and unto Thee do we send up glory: to the Father, and to the Son, and to the Holy Spirit, now and ever, and unto the ages of ages.

People: *Amen.*

The Eleventh Gospel

Deacon: That He will vouchsafe unto us the hearing of the Holy Gospel, let us pray unto the Lord God.

People: *Lord, have mercy.* **(x3)**

Deacon: Wisdom. Stand up. Let us hear the Holy Gospel.

Priest: Peace be unto all.

People: *And with thy spirit.*

Priest: The Reading is from the Holy Gospel according to John.

People: *Glory to Thy Passion, O Lord, glory to Thee.*

Deacon: Let us attend.

John §62 [19:38-42].

And after this Joseph of Arimathaea, being a disciple of Jesus, but secretly for fear of the Jews, besought Pilate that he might take away the body of Jesus: and Pilate gave him leave. He came therefore, and took the body of Jesus. And there came also Nicodemus, which at the first came to Jesus by night, and brought a mixture of myrrh and aloes, about a hundred pound weight. Then took they the body of Jesus, and wound it in linen clothes with the spices, as the manner of the Jews is to bury. Now in the place where he was crucified there was a garden; and in the garden a new sepulchre, wherein was never man yet laid. There laid they Jesus therefore because of the Jews' preparation day; for the sepulchre was nigh at hand.

People: *Glory to Thy Long suffering, O Lord, glory to Thee.*

The Aposticha

Tone 1   Magnificent, happy and earthy.   *C, D, Eb, F, G, A, Bb, C.*

The whole creation was changed by fear, when it saw Thee, O Christ, hanging on the Cross. The sun was darkened and the foundations of the earth were shaken; all things suffered with the Creator of all. Of Thine own will Thou hast endured this for our sakes: O Lord, glory to Thee.

Chorus: *They parted My garments amongst them, and cast lots upon My vesture.*

Reader: Why does the impious and transgressing people imagine vain things? Why have they condemned to death the Life of all? O mighty wonder. The Creator of the world is delivered into the hands of lawless men, and He Who loves mankind is raised upon the Cross, that He may free the prisoners in hell, who cry: O long suffering Lord, glory to Thee.

Chorus: *They gave Me gall to eat. And in My thirst they gave Me vinegar to drink.*

Reader: Today the most pure Virgin saw Thee hanging on the Cross, O Word; and with a mother's love she wept and bitterly her heart was wounded. She groaned in anguish from the depth of her soul, and in her grief she struck her face and tore her hair. And, beating her breast, she cried lamenting: "Woe is me, my divine Child. Woe is me, Thou Light of the world. Why dost Thou vanish from my sight, O Lamb of God?" Then the hosts of angels were seized with trembling, and they said: "O Lord beyond our understanding, glory to Thee."

Chorus: *God is our King before the ages. He has worked salvation in the midst of the earth.*

Reader: Seeing Thee hanging on the Cross, O Christ the Creator and God of all, bitterly Thy Virgin Mother cried: "O my Son, where is the beauty of Thy form? I cannot bear to look upon Thee crucified unjustly. Make haste, then, to arise, that I too may see Thy Resurrection on the third day from the dead."

Chorus: *Glory be be to the Father and to the Son and to the Holy Spirit;*

Tone 8   Humility, tranquillity, repose, suffering, pleading.   *C, D, Eb, F, G, A, Bb, C.*

Reader: O Lord, when Thou hast ascended on the Cross, fear and trembling seized all the creation. Thou hast not suffered the earth to swallow those that crucified Thee; but Thou hast commanded hell to render up its prisoners, for the regeneration of mortal men. O Judge of the living and the dead, Thou hast come to bring, not death, but life. O Thou Who lovest mankind, glory be to Thee.

Chorus: *Both now and forever and unto the ages of ages. Amen.*

Reader: Already the unjust judges have dipped their pens in ink, and Jesus is sentenced and condemned to the Cross; the creation suffers, seeing the Lord crucified. O loving Master, Who in Thy bodily nature hast suffered for my sake, glory be to Thee.

The Twelfth Gospel

Deacon: That He will vouchsafe unto us the hearing of the Holy Gospel, let us pray unto the Lord God.

People: *Lord, have mercy.* (x3)

Deacon: Wisdom. Stand up. Let us hear the Holy Gospel.

Priest: Peace be unto all.

People: *And with thy spirit.*

Priest: The Reading is from the Holy Gospel according to Matthew.

People: *Glory to Thy Passion, O Lord, glory to Thee.*

Deacon: Let us attend.

Matthew §114 [27:62-66].

Now the next day, that followed the day of the preparation, the chief priests and Pharisees came together unto Pilate, Saying, "Sir, we remember that that deceiver said, while he was yet alive, after three days I will rise again. Command therefore that the sepulchre be made sure until the third day, lest his disciples come by night, and steal him away, and say unto the people, 'He is risen from the dead': so the last error shall be worse than the first." Pilate said unto them, "You have a watch: go your way, make it as sure as you can." So they went, and made the sepulchre sure, sealing the stone, and setting a watch.

People: *Glory to Thy Long suffering, O Lord, glory to Thee.*

Reader: It is good to give praise unto the Lord, and to chant unto Thy name, O Most High, to proclaim in the morning Thy mercy, and Thy truth by night.

Trisagion

Holy God, Holy Mighty, Holy Immortal, have mercy on us. (x3)

Glory be be to the Father and to the Son and to the Holy Spirit;
Both now and forever and unto the ages of ages. Amen.

O Most Holy Trinity, have mercy on us.

O Lord, cleanse us from our sins.

O Master, pardon our iniquities.

O Holy One, visit and heal our infirmities, for Thy names sake.

Lord, have mercy. (x3)

Glory be be to the Father and to the Son and to the Holy Spirit;
Both now and forever and unto the ages of ages. Amen.

People: Our Father, Who art in Heaven, hallowed be Thy Name. Thy Kingdom come, Thy will be done, on earth as it is in Heaven. Give us this day our daily bread, and forgive us our trespasses, as we forgive those who trespass against us; and lead us not into temptation, but deliver us from the evil one.

Priest: For Thine is the Kingdom, and the power, and the glory; of the Father, and of the Son, and of the Holy Spirit, now and ever, and unto the ages of ages.

People: Amen.

Kathisma

Tone 4   Festive, joyous and expressing deep piety.   *C, D, Eb, F, G, A, Bb, C.*

Thou hast redeemed us from the curse of the law by Thy precious Blood. Having been nailed to the Cross and pierced with a spear, Thou hast poured forth immortality upon mankind. O our Saviour, glory to Thee.

Augmented Ektenia

Deacon: Have mercy on us, O God, according to Thy great mercy, we pray Thee, hearken and have mercy.

People: Lord, have mercy. (**x3**)

Deacon: Again we pray for this land and its Orthodox people, and for their salvation.

People: Lord, have mercy. (**x3**)

Deacon: Again we pray For our Patriarch Bartholomew; for our Archbishop Nikitas and all our brethren in Christ.

People: Lord, have mercy. (**x3**)

Deacon: Again we pray to the Lord our God that He may deliver His people from enemies visible and invisible, and confirm in us oneness of mind, brotherly love and piety.

People: Lord, have mercy. (**x3**)

Deacon: Again we pray for the blessed and ever memorable, holy Orthodox patriarchs; for our royal family; and for the founders of this *[holy temple / monastery]*: and for all our fathers and brethren gone to their rest before us, and the Orthodox here and everywhere laid to rest.

People: Lord, have mercy. (**x3**)

Deacon: Again we pray for them that bring offerings and do good works in this holy and all venerable temple; for them that minister and them that chant, and for all the people here present, that await of Thee great and abundant mercy.

People: Lord, have mercy. (**x3**)

Priest: For a merciful God art Thou, and the Lover of mankind, and unto Thee do we send up glory: to the Father, and to the Son, and to the Holy Spirit, now and ever, and unto the ages of ages.

People: Amen.

Dismissal

Deacon: Wisdom.

People: *Holy Father bless.*

Priest: He that is, is blessed, Christ our God, always, now and ever, and unto the ages of ages.

People: *Amen.*

Reader: Establish, O God, the holy Orthodox Faith of Orthodox Christians unto the ages of ages.

People: *Amen.*

Priest: O most holy Theotokos, save us.

Reader: Greater in honour than the Cherubim and beyond compare more glorious than the Seraphim; without corruption thou gavest birth to God the Word, truly the Theotokos, we magnify thee.

Priest: *Glory to Thee, O Christ God and our hope, glory to Thee.*

Reader: *Glory be be to the Father and to the Son and to the Holy Spirit;*

Both now and forever and unto the ages of ages. Amen.

Lord have mercy. **(x3)**

Holy Father, bless.

Priest: May Christ our true God, Who for the salvation of the world endured spitting, scourging, buffeting, the Cross, and death, through the intercessions of His most pure Mother; of *[patron of the church Saint …]* and of all the saints: have mercy on us and save us, for He is good and loveth mankind.

People: *Amen.*

Priest: Through the prayers of our Holy Fathers, O Lord Jesus Christ our God, have mercy on us and save us.

People: *Amen.*

[The First Hour is not said at the end of Orthros, but on Friday morning in the normal Office of the Hours.]

[Priest in dark epitrachelion.

Epitaphion on Prothesis table.]

The Blessing

[Priest and Deacon before Holy Table.]

Both: How beloved are Thy dwellings, O Lord of hosts; my soul longeth and fainteth for the courts of the Lord. As the hart panteth after the fountains of water, so panteth my soul after Thee, O God. *[bow]* **(x3)**

[Priest kisses Gospel and Holy Table. Kisses cross on epitrachelion and blesses it.]
[Deacon kisses south west corner of Holy Table.]

Priest: Let us pray to the Lord. Lord, have mercy. Blessed is God, who poureth out His grace upon His priests, as oil of myrrh upon the head, which runneth down upon the beard, upon the beard of Aaron, which runneth down to the fringe of his raiment, always, now and forever, and unto the ages of ages. Amen.

Priest: Blessed is our God, always, now and forever, and unto the ages of ages.
People: *Amen.*

Reader: Come, let us worship God, our King.

Come, let us worship and fall down before Christ, our King and our God.

Come, let us worship and fall down before Christ Himself, our King and our God.

Psalm 103
Of David. Concerning The Formation Of The World.

Bless the Lord, O my soul. O Lord my God, Thou hast been exceedingly magnified. Confession and majesty hast Thou put on, Who covered Thyself with light as with a garment, Who stretched out the heaven as it were a curtain; Who supports His chambers in the waters, Who appoints the clouds for His ascent, Who walks upon the wings of the winds, Who makes His angels spirits, and His ministers a flame of fire, Who establishes the earth in the sureness thereof; it shall not be turned back for ever and ever. The abyss like a garment is His mantle; upon the mountains shall the waters stand. At Thy rebuke they will flee, at the voice of Thy thunder shall they be afraid.

The mountains rise up and the plains sink down to the place where Thou hast established them. Thou appointed a boundary that they shall not pass, neither return to cover the earth. He sends forth springs in the valleys; between the mountains will the waters run. They shall give drink to all the beasts of the field; the wild asses will wait to quench their thirst. Beside them will the birds of the heaven lodge, from the midst of the rocks will they give voice. He waters the mountains from His chambers; the earth shall be satisfied with the fruit of Thy works.

He causes the grass to grow for the cattle, and green herb for the service of men, To bring forth bread out of the earth; and wine makes glad the heart of man. To make his face cheerful with oil; and bread strengthens mans heart. The trees of the plain shall be satisfied, the cedars of Lebanon, which Thou hast planted. There will the sparrows make their nests; the house of the heron is chief among them. The high mountains are a refuge for the harts, and so is the rock for the hares. He has made the moon for seasons; the sun knows his going down. Thou appointed the darkness, and there was the night, wherein all the beasts of the forest will go abroad. Young lions roaring after their prey, and seeking their food from God. The sun arises, and they are gathered together, and they lay them down in their dens.

But man shall go forth unto his work, and to his labour until the evening. How magnified are Thy works, O Lord. In wisdom hast Thou made them all; the earth is filled with Thy creation. So is this great and spacious sea, therein are things creeping innumerable, small living creatures with the great. There go the ships; there this dragon, whom Thou hast made to play therein. All things wait on Thee, to give them their food in due season; when Thou gavest it to them, they will gather it. When Thou opened Thy hand, all things shall be filled with goodness; when Thou turned away Thy face, they shall be troubled. Thou wilt take their spirit, and they shall cease; and to their dust shall they return. Thou wilt send forth Thy Spirit, and they shall be created; and Thou shalt renew the face of the earth.

Let the glory of the Lord be unto the ages; the Lord will rejoice in His works. Who looks on the earth and makes it tremble, Who touches the mountains and they smoke. I will sing unto the Lord throughout my life, I will chant to my God for as long as I have my being. May my words be sweet unto Him, and I will rejoice in the Lord. O that sinners would cease from the earth, and they that work iniquity, that they should be no more. Bless the Lord, O my soul. The sun knows his going down, Thou appointed the darkness, and there was the night. How magnified are Thy works, O Lord. In wisdom hast Thou made them all.

After The Psalm

Glory be to the Father and to the Son and to the Holy Spirit;

Both now and forever, and unto the ages of ages. Amen.

Alleluia, alleluia, alleluia. Glory to Thee, O God. **(x3)**

O our God and our Hope, glory to Thee.

The Litany Of Peace

Deacon: In peace, let us pray to the Lord.

People: *Lord, have mercy.*

Deacon: For the peace from above, and for the salvation of our souls, let us pray to the Lord.

People: *Lord, have mercy.*

Deacon: For the peace of the whole world, for the good estate of the holy churches of God, and for the union of all men, let us pray to the Lord.

People: *Lord, have mercy.*

Deacon: For this Holy House, and for those who with faith, reverence, and fear of God, enter therein, let us pray to the Lord.

People: *Lord, have mercy.*

Deacon: For our father and Archbishop Nikitas, for the venerable Priesthood, the Diaconate in Christ, for all the clergy and the people, let us pray to the Lord.

People: *Lord, have mercy.*

Deacon: For Her Majesty, the Queen, for the First Minister, for all civil authorities, and for our Armed Forces, let us pray to the Lord.

People: *Lord, have mercy.*

Deacon: That He will aid them and grant them victory over every enemy and adversary, let us pray to the Lord.

People: *Lord, have mercy.*

Deacon: For this city, and for every city and land, and for the faithful who dwell therein, let us pray to the Lord.

People: *Lord, have mercy.*

Deacon: For healthful seasons, for abundance of the fruits of the earth, and for peaceful times, let us pray to the Lord.

People: *Lord, have mercy.*

Deacon: For travellers by sea, by land, and by air; for the sick and the suffering; for captives and their salvation, let us pray to the Lord.

People: *Lord, have mercy.*

Deacon: For our deliverance from all tribulation, wrath, danger, and necessity, let us pray to the Lord.

People: *Lord, have mercy.*

Deacon: Help us; save us; have mercy on us; and keep us, O God, by Thy grace.

People: *Lord, have mercy.*

Deacon: Calling to remembrance our all holy, immaculate, most blessed and glorious Lady Theotokos and ever virgin Mary, with all the Saints: let us commend ourselves and each other, and all our life unto Christ our God.

People: *To Thee, O Lord.*

Priest: For to Thou art due all glory, honour, and worship: to the Father, and to the Son, and to the Holy Spirit; Both now and forever and unto the ages of ages.

People: *Amen.*

[Deacon or Priest does the Great censing whilst:]

Psalm 140

Chorus: Lord, I have cried to Thee: hear me. Hear me, O Lord.

Lord, I have cried to Thee: hear me. Receive the voice of my prayer.

When I call upon Thee, hear me, O Lord. Let my prayer arise as incense in Thy sight,

And let the lifting up of my hands be an evening sacrifice. Hear me, O Lord.

[Priest kisses cross on Phelonion and blesses it:]

Priest: *[soto voce]* Let us pray to the Lord. Lord, have mercy. Thy priests, O Lord, shall be clothed with righteousness, and Thy holy ones shall rejoice with joy, always, both now and forever, and unto the ages of ages. Amen.

Kekragarion
Sticheroi From Psalm 140

- Set, O Lord, a watch before my mouth, and a door of enclosure round about my lips.

- Incline not my heart to words of evil, to make excuses for sins.

- Those that work iniquity; I will not join with their number.

- The righteous man will chasten me with mercy and reprove me; as for the oil of the sinner, let it not anoint my head.

- For yet more is my prayer in the presence of their pleasures; their judges have been swallowed up by the rock.

- They shall hear my words, for they be sweetened; as a clod of earth is broken upon the earth, so have their bones been scattered into hades.

- To Thee O Lord are mine eyes. In Thee have I hoped; take not my soul away.

- Keep me from the snare which they have laid for me, and from the stumbling blocks of them that work iniquity.

- The sinners shall fall into their own net; I am alone until I pass by.

Sticheroi From Psalm 141

- With my voice to the Lord have I cried, with my voice have I made supplication.

- I will pour out before Him my supplications; my afflictions will I declare before Him.

- When my spirit was fainting within me, then Thou knewest my paths.

- In this way wherein I have walked they hid for me a snare.

- I looked on my right hand, and beheld, and there was none that knew me.

- Flight has failed me, and there is none that watches out for my soul.

- I cried to Thee, O Lord; I said: Thou art my hope, my portion in the land of the living.

- Attend unto my supplication, for I am brought very low.

- Deliver me from them that persecute me, for they are stronger than I.

- Bring my soul out of prison. That I may confess Thy name.

Stichera

Reader: The whole creation, O Christ, hath been transfigured by fear at beholding Thee suspended on the Cross. The Sun was darkened, the foundations of the earth were troubled, and everything suffered with the Creator of all. Wherefore, O Thou who didst endure this willingly for us, O Lord, glory to Thee.

Chorus: *The righteous shall patiently wait for me until Thou shalt reward me.*

Stichera

Reader: Why doth the law transgressing people of false worship meditate in falsehood? Why was he condemned to death who is the life of all? What great wonder that the Creator of the world hath been delivered into the hands of the wicked, and the lover of mankind hath been elevated on a tree to deliver those who are bound in Hades, who cry, "O long suffering Father, glory to Thee."

Sticheroi From Psalm 129

Chorus: *Out of the depths have I cried unto Thee, O Lord. O Lord, hear my voice.*

Reader: Today the blameless Virgin hath seen Thee, O Word, suspended on the Cross, and her heart was wounded with mourning from parental emotions. She sighed disconsolantely from the depth of her soul. She pulled her hair and cheeks bitterly. She smote her breast crying with copious tears, "Woe is me, O my Divine Son. Woe is me, O Light of the wold. Now hast Thou disappeared before mine eyes, O Lamb of God." Then the incorporeal hosts were engulfed with trembling, crying, "O incomprehensible Lord, glory to Thee."

Chorus: *Let Thine ears be attentive to the voice of my supplication.*

Reader: O Christ, God of all creation and its Maker, she who without seed gave Thee birth, seeing Thee suspended on a tree, cried bitterly, "Whither hath the beauty of Thy countenance disappeared, O my Son? I cannot endure the sight of Thine unjust crucifixion. Arise soon, that I may behold Thy third day resurrection from the dead."

Chorus: *If Thou should mark iniquities, O Lord; O Lord, who shall stand? For with Thee there is forgiveness.*

Reader: Today the Lord of creation standeth before Pilate, and the Creator of all is delivered up to crucifixion, offered as a lamb of His own will. He is fastened with nails, pierced with a spear, and a sponge is brought near to Him who rained manna. The Redeemer of the world is smitten on His cheek, and the Redeemer of all is ridiculed by His own servants. What love the Master showed to mankind. For He prayed to His Father on behalf of His crucifiers, saying, "Remit them this sin, for the transgressors of the law know not what they unjustly do."

Chorus: *Glory be to the Father, and to the Son, and to the Holy Spirit;*

Reader: Oh, how the assembly of the law transgressors condemned to death the King of creation, not being ashamed nor abashed by His benevolences, of which He has assured them formerly, calling them to their remembrance, saying, "My people, what have I done to thee? Have I not showered Judaism with wonders? Have I not raised the dead by only a word? Have I not healed every sickness and every weakness? With what, then, hast thou rewarded me? And why forgetest thou me? For healing, thou hast inflicted wounds upon me; and for raising the dead, thou dost cause me, the benevolent, to die suspended upon a tree as an evil doer;

the Giver of the Law, as a law transgressor; and the King of all, as one who is condemned." Wherefore, O long suffering Lord, glory to Thee.

Chorus: *Both now and forever, and unto the ages of ages. Amen.*

Theotokion

Reader: Today is beheld the working of a dread and strange mystery; for He who is inapprehensible is laid hold of; and He who released Adam is chained. He who trieth the hearts and reigns is tried faslely, and He who looketh into the depths is locked in prison. He before whom the heavenly powers stand trembling, standeth before Pilate. The Creator is smitten by the hand of His creatures. The Judge of the living and the dead is condemned to death on a tree; and the Destroyer of Hades is enfolded in the grave. Wherefore, O Thou who didst of Thy compassion bear all these things. Saving all from the curse, O long suffering Lord, glory to Thee.

[Whilst:

Priest kisses Gospel and Holy Table. Gives Gospel to Deacon. Deacon kisses Priests hand and places Orarion over Gospel. Deacon leads Priest(s) via North Door for the entrance. Deacon holds orarion with right hand and Gospel with left, points orarion toward the Holy Doors and says to Priest:]

The Holy Entrance

Deacon: *(Soto voce)* Let us pray to the Lord. Lord have mercy.

Priest: *(Soto voce)* In the evening and in the morning and at noon we praise Thee, we bless Thee, we give thanks unto Thee, and we pray unto Thee, O Master of all, Lord Who lovest mankind; Direct our prayer as incense before Thee, and incline not our hearts unto words of thought of evil, but deliver us from all who seek after our souls. For unto Thee, O Lord, Lord are our eyes, and in Thee have we hoped. Put us not to shame, O our God. For unto Thee are due all glory, honour and worship, to the Father, the Son and the Holy Spirit, both now and forever, and to the ages of ages.

Deacon: Amen.

[Censing]

Deacon: *(Soto voce)* Father, bless the Holy Entrance.

Priest: *(Soto voce)* Blessed is the Entrance to Thy Holy place; both now and forever, and unto the ages of ages. Amen.

Deacon: *(Aloud)* *Wisdom. Stand up.*

O Gladsome Light

O Gladsome Light of the holy glory of the immortal Father; Heavenly holy, blessed Jesus Christ.

Now that we have come to the setting of the sun, and behold the Evening Light.

We praise God; Father, Son and Holy Spirit.

For meet it is at all time to worship Thee, with voices of praise;

O Son of God and Giver of Life. Therefore all the world doth glorify Thee.

The First Reading

Priest: The Evening Prokeimenon.

Reader: They parted my garments among them, and upon my vesture did they cast lots.

People: *They parted my garments among them, and upon my vesture did they cast lots.*

Reader: My God, my God, look upon me; why hast Thou forsaken me?

People: *They parted my garments among them, and upon my vesture did they cast lots.*

Reader: They parted my garments among them | and upon my vesture did they cast lots.

Deacon: Wisdom.

Reader: The reading is from the book of Exodus (33:11-23).

Deacon: Let us attend.

Reader: And the LORD spake unto Moses face to face, as a man speaketh unto his friend. And he turned again into the camp: but his servant Joshua, the son of Nun, a young man, departed not out of the tabernacle. And Moses said unto the LORD, See, thou sayest unto me, Bring up this people: and thou hast not let me know whom thou wilt send with me. Yet thou hast said, I know thee by name, and thou hast also found grace in my sight. Now therefore, I pray thee, if I have found grace in thy sight, shew me now thy way, that I may know thee, that I may find grace in thy sight: and consider that this nation is thy people. And he said, My presence shall go with thee, and I will give thee rest. And he said unto him, If thy presence go not with me, carry us not up hence. For wherein shall it be known here that I and thy people have found grace in thy sight? Is it not in that thou goest with us? So shall we be separated, I and thy people, from all the people that are upon the face of the earth. And the LORD said unto Moses, I will do this thing also that thou hast spoken: for thou hast found grace in my sight, and I know thee by name. And he said, I beseech thee, shew me thy glory. And he said, I will make all my goodness pass before thee, and I will proclaim the name of the LORD before thee; and will be gracious to whom I will be gracious, and will shew mercy on whom I will shew mercy. And he said, Thou cannot see my face: for there shall no man see me, and live. And the LORD said, Behold, there is a place by me, and thou shalt stand upon a rock: And it shall come to pass, while my glory passeth by, that I will put thee in a cleft of the rock, and will cover thee with my hand while I pass by: And I will take away mine hand, and thou shalt see my back parts: but my face shall not be seen.

The Second Reading

Priest: The Evening Prokeimenon.

Reader: Plead Thou my cause, O Lord, with them that strive with me.

People: *Plead Thou my cause, O Lord, with them that strive with me.*

Reader: They rewarded me evil for good.

People: *Plead Thou my cause, O Lord, with them that strive with me.*

Reader: Plead Thou my cause, O Lord | with them that strive with me.

Deacon: Wisdom.

Reader: The reading is from the book of Job (42:12-17).

Deacon: Let us attend.

Reader: Yes, the Lord blessed the last years of Job more than the ones before, and his livestock was: fourteen thousand sheep, six thousand camels, a thousand yoke of oxen, a thousand female donkeys at pasture. And there were born to him seven sons and three daughters, and he called the first Day and the second Cassia and the third Horn of Amaltheia. And there were not found women more excellent than Job's daughters beneath heaven, and their father gave them an inheritance along with their brothers. Now Job lived after his calamity one hundred and seventy years, and all the years he lived were two hundred and forty-eight years. And Job saw his sons and the sons of his sons, a fourth generation, and Job died, old and full of days. And it is written that he will rise again with those the Lord raises up. This man is interpreted from the Syriac book as living in the land of Ausitis, on the borders of Idumea and Arabia, and previously his name was Iobab; now he took an Arabian wife and fathered a son, whose name was Ennon, and he in turn had as father Zare, a son of the sons of Esau, and as mother Bosorra, so that he was the fifth from Abraam.

The Third Reading

Priest: The Evening Prokeimenon.

Reader: O Lord, our Lord, how admirable is Thy Name in all the earth.

People: *O Lord, our Lord, how admirable is Thy Name in all the earth.*

Reader: Thy magnificence is elevated above the heavens.

People: *O Lord, our Lord, how admirable is Thy Name in all the earth.*

Reader: O Lord, our Lord, how admirable is Thy Name | in all the earth.

Deacon: Wisdom.

Reader: The reading is from the book of Isaiah (52:13-15; 53:1-12; 54:1).

Deacon: Let us attend.

Reader: See, my servant shall understand and he shall be exalted and glorified exceedingly. Just as many shall be astonished at you, so shall your appearance be without glory from men, and your glory be absent from the men, so shall many nations be astonished at him, and kings shall shut their mouth, because those who were not informed about him shall see and those who did not hear shall understand. Lord, who has believed our report? And to whom has the arm of the Lord been revealed? He grew up before him like a child, like a root in a thirsty land; he has no form or glory, and we saw him, and he had no form or beauty. But his form was without honour, failing beyond all men, a man being in calamity and knowing how to bear sickness; because his face is turned away, he was dishonoured and not esteemed. This one bears our sins and suffers pain for us, and we accounted him to be in trouble and calamity and ill treatment. But he was wounded because of our acts of lawlessness and has been weakened because of our sins; upon him was the discipline of our peace; by his bruise we were healed. All we like sheep have gone astray; a man has strayed in his own way, and the Lord gave him over to our sins. And he, because he has been ill treated, does not open his mouth; like a sheep he was led to the slaughter, and as a lamb is silent before the one shearing it, so he does not open his mouth. In his humiliation his judgment was taken away. Who will describe his generation? Because his life is being taken from the earth, he was led to death on account of the acts of lawlessness of my people. And I will give the wicked for his burial and the rich for his death, because he committed no lawlessness, nor was deceit found in his mouth. And the Lord desires to cleanse him from his blow. If you offer for sin, your soul shall see a long lived offspring. And the Lord wishes to take away from the pain of his soul, to show him light and fill him with understanding, to justify a righteous one who is well subject to many, and he himself shall bear their sins. Therefore he shall inherit many and he shall divide the spoils of the strong, because his soul was given over to death, and he was reckoned among the lawless, and he bore the sins of many, and because of their sins he was given over. O barren one who does not bear; break forth, and shout, Rejoice, you who are not in labour. Because more are the children of the desolate woman than of her that has a husband, for the Lord has spoken.

The Epistle

Priest: The Evening Prokeimenon.

Reader: They have laid me in the lower pits, in the dark places.
People: *They have laid me in the lower pits, in the dark places.*
Reader: O Lord, the God of my salvation, I have cried day and night before Thee.
People: *They have laid me in the lower pits, in the dark places.*
Reader: They have laid me in the lower pits | in the dark places.

Deacon: Wisdom.
Reader: The reading is from the First Epistle of the Apostle Paul to the Corinthians (1:18-31; 2:1-2).
Deacon: Let us attend.
Reader: For the preaching of the cross is to them that perish foolishness; but unto us which are saved it is the power of God. For it is written, "I will destroy the wisdom of the wise, and will bring to nothing the understanding of the prudent." Where is the wise? Where is the scribe? Where is the disputer of this world? Hath not God made foolish the wisdom of this world? For after that in the wisdom of God the world by wisdom knew not God, it pleased God by the foolishness of preaching to save them that believe. For the Jews require a sign, and the Greeks seek after wisdom: But we preach Christ crucified, unto the Jews a stumblingblock, and unto the Greeks foolishness; But unto them which are called, both Jews and Greeks, Christ the power of God, and the wisdom of God. Because the foolishness of God is wiser than men; and the weakness of God is stronger than men. For you see your calling, brethren, how that not many wise men after the flesh, not many mighty, not many noble, are called: But God hath chosen the foolish things of the world to confound the wise; and God hath chosen the weak things of the world to confound the things which are mighty; And base things of the world, and things which are despised, hath God chosen, yea, and things which are not, to bring to nought things that are; That no flesh should glory in his presence. But of him are you in Christ Jesus, who of God is made unto us wisdom, and righteousness, and sanctification, and redemption: That, according as it is

written, He that glorieth, let him glory in the Lord. And I, brethren, when I came to you, came not with excellency of speech or of wisdom, declaring unto you the testimony of God. For I determined not to know any thing among you, save Jesus Christ, and him crucified.

Priest: Peace be with you who read.

Reader: And with thy spirit.

Chorus: *Halleluiah. Halleluiah. Halleluiah.*

The Gospel

Priest: Wisdom, stand up. Let us listen to the Holy Gospel. Peace be with you all.

People: *And with thy spirit.*

Deacon or junior Priest: The Reading is from the Holy Gospel according to Matthew.

People: *Glory to Thee, O Lord, glory to Thee.*

Priest: Let us attend.

Deacon or junior Priest: When the morning was come, all the chief priests and elders of the people took counsel against Jesus to put him to death: And when they had bound him, they led him away, and delivered him to Pontius Pilate the governor. Then Judas, which had betrayeth him, when he saw that he was condemned, repented himself, and brought again the thirty pieces of silver to the chief priests and elders, Saying, I have sinned in that I have betrayed the innocent blood. And they said, What is that to us? See thou to that. And he cast down the pieces of silver in the temple, and departed, and went and hanged himself. And the chief priests took the silver pieces, and said, It is not lawful for to put them into the treasury, because it is the price of blood. And they took counsel, and bought with them the potter's field, to bury strangers in. Wherefore that field was called, The field of blood, unto this day. Then was fulfilled that which was spoken by Jeremiah the prophet, saying, And they took the thirty pieces of silver, the price of him that was valued, whom they of the children of Israel did value; And gave them for the potters field, as the Lord appointed me.

And Jesus stood before the governor: and the governor asked him, saying, Art thou the King of the Jews? And Jesus said unto him, Thou sayest I am. And when he was accused of the chief priests and elders, he answered nothing. Then said Pilate unto him, Hearest thou not how many things they witness against thee? And he answered him to never a word; insomuch that the governor marvelled greatly. Now at that feast the governor was wont to release unto the people a prisoner, whom they would. And they had then a notable prisoner, called Barabbas. Therefore when they were gathered together, Pilate said unto them, Whom will you that I release unto you? Barabbas, or Jesus which is called Christ? For he knew that for envy they had delivered him. When he was set down on the judgment seat, his wife sent unto him, saying, Have thou nothing to do with that just man: for I have suffered many things this day in a dream because of him. But the chief priests and elders persuaded the multitude that they should ask Barabbas, and destroy Jesus. The governor answered and said unto them, Whether of the twain will you that I release unto you? They said, Barabbas. Pilate saith unto them, What shall I do then with Jesus which is called Christ? They all said unto him, "Let him be crucified." And the governor said, "Why, what evil hath he done?" But they cried out the more, saying, "Let him be crucified." When Pilate saw that he could prevail nothing, but that rather a tumult was made, he took water, and washed his hands before the multitude, saying, I am innocent of the blood of this just person: see you to it. Then answered all the people, and said, "His blood be on us, and on our children."

Then released he Barabbas unto them: and when he had scourged Jesus, he delivered him to be crucified. Then the soldiers of the governor took Jesus into the common hall, and gathered unto him the whole band of soldiers. And they stripped him, and put on him a scarlet robe. And when they had platted a crown of thorns, they put it upon his head, and a reed in his right hand: and they bowed the knee before him, and mocked him, saying, "Hail, King of the Jews." And they spit upon him, and took the reed, and smote him on the head. And after that they had mocked him, they took the robe off from him, and put his own raiment on him, and led him away to crucify him. And as they came out, they found a man of Cyrene, Simon by name: him they compelled to bear his cross. And when they were come unto a place called Golgotha, that is to say, a place of a skull, They gave him vinegar to drink mingled with gall: and when he had tasted thereof, he would not drink. And they crucified him, and parted his garments, casting lots: that it might be fulfilled which was spoken by the prophet, "They parted my garments among them, and upon my vesture did they cast lots." And sitting down they watched him there; And set up over his head his accusation written, THIS IS JESUS THE KING OF THE JEWS. Then were there two thieves crucified with him, one on the right hand, and another on the left.

Luke (23:39-43)

And one of the malefactors which were hanged railed on him, saying, "If thou be Christ, save thyself and us." But the other answering rebuked him, saying, "Dost not thou fear God, seeing thou art in the same condemnation? And we indeed justly; for we receive the due reward of our deeds: but this man hath done nothing amiss." And he said unto Jesus, "Lord, remember me when thou comest into thy kingdom." And Jesus said unto him, "Verily I say unto thee, To day shalt thou be with me in paradise."

Matthew (27:39-54)

And they that passed by reviled him, wagging their heads, And saying, "Thou that destroyest the temple, and buildest it in three days, save thyself. If thou be the Son of God, come down from the cross." Likewise also the chief priests mocking him with the scribes and elders, said, "He saved others; himself he cannot save. If he be the King of Israel, let him now come down from the cross, and we will believe him. He trusted in God; let him deliver him now, if he will have him: for he said, I am the Son of God." The thieves also, which were crucified with him, cast the same in his teeth. Now from the sixth hour there was darkness over all the land unto the ninth hour. And about the ninth hour Jesus cried with a loud voice, saying, "Eli, Eli, lama sabachthani?" That is to say, "My God, my God, why hast thou forsaken me?" Some of them that stood there, when they heard that, said, "This man calleth for Elijah." And straightway one of them ran, and took a sponge, and filled it with vinegar, and put it on a reed, and gave him to drink. The rest said, "Let be, let us see whether Elijah will come to save him."

Jesus, when he had cried again with a loud voice, yielded up the ghost. And, behold, the veil of the temple was rent in twain from the top to the bottom; and the earth did quake, and the rocks rent, and the graves were opened; and many bodies of the saints which slept arose and came out of the graves after his resurrection, and went into the holy city, and appeared unto many.

Now when the centurion, and they that were with him, watching Jesus, saw the earthquake, and those things that were done, they feared greatly, saying, "Truly this was the Son of God."

John (19:31-37)

The Jews therefore, because it was the preparation, that the bodies should not remain upon the cross on the sabbath day, (for that sabbath day was an high day,) besought Pilate that their legs might be broken, and that they might be taken away. Then came the soldiers, and broke the legs of the first, and of the other which was crucified with him. But when they came to Jesus, and saw that he was dead already, they brake not his legs: But one of the soldiers with a spear pierced his side, and forthwith came there out blood and water. And he that saw it bare record, and his record is true: and he knoweth that he saith true, that you might believe. For these things were done, that the scripture should be fulfilled, A bone of him shall not be broken. And again another scripture saith, They shall look on him whom they pierced.

Matthew (27:55-61)

And many women were there beholding afar off, which followed Jesus from Galilee, ministering unto him: Among which was Mary Magdalene, and Mary the mother of James and Joses, and the mother of Zebedee's children. When the even was come, there came a rich man of Arimathaea, named Joseph, who also himself was Jesus' disciple: He went to Pilate, and begged the body of Jesus. Then Pilate commanded the body to be delivered.

[Senior Priest and Deacon exit via North Door to the solea, with a white linen shroud. Senior Priest (assisted by Deacon) removes the body from the cross, wraps it in white shroud and carries it through Holy Doors.
If only one Priest is serving he interrupts his reading of the Gospel to do this, then continues reading.]

Deacon or junior Priest: And when Joseph had taken the body, he wrapped it in a clean linen cloth, and laid it in his own new tomb, which he had hewn out in the rock: and he rolled a great stone to the door of the sepulchre, and departed. And there was Mary Magdalene, and the other Mary, sitting over against the sepulchre.

People: *Glory to Thee, O Lord, glory to Thee.*

The Litany Of Fervent Supplication

Deacon: Let us all say with our whole soul, and with our whole mind let us say:

People: *Lord, have mercy.*

Deacon: Lord Almighty, God of our Fathers, we pray Thee, hearest and have mercy.

People: *Lord, have mercy.*

Deacon: Have mercy on us, O God, according to Thy great mercy, we pray Thee; hear us and have mercy.

People: *Lord, have mercy.* **(x3)**

Deacon: Also we pray for our Archbishop Nikitas.

People: *Lord, have mercy.* **(x3)**

Deacon: For our Sovereign Lady, Queen <u>Elizabeth</u>, the Royal family, our Welsh Assembly Government, and all in authority, let us pray to the Lord.

People: *Lord, have mercy.* **(x3)**

Deacon: Also we pray for mercy, life, peace, health, salvation, visitation, pardon and forgiveness of sins for the servants of God, all devout and Orthodox Christians, those who dwell in or visit this city or town and parish, the wardens and members of this church and their families and all who have asked for our prayers, unworthy though we are.

People: *Lord, have mercy.* **(x3)**

Deacon: Also we pray for the blessed and ever remembered founders of this holy church, and for all our brothers and sisters who have gone to their rest before us, and who lie here asleep in the true faith; and for the Orthodox everywhere *[and the servants of God N and N – (names given before the service)]* and that they may be pardoned all their offences, both voluntary and involuntary.

People: *Lord, have mercy.* **(x3)**

Deacon: Also we pray for those who bring offerings, those who care for the beauty of this holy and venerable house, for those who labour in its service, for those who sing, and for the people here present, who await Thy great and rich mercy.

People: *Lord, have mercy.* **(x3)**

Priest: For Thou, O God, art merciful and love mankind, and to Thee we givest glory, to the Father, the Son and the Holy Spirit, both now and forever, and unto the ages of ages.

People: *Amen.*

The Evening Prayer

Reader: Vouchsafe, O Lord, to keep us this evening without sin. Blessed art Thou, O Lord, the God of our fathers, and praised and glorified is Thy name unto the ages. Amen.

Let Thy mercy, O Lord, be upon us, according as we have hoped in Thee.

Blessed art Thou, O Lord, teach me Thy statutes.
Blessed art Thou, O Master, give me understanding of Thy statutes.
Blessed art Thou, O Holy One, enlighten me by Thy statutes.

O Lord, Thy mercy endures forever; disdain not the work of Thy hands. To Thee is due praise, to Thee is due song, to Thee is due glory, to the Father, and to the Son, and to the Holy Spirit; both now and forever, and unto the ages of ages. Amen.

The Litany Of Supplication

Deacon: Let us complete our evening prayer unto the Lord.

People: *Lord, have mercy.*

Deacon: Help us; save us; have mercy on us; and keep us, O God, by Thy grace.

People: *Lord, have mercy.*

Deacon: That the whole evening may be perfect, holy, peaceful and sinless, let us ask of the Lord.

People: *Grant this, O Lord.*

Deacon: An angel of peace, a faithful guide, a guardian of our souls and bodies, let us ask of the Lord.

People: *Grant this, O Lord.*

Deacon: Pardon and remission of our sins and transgressions, let us ask of the Lord.

People: *Grant this, O Lord.*

Deacon: All things good and profitable for our souls and peace for the world, let us ask of the Lord.

People: *Grant this, O Lord.*

Deacon: That we may complete the remaining time of our life in peace and repentance, let us ask of the Lord.

People: *Grant this, O Lord.*

Deacon: A Christian ending to our life, painless, blameless, peaceful, and a good defence before the fearful judgement seat of Christ, let us ask of the Lord.

People: *Grant this, O Lord.*

Deacon: Calling to remembrance our all holy, immaculate, most blessed and glorious Lady Theotokos and ever virgin Mary, with all the Saints: let us commend ourselves and one another, and all our life to Christ our God.

People: *To Thee, O Lord.*

Priest: For Thou art a good God and lovest mankind, and to Thee we ascribe glory: to the Father, and to the Son, and to the Holy Spirit; both now and forever, and to the ages of ages.

People: *Amen.*

Priest: Peace be with you all.

People: *And with thy spirit.*

Deacon: Let us bow our heads unto the Lord.

People: *To Thee, O Lord.*

Priest: *(speaking voice)* O Lord our God, Who didst bow the heavens and come down for the salvation of mankind: Look upon Thy servants and Thine inheritance; for to Thee, the fearful Judge Who yet loves mankind, have Thine servants bowed their heads and submissively inclined their necks, awaiting not help from men but entreating Thy mercy and looking confidently for Thy salvation. Guard them at all times, both during this present evening and in the approaching night, from every foe, from all adverse powers of the devil, and from vain thoughts and from evil imaginations.

(aloud) Blessed and glorified be the might of Thy kingdom: of the Father, and of the Son, and of the Holy Spirit; both now and forever, and unto the ages of ages.

People: *Amen.*

Silent Procession With Epitaphios

a) *People kneel.*

b) *Acolytes with candles and exaptera.*

c) *Deacon, censing epitaphios.*

d) *Priests in exorasson and epitrachelion.*

e) *Senior Priest under epitaphios carrying Gospel.*

f) *If only one Priest then he carriers the epitaphios.*

g) *Three times around bier, then place epitaphios on it with the head of Christ to the north.*

h) *Priest places Gospel in the middle of epitaphios.*

i) *Priest sprinkles blossoms upon epitaphios, makes 3 prostrations before bier and venerates it and Gospel.*

j) *Remaining clergy make 3 prostrations and venerate epitaphios and Gospel, two by two.*

k) *The people do the same.*

l) *Clergy re-enter the Sanctuary.*

Aposticha

Tone 2   *Majesty, gentleness, hope, repentance and sadness.*   *E, F, G, Ab, B, C.*

Reader: O Christ, Life of all, when Joseph of Ramah brought Thee down dead from the Cross, he laid Thee in balms and linen, hastening anxiously to kiss Thy lips and bury Thy pure body free of corruption. But he was reverent with fear as he cried to Thee with joy, "Glory be to Thy condescension, O Lover of mankind."

Chorus: The Lord is King, He is clothed with majesty.

Reader: Hades, made ridiculous at seeing Thee, O Deliverer of all, placed in a new tomb for the sake of all, trembled with fear. Its locks were shattered; its doors broken; the tombs were opened; and the dead awoke. Then Adam cried to Thee with joy and gratitude, "Glory be to Thy condescension, O Lover of mankind."

Chorus: For He established the world which shall not be shaken

Reader: O Christ, who in Thy divine nature art boundless and infinite, when Thou wast enclosed in the grace by Thine own will after the flesh, Thou didst close the chambers of death and Hades, and didst demolish all its kingdoms. Then Thou preparedst this Sabbath for Thy glory, Thine illumination, and Thy divine blessing.

Chorus: Holiness becomes Thine house, O Lord, to the length of days.

Reader: The angelic hosts, O Christ,, beholding those lawless ones victimise Thee as a criminal, and seeing the tombstone sealed by the hands of those who pierced Thy side, were frightened at Thine ineffable long suffering. But, rejoicing at our salvation, they cried unto Thee, "Glory be to Thy condescension, O Lover of mankind."

Chorus: *Glory be to the Father, and to the Son, and to the Holy Spirit;*
Both now and forever, and unto the ages of ages. Amen.

Tone 5   Stimulating, dancing, and rhythmical.   *C, D, Eb, F, G, A, Bb, C.*

Reader: O Thou who puttest on light like a robe, when Joseph, with Nicodemus, brought Thee down from the tree and beheld Thee dead, naked and unburied, he mourned outwardly and grievously, crying to Thee with sighs, and saying, "Woe is me, O sweet Jesus, whom but a while ago, when the sun beheld Thee suspended upon the Cross, it was shrouded in darkness; the earth quaked with fear, and the veil of the Temple was rent asunder. Albeit, I see that Thou willingly endurest death for my sake. How then shall I array Thee, my God? How shall I wrap Thee with linen? Or what dirges shall I chant for Thy funeral? Wherefore, O compassionate Lord, I magnify Thy Passion, and praise Thy Burial with Thy Resurrection, crying, "Lord, glory to Thee."

Hymn Of Simeon The God Receiver

Reader: Lord, now lettest Thou Thy servant depart in peace, according to Thy word, for mine eyes have seen Thy salvation, which Thou hast prepared before the face of all peoples; a light of revelation for the Gentiles, and the glory of Thy people Israel.

Trisagion Prayers

Holy God, Holy Mighty, Holy Immortal, have mercy on us. **(x3)**
  Glory be to the Father, and to the Son, and to the Holy Spirit;
  Both now and forever, and unto the ages of ages. Amen.

O Most Holy Trinity, have mercy on us.

O Lord, cleanse us from our sins.

O Master, pardon our iniquities.

O Holy One, visit and heal our infirmities, for Thy names sake.

Lord have mercy. **(x3)**
    Glory be to the Father and to the Son and to the Holy Spirit;
    Both now and forever, and unto the ages of ages. Amen.

People: *Our Father, Who art in Heaven, hallowed be Thy Name. Thy Kingdom come, Thy will be done, on earth as it is in Heaven. Give us this day our daily bread, and forgive us our trespasses, as we forgive those who trespass against us; and lead us not into temptation, but deliver us from the evil one. Amen.*
O Lord, Jesus Christ, Son of God, have mercy on us.

Priest: For Thine is the kingdom, the power, and the glory, of the Father, and the Son and the Holy Spirit, both now and ever, and to the ages of ages.

People: *Amen.*

Apolytikia

Tone 2   Majesty, gentleness, hope, repentance and sadness.   *E, F, G, Ab, B, C.*

The pious Joseph, having brought down Thy pure body from the tree, wrapped it in pure linen, embalmed it with ointment, and arrayed it in a new tomb.

Verily, the angel came to the tomb and said to the ointment bearing women, "Ointment is meet for the dead, but Christ hath shown Himself to be free from corruption."

The Dismissal

Deacon: Wisdom.

People: *Holy Father, bless.*

Priest: Christ our God, the Existing One, is blessed, always, now and forever, and unto the ages of ages.

People: *Amen.*

Reader: Preserve, O god, the holy Orthodox faith and all Orthodox Christians, unto the ages of ages.

People: *Amen.*

Priest: Most holy Theotokos, save us.

Reader: Greater in honour than the Cherubim and beyond compare more glorious than the Seraphim; without corruption thou gavest birth to God the Word, truly the Theotokos, we magnify thee.

Priest: Glory to Thee, O Christ, our God and our hope, glory to Thee.

Reader: *Glory be to the Father, and to the Son, and to the Holy Spirit;*

Both now and forever, and unto the ages of ages. Amen.

Lord, have mercy. **(x3)**

Holy Father, bless.

Priest: May He who didst endure spitting, scourges, reviling, and death for our salvation, Christ our true God, through the intercessions of His all immaculate and all blameless holy Mother; of *[patronal saint(s)]* to whom the church is dedicated, of all the saints; have mercy on us, and save us, forasmuch as He is good and loveth mankind.

Priest: Through the prayers of our holy Fathers; O Lord Jesus Christ our God; have mercy on us and save us.

People: *Amen.*

[People come forward to venerate the epitaphios.

Chorus repeat as many times as necessary:]

Apolytikia

Tone 2   Majesty, gentleness, hope, repentance and sadness.   *E, F, G, Ab, B, C.*

The pious Joseph, having brought down Thy pure body from the tree, wrapped it in pure linen, embalmed it with ointment, and arrayed it in a new tomb.

Verily, the angel came to the tomb and said to the ointment bearing women, "Ointment is meet for the dead, but Christ hath shown Himself to be free from corruption."

[For Friday Evening]

The Trisagion Prayers

Priest: Blessed is our God, always, now and ever, and unto the ages of ages.

People: *Amen.*

Priest: Glory to Thee, our God, glory to Thee.

O Heavenly King, Comforter, Spirit of Truth, Who art everywhere present and fillest all things, Treasury of blessings and Giver of life: Come and abide in us and cleanse us from every impurity and save our souls, O Good One.

Reader: Holy God, Holy Mighty, Holy Immortal, have mercy on us. **(x3)**

Glory be to the Father, and to the Son, and to the Holy Spirit;

Both now and forever, and unto the ages of ages. Amen.

O Most Holy Trinity, have mercy on us.

O Lord, cleanse us from our sins.

O Master, pardon our iniquities.

O Holy One, visit and heal our infirmities, for Thy names sake.

Lord have mercy. **(x3)**

Glory be be to the Father and to the Son and to the Holy Spirit;

Both now and forever, and unto the ages of ages. Amen.

People: *Our Father, Who art in Heaven, hallowed be Thy Name. Thy Kingdom come, Thy will be done, on earth as it is in Heaven. Give us this day our daily bread, and forgive us our trespasses, as we forgive those who trespass against us; and lead us not into temptation, but deliver us from the evil one.*

Priest: For Thine is the kingdom and the power and the glory of the Father and of the Son and of the Holy Spirit; both now and forever and unto the ages of ages.

People: Amen.

Lord, have mercy. **(x3)**

> *Glory be be to the Father and to the Son and to the Holy Spirit;*
>
> *Both now and forever and unto the ages of ages. Amen.*

Troparion

Reader: O Lord, save Thy people and bless Thine inheritance. Grant victory unto Orthodox Christians over their enemies, and by the power of Thy Cross do Thou preserve Thy commonwealth.

Chorus: *Glory be to the Father and to the Son and to the Holy Spirit,*

Reader: O Thou Who wast lifted up willingly upon the Cross, bestow Thy mercies upon the new community named after Thee, O Christ God; gladden with Thy power the Orthodox Christians, granting them victory over enemies; may they have as Thy help the weapon of peace, the invincible trophy.

Chorus: *Both now and forever and unto the ages of ages. Amen.*

Reader: O Awesome intercession that cannot be put to shame, O good one, disdain not our prayer; O all hymned Theotokos, establish the commonwealth of the Orthodox, save the Orthodox Christians, and grant unto them victory from heaven, for thou didst bring forth God, O thou only blessed one.

Augmented Ektenia

Priest: Have mercy on us O God according to Thy great mercy; we pray Thee hearken and have mercy.

People: *Lord, have mercy.* **(x3)**

Priest: Again we pray for all the brethren and for all Christians.

People: *Lord, have mercy.* **(x3)**

Priest: Again we pray for His Holiness Patriarch Bartholomew; and for our Archbishop Nikitas.

People: *Lord, have mercy.* **(x3)**

Priest: For a merciful God art Thou, and the Lover of mankind, and unto Thee do we send up glory: to the Father, and to the Son, and to the Holy Spirit, both now and forever, and unto the ages of ages.

People: *Amen. Holy Father bless.*

Priest: Glory to the holy, and consubstantial, and life creating, and indivisible Trinity, always, now and ever, and unto the ages of ages.

People: *Amen.*

The Six Psalms

[From Doxology] **Reader:** Glory to God in the highest, and on earth peace, good will amongst men. **(x3)**

[From Ps 50] ***Chorus:*** *O Lord, Thou shalt open my lips, and my mouth shall declare Thy praise.* **(x2)**

Psalm 3

Reader: O Lord, why are they multiplied that afflict me? Many rise up against me. Many say unto my soul: There is no salvation for him in his God. But Thou, O Lord, art my helper, my glory, and the lifter up of my head. I cried unto the Lord with my voice, and He heard me out of His holy mountain. I laid me down and slept; I awoke, for the Lord will help me. I will not be afraid of ten thousands of people that set themselves against me round about. Arise, O Lord, save me, O my God, for Thou hast smitten all who without cause are mine enemies; the teeth of sinners hast Thou broken. Salvation is of the Lord, and Thy blessing is upon Thy people. I laid me down and slept; I awoke, for the Lord will help me.

Psalm 37

O Lord, rebuke me not in Thine anger, nor chasten me in Thy wrath. For Thine arrows are fastened in me, and Thou hast laid Thy hand heavily upon me. There is no healing in my flesh in the face of Thy wrath; and there is no peace in my bones in the face of my sins. For mine iniquities are risen higher than my head; as a heavy burden have they pressed heavily upon me. My bruises are become noisome and corrupt in the face of my folly. I have been wretched and utterly bowed down until the end; all the day long I went with downcast face. For my loins are filled with mockings, and there is no healing in my flesh. I am afflicted and exceedingly humbled, I have roared from the groaning of my heart. O Lord, before Thee is all my desire, and my groaning is not hid from Thee. My heart is troubled, my strength hath failed me; and the light of mine eyes, even this is not with me. My friends and my neighbours drew nigh over against me and stood, and my nearest of kin stood afar off. And they that sought after my soul used violence; and they that sought evils for me spake vain things, and craftinesses all the day long did they meditate. But as for me, like a deaf man I heard them not, and was as a speechless man that openeth not his mouth. And I became as a man that heareth not, and that hath in his mouth no reproofs. For in Thee have I hoped, O Lord; Thou wilt hearken unto me, O Lord my God. For I said: Let never mine enemies rejoice over me; yea, when my feet were shaken, those men spake boastful words against me. For I am ready for scourges, and my sorrow is continually before me. For I will declare mine iniquity, and I will take heed concerning my sin. But mine enemies live and are made stronger than I, and they that hated me unjustly are multiplied. They that render me evil for good slandered me, because I pursued goodness. Forsake me not, O Lord my God, depart not from me. Be attentive unto my help, O Lord of my salvation.

Psalm 62

O God, Thou art my God; early will I seek Thee; my soul thirsts for Thee; My flesh longs for Thee in a dry and thirsty land where there is no water. So I have looked for Thee in the sanctuary, to see Thy power and Thy glory. Because Thy loving kindness is better than life, my lips shall praise Thee. Thus I will bless Thee while I live; I will lift up my hands in Thy name. My soul shall be satisfied as with marrow and fatness, and my mouth shall praise Thee with joyful lips. When I remember Thee on my bed, I meditate on Thee in the night watches. Because Thou hast been my help, therefore in the shadow of Thy wings I will rejoice. My soul follows close behind Thee; Thy right hand upholds me. But those who seek my life, to destroy it, shall go into the lower parts of the earth. They shall fall by the sword; they shall be a portion for jackals. But the king shall rejoice in God; everyone who swears by Him shall glory; but the mouth of those who speak lies shall be stopped.

At the dawn I meditated on Thee. For Thou art become my helper; in the shelter of Thy wings will I rejoice. My soul hath cleaved after Thee, Thy right hand hath been quick to help me.

After The Psalm

Glory be to the Father and to the Son and to the Holy Spirit,
Both now and forever and unto the ages of ages. Amen.

Halleluiah, Halleluiah, Halleluiah. Glory to Thee, O God. **(x3)**
Lord. have mercy. **(x3)**

Glory be to the Father and to the Son and to the Holy Spirit,
Both now and forever and unto the ages of ages. Amen.

Psalm 87

O Lord God of my salvation, by day have I cried and by night before Thee. Let my prayer come before Thee, bow down Thine ear unto my supplication. For filled with evils is my soul, and my life unto hades hath drawn nigh. I am counted with them that go down into the pit; I am become as a man without help, free amongst the dead. Like the bodies of the slain that sleep in the grave, whom Thou rememberest no more, and they are cut off from Thy hand. They laid me in the lowest pit, in darkness and in the shadow of death. Against me is Thine anger made strong, and all Thy billows hast Thou brought upon me. Thou hast removed my friends afar from me; they have made me an abomination unto themselves. I have been delivered up, and have not come forth; mine eyes are grown weak from poverty. I have cried unto Thee, O Lord, the whole day long; I have stretched out my hands unto Thee. Nay, for the dead wilt Thou work wonders? Or shall physicians raise them up that they may give thanks unto Thee? Nay, shall any in the grave tell of Thy mercy, and of Thy truth in that destruction? Nay, shall Thy wonders be known in that darkness, and Thy righteousness in that land that is forgotten? But as for me, unto Thee, O Lord, have I cried; and in the morning shall my prayer come before Thee. Wherefore, O Lord, dost Thou cast off my soul and turnest Thy face away from me? A poor man am I, and in troubles from my youth; yea, having been exalted, I was humbled and brought to distress. Thy furies have passed upon me, and Thy terrors have sorely troubled me. They came round about me like water, all the day long they compassed me about together. Thou hast removed afar from me friend and neighbour, and mine acquaintances because of my misery. O Lord God of my salvation, by day have I cried and by night before Thee. Let my prayer come before Thee, bow down Thine ear unto my supplication.

Psalm 102

Bless the Lord, O my soul, and all that is within me bless His holy name. Bless the Lord, O my soul, and forget not all that He hath done for thee, Who is gracious unto all thine iniquities, Who healeth all thine infirmities, Who redeemeth thy life from corruption, Who crowneth thee with mercy and compassion, Who fulfilleth thy desire with good things; thy youth shall be renewed as the eagles. The Lord performeth deeds of mercy, and executeth judgement for all them that are wronged. He hath made His ways known unto Moses, unto the sons of Israel the things that He hath willed. Compassionate and merciful is the Lord, long suffering and plenteous in mercy; not unto the end will He be angered, neither unto eternity will He be wroth. Not according to our iniquities hath He dealt with us, neither according to our sins hath He rewarded us. For according to the height of heaven from the earth, the Lord hath made His mercy to prevail over them that fear Him. As far as the east is from the west, so far hath He removed our iniquities from us. Like as a father hath compassion upon his sons, so hath the Lord had compassion upon them that fear Him; for He knoweth whereof we are made, He hath remembered that we are dust. As for man, his days are as the grass; as a flower of the field, so shall he blossom forth. For when the wind is passed over it, then it shall be gone, and no longer will it know the place thereof. But the mercy of the Lord is from eternity, even unto eternity, upon them that fear Him. And His righteousness is upon sons of sons, upon them that keep His testament and remember His commandments to do them. The Lord in heaven hath prepared His throne, and His kingdom ruleth over all. Bless the Lord, all you His angels, mighty in strength, that perform His word, to hear the voice of His words. Bless the Lord, all you His hosts, His ministers that do His will. Bless the Lord, all you His works, in every place of His dominion. Bless the Lord, O my soul. In every place of His dominion, bless the Lord, O my soul.

Psalm 142

O Lord, hear my prayer, give ear unto my supplication in Thy truth; hearken unto me in Thy righteousness. And enter not into judgement with Thy servant, for in Thy sight shall no man living be justified. For the enemy hath persecuted my soul; he hath humbled my life down to the earth. He hath seated me in darkness as those that have been long dead, and my spirit within me is become despondent; within me my heart is troubled. I remembered days of old, I meditated on all Thy works, I pondered on the creations of Thy hands. I stretched forth my hands unto Thee; my soul thirsteth after thee like a waterless land. Quickly hear me, O Lord; my spirit hath fainted away. Turn not Thy face away from me, lest I be like unto them that go down into the pit. Cause me to hear Thy mercy in the morning; for in Thee have I put my hope. Cause me to know, O Lord, the way wherein I should walk; for unto Thee have I lifted up my soul. Rescue me from mine enemies, O Lord; unto Thee have I fled for refuge. Teach me to do Thy will, for Thou art my God. Thy good Spirit shall lead me in the land of uprightness; for Thy names sake, O Lord, shalt Thou quicken me. In Thy righteousness shalt Thou bring my soul out of affliction, and in Thy mercy shalt Thou utterly destroy mine enemies. And Thou shalt cut off all them that afflict my soul, for I am Thy servant.

Chorus: *Hearken unto me, O Lord, in Thy righteousness, and enter not into judgement with Thy servant.* (x2)

Reader: Thy good Spirit shall lead me in the land of uprightness.

After The Psalm

Glory be to the Father and to the Son and to the Holy Spirit,
Both now and forever and unto the ages of ages. Amen.

Halleluiah, Halleluiah, Halleluiah. Glory to Thee, O God. *(cross and bow)* **(x3)**
O our God and our hope, glory to Thee.

Great Litany

Deacon: In peace let us pray to the Lord.

People: *Lord, have mercy.*

Deacon: For the peace from above, and the salvation of our souls; let us pray to the Lord.

People: *Lord, have mercy.*

Deacon: For the peace of the whole world, the good estate of the holy churches of God, and the union of all, let us pray to the Lord.

People: *Lord, have mercy.*

Deacon: For this holy temple, and for them that with faith, reverence, and the fear of God enter herein, let us pray to the Lord

People: *Lord, have mercy.*

Deacon: Again we pray for our His Holiness Patriarch Bartholomew; for our Archbishop Nikitas, whose diocese this is; for the venerable priesthood, the diaconate in Christ, for all the clergy and people, let us pray to the Lord.

People: *Lord, have mercy.*

Deacon: For this land, the Royal family, the authorities and armed forces, let us pray to the Lord.

People: *Lord, have mercy.*

Deacon: For seasonable weather, an abundance of the fruits of the earth, and peaceful times, let us pray to the Lord.

People: *Lord, have mercy.*

Deacon: For travellers by sea, land and air; for the sick, the suffering, the imprisoned, and for their salvation, let us pray to the Lord.

People: *Lord, have mercy.*

Deacon: That we may be delivered from all tribulation, wrath, and necessity, let us pray to the Lord.

People: *Lord, have mercy.*

Deacon: Help us, save us, have mercy on us, and keep us, O God, by Thy grace.

People: *Lord, have mercy.*

Deacon: Calling to remembrance our most holy, most pure, most blessed, glorious Lady Theotokos and Ever Virgin Mary with all the saints, let us commit ourselves and one another and all our life unto Christ our God.

People: *To Thee O Lord.*

Deacon: For unto Thee is due all glory, honour and worship; to the Father, and to the Son, and to the Holy Spirit, both now and ever, and unto the ages of ages.

People: *Amen.*

God Is The Lord

Chorus: *God is the Lord and has revealed Himself to us. Blessed is He who cometh in the Name of the Lord.*

Reader: Give thanks to the Lord, for He is good; and His steadfast love endures forever.

Chorus: *God is the Lord and has revealed Himself to us. Blessed is He who cometh in the Name of the Lord.*

Reader: All nations surrounded me; in the Name of the Lord, I withstood them.

Chorus: *God is the Lord and has revealed Himself to us. Blessed is He who cometh in the Name of the Lord.*

Reader: I shall not die, but live, and recount the deeds of the Lord.

Chorus: *God is the Lord and has revealed Himself to us. Blessed is He who cometh in the Name of the Lord.*

Reader: The stone which the builders rejected has become the chief cornerstone.

This is the Lords doing and is marvellous in our eyes.

Chorus: *God is the Lord and has revealed Himself to us. Blessed is He who cometh in the Name of the Lord.*

Apolytikion

Tone 2   *Majesty, gentleness, hope, repentance and sadness.*   E, F, G, Ab, B, C.

Reader: The Noble Joseph, taking Thy most pure body down from the Tree and having wrapped it in pure linen and spices, laid it in a new tomb.

Chorus: *Glory be to the Father and to the Son and to the Holy Spirit,*

Reader: When Thou didst descend unto death, O Life Immortal, then didst Thou slay hell with the lightning of Thy divinity. And when Thou didst also raise the dead out of the nethermost depths, all the hosts of the heavens cried out: O Life Giver, Christ our God, glory be to Thee.

Chorus: *Both now and forever and unto the ages of ages. Amen.*

Reader: Unto the myrrh bearing women did the angel cry out as he stood by the grave: Myrrh is meet for the dead, but Christ hath proved a stranger to corruption.

Little Litany

Deacon: Again and again, in peace let us pray to the Lord.

People: *Lord, have mercy.*

Deacon: Help us, save us, have mercy on us, and keep us, O God, by Thy grace.

People: *Lord, have mercy.*

Deacon: Calling to remembrance our most holy, most pure, most blessed, glorious Lady Theotokos and Ever Virgin Mary with all the saints, let us commit ourselves and one another and all our life unto Christ our God.

People: *To Thee, O Lord.*

Priest: For blessed is thy name and glorified is Thy Kingdom, of the Father, and of the Son, and of the Holy Spirit, both now and ever, and unto the ages of ages.

People: *Amen.*

Kathisma From The Triodion

Tone 1   Magnificent, happy and earthy.   *C, D, Eb, F, G, A, Bb, C.*

Reader: Joseph begged Thy holy body from Pilate and, anointing it with sweet smelling spices, he wrapped it in clean linen and laid it in a new tomb; and early in the morning the women bearing myrrh cried out: "As Thou hast foretold, O Christ, show to us the Resurrection."

Chorus: *Glory be to the Father, and to the Son, and to the Holy Spirit;*
Both now and forever, and unto the ages of ages. Amen.

Reader: The angelic Chorus' are filled with wonder, beholding Him Who rests in the bosom of the Father laid in the tomb as one dead, though He is immortal. The ranks of the angels surround Him, and with the dead in hell they glorify Him as Creator and Lord.

Psalm 50

Reader: Have mercy on me, O God, according to Thy great mercy; and according to the multitude of Thy compassions blot out my transgression. Wash me thoroughly from mine iniquity, and cleanse me from my sin. For I acknowledge mine iniquity, and my sin is ever before me. Against Thee, Thee only have I sinned, and done evil in Thy sight, that Thou mayest be found just when Thou speakest, and victorious when Thou art judged. For behold, I was conceived in iniquity, and in sin my mother bore me. For behold, Thou hast loved truth; Thou hast made known to me the hidden and secret things of Thy wisdom. Thou shalt sprinkle me with hyssop, and I shall be made clean; Thou shalt wash me, and I shall be whiter than snow. Make me to hear joy and gladness; that the humbled bones may rejoice. Turn Thy face away from my sins, and blot out all mine iniquities.

Create in me a clean heart, O God, and renew a steadfast spirit within me. Cast me not away from Thy presence, and take not Thy Holy Spirit from me. Restore to me the joy of Thy salvation, and establish me with Thy governing Spirit. I shall teach transgressors Thy ways, and the ungodly shall turn back to Thee. Deliver me from blood guiltiness, O God, the God of my salvation; my tongue shall joyfully declare Thy righteousness. Lord, open my lips, and my mouth shall declare Thy praise. For if Thou hadst desired sacrifice, I would give it; Thou dost not delight in burned offerings. A sacrifice to God is a broken spirit; God will not despise a broken and a humbled heart. Do good, O Lord, in Thy good pleasure to Zion, and let the walls of Jerusalem be builded. Then Thou shalt be pleased with a sacrifice of righteousness, with oblation and whole burned offerings. Then shall they offer bulls on Thine altar.

The Canon Of Holy Saturday
Ode I

Eirmos

Tone 6   Rich texture, funereal character, sorrowful tone.   *D, Eb, F##, G, A, Bb, C##, D.*

Reader: He Who in ancient times hid the pursuing tyrant beneath the waves of the sea, is hidden beneath the earth by the children of those whom once He saved. But let us, like the maidens, sing unto the Lord, for gloriously is He glorified.

Chorus: *Glory to Thee, our God, glory to Thee.*

Reader: O Lord my God, I will sing to Thee a funeral hymn, a song at Thy burial: for by Thy burial Thou hast opened for me the gates of life, and by Thy death Thou hast slain death and hades.

Chorus: *Glory be to the Father and to the Son and to the Holy Spirit,*

Reader: All things above and all beneath the earth quaked with fear at Thy death, as they beheld Thee, O my Saviour, upon Thy throne on high and in the tomb below. For seeing Thou wert mortal is beyond understanding, O Author of life.

Chorus: *Both now and forever and unto the ages of ages. Amen.*

Reader: To fill all things with Thy glory, Thou hast gone down into the nethermost parts of the earth: for my substance that is in Adam is not hidden from Thee, but when buried, Thou dost restore me from corruption, O Lover of mankind.

Katavasia

Tone 6   Rich texture, funereal character, sorrowful tone.   *D, Eb, F##, G, A, Bb, C##, D.*

Chorus: *He Who in ancient times hid the pursuing tyrant beneath the waves of the sea, is hidden beneath the earth by the children of those whom once He saved. But let us, like the maidens, sing unto the Lord, for gloriously is He glorified.*

Ode III

Eirmos

Tone 6   Rich texture, funereal character, sorrowful tone.   *D, Eb, F##, G, A, Bb, C##, D.*

Reader: When the creation beheld Thee, Who hast hung the whole earth freely upon the waters, hanging on Golgotha, it was seized with horror and cried aloud: "There is none holy beside Thee, O Lord."

Chorus: *Glory to Thee, our God, glory to Thee.*

Reader: Images of Thy burial hast Thou disclosed in a multitude of visions; and now, as the God Man, Thou hast revealed Thy secrets unto those in hades, O Master, who cry aloud: "There is none holy beside Thee, O Lord."

Chorus: *Glory be to the Father and to the Son and to the Holy Spirit,*

Reader: Thou hast stretched out Thine arms and united all that of old was separated; clothed in a winding sheet, O Saviour, and buried in a tomb, Thou hast loosed the captives, who cry aloud: "There is none holy beside Thee, O Lord."

Chorus: *Both now and forever and unto the ages of ages. Amen.*

Reader: By a tomb and seals, O Uncontainable One, wast Thou held of Thine own will; but through Thine energies Thou hast showed Thy power by Divine action to those who sing: "There is none holy beside Thee, O Lord, Lover of mankind.

Katavasia

Tone 6   *Rich texture, funereal character, sorrowful tone.*   *D, Eb, F##, G, A, Bb, C##, D.*

Chorus: *When the creation beheld Thee, Who hast hung the whole earth freely upon the waters, hanging on Golgotha, it was seized with horror and cried aloud: "There is none holy beside Thee, O Lord."*

Little Litany

Deacon: Again and again, in peace let us pray to the Lord.

People: *Lord, have mercy.*

Priest: Help us, save us, have mercy on us, and keep us, O God, by Thy grace.

People: *Lord, have mercy.*

Priest: Calling to remembrance our most holy, most pure, most blessed, glorious Lady Theotokos and Ever Virgin Mary with all the saints, let us commit ourselves and one another and all our life unto Christ our God.

People: *To Thee, O Lord.*

Priest: For Thou art the King of peace, O Christ our God, and to Thee we ascribe glory, together with Thine eternal Father, and Thy most holy, good and life creating Spirit, now and ever, and unto the ages of ages.

People: *Amen.*

Kathisma

Tone 1   *Magnificent, happy and earthy.*   *C, D, Eb, F, G, A, Bb, C.*

Chorus: *The soldiers keeping watch over Thy tomb, O Saviour, became as dead men from the shining brightness at the appearing of the angel, who proclaimed to the women the Resurrection. We glorify Thee as the Destroyer of corruption; we fall down before Thee, risen from the tomb, our only God.*

Ode IV

Eirmos

Tone 6   Rich texture, funereal character, sorrowful tone.   *D, Eb, F##, G, A, Bb, C##, D.*

Reader: Foreseeing Thy divine self emptying upon the Cross, Habakkuk, amazed, cried out: "Thou hast cut asunder the strength of the mighty, O Good One, and preached to those in hades, as the Almighty One. *"*

Chorus: Glory to Thee, our God, glory to Thee.

Reader: Today Thou hast sanctified the seventh day, which anciently Thou didst bless by resting from Thy works. Thou bringest all things into being and renewest all things, observing the Sabbath, O my Saviour, and restoring all.

Chorus: Glory be to the Father and to the Son and to the Holy Spirit,

Reader: By Thy greater power, Thou hast conquered; from the flesh Thy soul was parted, yet Thou hast burst asunder both bonds, death and hades, O Word, by Thy might.

Chorus: Both now and forever and unto the ages of ages. Amen.

Reader: Hades was embittered when it met Thee, O Word, for it saw a mortal deified, striped with wounds, yet all powerful; and it shrank back in terror at this sight.

Katavasia

Tone 6   Rich texture, funereal character, sorrowful tone.   *D, Eb, F##, G, A, Bb, C##, D.*

Chorus: Foreseeing Thy divine self emptying upon the Cross, Habakkuk, amazed, cried out: "Thou hast cut asunder the strength of the mighty, O Good One, and preached to those in hades, as the Almighty One.

Ode V

Eirmos

Tone 6   Rich texture, funereal character, sorrowful tone.   *D, Eb, F##, G, A, Bb, C##, D.*

Reader: Thy Theophany, O Christ, the Unwaning Light, that mercifully came to pass for us, Isaiah, keeping watch, beheld out of the night, and he cried aloud: "The dead shall arise, and those in the tombs shall be raised up, and all that are born of earth shall rejoice."

Chorus: Glory to Thee, our God, glory to Thee.

Reader: Thou makest new those of earth, O Creator, becoming a thing of dust, and the winding sheet and tomb reveal, O Word, the mystery that is within Thee; for the noble counsellor typifies the counsel of Him that begat Thee, Who hath majestically refashioned me in Thee.

Chorus: *Glory be to the Father and to the Son and to the Holy Spirit,*

Reader: By Thy death dost Thou transform mortality and by Thy burial, corruption, for Thou makest incorruptible, by divine majesty, the nature Thou hast taken, rendering it immortal; for Thy flesh saw not corruption, O Master, nor was Thy soul left in hades as that of a stranger.

Chorus: *Both now and forever and unto the ages of ages. Amen.*

Reader: Coming forth from an unwedded Mother, and wounded in Thy side with a spear, O my Maker, Thou hast brought to pass the re-creation of Eve. Becoming Adam, Thou hast in ways surpassing nature slept a nature restoring sleep, raising life from sleep and from corruption, for Thou art the Almighty.

Katavasia

Tone 6   Rich texture, funereal character, sorrowful tone.   *D, Eb, F##, G, A, Bb, C##, D.*

Chorus: *Thy Theophany, O Christ, the Unwaning Light, that mercifully came to pass for us, Isaiah, keeping watch, beheld out of the night, and he cried aloud: "The dead shall arise, and those in the tombs shall be raised up, and all that are born of earth shall rejoice."*

Ode VI

Eirmos

Tone 6   Rich texture, funereal character, sorrowful tone.   *D, Eb, F##, G, A, Bb, C##, D.*

Reader: Caught but not held in the belly of the whale was Jonah; for, bearing the image of Thee, Who hast suffered and wast given to burial, he came forth from the monster as from a bridal chamber, and he called out to the watch: "O you who keep guard falsely and in vain, you have forsaken thine own mercy."

Chorus: *Glory to Thee, our God, glory to Thee.*

Reader: Torn wast Thou, but not separated, O Word, from the flesh of which Thou hadst partaken; for though Thy temple was destroyed at the time of Thy Passion, yet the Substance of Thy Godhead and of Thy flesh is but one. For in both Thou art one Son, the Word of God, both God and man.

Chorus: *Glory be to the Father and to the Son and to the Holy Spirit,*

Reader: Fatal to man, but not to God, was the sin of Adam; for though the earthly substance of Thy flesh suffered, yet the Godhead remained impassable; that which in Thy nature was corruptible Thou hast transformed to incorruption, and a fountain of life incorruptible hast Thou revealed by Thy Resurrection.

Chorus: *Both now and forever and unto the ages of ages. Amen.*

Reader: Hades reigneth, but not for ever over the race of man; for Thou, laid in a tomb, O Sovereign Lord, hast burst asunder the bars of death with Thy life giving hand, and Thou hast proclaimed to those who slept from the ages the true redemption, O Saviour, Who art become the First born from the dead.

Katavasia

Tone 6   Rich texture, funereal character, sorrowful tone.   *D, Eb, F##, G, A, Bb, C##, D.*

Chorus: *Caught but not held in the belly of the whale was Jonah; for, bearing the image of Thee, Who hast suffered and wast given to burial, he came forth from the monster as from a bridal chamber, and he called out to the watch: "O you who keep guard falsely and in vain, you have forsaken thine own mercy."*

Little Litany

Deacon: Again and again, in peace let us pray to the Lord.

People: *Lord, have mercy.*

Priest: Help us, save us, have mercy on us, and keep us, O God, by Thy grace.

People: *Lord, have mercy.*

Priest: Calling to remembrance our most holy, most pure, most blessed, glorious Lady Theotokos and Ever Virgin Mary with all the saints, let us commit ourselves and one another and all our life unto Christ our God.

People: *To Thee, O Lord.*

Priest: For Thou art the King of peace, O Christ our God, and to Thee we ascribe glory, together with Thine eternal Father, and Thy most holy, good and life creating Spirit, now and ever, and unto the ages of ages.

People: *Amen.*

Kontakion Of Holy Saturday

Tone 6   Rich texture, funereal character, sorrowful tone.   *D, Eb, F##, G, A, Bb, C##, D.*

Reader: He that shut up the abyss is seen as one dead, and like a mortal, the Immortal One is wrapped in linen and myrrh, and placed in a grave. And women came to anoint Him, weeping bitterly and crying out: This is the most blessed Sabbath day wherein Christ, having slept, shall arise on the third day.

Oikos Of Holy Saturday

Chorus: *He Who sustaineth all things was lifted upon the Cross, and all creation wept, seeing Him hanging naked on the Tree. The sun hid its rays, and the stars cast aside their light; the earth shook in much fear, and the sea fled, and the rocks were rent, and many graves were opened and the bodies of the saints arose. Hades groaned below, and the Jews conspired to spread slander against Christs' Resurrection. But the women cried aloud: "This is the most blessed Sabbath day wherein Christ, having slept, shall arise on the third day."*

Synaxarion Of Great And Holy Saturday

Reader: On the Great Holy Saturday, we celebrate the burial of the divine body, and the descent of our Lord and Saviour Jesus Christ to Hades, through which He restored our kind from corruption and transplanted it to eternal life. On the following day, which was Saturday, and which fell on the twenty fourth of March, the enemies of God, the high priests and Pharisees, came to Pilate and asked him to seal the tomb until the third day, lest the Disciples come at night, as they claimed, and steal the buried body, and then preach amongst the people, proclaiming the truth of the Resurrection, which that deceiver had foretold when He was alive, and the last error should be worse than the first. Thus they obtained permission to seal the tomb, and so they went and sealed it and place a guard upon it from amongst the soldiers who were guarding the city.

[St Matthew 27:62-66]

Chorus: *Wherefore, by Thine ineffable condescension, O Christ our God, have mercy upon us. Amen.*

Ode VII

Eirmos

Tone 6   Rich texture, funereal character, sorrowful tone.   *D, Eb, F##, G, A, Bb, C##, D.*

Reader: O ineffable wonder. He Who delivered the holy Children from the fiery furnace is laid a corpse without breath in the tomb, for the salvation of us who sing: "O God our Redeemer, blessed art Thou."

Chorus: *Glory to Thee, our God, glory to Thee.*

Reader: Wounded in the heart was hades when it received Him Who was wounded in the side by a spear, and consumed by divine fire it groaned aloud at the salvation of us who sing: "O God our Redeemer, blessed art Thou."

Chorus: *Glory to Thee, our God, glory to Thee.*

Reader: O wealthy tomb. For it received within itself the Creator, as one asleep, and it was shown to be a divine treasury of life, for the salvation of us who sing: "O God our Redeemer, blessed art Thou."

Chorus: *Glory be to the Father, and to the Son, and to the Holy Spirit;*

Reader: In accordance with the law of the dead, the Life of all submitteth to be laid in the tomb, and He showeth it to be a source of awakening, for the salvation of us who sing: "O God our Redeemer, blessed art Thou."

Chorus: *Both now and forever, and unto the ages of ages. Amen.*

Reader: Whether in hades or in the tomb or in Eden, the Godhead of Christ was indivisibly one with the

Father and the Spirit, for the salvation of us who sing: "O God our Redeemer, blessed art Thou."

Katavasia

Tone 6   Rich texture, funereal character, sorrowful tone.   *D, Eb, F##, G, A, Bb, C##, D.*

Chorus: *O ineffable wonder. He Who delivered the holy Children from the fiery furnace is laid a corpse without breath in the tomb, for the salvation of us who sing: "O God our Redeemer, blessed art Thou."*

Ode VIII

Eirmos

Tone 6   Rich texture, funereal character, sorrowful tone.   *D, Eb, F##, G, A, Bb, C##, D.*

Reader: Be you astonished and afraid, O heaven, and let the foundations of the earth be shaken; for lo, He Who dwelleth on high is numbered with the dead and lodgeth as a stranger in a narrow tomb. Him do you children bless, you priests praise, and you people supremely exalt unto all ages.

Chorus: *Glory to Thee, our God, glory to Thee.*

Reader: The most pure Temple is destroyed, but raiseth up the fallen tabernacle. For the second Adam, He Who dwelleth on high, hath come down to the first Adam, even into the chambers of hades. Him do you children bless, you priests praise, and you people supremely exalt unto all ages.

Chorus: *Glory be to the Father, and to the Son, and to the Holy Spirit;*

Reader: The disciples' courage failed, but Joseph of Arimathea was bolder; for, seeing the God of all a corpse and naked, he asked for the body and buried Him, crying: "Him do you children bless, you priests praise, and you people supremely exalt unto all ages."

Chorus: *Both now and forever, and unto the ages of ages. Amen.*

Reader: O new wonders. O what goodness. O ineffable forbearance. For of His own will He Who dwelleth on high is sealed beneath the earth, and God is falsely accused as a deceiver. Him do you children bless, you priests praise, and you people supremely exalt unto all ages.

Chorus: *We praise, we bless, we worship the Lord; praising and supremely exalting Him unto all ages.*

Katavasia

Tone 6   Rich texture, funereal character, sorrowful tone.   *D, Eb, F##, G, A, Bb, C##, D.*

Reader: Be you astonished and afraid, O heaven, and let the foundations of the earth be shaken; for lo, He Who dwelleth on high is numbered with the dead and lodgeth as a stranger in a narrow tomb. Him do you children bless, you priests praise, and you people supremely exalt unto all ages.

Ode IX

Deacon: The Theotokos and Mother of the Light, let us honour and magnify in song.

Eirmos

Tone 6   Rich texture, funereal character, sorrowful tone.   *D, Eb, F##, G, A, Bb, C##, D.*

Reader: Weep not for Me, O Mother, beholding in the tomb the Son Whom thou hast conceived without seed in the womb; for I shall arise and shall be glorified, and as God I shall exalt with glory unceasing those that with faith and love magnify thee.

Chorus: Glory to Thee, our God, glory to Thee.

Reader: At Thy strange birth, O Son without beginning, I was blessed in ways surpassing nature, for I was spared all travail. But now, beholding Thee, my God, a lifeless corpse, I am pierced with the sword of bitter grief. But arise, that I may be magnified.

Chorus: Glory be to the Father and to the Son and to the Holy Spirit,

Reader: The earth covereth Me as I desire, O Mother, but the gatekeepers of hades tremble as they see Me, clothed in the bloodstained garment of vengeance; for on the Cross as God have I struck down Mine enemies, and I shall rise again and magnify thee.

Chorus: Both now and forever and unto the ages of ages. Amen.

Reader: Let creation rejoice, let all that are born of earth be glad, for the enemy, hades, hath been despoiled; let the women come with myrrh to meet Me, for I am delivering Adam and Eve with all their offspring, and on the third day I shall rise again.

Katavasia

Tone 6   Rich texture, funereal character, sorrowful tone.   *D, Eb, F##, G, A, Bb, C##, D.*

Chorus: Weep not for He, O Mother, beholding in the tomb the Son Whom thou hast conceived without seed in the womb; for I shall arise and shall be glorified, and as God I shall exalt with glory unceasing those that with faith and love magnify thee.

The Lamentations Service for Holy Saturday Matins

[Lamentations consist of verses (troparia) called the "Praises" interspersed with verses of the 118th Psalm (17th Kathisma), which is divided into three parts (stases). In the Greek practice, the priest chants the Psalm verses, followed by the Chorus or cantor singing the Praises in a special sweet melody, imbued with an ineffable feeling of sorrow for a son, yet radiantly coloured by a sacred love for His Divinity.]

[Clergy come out from the sanctuary and stand in front of the Epitaphios. The priest and the deacon, or the deacon alone, censes the Epitaphios from the four sides and then the sanctuary and then the whole Church, whilst:]

First Stasis

Tone 5   Stimulating, dancing, and rhythmical.   C, D, Eb, F, G, A, Bb, C.

Priest: Thou who art the Life wast laid in a tomb, O Christ; and the hosts of angels were amazed and glorified Thy self abasement.

Extremely Mournful

Chorus: *O Life, how canst Thou die? How canst Thou dwell in a tomb? Yet Thou dost destroy deaths kingdom and raise the dead from hell.*

Reader: For they that work wickedness have not walked in His ways.

Chorus: *We magnify Thee, Jesus our King: we honour Thy burial and Thy sufferings, whereby Thou hast saved us from corruption.*

Reader: Thou hast commanded us to keep Thy precepts diligently.

Chorus: *O Jesus, King of all, who hast set measures to the earth, Thou dost go this day to dwell in a narrow grave, raising up the dead from their tombs.*

Reader: O that my ways were directed to keep Thy statutes.

Chorus: *O Jesus, my Christ and King of all, why hast Thou come to those in hell? Is it to set free the race of mortal men?*

Reader: Then shall I not be ashamed, when I give heed unto all Thy commandments.

Chorus: *The Master of all is seen lying dead, and in a new tomb He is laid, who empties the tombs of the dead.*

Reader: I will praise Thee with uprightness of heart, when I shall have learned the judgements of Thy righteousness.

Chorus: *Thou who art Life wast laid in a tomb, O Christ: by Thy death Thou hast destroyed death and art become a fountain of life for the world.*

Reader: I will keep Thy statutes: O forsake me not utterly.

Chorus: *Numbered with the transgressors, O Christ, Thou dost free us all from the guilt brought upon us of old by the deceiver.*

Reader: Wherewithal shall a young man cleanse his way? By keeping Thy words.

Chorus: *Fairer in His beauty than all mortal men, He appears now as a corpse without form or comeliness, He who has made beautiful the nature of all things.*

Reader: With my whole heart have I sought Thee: O let me not wander from Thy commandments.

Chorus: *How could hell endure Thy coming, O Saviour? Was it not shattered and struck blind by the dazzling radiance of Thy light?*

Reader: Thy words have I hid in my heart, that I might not sin against Thee.

Chorus: *O Jesus, my sweetness and light of salvation, how art Thou hidden in a dark tomb? O forbearance ineffable, beyond all words.*

Reader: Blessed art Thou, O Lord: teach me Thy statutes.

Chorus: *The spiritual powers and the angelic hosts are amazed, O Christ, at the mystery of Thy burial past utterance and speech.*

Reader: With my lips have I declared all the judgements of Thy mouth.

Chorus: *O strange wonder, new to man. He who granted me the breath of life is carried lifeless in Josephs hands to burial.*

Reader: I have rejoiced in the way of Thy testimonies, as much as in all riches.

Chorus: *Thou hast gone down into the tomb, O Christ, yet wast Thou never parted from Thy Fathers side. O marvellous wonder.*

Reader: I will meditate on Thy precepts, and I will understand Thy ways.

Chorus: *Though Thou wast shut within the narrowest of sepulchres, O Jesus, all creation knew Thee as true King of heaven and earth.*

Reader: My study shall be in Thy statutes : I will not forget Thy words.

Chorus: *When Thou wast laid in a tomb, O Christ the Creator, the foundations of hell were shaken and the graves of mortal men were opened*

Reader: O reward Thy servant: give me life, and I shall keep Thy words.

Chorus: *He who holds the earth in the hollow of His hand is held fast by the earth; put to death according to the flesh, He delivers the dead from the grasping hand of hell.*

Reader: Open Thou mine eyes, that I may behold the wondrous things of Thy law.

Chorus: *O Saviour, my Life, dying Thou hast gone to dwell amongst the dead: yet Thou hast shattered the bars of hell and arisen from corruption.*

Reader: I am but a sojourner upon the earth: hide not Thy commandments from me.

Chorus: *The flesh of God is hidden now beneath the earth, like a candle underneath a bushel, and it drives away the darkness in hell.*

Reader: My soul is consumed with the longing that it has for Thy judgements at all times.

Chorus: *The multitude of the heavenly powers makes haste with Joseph and Nicodemus, and within a narrow sepulchre they enclose Thee whom nothing can contain.*

Reader: Thou hast rebuked the proud: and cursed are they that do err from Thy commandments.

Chorus: *With Thine own consent slain and laid beneath the earth, O my Jesus, Fountain of Life, Thou hast brought me back to life when I was dead through bitter sin.*

Reader: Remove from me reproach and contempt; for I have sought Thy testimonies.

Chorus: *The whole creation was altered by Thy Passion: for all things suffered with Thee, knowing, O Word, that Thou holdest all in unity.*

Reader: Princes also did sit and speak against me: but Thy servant did meditate on Thy statutes.

Chorus: *All devouring hell received within himself the Rock of Life, and cast forth all the dead that he had swallowed since the beginning of the world.*

Reader: Thy testimonies also are my study: and Thy statutes are my counsellors.

Chorus: *Thou wast laid in a new tomb, O Christ, and hast made new the nature of mortal man, rising from the dead by Thy divine power.*

Reader: My soul has cleaved unto the dust: quicken Thou me according to Thy word.

Chorus: *To earth hast Thou come down, O Master, to save Adam: and not finding him on earth, Thou hast descended into hell, seeking him there.*

Reader: I have declared my ways, and Thou heardest me: teach me Thy statutes.

Chorus: *The whole earth quaked with fear, O Word, and the daystar hid its rays, when Thy great Light was hidden in the earth.*

Reader: Make me to understand the way of Thy precepts: so shall I talk of Thy wondrous works.

Chorus: *Willingly Thou diest as a mortal man, O Saviour, but as God Thou dost raise up the dead from the grave and from the depths of sin.*

Reader: My soul is grown drowsy from heaviness: strengthen me with Thy words.

Chorus: *Tears of lamentation the pure Virgin shed over Thee, Jesus, and with a mothers grief she cried: "How shall I bury Thee, my Son?"*

Reader: Remove from me the way of lying: and take pity on me with Thy law.

Chorus: *Buried in the earth like a grain of wheat, Thou hast yielded a rich harvest, raising to life the mortal sons of Adam.*

Reader: I have chosen the way of truth: Thy judgements have I not forgotten.

Chorus: *Now art Thou hidden like the setting sun beneath the earth and covered by the night of death: but, O Saviour, rise in brighter dawn.*

Reader: I have stuck unto Thy testimonies: O Lord, put me not to shame.

Chorus: *As the moon hides the circle of the sun, O Saviour, now the grave has hidden Thee, bodily eclipsed in death.*

Reader: I have run the way of Thy commandments: for Thou hast enlarged my heart.

Chorus: *Christ the Life, by tasting death, has delivered mortal men from death, and now gives life to all.*

Reader: Teach me, O Lord, the way of Thy statutes; and I shall seek it always.

Chorus: *Adam was slain of old through envy, but by Thy dying Thou hast brought him back to life, O Saviour, revealed in the flesh as the new Adam.*

Reader: Give me understanding, and I shall seek Thy law; yea, I shall observe it with my whole heart.

Chorus: *When the ranks of angels saw Thee, O Saviour, laid out dead for our sake, they were filled with wonder and veiled their faces with their wings.*

Reader: Make me to go in the path of Thy commandments; for therein do I delight.

Chorus: *Taking Thee down dead from the Tree, O Word, Joseph now has laid Thee in a tomb: but rise up as God to save us all.*

Reader: Incline my heart unto Thy testimonies, and not to covetousness.

Chorus: *Thou art the Joy of the angels, O Saviour, but now Thou art become the cause of their grief, as they see Thee in the flesh a lifeless corpse.*

Reader: Turn away mine eyes from beholding vanity, and quicken Thou me in Thy way.

Chorus: *Uplifted on the Cross, Thou hast uplifted with Thyself all living men; and then descending beneath the earth, Thou raisest all that lie buried there.*

Reader: Stablish Thy word in Thy servant, that I may fear Thee.

Chorus: *As a lion hast Thou fallen asleep in the flesh, O Saviour, and as a young lion hast Thou risen from the dead, putting off the old age of the flesh.*

Reader: Take away my reproach which I fear: for Thy judgements are good.

Chorus: *O Thou who hast fashioned Eve from Adams side, Thy side was pierced and from it flowed streams of cleansing.*

Reader: Behold, I have longed after Thy precepts: quicken me in Thy righteousness.

Chorus: *Of old the lamb was sacrificed in secret; but Thou, long suffering Saviour, wast sacrificed beneath the open sky and hast cleansed the whole creation.*

Reader: Let Thy mercy come also upon me, O Lord, even Thy salvation, according to Thy word.

Chorus: *Who can describe this strange and terrible thing? The Lord of Creation today accepts the Passion and dies for our sake.*

Reader: So shall I give an answer to them that reproach me: for I trust in Thy word.

Chorus: *"How do we see the Giver of Life now dead?" the angels cried in amazement. "How is God enclosed within a tomb?"*

Reader: And take not the word of truth utterly out of my mouth; for I have hoped in Thy judgements.

Chorus: *Pierced by a spear, O Saviour, from Thy side Thou pourest out life upon Eve, the mother of all the living, who banished me from life; and Thou quickenest me also with her.*

Reader: So shall I keep Thy law continually for ever and ever.

Chorus: *Stretched out upon the Wood, Thou hast drawn mortal men to unity; pierced in Thy life giving side, O Jesus, Thou art become a fountain of forgiveness unto all.*

Reader: And I walked at liberty: for I have sought Thy precepts.

Chorus: *With fear and reverence noble Joseph lays Thee out for burial as a corpse, O Saviour, and he looks with wonder on Thy dread form.*

Reader: I spoke of Thy testimonies also before kings, and was not ashamed.

Chorus: *Of Thine own will descending as one dead beneath the earth, O Jesus, Thou leadest up the fallen from earth to heaven.*

Reader: And my study was in Thy commandments, which I have exceedingly loved.

Chorus: *Dead in outward appearance, yet alive as God, O Jesus, Thou leadest up the fallen from earth to heaven.*

Reader: My hands also have I lifted up unto Thy commandments, which I have loved.

Chorus: *Dead in outward appearance, yet alive as God, Thou hast restored dead mortals to life and slain him that slew me.*

Reader: And I have meditated in Thy statutes.

Chorus: *How great the joy, how full the gladness, that Thou hast brought to those in hell, shining as lightning in its gloomy depths.*

Reader: Remember Thy words unto Thy servant, in which Thou hast caused me to hope.

Chorus: *I venerate Thy Passion, I sing the praises of Thy burial, and I magnify Thy power, O loving Lord: through them I am set free from corrupting passions.*

Reader: This is my comfort in my affliction: for Thy word has quickened me.

Chorus: *A sword was sharpened against Thee, O Christ: but the sword of the strong was blunted, and the sword that guards Eden was turned back.*

Reader: The proud have exceedingly transgressed: yet have I not turned aside from Thy law.

Chorus: *The Ewe, seeing her Lamb slaughtered, was pierced with anguish : and she cried aloud in grief, calling the flock to lament with her.*

Reader: I remembered Thy judgements of old, O Lord; and was comforted.

Chorus: *Though Thou art buried in a grave, though Thou goest down to hell, O Saviour Christ, yet hast Thou emptied the graves and stripped hell naked.*

Reader: Discouragement has taken hold upon me, because of the wicked that forsake Thy law.

Chorus: *Willingly, O Saviour, Thou hast gone down beneath the earth, and Thou hast restored the dead to life, leading them back to the glory of the Father.*

Reader: Thy statutes have been my songs in the house of my pilgrimage.

Chorus: *One of the Trinity endures a shameful death in the flesh on our account; the sun trembles and the earth quakes.*

Reader: I have remembered Thy Name, O Lord, in the night, and have kept Thy law.

Chorus: *Offspring from a bitter source, the children of the tribe of Judah have cast into a pit Jesus who fed them with manna.*

Reader: This has been my reward, because I sought Thy precepts.

Chorus: *The Judge stood as one accused before the judgement seat of Pilate, and He was condemned to an unjust death upon the wood of the Cross.*

Reader: Thou art my portion, O Lord: I have said that I would keep Thy law.

Chorus: *O arrogant Israel, O people guilty of blood, why hast thou set free Barabbas but delivered the Saviour to be crucified?*

Reader: I entreated Thy favour with my whole heart: be merciful unto me according to Thy word.

Chorus: *With Thy hand Thou hast fashioned Adam from the earth; and for his sake Thou hast become by nature man and wast of Thine own will crucified.*

Reader: I thought on Thy ways, and turned my feet unto Thy testimonies.

Chorus: *In obedience to Thine own Father, O Word, Thou hast descended to dread hell and raised up the race of mortal men.*

Reader: I made ready, and I was not troubled: that I might keep Thy commandments.

Chorus: *"Woe is me, Light of the world. Woe is me, my Light. Jesus, my hearts desire." cried the Virgin in her bitter grief.*

Reader: The cords of the wicked have entangled me: but I have not forgotten Thy law.

Chorus: *O bloodthirsty people, jealous and vengeful. May the very grave clothes and the napkin put you to shame at Christs' Resurrection.*

Reader: At midnight I rose to give thanks unto Thee because of the judgements of Thy righteousness.

Chorus: *Come, evil disciple, murderer of thy Lord, and show me the manner of thy wickedness, how thou hast become Christs' betrayer.*

Reader: I am a companion of all them that fear Thee and keep Thy commandments.

Chorus: *O blind fool, utterly wicked, implacable in hatred, thou dost make a pretence of love for men, yet thou hast sold for money the sweet Myrrh.*

Reader: The earth, O Lord, is full of Thy mercy: teach me Thy statutes.

Chorus: *What price hast thou received for the heavenly Myrrh? What wast thou given in exchange for Him who is precious? Thou hast gained folly and madness, O accursed Satan.*

Reader: Thou hast dealt well with Thy servant, O Lord, according unto Thy word.

Chorus: *If thou lovest the poor and dost grieve over the ointment emptied out in cleansing propitiation for a soul, how canst thou sell the Giver of Light for gold?*

Reader: Teach me goodness, discipline and knowledge: for I have believed in Thy commandments.

Chorus: *"O my God and Word, my Joy, how shall I endure Thy three days in the tomb? Now is my heart torn in pieces by a mothers grief."* Before I was humbled I went astray: but now have I kept Thy word.

Reader: "Who shall give me water and springs of tears," cried the Virgin Bride of God, "that I may weep for my sweet Jesus?"

Chorus: *Thou art good, O Lord: in Thy goodness teach me Thy statutes.*

Reader: "O hills and valleys, the multitude of men, and all creation, weep and lament with me, the Mother of our God."

Chorus: *The injustice of the proud is multiplied against me: but I shall seek Thy commandments with my whole heart.*

Reader: "When shall I see Thee, Saviour, Light eternal, the joy and gladness of my heart?" cried the Virgin in her bitter grief.

Chorus: *Their heart is curdled like milk; but my study has been in Thy law.*

Reader: Thy side was pierced, O Saviour, like the rock of flint in the wilderness; but Thou hast poured forth a stream of living water, for Thou art the Fount of Life.

Chorus: *It is good for me that Thou hast humbled me: that I might learn Thy statutes.*

Reader: Out of Thy side, as from a single source, there flows a double stream; and drinking from it we gain immortal life.

Chorus: *The law of Thy mouth is better unto me than thousands of gold and silver pieces.*

Reader: Of Thine own will, O Word, Thou wast laid dead in the tomb: yet dost Thou live, my Saviour, and, as Thou hast foretold, Thou shalt raise up mortal men by Thy Resurrection.

Chorus: *Glory be to the Father and to the Son and to the Holy Spirit,*

Reader: O Word and God of all, in our hymns we praise Thee with the Father and Thy Holy Spirit, and we glorify Thy divine burial.

Chorus: *Both now and forever and unto the ages of ages. Amen.*

Theotokion

Reader: O pure Theotokos; we bless thee and with faith we honour the three day burial of thy Son and our God.

Chorus: *Thou who art Life wast laid in a tomb, O Christ, and the hosts of angels were amazed and glorified Thy self abasement.*

People: *Amen.*

Little Litany

Deacon: Again and again, in peace let us pray to the Lord.

People: *Lord, have mercy.*

Priest: Help us, save us, have mercy on us, and keep us, O God, by Thy grace.

People: *Lord, have mercy.*

Priest: Calling to remembrance our most holy, most pure, most blessed, glorious Lady Theotokos and Ever Virgin Mary with all the saints, let us commit ourselves and one another and all our life unto Christ our God.

People: *To Thee, O Lord.*

Priest: For Thou art the King of peace, O Christ our God, and to Thee we ascribe glory, together with Thine eternal Father, and Thy most holy, good and life creating Spirit, now and ever, and unto the ages of ages.

People: *Amen.*

Second Stasis

Tone 5   Stimulating, dancing, and rhythmical.   *C, D, Eb, F, G, A, Bb, C.*

Priest: It is right to magnify Thee, Giver of Life, who hast stretched out Thine arms upon the Cross and broken the power of the enemy.

Chorus: Thy hands have made me and fashioned me: give me understanding, and I shall learn Thy commandments.

Reader: It is right to magnify Thee, Creator of all, for through Thy Passion we are freed from passions and corruption.

Chorus: They that fear Thee shall be glad when they see me: because I have hoped in Thy words.

Reader: The earth trembled with fear, O Saviour Christ, and the sun hid itself, seeing Thee, the Light that knows no evening, sinking in Thy body down into the tomb.

Chorus: I know, O Lord, that Thy judgements are right, and that with truth Thou hast humbled me.

Reader: Thou hast slept, O Christ, a life giving sleep in the tomb, and aroused mankind from the heavy slumber of sin.

Chorus: O let Thy merciful kindness be for my comfort, according to Thy word unto Thy servant.

Reader: "Alone amongst women without pain I bore Thee, my Child', said the Holy Virgin. "But now at Thy Passion I suffer unbearable pain." Let Thy tender mercies come unto me, and I shall live: for Thy law is my study.

Chorus: The seraphim, O Saviour, beheld Thee on high, united inseparably with the Father, yet they saw Thee below lying dead in the tomb; and they trembled with fear.

Reader: Let the proud be ashamed, for they have transgressed against me unjustly: but I shall meditate on Thy commandments.

Chorus: *The veil of the temple is rent in twain at Thy Crucifixion, O Word, and the lights of heaven hide their radiance, when Thou, the Sun, art hidden beneath the earth.*

Reader: Let those that fear Thee turn unto me, and those that know Thy testimonies.

Chorus: *He who at the beginning by His will alone set the earth upon its course, now descends dead beneath the earth. Tremble, O heaven, at this sight.*

Reader: Let my heart be blameless in Thy statutes: that I be not ashamed.

Chorus: *O Thou who hast fashioned Adam with Thine own hand, Thou hast gone down beneath the earth, to raise up fallen men by Thine almighty power.*

Reader: My soul faints for Thy salvation: and I have hoped in Thy words.

Chorus: *Come, and as the women bearing myrrh let us sing a holy lament to the dead Christ, that like them we too may hear Him say "Rejoice.'*

Reader: Mine eyes have grown dim with waiting for Thy word; they say: when wilt Thou comfort me?

Chorus: *Thou art in very truth, O Word, the myrrh that never fails: yet the women with their spices brought myrrh to Thee, the living God, to anoint Thee as a corpse.*

Reader: For I am become like a wineskin in the frost; yet have I not forgotten Thy statutes.

Chorus: *Through Thy burial, O Christ, Thou dost destroy the palaces of hell: by Thy death Thou slayest death, and dost deliver from corruption the children of the earth.*

Reader: How many are the days of Thy servant? When wilt Thou execute judgement on them that persecute me?

Chorus: *Source of the river of life, the Wisdom of God descends into the tomb and gives life to all those in the depths of hell.*

Reader: The transgressors told me idle tales, which are not after Thy law, O Lord.

Chorus: *"To renew the broken nature of mortal men, willingly have I been wounded in the flesh by death. O Mother, do not strike thy breast in grief." All Thy commandments are true: they persecute me wrongfully; help Thou me.*

Reader: O Morning Star of righteousness, Thou art gone down beneath the earth and hast raised up the dead as if from sleep, dispersing all the darkness of hell.

Chorus: *They had almost made an end of me upon earth; but I forsook not Thy commandments.*

Reader: The life giving Seed, twofold in nature, today is sown with tears in the furrows of the earth; but springing up He shall bring joy to the world.

Chorus: *Quicken me according to Thy mercy; so shall I keep the testimonies of Thy mouth.*

Reader: Adam was afraid when God walked in Paradise, but now he rejoices when God descends to hell. Then he fell, but now he is raised up.

Chorus: *For ever, O Lord, Thy word endures in heaven.*

Reader: Seeing Thy body laid in the tomb, O Christ, Thy Mother brings Thee the offering of her tears, and she says: "Arise, my Child, as Thou hast foretold."

Chorus: *Thy truth also remains from one generation to another: Thou hast established the earth, and it abides.*

Reader: Joseph hid Thee reverently in a new tomb, O Saviour, and lamenting sang to Thee a funeral hymn fitting for God.

Chorus: *The day continues according to Thine ordinance: for all things are Thy servants.*

Reader: Seeing Thee, O Word, pierced with nails upon the Cross, Thy Mother was wounded in her soul with the nails and arrows of bitter grief.

Chorus: *Unless Thy law had been my study, I should have perished in my humiliation.*

Reader: Thy Mother saw Thee drink the bitter vinegar, O Sweetness of the world, and her cheeks were wet with bitter tears. I shall never forget Thy precepts: for with them Thou hast quickened me.

Chorus: *"I am grievously wounded and my heart is torn, O Word, as I behold Thee slain unjustly', said the All pure Virgin weeping.*

Reader: I am Thine, save me; for I have sought Thy precepts.

Chorus: *"How shall I close Thy sweet eyes and Thy lips, O Word? And how shall I lay Thee out for burial as a corpse?" cried Joseph trembling. Sinners have waited for me to destroy me: but I have understood Thy testimonies.*

Reader: Joseph and Nicodemus now sing hymns of burial to the dead Christ; and with them sing the seraphim.

Chorus: *I have seen the outcome of all perfection: but Thy commandment is exceeding broad.*

Reader: O Saviour, Sun of Righteousness, Thou dost set beneath the earth: therefore the Moon, Thy Mother, is eclipsed in grief, seeing Thee no more.

Chorus: *O how I have loved Thy law, O Lord. It is my meditation all the day.*

Reader: Hell trembled, O Saviour, when he saw Thee, the Giver of Life, despoiling him of his wealth and raising up the dead from every age.

Chorus: *Thou through Thy commandment hast made me wiser than mine enemies: for it is mine for ever.*

Reader: After the night the sun shines out again in brightness; and after death do Thou, O Word, arise once more and shine in Thy glory, as a bridegroom coming from his chamber.

Chorus: *I have more understanding than all my teachers: for Thy testimonies are my meditation.*

Reader: When she received Thee in her bosom, O Creator and Saviour, the earth shook in fear, and with her quaking she awoke the dead.

Chorus: *I understand more than my elders, because I have sought Thy commandments.*

Reader: In a new and strange way Nicodemus and noble Joseph buried Thee with spices, and they cried aloud: "Tremble, all the earth."

Chorus: *I have restrained my feet from every evil way, that I might keep Thy words.*

Reader: Thou hast gone down beneath the earth, O Creator of light, and with Thee the suns light has also set; creation is seized with trembling and proclaims Thee the Maker of all.

Chorus: *I have not departed from Thy judgements: for Thou hast taught me.*

Reader: A stone hewn from the rock covers the Cornerstone; and a mortal man now buries God in the grave as one dead. Tremble, O earth.

Chorus: *How sweet are Thy words unto my taste. yea, sweeter than honey to my mouth.*

Reader: "Behold the disciple whom Thou hast loved and Thine own Mother, O my sweetest Child, and do Thou speak to them," cried the pure Virgin weeping.

Chorus: *Through Thy commandments I have gained understanding: therefore have I hated every evil way.*

Reader: Since Thou art Life giver, O Word, when stretched out upon the Cross, Thou hast not slain the Jews but raised their forefathers from the dead.

Chorus: *Thy law is a lamp unto my feet, and a light unto my path.*

Reader: At Thy Passion, O Word, there was neither form nor beauty in Thee: but Thou hast risen in glory, and with Thy divine light Thou hast given beauty to mortal men. I have sworn, and am steadfastly purposed, that I shall keep the judgements of Thy righteousness.

Chorus: *Daystar without evening, Thou hast gone down in the flesh neath the earth; and the sun grew dark at height of noon day, for could not bear to look upon Thee.*

Reader: I have been very greatly humbled : quicken me, O Lord, according unto Thy word.

Chorus: *The sun and moon grew dark together, O Saviour, like faithful servants clothed in black robes of mourning.*

Reader: Accept, I beseech Thee, the free will offerings of my mouth, O Lord, and teach me Thy judgements.

Chorus: *"The centurion knew Thee to be God, though Thou wast dead. How, then, my God, shall I touch Thee with my hands? I am afraid," cried Joseph.*

Reader: My soul is continually in Thy hands: yet have I not forgotten Thy law.

Chorus: *Adam slept, and from his side there came death; now Thou dost sleep, O Word of God, and from Thy side there flows a fountain of life for the world.*

Reader: Sinners have laid a snare for me: yet have I not gone astray from Thy commandments.

Chorus: *Thou hast slept a little while, and brought the dead to life; Thou hast arisen, O loving Lord, and raised up those that from the beginning of time had fallen asleep.*

Reader: Thy testimonies have I received as a heritage for ever: for they are the rejoicing of my heart.

Chorus: *O life giving Vine, Thou wast lifted up from the earth, yet hast Thou poured out the wine of salvation. I glorify Thy Passion and Thy Cross.*

Reader: I have inclined my heart to perform Thy statutes: for therein is an everlasting reward.

Chorus: *When the chief captains of the heavenly hosts saw Thee, Saviour, stripped, bloodstained and condemned, how could they bear the boldness of Thy crucifiers?*

Reader: I have hated transgressors: but Thy law have I loved.

Chorus: *Perverse and crooked people of the Hebrews, you knew how the temple would be raised again: why then did you condemn Christ?*

Reader: Thou art my helper and defender: I have hoped in Thy words.

Chorus: *In a robe of mockery you clothe Him who ordered all things, who adorned the heavens with stars and the earth with wonders.*

Reader: Depart from me, you evildoers: for I shall seek the commandments of my God.

Chorus: *Wounded in Thy side, O Word, through the life giving drops of Thy blood as the pelican Thou hast restored Thy dead children to life.*

Reader: Uphold me according unto Thy word, and give me life: and turn me not away in shame from mine expectation.

Chorus: *Of old Joshua made the sun stand still, as he smote the heathen tribes; but Thou hast blotted out its light, whilst casting down the prince of darkness.*

Reader: Help me, and I shall be saved: and my study shall be ever in Thy statutes.

Chorus: *Without leaving Thy Fathers side, O merciful Christ, Thou hast consented in Thy love to become a mortal man, and Thou hast gone down to hell.*

Reader: Thou hast brought to nothing all them that depart from Thy statutes: for their inward thought is unrighteous.

Chorus: *He who hung the earth upon the waters is hung upon the Cross. As a lifeless corpse He is laid in the earth, and it quakes in terror, unable to endure His presence.*

Reader: I have regarded all the wicked of the earth as transgressors: therefore I love Thy testimonies.

Chorus: *"Woe is me, my Son." laments the Virgin. "I see Thee now condemned upon the Cross, whom I had hoped to see enthroned as King." Nail my flesh with the fear of Thee: for I am afraid of Thy judgements.*

Reader: "Such were the tidings Gabriel brought me when he flew down from heaven: for he said that the Kingdom of my Son Jesus would be eternal."

Chorus: *I have done judgement and justice: O give me not over unto mine oppressors.*

Reader: "Alas. the prophecy of Simeon has been fulfilled: for Thy sword has pierced my heart, Emmanuel."

Chorus: *Be surety for Thy servant for good: let not the proud accuse me falsely.*

Reader: Be ashamed, O Jews, for the Life giver raised thy dead, yet you slew Him out of envy.

Chorus: *Mine eyes have failed with waiting for Thy salvation, and for the word of Thy righteousness.*

Reader: Seeing Thee, my Christ, the Light invisible, hidden lifeless in the tomb, the sun trembled and darkened its light.

Chorus: *Deal with Thy servant according unto Thy mercy, and teach me Thy statutes.*

Reader: Thine all blameless Mother wept bitterly, O Word, when she beheld Thee in the grave, God ineffable and without beginning.

Chorus: *I am Thy servant; give me understanding, that I may know Thy testimonies.*

Reader: Thine undefiled Mother, seeing Thy death, O Christ, cried to Thee in bitter sorrow: "Tarry not, O Life, amongst the dead."

Chorus: *It is time for the Lord to act: for they have made void Thy law.*

Reader: Cruel hell trembled when he saw Thee, O immortal Sun of glory, and in haste he yielded up his prisoners.

Chorus: *Therefore have I loved Thy commandments above gold or topaz.*

Reader: Great and fearful is the sight now before our eyes, O Saviour: for of His own will the Cause of life submits to death, that He may give life to all.

Chorus: *Therefore I walked uprightly according unto all Thy commandments: and I hated every evil way.*

Reader: Thy side is pierced, O Master, and Thy hands are transfixed with nails; so Thou healest the wound of our first parents and the sinful greed of their hands.

Chorus: *Thy testimonies are wonderful: therefore has my soul sought them.*

Reader: Once they wept in every house for Rachels child; and now the company of Christs' disciples with His Mother lament for the Virgins Son.

Chorus: *The revelation of Thy words shall give light and understanding unto the simple.*

Reader: With their hands they struck Christ in the face, though He it was who formed man with His hand and crushed the teeth of the beast.

Chorus: *I opened my mouth, and drew in my breath: for I longed for Thy commandments.*

Reader: In our hymns, O Christ, with all the faithful we worship now Thy Crucifixion and Thy Sepulchre, for by Thy burial we are set free from death.

Chorus: *Glory be to the Father and to the Son and to the Holy Spirit,*

Reader: O God without beginning, Word co-eternal, and Holy Spirit, in Thy love strengthen the power of our rulers against their enemies.

Chorus: *Both now and forever and unto the ages of ages. Amen.*

Theotokion

Reader: O Virgin pure and undefiled, who hast given birth to our Life, bring to an end the scandals of the churches and in thy love grant her peace.

Chorus: *It is right to magnify Thee, Giver of Life, who hast stretched Thine arms upon the Cross and broken the power of the enemy.*

People: *Amen.*

Little Litany

Deacon: Again and again, in peace let us pray to the Lord.

People: *Lord, have mercy.*

Deacon: Help us, save us, have mercy on us, and keep us, O God, by Thy grace.

People: *Lord, have mercy.*

Deacon: Calling to remembrance our most holy, most pure, most blessed, glorious Lady Theotokos and Ever Virgin Mary with all the saints, let us commit ourselves and one another and all our life unto Christ our God.

People: *To Thee, O Lord.*

Priest: For holy art Thou, our God, Who does rest upon the glorious throne of the cherubim, and to Thee we ascribe glory, together with Thine eternal Father and Thy most holy, good and life creating Spirit, both now and ever, and unto the ages of ages.

People: *Amen.*

Third Stasis

Tone 3   *Arrogant, brave, and mature atmosphere.*   *F, G, A, A#, C, D, E, F.*

Priest: Every generation, O my Christ, offers praises at Thy burial.

Reader: Look Thou upon me, and be merciful unto me, according the judgement of those that love Thy Name.

Chorus: *Taking Thee down from the Tree, Joseph of Arimathaea lay Thee in a sepulchre.*

Reader: Order my steps in Thy word: and let not any iniquity have dominion over me.

Chorus: *Providently bringing Thee sweet spices, O my Christ, the Myrrh bearers drew near.*

Reader: Deliver me from the false accusation of men: so shall I keep Thy commandments.

Chorus: *Come, and with the whole creation let us offer a funeral hymn to the Creator.*

Reader: Make Thy face to shine upon Thy servant; and teach me Thy statutes.

Chorus: *Understanding what we do, with the Myrrh bearers let us all anoint the Living as a corpse.*

Reader: Rivers of water have run down from mine eyes, because I kept not Thy law.

Chorus: *O thrice blessed Joseph, bury the body of Christ, the Giver of Life.*

Reader: Righteous art Thou, O Lord, and upright are Thy judgements.

Chorus: *Those He fed with manna have lifted up their heel against their Benefactor.*

Reader: Thy testimonies that Thou hast commanded are righteous and very faithful.

Chorus: *Those He fed with manna offer to the Saviour vinegar and gall.*

Reader: My zeal has consumed me, because mine enemies have forgotten Thy words.

Chorus: *O the folly of those who killed the prophets and slew Christ.*

Reader: Thy word is tried in the fire to the uttermost: therefore has Thy servant loved it.

Chorus: *Like a foolish servant, the disciple has betrayed the Abyss of Wisdom.*

Reader: I am young and despised: yet have I not forgotten Thy statutes.

Chorus: *Judas the traitor has sold his Deliverer and himself become a captive.*

Reader: Thy righteousness is an everlasting righteousness, and Thy law is. truth.

Chorus: *As Solomon said, the mouth of the transgressing Hebrews is a deep pit.*

Reader: Trouble and anguish have taken hold on me: yet Thy commandments are my study.

Chorus: *In the crooked paths of the transgressing Hebrews there are thorns and snares.*

Reader: The righteousness of Thy testimonies is everlasting: give me understanding, and I shall live.

Chorus: *Joseph and Nicodemus bury the Creator with the honours that befit the dead.*

Reader: I cried with my whole heart; hear me, O Lord: I shall seek Thy statutes.

Chorus: *Life giver and Saviour, Thou hast destroyed hell: to Thy power be glory.*

Reader: I cried unto Thee; save me, and I shall keep Thy testimonies.

Chorus: *When she saw Thee lying dead, O Word, the all pure Virgin wept with a mothers grief.*

Reader: I rose up before it was dawn, and cried: I have hoped in Thy word.

Chorus: *"O my sweet springtime, O my sweetest Child, where has all Thy beauty gone?"*

Reader: Mine eyes woke before the morning: that I might meditate in Thy words.

Chorus: *When Thou, O Word, wast dead, Thine all pure Mother raised a lamentation for Thee.*

Reader: Hear my voice according unto Thy loving kindness, O Lord quicken me according to Thy judgement.

Chorus: *The women came with myrrh to anoint Christ, the Myrrh of Cod.*

Reader: They draw nigh that persecute me unlawfully: they are far from Thy Law.

Chorus: *By dying, O my God, Thou puttest death to death through Thy divine power.*

Reader: Thou art near, O Lord; and all Thy ways are truth.

Chorus: *The deceiver is deceived, and those he misled are set free by Thy wisdom, O my God.*

Reader: Concerning Thy testimonies, I have known of old that Thou hast founded them for ever.

Chorus: *The traitor was cast down to the depths of hell, and to the pit of destruction.*

Reader: Behold my humiliation, and deliver me: for I have not forgotten Thy law.

Chorus: *Thorns and snares beset the path of Judas the foolish and the thrice wretched.*

Reader: Judge my cause, and deliver me: quicken me according to Thy word.

Chorus: *All that crucified Thee shall be destroyed together, O Word, Thou Son of God and King of all.*

Reader: Salvation is far from the wicked: for they have not sought Thy statutes.

Chorus: *In the pit of destruction shall all the men of blood be destroyed together.*

Reader: Many are Thy tender mercies, O Lord: quicken me according to Thy judgement.

Chorus: *O Son of God and King of all, my God and my Creator, how hast Thou accepted suffering?*

Reader: Many are they that persecute and afflict me: yet have I not turned aside from Thy testimonies.

Chorus: *As the mother of a foal, the Virgin gazed on Thee in grief when she saw Thee hanging on the Tree.*

Reader: I beheld the foolish and was grieved; because they kept not Thy words.

Chorus: *Joseph and Nicodemus bury the body that is the Source of life.*

Reader: See how I have loved Thy commandments: quicken me, O Lord, in Thy mercy.

Chorus: *Pierced to the heart, the Virgin shed warm tears and cried aloud.*

Reader: The beginning of Thy words is truth: and every one of Thy righteous judgements endures for ever.

Chorus: *"O Light of mine eyes, my sweetest Child, how art Thou hidden now in the sepulchre?"*

Reader: Princes have persecuted me without a cause: but my heart stands in awe of Thy words.

Chorus: *"Weep not, O Mother, for I suffer this to set at liberty Adam and live."*

Reader: I shall rejoice at Thy words, as one that finds great spoil.

Chorus: *"O my Son, I glorify Thy supreme compassion, that causes Thee to suffer so."*

Reader: I have hated and abhorred injustice: but Thy law have I loved.

Chorus: *Thou hast drunk vinegar and gall, in Thy compassion, to loose us from the guilt of the forbidden fruit.*

Reader: Seven times a day have I praised Thee because of the judgements of Thy righteousness.

Chorus: *Thou art nailed upon the Cross, who of old hast sheltered Thy people with a pillar of cloud.*

Reader: Great peace have they that love Thy law: and for them there is no stumbling block.

Chorus: *The women bearing myrrh came, O Saviour, to Thy tomb and offered Thee sweet spices.*

Reader: Lord, I have looked for Thy salvation, and loved Thy commandments.

Chorus: *Arise, O merciful Lord, and raise us from the depths of hell,*

Reader: My soul has kept Thy testimonies: and exceedingly loved them.

Chorus: *"Arise, O Giver of Life', the Mother who bore Thee said with tears.*

Reader: I have kept Thy commandments and Thy testimonies: for all my ways are before Thee, O Lord.

Chorus: *Make haste to arise, O Word, and take away the sorrow of Thy Virgin Mother.*

Reader: Let my prayer draw near to Thee, O Lord; give me understanding according to Thy word.

Chorus: *All the powers of heaven were filled with fear and wonder when they saw Thee dead.*

Reader: Let my supplication come before Thee, O Lord: deliver me according to Thy word.

Chorus: *With love and fear we honour Thy Passion: grant us the forgiveness of our sins.*

Reader: Let my lips speak of Thy praise: for Thou hast taught me Thy statutes.

Chorus: *Strange and dreadful wonder. How art Thou now hidden in the earth, O Word of God?*

Reader: Let my tongue speak of Thy words: for all Thy commandments are righteousness.

Chorus: *Joseph once fled with Thee, O Saviour, and now another Joseph buries Thee.*

Reader: Let Thine hand be near to save me: for I have chosen Thy commandments.

Chorus: *Thine all holy Mother weeps for Thee lamenting, O my Saviour, at Thy death.*

Reader: I have longed for Thy salvation, O Lord; and Thy law is my study.

Chorus: *The spiritual powers tremble at Thy strange and fearful burial, O Maker of all.*

Reader: My soul shall live, and it shall praise Thee: and Thy judgements shall help me.

[Priest sprinkles Epitaphion and the entire church with rose water.

Repeat as many times as necessary:]

Chorus: *Early in the morning the myrrh bearers came to Thee and sprinkled myrrh upon Thy tomb.*

[When sprinkling is finished continue:]

Reader: I have gone astray like a lost sheep: seek Thy servant, for I have not forgotten Thy commandments.

Chorus: *By Thy Resurrection give peace to the Church and salvation to Thy people.*

Chorus: *Glory be to the Father and to the Son and to the Holy Spirit,*

Reader: O my God in Trinity, Father, Son and Spirit, grant Thy mercy to the world.

Chorus: *Both now and forever and unto the ages of ages. Amen.*

Theotokion

Reader: O Virgin, grant to us thy servants to behold the Resurrection of thy Son.

Chorus: *Each generation offers, my Christ, for Thine entombment, its praises in hymns and songs.*

People: *Amen.*

[People extinguish their candles.]

Little Litany

Deacon: Again and again, in peace let us pray to the Lord.

People: *Lord, have mercy.*

Priest: Help us, save us, have mercy on us, and keep us, O God, by Thy grace.

People: *Lord, have mercy.*

Priest: Calling to remembrance our most holy, most pure, most blessed, glorious Lady Theotokos and Ever Virgin Mary with all the saints, let us commit ourselves and one another and all our life unto Christ our God.

People: *To Thee, O Lord.*

Priest: For Thou art the King of peace, O Christ our God, and to Thee we ascribe glory, together with Thine eternal Father, and Thy most holy, good and life creating Spirit, now and ever, and unto the ages of ages.

People: *Amen.*

Evlogitaria

Tone 5 Stimulating, dancing, and rhythmical.   C, D, Eb, F, G, A, Bb, C.

Chorus: *Blessed art Thou, O Lord, teach me Thy statutes.*

Reader: The assembly of angels was amazed, beholding Thee numbered amongst the dead; yet, O Saviour, destroying the stronghold of death, and with Thyself raising up Adam, and freeing all from hades.

Chorus: *Blessed art Thou, O Lord, teach me Thy statutes.*

Reader: Why mingle you myrrh with tears of pity, O you women disciples? Thus the radiant angel within the tomb addressed the myrrh bearing women; behold the tomb and understand, for the Saviour is risen from the tomb.

Chorus: *Blessed art Thou, O Lord, teach me Thy statutes.*

Reader: Very early the myrrh bearing women hastened unto Thy tomb, lamenting, but the angel stood before them and said: the time for lamentation is passed, weep not, but tell of the Resurrection to the apostles.

Chorus: *Blessed art Thou, O Lord, teach me Thy statutes.*

Reader: The myrrh bearing women, with myrrh came to Thy tomb, O Saviour, bewailing, but the angel addressed them, saying: Why number you the living amongst the dead, for as God He is risen from the tomb.

Chorus: *Glory be to the Father, and to the Son, and to the Holy Spirit;*

Reader: Let us worship the Father, and His Son, and the Holy Spirit, the Holy Trinity; one in essence, crying with the Seraphim: Holy, Holy, Holy art Thou, O Lord.

Chorus: *Both now and forever, and unto the ages of ages. Amen.*

Reader: In bringing forth the Giver of life, thou hast delivered Adam from sin, O Virgin, and hast brought joy to Eve instead of sorrow; and those fallen from life have thereunto been restored, by Him Who of thee was incarnate, God and man.

Chorus: *Halleluiah, Halleluiah, Halleluiah. Glory to Thee, O God. (x3)*

Reader: O our God and our Hope, glory to Thee.

Little Litany

Deacon: Again and again, in peace let us pray to the Lord.

People: *Lord, have mercy.*

Deacon: Help us, save us, have mercy on us, and keep us, O God, by Thy grace.

People: *Lord, have mercy.*

Deacon: Calling to remembrance our most holy, most pure, most blessed, glorious Lady Theotokos and Ever Virgin Mary with all the saints, let us commit ourselves and one another and all our life unto Christ our God.

People: *To Thee, O Lord.*

Priest: For all the powers of heaven praise Thee, and unto Thee we ascribe glory to the Father, and to the Son, and to the Holy Spirit, both now and ever, and unto the ages of ages.

People: *Amen.*

Exaposteilarion

Tone 2   *Majesty, gentleness, hope, repentance and sadness.*   *E, F, G, Ab, B, C.*

Chorus: *Holy is the Lord our God.* **(x3)**

[Priest puts on all his vestments whilst:]

Lauds (The Praises)

Psalm 148

Tone 2   *Majesty, gentleness, hope, repentance and sadness.*   *E, F, G, Ab, B, C.*

Chorus: *Let every breath praise the Lord. Praise the Lord. Praise the Lord from the heavens; praise Him in the heights. To Thee, O God, is due our song. Praise Him, all His angels; praise Him, all His hosts. To Thee, O God, is due our song.*

Idiomelons

Tone 2   *Majesty, gentleness, hope, repentance and sadness.*   *E, F, G, Ab, B, C.*

Chorus: *Praise God in His sanctuary, praise Him in the firmament of His power.*

Reader: Today a tomb hold him who holds all creation in his palm. A stone covers him who covered the heavens with glory. Life sleeps and Hell trembles and Adam is being released from his bonds. Glory to Thy dispensation, through which Thou hast accomplished all things and granted us an eternal Sabbath rest, Thy resurrection from the dead.

Chorus: *Praise Him for His mighty acts, praise Him according to His excellent greatness.*

Reader: What is this sight that is seen? What is this present rest? The king of the ages, having accomplished His dispensation through suffering, takes His Sabbath rest in a tomb, granting us a new Sabbath rest. To Him let us cry, 'Arise, O God, judge the earth, for Thou art king for ever, and without measure is Thy great mercy.

Chorus: *Praise Him with the sound of trumpet. Praise Him with the psaltery and harp.*

Reader: Come, let us see our life lying in a tomb, that he may give life to all those who lie in the tombs. Come today, as we contemplate the Sleeping one from Judah, let us prophetically cry out to him, 'Taking Thine rest, Thou layest down like a lion. Who shall rouse Thee, O King? But arise by Thine own will, who gave Thyself willingly for us. Lord, glory to Thee.

Chorus: *Praise Him with the timbrel and dance: praise Him with stringed instruments and organs.*

Reader: Joseph asked for the body of Jesus, and laid it in his new grave; for it was right that he should come forth from a tomb as from a bridal chamber. Thou smashed the might of death and opened the gates of Paradise for humankind; glory to Thee.

Doxasticon

Tone 6   Rich texture, funereal character, sorrowful tone.   *D, Eb, F##, G, A, Bb, C##, D.*

Chorus: *Glory be to the Father and to the Son and to the Holy Spirit;*

Reader: Great Moses mystically prefigured this present day when he said, 'And God blessed the seventh day'. For this is the blessed Sabbath, this the day of rest on which the only begotten Son of God rested from all his works. Through the dispensation in accordance with death, he kept the Sabbath in the flesh, and, returning once again to what he was, through the Resurrection he has granted us eternal life, for he alone is good and loves humankind.

Chorus: *Both now and forever and unto the ages of ages. Amen.*

Theotokion

Reader: O Virgin Mother of God, thou art most blessed, for through him who took flesh from thee, Hell has been captured, Adam recalled, the curse slain, Eve set free, death put to death, and we given life. Therefore in praise we cry: Blessed art Thou, Christ our God, who hast been thus well pleased, glory to Thee.

[Prepare people for procession whilst:]

Great Doxology

Glory to God, Who has shown us the Light. Glory to God in the highest, and on earth, peace, good will toward men. We praise Thee. We bless Thee. We worship Thee. We glorify Thee and give thanks to Thee for Thy great glory. O Lord God, Heavenly King, God the Father Almighty. O Lord, the Only Begotten Son, Jesus Christ, and the Holy Spirit. \

O Lord God, Lamb of God, Son of the Father, Who takes away the sins of the world, have mercy on us. Thou, Who takes away the sins of the world, receive our prayer. Thou, Who sittest at the right hand of God the Father, have mercy on us. /

For Thou alone art holy, and Thou alone art Lord. Thou alone, O Lord Jesus Christ, are most high in the glory of God the Father. Amen. I shall give thanks to Thee every day and praise Thy Name forever and ever, Lord. Every day shall I bless Thee and praise Thy name forever, and to the ages of ages. Amen. \

Vouchsafe, O Lord, to keep us this day without sin. Blessed art Thou, O Lord, the God of our fathers, and praised and glorified is Thy Name forever. Amen. Let Thy mercy be upon us, O Lord, even as we have set our hope on Thee.

Blessed art Thou, O Master; teach me Thy statutes.

Blessed art Thou, O Lord; enlighten me with Thy commandments.

Blessed art Thou, O Holy One; make me to understand Thy precepts.

Lord, Thou hast been our refuge from generation to generation. I said, *"Lord, have mercy on me. Heal my soul, for I have sinned against Thee."* \

Lord, I flee to Thee for refuge. Teach me to do Thy will, for Thou art my God. For with Thee is the fountain of Life, and in Thy light we shall see light. Continue Thy loving kindness to those who know Thee.

Holy God, Holy Strong, Holy Immortal, have mercy on us.

Holy God, Holy Strong, Holy Immortal, have mercy on us.

Holy God, Holy Strong, Holy Immortal, have mercy on us.

  Glory be to the Father, and to the Son, and to the Holy Spirit;

  Both now and ever, and unto the ages of ages. Amen.

Holy Immortal, have mercy on us.

Holy God, Holy Strong, Holy Immortal, have mercy on us. \

  [Repeat whilst:]

[Order Of Procession Around The Outside Of The Church:

  (i)   Cross.

  (ii)   Acolytes with Candles.

  (ii)   Chorus.

  (iii)   Deacon with incense.

  (iv)   Clergy with Epitaphios.

  (v)   Congregation with lighted candles.

Procession returns to the interior of the church under the Epitaphios, whilst:]

Idiomel

[By George Of The Holy City]

Tone 5   *Stimulating, dancing, and rhythmical.*   *C, D, Eb, F, G, A, Bb, C.*

When Joseph saw that the sun had hidden its rays and the veil of the temple had been rent in two at the death of the Saviour, he approached Pilate and entreated him, saying, 'Give me this stranger, who since infancy has been a stranger in the world. Give me this stranger, whom members of his own race hated and slew as a stranger. Give me this stranger, whom I welcome as a stranger as I see the strangeness of his death. Give me this stranger, who knew how to welcome as strangers the poor and those who were strangers. Give me this stranger, whom Hebrews out of envy have made a stranger to the world. Give me this stranger, that I may hide in a tomb one who as a stranger has no place to lay his head. Give me this stranger, whose his mother when she saw him slain cried out, 'O my Son and my God, though I am wounded to the core and torn to the heart as I see Thee dead, yet confident in Thy resurrection, I magnify Thee'.' When he had with words like this entreated Pilate, the noble Joseph takes the Saviour's body, and having in fear wrapped it in a winding sheet with myrrh, he placed in a tomb the One who grants the world eternal life and his great mercy.

[When all people back in church the Priest stops before the Holy Doors with the Epitaphios:]

Priest: Let us attend. Peace be with you all.

Reader: And with thy spirit.

Priest: Wisdom.

[Priest takes Epitaphios into the altar and carries it 3 times around the Holy Table. Then sets it on the Holy Table where it remains.]

Apolytikia

Tone 2   Majesty, gentleness, hope, repentance and sadness.   *E, F, G, Ab, B, C.*

Reader: When Thou went down to death, O immortal life, then Thou slew Hell with the lightning flash of Thy Godhead; but when from the depths below the earth Thou raised the dead, all the Powers beyond the heavens cried out: Giver of life, Christ our God, glory to Thee.

Chorus: *The noble Joseph, taking down Thy most pure Body from the Tree, wrapped it in a clean shroud with sweet spices and laid it for burial in a new grave.*

Reader: The Angel standing by the grave cried to the women bearing myrrh: Myrrh is fitting for the dead, but Christ has shown himself a stranger to corruption.

Prokeimenon

Deacon: Let us attend. The Prokeimenon.

Reader: Arise, O Lord, help us, and redeem us for Thy name's sake.

People: *Arise, O Lord, help us, and redeem us for Thy name's sake.*

Reader: O God, with our ears have we heard, for our fathers have told us.

People: *Arise, O Lord, help us, and redeem us for Thy name's sake.*

Reader: Arise, O Lord, help us, and redeem us | for Thy name's sake.

Prophecy

Deacon: Wisdom.

Reader: The reading is from the Prophet Ezekiel. *[37:1-14]*

Deacon: Let us attend.

Reader: The hand of the Lord came upon me, and the Lord brought me forth by the Spirit, and set me in the midst of the plain, and it was full of human bones. And He led me round about them every way. And behold, there were very many on the face of the plain, very dry. And He said to me, Son of man, shall these bones live? And I said, O Lord God, Thou knowest this. And He said to me, Prophesy upon these bones, and thou shalt say to them, you dry bones, hear the word of the Lord. Thus saith Adonai the Lord to these bones: Behold, I shall bring upon you the breath of life; and I shall lay sinews upon ye, and shall bring up flesh upon ye, and shall spread skin upon ye, and I shall put My Spirit into ye, and you shall live; and you shall know that I am the Lord. So I prophesied as the Lord commanded me. And it came to pass while I was prophesying, that behold, there was an earthquake, and the bones came together, bone to bone, each one to his joint. And I looked, and behold, sinews came upon them, and flesh grew and came upon them, and skin was spread upon them above, but there was no breath in them. And He said to me, Prophesy to the wind, prophesy, son of man, and say to the wind, Thus saith Adonai the Lord: Come from the four winds, O breath, and breathe upon these dead, and let them live. So I prophesied as He commanded me, and the breath entered into them, and they lived, and stood upon their feet, a very great assembly. And the Lord spoke to me, saying, Son of man, these bones are the whole house of Israel: and they say, Our bones have become dry, our hope hath perished, we are quite spent. Therefore prophesy, son of man, and say, Thus saith Adonai the Lord: Behold, I shall open thy tombs, My people, and shall bring you up out of thy tombs, and I shall bring you into the land of Israel. And you shall know that I am the Lord, when I have opened thy graves, that I may bring you up from thy graves, My people; and I shall put My Spirit within ye, and you shall live. And I shall place you upon thine own land; and you shall know that I am the Lord; I have spoken, and shall do it, saith Adonai the Lord.

Prokeimenon

Deacon: Let us attend. The Prokeimenon.

Reader: Arise, O Lord my God, let Thy hand be lifted high; forget not Thy paupers to the end.

People: *Arise, O Lord my God, let Thy hand be lifted high; forget not Thy paupers to the end.*

Reader: I shall confess Thee, O Lord with my whole heart; I shall tell of all Thy wonders.

People: *Arise, O Lord my God, let Thy hand be lifted high; forget not Thy paupers to the end.*

Reader: Arise, O Lord my God, let Thy hand be lifted high | forget not Thy paupers to the end.

Epistle

Deacon: Wisdom.

Reader: The reading is from the first letter of the Blessed Holy Apostle Paul to the Corinthians and the letter to the Galatians. *[1 Corinthians 5:6-8; Galatians 3:13-14].*

Deacon: Let us attend.

Reader: Brethren: Thy glorying is not good. Know you not that a little leaven leaveneth the whole lump? Purge out therefore the old leaven, that you may be a new lump, as you are unleavened. For even Christ our passover is sacrificed for us: Therefore let us keep the feast, not with old leaven, neither with the leaven of malice and wickedness; but with the unleavened bread of sincerity and truth. Christ hath redeemed us from the curse of the law, being made a curse for us: for it is written, Cursed is every one that hangeth on a tree:

That the blessing of Abraham might come on the Gentiles through Jesus Christ; that we might receive the promise of the Spirit through faith.

Priest: Peace be with thy spirit.

Reader: And with thy spirit.

Halleluiarion

People: *Halleluiah, Halleluiah, Halleluiah.*

Reader: As smoke vanisheth, so let them vanish; as wax melteth before the fire.

People: *Halleluiah, Halleluiah, Halleluiah.*

Reader: So let sinners perish at the presence of God.

People: *Halleluiah, Halleluiah, Halleluiah.*

The Gospel

Deacon: Wisdom. Stand up. Let us hear the Holy Gospel.

Priest: Peace be with you all.

People: *And with thy spirit.*

Priest: The Reading is from the Holy Gospel according to Matthew.

People: *Glory to Thee, O Lord, glory to thee.*

Deacon: Let us attend.

Priest: On the next day, that followed the day of the preparation, the chief priests and Pharisees came together unto Pilate, Saying, Sir, we remember that that deceiver said, while he was yet alive, After three days I shall rise again. Command therefore that the sepulchre be made sure until the third day, lest his disciples come by night, and steal him away, and say unto the people, He is risen from the dead: so the last error shall be worse than the first. Pilate said unto them, you have a watch: go thy way, make it as sure as you can. So they went, and made the sepulchre sure, sealing the stone, and setting a watch.

People: *Glory to Thee, O Lord, glory to thee.*

Augmented Ektenia

Deacon: Let us all say with our whole soul and with our whole mind, let say:

People: *Lord, have mercy.*

Deacon: O Lord Almighty, the God of our fathers, we pray Thee hearken and have mercy.

People: *Lord, have mercy.*

Deacon: Have mercy on us, O God, according to Thy great mercy, we pray Thee, hearken and have mercy.

People: *Lord, have mercy.* **(x3)**

Deacon: Again we pray for our Archbishop Nikitas and all our brethren in Christ.

People: *Lord, have mercy.* **(x3)**

Deacon: Again we pray for mercy, life, peace, health, salvation and visitation and pardon and forgiveness of since for *[the servants of God N, N]* and all Orthodox Christians of true worship, who live and dwell in this community.

People: *Lord, have mercy.* **(x3)**

Deacon: Again we pray for the blessed and ever memorable, holy Orthodox patriarchs; for pious kings and right believing queens; and for the founders of this holy temple (if it be a monastery: this holy monastery): and for all our fathers and brethren gone to their rest before us, and the Orthodox here and everywhere laid to rest.

People: *Lord, have mercy.* **(x3)**

Deacon: Again we pray for them that bring offerings and do good works in this holy and all venerable temple; for them that minister and them that chant, and for all the people here present, that await of Thee great and abundant mercy.

People: *Lord, have mercy.* **(x3)**

Priest: For a merciful God art Thou, and the Lover of mankind, and unto Thee do we send up glory: to the Father, and to the Son, and to the Holy Spirit, both now and ever, and unto the ages of ages.

People: *Amen.*

Litany Of Supplication

Deacon: Let us complete our morning prayer unto the Lord.

People: *Lord, have mercy.*

Deacon: Help us, save us, have mercy on us, and keep us, O God, by Thy grace.

People: *Lord, have mercy.*

Deacon: That the whole day may be perfect, holy, peaceful and sinless, let us ask of the Lord.

People: *Grant this, O Lord.*

Deacon: An angel of peace, a faithful guide, a guardian of our souls and bodies, let us ask of the Lord.

People: *Grant this, O Lord.*

Deacon: Pardon and remission of our sins and offences, let us ask of the Lord.

People: *Grant this, O Lord.*

Deacon: Things good and profitable for our souls, and peace for the world, let us ask of the Lord.

People: *Grant this, O Lord.*

Deacon: That we may complete the remaining time of our life in peace and repentance let us ask of the Lord

People: *Grant this, O Lord.*

Deacon: A Christian ending to our life, painless, blameless, peaceful, and a good defence before the dread judgement seat of Christ, let us ask.

People: *Grant this, O Lord.*

Deacon: Calling to remembrance our most holy, most pure, most blessed, glorious Lady Theotokos and Ever Virgin Mary with all the saints, let us commit ourselves and one another and all our life unto Christ our God.

People: *To Thee, O Lord.*

Priest: For Thou art a God of mercy, compassion and love for mankind, and unto Thee do we send up glory: to the Father, and to the Son, and to the Holy Spirit, both now and ever, and unto the ages of ages.

People: *Amen.*

Priest: Peace be with you all.

People: *And with thy spirit.*

Deacon: Let us bow down our heads unto the Lord.

People: *To Thee, O Lord.*

Priest: O holy Lord, who dwelleth on high and regardest the humble of heart and with Thine all seeing eye dost behold all creation, unto Thee have we bowed the neck of our soul and body, and we entreat Thee: O Holy of holies, stretch forth Thine invisible hand from Thy holy dwelling place and bless us all. And if in aught we have sinned, whether voluntarily or involuntarily, forgive, inasmuch as Thou art a good God, and lovest mankind, vouchsafing unto us Thine earthly and heavenly good things.

For Thine it is to show mercy and to save us, O our God, and unto Thee do we send up glory: to the Father, and to the Son, and to the Holy Spirit, both now and ever, and unto the ages of ages.

People: *Amen.*

Prayer Before The Holy Doors

Deacon: Wisdom.

People: *Holy Father bless.*

Priest: He that is is blessed, Christ our God, always, now and ever, and unto the ages of ages.

People: *Amen. Establish, O God, the holy Orthodox Faith of Orthodox Christians unto the ages of ages.*

Priest: O most holy Theotokos, save us.

Reader: Greater in honour than the Cherubim and beyond compare more glorious than the Seraphim; without corruption thou gavest birth to God the Word, truly the Theotokos, we magnify thee.

Priest: Glory to Thee, O Christ God, our hope, glory to Thee.

Reader: *Glory be to the Father and to the Son and to the Holy Spirit,*

Both now and forever and unto the ages of ages. Amen.

Lord have mercy. **(x3)**

Holy Father, bless.

The Dismissal

Priest: May Christ our true God, Who for us men and for our salvation did deign to suffer the dread passion, and the life creating Cross and voluntary burial in the flesh, through the intercessions of His most pure Mother; of *[patron of the church Saint ...]* and of all the saints: have mercy on us and save us, for He is good and loveth mankind.

People: *Amen.*

[Congregation come up to venerate the Epitaphios. Whilst:]

Tone 5   *Stimulating, dancing, and rhythmical.*   *C, D, Eb, F, G, A, Bb, C.*

Come and let us bless Joseph of everlasting memory, who came to Pilate by night and begged for the Life of People: 'Give me this stranger, Who has no place to lay His head. Give me this stranger, Whom His evil disciple delivered to death. Give me this stranger, Whom His Mother saw hanging on the Cross, and with a mother's sorrow she cried weeping: "Woe is me, O my Child. Woe is me, Light of mine eyes and beloved fruit of my womb. For what Symeon foretold in the temple is come to pass today: a sword pierces my heart, but do Thou change my grief to gladness by Thy Resurrection." '

We venerate Thy Passion, O Christ.

We venerate Thy Passion, O Christ.

We venerate Thy Passion, O Christ and Thy Holy Resurrection.

[The reader immediately begins the first hour.]

Reader:

Come, let us worship God, our King.

Come, let us worship and fall down before Christ, our King and our God.

Come, let us worship and fall down before Christ Himself, our King and our God.

Psalm 5

Unto my words give ear, O Lord, hear my cry. Attend unto the voice of my supplication, O my King and my God; for unto Thee shall I pray, O Lord. In the morning shalt Thou hear my voice. In the morning shall I stand before Thee, and Thou shalt look upon me; for not a God that willest iniquity art Thou. He that worketh evil shall not dwell near Thee nor shall transgressors abide before Thine eyes. Thou hast hated all them that work iniquity; Thou shalt destroy all them that speak a lie. A man that is bloody and deceitful shall the Lord abhor. But as for me, in the multitude of Thy mercy shall I go into Thy house; I shall worship toward Thy holy temple in fear of Thee. O Lord, guide me in the way of Thy righteousness; because of mine enemies, make straight my way before Thee, For in their mouth there is no truth; their heart is vain. Their throat is an open sepulchre, with their tongues have they spoken deceitfully; judge them, O God. Let them fall down on account of their own devisings; according to the multitude of their ungodliness, cast them out, for they have embittered Thee, O Lord. And let all them be glad that hope in Thee; they shall rejoice, and Thou shalt dwell amongst them. And all shall glory in Thee that love Thy name, for Thou shalt bless the righteous. O Lord, as with a shield of Thy good pleasure hast Thou crowned us.

Psalm 89

Lord, Thou hast been our refuge in generation and generation. Before the mountains came to be and the earth was formed and the world, even from everlasting to everlasting art Thou. Turn not man away unto lowliness; yea, Thou hast said: Turn back you sons of men. For a thousand years in Thine eyes, O Lord, are but as yesterday that is past, and as a watch in the night. Things of no account shall their years be; in the morning like grass shall man pass away. In the morning shall he bloom and pass away. In the evening shall he fall and grow withered and dry. For we have fainted away in Thy wrath, and in Thine anger have we been troubled. Thou hast set our iniquities before us; our lifespan is in the light of Thy countenance. For all our days are faded away, and in Thy wrath are we fainted away; our years have, like a spider, spun out their tale. As for the days of our years, in their span, they be threescore years and ten. And if we be in strength, mayhap fourscore years; and what is more than these is toil and travail. For mildness is come upon us, and we shall be chastened. Who knoweth the might of Thy wrath? And out of fear of Thee, who can recount Thine anger? So make Thy right hand known to me, and to them that in their heart are instructed in wisdom. Return, O Lord; how long? And be Thou entreated concerning Thy servants. We were filled in the morning with Thy mercy, O Lord, and we rejoiced and were glad. In all our days, let us be glad for the days wherein Thou didst humble us, for the years wherein we saw evils. And look upon Thy servants, and upon Thy works, and do Thou guide their sons. And let the brightness of the Lord our God be upon us, and the works of our hands do Thou guide aright upon us, yea, the works of our hands do Thou guide aright.

Psalm 100

Of mercy and judgement shall I sing to Thee, O Lord; I shall chant and have understanding in a blameless path. When wilt Thou come unto me? I have walked in the innocence of my heart in the midst of my house. I have no unlawful thing before mine eyes; the workers of transgressions I have hated. A crooked heart hath not cleaved unto me; as for the wicked man who turned from me, I knew him not. Him that privily talked against his neighbour did I drive away from me. With him whose eye was proud and his heart insatiate, I did not eat. Mine eyes were upon the faithful of the land, that they might sit with me; the man that walked in the blameless path, he ministered unto me. The proud doer dwelt not in the midst of my house; the speaker of unjust things prospered not before mine eyes. In the morning I slew all the sinners of the land, utterly to destroy out of the city of the Lord all them that work iniquity.

After The Psalm

Glory be to the Father, and to the Son, and to the Holy Spirit;
Both now and forever, and unto the ages of ages. Amen.
Halleluiah, Halleluiah, Halleluiah. Glory to Thee, O God. **(x3)**

Lord, have mercy. **(x3)**

The Noble Joseph, taking Thy most pure body down from the Tree and having wrapped it in pure linen and spices, laid it in a new tomb

Glory be to the Father and to the Son and to the Holy Spirit;

When Thou didst descend unto death, O Life Immortal, then didst Thou slay hell with the lightning of Thy divinity. And when Thou didst also raise the dead out of the nethermost depths, all the hosts of the heavens cried out: O Life Giver, Christ our God, glory be to Thee.

Both now and forever, and unto the ages of ages. Amen.

Theotokion

What shall we call thee, O thou who art full of grace? Heaven, for from thee hast dawned forth the Sun of Righteousness. Paradise, for from thee hath blossomed forth the flower of immortality. Virgin, for thou hast remained incorrupt. Pure Mother, for thou hast held in thy holy embrace the Son, the God of all. Do thou entreat Him to save our souls.

My steps do Thou direct according to thy saying, and let no iniquity have dominion over me. Deliver me from the false accusations of men, and I shall keep Thy commandments. Make Thy face to shine upon Thy servant, and teach me Thy statutes.

Let my mouth be filled with Thy praise, that I may hymn Thy glory and Thy majesty all the day long.

Holy God, Holy Mighty, Holy Immortal, have mercy on us. **(x3)**

Glory be to the Father and to the Son and to the Holy Spirit,
Both now and forever and unto the ages of ages. Amen.

O Most Holy Trinity, have mercy on us.
O Lord, cleanse us from our sins.
O Master, pardon our iniquities.
O Holy One, visit and heal our infirmities, for Thy names sake.

Lord have mercy. **(x3)**

Glory be to the Father and to the Son and to the Holy Spirit,
Both now and forever and unto the ages of ages. Amen.

People: *Our Father, Who art in Heaven, hallowed be Thy Name. Thy Kingdom come, Thy will be done, on earth as it is in Heaven. Give us this day our daily bread, and forgive us our trespasses, as we forgive those who trespass against us; and lead us not into temptation, but deliver us from the evil one.*
Priest: For Thine is the kingdom and the power, and the glory: of the Father and of the Son, and of the Holy Spirit, both now and ever, and unto the ages of ages.
People: *Amen.*

Reader: He that shut up the abyss is seen as one dead, and like a mortal, the Immortal One is wrapped in linen and myrrh, and placed in a grave. And women came to anoint Him, weeping bitterly and crying out: This is the most blessed Sabbath day wherein Christ, having slept, shall arise on the third day.

Lord, have mercy. **(x40)**

The Prayer Of The Hours

At all times and in every hour, Thou art worshipped and glorified in heaven and on earth, Christ our God. Long in patience, great in mercy and compassion, Thou lovest the righteous and showest mercy to sinners. Thou callest all to salvation through the promise of good things to come. Lord, receive our prayers at the present time. Direct our lives according to Thy commandments. Sanctify our souls. Purify our bodies. Set our minds aright. Cleanse our thoughts, and deliver us from all sorrow, evil and distress. Surround us with Thy holy angels, that, guarded and guided by their host, we may arrive at the unity of the faith and the understanding of Thine ineffable glory. For Thou art blessed to the ages of ages. Amen.

Lord, have mercy. **(x3)**

Glory be to the Father and to the Son and to the Holy Spirit,
Both now and forever and unto the ages of ages. Amen.

Greater in honour than the Cherubim and beyond compare more glorious than the Seraphim; without corruption thou gavest birth to God the Word, truly the Theotokos, we magnify thee.
Holy Father bless.

Priest: God be gracious unto us and bless us, and cause Thy face to shine upon us and have mercy on us.
People: *Amen.*

Kontakion For The Annunciation

Tone 8   Humility, tranquillity, repose, suffering, pleading.   *C, D, Eb, F, G, A, Bb, C.*
To Thee, the Champion Leader, we Thy servants dedicate a feast of victory and of thanksgiving as ones rescued out of sufferings, O Theotokos: but as Thou art one with might, which is invincible, from all dangers that can be, do Thou deliver us, that we may cry to Thee: Rejoice, Thou Bride Unwedded.

Glory be to the Father, and to the Son, and to the Holy Spirit;
Both now and ever, and unto the ages of ages. Amen.

Lord, have mercy. **(x3)**

Holy Father, bless.

Priest: May Christ our true God, through the intercessions of His most pure Mother, of our holy and God bearing fathers, and of all the saints, have mercy on us and save us, for He is good and the Lover of mankind.
People: *Amen*

[End of the First Hour.]

Pascha

Also known in the West as Easter.

Until The Ascension.

(a)   Iconostasis doors remain open.

(b)   No fasting on Wednesdays and Fridays.

(c)   If a death occurs, the funeral service for Bright Week is celebrated instead of the normal one.

(d)   The troparion *"O Heavenly King..."* is replaced with *"Christ is risen from the dead..."*.

(e)   <u>Divine Liturgy.</u> Instead of *"We have seen the true light"*, sing: *"Christ is risen from the dead..."*

(f)   <u>Hours</u> and are replaced with <u>The Paschal Hours</u>.

Rush Procession – Saturday Night

[Priest may start from the distribution of the light.]

Priest: Blessed is our God, always, now and ever, and unto ages of ages. *[then the great censing]*

People: *Amen.*

Priest: Glory to Thee our God, glory to Thee.

Priest: O Heavenly King, the Comforter, the Spirit of Truth; who art everywhere present and fillest all things; Treasury of blessings, and giver of life: come and abide in us, and cleanse us from every impurity, and save our souls, O Good One.

People: *Amen.*

People: Holy God, Holy Strong, Holy Immortal, have mercy on us. **(x3)**

Glory be to the Father and to the Son and to the Holy Spirit;
Both now and forever and unto the ages of ages. Amen.

O Most Holy Trinity, have mercy on us.

O Lord, cleanse us from our sins.

O Master, pardon our iniquities.

O Holy One, visit and heal our infirmities, for Thy names sake.

Lord, have mercy. **(x3)**

Glory be to the Father and to the Son and to the Holy Spirit;
Both now and forever and to the ages of ages. Amen.

The Lords Prayer

People: , hallowed be Thy Name; Thy Kingdom come; Thy will be done, on earth as it is in Heaven. *Give us this day our daily bread; and forgive us our trespasses, as we forgive those who trespass against us. And lead us not into temptation, but deliver us from the evil one.*

Priest: For Thine is the kingdom and the power and the glory, of the Father, and of the Son, and of the Holy Spirit. Both now and forever, and unto ages of ages.

People: Amen.

Lord have mercy **(x12)**

Glory be to the Father and to the Son and to the Holy Spirit;
Both now and forever and to the ages of ages. Amen.

Come, let us worship God, our King.

Come, let us worship and fall down before Christ, our King and our God.

Come, let us worship and fall down before Christ Himself, our King and our God.

Psalm 50

Reader: Have mercy on me, O God, according to Thy great mercy; and according to the multitude of Thy compassions blot out my transgression. Wash me thoroughly from mine iniquity, and cleanse me from my sin. For I acknowledge mine iniquity, and my sin is ever before me. Against Thee, Thee only have I sinned, and done evil in Thy sight, that Thou mayest be found just when Thou speakest, and victorious when Thou art judged. For behold, I was conceived in iniquity, and in sin my mother bore me. For behold, Thou hast loved truth; Thou hast made known to me the hidden and secret things of Thy wisdom. Thou shalt sprinkle me with hyssop, and I shall be made clean; Thou shalt wash me, and I shalt be whiter than snow. Make me to hear joy and gladness; that the humbled bones may rejoice. Turn Thy face away from my sins, and blot out all mine iniquities.

Create in me a clean heart, O God, and renew a steadfast spirit within me. Cast me not away from Thy presence, and take not Thy Holy Spirit from me. Restore to me the joy of Thy salvation, and establish me with Thy governing Spirit. I shall teach transgressors Thy ways, and the ungodly shall turn back to Thee. Deliver me from blood guiltiness, O God, the God of my salvation; my tongue shall joyfully declare Thy righteousness. Lord, open my lips, and my mouth shall declare Thy praise. For if Thou hadst desired sacrifice, I would give it; Thou dost not delight in burned offerings. A sacrifice to God is a broken spirit; God shall not despise a broken and a humbled heart. Do good, O Lord, in Thy good pleasure to Zion, and let the walls of Jerusalem be builded. Then Thou shalt be pleased with a sacrifice of righteousness, with oblation and whole burned offerings. Then shall they offer bulls on Thine altar.

Canon of Great and Holy Friday
Ode 1

Eirmos

Tone 6   *Rich texture, funereal character, sorrowful tone.*   *D, Eb, F##, G, A, Bb, C##, D.*

Reader: The children of those who were saved, hid under ground the God who made the persecuting giant of old to disappear in the waves of the sea. As for us, however, let us praise the Lord as did the youths; for in glory has he been glorified.

Chorus: *Glory to Thee, Our God, Glory to Thee.*

Reader: O Lord my God, I shall praise Thy burial with funeral dirges, and indite unto Thee paeans, O Thou through whose Burial the entrance of life hath opened for me; and who by death caused death and hades to die.

Chorus: *Glory be to the Father and to the Son and to the Holy Spirit.*

Reader: Verily, the super terrestrial, and those below the earth, beholding Thee on Thy throne on high and in the grave below, were amazed, trembling at Thy death; for Thou O Element of life, was seen to be dead in a manner transcending the mind.

Chorus: *Both now and forever and unto ages of ages, Amen.*

Reader: To the depths of the earth Thou descendest to fill all with Thy glory; for my person that is in Adam was not hidden from Thee; and when Thou wast buried Thou didst renew me, who was corrupt, O Lover of mankind.

Eirmos

Tone 6   Rich texture, funereal character, sorrowful tone.   *D, Eb, F##, G, A, Bb, C##, D.*

The children of those who were saved, hid under ground the God who made the persecuting giant of old to disappear in the waves of the sea. As for us, however, let us praise the Lord as did the youths; for in glory has he been glorified.

Ode 3

Eirmos

Verily, creation, having beheld Thee suspended on Golgotha, O Thou who didst suspend the whole earth on the waters without hinges, was overtaken with great surprise, crying aloud, There is none holy save Thee, O Lord.

Chorus: *Glory to Thee, Our God, Glory to Thee.*

Reader: Thou hast revealed, O Master, numerous sights as signs of Thy burial. But now Thou hast revealed Thy hidden things as God and Man to those who are in hades also, who shouted, saying, "There is none holy save Thee, O Lord."

Chorus: *Glory be to the Father and to the Son and to the Holy Spirit.*

Reader: Thou hast stretched forth Thy hands, O Saviour, and gathered the things dispersed of old; and by Thy burial in the linen and the grave Thou hast loosed the captives, who shout, "There is none holy save Thee, O Lord."

Chorus: *Both now and forever and unto ages of ages, Amen.*

Reader: A grave and seals contained Thee by Thy will, O uncontainable; for by deeds, O Lover of mankind, Thou hast made Thy power known by a divine act to those who sing, "There is none holy save Thee, O Lord."

Eirmos

Verily, creation, having beheld Thee suspended on Golgotha, O Thou who didst suspend the whole earth on the waters without hinges, was overtaken with great surprise, crying aloud, There is none holy save Thee, O Lord.

Ode 4

Eirmos

Verily, Habakkuk, O good One, foresaw Thy divine condescension even to the Cross; and was dazzled as he cried, Thou abolishest the prestige of the mighty, when Thou didst appear in hades, since Thou art Almighty.

Chorus: *Glory to Thee, Our God, Glory to Thee.*

Reader: Thou hast blessed, O Saviour, this seventh day, which Thou hadst blessed at the beginning with rest from work; for Thou hast brought out everything, renewing it and restoring it to its former state, thus keeping the Sabbath.

Chorus: *Glory be to the Father and to the Son and to the Holy Spirit.*

Reader: Thy soul, by the power of the best, hath vanquished the body, O Word, breaking the bonds of hades and death together by Thy might.

Chorus: *Both now and forever and unto ages of ages, Amen.*

Reader: Hades in welcoming, O Word, murmured at beholding a deified Man marked with wounds, who is yet Almighty. Wherefore, at that terrible sight it shouted in fear.

Eirmos

Verily, Habakkuk, O good One, foresaw Thy divine condescension even to the Cross; and was dazzled as he cried, Thou abolishest the prestige of the mighty, when Thou didst appear in hades, since Thou art Almighty.

Ode 5

Eirmos

When Isaiah, O Christ, saw Thy light, that sets not, the light of Thy divine appearance coming to us in pity, he rose up early, crying, The dead shall rise, and they who are in the tombs shall awake, and all those on the earth shall rejoice.

Chorus: *Glory to Thee, Our God, Glory to Thee.*

Reader: When Thou becamest earthly, O Creator, Thou didst renew those who are earthly. And the linen and the grave explained Thy hidden mystery, O Word; for the honourable Joseph, of sound belief, fulfilled Thy Fathers plan, through whom Thou hast renewed me by the might of His greatness.

Chorus: *Glory be to the Father and to the Son and to the Holy Spirit.*

Reader: Thou hast transported the dead by death, and the corrupt by burial, for as becometh God Thou hast made the body which Thou didst create incorrupt and deathless, for Thy body, O Master, did not see corruption, and Thy soul in a strange manner was not left in hades.

Chorus: *Both now and forever and unto ages of ages, Amen.*

Reader: Thou didst come from a Virgin who knew no travail. Thy side, O my Creator, was pierced with a spear, by which Thou didst accomplish the recreation of Eve, having Thyself become Adam. Supernaturally Thou didst fall into a sleep that renewed nature, raising life from sleep and corruption; for Thou art Almighty.

Eirmos

When Isaiah, O Christ, saw Thy light, that sets not, the light of Thy divine appearance coming to us in pity, he rose up early, crying, The dead shall rise, and they who are in the tombs shall awake, and all those on the earth shall rejoice.

Ode 6

Eirmos

Verily, Jonah the Prophet was caught but not held in the belly of the whale. But being a sign of Thee, O Thou who didst suffer and were delivered to burial, he came out of the whale as out of a chamber, and cried unto the watchmen, In vain do you watch, O watchmen; for you have neglected mercy.

Chorus: *Glory to Thee, Our God, Glory to Thee.*

Reader: Thou wast killed, O Word, but wast not separated from the body which Thou didst share with us; for even though Thy temple was dissolved at the time of the Passion, the Person of Thy Divinity and Humanity is one only and in both Thou art still a single Son, the Word of God, God and man.

Chorus: *Glory be to the Father and to the Son and to the Holy Spirit.*

Reader: The fall of Adam resulted in the death of a Man, not God; for though the substance of Thine earthly body suffered, Thy Divinity hath remained passionless, transforming the corrupt to incorruptibility. And by Thy Resurrection Thou hast uncovered the incorrupt fountain of life.

Chorus: *Both now and forever and unto ages of ages, Amen.*

Reader: Verily, hades ruled the race of man, but not forever; for Thou, O mighty One, when Thou wast placed in the grave didst demolish the locks of death with the palm of Thy hand, O Element of Life, proclaiming to those sitting yonder from the ages a true salvation, having become, O Saviour, the First born of the dead.

Eirmos

Verily, Jonah the Prophet was caught but not held in the belly of the whale. But being a sign of Thee, O Thou who didst suffer and were delivered to burial, he came out of the whale as out of a chamber, and cried unto the watchmen, In vain do you watch, O watchmen; for you have neglected mercy.

Ode 7

Eirmos

An ineffable wonder. He who saved the righteous youths from the fire of the furnace, has been placed in the grave, a breathless corpse, for our salvation and deliverance, who sing, Blessed art Thou, O delivering God.

Chorus: *Glory to Thy holy resurrection, O Lord.*

Reader: Verily, hades was pierced and destroyed by the divine fire when it received in its heart Him who was pierced in His side with a spear for our salvation, who sing, "Blessed art Thou, O delivering God."

Chorus: *Glory to Thy holy resurrection, O Lord.*

Reader: The tomb is happy, having become divine when it received within it the Treasure of life, the Creator, as one who slumbereth for our salvation, who sing, "Blessed art Thou, O delivering God."

Chorus: *Glory be to the Father and to the Son and to the Holy Spirit.*

Reader: The Life of all was willing to lie in a grave, in accordance with the law of the dead, making it appear as the fountain of the resurrection of our salvation, who sing, "Blessed art Thou, O delivering God."

Chorus: *Both now and forever and unto ages of ages, Amen.*

Reader: The Godhead of Christ was one without separation in hades, in the tomb, in Eden, and with the Father and the Spirit, for our salvation, who sing, "Blessed art Thou, O delivering God."

Eirmos

An ineffable wonder. He who saved the righteous youths from the fire of the furnace, has been placed in the grave, a breathless corpse, for our salvation and deliverance, who sing, Blessed art Thou, O delivering God.

Ode 8

Eirmos

Be thou amazed, O heaven, and let the foundations of the earth quake; for behold, he who dwells in the highest has been accounted among the dead, and has been Guest in a humble tomb. Wherefore, O you youths, bless him. Praise him, you Priests; and you nations, exalt him more and more unto all the ages.

Chorus: *Glory to Thy holy resurrection, O Lord.*

Reader: The pure Temple hath been destroyed, then rising, He raised with Him the fallen tabernacle; for the second Adam who dwelleth in the highest hath descended unto the first Adam in the uttermost chambers of hades. Wherefore, you youths, bless Him. Praise Him, you priests; and you nations, exalt Him more and more unto all ages.

Chorus: *Glory be to the Father and to the Son and to the Holy Spirit.*

Reader: The courage of the Disciples hath come to its end. But Joseph of Ramah hath shown great valour; for beholding the God of all dead and naked, he sought Him and arrayed Him, shouting "O you youths, bless Him. Praise Him, you priests; and you nations, exalt Him more and more unto all ages."

Chorus: *Both now and forever and unto ages of ages, Amen.*

Reader: O what dazzling wonders. O what endless goodness. O what ineffable endurance. For He that dwelleth in the highest is sealed up under the earth by His own will. God is slandered as a misleader. Wherefore, you youths, bless Him. Praise Him, you priests; and you nations, exalt Him more and more unto all ages.

Eirmos

Be thou amazed, O heaven, and let the foundations of the earth quake; for behold, he who dwells in the highest has been accounted among the dead, and has been Guest in a humble tomb. Wherefore, O you youths, bless him. Praise him, you Priests; and you nations, exalt him more and more unto all the ages.

Ode 9

Eirmos *[male singer]*

Mourn not for me, Mother, as thou behold me in the grave; for I thy Son, whom Thou didst conceive in thy womb without seed, shall rise and shall be glorified. And being God, I shall ceaselessly exalt and ennoble those who in faith and longing magnify thee.

Chorus: *Glory to Thy holy resurrection, O Lord.*

[female singer]

My eternal Son, I escaped sufferings at Thy strange birth and was supernaturally blessed. And now, beholding Thee, O my Son, dead and breathless, I am pierced with the spear of bitter sorrow. But arise Thou, that I may be magnified by Thee.

Chorus: *Glory be to the Father and to the Son and to the Holy Spirit.*

[male singer]

The earth, O my mother, hath hidden me by mine own will. And the gate keepers of hades trembled at beholding me clothed with a robe spattered with revenge; for I being God, have vanquished mine enemies with the Cross, and I shall rise again and magnify thee.

Chorus: *Both now and forever and unto ages of ages, Amen.*

[male singer]

Let all creation rejoice, and all the earthly be glad, for hades and the enemy have been spoiled. Let the women meet me with spices; for I redeem Adam and all their descendants, and shall rise on the third day.

Eirmos *[male singer]*

Mourn not for me, Mother, as thou behold me in the grave; for I thy Son, whom Thou didst conceive in thy womb without seed, shall rise and shall be glorified. And being God, I shall ceaselessly exalt and ennoble those who in faith and longing magnify thee.

[Darken the Church.]

The Trisagion Prayers

Reader: Holy God, Holy Mighty, Holy Immortal, have mercy on us. **(x3)**

Chorus: *Glory be to the Father, and to the Son, and to the Holy Spirit.*
Both now and forever, and unto ages of ages. Amen.

O Most Holy Trinity, have mercy on us.

O Lord, cleanse us from our sins.

O Master, pardon our iniquities.

O Holy One, visit and heal our infirmities, for Thy names sake.

Lord, have mercy. **(x3)**

Chorus: *Glory be to the Father, and to the Son, and to the Holy Spirit.*
Both now and forever, and unto ages of ages. Amen.

The Lords Prayer

People: *Our Father, who art in Heaven, hallowed be Thy Name; Thy Kingdom come; Thy will be done, on earth as it is in Heaven. Give us this day our daily bread; and forgive us our trespasses, as we forgive those who trespass against us. And lead us not into temptation, but deliver us from the evil one.*

Priest: For Thine is the kingdom and the power and the glory, of the Father, and of the Son, and of the Holy Spirit. Both now and forever, and unto ages of ages.

People: *Amen.*

Resurrectional Apolytikion

Tone 2   *Majesty, gentleness, hope, repentance and sadness.*   *E, F, G, Ab, B, C.*

When Thou didst submit Thyself unto death, O Thou deathless and immortal one, then Thou didst destroy Hell with Thy Godly power, and when Thou didst raise the dead from beneath the earth, all the powers of heaven did cry aloud unto Thee O Christ Thou giver of life glory to Thee.

Augmented Ektenia

Priest: Have mercy on us, O God, according to Thy great mercy, we pray Thee; hearken and have mercy.

People: *Lord, have mercy.* (**x3**)

Priest: Again we pray that he shall keep this holy church and this city and ever city and countryside from wrath, famine, plague, earthquake, flood, file, the sword, foreign invasion, civil war and sudden death; that our good God, who loves mankind, shall be gracious, favourable and conciliatory and turn away and dispel all the wrath stirred up against us and all sickness, and may deliver us from his righteous chastisement which impends against us, and have mercy on us.

People: *Lord, have mercy.* (**x3**)

Priest: Hear us, O God our Saviour, the Hope of all the ends of the earth and of those who are far off upon the sea; and be gracious, O Master, upon our sins, and have mercy on us. For Thou art a merciful God and lovest mankind, and unto Thee we ascribe Glory be to the Father and to the Son and to the Holy Spirit, both now and forever and unto the ages of ages.

People: *Amen.*

Priest: Glory to Thee, O Christ our God and our Hope, glory to Thee.

Chorus: *Glory be to the Father, and to the Son, and to the Holy Spirit.*

Both now and forever, and unto ages of ages. Amen.

Lord, have mercy. (**x3**)

Holy Father, bless.

Priest: May He who rose from again from the dead, Christ our true God, through the intercessions of His all immaculate and all blameless holy Mother, of Saint *[patron of the church]*; of the holy and righteous ancestors of God, Joachim and Anna and of all the Saints: have mercy on us and save us, forasmuch as He is good and loveth mankind.

Through the prayers of our Holy Father, Lord Jesus Christ our God, have mercy on us and save us.

THE RESURRECTION SERVICE

Priest: Come ye, take light from the Light that is never over taken by night.

Come and glorify Christ, risen from the dead.

(The Faithful receive the light for their candles)

Chorus: *Come ye, take light from the Light that is never overtaken by night.*

Come and glorify Christ, risen from the dead.

[as many times until all have received.]

[Priest re-enters the sanctuary through the holy doors and, still holding the Paschal candle in his right hand, takes up the Gospel book in his left arm.]

Priest: "Thy resurrection", O Christ our Saviour, the angels in heaven sing.

Enable us on earth to glorify Thee with purity of heart.

THE PROCESSION AROUND THE OUTSIDE OF THE CHURCH

Tone 6   *Rich texture, funereal character, sorrowful tone.*   D, Eb, F##, G, A, Bb, C##, D.

Chorus: "Thy resurrection", O Christ our Saviour, the angels in heaven sing.

Enable us on earth to glorify Thee with purity of heart.

AT THE ENTRANCE DOOR

Little Litany

Deacon: And that we may be accounted worthy to hear the Holy Gospel, let us pray to the Lord.

People: *Lord, have mercy.* **(x3)**

Deacon: Wisdom. Stand upright. Let us hear the Holy Gospel.

[The Priest turns to face the people and blesses them, saying:]

Priest: Peace be with you all.

People: *And with thy Spirit.*

Priest: The reading is from the Holy Gospel according to Saint Mark 16:1-8.

People: *Glory to Thee, O Lord, Glory to Thee.*

Deacon: Let us attend.

Priest: And when the Sabbath was past, Mary Magdalene, and Mary the mother of James, and Salome brought sweet spices, that coming, they might anoint Jesus. And very early in the morning, the first day of the week, they come to the sepulchre, the sun being no now risen. And they said one to another: Who shall roll us back the stone from the door of the sepulchre? And looking, they saw the stone rolled back. For it was very great. And entering into the sepulchre, they saw a young man sitting on the right side, clothed with a white robe: and they were astonished. Who says to them: Be not frightened; you seek Jesus of Nazareth, who was crucified: He is risen, He is not here, behold the place where they laid Him. But go, tell His disciples and Peter that He goes before you in Galilee; there you shall see Him, as He told you. But they going out, fled from the sepulchre. For a trembling and fear had seized them: and they said nothing to any man; for they were afraid.

People: *Glory to Thee, O Lord, Glory to Thee.*

PASCHAL ORTHROS

[Making the Sign of the Cross with the Censer, the Priest says:]

Priest: Glory to the Holy, consubstantial, life giving and undivided Trinity.

Both now and forever and unto the ages of ages.

People: Amen.

All clergy: Christ is risen from the dead, trampling down death by death;
And upon those in the tombs, bestowing life. **(x3)**

Priest: Let God arise and let His enemies be scattered;
And let those who hate Him flee from His face.

People: *Christ is risen from the dead, trampling down death by death;*
And upon those in the tombs, bestowing life.

Priest: As smoke vanishes, so let them vanish away; as wax melts before the fire.

Russian Kristos voss kreysyey iz myert vikh. Smyertee oh smyert poh prav.
Ee sooshim vogrow byekh zhivawt darowvav.

Priest: Then shall the ungodly perish in the presence of God. But the righteous shall rejoice.

Greek Χριστὸς ἀνέστη ἐκ νεκρῶν, θανάτῳ θάνατον πατήσας,
καὶ τοῖς ἐν τοῖς μνήμασι, ζωὴν χαρισάμενος.

Priest: This is the day that the Lord has made; let us rejoice and be glad in it.

People: *Christ is risen from the dead, trampling down death by death;*
And upon those in the tombs, bestowing life.

Priest: Glory be to the Father and to the Son and to the Holy Spirit.

Russian Kristos voss kreysyey iz myert vikh. Smyertee oh smyert poh prav.
Ee sooshim vogrow byekh zhivawt darowvav.

Priest: Both now and forever and unto ages of ages, Amen.

Greek Χριστὸς ἀνέστη ἐκ νεκρῶν, θανάτῳ θάνατον πατήσας,
καὶ τοῖς ἐν τοῖς μνήμασι, ζωὴν χαρισάμενος.

Romanian Kristos aa inveeat din morts koo, mortay mortay kakoond.
Shay chaylore deem ormintay veeaatsay, daaroo indoolay.

Priest: Christ is risen from the dead, trampling down death by death and upon those in the tombs...

People: *... bestowing life.*

Litany of Peace (Great Ektenia)

Deacon: In peace, let us pray to the Lord.

People: *Lord, have mercy.*

Deacon: For the peace from above and for the salvation of our souls, let us pray to the Lord.

People: *Lord, have mercy.*

Deacon: For the peace of the whole world, for the good estate of the holy churches of God, and for the union of all men, let us pray to the Lord.

People: *Lord, have mercy.*

Deacon: For this holy house and for those who with faith, reverence, and fear of God enter therein, let us pray to the Lord.

People: *Lord, have mercy.*

Deacon: For our Archbishop Nikitas for the honourable Presbyter, the Diaconate in Christ, for all the Clergy and the people, let us pray to the Lord.

People: *Lord, have mercy.*

Deacon: For the Royal Family, our civil authorities, and our armed forces everywhere, let us pray to the Lord.

People: *Lord, have mercy.*

Deacon: For this [city / town / village] and every [city / town / village] and country, and for the faithful who dwell therein, let us pray to the Lord.

People: *Lord, have mercy.*

Deacon: For healthful seasons, for abundance of the fruits of the earth, and for peaceful times, let us pray to the Lord.

People: *Lord, have mercy.*

Deacon: For travellers by sea, by land, and by air, for the sick and the suffering, for captives and their salvation, let us pray to the Lord.

People: *Lord, have mercy.*

Deacon: For our deliverance from all tribulation, wrath, danger, and necessity, let us pray to the Lord.

People: *Lord, have mercy.*

Deacon: Help us; save us; have mercy on us; and keep us, O God, by Thy grace.

People: *Lord, have mercy.*

Deacon: Calling to remembrance our all holy, immaculate, most blessed and glorious Lady Theotokos and ever Virgin Mary, with all the saints, let us commend ourselves and each other, and all our life, unto Christ our God.

People: *To Thee, O Lord.*

Priest: For unto Thou art due all glory, honour, and worship, to the Father, and to the Son, and to the Holy Spirit, Both now and forever, and unto the ages of ages.

People: *Amen.*

Dialogue With The Door Keeper – Psalm 23

Priest: Lift up thy gates O you princes. And be lifted up, O everlasting gates;

That the King of Glory shall enter in.

Door Keeper: Who is the King of Glory?

Priest: The Lord strong and mighty; the Lord, mighty in war.   **(Knock 3 times)**

Lift up thy gates O you princes. And be lifted up, O everlasting gates;

That the King of Glory shall enter in.

Door Keeper: Who is the King of Glory?

Priest: The Lord strong and mighty; the Lord, mighty in war.   **(Knock 3 times)**

Lift up thy gates O you princes. And be lifted up, O everlasting gates;

That the King of Glory shall enter in.

Door Keeper: Who is the King of Glory?

Priest: The Lord of hosts, He is the King Of Glory.

[The doors are opened and the Clergy and Faithful re-enter. Bells ring.]

[Start when back at the Readers stand:]

Canon Of Pascha
By John of Damascus
Ode 1

Eirmos

Tone 1   Magnificent, happy and earthy.   *C, D, Eb, F, G, A, Bb, C.*

It is the day of the Resurrection, be illumined, people, Pascha, the Lord's Pascha. From death unto life, from the earth to heaven has Christ Our God led us singing the song of victory.

Chorus: *Glory to Thy Holy Resurrection, O Lord.*

Troparia

Let us cleanse our senses, that we may behold Christ shining like lightning, with Resurrection's unapproachable Light. We shall hear Him clearly say rejoice as we sing the song of victory.

Chorus: *Glory be to the Father and to the Son and to the Holy Spirit.*

Both now and forever and unto ages of ages, Amen.

Let the heavens rejoice, and the earth be glad, as it is truly meet. Let the whole world feast, visible and invisible, for Christ is risen to everlasting joy.

People: *Christ is risen from the dead trampling down death by death;*

and upon those in the tombs bestowing life.

Russian	Kristos voss kreysyey iz myert vikh. Smyertee oh smyert poh prav.
	Ee sooshim vogrow byekh zhivawt darowvav.
Greek	Χριστὸς ἀνέστη ἐκ νεκρῶν, θανάτῳ θάνατον πατήσας,
	καὶ τοῖς ἐν τοῖς μνήμασι, ζωὴν χαρισάμενος.
Romanian	Kristos aa inveeat din morts koo, mortay mortay kakoond.
	Shay chaylore deem ormintay veeaatsay, daaroo indoolay.

(Chant)

Jesus having risen from the grave, as he foretold. Has granted us life everlasting, and great mercy.

The Little Litany

Deacon: Again and again in peace, let us pray to the Lord.

People: *Lord, have mercy.*

Deacon: Help us; save us; have mercy on us; and keep us, O God, by Thy grace.

People: *Lord, have mercy.*

Deacon: Calling to remembrance our all holy, immaculate, most blessed and glorious Lady Theotokos and ever virgin Mary, with all the Saints, let us commend ourselves and each other, and all our life unto Christ our God.

People: *To Thee, O Lord.*

Priest: For Thine is the might, and Thine is the kingdom and the power and the glory of the Father, and of the Son, and of the Holy Spirit, both now and ever, and unto ages of ages.

People: *Amen.*

Ode 3

Eirmos

Tone 1   Magnificent, happy and earthy.   C, D, Eb, F, G, A, Bb, C.

Come let us drink, not miraculous water drawn forth from a barren stone, but a new vintage from the fount of incorruption, spring from the tomb of Christ. In him we are established.

Glory to Thy holy resurrection, O Lord.

Troparion

Now all is filled with light: heaven and earth and the lower regions. Let all creation celebrate the rising of Christ. In him we are established.

Chorus: *Glory be to the Father and to the Son and to the Holy Spirit.*

Both now and forever and unto ages of ages, Amen.

Yesterday I was buried with Thee, O Christ. Today I arise with Thee in Thine resurrection. Yesterday I was crucified with Thee. Glorify me with Thee, O Saviour, in Thy kingdom.

People: *Christ is risen from the dead trampling down death by death;*

and upon those in the tombs bestowing life.

Russian   Kristos voss kreysyey iz myert vikh. Smyertee oh smyert poh prav.

Ee sooshim vogrow byekh zhivawt darowvav.

Greek   Χριστὸς ἀνέστη ἐκ νεκρῶν, θανάτῳ θάνατον πατήσας,

καὶ τοῖς ἐν τοῖς μνήμασι, ζωὴν χαρισάμενος.

Romanian   Kristos aa inveeat din morts koo, mortay mortay kakoond.

Shay chaylore deem ormintay veeaatsay, daaroo indoolay.

(Chant)

Jesus having risen from the grave, as he foretold. Has granted us life everlasting, and great mercy.

The Little Litany

Deacon: Again and again in peace, let us pray to the Lord.

People: Lord, have mercy.

Deacon: Help us; save us; have mercy on us; and keep us, O God, by Thy grace.

People: Lord, have mercy.

Deacon: Calling to remembrance our all holy, immaculate, most blessed and glorious Lady Theotokos and ever virgin Mary, with all the Saints, let us commend ourselves and each other, and all our life unto Christ our God.

People: To Thee, O Lord.

Priest: For Thou art holy, our God, and unto Thee do we ascribe Glory be to the Father, and to the Son, and to the Holy Spirit, now and ever, and unto ages of ages.

People: Amen.

Paschal Hypakoe

Tone 4   Festive, joyous and expressing deep piety.   *C, D, Eb, F, G, A, Bb, C.*

They who were with Mary came before the dawn, found the stone rolled away from the sepulchre, and heard the angels say unto them, Why seek you him as man with the dead, who dwells in light eternal? Behold the grave wrappings; make haste and declare to the world that the Lord is risen, and has caused death to die; for he is the Son of God, the Saviour of mankind.

Ode 4

Eirmos

Tone 6   Rich texture, funereal character, sorrowful tone.   *D, Eb, F##, G, A, Bb, C##, D.*

The inspired prophet Habakkuk now stands with us in holy vigil. He is like a shining angel who cries with a piercing voice. Today salvation has come to the world. For Christ is risen as all powerful.

Chorus: *Glory to Thy holy resurrection, O Lord.*

Troparia

Christ appeared as a male child, the son that opens a virgin womb. He is called the lamb as one destined to be our food, unblemished for he has not tasted of defilement and perfect for he is our true God.

Chorus: *Glory to Thy holy resurrection, O Lord.*

Christ, the crown with which we are blessed, has appeared as a yearling lamb. Freely he has given himself as our cleansing paschal sacrifice. From the tomb he has shown forth once again, our radiant sun of righteousness.

Chorus: *Glory be to the Father and to the Son and to the Holy Spirit.*
          Both now and forever and unto ages of ages, Amen.

David the ancestor of God, leaped and danced before the ark which prefigured Thee. Now let us the holy people of God, seeing the fulfilment of all figures, rejoice in piety, for Christ is risen as all powerful.

People:	*Christ is risen from the dead trampling down death by death;*
	and upon those in the tombs bestowing life.
Russian	Kristos voss kreysyey iz myert vikh. Smyertee oh smyert poh prav.
	Ee sooshim vogrow byekh zhivawt darowvav.
Greek	Χριστὸς ἀνέστη ἐκ νεκρῶν, θανάτῳ θάνατον πατήσας,
	καὶ τοῖς ἐν τοῖς μνήμασι, ζωὴν χαρισάμενος.
Romanian	Kristos aa inveeat din morts koo, mortay mortay kakoond.
	Shay chaylore deem ormintay veeaatsay, daaroo indoolay.

(Chant)

Jesus having risen from the grave, as he foretold. Has granted us life everlasting, and great mercy.

The Little Litany

Deacon: Again and again in peace, let us pray to the Lord.

People: *Lord, have mercy.*

Deacon: Help us; save us; have mercy on us; and keep us, O God, by Thy grace.

People: Lord, have mercy.

Deacon: Calling to remembrance our all holy, immaculate, most blessed and glorious Lady Theotokos and ever virgin Mary, with all the Saints, let us commend ourselves and each other, and all our life unto Christ our God.

People: To Thee, O Lord.

Priest: For Thou art holy, our God, and unto Thee do we ascribe Glory be to the Father, and to the Son, and to the Holy Spirit, now and ever, and unto ages of ages.

People: Amen.

Ode 5

Eirmos

Tone 1   Magnificent, happy and earthy.   *C, D, Eb, F, G, A, Bb, C.*

Let us a rise at the rising of the sun and bring to the master a hymn in stead of myrrh and we shall see Christ, the sun of righteousness, who causes life to dawn for all.

Chorus: Glory to Thy holy resurrection, O Lord.

Troparia

The souls bound in the chains of hell O Christ, seeing Thy compassion without measure, pressed onward to the light with joyful steps, praising the eternal Pascha.

Chorus: Glory be to the Father and to the Son and to the Holy Spirit.
Both now and forever and unto ages of ages, Amen.

Let us go with lamps in hand to meet Christ, who comes from the tomb like a bridegroom, and with festive ranks of angels we celebrate the saving Pascha of God.

Paschal Troparion

People: Christ is risen from the dead trampling down death by death,
and upon those in the tombs bestowing life.

Russian   Kristos voss kreysyey iz myert vikh. Smyertee oh smyert poh prav.
Ee sooshim vogrow byekh zhivawt darowvav.

Greek   Χριστὸς ἀνέστη ἐκ νεκρῶν, θανάτῳ θάνατον πατήσας,
καὶ τοῖς ἐν τοῖς μνήμασι, ζωὴν χαρισάμενος.

Romanian   Kristos aa inveeat din morts koo, mortay mortay kakoond.
Shay chaylore deem ormintay veeaatsay, daaroo indoolay.

(Chant)

Jesus having risen from the grave, as he foretold. Has granted us life everlasting, and great mercy.

The Little Litany

Deacon: Again and again in peace, let us pray to the Lord.

People: *Lord, have mercy.*

Deacon: Help us; save us; have mercy on us; and keep us, O God, by Thy grace.

People: *Lord, have mercy.*

Deacon: Calling to remembrance our all holy, immaculate, most blessed and glorious Lady Theotokos and ever virgin Mary, with all the Saints, let us commend ourselves and each other, and all our life unto Christ our God.

People: *To Thee, O Lord.*

Priest: For sanctified and glorified is Thine all honourable and majestic name of the Father and of the Son and of the Holy Spirit; both now and forever, and unto the ages of ages.

People: *Amen.*

Ode 6

Eirmos

Tone 6   Rich texture, funereal character, sorrowful tone.   D, Eb, F##, G, A, Bb, C##, D.

Thou did descend, O Christ, to the depths of the earth. Thou did break the ever lasting bars which had held deaths captives, and like Jonah from the whale on the third day, Thou did arise from the grave.

Chorus: *Glory to Thy holy resurrection, O Lord.*

Troparia

Thou didst arise, O Christ, and yet the tomb remained sealed, as at Thy birth the virgins womb remained unharmed, and Thou hast opened for us the gates of paradise.

Chorus: *Glory be to the Father and to the Son and to the Holy Spirit.*
Both now and forever and unto ages of ages, Amen.

O my Saviour, as God Thou did bring thyself freely to the Father, a victim living and unsacrificed, resurrecting Adam, the father of us all, when Thou arose from the grave.

Paschal Troparion

People: *Christ is risen from the dead trampling down death by death;*
and upon those in the tombs bestowing life.

Russian Kristos voss kreysyey iz myert vikh. Smyertee oh smyert poh prav.
Ee sooshim vogrow byekh zhivawt darowvav.

Greek Χριστὸς ἀνέστη ἐκ νεκρῶν, θανάτῳ θάνατον πατήσας,
καὶ τοῖς ἐν τοῖς μνήμασι, ζωὴν χαρισάμενος.

Romanian Kristos aa inveeat din morts koo, mortay mortay kakoond.
Shay chaylore deem ormintay veeaatsay, daaroo indoolay.

(Chant)

Jesus having risen from the grave, as he foretold. Has granted us life everlasting, and great mercy.

The Little Litany

Deacon: Again and again in peace, let us pray to the Lord.

People: *Lord, have mercy.*

Deacon: Help us; save us; have mercy on us; and keep us, O God, by Thy grace.

People: *Lord, have mercy.*

Deacon: Calling to remembrance our all holy, immaculate, most blessed and glorious Lady Theotokos and ever virgin Mary, with all the Saints, let us commend ourselves and each other, and all our life unto Christ our God.

People: *To Thee, O Lord.*

Priest: For Thou art the king of peace and the Saviour of our souls, and unto Thee we ascribe glory to the Father, and to the Son, and to the Holy Spirit; both now and forever, and unto ages of ages.

People: *Amen.*

Kontakion

Tone 8   *Humility, tranquillity, repose, suffering, pleading.*   *C, D, Eb, F, G, A, Bb, C.*

Reader: Though Thou, O deathless One, didst descend into the grave, Thou didst destroy the power of hell and, as Victor, Thou didst rise again, O Christ our God. Thou didst greet the ointment bearing women, saying, "Rejoice. Thou didst bestow peace upon Thy Disciples, and resurrection upon those that are fallen."

Oikos

Reader *[Chant, don't sing]*:   To the Sun before the sun, as it set for a time in the grave, the ointment bearing maidens came at dawn, seeking him as they would the day. And they shouted one to another, Come, let us, O friends, anoint with spices the life bearing body, now buried; the body that raises fallen Adam, lying in the sepulchre. Come, let us hasten, as did the Magi, and fall down in worship; let us offer of our spices like unto their offerings, to him who is no longer wrapped in swaddling clothes, but in finest linen. Let us lament; let us weep and let us cry, Master, arise O Thou who dost resurrect the fallen.

Synaxarion

Reader *[plain reading]*:   On the Holy and Great Sunday of Pascha we celebrate the life giving Resurrection of our Lord and God and Saviour Jesus Christ; for Christ alone did descend with condescension to fight hades; and he ascended, bringing the abundant spoils of victory which he had snatched.

Mary the Magdalene and the rest of the women who were present at the Saviour's burial on Friday evening, returned that very day from Golgotha to the city and prepared ointment and spices, that they might come later and anoint the body of Jesus. They rested the next day, Saturday, in fulfilment of the commandment. And on the following day, which was Sunday and which the Evangelists call the first day of the week, which fell on the twenty fifth of March, or thirty six hours after the Death of life giving Jesus, the women came to the sepulchre with their prepared ointments. And as they were pondering the difficulty of rolling the stone from the gate of the sepulchre, a great earthquake took place, an angel of the Lord came down, whose appearance was like lightning and his clothes like snow, and rolled away the stone and sat thereon. The guards trembled with fear, became like dead, and fled. But the women entered the sepulchre and found not Jesus. But they found two other angels in the form of men dressed in white raiment who proclaimed to them the Resurrection of the Saviour. commanding them to hasten and give the good news to the Disciples. In the meantime Peter and John, who had received the report from Mary the Magdalene, hastened and entered the tomb and found there only the linen clothes. They returned with great joy to the city, and began to preach the supernatural Resurrection of Christ, having seen him alive in truth five times that very day.

For this joyful Resurrection we therefore Celebrate today, kissing one another in Christ with the brotherly kiss, illustrating thereby the dissolution of the enmity that was between us and God, and our reconciliation through Christ. This Feast was called Passover from the Jewish name; for Christ by his Passion and Resurrection translated us from the curse of Adam and the bondage of Satan to the ancient liberty and bliss. As for the day of the week, which is called in Hebrew, the first day, being dedicated to our Lord for his glorification and magnification, is called in Greek Kyriake, or the Lords Day. The Disciples transferred to it the dignity of the Sabbath after the law of the Old Testament, and prescribed that it be a holiday and a day of rest. To Him be glory and power forever and ever. Amen.

Tone 2   Majesty, gentleness, hope, repentance and sadness.   *E, F, G, Ab, B, C.*

Having beheld the Resurrection of Christ, Let us worship the Holy Lord Jesus, the only sinless one. We venerate Thy cross, O Christ, and we praise and glorify Thy holy Resurrection for Thou art our God and we know no other than Thee. We call on Thy Name, Come all you faithful. Let us venerate Christ holy Resurrection, for Behold through the cross joy has come into all the world. Let us ever bless the Lord, Praising His Resurrection for by enduring the cross for us He has destroyed death by death. Jesus has Risen from the tomb as he foretold, Granting us eternal life, and great mercy.

(Chant)

Jesus having risen from the grave as he foretold. Has granted us life everlasting and great mercy. **(x3)**

Ode 7

Eirmos

Tone 6   Rich texture, funereal character, sorrowful tone.   *D, Eb, F##, G, A, Bb, C##, D.*

He who saved the three young men in the furnace became incarnate and suffered as a mortal man. Through his sufferings he clothed what is mortal in the robe of immortality. He alone is blessed and most glorious, God of our fathers.

Chorus: *Glory to Thy holy resurrection, O Lord.*

Troparion

The Godly women had hastened to Thee with myrrh, O Christ. In tears they had sought Thee as a dead man, but in joy they worshipped Thee as the living God and proclaimed the mystical Pascha to Thy disciples.

Chorus: *Glory to Thy holy resurrection, O Lord.*

We celebrate the death of death and the overthrow of hell, the beginning of another life which is eternal, and in exaltation we sing the praises of its source. He alone is blessed and most glorious, the God of our fathers.

Chorus: *Glory be to the Father and to the Son and to the Holy Spirit.*
Both now and forever and unto ages of ages, Amen.

This is the bright and saving night, sacred and supremely festal. It heralds the radiant day of the resurrection, on which the timeless light shown forth from the tomb of all.

Paschal Troparion

People:	*Christ is risen from the dead trampling down death by death;*
	and upon those in the tombs bestowing life.
Russian	Kristos voss kreysyey iz myert vikh. Smyertee oh smyert poh prav.
	Ee sooshim vogrow byekh zhivawt darowvav.
Greek	Χριστὸς ἀνέστη ἐκ νεκρῶν, θανάτῳ θάνατον πατήσας,
	καὶ τοῖς ἐν τοῖς μνήμασι, ζωὴν χαρισάμενος.
Romanian	Kristos aa inveeat din morts koo, mortay mortay kakoond.
	Shay chaylore deem ormintay veeaatsay, daaroo indoolay.

(Chant)
Jesus having risen from the grave, as he foretold. Has granted us life everlasting, and great mercy.

The Little Litany

Deacon: Again and again in peace, let us pray to the Lord.

Reader: *Lord, have mercy.*

Deacon: Help us; save us; have mercy on us; and keep us, O God, by Thy grace.

Reader: *Lord, have mercy.*

Deacon: Calling to remembrance our all holy, immaculate, most blessed and glorious Lady Theotokos and ever virgin Mary, with all the Saints, let us commend ourselves and each other, and all our life unto Christ our God.

Reader: *To Thee, O Lord.*

Priest: For Thou art holy, our God, and unto Thee do we ascribe Glory be to the Father, and to the Son, and to the Holy Spirit, now and ever, and unto ages of ages.

Reader: *Amen.*

Ode 8

Eirmos

Tone 1   *Magnificent, happy and earthy.*   *C, D, Eb, F, G, A, Bb, C.*

This is the chosen and holy day, first of Sabbaths king and Lord of days. The feast of feasts, holy day of holy days: on this day we bless Christ for evermore.

Chorus: *Glory to Thy holy resurrection, O Lord.*

Troparion

Come on this chosen day of the resurrection. Let us partake of the new fruit of the vine. Let us share in the divine rejoicing of the kingdom of Christ. Praising him as God forever more.

Chorus: *Glory to Thy holy resurrection, O Lord.*

Lift up thine eyes, O Zion, round about and see: thy children like divinely shining stars assemble from the north, the south, the east, and the west to bless Christ in you forever more. O most holy Trinity our God, glory to Thee.

Chorus: *Glory be to the Father and to the Son and to the Holy Spirit.*
           Both now and forever and unto ages of ages, Amen.

O Father Almighty, the Word, and the Spirit, one nature in three persons, surpassing essence and divinity. In Thee have we been baptised, and Thee we bless forever more.

Chorus: *We praise, we bless and we worship the Lord.*

Eirmos

This is the chosen and holy day, first of Sabbaths king and Lord of days. The feast of feasts, holy day of holy days: on this day we bless Christ for evermore.

Paschal Troparion

People: *Christ is risen from the dead trampling down death by death;*
           and upon those in the tombs bestowing life.

Russian   Kristos voss kreysyey iz myert vikh. Smyertee oh smyert poh prav.
           Ee sooshim vogrow byekh zhivawt darowvav.

Greek   Χριστὸς ἀνέστη ἐκ νεκρῶν, θανάτῳ θάνατον πατήσας,
           καὶ τοῖς ἐν τοῖς μνήμασι, ζωὴν χαρισάμενος.

Romanian Kristos aa inveeat din morts koo, mortay mortay kakoond.

Shay chaylore deem ormintay veeaatsay, daaroo indoolay.

(Chant)

Jesus having risen from the grave, as he foretold. Has granted us life everlasting, and great mercy.

The Little Litany

Deacon: Again and again in peace, let us pray to the Lord.

People: *Lord, have mercy.*

Deacon: Help us; save us; have mercy on us; and keep us, O God, by Thy grace.

People: *Lord, have mercy.*

Deacon: Calling to remembrance our all holy, immaculate, most blessed and glorious Lady Theotokos and ever virgin Mary, with all the Saints, let us commend ourselves and each other, and all our life unto Christ our God.

People: *To Thee, O Lord.*

Priest: For blessed is Thy Name, and glorified is Thy Kingdom of the Father, and of the Son, and of the Holy Spirit, now and ever, and until the ages of ages.

People: *Amen.*

Deacon: Let us magnify the Theotokos and Mother of the Light, honouring her with hymns.

Ode 9

Megalynarion

Tone 1   Magnificent, happy and earthy.   *C, D, Eb, F, G, A, Bb, C.*

Magnify, O my soul, Him who died of His own free will, and was buried, and did rise from the tomb on the third day.

Eirmos

Shine, shine you new Jerusalem, for the glory of the Lord is dawning upon ye. Exult and be glad O Zion, and O Virgin Theotokos, be radiant in the rising of thy son.

Megalynarion

Chorus: *Magnify, O my soul, the Life giving Christ; who is risen from the tomb on the third day.*

Eirmos

Shine, shine you new Jerusalem, for the glory of the Lord is dawning upon ye. Exult and be glad O Zion, and O Virgin Theotokos, be radiant in the rising of thy son.

Megalynarion

Chorus: *Verily, Christ is a new Pascha, a living Sacrifice, the Lamb of God who bears the sin of the world.*

Troparion

How noble, O how dear, how sweet is Thy voice O Christ; for Thou hast made us a promise, that Thou shalt be with us to the end of time; a promise to which we believers hold and an anchor for our hopes, as we sing rejoicing.

Megalynarion

Chorus: *Today does all creation rejoice and is glad; for Christ is risen, and hades He has despoiled.*

Troparion

How noble, O how dear, how sweet is Thy voice O Christ; for Thou hast made us a promise, that Thou shalt be with us to the end of time; a promise to which we believers hold and an anchor for our hopes, as we sing rejoicing.

Chorus: *Glory be to the Father and to the Son and to the Holy Spirit.*

Megalynarion

Chorus: *Magnify, O my soul, the might of the indivisible and three personned Godhead.*

Troparion

O Christ, the perfect, most exalted Pascha; O wisdom of God, his word and his power. Grant that we may partake of Thee more perfectly, in Thy kingdoms day which does not set.

Chorus: *Both now and forever and unto ages of ages. Amen.*

Megalynarion

Chorus: *Rejoice, O Virgin, rejoice; rejoice, O blessed one; rejoice, O glorified one; for thy Son is risen from the tomb on the third day.*

Troparion

O Christ, the perfect, most exalted Pascha; O wisdom of God, his word and his power. Grant that we may partake of Thee more perfectly, in Thy kingdoms day that sets not.

Megalynarion

Chorus: *The Angel cried out to the Lady full of grace: O Pure Virgin rejoice and again I say rejoice; behold thy son is risen from his three days in the tomb.*

Katavasia

Shine, Shine you new Jerusalem. For the glory of the Lord is dawning upon ye. Exult and be glad Zion, and O Virgin Theotokos. Be radiant in the rising of thy Son.

Paschal Troparion

People: *Christ is risen from the dead trampling down death by death;*

and upon those in the tombs bestowing life.

Russian Kristos voss kreysyey iz myert vikh. Smyertee oh smyert poh prav.

Ee sooshim vogrow byekh zhivawt darowvav.

Greek Χριστὸς ἀνέστη ἐκ νεκρῶν, θανάτῳ θάνατον πατήσας,

καὶ τοῖς ἐν τοῖς μνήμασι, ζωὴν χαρισάμενος.

Romanian Kristos aa inveeat din morts koo, mortay mortay kakoond.

Shay chaylore deem ormintay veeaatsay, daaroo indoolay.

(Chant)

Jesus having risen from the grave, as he foretold. Has granted us life everlasting, and great mercy.

The Little Litany

Deacon: Again and again, in peace, let us pray to the Lord.

People: *Lord, have mercy.*

Deacon: Help us; save us; have mercy on us; and keep us, O God, by Thy grace.

People: *Lord, have mercy.*

Deacon: Calling to remembrance our all holy, immaculate, most blessed and glorious Lady Theotokos and ever Virgin Mary, with all the Saints, let us commend ourselves and each other, and all our life unto Christ our God.

People: *To Thee, O Lord.*

Priest: For all the powers of heaven praise Thee, and unto Thee we ascribe glory to the Father, and to the Son, and to the Holy Spirit, now and forever, and unto ages of ages.

People: *Amen.*

Exaposteilarion

Tone 2   Majesty, gentleness, hope, repentance and sadness.   *E, F, G, Ab, B, C.*

When Thou didst fall asleep in the body as mortal, O Thou who art Lord and King, Thou didst abolish death. And on the third day Thou didst surely rise, verily raising Adam from corruption, O Thou incorruptible Pascha, O Salvation of the world. **(x3)**

Praises

Tone 1   Magnificent, happy and earthy.   *C, D, Eb, F, G, A, Bb, C.*

Chorus: *Praise Him for His mighty acts. Praise Him according to the multitude of His greatness.*

Reader: O Christ, Thy saving Passion do we praise; and Thy Resurrection do we glorify.

Chorus: *Praise Him with the sound of the trumpet. Praise Him with the psaltery and harp.*

Reader: O Thee who did submit to the Cross and did abolish death, who did arise from the dead, preserve our lives, O Lord, since Thou alone are almighty.

Chorus: *Praise Him with timbrel and dance. Praise Him with strings and flute.*

Reader: O Christ, who as a Destroyer did invade hades, and who did raise man by Thy Resurrection make us worthy to praise Thee with pure hearts, and to glorify Thee.

Chorus: *Praise Him with tuneful cymbals. Praise Him with cymbals of jubilation. Let everything that has breath praise the Lord.*

Reader: O Christ, we praise Thee, glorifying Thy condescension, which becomes God. O Thou who were born of a Virgin and were yet inseparable from the bosom of the Father; who did suffer like man, did submit to the Cross willingly, did arise from the tomb as from a chamber, that Thou might save the world, glory to Thee, O Lord.

The Stichera Of Pascha With Verses

Tone 5   Stimulating, dancing, and rhythmical.   C, D, Eb, F, G, A, Bb, C.

Chorus: *Let God arise, and let his enemies be scattered; and let them who hate him flee from before his face.*

Reader: Today a sacred Pascha is revealed to us. A new and Holy Pascha. A mystical Pascha, a Pascha worthy of veneration. A Pascha which is Christ, the redeemer. A blameless Pascha of the faithful. A Pascha which has opened for us the gates of paradise. A Pascha which sanctifies all the faithful.

Chorus: *As smoke vanishes so let them vanish away, as wax melts from the presence of the fire.*

Reader: Come from that scene O women bearers of glad tidings and say to Zion: receive from us the glad tiding of joy of Christ's resurrection: exult and be glad, and rejoice O Jerusalem, seeing Christ the king who comes forth from the tomb, like a bridegroom in procession.

Chorus: *So the sinners shall perish before the face of God, but let the righteous be glad.*

Reader: The myrrh bearing women at breaking of dawn drew near to the tomb of the life giver. There they found an angel sitting up on the stone, he greeted them with these words: Why do you seek the living among the dead? Why do you mourn the incorrupt amid corruption? Go proclaim the glad tidings to his disciples.

Chorus: *This is the day which the Lord has made. Let us rejoice and be glad in it.*

Reader: Pascha of beauty. The Pascha of the Lord. A Pascha worthy of all honour has dawned for us. Pascha. Let us embrace each other joyously. Pascha, ransom from affliction. For today as from a bridal chamber Christ has shone forth from the tomb. And filled the women with joy saying: Proclaim the glad tiding to the Apostles.

Chorus: *Glory be to the Father and to the Son and to the Holy Spirit.*

Both now and forever and unto ages of ages, Amen.

Doxasticon

Tone 5 Stimulating, dancing, and rhythmical.   C, D, Eb, F, G, A, Bb, C.

This is the day of Resurrection. Let us be illumined by the feast. Let us embrace each other. Let us call brothers even those that hate us and forgive all by the resurrection, and so let us cry:

People: *Christ is risen from the dead trampling down death by death;*

and upon those in the tombs bestowing life.

Russian Kristos voss kreysyey iz myert vikh. Smyertee oh smyert poh prav.

Ee sooshim vogrow byekh zhivawt darowvav.

Greek Χριστὸς ἀνέστη ἐκ νεκρῶν, θανάτῳ θάνατον πατήσας,

καὶ τοῖς ἐν τοῖς μνήμασι, ζωὴν χαρισάμενος.

Romanian Kristos aa inveeat din morts koo, mortay mortay kakoond.

Shay chaylore deem ormintay veeaatsay, daaroo indoolay.

The Catechetical Homily Of Our Father John Chrysostom, Archbishop Of Constantinople

[For the Holy and Light bearing Day of the Holy and Saving Resurrection of Christ our God.]

Reader: Holy Father, Bless.

Priest: If any be pious and a lover of God, let him partake of this good and radiant festival. If any be a wise servant, let him rejoicing enter into the joy of his Lord. If any have wearied himself in fasting, let him now partake of his recompense. If any have wrought from the first hour, let him receive today his rightful due. If any have come after the third hour, let him feast with thanksgiving. If any have arrived at the sixth hour, let him have no misgivings, for he shall in no wise suffer loss. If any have delayed until the ninth hour, let him draw near, not wavering. If any have arrived only at the eleventh hour, let him not fear for his tardiness. For the Master, who loves his honour, accepts the last even as the first. He giveth rest to the one who came at the eleventh hour, as to the one who wrought from the first. And He has mercy on the one that delays, and he cares for the first. To the one He giveth, and on the other He bestows gifts. He both accepts the works, and welcomes the intention; He honours the acts, and praises the purpose. Enter you all, therefore, into the joy of our Lord. you first and you second, partake of the reward. you rich and you poor, dance thy joy together. you that abstain and you slothful, honour the day. you that have fasted, and you that have not fasted, be glad today. The table is laden; do you all fare sumptuously. The calf is fatted; let none go away hungered. Partake you all of the banquet of faith. Partake you all of the riches of loving kindness. Let none lament his neediness, for the common kingdom has been revealed. Let none grieve for his offences, for pardon has shone forth from the grave. Let none fear death, for the Saviour's death has set us free. He that was held by it has quenched it. He that descended into Hell has despoiled Hell. He embittered it, which had tasted of His flesh, and Isaiah, anticipating this says:

Priest: Hell was embittered

Reader: Epichranthé.

Priest: When it met Thee below. He was embittered

Reader: Epichranthé.

Priest: for he was overthrown. He was embittered

Reader: Epichranthé.

Priest: for he was deceived. He was embittered

Reader: Epichranthé.

Priest: for he was slain. He was embittered

Reader: Epichranthé.

Priest: for he was cast down. He was embittered

Reader: Epichranthé.

Priest: for he was fettered. He took a body and encountered God. He took earth and met heaven. He took what it saw and fell upon what it saw not. Where is thy sting, O Death? O Hell, where is thy victory?

Priest: Arisen is Christ

Reader: Anesté.

Priest: and thou art overthrown. Arisen is Christ

Reader: Anesté.

Priest: and the demons are fallen. Arisen is Christ

Reader: Anesté.

Priest: and the angels rejoice. Arisen is Christ

Reader: Anesté.

Priest: and life prevaileth, Arisen is Christ

Reader: Anesté.

Priest: and there is none dead in the tomb. For Christ, in arising from the dead is become the first fruits of those that have fallen asleep. To Him be glory and might unto ages of ages. Amen.

Dismissal Hymn Of St John Chrysostom

Tone 8   *Humility, tranquillity, repose, suffering, pleading.*   *C, D, Eb, F, G, A, Bb, C.*
Grace shining forth from thy mouth like a beacon has illumined the universe, and disclosed to the world treasures of uncovetousness, and shown us the heights of humility; but whilst instructing us by thy words; O Father John Chrysostom, intercede with the Word, Christ our God. O save our souls.

Divine Liturgy Of St John Chrysostom

(Long Introduction)

Priest: Glory to the holy, consubstantial, life giving and undivided Trinity, always, now and forever and to the ages of ages.

People: *Amen.*

Priest & All: Christ is risen from the dead, trampling down death by death,
and upon those in the tombs bestowing life.

People: Kristos voss kreysyey iz myert vikh. Smyertee oh smyert poh prav.
Ee sooshim vogrow byekh zhivawt darowvav.

People: Χριστὸς ἀνέστη ἐκ νεκρῶν, θανάτῳ θάνατον πατήσας,
καὶ τοῖς ἐν τοῖς μνήμασι, ζωὴν χαρισάμενος.

Priest: Let God arise and let His enemies be scattered and let those who hate
Him flee from His face.

People: Christ is risen from the dead, trampling down death by death,
and upon those in the tombs bestowing life.

Priest: They shall vanish as smoke vanishes and melt as wax melts.

People: Kristos voss kreysyey iz myert vikh. Smyertee oh smyert poh prav.
Ee sooshim vogrow byekh zhivawt darowvav.

Priest: Thus shall the ungodly perish in the presence of God, but the righteous shall rejoice.

People: Χριστὸς ἀνέστη ἐκ νεκρῶν, θανάτῳ θάνατον πατήσας,
καὶ τοῖς ἐν τοῖς μνήμασι, ζωὴν χαρισάμενος.

Priest: This is the day that the Lord has made, let us rejoice and be glad in it.

People: Christ is risen from the dead, trampling down death by death,
and upon those in the tombs bestowing life.

Priest: Glory be to the Father and to the Son and to the Holy Spirit.

People: Kristos voss kreysyey iz myert vikh. Smyertee oh smyert poh prav.
Ee sooshim vogrow byekh zhivawt darowvav.

Priest: Both Now and forever and to the ages of ages.

People: Χριστὸς ἀνέστη ἐκ νεκρῶν, θανάτῳ θάνατον πατήσας,
καὶ τοῖς ἐν τοῖς μνήμασι, ζωὴν χαρισάμενος.

First Antiphon

Reader: Shout with jubilation unto the Lord, all the earth.

People: At the prayers of the Mother of God, O Saviour, save us.

Reader: Chant you unto His Name, give glory in praise of Him.

People: At the prayers of the Mother of God, O Saviour, save us.

Reader: Say unto God: How awesome are Thy works.
In the multitude of Thy power shall Thine enemies be proved false unto Thee.

People: At the prayers of the Mother of God, O Saviour, save us.

Reader:	Let all the earth worship and chant unto Thee.
	Let them chant unto Thy Name O Most High,
People:	*At the prayers of the Mother of God, O Saviour, save us.*
Reader:	Glory be to the Father, and to the Son, and to the Holy Spirit.
	Both now and forever, and unto the ages of ages. Amen.
People:	*At the prayers of the Mother of God	O Saviour, save us.*

Second Antiphon

Reader:	May God have mercy upon us and bless us.
	May He cause His face to shine upon us, and have mercy on us.
People:	*Save us, O Son of God risen from the dead; Save us who sing to Thee: Halleluiah.*
Reader:	That Thy way may be known upon earth, Thy salvation among all nations.
	Let the peoples give thanks to Thee, O God, let all the peoples give thanks to Thee.
People:	*Save us, O Son of God risen from the dead; Save us who sing to Thee: Halleluiah.*
Reader:	Let the peoples give Thee praise. O God let all the peoples praise Thee.
People:	*Save us, O Son of God risen from the dead; Save us who sing to Thee: Halleluiah.*
Reader:	May God bless us, and may all the ends of the earth fear Him
People:	*Save us, O Son of God risen from the dead; Save us who sing to Thee: Halleluiah.*
Reader:	Glory be to the Father, and to the Son, and to the Holy Spirit.
Priest:	Both now and forever, and unto the ages of ages. Amen.

Third Antiphon

Reader:	Let God arise, and let his enemies be scattered;
	And let those who hate Him flee from His face.
Chorus:	*Christ is risen from the dead, trampling down death by death,*
	and upon those in the tombs bestowing life.

Reader:	As smoke vanishes, let them vanish; as wax melts before the fire.
Russian	*Kristos voss kreysyey iz myert vikh. Smyertee oh smyert poh prav.*
	Ee sooshim vogrow byekh zhivawt darowvav.

Reader:	So let the sinners perish before God, but let the righteous rejoice.
Greek	Χριστὸς ἀνέστη ἐκ νεκρῶν, θανάτῳ θάνατον πατήσας,
	καὶ τοῖς ἐν τοῖς μνήμασι, ζωὴν χαρισάμενος.

Reader:	This is the day which the Lord has made; let us rejoice and be glad in it.
People:	*Christ is risen from the dead trampling down death by death;*
	and upon those in the tombs bestowing life.

Russian Kristos voss kreysyey iz myert vikh. Smyertee oh smyert poh prav.

Ee sooshim vogrow byekh zhivawt darowvav.

Greek Χριστὸς ἀνέστη ἐκ νεκρῶν, θανάτῳ θάνατον πατήσας,

καὶ τοῖς ἐν τοῖς μνήμασι, ζωὴν χαρισάμενος.

Romanian Kristos aa inveeat din morts koo, mortay mortay kakoond.

Shay chaylore deem ormintay veeaatsay, daaroo indoolay.

Entrance Hymn

Reader: In the gathering places bless God the Lord from the springs of Israel.

People: *Save us, O Son of God risen from the dead, as we sing to Thee: Halleluiah.*

After the Little Entrance *(Priest enters)*:

Reader: Christ is risen from the dead, trampling down death by death,

and upon those in the tombs bestowing life.

Russian Kristos voss kreysyey iz myert vikh. Smyertee oh smyert poh prav.

Ee sooshim vogrow byekh zhivawt darowvav.

Greek Χριστὸς ἀνέστη ἐκ νεκρῶν, θανάτῳ θάνατον πατήσας,

καὶ τοῖς ἐν τοῖς μνήμασι, ζωὴν χαρισάμενος.

[No Saints of the day during Pascha entire season or any Great Feast or a major Saints day.]

Paschal Hypakoe

Tone 4   Festive, joyous and expressing deep piety.   *C, D, Eb, F, G, A, Bb, C.*

They who were with Mary came before the dawn, found the stone rolled away from the sepulchre, and heard the angels say unto them, Why seek you him as man with the dead, who dwells in light eternal? Behold the grave wrappings; make haste and declare to the world that the Lord is risen, and has caused death to die; for he is the Son of God, the Saviour of mankind.

Glory be to the Father, and to the Son, and to the Holy Spirit;

Kontakion

Tone 8   Humility, tranquillity, repose, suffering, pleading.   *C, D, Eb, F, G, A, Bb, C.*

Though Thee, O deathless One, did descend into the grave, Thou didst destroy the power of hell and, as Victor, Thou didst rise again, O Christ our God. Thou didst greet the ointment bearing women, saying, Rejoice. Thou didst bestow peace upon Thy Disciples, and resurrection upon those that are fallen.

*Both now and forever, and unto the ages of ages. **Amen.***

Instead of the Trisagion Hymn ("Holy God")

People: As many as have been baptised into Christ, have put on Christ. Halleluiah. **(x3)**

Glory be to the Father, and to the Son, and to the Holy Spirit;

Both now and forever, and unto the ages of ages. Amen.

Have put on Christ. Halleluiah.

Priest: Dynamis.

People: As many as have been baptised into Christ, have put on Christ. Halleluiah.

Prokeimenon

Reader: This is the day that the Lord has made, let us rejoice and be glad in it.

People: *This is the day that the Lord has made, let us rejoice and be glad in it.*

Reader: O give thanks to the Lord for He is good; for His mercy endures forever.

People: *This is the day that the Lord has made, let us rejoice and be glad in it.*

Reader: This is the day that the Lord has made | let us rejoice and be glad in it.

The Reading Is From The Blessed Apostle Lukes Acts Of The Apostles 1:1-8.

In the first book, O Theophilos, I have dealt with all that Jesus began to do and teach, until the day when he was taken up, after he had given commandment through the Holy Spirit to the apostles whom he had chosen. To them he presented himself alive after his passion by any proofs, appearing to them during forty days, and speaking of the kingdom of God. And while staying with them he charged them not to depart from Jerusalem, but to wait for the promise of the Father, which, he said, "You heard from me, for John baptised with water, but before many days you shall be baptised with the Holy Spirit."

So when they had come together, they asked him, "Lord, willest Thou at this time restore the kingdom of Israel?" He said to them, "It is not for you to know times or seasons which the Father has fixed by his own authority. But you shall receive power when the Holy Spirit has come upon ye; and you shall be my witnesses in Jerusalem and in all Judea and Samaria and to the end of the earth."

Priest: Peace be with thee who readest.

Reader: And with thy spirit.

Halleluiarion

People: *Halleluiah, Halleluiah, Halleluiah.*

Reader: Thou, O Lord shall rise up and have pity upon Zion;

For it is time to have compassion on her, yea the time is come.

People: *Halleluiah, Halleluiah, Halleluiah.*

Reader: The Lord from Heaven has looked upon the earth;

To hear the groaning of them that be in fetters, to loose the sons of the slain.

People: *Halleluiah, Halleluiah, Halleluiah.*

The Reading Is From The Gospel According To St John 1:1-17.

In the beginning was the Word, and the Word was with God, and the Word was God. He was in the beginning with God; all things were made through him, and without him was not anything made that was made. In him was life, and the life was the light of men. The light shines in the darkness, and the darkness has not overcome it....

There was a man sent from God, whose name was John. He came for testimony, to bear witness to the light, that all might believe through him. He was not the light, but came to bear witness to the light. The true light that enlightens every man was coming into the world. He was in the world, and the world was made through him, yet the world knew him not. He came to his own home, and his own people received him not. But to all who received him, who believed in his name, he gave power to become children of God; who were born, not of blood nor of the will of the flesh nor of the will of man, but of God.

And the Word became flesh and dwelt among us, full of grace and truth; we have beheld his glory, glory as of the only Son from the Father. (John bore witness to him, and cried, "This was he of whom I said, 'He who comes after me ranks before me, for he was before me.'") And from his fullness have we all received, grace upon grace. For the law was given through Moses; grace and truth came through Jesus Christ. No one has ever seen God; the only Son, who is in the bosom of the Father, he has made him known.

Instead of "It is truly right... "

The Megalynarion

Chorus: *The angel cried out to the Lady full of grace: O Pure Virgin rejoice and again I say rejoice; behold thy son is risen from his three days in the tomb.*

Reader: Shine, shine you new Jerusalem, for the glory of the Lord is dawning upon ye. Exult and be glad O Zion, and O Virgin Theotokos, be radiant in the rising of thy son.

Konoinikon:

   Tone 8   Humility, tranquillity, repose, suffering, pleading.   C, D, Eb, F, G, A, Bb, C.

Receive the Body of Christ, and taste of Him who is the Fountain of immortality. Halleluiah.

Post Communion:

Instead of "We have seen the true Light...", sing ONCE:

Christ is risen from the dead, trampling down death by death, and upon those in the tombs bestowing life.

Dismissal:

Instead of "Blessed be the name of the Lord":

Paschal Troparion

People: Christ is risen from the dead trampling down death by death,

            and upon those in the tombs bestowing life.

Russian	Kristos voss kreysyey iz myert vikh. Smyertee oh smyert poh prav.
	Ee sooshim vogrow byekh zhivawt darowvav.
Greek	Χριστὸς ἀνέστη ἐκ νεκρῶν, θανάτῳ θάνατον πατήσας,
	καὶ τοῖς ἐν τοῖς μνήμασι, ζωὴν χαρισάμενος.
Romanian	Kristos aa inveeat din morts koo, mortay mortay kakoond.
	Shay chaylore deem ormintay veeaatsay, daaroo indoolay.

The Blessing of the Eggs and Cheese is recited before the dismissal.

Dismissal

After the long prayer by the Priest, long dismissal:

Priest: Christ is risen.

People: *He is risen indeed.*

Priest: Christos Anesti.

People: *Alithos anesti.*

Priest: Kristos Voskresey.

People: *Voyistino Voskresey.*

Priest: Glory to his resurrection on the third day.

People: *We worship his resurrection on the third day.*

Priest: To him be the glory, dominion, honour and worship to the ages of ages.

People: *Amen.*

Troparion	Christ is risen from the dead, trampling down death by death,
	and upon those in the tombs bestowing life.
Russian	Kristos voss kreysyey iz myert vikh. Smyertee oh smyert poh prav.
	Ee sooshim vogrow byekh zhivawt darowvav.
Greek	Χριστὸς ἀνέστη ἐκ νεκρῶν, θανάτῳ θάνατον πατήσας,
	καὶ τοῖς ἐν τοῖς μνήμασι, ζωὴν χαρισάμενος.
Romanian	Kristos aa inveeat din morts koo, mortay mortay kakoond.
	Shay chaylore deem ormintay veeaatsay, daaroo indoolay.

Priest:	**English**	Christ is risen.	*People:*	*He is risen indeed.*
Priest:	**Greek**	Christos Anesti.	*People:*	*Alithos anesti.*
Priest:	**Russian**	Kristos Voskresey.	*People:*	*Voyistino Voskresey.*
Priest:	**Romanian**	Kristos aa inveeat.	*People:*	Add-evar-at aainveeat.
Priest:	**Albanian**	Kristi Unjhal.	*People:*	Vertet Unjhal.
Priest:	**Welsh**	Atgyfododd Crist.	*People:*	Atgyfododd yn wir.

Priest: Glory to the Holy, Consubstantial, Life giving and undivided Trinity, always, now and ever, and unto ages of ages.

People: Amen.

[Bearing the Paschal Candle, the Priest then leads the singing of the Paschal Apolytikion and censes the Altar as follows:]

Priest: Christ is risen from the dead, trampling down Death by death;
And upon those in the tombs bestowing life.

Russian Kristos voss kreysyey iz myert vikh. Smyertee oh smyert poh prav.
Ee sooshim vogrow byekh zhivawt darowvav.

Greek Χριστὸς ἀνέστη ἐκ νεκρῶν, θανάτῳ θάνατον πατήσας,
καὶ τοῖς ἐν τοῖς μνήμασι, ζωὴν χαρισάμενος.

[Censing the west side of the Altar]

Priest: Let God arise, and let His enemies be scattered;
And let those who hate Him flee from before His face.

People: *Christ is risen from the dead, trampling down Death by death;*
And upon those in the tombs, bestowing life.

[Censing the south side of the Altar:]

Priest: As smoke vanisheth, so let them vanish; as wax melteth before the fire.

Russian Kristos voss kreysyey iz myert vikh. Smyertee oh smyert poh prav.
Ee sooshim vogrow byekh zhivawt darowvav.

[Censing the east side of the Altar:]

Priest: So let sinners perish at the presence of God, and let the righteous be glad.

Greek Χριστὸς ἀνέστη ἐκ νεκρῶν, θανάτῳ θάνατον πατήσας,
καὶ τοῖς ἐν τοῖς μνήμασι, ζωὴν χαρισάμενος.

[Censing the north side of the Altar:]

Priest: This is the day which the Lord hath made; let us rejoice and be glad therein.

People: *Christ is risen from the dead, trampling down Death by death;*
And upon those in the tombs, bestowing life.

[Censing the Prothesis and the remainder of the Sanctuary:]

Priest: Glory be to the Father, and to the Son, and to the Holy Spirit.

Russian   Kristos voss kreysyey iz myert vikh. Smyertee oh smyert poh prav.

Ee sooshim vogrow byekh zhivawt darowvav.

[Censing the Iconostasis from the Royal Doors:]

Priest: Both now and forever, and unto the ages of ages. Amen.

Greek   Χριστὸς ἀνέστη ἐκ νεκρῶν, θανάτῳ θάνατον πατήσας,

καὶ τοῖς ἐν τοῖς μνήμασι, ζωὴν χαρισάμενος.

[The Priest completes the censing while singing:]

Priest: Christ is risen from the dead, trampling down Death by death; and upon those in the tombs...

People: ...bestowing life.

[Psalm 103 is omitted.]

The Great Litany

Deacon: In peace, let us pray to the Lord.

People: *Lord, have mercy.*

Deacon: For the peace from above, and for the salvation of our souls, let us pray to the Lord.

People: *Lord, have mercy.*

Deacon: For the peace of the whole world, for the good estate of the holy churches of God, and for the union of all men, let us pray to the Lord.

People: *Lord, have mercy.*

Deacon: For this Holy House, and for those who with faith, reverence, and fear of God, enter therein, let us pray to the Lord.

People: *Lord, have mercy.*

Deacon: For our Archbishop Nikitas, for the venerable Priesthood, the Diaconate in Christ, for all the clergy and the people, let us pray to the Lord.

People: *Lord, have mercy.*

Deacon: For Elizabeth The Queen and the Royal Family, for all civil authorities, and for our Armed Forces everywhere, let us pray to the Lord.

People: *Lord, have mercy.*

Deacon: That He shall aid them and grant them victory over every enemy and adversary, let us pray to the Lord.

People: *Lord, have mercy.*

Deacon: For this *[city / town / village]*, and for every *[city / town / village]* and land, and for the faithful who dwell therein, let us pray to the Lord.

People: *Lord, have mercy.*

Deacon: For healthful seasons, for abundance of the fruits of the earth, and for peaceful times, let us pray to the Lord.

People: *Lord, have mercy.*

Deacon: For travellers by sea, by land, and by air; for the sick and the suffering; for captives and their salvation, let us pray to the Lord.

People: *Lord, have mercy.*

Deacon: For our deliverance from all tribulation, wrath, danger, and necessity, let us pray to the Lord.

People: *Lord, have mercy.*

Deacon: Help us; save us; have mercy on us; and keep us, O God, by Thy grace.

People: *Lord, have mercy.*

Deacon: Calling to remembrance our all holy, immaculate, most blessed and glorious Lady Theotokos and ever virgin Mary, with all the Saints: let us commend ourselves and each other, and all our life unto Christ our God.

People: *To Thee, O Lord.*

Priest: For unto Thee are due all glory, honour, and worship: to the Father, and to the Son, and to the Holy Spirit; now and forever and unto ages of ages.

People: *Amen.*

Lord, I Have Cried.

Lord, I have cried to Thee: hear me. Hear me, O Lord.

Lord, I have cried to Thee: hear me. Receive the voice of my prayer.

When I call upon Thee, hear me, O Lord. Let my prayer arise as incense in Thy sight,

And let the lifting up of my hands be an evening sacrifice. Hear me, O Lord.

Kekragarion
Sticheroi From Psalm 140

• Set, O Lord, a watch before my mouth, and a door of enclosure round about my lips.

• Incline not my heart to words of evil, to make excuses for sins.

• Those that work iniquity; I shall not join with their number.

• The righteous man shall chasten me with mercy and reprove me; as for the oil of the sinner, let it not anoint my head.

• For yet more is my prayer in the presence of their pleasures; their judges have been swallowed up by the rock.

• They shall hear my words, for they be sweetened; as a clod of earth is broken upon the earth, so have their bones been scattered into hades.

• To Thee O Lord are mine eyes. In Thee have I hoped; take not my soul away.

• Keep me from the snare which they have laid for me, and from the stumbling blocks of them that work iniquity.

• The sinners shall fall into their own net; I am alone until I pass by.

Sticheroi From Psalm 141

- With my voice to the Lord have I cried, with my voice have I made supplication.

- I shall pour out before Him my supplications; my afflictions shall I declare before Him.

- When my spirit was fainting within me, then Thou knewest my paths.

- In this way wherein I have walked they hid for me a snare.

- I looked on my right hand, and beheld, and there was none that knew me.

- Flight has failed me, and there is none that watches out for my soul.

- I cried to Thee, O Lord; I said: Thou art my hope, my portion in the land of the living.

- Attend unto my supplication, for I am brought very low.

- Deliver me from them that persecute me, for they are stronger than I.

- Bring my soul out of prison.

- That I may confess Thy name.

- The righteous shall patiently wait for me until Thou shalt reward me.

Sticheroi From Psalm 129

- Out of the depths have I cried unto Thee, O Lord. O Lord, hear my voice.

- Let Thine ears be attentive to the voice of my supplication.

- If Thou should mark iniquities, O Lord; O Lord, who shall stand? For with Thee there is forgiveness.

- For Thy name's sake have I patiently waited for Thee, O Lord; my soul has patiently waited for Thy word, my soul has hoped in the Lord.

For The Resurrection

Tone 2   Majesty, gentleness, hope, repentance and sadness.   *E, F, G, Ab, B, C.*

Chorus: *From the morning watch until night, from the morning watch let Israel hope in the Lord.*

Reader: Come ye, let us worship Him Who was born of the Father before all time, the Word of God, incarnate of the Virgin Mary; for He did submit to crucifixion by His own choice, was delivered to burial as He Himself willed, rose from the dead, and saved me, who was lost.

Chorus: *For with the Lord there is mercy and with Him is abundant redemption, and He shall deliver Israel from all his iniquities.*

Reader: Verily, Christ our Saviour nailed to His Cross the handwriting of the decree, and did expunge it. And He abolished the might of Death. Let us therefore adore His third day Resurrection.

Sticheroi From Psalm 116

Chorus: *Praise the Lord, all you nations; praise Him, all you people.*

Reader: Come, let us with the archangels praise the Resurrection of Christ; for He is the Redeemer and Saviour of our souls, and He it is Who shall come with fearful magnificence and glorious might to judge the world which He hath created.

Chorus: *For His mercy is great toward us, and the truth of the Lord endureth forever.*

Reader: O Thou Who wast crucified and wast buried, the angel did proclaim Thee, that Thou art the Master, saying to the women, Come you and behold where the Lord was laid; for He is risen as He said; for He is the Almighty One, and therefore, do we worship Thee, O Thou Who alone art deathless; O Christ, Giver of life, have mercy upon us.

Chorus: *Glory to the Father, and to the Son, and to the Holy Spirit.*

Reader: Come, let us all sing with our mouths a song of salvation. Let us kneel down in the house of the Lord, saying, "O Thou who wast crucified on a Tree, who didst rise from the dead, and who still remainest in the bosom of the Father, forgive us our sins."

Chorus: *Both now and forever, and unto ages of ages. Amen.*

Theotokion For The Resurrection

Tone 2   Majesty, gentleness, hope, repentance and sadness.   *E, F, G, Ab, B, C.*

O Virgin, verily, the shadow of the law hath been annulled by the coming of thy grace; for as the bush was burning but not consumed, so didst thou give birth while yet a Virgin. And instead of the pillar of fire, the Sun of justice shone forth; and instead of Moses, Christ the Saviour of our souls.

The Holy Entrance

Deacon: Let us pray to the Lord.

People: *Lord, have mercy.*

Priest: In the evening and in the morning and at noonday we praise Thee, we bless Thee, we give thanks unto Thee, and we pray unto Thee, O Master of all, Lord Who lovest mankind: Direct our prayer as incense before Thee, and incline not our hearts unto words or thoughts of evil, but deliver us from all who seek after our souls. For unto Thee, O Lord, Lord, are our eyes, and in Thee have we hoped. Put us not to shame, O our God. For unto Thee are due all glory, honour, and worship: to the Father and to the Son and to the Holy Spirit, now and ever, and unto ages of ages.

People: *Amen.*

(The clergy process to the centre of the solea and:)

Deacon: *[soto voce]* Father, bless the Holy Entrance.

Priest: *[soto voce]* Blessed is the entrance to Thy Holy Place, always, now and forever, and unto the ages of ages. Amen.

[After the Chorus has finished:]

Deacon: *[aloud]* Wisdom. Let us attend.

O Gladsome Light

O Gladsome Light of the holy glory of the immortal Father.

Heavenly holy, blessed Jesus Christ;

Now that we have come to the setting of the sun, and behold the Evening Light;

We praise God; Father, Son and Holy Spirit.

For meet it is at all time to worship Thee, with voices of praise;

O Son of God and Giver of Life. Therefore all the world doth glorify Thee.

Deacon: The Evening Prokeimenon.

The Great Prokeimenon

Tone 7   *Manly character and strong melody.*   *F, G, A, A#, C, D, E, F.*

Reader: Who is so great a god as our God? Thou art the God Who worketh wonders.

Chorus: *Who is so great a god as our God? Thou art the God Who worketh wonders.*

Reader: Thou hast made Thy power known among the peoples;

With Thine arm hast Thou redeemed Thy people.

Chorus: *Who is so great a god as our God? Thou art the God Who worketh wonders.*

Reader: And I said: Now have I made a beginning;

This change hath been wrought by the right hand of the Most High.

Chorus: *Who is so great a god as our God? Thou art the God Who worketh wonders.*

Reader: I remembered the works of the Lord.

For I shall remember Thy wonders from the beginning.

Chorus: *Who is so great a god as our God? Thou art the God Who worketh wonders.*

Reader: Who is so great a god as our God? | Thou art the God Who worketh wonders.

The Paschal Agape Gospel

Deacon: And that we may be accounted worthy to hear the Holy Gospel, let us pray to the Lord God.

People: *Lord, have mercy.* **(x3)**

Deacon: Wisdom. Attend. Let us hear the Holy Gospel.

Priest: Peace be with you all.

People: *And with thy spirit.*

Priest: The Reading from the Holy Gospel according to Saint John.

People: *Glory to Thee, O Lord, glory to Thee.*

Deacon: Let us attend.

The Holy Gospel According To Saint John 20:19-25.

[The Gospel reading is done in as many languages as the clergy and people can manage. Here are some examples.]

Czech

Téhož dne večer byli učedníci pohromadě za zamčenými dveřmi, protože se báli, že teď přijdou Židé na ně. Pojednou stál Ježíš mezi nimi a řekl: "Pokoj vám." Potom jim ukázal rány v rukou a v boku. To byla radost pro učedníky, že zase vidí svého Pána.

Ježíš opakoval: "Pokoj vám." a pokračoval: "Otec vyslal mne a já vysílám vás." Dýchl na ně a řekl: "Přijměte svatého Ducha. Komu budete zvěstovat odpuštění hříchů a přijme je, tomu bude odpuštěno. Komu tu zvěst zadržíte, zůstává ve svém hříchu."

Toho večera chyběl mezi učedníky Tomáš, kterému přezdívali Dvojče. Ostatní mu o setkání s Ježíšem vyprávěli, ale on pochyboval: "Neuvěřím, dokud neuvidím a neohmatám rány na jeho rukou a boku."

French

Ce même dimanche, dans la soirée, les disciples étaient dans une maison dont ils avaient verrouillé les portes, parce qu'ils avaient peur des chefs des Juifs. Jésus vint: il se trouva là, au milieu d'eux, et il leur dit: Que la paix soit avec vous. Tout en disant cela, il leur montra ses mains et son côté. Les disciples furent remplis de joie parce qu'ils voyaient le Seigneur.

Que la paix soit avec vous, leur ditil de nouveau. Comme mon Père m'a envoyé, moi aussi je vous envoie. Après avoir dit cela, il souffla sur eux et continua: Recevez l'Esprit Saint. Ceux à qui vous remettrez leurs péchés en seront effectivement tenus quittes; et ceux à qui vous les retiendrez en resteront chargés.

L'un des Douze, Thomas, surnommé le Jumeau, n'était pas avec eux lors de la venue de Jésus. Les autres disciples lui dirent: Nous avons vu le Seigneur. Mais il leur répondit: Si je ne vois pas la marque des clous dans ses mains, si je ne mets pas mon doigt à la place des clous, et si je ne mets pas la main dans son côté, je ne croirai pas.

Welsh

Yna, a hi yn hwyr y dydd cyntaf hwnnw o'r wythnos, a'r drysau yn gauad lle yr oedd y disgyblion wedi ymgasglu ynghyd rhag ofn yr Iuddewon, daeth yr Iesu, ac a safodd yn y canol, ac a ddywedodd wrthynt, Tangnefedd i chi. Ac wedi iddo ddywedyd hyn, efe a ddangosodd iddynt ei ddwylaw a'i ystlys. Yna y disgyblion a lawenychasant pan welsant yr Arglwydd.

Yna y dywedodd yr Iesu wrthynt drachefn, Tangnefedd i chi: megis y danfonodd y Tad fi, yr wyf finnau yn eich danfan chi. Ac wedi iddo ddywedyd hyn, efe a anadlodd arnynt, ac a ddywedodd wrthynt, Derbyniwch yr Ysbryd Glân. Pwy bynnag y maddeuwch eu pechodau, maddau iddynt; â'r eiddo pwy bechodau i cadw, hwy i cadw.

Eithr Thomas, un o'r deuddeg, yr hwn a elwir Didymus, nid oedd gyd â hwynt pan ddaeth yr Iesu. Y disgyblion eraill gan hynny a ddywedasant wrtho, Ni a welsom yr Arglwydd. Yntau a ddywedodd wrthynt, Oni chaf weled yn ei ddwylaw ef ôl yr hoelion, a dodi fy llaw yn ei ystlys ef, ni chredaf fi.

English

On the evening of that day, the first day of the week, the doors being shut where the Disciples were, for fear of the Jews, Jesus came and stood among them and said to them, "Peace be with ye." When He had said this, He showed them His hands and His side. Then the Disciples were glad when they saw the Lord.

Jesus said to them again, "Peace be with ye. As the Father has sent Me, even so I send ye." And when He had said this, He breathed on them, and said to them, "Receive the Holy Spirit. If you forgive the sins of any, they are forgiven; if you retain the sins of any, they are retained."

Now Thomas, one of the twelve, called the Twin, was not with them when Jesus came. So the other Disciples told him, "We have seen the Lord." But he said to them, "Unless I see in His hands the print of the nails, and place my finger in the mark of the nails, and place my hand in His side, I shall not believe."

People: *Glory to Thee, O Lord, glory to Thee.*

The Litany Of Fervent Supplication

Deacon: Let us say with our whole soul, and with our whole mind, let us say.

People: *Lord, have mercy.*

Deacon: O Lord Almighty, the God of our Fathers, we pray Thee, hearken and have mercy.

People: *Lord, have mercy.*

Deacon: Have mercy on us, O God, according to Thy great mercy, we pray Thee, hearken and have mercy.

People: *Lord, have mercy.* **(x3)**

Deacon: Again we pray for all pious and Orthodox Christians.

People: *Lord, have mercy.* **(x3)**

Deacon: Again we pray for our Archbishop <u>Nikitas</u>.

People: *Lord, have mercy.* **(x3)**

Deacon: Again we pray for our brethren: the priests, hieromonks, deacons, hierodeacons and monastics and all our brotherhood in Christ.

People: *Lord, have mercy.* **(x3)**

Deacon: Again we pray for mercy, life, peace, health, salvation and visitation and pardon and remission of sins for (the servants of God, *[Names]*, and) all Orthodox Christians of true worship, who live and dwell in this community.

People: *Lord, have mercy.* **(x3)**

Deacon: Again we pray for the blessed and ever memorable founders of this holy church and (for the departed servants of God, *[Names]*, and) all our fathers and brethren, the Orthodox departed this life before us, who here and in all the world lie asleep in the Lord.

People: *Lord, have mercy.* **(x3)**

Deacon: Again we pray for those who bear fruit and do good works in this holy and all venerable temple, those who serve and those who sing, and for all the people here present, who await Thy great and rich mercy.

People: *Lord, have mercy.* **(x3)**

Priest: For Thou art a merciful God and lovest mankind, and unto Thee we ascribe glory: to the Father, and to the Son, and to the Holy Spirit; now and ever, and unto ages of ages.

People: Amen.

The Evening Prayer

Reader: Vouchsafe, O Lord, to keep us this evening without sin. Blessed art Thou, O Lord, the God of our fathers, and praised and glorified is Thy Name forever. Amen. Let Thy mercy be upon us, O Lord, even as we have set our hope on Thee.

Blessed art Thou, O Lord; teach me Thy statutes.

Blessed art Thou, O Master; make me to understand Thy statutes.

Blessed art Thou, O Holy One; enlighten me with Thy statutes.

Thy mercy, O Lord, endureth forever. O despise not the works of Thy hands. To Thee belongeth worship, to Thee belongeth praise, to Thee belongeth glory: to the Father and to the Son and to the Holy Spirit, now and ever, and unto ages of ages. Amen.

The Litany Of Supplication

Deacon: Let us complete our evening prayer unto the Lord.

People: Lord, have mercy.

Deacon: Help us; save us; have mercy on us; and keep us, O God, by Thy grace.

People: Lord, have mercy.

Deacon: That the whole evening may be perfect, holy, peaceful and sinless, let us ask of the Lord.

People: Grant this, O Lord.

Deacon: An angel of peace, a faithful guide, a guardian of our souls and bodies, let us ask of the Lord.

People: Grant this, O Lord.

Deacon: Pardon and remission of our sins and transgressions, let us ask of the Lord.

People: Grant this, O Lord.

Deacon: All things good and profitable for our souls and peace for the world, let us ask of the Lord.

People: Grant this, O Lord.

Deacon: That we may complete the remaining time of our life in peace and repentance, let us ask of the Lord.

People: Grant this, O Lord.

Deacon: A Christian ending to our life, painless, blameless, peaceful, and a good defence before the fearful judgement seat of Christ, let us ask of the Lord.

People: Grant this, O Lord.

Deacon: Calling to remembrance our all holy, immaculate, most blessed and glorious Lady Theotokos and ever virgin Mary, with all the Saints: let us commend ourselves and each other, and all our life unto Christ our God.

People: To Thee, O Lord.

Priest: For Thou art a good God and lovest mankind, and unto Thee we ascribe glory: to the Father, and to the Son, and to the Holy Spirit; now and ever, and unto ages of ages.

People: Amen.

The Peace

Priest: Peace be with you all.

People: And with thy spirit.

Deacon: Let us bow down our heads unto the Lord.

People: To Thee, O Lord.

[All bow their heads as the priest says the following prayer:]

Priest: O Lord our God, Who didst bow the heavens and come down for the salvation of mankind: Look upon Thy servants and Thine inheritance; for unto Thee, the fearful Judge Who yet lovest mankind, have Thy servants bowed their heads and submissively inclined their necks, awaiting not help from men but entreating Thy mercy and looking confidently for Thy salvation. Guard them at all times, both during this present evening and in the approaching night, from every foe, from all adverse powers of the devil, and from vain thoughts and from evil imaginations. Blessed and glorified be the might of Thy kingdom: of the Father, and of the Son, and of the Holy Spirit; now and ever, and unto ages of ages.

People: Amen.

[It is customary to hold a procession around the church at this time. During this the Chorus sings the Apostichon and Paschal Stichera:]

Apostichon For The Resurrection

Tone 2   Majesty, gentleness, hope, repentance and sadness.   *E, F, G, Ab, B, C.*

Thy Resurrection, O Christ Saviour, hath illumined the whole universe. Thou hast renewed Thy creation. O Lord Almighty, glory to Thee.

The Paschal Stichera

Tone 5   Stimulating, dancing, and rhythmical.   *C, D, Eb, F, G, A, Bb, C.*

Chorus: Let God arise, and let His enemies be scattered, and let those who hate Him flee from before His face.

Reader: Today Christ, our saving Pascha, hath been revealed unto us a noble Pascha; the Pascha new and holy; the mystical Pascha; the Pascha all august; the blameless Pascha; the great Pascha; the Pascha of the faithful; the Pascha which openeth unto us the gates of paradise; the Pascha which sanctifieth all the faithful.

Chorus: As smoke vanisheth, so let them vanish; as wax melteth before the fire.

Reader: O come from the vision, you women, heralds of good tidings, and say you unto Zion, Receive from us the glad tidings of the joy of the Resurrection of Christ. Rejoice, O Jerusalem, and leap for joy, in that thou beholdest Christ the King like a bridegroom come forth from the grave.

Chorus: *So let sinners perish at the presence of God, and let the righteous be glad.*

Reader: When the ointment bearing women stood, very early in the morning, before the tomb of the Life giver, they found an angel sitting upon the stone. And he cried out unto them, saying, Why seek you the Living among the dead? Why mourn you the Incorruptible amidst corruption? Go, proclaim the glad tidings to His Disciples.

Chorus: *This is the day which the Lord hath made; let us rejoice and be glad therein.*

Reader: The joyful Pascha, the Pascha of the Lord, the Pascha all majestic hath shone upon us. The Pascha in which we embrace one another with joy. O what a Pascha, delivering from sorrow. For today from the tomb, as from a chamber Christ shone, and hath filled the women with joy, saying: Proclaim the glad tidings to the Apostles.

Glory to the Father, and to the Son, and to the Holy Spirit.

The Doxasticon For Pascha

Tone 5   Stimulating, dancing, and rhythmical.   *C, D, Eb, F, G, A, Bb, C.*

Today is the Day of Resurrection. Let us shine with the Feast. Let us embrace one another. Let us say, Brethren. And because of the Resurrection, let us forgive all things to those who hate us, and in this wise, exclaim: Christ is risen from the dead; trampling Death by death, and upon those in the tombs bestowing life.

Both now and forever, and unto ages of ages. Amen.

Paschal Apolytikion

Troparion	Christ is risen from the dead, trampling down death by death, and upon those in the tombs bestowing life.
Russian	Kristos voss kreysyey iz myert vikh. Smyertee oh smyert poh prav. Ee sooshim vogrow byekh zhivawt darowvav.
Greek	Χριστὸς ἀνέστη ἐκ νεκρῶν, θανάτῳ θάνατον πατήσας, καὶ τοῖς ἐν τοῖς μνήμασι, ζωὴν χαρισάμενος.
Romanian	Kristos aa inveeat din morts Koo, mortay mortay kakoond Shay chaylore deem ormintay veeaatsay, daaroo indoolay.

[At the conclusion of the Paschal Apolytikion, the clergy and acolytes return to the solea, where the priest immediately offers The Dismissal.]

The Dismissal

Priest: Glory to Thee, O Christ our God and our hope, glory to Thee.

Chorus: *Glory be to the Father, and to the Son, and to the Holy Spirit; Both now and forever, and unto the ages of ages. Amen.*

Lord, have mercy (x3).

Holy Father, bless.

Priest: May He Who is risen from the dead, trampling down Death by death, and upon those in the tombs bestowing life, Christ our true God, through the intercessions of His all immaculate and all blameless holy Mother; by the might of the Precious and Life giving Cross; by the protection of the honourable Bodiless Powers of Heaven; at the supplication of the honourable, glorious Prophet, Forerunner and Baptist John; of the holy, glorious and all laudable apostles; of the holy, glorious and right victorious Martyrs; of our venerable and God bearing Fathers; of *[Saint N]*, the patron and protector of this holy community; of the holy and righteous ancestors of God, Joachim and Anna; of the holy, glorious and righteous saints, whose memories we celebrate today, and of all the saints: have mercy on us and save us, forasmuch as He is good and loveth mankind.

Priest:	**English**	Christ is risen.	*People:*	*He is risen indeed.*
Priest:	**Greek**	Christos Anesti.	*People:*	*Alithos anesti.*
Priest:	**Russian**	Kristos Voskresey.	*People:*	*Voyistino Voskresey.*
Priest:	**Romanian**	Kristos aa inveeat.	*People:*	Add-evar-at aainveeat.
Priest:	**Albanian**	Kristi Unjhal.	*People:*	Vertet Unjhal.
Priest:	**Welsh**	Atgyfododd Crist.	*People:*	Atgyfododd yn wir.

Priest: Glory to His Holy Third day Resurrection.

People: *We adore His Holy Third day Resurrection.*

Priest: Christ is risen from the dead, trampling down Death by death, and upon those in the tombs…

People: *…bestowing life.*

Troparion Christ is risen from the dead, trampling down death by death,

and upon those in the tombs bestowing life.

Russian Kristos voss kreysyey iz myert vikh. Smyertee oh smyert poh prav.

Ee sooshim vogrow byekh zhivawt darowvav.

Greek Χριστὸς ἀνέστη ἐκ νεκρῶν, θανάτῳ θάνατον πατήσας,

καὶ τοῖς ἐν τοῖς μνήμασι, ζωὴν χαρισάμενος.

Romanian Kristos aa inveeat din morts Koo, mortay mortay kakoond

Shay chaylore deem ormintay veeaatsay, daaroo indoolay.

[Daily Epistle / Gospel required.]

Priest: Blessed is our God, always, now and ever, and unto the ages of ages.

People: *Amen.*

Priest: Glory to Thee, our God, glory to Thee.

People: *Christ is risen from the dead trampling down death by death,*

and upon those in the tombs bestowing life.

Russian   Kristos voss kreysyey iz myert vikh. Smyertee oh smyert poh prav.

Ee sooshim vogrow byekh zhivawt darowvav.

Greek   Χριστὸς ἀνέστη ἐκ νεκρῶν, θανάτῳ θάνατον πατήσας,

καὶ τοῖς ἐν τοῖς μνήμασι, ζωὴν χαρισάμενος.

Reader: *Glory be to the Father, and to the Son, and to the Holy Spirit;*

Both now and forever, and unto the ages of ages. Amen.

O Most Holy Trinity, have mercy on us.

O Lord, cleanse us from our sins.

O Master, pardon our iniquities.

O Holy One, visit and heal our infirmities, for Thy names sake.

Lord have mercy. **(x3)**

Glory be to the Father and to the Son and to the Holy Spirit;

Both now and forever, and unto the ages of ages. Amen.

People: *Our Father, who art in heaven, hallowed be Thy name. Thy Kingdom come. Thy will be done, on earth as it is in heaven. Give us this day our daily bread; and forgive us our trespasses, as we forgive those who trespass against us; and lead us not into temptation, but deliver us from the evil one.*

Priest: For Thine is the kingdom, the power, and the glory, of the Father, and the Son and

the Holy Spirit, both now and forever, and to the ages of ages.

People: *Amen.*

Lord, have mercy. **(x12)**

Glory be to the Father and to the Son and to the Holy Spirit;

Both now and forever and unto the ages of ages. Amen.

Come, let us worship God, our King.

Come, let us worship and fall down before Christ, our King and our God.

Come, let us worship and fall down before Christ Himself, our King and our God.

Psalm 19

The Lord hear thee in the day of affliction; the name of the God of Jacob defend thee. Let Him send forth unto thee help from His sanctuary, and out of Zion let Him help thee. Let Him remember every sacrifice of thine, and thy whole burnt offering let Him fatten. The Lord grant thee according to thy heart, and fulfil all thy purposes. We shall rejoice in Thy salvation, and in the name of the Lord our God shall we be magnified. The Lord fulfil all thy requests. Now have I known that the Lord hath saved His anointed one; He shall hearken unto him out of His holy heaven; in mighty deeds is the salvation of His right hand. Some trust in chariots, and some in horses, but we shall call upon the name of the Lord our God. They have been fettered and have fallen, but we are risen and are set upright. O Lord, save the king, and hearken unto us in the day when we call upon Thee.

Psalm 20

O Lord, in Thy strength the king shall be glad, and in Thy salvation shall he exceedingly rejoice. The desire of his heart hast Thou granted unto him, and hast not denied him the requests of his lips. Thou wentest before him with the blessings of goodness, Thou hast set upon his head a crown of precious stone. He asked life of Thee, and Thou gavest him length of days unto the ages of ages. Great is his glory in Thy salvation; glory and majesty shalt Thou lay upon him. For Thou shalt give him blessing for ever and ever, Thou shalt gladden him in joy with Thy countenance. For the king hopeth in the Lord, and through the mercy of the Most High shall he not be shaken. Let Thy hand be found on all Thine enemies; let Thy right hand find all that hate Thee. For Thou wilt make them as an oven of fire in the time of Thy presence; the Lord in His wrath shall trouble them sorely and fire shall devour them. Their fruit wilt Thou destroy from the earth, and their seed from the sons of men. For they have intended evil against Thee, they have devised counsels which they shall not be able to establish. For Thou shalt make them turn their backs; amongst those that are Thy remnant, Thou shalt make ready their countenance. Be Thou exalted, O Lord, in Thy strength; we shall sing and chant of Thy mighty acts.

After The Psalm

Glory be to the Father and to the Son and to the Holy Spirit,
Both now and forever and unto the ages of ages. Amen.

Holy God. Holy Mighty. Holy Immortal. Have mercy on us. **(x3)**

Glory be to the Father and to the Son and to the Holy Spirit,
Both now and forever and unto the ages of ages. Amen.

O Most Holy Trinity, have mercy on us.

O Lord, cleanse us from our sins.

O Master, pardon our iniquities.

O Holy One, visit and heal our infirmities, for Thy names sake.

Lord have mercy. **(x3)**

Glory be to the Father and to the Son and to the Holy Spirit;

Both now and forever, and unto the ages of ages. Amen.

People: *Our Father, who art in heaven, hallowed be Thy name. Thy Kingdom come. Thy will be done, on earth as it is in heaven. Give us this day our daily bread; and forgive us our trespasses, as we forgive those who trespass against us; and lead us not into temptation, but deliver us from the evil one.*

Priest: For Thine is the kingdom, the power, and the glory, of the Father, and the Son and

the Holy Spirit, both now and forever, and to the ages of ages.

People: *Amen.*

Apolytikion Of The Exaltation Of The Holy Cross

Tone 1   Magnificent, happy and earthy.   *C, D, Eb, F, G, A, Bb, C.*

Reader: O Lord, save Thy people and bless Thine inheritance. Grant victories to the Orthodox Christians over their adversaries. And by virtue of Thy Cross, preserve Thy commonwealth.

Glory be to the Father and to the Son and to the Holy Spirit;

Do Thou, Who of Thine own good will wast lifted up upon the Cross, O Christ our God, bestow thy bounties upon the new Nation which is called by Thy Name; make glad in Thy might those who lawfully govern, that with them we may be led to victory over our adversaries, having in Thine aid a weapon of peace and a trophy invincible.

Both now and forever, and unto the ages of ages. Amen.

Kontakion

Tone 8   Humility, tranquillity, repose, suffering, pleading.   *C, D, Eb, F, G, A, Bb, C.*

O Champion dread, who cannot be put to confusion, despise not our petitions, O Good and all praised Theotokos; establish the way of the Orthodox; save those who have been called upon to govern us, leading us all to that victory which is from heaven, for thou art she who gavest birth to God, and alone art blessed.

Little Litany

Priest: Have mercy on us, O God, according to thy great goodness, we pray Thee; hearken and have mercy.

People: *Lord, have mercy.* **(x3)**

Priest: Again we pray for all pious and Orthodox Christians.

People: *Lord, have mercy.* **(x3)**

Priest: Again we pray for our Archbishop Nikitas, and all our brotherhood in Christ.

People: *Lord, have mercy.* **(x3)**

Priest: For Thou art a merciful God and lovest mankind, and unto Thee we ascribe glory: to the Father, and to the Son, and to the Holy Spirit: now and ever, and unto the ages of ages.

People: *Amen. Holy Father, bless.*

Priest: Glory to the Holy, Consubstantial, Life creating and Undivided Trinity, always: now and forever, and unto the ages of ages.

People: *Amen.*

Doxology – excerpt Glory to God in the highest and on earth peace good will toward men. **(x3)**

Psalm 50 – excerpt O Lord, open my lips, and my mouth shall proclaim Thy praise. **(x2)**

Psalm 3

Lord, how they have increased who trouble me. Many are they who rise up against me. Many are they who say of me, "There is no help for him in God." But Thou, O Lord, art a shield for me, my glory and the One Who lifts up my head. I cried to the Lord with my voice, and He heard me from His holy hill. I lay down and slept; I awoke, for the Lord sustained me. I shall not be afraid of ten thousands of people who have set themselves against me all around. Arise, O Lord; save me, O my God. For Thou hast struck all mine enemies on the cheekbone; Thou hast broken the teeth of the ungodly. Salvation belongs to the Lord. Thy blessing is upon Thy people.

Psalm 37

O Lord, do not rebuke me in Thy wrath, nor chasten me in Thy hot displeasure. For Thine arrows deeply pierce me, and Thine hand presses me down. There is no soundness in my flesh because of Thine anger, Nor is there any health in my bones because of my sin. For mine iniquities have gone over my head; like a heavy burden they are too heavy for me. My wounds are foul and festering because of my foolishness. I am troubled, I am bowed down greatly; I go mourning all the day long. For my loins are full of inflammation, and there is no soundness in my flesh. I am feeble and severely broken; I groan because of the turmoil of my heart. Lord, all my desire is before Thee; and my sighing is not hidden from Thee. My heart pants, my strength fails me; as for the light of mine eyes, it also has gone from me. My loved ones and my friends stand aloof from my plague, and my kinsmen stand afar off. Those also who seek my life lay snares for me; those who seek my hurt speak of destruction, and plan deception all the day long. But I, like a deaf man, do not hear; and I am like a mute who does not open his mouth. Thus I am like a man who does not hear, and in whose mouth is no response. For in Thee, O Lord, I hope; Thou wilt hear, O Lord my God. For I said, "Hear me, lest they rejoice over me, lest, when my foot slips, they magnify themselves against me." For I am ready to fall, and my sorrow is continually before me. For I shall declare mine iniquity; I shall be in anguish over my sin. But mine enemies are vigorous, and they are strong; and those who wrongfully hate me have multiplied. Those also who render evil for good, they are mine adversaries, because I follow what is good. Do not forsake me, O Lord; O my God, be not far from me. Make haste to help me, O Lord, my salvation.

Psalm 62

O God, Thou art my God; early shall I seek Thee; my soul thirsts for Thee; My flesh longs for Thee in a dry and thirsty land where there is no water. So I have looked for Thee in the sanctuary, to see Thy power and Thy glory. Because Thy loving kindness is better than life, my lips shall praise Thee. Thus I shall bless Thee while I live; I shall lift up my hands in Thy name. My soul shall be satisfied as with marrow and fatness, and my mouth shall praise Thee with joyful lips. When I remember Thee on my bed, I meditate on Thee in the night watches. Because Thou hast been my help, therefore in the shadow of Thy wings I shall rejoice. My soul follows close behind Thee; Thy right hand upholds me. But those who seek my life, to destroy it, shall go into the lower parts of the earth. They shall fall by the sword; they shall be a portion for jackals. But the king shall rejoice in God; everyone who swears by Him shall glory; but the mouth of those who speak lies shall be stopped.

After The Psalm

Glory be to the Father and to the Son and to the Holy Spirit,
Both now and forever and unto the ages of ages. Amen.

Halleluiah, Halleluiah, Halleluiah. Glory to Thee, O God. **(x3)**

Lord have mercy. **(x3)**

Glory be to the Father and to the Son and to the Holy Spirit,
Both now and forever and unto the ages of ages. Amen.

Psalm 87

O Lord, God of my salvation, I have cried out day and night before Thee. Let my prayer come before Thee; incline Thine ear to my cry. For my soul is full of troubles, and my life draws near to the grave. I am counted with those who go down to the pit; I am like a man who has no strength, Adrift among the dead, like the slain who lie in the grave, whom Thou rememberest no more, and who are cut off from Thine hand. Thou hast laid me in the lowest pit, in darkness, in the depths. Thy wrath lies heavy upon me, and Thou hast afflicted me with all Thy waves. Thou hast put away mine acquaintances far from me; Thou hast made me an abomination to them; I am shut up, and I cannot get out; Mine eye wastes away because of affliction. Lord, I have called daily upon Thee; I have stretched out my hands to Thee. Willest Thou work wonders for the dead? Shall the dead arise and praise Thee? Shall Thy loving kindness be declared in the grave? Or Thy faithfulness in the place of destruction? Shall Thy wonders be known in the dark? And Thy righteousness in the land of forgetfulness? But to Thee I have cried out, O Lord, and in the morning my prayer comes before Thee. Lord, why dost Thou cast off my soul? Why dost Thou hide Thy face from me? I have been afflicted and ready to die from my youth up; I suffer Thy terrors; I am distraught. Thy fierce wrath has gone over me; Thy terrors have cut me off. They came around me all day long like water; they engulfed me altogether. Loved one and friend Thou hast put far from me, and mine acquaintances into darkness.

Psalm 102

Bless the Lord O my soul; and all that is within me, bless His holy name. Bless the Lord O my soul, and forget not all His benefits: Who forgives all thine iniquities, Who heals all thy diseases, Who redeems thy life from destruction, Who crowns thee with loving kindness and tender mercies, Who satisfies thy mouth with good things, so that thine youth is renewed like the eagles. The Lord executes righteousness and justice for all who are oppressed. He made known His ways to Moses, His acts to the children of Israel. The Lord is merciful and gracious, slow to anger, and abounding in mercy. He shall not always strive with us, nor shall He keep His anger forever. He has not dealt with us according to our sins, nor punished us according to our iniquities. For as the heavens are high above the earth, so great is His mercy toward those who fear Him; As far as the east is from the west, so far has He removed our transgressions from us. As a father pities his children, so the Lord pities those who fear Him. For He knows our frame; He remembers that we are dust. As for man, his days are like grass; as a flower of the field, so he flourishes. For the wind passes over it, and it is gone, and its place remembers it no more. But the mercy of the Lord is from everlasting to everlasting on those who fear Him, and His righteousness to childrens children, To such as keep His covenant, and to those who remember His commandments to do them. The Lord has established His throne in heaven, and His kingdom rules overall. Bless the Lord you His angels, who excel in strength, who do His word, heeding the voice of His word. Bless the Lord all you His hosts, you ministers of His, who do His pleasure. Bless the Lord all His works, in all places of His dominion. Bless the Lord O my soul.

Psalm 142

Lord, hear my prayer; in Thy truth give ear to my supplications; in Thy righteousness hear me. Enter not into judgement with Thy servant, for no one living is justified in Thy sight. For the enemy has pursued my soul; has crushed my life to the ground. He has made me to dwell in darkness, like those that have long been dead, and my spirit within me is overwhelmed; my heart within me is distressed. I remembered the days of old, I meditated on all Thy works, I pondered on the creations of Thine hands. I stretched forth my hands to Thee; my soul longs for Thee like a thirsty land. Lord, hear me quickly; my spirit fails. Turn not Thy face away from me, lest I be like those who go down into the pit. Let me hear Thy mercy in the morning; for in Thee have I put my trust. Lord, teach me to know the way wherein I should walk; for I lift up my soul to Thee. Rescue me, Lord, from mine enemies, to Thee have I fled for refuge. Teach me to do Thy will, for Thou art my God. Thy good Spirit shall lead me on a level path. Lord, for Thy names sake Thou shalt preserve my life. In Thy righteousness Thou shalt bring my soul out of trouble, and in Thy mercy Thou shalt utterly destroy my enemies. And Thou shalt destroy all those who afflict my soul, for I am Thy servant.

After The Psalm

> *Glory be to the Father and to the Son and to the Holy Spirit,*
>
> *Both now and forever and unto the ages of ages. Amen.*

Halleluiah, Halleluiah, Halleluiah. Glory to Thee, O God. **(x3)**

O Lord our Hope, glory to Thee.

The Great Litany

Priest: In peace, let us pray to the Lord.

People: Lord, have mercy.

Priest: For the peace from above and the salvation of our souls, let us pray to the Lord.

People: Lord, have mercy.

Priest: For the peace of the whole world, the good estate of the holy churches of God, and the union of all men, let us pray to the Lord.

People: Lord, have mercy.

Priest: For this holy house, and those who with faith, reverence and the fear of God enter therein, let us pray to the Lord.

People: Lord, have mercy.

Priest: For our Archbishop Nikitas, the honourable presbytery, the diaconate in Christ, all the clergy and the people, let us pray to the Lord.

People: Lord, have mercy.

Priest: For our Queen Elizabeth, the First Minister, the Welsh Assembly Government, civil authorities and armed forces, let us pray to the Lord.

People: Lord, have mercy.

Priest: For this town, and every city and the countryside, and the faithful who dwell therein, let us pray to the Lord.

People: Lord, have mercy.

Priest: For healthful seasons, abundant of the fruits of the earth and peaceful times, let us pray to the Lord.

People: Lord, have mercy.

Priest: For travellers by sea, by land and by air, the sick, the suffering, captives and their salvation, let us pray to the Lord.

People: Lord, have mercy.

Priest: For our deliverance from all tribulation, wrath, danger and necessity, let us pray to the Lord.

People: Lord, have mercy.

Priest: Help us; save us; have mercy on us; and keep us, O God, by Thy grace.

People: Lord, have mercy.

Priest: Calling to remembrance our all-holy, immaculate, most blessed and glorious Lady Theotokos and ever Virgin Mary, with all the saints, let us commend ourselves and each other and all our life unto Christ our God.

People: *To Thee, O Lord.*

Priest: For unto Thee are due all glory, honour and worship: to the Father, and to the Son, and to the Holy Spirit: now and forever, and unto the ages of ages.

People: *Amen.*

God Is The Lord - Paschal

People: *God is the Lord, Who hath shown us light. Blessed is He that cometh in the Name of the Lord.*

Reader: Give thanks to the Lord, for He is good; and His steadfast love endures forever.

People: *God is the Lord, Who hath shown us light. Blessed is He that cometh in the Name of the Lord.*

Reader: All nations surrounded me; in the Name of the Lord, I withstood them.

People: *God is the Lord, Who hath shown us light. Blessed is He that cometh in the Name of the Lord.*

Reader: I shall not die, but live, and recount the deeds of the Lord.

People: *God is the Lord, Who hath shown us light. Blessed is He that cometh in the Name of the Lord.*

Reader: The stone that the builders rejected has become the chief cornerstone.

This is the Lords doing and is marvellous in our eyes.

People: *God is the Lord, Who hath shown us light. Blessed is He that cometh in the Name of the Lord.*

Reader: In that we have beheld the Resurrection of Christ, let us bow down before the Holy Lord Jesus, the only sinless One. Thy Cross do we adore, O Christ, and Thy holy Resurrection we praise and glorify: for Thou art our God, and we know none other beside Thee; we call upon Thy Name. O come, all you faithful, let us adore Christ's holy Resurrection. For lo, through the Cross is joy come into all the world. Ever blessing the Lord, let us sing His Resurrection: for in that He endured the Cross he hath destroyed death by death.

Psalm 50

Reader: Have mercy on me, O God, according to Thy great mercy; and according to the multitude of Thy compassions blot out my transgression. Wash me thoroughly from mine iniquity, and cleanse me from my sin. For I acknowledge mine iniquity, and my sin is ever before me. Against Thee, Thee only have I sinned, and done evil in Thy sight, that Thou mayest be found just when Thou speakest, and victorious when Thou art judged. For behold, I was conceived in iniquity, and in sin my mother bore me. For behold, Thou hast loved truth; Thou hast made known to me the hidden and secret things of Thy wisdom. Thou shalt sprinkle me with hyssop, and I shall be made clean; Thou shalt wash me, and I shalt be whiter than snow. Make me to hear joy and gladness; that the humbled bones may rejoice. Turn Thy face away from my sins, and blot out all mine iniquities. Create in me a clean heart, O God, and renew a steadfast spirit within me. Cast me not away from Thy presence, and take not Thy Holy Spirit from me. Restore to me the joy of Thy salvation, and establish me with Thy governing Spirit. I shall teach transgressors Thy ways, and the ungodly shall turn back to Thee. Deliver me from blood guiltiness, O God, the God of my salvation; my tongue shall joyfully declare Thy righteousness. Lord, open my lips, and my mouth shall declare Thy praise. For if Thou hadst desired sacrifice,

I would give it; Thou dost not delight in burned offerings. A sacrifice to God is a broken spirit; God shall not despise a broken and a humbled heart. Do good, O Lord, in Thy good pleasure to Zion, and let the walls of Jerusalem be builded. Then Thou shalt be pleased with a sacrifice of righteousness, with oblation and whole burned offerings. Then shall they offer bulls on Thine altar.

The Synaxarion

Reader: Bless, Father, the reading from the Synaxarion.

Priest: Blessed is our God, always now and ever and unto the ages of ages.

Reader: *[reads the appointed section from the Synaxarion]*

Priest: Through the prayers of Thy saints, O Lord Jesus Christ our God, have mercy on us and save us.

People: *Amen.*

Priest: The Theotokos and Mother of the Light, let us honour and magnify in song.

The Magnificat (Luke 1:46-55).

Reader: My soul magnifies the Lord, and my spirit has rejoiced in God my Saviour.

Chorus: *Greater in honour than the Cherubim and beyond compare more glorious than the Seraphim; without corruption thou gavest birth to God the Word, truly the Theotokos, we magnify thee.*

Reader: For He has regarded the lowly state of His maidservant;
For behold, henceforth all generations shall call me blessed.

Chorus: *Greater in honour than the Cherubim and beyond compare more glorious than the Seraphim; without corruption thou gavest birth to God the Word, truly the Theotokos, we magnify thee.*

Reader: For He who is mighty has done great things for me, and holy is His name.
And His mercy is on those who fear Him from generation to generation.

Chorus: *Greater in honour than the Cherubim and beyond compare more glorious than the Seraphim; without corruption thou gavest birth to God the Word, truly the Theotokos, we magnify thee.*

Reader: He has shown strength with His arm;
He has scattered the proud in the imagination of their hearts.

Chorus: *Greater in honour than the Cherubim and beyond compare more glorious than the Seraphim; without corruption thou gavest birth to God the Word, truly the Theotokos, we magnify thee.*

Reader: He has put down the mighty from their thrones, and exalted the lowly.
He has filled the hungry with good things, and the rich He has sent empty away.

Chorus: *Greater in honour than the Cherubim and beyond compare more glorious than the Seraphim; without corruption thou gavest birth to God the Word, truly the Theotokos, we magnify thee.*

Reader: He has helped His servant Israel, in remembrance of His mercy, as He spoke to our fathers, to Abraham and to his seed forever.

Chorus: *Greater in honour than the Cherubim and beyond compare more glorious than the Seraphim; without corruption thou gavest birth to God the Word, truly the Theotokos, we magnify thee.*

Megalynarion

Chorus: *The Angel cried out to the Lady full of grace: O Pure Virgin rejoice and again I say rejoice; behold thy son is risen from his three days in the tomb.*

Eirmos

Shine, shine you new Jerusalem, for the glory of the Lord is dawning upon ye. Exult and be glad O Zion, and O Virgin Theotokos, be radiant in the rising of thy son.

Katavasia *[male singer]*

[Typikon: Eirmos of the 9ᵗʰ Ode of the last Menaion Canon is to be chanted as the concluding Katavasia.]

Mourn not for me, Mother, as thou behold me in the grave; for I thy Son, whom Thou didst conceive in thy womb without seed, shall rise and shall be glorified. And being God, I shall ceaselessly exalt and ennoble those who in faith and longing magnify thee.

Little Litany

Priest: Again and again in peace, let us pray to the Lord.

People: *Lord, have mercy.*

Priest: Help us; save us; have mercy on us; and keep us, O God, by Thy grace.

People: *Lord, have mercy.*

Priest: Calling to remembrance our all holy, immaculate, most blessed and glorious Lady Theotokos and ever Virgin Mary, with all the saints, let us commend ourselves and each other and all our life unto Christ our God.

People: *To Thee, O Lord.*

Priest: For all the powers of heaven praise Thee and unto Thee do they ascribe glory: to the Father and to the Son and to the Holy Spirit, now and ever and unto ages of ages.

People: *Amen.*

Lauds - The Praises

[Psalms always sung]

Psalm 148

Praise the Lord. Praise the Lord from the heavens; praise Him in the heights. Praise Him, all His angels; praise Him, all His hosts. Praise Him, sun and moon; praise Him, all you stars of light. Praise Him, you heavens of heavens, and you waters above the heavens. Let them praise the name of the Lord, for He commanded and they were created. He has also established them forever and ever; He has made a decree that shall not pass away. Praise the Lord from the earth, you great sea creatures and all the depths; Fire and hail, snow and clouds; stormy wind, fulfilling His word; Mountains and all hills; fruitful trees and all cedars; Beasts and all cattle; creeping things and flying fowl; Kings of the earth and all peoples; princes and all judges of the earth; Both young men and maidens; old men and children. Let them praise the name of the Lord, for His name alone is exalted; His glory is above the earth and heaven. And He has exalted the horn of His people, the praise of all His saints - of the children of Israel, a people near to Him. Praise the Lord.

Psalm 149

Praise the Lord. Sing to the Lord a new song, and His praise in the congregation of saints. Let Israel rejoice in their Maker; let the children of Zion be joyful in their King. Let them praise His name with the dance; let them sing praises to Him with the timbrel and harp. For the Lord takes pleasure in His people; He shall beautify the humble with salvation. Let the saints be joyful in glory; let them sing aloud on their beds. Let the high praises of God be in their mouth, and a two edged sword in their hand, To execute vengeance on the nations, and punishments on the peoples; To bind their kings with chains, and their nobles with fetters of iron; To execute on them the written judgement; this honour have all His saints. Praise the Lord.

Psalm 150

Praise the Lord. Praise God in His sanctuary; praise Him in His mighty firmament. Praise Him for His mighty acts; praise Him according to His excellent greatness. Praise Him with the sound of the trumpet; praise Him with the lute and harp. Praise Him with the timbrel and dance; praise Him with stringed instruments and flutes. Praise Him with loud cymbals; praise Him with high sounding cymbals. Let everything that has breath praise the Lord. Praise the Lord.

Lesser Doxology

Glory to God, Who has shown us the Light. Glory to God in the highest, and on earth, peace, good will toward men. We praise Thee. We bless Thee. We worship Thee. We glorify Thee and give thanks to Thee for Thy great glory. O Lord God, Heavenly King, God the Father Almighty. O Lord, the Only Begotten Son, Jesus Christ, and the Holy Spirit. \

O Lord God, Lamb of God, Son of the Father, Who takes away the sins of the world, have mercy on us. Thou, Who takes away the sins of the world, receive our prayer. Thou, Who sittest at the right hand of God the Father, have mercy on us. /

For Thou alone art holy, and Thou alone art Lord. Thou alone, O Lord Jesus Christ, are most high in the glory of God the Father. Amen. I shall give thanks to Thee every day and praise Thy Name forever and ever. Lord, Thou hast been our refuge from generation to generation. I said, *"Lord, have mercy on me. Heal my soul, for I have sinned against Thee."* \

Lord, I flee to Thee. Teach me to do Thy will, for Thou art my God. For with Thee is the fountain of Life, and in Thy light we shall see light. Continue Thy loving kindness to those who know Thee. Vouchsafe, O Lord, to keep us this day without sin. Blessed art Thou, O Lord, the God of our fathers, and praised and glorified is Thy Name forever. Amen. Let Thy mercy be upon us, O Lord, even as we have set our hope on Thee. Blessed art Thou, O Master; teach me Thy statutes. Blessed art Thou, O Lord; enlighten me with Thy commandments. Blessed art Thou, O Holy One; make me to understand Thy precepts. Thy mercy endures forever, O Lord. Do not despise the works of Thine hands. To Thee belongs worship, to Thee belongs praise, to Thee belongs glory: to the Father and to the Son and to the Holy Spirit, both now and forever and unto the ages of ages. Amen. \

The Litany Of Supplication

Priest: Let us complete our morning prayer unto the Lord.

People: *Lord, have mercy.*

Priest: Help us; save us; have mercy on us; and keep us, O God, by Thy grace.

People: *Lord, have mercy.*

Priest: That this whole day may be perfect, holy, peaceful and sinless, let us ask of the Lord.

People: *Grant this, O Lord.*

Priest: An angel of peace, a faithful guide, a guardian of our souls and bodies, let us ask of the Lord.

People: *Grant this, O Lord.*

Priest: Pardon and forgiveness of our sins and transgressions, let us ask of the Lord.

People: *Grant this, O Lord.*

Priest: All things good and profitable for our souls and peace for the world, let us ask of the Lord.

People: *Grant this, O Lord.*

Priest: That we may complete the remaining time of our life in peace and repentance, let us ask of the Lord.

People: *Grant this, O Lord.*

Priest: A Christian ending to our life, painless, blameless, peaceful and a good defence before the fearful judgement seat of Christ, let us ask.

People: *Grant this, O Lord.*

Priest: Calling to remembrance our all holy, immaculate, most blessed and glorious Lady Theotokos and ever Virgin Mary, with all the saints, let us commend ourselves and each other and all our life unto Christ our God.

People: *To Thee, O Lord.*

Priest: For Thou art the God of mercy and compassions and love toward mankind, and unto Thee we ascribe glory: to the Father and to the Son and to the Holy Spirit, now and forever and unto the ages of ages.

People: *Amen.*

Priest: Peace be with you all.

People: *And with thy spirit.*

Priest: Let us bow down our heads to the Lord.

People: *To Thee, O Lord.*

Priest: [Soto voce] Lord, our God, dwelling on high and beholding things below, who for the salvation of mankind sent forth Thine only begotten Son, our Lord and God, Jesus Christ, look upon Thy servants the Catechumens, who have bowed their necks to Thee and count them worthy in due time of the washing of rebirth, the forgiveness of sins and the garment of incorruption, unite them to Thy holy, Catholic and Apostolic Church, and number them with Thy chosen flock.

Priest: *[aloud]* For Thine it is to show mercy and to save us, O our God, and unto Thee we ascribe glory to the Father and to the Son and to the Holy Spirit, now and ever and unto the ages of ages.

People: *Amen.*

Priest: It is a good thing to confess unto the Lord, to sing praise to Thy name, O Most High, to declare Thy mercy in the morning and Thy truth by night.

Reader: Holy God. Holy Mighty. Holy Immortal. Have mercy on us. **(x3)**

Glory be to the Father and to the Son and to the Holy Spirit,
Both now and forever and unto the ages of ages. Amen.

O Most Holy Trinity, have mercy on us.

O Lord, cleanse us from our sins.

O Master, pardon our iniquities.

O Holy One, visit and heal our infirmities, for Thy names sake.

Lord have mercy. **(x3)**

Glory be to the Father and to the Son and to the Holy Spirit;
Both now and forever, and unto the ages of ages. Amen.

People: *Our Father, who art in heaven, hallowed be Thy name. Thy Kingdom come. Thy will be done, on earth as it is in heaven. Give us this day our daily bread; and forgive us our trespasses, as we forgive those who trespass against us; and lead us not into temptation, but deliver us from the evil one.*

Priest: For Thine is the kingdom, the power, and the glory, of the Father, and the Son and the Holy Spirit, both now and forever, and to the ages of ages.

People: *Amen.*

The Troparia Of The Day And Season

[see Pentecostarion for rubrics]

The Epistle

[Only read at Orthros if the Divine Liturgy does not follow.]

Priest: Wisdom.

Reader: The reading is from the _____

Priest: Let us attend.

Reader: *[chants the appointed Epistle]*

Priest: Peace be to thee that readest.

Reader: And to thy spirit.

Halleluiarion

People: *Halleluiah, Halleluiah, Halleluiah.*

Reader: *[Response of the week.]*

People: *Halleluiah, Halleluiah, Halleluiah.*

Reader: *[Response of the week.]*

People: *Halleluiah, Halleluiah, Halleluiah.*

The Gospel

Priest: Wisdom. Stand upright. Let us hear the holy Gospel. Peace be with you all.

People: *And to thy spirit.*

Priest: The reading is from the holy Gospel according to *N.*

People: *Glory to thee, O Lord. Glory to thee.*

Priest: *[Gospel of the day]*

People: *Glory to thee, O Lord. Glory to thee.*

The Augmented Ektenia

Priest: Have mercy upon us, O God, according to Thy great mercy, we pray Thee, hearken and have mercy.

People: *Lord, have mercy.* **(x3)**

Priest: Again we pray for our Archbishop Nikitas.

People: *Lord, have mercy.* **(x3)**

Priest: Again we pray our brethren: the priests, hieromonks, deacons, hierodeacons and monastics, and all our brotherhood in Christ.

People: *Lord, have mercy.* **(x3)**

Priest: Again we pray mercy, life, peace, health, salvation and visitation and pardon and forgiveness of sins for (*the servants of God, N, N., and*) all pious and Orthodox Christians who live and dwell in this community, the parishioners, members of the parish council, donors and benefactors of this holy church.

People: *Lord, have mercy.* **(x3)**

Priest: Again we pray for the blessed and ever memorable founders of this holy church (*and for the servants of God, N, N.,*) and for all our fathers and brethren, the Orthodox Christians departed this life before us, who here and in all the world lie asleep in the Lord.

People: *Lord, have mercy.* **(x3)**

Priest: Again we pray for those who bear fruit and do good works in this holy and all venerable temple; for those who serve and those who sing; and for all the people here present, who await Thy great and rich mercy.

People: *Lord, have mercy.* **(x3)**

Priest: For Thou art a merciful God and lovest mankind, and to Thee we ascribe glory to the Father and to the Son and to the Holy Spirit: now and ever, and unto the ages of ages.

People: *Amen.*

Priest: Glory to Thee, O Christ our God and our Hope, glory to Thee.

People: *Glory be to the Father and to the Son and to the Holy Spirit;*

Both now and forever and unto the ages of ages. Amen.

Lord, have mercy. (x3)

Holy Father, bless.

Priest: May He who rose from again from the dead, trampling down death by death and upon those in the tombs bestowing life, Christ our true God, through the intercessions of His all immaculate and all blameless holy Mother; of *[patron saint of the church]*; of the holy and righteous ancestors of God, Joachim and Anna; of *[Saints of the day]* whose memory we celebrate and of all the saints: have mercy on us, and save us, forasmuch as he is good and loveth mankind.

People: *Amen.*

Priest: Christ is risen.

People: *He is risen indeed.*

Priest: Christos Anesti.

People: *Alithos anesti.*

Priest: Kristos Voskresey.

People: *Voyistino Voskresey.*

Priest: Glory to his resurrection on the third day.

People: *We worship his resurrection on the third day.*

Priest: Christ is risen from the dead, trampling down by death and upon those in the tombs …

People: *… bestowing life.*

[Daily Epistle and Gospel required.]

Reader: In the Name of the Father and of the Son and of the Holy Spirit.

People: *Amen.*

People: Christ is risen from the dead trampling down death by death,

and upon those in the tombs bestowing life.

Russian Kristos voss kreysyey iz myert vikh. Smyertee oh smyert poh prav.

Ee sooshim vogrow byekh zhivawt darowvav.

Greek Χριστὸς ἀνέστη ἐκ νεκρῶν, θανάτῳ θάνατον πατήσας,

καὶ τοῖς ἐν τοῖς μνήμασι, ζωὴν χαρισάμενος.

Glory be to the Father, and to the Son, and to the Holy Spirit;

Both now and forever, and unto the ages of ages. Amen.

O Most Holy Trinity, have mercy on us.

O Lord, cleanse us from our sins.

O Master, pardon our iniquities.

O Holy One, visit and heal our infirmities, for Thy names sake.

Lord have mercy. **(x3)**

Glory be to the Father and to the Son and to the Holy Spirit;

Both now and forever, and unto the ages of ages. Amen.

People: *Our Father, Who art in Heaven, hallowed be Thy Name. Thy Kingdom come, Thy will be done, on earth as it is in Heaven. Give us this day our daily bread, and forgive us our trespasses, as we forgive those who trespass against us; and lead us not into temptation, but deliver us from the evil one. Amen.*

Reader: Through the prayers of our holy fathers, O Lord Jesus Christ our God, have mercy upon us and save us.

People: *Amen.*

Troparion Of The Holy And Life Giving Cross

Tone 2 *Majesty, gentleness, hope, repentance and sadness.* *E, F, G, Ab, B, C.*

O Lord, save Thy people, And bless Thine inheritance. Grant victories to the Orthodox Christians over their adversaries. And by virtue of Thy Cross, Preserve Thy habitation.

Chorus: *Glory be to the Father and to the Son and to the Holy Spirit;*

Kontakion Of The Cross

Tone 4   Festive, joyous and expressing deep piety.   *C, D, Eb, F, G, A, Bb, C.*

Reader: Do Thou, who of Thy good will was lifted up on the Cross, O Christ our God, bestow Thy bounties upon the new nation which is called by Thy name. Make glad in Thy might those who lawfully govern, that with them we may be led to victory over our adversaries, having in Thine aid a weapon of peace and an invincible trophy.

Chorus: *Both now and forever and unto the ages of ages. Amen.*

Theotokion

O Champion dread, who cannot be put to confusion, despise not our petitions, O Good and All praised Theotokos; establish the way of the Orthodox; save those who have been called upon to govern us, leading us all to that victory which is from heaven, for thou art she who gavest birth to God, and alone art blessed.

Lord have mercy. **(x12)**

Doxology – excerpt Glory to God in the highest and on earth peace good will toward men. **(x3)**

Psalm 50 – excerpt O Lord, open my lips, and my mouth shall proclaim Thy praise. **(x2)**

Psalm 3

Lord, how they have increased who trouble me. Many are they who rise up against me. Many are they who say of me, "There is no help for him in God." But Thou, O Lord, art a shield for me, my glory and the One Who lifts up my head. I cried to the Lord with my voice, and He heard me from His holy hill. I lay down and slept; I awoke, for the Lord sustained me. I shall not be afraid of ten thousands of people who have set themselves against me all around. Arise, O Lord; save me, O my God. For Thou hast struck all mine enemies on the cheekbone; Thou hast broken the teeth of the ungodly. Salvation belongs to the Lord. Thy blessing is upon Thy people.

Psalm 37

O Lord, do not rebuke me in Thy wrath, nor chasten me in Thy hot displeasure. For Thine arrows deeply pierce me, and Thine hand presses me down. There is no soundness in my flesh because of Thine anger, Nor is there any health in my bones because of my sin. For mine iniquities have gone over my head; like a heavy burden they are too heavy for me. My wounds are foul and festering because of my foolishness. I am troubled, I am bowed down greatly; I go mourning all the day long. For my loins are full of inflammation, and there is no soundness in my flesh. I am feeble and severely broken; I groan because of the turmoil of my heart. Lord, all my desire is before Thee; and my sighing is not hidden from Thee. My heart pants, my strength fails me; as for the light of mine eyes, it also has gone from me. My loved ones and my friends stand aloof from my plague, and my kinsmen stand afar off. Those also who seek my life lay snares for me; those who seek my hurt speak of destruction, and plan deception all the day long. But I, like a deaf man, do not hear; and I am like a mute who does not open his mouth. Thus I am like a man who does not hear, and in whose mouth is no response. For in Thee, O Lord, I hope; Thou wilt hear, O Lord my God. For I said, "*Hear me, lest they rejoice over me, lest, when my foot slips, they magnify themselves against me.*" For I am ready to fall, and my sorrow is continually before me. For I shall declare mine iniquity; I shall be in anguish over my sin. But mine enemies are vigorous, and they are strong; and those who wrongfully hate me have multiplied. Those also who render evil for good, they are mine adversaries, because I follow what is good. Do not forsake me, O Lord; O my God, be not far from me. Make haste to help me, O Lord, my salvation.

Psalm 62

O God, Thou art my God; early shall I seek Thee; my soul thirsts for Thee; My flesh longs for Thee in a dry and thirsty land where there is no water. So I have looked for Thee in the sanctuary, to see Thy power and Thy glory. Because Thy loving kindness is better than life, my lips shall praise Thee. Thus I shall bless Thee while I live; I shall lift up my hands in Thy name. My soul shall be satisfied as with marrow and fatness, and my mouth shall praise Thee with joyful lips. When I remember Thee on my bed, I meditate on Thee in the night watches. Because Thou hast been my help, therefore in the shadow of Thy wings I shall rejoice. My soul follows close behind Thee; Thy right hand upholds me. But those who seek my life, to destroy it, shall go into the lower parts of the earth. They shall fall by the sword; they shall be a portion for jackals. But the king shall rejoice in God; everyone who swears by Him shall glory; but the mouth of those who speak lies shall be stopped.

After The Psalm

Glory be to the Father and to the Son and to the Holy Spirit,
Both now and forever and unto the ages of ages. Amen.

Halleluiah, Halleluiah, Halleluiah. Glory to Thee, O God. **(x3)**
Lord have mercy. **(x3)**

Glory be to the Father and to the Son and to the Holy Spirit,
Both now and forever and unto the ages of ages. Amen.

Psalm 87

O Lord, God of my salvation, I have cried out day and night before Thee. Let my prayer come before Thee; incline Thine ear to my cry. For my soul is full of troubles, and my life draws near to the grave. I am counted with those who go down to the pit; I am like a man who has no strength, Adrift among the dead, like the slain who lie in the grave, whom Thou rememberest no more, and who are cut off from Thine hand. Thou hast laid me in the lowest pit, in darkness, in the depths. Thy wrath lies heavy upon me, and Thou hast afflicted me with all Thy waves. Thou hast put away mine acquaintances far from me; Thou hast made me an abomination to them; I am shut up, and I cannot get out; Mine eye wastes away because of affliction. Lord, I have called daily upon Thee; I have stretched out my hands to Thee. Willest Thou work wonders for the dead? Shall the dead arise and praise Thee? Shall Thy loving kindness be declared in the grave? Or Thy faithfulness in the place of destruction? Shall Thy wonders be known in the dark? And Thy righteousness in the land of forgetfulness? But to Thee I have cried out, O Lord, and in the morning my prayer comes before Thee. Lord, why dost Thou cast off my soul? Why dost Thou hide Thy face from me? I have been afflicted and ready to die from my youth up; I suffer Thy terrors; I am distraught. Thy fierce wrath has gone over me; Thy terrors have cut me off. They came around me all day long like water; they engulfed me altogether. Loved one and friend Thou hast put far from me, and mine acquaintances into darkness.

Psalm 102

Bless the Lord O my soul; and all that is within me, bless His holy name. Bless the Lord O my soul, and forget not all His benefits: Who forgives all thine iniquities, Who heals all thy diseases, Who redeems thy life from destruction, Who crowns thee with loving kindness and tender mercies, Who satisfies thy mouth with good things, so that thine youth is renewed like the eagles. The Lord executes righteousness and justice for all who are oppressed. He made known His ways to Moses, His acts to the children of Israel. The Lord is merciful and gracious, slow to anger, and abounding in mercy. He shall not always strive with us, nor shall He keep His anger forever. He has not dealt with us according to our sins, nor punished us according to our iniquities. For as the heavens are high above the earth, so great is His mercy toward those who fear Him; As far as the east is from the west, so far has He removed our transgressions from us. As a father pities his children, so the Lord pities those who fear Him. For He knows our frame; He remembers that we are dust. As for man, his days are like grass; as a flower of the field, so he flourishes. For the wind passes over it, and it is gone, and its place remembers it no more. But the mercy of the Lord is from everlasting to everlasting on those who fear Him, and His righteousness to childrens children, To such as keep His covenant, and to those who remember His commandments to do them. The Lord has established His throne in heaven, and His kingdom rules overall. Bless the Lord you His angels, who excel in strength, who do His word, heeding the voice of His word. Bless the Lord all you His hosts, you ministers of His, who do His pleasure. Bless the Lord all His works, in all places of His dominion. Bless the Lord O my soul.

Psalm 142

Lord, hear my prayer; in Thy truth give ear to my supplications; in Thy righteousness hear me. Enter not into judgement with Thy servant, for no one living is justified in Thy sight. For the enemy has pursued my soul; he has crushed my life to the ground. He has made me to dwell in darkness, like those that have long been dead, and my spirit within me is overwhelmed; my heart within me is distressed. I remembered the days of old, I meditated on all Thy works, I pondered on the creations of Thine hands. I stretched forth my hands to Thee; my soul longs for Thee like a thirsty land. Lord, hear me quickly; my spirit fails. Turn not Thy face away from me, lest I be like those who go down into the pit. Let me hear Thy mercy in the morning; for in Thee have I put my trust. Lord, teach me to know the way wherein I should walk; for I lift up my soul to Thee. Rescue me, Lord, from mine enemies, to Thee have I fled for refuge. Teach me to do Thy will, for Thou art my God. Thy good Spirit shall lead me on a level path. Lord, for Thy names sake Thou shalt preserve my life. In Thy righteousness Thou shalt bring my soul out of trouble, and in Thy mercy Thou shalt utterly destroy my enemies. And Thou shalt destroy all those who afflict my soul, for I am Thy servant.

After The Psalm

Glory be to the Father and to the Son and to the Holy Spirit,
Both now and forever and unto the ages of ages. Amen.

Halleluiah, Halleluiah, Halleluiah. Glory to Thee, O God. **(x3)**
O Lord our Hope, glory to Thee.

Lord have mercy. **(x40)**

God Is The Lord

People: *God is the Lord, Who has shown us light. Blessed is He who comes in the Name of the Lord.*

Reader: Give thanks to the Lord, for He is good; and His steadfast love endures forever.

People: *God is the Lord, Who has shown us light. Blessed is He who comes in the Name of the Lord.*

Reader: All nations surrounded me; in the Name of the Lord, I withstood them.

People: *God is the Lord, Who has shown us light. Blessed is He who comes in the Name of the Lord.*

Reader: I shall not die, but live, and recount the deeds of the Lord.

People: *God is the Lord, Who has shown us light. Blessed is He who comes in the Name of the Lord.*

Reader: The stone that the builders rejected has become the chief cornerstone.

This is the Lords doing and is marvellous in our eyes.

People: *God is the Lord, Who has shown us light. Blessed is He who comes in the Name of the Lord.*

Reader: In that we have beheld the Resurrection of Christ, let us bow down before the Holy Lord Jesus, the only sinless One. Thy Cross do we adore, O Christ, and Thy holy Resurrection we praise and glorify: for Thou art our God, and we know none other beside Thee; we call upon Thy Name. O come, all you faithful, let us adore Christ's holy Resurrection. For lo, through the Cross is joy come into all the world. Ever blessing the Lord, let us sing His Resurrection: for in that He endured the Cross he hath destroyed death by death.

Psalm 50

Have mercy on me, O God, according to Thy great mercy; and according to the multitude of Thy compassions blot out my transgression. Wash me thoroughly from mine iniquity, and cleanse me from my sin. For I acknowledge mine iniquity, and my sin is ever before me. Against Thee, Thee only have I sinned, and done evil in Thy sight, that Thou mayest be found just when Thou speakest, and victorious when Thou art judged. For behold, I was conceived in iniquity, and in sin my mother bore me. For behold, Thou hast loved truth; Thou hast made known to me the hidden and secret things of Thy wisdom. Thou shalt sprinkle me with hyssop, and I shall be made clean; Thou shalt wash me, and I shalt be whiter than snow. Make me to hear joy and gladness; that the humbled bones may rejoice. Turn Thy face away from my sins, and blot out all mine iniquities.

Create in me a clean heart, O God, and renew a steadfast spirit within me. Cast me not away from Thy presence, and take not Thy Holy Spirit from me. Restore to me the joy of Thy salvation, and establish me with

Thy governing Spirit. I shall teach transgressors Thy ways, and the ungodly shall turn back to Thee. Deliver me from blood guiltiness, O God, the God of my salvation; my tongue shall joyfully declare Thy righteousness. Lord, open my lips, and my mouth shall declare Thy praise. For if Thou hadst desired sacrifice, I would give it; Thou dost not delight in burned offerings. A sacrifice to God is a broken spirit; God shall not despise a broken and a humbled heart. Do good, O Lord, in Thy good pleasure to Zion, and let the walls of Jerusalem be builded. Then Thou shalt be pleased with a sacrifice of righteousness, with oblation and whole burned offerings. Then shall they offer bulls on Thine altar.

The Synaxarion For Today *(The Prologue Of Ohrid)]*

The Magnificat (Luke 1:46-55).

Reader: My soul magnifies the Lord, and my spirit has rejoiced in God my Saviour.

Chorus: Greater in honour than the Cherubim and beyond compare more glorious than the Seraphim; without corruption thou gavest birth to God the Word, truly the Theotokos, we magnify thee.

Reader: For He has regarded the lowly state of His maidservant; for behold, henceforth all generations shall call me blessed.

Chorus: Greater in honour than the Cherubim and beyond compare more glorious than the Seraphim; without corruption thou gavest birth to God the Word, truly the Theotokos, we magnify thee.

Reader: For He who is mighty has done great things for me, and holy is His name. And His mercy is on those who fear Him from generation to generation.

Chorus: Greater in honour than the Cherubim and beyond compare more glorious than the Seraphim; without corruption thou gavest birth to God the Word, truly the Theotokos, we magnify thee.

Reader: He has shown strength with His arm; he has scattered the proud in the imagination of their hearts.

Chorus: Greater in honour than the Cherubim and beyond compare more glorious than the Seraphim; without corruption thou gavest birth to God the Word, truly the Theotokos, we magnify thee.

Reader: He has put down the mighty from their thrones, and exalted the lowly. He has filled the hungry with good things, and the rich He has sent empty away.

Chorus: Greater in honour than the Cherubim and beyond compare more glorious than the Seraphim; without corruption thou gavest birth to God the Word, truly the Theotokos, we magnify thee.

Reader: He has helped His servant Israel, in remembrance of His mercy, as He spoke to our fathers, to Abraham and to his seed forever.

Chorus: Greater in honour than the Cherubim and beyond compare more glorious than the Seraphim; without corruption thou gavest birth to God the Word, truly the Theotokos, we magnify thee.

Megalynarion For Pascha

Chorus: *The Angel cried out to the Lady full of grace: O Pure Virgin rejoice and again I say rejoice; behold thy son is risen from his three days in the tomb.*

Katavasia

Reader: Shine, Shine you new Jerusalem. For the glory of the Lord is dawning upon ye. Exult and be glad Zion, and O Virgin Theotokos. Be radiant in the rising of thy Son.

Lord have mercy. **(x3)**

Lauds - The Praises

[Monday, Thursday, Sunday]   **Psalm 148**

Praise the Lord. Praise the Lord from the heavens; praise Him in the heights. Praise Him, all His angels; praise Him, all His hosts. Praise Him, sun and moon; praise Him, all you stars of light. Praise Him, you heavens of heavens, and you waters above the heavens. Let them praise the name of the Lord, for He commanded and they were created. He has also established them forever and ever; He has made a decree that shall not pass away. Praise the Lord from the earth, you great sea creatures and all the depths; Fire and hail, snow and clouds; stormy wind, fulfilling His word; Mountains and all hills; fruitful trees and all cedars; Beasts and all cattle; creeping things and flying fowl; Kings of the earth and all peoples; princes and all judges of the earth; Both young men and maidens; old men and children. Let them praise the name of the Lord, for His name alone is exalted; His glory is above the earth and heaven. And He has exalted the horn of His people, the praise of all His saints - of the children of Israel, a people near to Him. Praise the Lord.

[Tuesday, Friday, Sunday]   **Psalm 149**

Praise the Lord. Sing to the Lord a new song, and His praise in the congregation of saints. Let Israel rejoice in their Maker; let the children of Zion be joyful in their King. Let them praise His name with the dance; let them sing praises to Him with the timbrel and harp. For the Lord takes pleasure in His people; He shall beautify the humble with salvation. Let the saints be joyful in glory; let them sing aloud on their beds. Let the high praises of God be in their mouth, and a two edged sword in their hand, To execute vengeance on the nations, and punishments on the peoples; To bind their kings with chains, and their nobles with fetters of iron; To execute on them the written judgement; this honour have all His saints. Praise the Lord.

[Wednesday, Saturday, Sunday]   **Psalm 150**

Praise the Lord. Praise God in His sanctuary; praise Him in His mighty firmament. Praise Him for His mighty acts; praise Him according to His excellent greatness. Praise Him with the sound of the trumpet; praise Him with the lute and harp. Praise Him with the timbrel and dance; praise Him with stringed instruments and flutes. Praise Him with loud cymbals; praise Him with high sounding cymbals. Let everything that has breath praise the Lord. Praise the Lord.

Chorus: *To Thee belongeth glory, O Lord our God, and unto Thee we ascribe glory to the Father and to the Son and to the Holy Spirit, both now and forever and unto the ages of ages. Amen.*

Lesser Doxology

Glory to God, Who has shown us the Light. Glory to God in the highest, and on earth, peace, good will toward men. We praise Thee. We bless Thee. We worship Thee. We glorify Thee and give thanks to Thee for Thy great glory. O Lord God, Heavenly King, God the Father Almighty. O Lord, the Only Begotten Son, Jesus Christ, and the Holy Spirit. \

O Lord God, Lamb of God, Son of the Father, Who takes away the sins of the world, have mercy on us. Thou, Who takes away the sins of the world, receive our prayer. Thou, Who sittest at the right hand of God the Father, have mercy on us. /

For Thou alone art holy, and Thou alone art Lord. Thou alone, O Lord Jesus Christ, are most high in the glory of God the Father. Amen. I shall give thanks to Thee every day and praise Thy Name forever and ever. Lord, Thou hast been our refuge from generation to generation. I said, *"Lord, have mercy on me. Heal my soul, for I have sinned against Thee."* \

Lord, I flee to Thee. Teach me to do Thy will, for Thou art my God. For with Thee is the fountain of Life, and in Thy light we shall see light. Continue Thy loving kindness to those who know Thee. Vouchsafe, O Lord, to keep us this day without sin. Blessed art Thou, O Lord, the God of our fathers, and praised and glorified is Thy Name forever. Amen. Let Thy mercy be upon us, O Lord, even as we have set our hope on Thee. Blessed art Thou, O Master; teach me Thy statutes. Blessed art Thou, O Lord; enlighten me with Thy commandments. Blessed art Thou, O Holy One; make me to understand Thy precepts. Thy mercy endures forever, O Lord. Do not despise the works of Thine hands. To Thee belongs worship, to Thee belongs praise, to Thee belongs glory: to the Father and to the Son and to the Holy Spirit, both now and forever and unto the ages of ages. Amen. \

Lord have mercy. **(x12)**

Holy God, Holy Mighty, Holy Immortal: have mercy on us. **(x3)**

Glory be to the Father, and to the Son, and to the Holy Spirit;
Both now and forever, and unto the ages of ages. Amen.

O Most Holy Trinity, have mercy on us.
O Lord, cleanse us from our sins.
O Master, pardon our iniquities.
O Holy One, visit and heal our infirmities, for Thy names sake.

Lord have mercy. **(x3)**

Glory be to the Father and to the Son and to the Holy Spirit;

Both now and forever, and unto the ages of ages. Amen.

People: *Our Father, Who art in Heaven, hallowed be Thy Name. Thy Kingdom come, Thy will be done, on earth as it is in Heaven. Give us this day our daily bread, and forgive us our trespasses, as we forgive those who trespass against us; and lead us not into temptation, but deliver us from the evil one. Amen.*

Reader: Through the prayers of our holy fathers, O Lord Jesus Christ our God, have mercy upon us and save us.

People: *Amen.*

The Apostle

Reader: The Reading is from the book of ...

Reader: *[Reads the Apostle.]*

The Daily Gospel

Reader: The Reading is From The Holy Gospel According To ...

People: *Glory to Thee, O Lord, glory to Thee.*

Reader: *[Reads The Gospel For The Day.]*

People: *Glory to Thee, O Lord, glory to Thee.*

Lord, have mercy. **(x40)**

People: Christ is risen from the dead trampling down death by death,

           and upon those in the tombs bestowing life.

Russian   Kristos voss kreysyey iz myert vikh. Smyertee oh smyert poh prav.

           Ee sooshim vogrow byekh zhivawt darowvav.

Greek   Χριστὸς ἀνέστη ἐκ νεκρῶν, θανάτῳ θάνατον πατήσας,

           καὶ τοῖς ἐν τοῖς μνήμασι, ζωὴν χαρισάμενος.

[Daily and seasonal variables required.]

Trisagion Prayers

Reader: Through the prayers of our holy fathers, Lord Jesus Christ our God, have mercy on us and save us.

People: Amen.

People: Christ is risen from the dead trampling down death by death, and upon those in the tombs bestowing life.

Russian Kristos voss kreysyey iz myert vikh. Smyertee oh smyert poh prav. Ee sooshim vogrow byekh zhivawt darowvav.

Greek Χριστὸς ἀνέστη ἐκ νεκρῶν, θανάτῳ θάνατον πατήσας, καὶ τοῖς ἐν τοῖς μνήμασι, ζωὴν χαρισάμενος.

Glory be to the Father, and to the Son, and to the Holy Spirit;
Both now and forever, and unto the ages of ages. Amen.

O Most Holy Trinity, have mercy on us.

O Lord, cleanse us from our sins.

O Master, pardon our iniquities.

O Holy One, visit and heal our infirmities, for Thy names sake.

Lord have mercy. **(x3)**

Glory be to the Father and to the Son and to the Holy Spirit;
Both now and forever, and unto the ages of ages. Amen.

People: Our Father, Who art in Heaven, hallowed be Thy Name. Thy Kingdom come, Thy will be done, on earth as it is in Heaven. Give us this day our daily bread, and forgive us our trespasses, as we forgive those who trespass against us; and lead us not into temptation, but deliver us from the evil one. Amen.

Reader: Through the prayers of our holy fathers, Lord Jesus Christ our God, have mercy on us and save us.

People: Amen.

Lord, have mercy. **(x12)**

Glory be to the Father and to the Son and to the Holy Spirit;
Both now and forever and unto the ages of ages. Amen.

Come, let us worship God, our King.

Come, let us worship and fall down before Christ, our King and our God.

Come, let us worship and fall down before Christ Himself, our King and our God.

Psalm 103 - Of David. Concerning The Formation Of The World.

Bless the Lord, O my soul. O Lord my God, Thou hast been exceedingly magnified. Confession and majesty hast Thou put on, Who covered Thyself with light as with a garment, Who stretched out the heaven as it were a curtain; Who supports His chambers in the waters, Who appoints the clouds for His ascent, Who walks upon the wings of the winds, Who makes His angels spirits, and His ministers a flame of fire, Who establishes the earth in the sureness thereof; it shall not be turned back for ever and ever. The abyss like a garment is His mantle; upon the mountains shall the waters stand. At Thy rebuke they shall flee, at the voice of Thy thunder shall they be afraid.

The mountains rise up and the plains sink down to the place where Thou hast established them. Thou appointed a boundary that they shall not pass, neither return to cover the earth. He sends forth springs in the valleys; between the mountains shall the waters run. They shall give drink to all the beasts of the field; the wild asses shall wait to quench their thirst. Beside them shall the birds of the heaven lodge, from the midst of the rocks shall they give voice. He waters the mountains from His chambers; the earth shall be satisfied with the fruit of Thy works.

He causes the grass to grow for the cattle, and green herb for the service of men, To bring forth bread out of the earth; and wine makes glad the heart of man. To make his face cheerful with oil; and bread strengthens mans heart. The trees of the plain shall be satisfied, the cedars of Lebanon, which Thou hast planted. There shall the sparrows make their nests; the house of the heron is chief among them. The high mountains are a refuge for the harts, and so is the rock for the hares. He has made the moon for seasons; the sun knows his going down. Thou appointed the darkness, and there was the night, wherein all the beasts of the forest shall go abroad. Young lions roaring after their prey, and seeking their food from God. The sun arises, and they are gathered together, and they lay them down in their dens.

But man shall go forth unto his work, and to his labour until the evening. How magnified are Thy works, O Lord. In wisdom hast Thou made them all; the earth is filled with Thy creation. So is this great and spacious sea, therein are things creeping innumerable, small living creatures with the great. There go the ships; there this dragon, whom Thou hast made to play therein. All things wait on Thee, to give them their food in due season; when Thou gavest it to them, they shall gather it. When Thou opened Thy hand, all things shall be filled with goodness; when Thou turned away Thy face, they shall be troubled. Thou wilt take their spirit, and they shall cease; and to their dust shall they return. Thou wilt send forth Thy Spirit, and they shall be created; and Thou shalt renew the face of the earth.

Let the glory of the Lord be unto the ages; the Lord shall rejoice in His works. Who looks on the earth and makes it tremble, Who touches the mountains and they smoke. I shall sing unto the Lord throughout my life, I shall chant to my God for as long as I have my being. May my words be sweet unto Him, and I shall rejoice in the Lord. O that sinners would cease from the earth, and they that work iniquity, that they should be no more.

Bless the Lord, O my soul. The sun knows his going down, Thou appointed the darkness, and there was the night. How magnified are Thy works, O Lord. In wisdom hast Thou made them all.

After The Psalm

Glory be to the Father and to the Son and to the Holy Spirit;
Both now and forever, and unto the ages of ages. Amen.

Halleluiah, Halleluiah, Halleluiah. Glory to Thee, O God. **(x3)**
Our hope, O Lord, glory to Thee.

Lord, have mercy. **(x12)**

Reader: Through the prayers of our holy fathers, Lord Jesus Christ our God, have mercy on us and save us.
People: Amen.

Psalm 140

Chorus: Lord, I have cried to Thee: hear me. Hear me, O Lord.

Lord, I have cried to Thee: hear me. Receive the voice of my prayer.

When I call upon Thee, hear me, O Lord. Let my prayer arise as incense in Thy sight,

And let the lifting up of my hands be an evening sacrifice. Hear me, O Lord.

Kekragarion
Sticheroi From Psalm 140

• Set, O Lord, a watch before my mouth, and a door of enclosure round about my lips.

• Incline not my heart to words of evil, to make excuses for sins.

• Those that work iniquity; I shall not join with their number.

• The righteous man shall chasten me with mercy and reprove me; as for the oil of the sinner, let it not anoint my head.

• For yet more is my prayer in the presence of their pleasures; their judges have been swallowed up by the rock.

• They shall hear my words, for they be sweetened; as a clod of earth is broken upon the earth, so have their bones been scattered into hades.

• To Thee O Lord are mine eyes. In Thee have I hoped; take not my soul away.

• Keep me from the snare which they have laid for me, and from the stumbling blocks of them that work iniquity.

• The sinners shall fall into their own net; I am alone until I pass by.

Sticheroi From Psalm 141

- With my voice to the Lord have I cried, with my voice have I made supplication.

- I shall pour out before Him my supplications; my afflictions shall I declare before Him.

- When my spirit was fainting within me, then Thou knewest my paths.

- In this way wherein I have walked they hid for me a snare.

- I looked on my right hand, and beheld, and there was none that knew me.

- Flight has failed me, and there is none that watches out for my soul.

- I cried to Thee, O Lord; I said: Thou art my hope, my portion in the land of the living.

- Attend unto my supplication, for I am brought very low.

- Deliver me from them that persecute me, for they are stronger than I.

- 10. Bring my soul out of prison. That I may confess Thy name.

[daily and seasonal Troparia]

- 9. The righteous shall patiently wait for me until Thou shalt reward me.

[daily and seasonal Troparia]

Sticheroi From Psalm 129

- 8. Out of the depths have I cried unto Thee, O Lord. O Lord, hear my voice.

[daily and seasonal Troparia]

- 7. Let Thine ears be attentive to the voice of my supplication.

[daily and seasonal Troparia]

- 6. If Thou should mark iniquities, O Lord; O Lord, who shall stand? For with Thee there is forgiveness.

[daily and seasonal Troparia]

- 5. For Thy name's sake have I patiently waited for Thee, O Lord; my soul has patiently waited for Thy word, my soul has hoped in the Lord.

[daily and seasonal Troparia]

- 4. From the morning watch until night, from the morning watch let Israel hope in the Lord.

[daily and seasonal Troparia]

- 3. For with the Lord there is mercy, and with Him is plenteous redemption; and He shall redeem Israel out of all his iniquities.

[daily and seasonal Troparia]

Sticheroi From Psalm 116

- 2. O praise the Lord, all you nations; praise Him, all you peoples.

[daily and seasonal Troparia]

- 1. For He has made His mercy to prevail over us, and the truth of the Lord abides forever.

[daily and seasonal Troparia]

Glory be to the Father and to the Son and to the Holy Spirit.

Both now and forever, and unto the ages of ages. Amen.

O Gladsome Light

O Gladsome Light of the holy glory of the immortal Father; Heavenly holy, blessed Jesus Christ.

Now that we have come to the setting of the sun, and behold the Evening Light.

We praise God; Father, Son and Holy Spirit.

For meet it is at all time to worship Thee, with voices of praise;

O Son of God and Giver of Life. Therefore all the world doth glorify Thee.

Prokeimenon

Reader: The Evening Prokeimenon.

[Saturday]   Tone 6   *Rich texture, funeral, sorrowful.*   *D, Eb, F##, G, A, Bb, C##, D.*

Reader: The Lord is clothed with strength and He has girded Himself.

People: *The Lord is King, He is clothed with majesty.*

Reader: For He established the world which shall not be shaken.

People: *The Lord is King, He is clothed with majesty.*

Reader: Holiness becomes Thine house, O Lord, to the length of days.

People: *The Lord is King, He is clothed with majesty.*

Reader: The Lord is King | *He is clothed with majesty.*

Lord, have mercy. **(x40)**

Reader: Through the prayers of our holy fathers, Lord Jesus Christ our God, have mercy on us and save us.

People: Amen.

Reader: Vouchsafe, O Lord, to keep us this evening without sin. Blessed art Thou, O Lord, the God of our fathers, and praised and glorified is Thy name unto the ages.

People: Amen.

Reader: Let Thy mercy, O Lord, be upon us, according as we have hoped in Thee.

Blessed art Thou, O Lord, teach me Thy statutes.

Blessed art Thou, O Master, give me understanding of Thy statutes.

Blessed art Thou, O Holy One, enlighten me by Thy statutes.

O Lord, Thy mercy endures forever; disdain not the work of Thy hands. To Thee is due praise, to Thee is due song, to Thee is due glory, to the Father, and to the Son, and to the Holy Spirit; both now and forever, and unto the ages of ages. Amen.

Reader: Through the prayers of our holy fathers, Lord Jesus Christ our God, have mercy on us and save us.

People: *Amen.*

Aposticha

Chorus: *The Lord is King, He is clothed with majesty.*

Reader: Let us glorify Christ risen from the dead; for He did take unto Himself a soul and a body; and He separated one from the other in the Passion, when His pure soul went down to Hades that He led captive; and the holy body saw no corruption in the grave, the body of the Redeemer, Saviour of our souls.

Chorus: *For He established the world which shall not be shaken.*

Reader: With psalms and songs of praise, O Christ, do we glorify Thy Resurrection from the dead, by which Thou didst deliver us from the rebellion of Hades. And since Thou art God, Thou didst grant us eternal life and the Great Mercy.

Chorus: *Holiness becomes Thine house, O Lord, to the length of days.*

Reader: O Lord of all, O incomprehensible One; O Maker of heaven and earth, when Thou didst suffer in Thy Passion on the Cross, Thou didst pour out for me passionlessness; and when Thou didst submit to burial and didst rise in glory, Thou didst raise Adam with Thee by a mighty hand. Wherefore, glory to Thy third day Resurrection by which Thou didst grant us eternal life and forgiveness of sins; for Thou alone art compassionate.

Chorus: *Glory be to the Father, and to the Son, and to the Holy Spirit;*
Both now and forever, and unto the ages of ages. Amen.

Hymn Of Simeon The God Receiver

Reader: Lord, now lettest Thou Thy servant depart in peace, according to Thy word, for mine eyes have seen Thy salvation, which Thou hast prepared before the face of all peoples; a light of revelation for the Gentiles, and the glory of Thy people Israel.

Trisagion Prayers

Holy God, Holy Mighty, Holy Immortal, have mercy on us. **(x3)**

Glory be to the Father, and to the Son, and to the Holy Spirit;
Both now and forever, and unto the ages of ages. Amen.

O Most Holy Trinity, have mercy on us.

O Lord, cleanse us from our sins.

O Master, pardon our iniquities.

O Holy One, visit and heal our infirmities, for Thy names sake.

Lord have mercy. **(x3)**

Glory be to the Father and to the Son and to the Holy Spirit;

Both now and forever, and unto the ages of ages. Amen.

People: Our Father, Who art in Heaven, hallowed be Thy Name. Thy Kingdom come, Thy will be done, on earth as it is in Heaven. Give us this day our daily bread, and forgive us our trespasses, as we forgive those who trespass against us; and lead us not into temptation, but deliver us from the evil one. Amen.

Reader: O Lord, Jesus Christ, Son of God, have mercy on us.

People: Amen.

Reader: Through the prayers of our holy fathers, Lord Jesus Christ our God, have mercy on us and save us.

People: Amen.

Resurrectional Apolytikion

Tone 8   Humility, tranquillity, repose, suffering, pleading.   *C, D, Eb, F, G, A, Bb, C.*

From the heights Thou didst descend, O compassionate One, and Thou didst submit to the three day burial, that Thou might deliver us from passion; Thou art our life and our Resurrection, O Lord, glory to Thee.

Chorus: *Glory be to the Father and to the Son and to the Holy Spirit;*

Resurrectional Theotokion

Tone 1   Magnificent, happy and earthy.   *C, D, Eb, F, G, A, Bb, C.*

As Gabriel cried aloud unto thee: "Rejoice, O Virgin," with that cry did the Lord of all become incarnate in thee, O holy ark, as spake the righteous David; and thou wast revealed, as more spacious than the heavens, in that thou bore thy Creator. Wherefore, glory to Him Who abided in thee; glory to Him Who came from thee; glory to Him, Who through thy birth giving hath set us free.

Chorus: *Both now and forever, and unto the ages of ages. Amen.*

Reader: Through the prayers of our holy fathers, Lord Jesus Christ our God, have mercy on us and save us.

People: Amen.

The Dismissal

People:	Christ is risen from the dead trampling down death by death,
	and upon those in the tombs bestowing life.
Russian	Kristos voss kreysyey iz myert vikh. Smyertee oh smyert poh prav.
	Ee sooshim vogrow byekh zhivawt darowvav.
Greek	Χριστὸς ἀνέστη ἐκ νεκρῶν, θανάτῳ θάνατον πατήσας,
	καὶ τοῖς ἐν τοῖς μνήμασι, ζωὴν χαρισάμενος.

[Count the Troparia available for today and used at the end of the Kekragarion]

Trisagion Prayers

Reader: Through the prayers of our holy fathers, Lord Jesus Christ our God, have mercy on us and save us.

People: Amen.

People: Christ is risen from the dead trampling down death by death,

and upon those in the tombs bestowing life.

Russian Kristos voss kreysyey iz myert vikh. Smyertee oh smyert poh prav.

Ee sooshim vogrow byekh zhivawt darowvav.

Greek Χριστὸς ἀνέστη ἐκ νεκρῶν, θανάτῳ θάνατον πατήσας,

καὶ τοῖς ἐν τοῖς μνήμασι, ζωὴν χαρισάμενος.

Glory be to the Father, and to the Son, and to the Holy Spirit;

Both now and forever, and unto the ages of ages. Amen.

O Most Holy Trinity, have mercy on us.

O Lord, cleanse us from our sins.

O Master, pardon our iniquities.

O Holy One, visit and heal our infirmities, for Thy names sake.

Lord have mercy. **(x3)**

Glory be to the Father and to the Son and to the Holy Spirit;

Both now and forever, and unto the ages of ages. Amen.

People: *Our Father, Who art in Heaven, hallowed be Thy Name. Thy Kingdom come, Thy will be done, on earth as it is in Heaven. Give us this day our daily bread, and forgive us our trespasses, as we forgive those who trespass against us; and lead us not into temptation, but deliver us from the evil one. Amen.*

Reader: Through the prayers of our holy fathers, Lord Jesus Christ our God, have mercy on us and save us.

People: Amen.

Lord, have mercy. **(x12)**

Glory be to the Father and to the Son and to the Holy Spirit;

Both now and forever and unto the ages of ages. Amen.

Come, let us worship God, our King.

Come, let us worship and fall down before Christ, our King and our God.

Come, let us worship and fall down before Christ Himself, our King and our God.

Psalm 103 - Of David. Concerning The Formation Of The World.

Bless the Lord, O my soul. O Lord my God, Thou hast been exceedingly magnified. Confession and majesty hast Thou put on, Who covered Thyself with light as with a garment, Who stretched out the heaven as it were a curtain; Who supports His chambers in the waters, Who appoints the clouds for His ascent, Who walks upon the wings of the winds, Who makes His angels spirits, and His ministers a flame of fire, Who establishes the earth in the sureness thereof; it shall not be turned back for ever and ever. The abyss like a garment is His mantle; upon the mountains shall the waters stand. At Thy rebuke they shall flee, at the voice of Thy thunder shall they be afraid.

The mountains rise up and the plains sink down to the place where Thou hast established them. Thou appointed a boundary that they shall not pass, neither return to cover the earth. He sends forth springs in the valleys; between the mountains shall the waters run. They shall give drink to all the beasts of the field; the wild asses shall wait to quench their thirst. Beside them shall the birds of the heaven lodge, from the midst of the rocks shall they give voice. He waters the mountains from His chambers; the earth shall be satisfied with the fruit of Thy works.

He causes the grass to grow for the cattle, and green herb for the service of men, To bring forth bread out of the earth; and wine makes glad the heart of man. To make his face cheerful with oil; and bread strengthens mans heart. The trees of the plain shall be satisfied, the cedars of Lebanon, which Thou hast planted. There shall the sparrows make their nests; the house of the heron is chief among them. The high mountains are a refuge for the harts, and so is the rock for the hares. He has made the moon for seasons; the sun knows his going down. Thou appointed the darkness, and there was the night, wherein all the beasts of the forest shall go abroad. Young lions roaring after their prey, and seeking their food from God. The sun arises, and they are gathered together, and they lay them down in their dens.

But man shall go forth unto his work, and to his labour until the evening. How magnified are Thy works, O Lord. In wisdom hast Thou made them all; the earth is filled with Thy creation. So is this great and spacious sea, therein are things creeping innumerable, small living creatures with the great. There go the ships; there this dragon, whom Thou hast made to play therein. All things wait on Thee, to give them their food in due season; when Thou gavest it to them, they shall gather it. When Thou opened Thy hand, all things shall be filled with goodness; when Thou turned away Thy face, they shall be troubled. Thou wilt take their spirit, and they shall cease; and to their dust shall they return. Thou wilt send forth Thy Spirit, and they shall be created; and Thou shalt renew the face of the earth.

Let the glory of the Lord be unto the ages; the Lord shall rejoice in His works. Who looks on the earth and makes it tremble, Who touches the mountains and they smoke. I shall sing unto the Lord throughout my life, I shall chant to my God for as long as I have my being. May my words be sweet unto Him, and I shall rejoice in the Lord. O that sinners would cease from the earth, and they that work iniquity, that they should be no more. Bless the Lord, O my soul. The sun knows his going down, Thou appointed the darkness, and there was the night. How magnified are Thy works, O Lord. In wisdom hast Thou made them all.

After The Psalm

> *Glory be to the Father and to the Son and to the Holy Spirit;*
> *Both now and forever, and unto the ages of ages. Amen.*

Halleluiah, Halleluiah, Halleluiah. Glory to Thee, O God. **(x3)**

Our Hope, O Lord, glory to Thee.

Lord, have mercy. **(x12)**

Reader: Through the prayers of our holy fathers, Lord Jesus Christ our God, have mercy on us and save us.
People: *Amen.*

Psalm 140

Chorus: Lord, I have cried to Thee: hear me. Hear me, O Lord.

Lord, I have cried to Thee: hear me. Receive the voice of my prayer.

When I call upon Thee, hear me, O Lord. Let my prayer arise as incense in Thy sight,

And let the lifting up of my hands be an evening sacrifice. Hear me, O Lord.

Kekragarion
Sticheroi From Psalm 140

• Set, O Lord, a watch before my mouth, and a door of enclosure round about my lips.

• Incline not my heart to words of evil, to make excuses for sins.

• Those that work iniquity; I shall not join with their number.

• The righteous man shall chasten me with mercy and reprove me; as for the oil of the sinner, let it not anoint my head.

• For yet more is my prayer in the presence of their pleasures; their judges have been swallowed up by the rock.

• They shall hear my words, for they be sweetened; as a clod of earth is broken upon the earth, so have their bones been scattered into hades.

• To Thee O Lord are mine eyes. In Thee have I hoped; take not my soul away.

• Keep me from the snare which they have laid for me, and from the stumbling blocks of them that work iniquity.

• The sinners shall fall into their own net; I am alone until I pass by.

Sticheroi From Psalm 141

- With my voice to the Lord have I cried, with my voice have I made supplication.

- I shall pour out before Him my supplications; my afflictions shall I declare before Him.

- When my spirit was fainting within me, then Thou knewest my paths.

- In this way wherein I have walked they hid for me a snare.

- I looked on my right hand, and beheld, and there was none that knew me.

- Flight has failed me, and there is none that watches out for my soul.

- I cried to Thee, O Lord; I said: Thou art my hope, my portion in the land of the living.

- Attend unto my supplication, for I am brought very low.

- Deliver me from them that persecute me, for they are stronger than I.

- 10. Bring my soul out of prison. That I may confess Thy name.

[daily and seasonal Troparia]

- 9. The righteous shall patiently wait for me until Thou shalt reward me.

[daily and seasonal Troparia]

Sticheroi From Psalm 129

- 8. Out of the depths have I cried unto Thee, O Lord. O Lord, hear my voice.

[daily and seasonal Troparia]

- 7. Let Thine ears be attentive to the voice of my supplication.

[daily and seasonal Troparia]

- 6. If Thou should mark iniquities, O Lord; O Lord, who shall stand? For with Thee there is forgiveness.

[daily and seasonal Troparia]

- 5. For Thy name's sake have I patiently waited for Thee, O Lord; my soul has patiently waited for Thy word, my soul has hoped in the Lord.

[daily and seasonal Troparia]

- 4. From the morning watch until night, from the morning watch let Israel hope in the Lord.

[daily and seasonal Troparia]

- 3. For with the Lord there is mercy, and with Him is plenteous redemption; and He shall redeem Israel out of all his iniquities.

[daily and seasonal Troparia]

Sticheroi From Psalm 116

- 2. O praise the Lord, all you nations; praise Him, all you peoples.

[daily and seasonal Troparia]

- 1. For He has made His mercy to prevail over us, and the truth of the Lord abides forever.

[daily and seasonal Troparia]

Glory be to the Father and to the Son and to the Holy Spirit.
Both now and forever, and unto the ages of ages. Amen.

O Gladsome Light

O Gladsome Light of the holy glory of the immortal Father;

Heavenly holy, blessed Jesus Christ.

Now that we have come to the setting of the sun, and behold the Evening Light.

We praise God; Father, Son and Holy Spirit.

For meet it is at all time to worship Thee, with voices of praise;

O Son of God and Giver of Life. Therefore all the world doth glorify Thee.

Prokeimenon

Reader: The Prokeimenon.

[Sunday]   Tone 8   *Humility, tranquillity, repose, suffering, pleading.*   *C, D, Eb, F, G, A, Bb, C.*

Reader: Behold now, bless the Lord, all you servants of the Lord.

People: *Behold now, bless the Lord, all you servants of the Lord.*

Reader: You that stand in the house of the Lord, in the courts of the house of our God.

People: *Behold now, bless the Lord, all you servants of the Lord.*

Reader: Behold now, bless the Lord | *all you servants of the Lord.*

[Monday]   Tone 4   *Festive, joyous and expressing deep piety.*   *C, D, Eb, F, G, A, Bb, C.*

Reader: The Lord shall hearken unto me when I cry unto Him.

People: *The Lord shall hearken unto me when I cry unto Him.*

Reader: When I called upon Thee, O God of my righteousness; Thou didst hearken unto me.

People: *The Lord shall hearken unto me when I cry unto Him.*

Reader: The Lord shall hearken unto me | *when I cry unto Him.*

[Tuesday]   Tone 1   *Magnificent, happy and earthy.*   *C, D, Eb, F, G, A, Bb, C.*

Reader: Thy mercy, O Lord, shall pursue me all the days of my life.

People: *Thy mercy, O Lord, shall pursue me all the days of my life.*

Reader: The Lord is my shepherd, and I shall not want.

In a place of green pasture, there has He made me to dwell.

People: *Thy mercy, O Lord, shall pursue me all the days of my life.*

Reader: Thy mercy, O Lord | *shall pursue me all the days of my life.*

[Wednesday]   Tone 5   *Stimulating, dancing, and rhythmical.*   *C, D, F, G, A, Bb, C.*

Reader: O God, in Thy name save me, and in Thy strength Thou judgest me.

People: *O God, in Thy name save me, and in Thy strength Thou judgest me.*

Reader: O God, hearken to my prayer, give ear to the words of my mouth.

People: *O God, in Thy name save me, and in Thy strength Thou judgest me.*

Reader: O God, in Thy name save me | *and in Thy strength Thou judgest me.*

[Thursday]   Tone 6   *Rich texture, funeral, sorrowful.*   *D, Eb, F##, G, A, Bb, C##, D.*

Reader: My help comes from the Lord, who has made the heaven and the earth.

People: *My help comes from the Lord, who has made the heaven and the earth.*

Reader: I lifted up my eyes to the mountains from where comes my help.

People: *My help comes from the Lord, who has made the heaven and the earth.*

Reader: My help comes from the Lord | *who has made the heaven and the earth.*

[Friday]   Tone 7   *Manly character and strong melody.*   *F, G, A, A#, C, D, E, F.*

Reader: O God, my helper art Thou, and Thy mercy shall go before me.

People: *O God, my helper art Thou, and Thy mercy shall go before me.*

Reader: Rescue me from mine enemies, O God; and from them that rise up against me redeem me.

People: *O God, my helper art Thou, and Thy mercy shall go before me.*

Reader: O God, my helper art Thou | *and Thy mercy shall go before me.*

[Saturday]   Tone 6   *Rich texture, funeral, sorrowful.*   *D, Eb, F##, G, A, Bb, C##, D.*

Reader: The Lord is clothed with strength and He has girded Himself.

People: *The Lord is King, He is clothed with majesty.*

Reader: For He established the world which shall not be shaken.

People: *The Lord is King, He is clothed with majesty.*

Reader: Holiness becomes Thine house, O Lord, to the length of days.

Reader: The Lord is King | *He is clothed with majesty.*

Reader: Vouchsafe, O Lord, to keep us this evening without sin. Blessed art Thou, O Lord, the God of our fathers, and praised and glorified is Thy name unto the ages. Amen.

Let Thy mercy, O Lord, be upon us, according as we have hoped in Thee.

Blessed art Thou, O Lord, teach me Thy statutes.

Blessed art Thou, O Master, give me understanding of Thy statutes.

Blessed art Thou, O Holy One, enlighten me by Thy statutes.

O Lord, Thy mercy endures forever; disdain not the work of Thy hands. To Thee is due praise, to Thee is due song, to Thee is due glory, to the Father, and to the Son, and to the Holy Spirit; both now and forever, and unto the ages of ages. Amen.

Lord, have mercy. **(x40)**

Reader: Through the prayers of our holy fathers, Lord Jesus Christ our God, have mercy on us and save us.

People: Amen.

Aposticha

Chorus: *The Lord is King, He is clothed with majesty.*

Reader: Let us glorify Christ risen from the dead; for He did take unto Himself a soul and a body; and He separated one from the other in the Passion, when His pure soul went down to Hades that He led captive; and the holy body saw no corruption in the grave, the body of the Redeemer, Saviour of our souls.

Chorus: *For He established the world which shall not be shaken.*

Reader: With psalms and songs of praise, O Christ, do we glorify Thy Resurrection from the dead, by which Thou didst deliver us from the rebellion of Hades. And since Thou art God, Thou didst grant us eternal life and the Great Mercy.

Chorus: *Holiness becomes Thine house, O Lord, to the length of days.*

Reader: O Lord of all, O incomprehensible One; O Maker of heaven and earth, when Thou didst suffer in Thy Passion on the Cross, Thou didst pour out for me passionlessness; and when Thou didst submit to burial and didst rise in glory, Thou didst raise Adam with Thee by a mighty hand. Wherefore, glory to Thy third day Resurrection by which Thou didst grant us eternal life and forgiveness of sins; for Thou alone art compassionate.

Chorus: *Glory be to the Father, and to the Son, and to the Holy Spirit;*
Both now and forever, and unto the ages of ages. Amen.

Reader: Lord, now lettest Thou Thy servant depart in peace, according to Thy word, for mine eyes have seen Thy salvation, which Thou hast prepared before the face of all peoples; a light of revelation for the Gentiles, and the glory of Thy people Israel.

Holy God, Holy Mighty, Holy Immortal, have mercy on us. **(x3)**

Glory be to the Father, and to the Son, and to the Holy Spirit;
Both now and forever, and unto the ages of ages. Amen.

O Most Holy Trinity, have mercy on us.
O Lord, cleanse us from our sins.
O Master, pardon our iniquities.
O Holy One, visit and heal our infirmities, for Thy names sake.

Lord have mercy. **(x3)**

Glory be to the Father and to the Son and to the Holy Spirit;
Both now and forever, and unto the ages of ages. Amen.

People: *Our Father, Who art in Heaven, hallowed be Thy Name. Thy Kingdom come, Thy will be done, on earth as it is in Heaven. Give us this day our daily bread, and forgive us our trespasses, as we forgive those who trespass against us; and lead us not into temptation, but deliver us from the evil one. Amen.*

Reader: O Lord, Jesus Christ, Son of God, have mercy on us.

People: *Amen.*

Reader: Through the prayers of our holy fathers, Lord Jesus Christ our God, have mercy on us and save us.

People: *Amen.*

Resurrectional Apolytikion

Tone 8   Humility, tranquillity, repose, suffering, pleading.   C, D, Eb, F, G, A, Bb, C.

From the heights Thou didst descend, O compassionate One, and Thou didst submit to the three day burial, that Thou might deliver us from passion; Thou art our life and our Resurrection, O Lord, glory to Thee.

Chorus: *Glory be to the Father and to the Son and to the Holy Spirit;*

Resurrectional Theotokion

Tone 1   Magnificent, happy and earthy.   C, D, Eb, F, G, A, Bb, C.

As Gabriel cried aloud unto thee: "Rejoice, O Virgin," with that cry did the Lord of all become incarnate in thee, O holy ark, as spake the righteous David; and thou wast revealed, as more spacious than the heavens, in that thou bore thy Creator. Wherefore, glory to Him Who abided in thee; glory to Him Who came from thee; glory to Him, Who through thy birth giving hath set us free.

Chorus: *Both now and forever, and unto the ages of ages. Amen.*

Reader: Lord, have mercy. **(x40)**

Reader: Through the prayers of our holy fathers, Lord Jesus Christ our God, have mercy on us and save us.

People: *Amen.*

The Dismissal

People:	Christ is risen from the dead trampling down death by death, and upon those in the tombs bestowing life.
Russian	Kristos voss kreysyey iz myert vikh. Smyertee oh smyert poh prav. Ee sooshim vogrow byekh zhivawt darowvav.
Greek	Χριστὸς ἀνέστη ἐκ νεκρῶν, θανάτῳ θάνατον πατήσας, καὶ τοῖς ἐν τοῖς μνήμασι, ζωὴν χαρισάμενος.

The Paschal Hours

Reader: In the Name of the Father, and of the Son, and of the Holy Spirit. Amen.

Paschal Apolytikion

Troparion Christ is risen from the dead, trampling down death by death,

and upon those in the tombs bestowing life.

Russian Kristos voss kreysyey iz myert vikh. Smyertee oh smyert poh prav.

Ee sooshim vogrow byekh zhivawt darowvav.

Greek Χριστὸς ἀνέστη ἐκ νεκρῶν, θανάτῳ θάνατον πατήσας,

καὶ τοῖς ἐν τοῖς μνήμασι, ζωὴν χαρισάμενος.

Having beheld the Resurrection of Christ, let us worship the holy Lord Jesus, the only Sinless One. We worship Thy Cross, O Christ, and Thy holy Resurrection we hymn and glorify; for Thou art our God, and we know none other beside Thee, we call upon Thy name. O come, all you faithful, let us worship Christs' Holy Resurrection, for behold, through the Cross joy hath come to all the world. Ever blessing the Lord, we hymn His Resurrection; for, having endured crucifixion, He hath destroyed death by death.

The Hypakoe

Tone 8   Humility, tranquillity, repose, suffering, pleading.   *C, D, Eb, F, G, A, Bb, C.*

Forestalling the dawn, the women came with Mary, and found the stone rolled away from the sepulchre, and heard from the angel: "Why seek you among the dead, as though He were mortal, Him Who liveth in everlasting light? Behold the grave clothes. Quickly go and proclaim to the world that the Lord is risen and hath slain death. For He is the Son of God Who saveth mankind."

Kontakion Of Pascha

Tone 8   Humility, tranquillity, repose, suffering, pleading.   *C, D, Eb, F, G, A, Bb, C.*

When Thou went down to death, O immortal life, then Thou slew Hell with the lightning flash of Thy Godhead; but when from the depths below the earth Thou raised the dead, O Christ God, proclaiming *"Rejoice"* to the myrrh bearing women, granting peace to Thine apostles and bestowing resurrection to the fallen.

Troparion Of The Resurrection

Tone 8   Humility, tranquillity, repose, suffering, pleading.   *C, D, Eb, F, G, A, Bb, C.*

In the grave bodily, but in hades with Thy soul as God; in Paradise with the thief, and on the throne with the Father and the Spirit wast Thou Who fillest all things, O Christ the Inexpressible.

Glory be to the Father, and to the Son, and to the Holy Spirit.

How life giving, how much more beautiful than Paradise, and truly more resplendent than any royal palace was Thy tomb shown to be, O Christ, the source of our resurrection.

Both now and forever, and unto the ages of ages. Amen.

O sanctified and divine tabernacle of the Most High, Rejoice. For through thee, O Theotokos, joy is given to them that cry: "Blessed art thou among women, O all spotless Lady."

Lord, have mercy. **(x40)**

Glory be to the Father, and to the Son, and to the Holy Spirit;
Both now and forever, and unto the ages of ages. Amen.

Greater in honour than the Cherubim and beyond compare more glorious than the Seraphim; without corruption thou gavest birth to God the Word, truly the Theotokos, we magnify thee.

Paschal Apolytikion

Troparion	Christ is risen from the dead, trampling down death by death, and upon those in the tombs bestowing life.
Russian	Kristos voss kreysyey iz myert vikh. Smyertee oh smyert poh prav. Ee sooshim vogrow byekh zhivawt darowvav.
Greek	Χριστὸς ἀνέστη ἐκ νεκρῶν, θανάτῳ θάνατον πατήσας, καὶ τοῖς ἐν τοῖς μνήμασι, ζωὴν χαρισάμενος.

Glory be to the Father, and to the Son, and to the Holy Spirit;
Both now and forever, and unto the ages of ages. Amen.

Lord, have mercy. **(x3)**

May Christ our true God, Who rose from the dead, and trampled down death by death and upon those in the tombs bestowed life, through the intercessions of His most pure Mother, and of all the saints, have mercy on us and save us, for He is good and the Lover of mankind. Amen.

Through the prayers of our holy fathers, O Lord Jesus Christ our God, have mercy on us and save us. Amen.

(Long Introduction to the Divine Liturgy)

Priest: Glory to the holy, consubstantial, life giving and undivided Trinity;

Always, now and forever and to the ages of ages.

People: *Amen.*

People: *Christ is risen from the dead, trampling down death by death,*

and upon those in the tombs bestowing life.

Russian Kristos voss kreysyey iz myert vikh. Smyertee oh smyert poh prav.

Ee sooshim vogrow byekh zhivawt darowvav.

Greek Χριστὸς ἀνέστη ἐκ νεκρῶν, θανάτῳ θάνατον πατήσας,

καὶ τοῖς ἐν τοῖς μνήμασι, ζωὴν χαρισάμενος.

Priest: Let God arise and let His enemies be scattered;

And let those who hate Him flee from His face.

People: *Christ is risen from the dead, trampling down death by death,*

and upon those in the tombs bestowing life.

Priest: They shall vanish as smoke vanishes and melt as wax melts.

People: Kristos voss kreysyey iz myert vikh. Smyertee oh smyert poh prav.

Ee sooshim vogrow byekh zhivawt darowvav.

Priest: Thus shall the ungodly perish in the presence of God, but the righteous shall rejoice.

People: Χριστὸς ἀνέστη ἐκ νεκρῶν, θανάτῳ θάνατον πατήσας,

καὶ τοῖς ἐν τοῖς μνήμασι, ζωὴν χαρισάμενος.

Priest: This is the day that the Lord has made, let us rejoice and be glad in it.

People: *Christ is risen from the dead, trampling down death by death,*

and upon those in the tombs bestowing life.

Priest: Glory be to the Father and to the Son and to the Holy Spirit.

Russian Kristos voss kreysyey iz myert vikh. Smyertee oh smyert poh prav.

Ee sooshim vogrow byekh zhivawt darowvav.

Priest: Both Now and forever and to the ages of ages.

Greek Χριστὸς ἀνέστη ἐκ νεκρῶν, θανάτῳ θάνατον πατήσας,

καὶ τοῖς ἐν τοῖς μνήμασι, ζωὴν χαρισάμενος.

First Antiphon

Reader: Shout with joy to God, all the earth; sing to His Name. Give glory to His praises.

People: *At the prayers of the Mother of God, O Saviour, save us.*

Reader: Say to God: "How awesome are Thy works. Let all the earth worship Thee, and sing to Thee.

Let it sing a song to Thy Name, O Most High."

People: *At the prayers of the Mother of God, O Saviour, save us.*

Reader: Glory be to the Father and to the Son and to the Holy Spirit.

Both now and forever and unto the ages of ages. Amen.

People: *At the prayers of the Mother of God | O Saviour, save us.*

Second Antiphon

Reader: May God have mercy upon us, and bless us;

And may He cause His face to shine upon us, and have mercy upon us.

People: *Save us, O Son of God, risen from the dead; Save us who sing to Thee: Halleluiah.*

Reader: That Thy way may be known upon earth. Thy salvation among all nations.

Let the peoples give thanks to Thee, O God, let all the peoples give thanks to Thee.

People: *Save us, O Son of God, risen from the dead; Save us who sing to Thee: Halleluiah.*

Reader: May God bless us, and may all the ends of the earth fear Him.

People: *Save us, O Son of God, risen from the dead; Save us who sing to Thee: Halleluiah.*

Reader: Glory be to the Father and to the Son and to the Holy Spirit.

Chorus: *Both now and forever and unto the ages of ages. Amen.*

Third Antiphon – Little Entrance

Reader: Let God arise, and let His enemies be scattered;

And let them that fear Him flee from before His face.

People: Christ is risen from the dead, trampling down death by death;

And upon those in the tombs, bestowing life.

Reader: As smoke vanisheth, so let them vanish; as wax melteth before the fire.

People: Kristos voss kreysyey iz myert vikh. Smyertee oh smyert poh prav.

Ee sooshim vogrow byekh zhivawt darowvav.

Reader: So let sinners perish at the presence of God; and let the righteous be glad.

People: Χριστὸς ἀνέστη ἐκ νεκρῶν, θανάτῳ θάνατον πατήσας,

καὶ τοῖς ἐν τοῖς μνήμασι, ζωὴν χαρισάμενος.

Reader: This is the day which the Lord hath made; let us rejoice and be glad therein.

People: Christ is risen from the dead, trampling down death by death;

And upon those in the tombs, bestowing life.

Eisodikon (Entrance Hymn) Of Pascha

Reader: In the gathering places bless God the Lord, from the springs of Israel.

People: *Save us, O Son of God risen from the dead. Save us who sing to You: Halleluiah.*

Megalynarion For Pascha   *(Instead of "It is truly meet...")*

Tone 1   Magnificent, happy and earthy.   *C, D, Eb, F, G, A, Bb, C.*

Chorus: *The angel spake to her that is full of grace, saying, O pure Virgin, rejoice; and I say also, Rejoice; for thy Son is risen from the tomb on the third day.*

Reader: Shine, shine you new Jerusalem, for the glory of the Lord is dawning upon ye. Exult and be glad O Zion, and O Virgin Theotokos, be radiant in the rising of thy son.

Konoinikon:

Tone 8   Humility, tranquillity, repose, suffering, pleading.   *C, D, Eb, F, G, A, Bb, C.*

Receive you the body of Christ; taste you the Fount of immortality.

Post-Communion:

Instead of "We have seen the true Light ..." sing ONCE:

Christ is risen from the dead, trampling down death by death, and upon those in the tombs bestowing life.

Instead of "Blessed be the name of the Lord"

English   Christ is risen from the dead, trampling down death by death,

And upon those in the tombs bestowing life.

Russian   Kristos voss kreysyey iz myert vikh. Smyertee oh smyert poh prav.

Ee sooshim vogrow byekh zhivawt darowvav.

Greek   Χριστὸς ἀνέστη ἐκ νεκρῶν, θανάτῳ θάνατον πατήσας,

καὶ τοῖς ἐν τοῖς μνήμασι, ζωὴν χαρισάμενος.

Dismissal

After the long prayer by the Priest, long dismissal:

Priest:	**English**	Christ is risen.	*People:*	*He is risen indeed.*
Priest:	**Greek**	Christos Anesti.	*People:*	*Alithos anesti.*
Priest:	**Russian**	Kristos Voskresey.	*People:*	*Voyistino Voskresey.*
Priest:	**Romanian**	Kristos aa inveeat.	*People:*	Add-evar-at aainveeat.
Priest:	**Albanian**	Kristi Unjhal.	*People:*	Vertet Unjhal.
Priest:	**Welsh**	Atgyfododd Crist.	*People:*	Atgyfododd yn wir.

Priest: Glory to his resurrection on the third day.

People: *We worship his resurrection on the third day.*

Priest: To him be the glory, dominion, honour and worship to the ages of ages. Amen.

Priest: Christ is risen from the dead, trampling down death by death, and upon those in the tombs...

People: *bestowing life.*

English Christ is risen from the dead, trampling down death by death,

And upon those in the tombs bestowing life.

Russian Kristos voss kreysyey iz myert vikh. Smyertee oh smyert poh prav.

Ee sooshim vogrow byekh zhivawt darowvav.

Greek Χριστὸς ἀνέστη ἐκ νεκρῶν, θανάτῳ θάνατον πατήσας,

καὶ τοῖς ἐν τοῖς μνήμασι, ζωὴν χαρισάμενος.

From The Second Monday After Pentecost Until 29th June

<u>Apostles Fast.</u>

Fish, wine and oil allowed on all days except on Wednesdays and Fridays.

[All variables already included.]

[Can be used as first part of a Vesperal Liturgy.

After Prokeimenon swap to Liturgy coming in at the Epistle.]

Trisagion Prayers

Priest: Blessed is our God, always, now and forever and unto the ages of ages.

People: Amen.

Reader: Come, let us worship God, our King.

Come, let us worship and fall down before Christ, our King and our God.

Come, let us worship and fall down before Christ Himself, our King and our God.

Psalm 103

Of David. Concerning The Formation Of The World.

Reader: Bless the Lord, O my soul. O Lord my God, Thou hast been exceedingly magnified. Confession and majesty hast Thou put on, Who covered Thyself with light as with a garment, Who stretched out the heaven as it were a curtain; Who supports His chambers in the waters, Who appoints the clouds for His ascent, Who walks upon the wings of the winds, Who makes His angels spirits, and His ministers a flame of fire, Who establishes the earth in the sureness thereof; it shall not be turned back for ever and ever. The abyss like a garment is His mantle; upon the mountains shall the waters stand. At Thy rebuke they shall flee, at the voice of Thy thunder shall they be afraid.

The mountains rise up and the plains sink down to the place where Thou hast established them. Thou appointed a boundary that they shall not pass, neither return to cover the earth. He sends forth springs in the valleys; between the mountains shall the waters run. They shall give drink to all the beasts of the field; the wild asses shall wait to quench their thirst. Beside them shall the birds of the heaven lodge, from the midst of the rocks shall they give voice. He waters the mountains from His chambers; the earth shall be satisfied with the fruit of Thy works.

He causes the grass to grow for the cattle, and green herb for the service of men, To bring forth bread out of the earth; and wine makes glad the heart of man. To make his face cheerful with oil; and bread strengthens mans heart. The trees of the plain shall be satisfied, the cedars of Lebanon, which Thou hast planted. There shall the sparrows make their nests; the house of the heron is chief among them. The high mountains are a refuge for the harts, and so is the rock for the hares. He has made the moon for seasons; the sun knows his going down. Thou appointed the darkness, and there was the night, wherein all the beasts of the forest shall go abroad. Young lions roaring after their prey, and seeking their food from God. The sun arises, and they are gathered together, and they lay them down in their dens.

But man shall go forth unto his work, and to his labour until the evening. How magnified are Thy works, O Lord. In wisdom hast Thou made them all; the earth is filled with Thy creation. So is this great and spacious sea, therein are things creeping innumerable, small living creatures with the great. There go the ships; there this dragon, whom Thou hast made to play therein. All things wait on Thee, to give them their food in due season; when Thou gavest it to them, they shall gather it. When Thou opened Thy hand, all things shall be filled with goodness; when Thou turned away Thy face, they shall be troubled. Thou wilt take their spirit, and they shall cease; and to their dust shall they return. Thou wilt send forth Thy Spirit, and they shall be created; and Thou shalt renew the face of the earth.

Let the glory of the Lord be unto the ages; the Lord shall rejoice in His works. Who looks on the earth and makes it tremble, Who touches the mountains and they smoke. I shall sing unto the Lord throughout my life, I shall chant to my God for as long as I have my being. May my words be sweet unto Him, and I shall rejoice in the Lord. O that sinners would cease from the earth, and they that work iniquity, that they should be no more. Bless the Lord, O my soul. The sun knows his going down, Thou appointed the darkness, and there was the night. How magnified are Thy works, O Lord. In wisdom hast Thou made them all.

After The Psalm

Glory be to the Father and to the Son and to the Holy Spirit;
Both now and forever, and unto the ages of ages. Amen.

Halleluiah, Halleluiah, Halleluiah. Glory to Thee, O God. **(x3)**
O our God and our hope, glory to Thee.

The Great Litany

Deacon: In peace, let us pray to the Lord.

People: *Lord, have mercy.*

Deacon: For the peace from above, and for the salvation of our souls, let us pray to the Lord.

People: *Lord, have mercy.*

Deacon: For the peace of the whole world, for the good estate of the holy churches of God, and for the union of all men, let us pray to the Lord.

People: *Lord, have mercy.*

Deacon: For this Holy House, and for those who with faith, reverence, and fear of God, enter therein, let us pray to the Lord.

People: *Lord, have mercy.*

Deacon: For our father and Archbishop Nikitas, for the venerable Priesthood, the Diaconate in Christ, for all the clergy and the people, let us pray to the Lord.

People: *Lord, have mercy.*

Deacon: For Her Majesty Elizabeth the Queen, for the First Minister, for all civil authorities, and for our Armed Forces, let us pray to the Lord.

People: *Lord, have mercy.*

Deacon: That He shall aid them and grant them victory over every enemy and adversary, let us pray to the Lord.

People: *Lord, have mercy.*

Deacon: For this city, and for every city and land, and for the faithful who dwell therein, let us pray to the Lord.

People: *Lord, have mercy.*

Deacon: For healthful seasons, for abundance of the fruits of the earth, and for peaceful times, let us pray to the Lord.

People: *Lord, have mercy.*

Deacon: For travellers by sea, by land, and by air; for the sick and the suffering; for captives and their salvation, let us pray to the Lord.

People: *Lord, have mercy.*

Deacon: For our deliverance from all tribulation, wrath, danger, and necessity, let us pray to the Lord.

People: *Lord, have mercy.*

Deacon: Help us; save us; have mercy on us; and keep us, O God, by Thy grace.

People: *Lord, have mercy.*

Deacon: Calling to remembrance our all holy, immaculate, most blessed and glorious Lady Theotokos and ever virgin Mary, with all the Saints: let us commend ourselves and each other, and all our life unto Christ our God.

People: *To Thee, O Lord.*

Priest: For to Thou art due all glory, honour, and worship: to the Father, and to the Son, and to the Holy Spirit; Both now and forever and unto the ages of ages.

People: *Amen.*

Psalm 140

Chorus: Lord, I have cried to Thee: hear me. Hear me, O Lord.

Lord, I have cried to Thee: hear me. Receive the voice of my prayer.

When I call upon Thee, hear me, O Lord. Let my prayer arise as incense in Thy sight,

And let the lifting up of my hands be an evening sacrifice. Hear me, O Lord.

Kekragarion
Sticheroi From Psalm 140

• Set, O Lord, a watch before my mouth, and a door of enclosure round about my lips.

• Incline not my heart to words of evil, to make excuses for sins.

• Those that work iniquity; I shall not join with their number.

• The righteous man shall chasten me with mercy and reprove me; as for the oil of the sinner, let it not anoint my head.

• For yet more is my prayer in the presence of their pleasures; their judges have been swallowed up by the rock.

• They shall hear my words, for they be sweetened; as a clod of earth is broken upon the earth, so have their bones been scattered into hades.

• To Thee O Lord are mine eyes. In Thee have I hoped; take not my soul away.

- Keep me from the snare which they have laid for me, and from the stumbling blocks of them that work iniquity.
- The sinners shall fall into their own net; I am alone until I pass by.

Sticheroi From Psalm 141

- With my voice to the Lord have I cried, with my voice have I made supplication.
- I shall pour out before Him my supplications; my afflictions shall I declare before Him.
- When my spirit was fainting within me, then Thou knewest my paths.
- In this way wherein I have walked they hid for me a snare.
- I looked on my right hand, and beheld, and there was none that knew me.
- Flight has failed me, and there is none that watches out for my soul.
- I cried to Thee, O Lord; I said: Thou art my hope, my portion in the land of the living.
- Attend unto my supplication, for I am brought very low.
- Deliver me from them that persecute me, for they are stronger than I.
- Bring my soul out of prison. That I may confess Thy name.
- The righteous shall patiently wait for me until Thou shalt reward me.

Sticheroi From Psalm 129

- Out of the depths have I cried unto Thee, O Lord. O Lord, hear my voice.
- Let Thine ears be attentive to the voice of my supplication.

Chorus: *If Thou should mark iniquities, O Lord; O Lord, who shall stand? For with Thee there is forgiveness.*

Reader: O strange wonder, great and marvellous. For the fount of life is laid within a sepulchre; a ladder to Heaven's heights doth the small grave become. Be glad, O Gethsemane, the sanctuary of her that gave birth to God. You faithful, let us cry out, possessing as our commander great Gabriel: "Maiden Full of Grace, rejoice thou, with thee is the Lord our God, Who abundantly granteth His Great Mercy to the world through thee."

Chorus: *For Thy name's sake have I patiently waited for Thee, O Lord; my soul has patiently waited for Thy word, my soul has hoped in the Lord.*

Reader: O strange wonder, great and marvellous. For the fount of life is laid within a sepulchre; a ladder to Heaven's heights doth the small grave become. Be glad, O Gethsemane, the sanctuary of her that gave birth to God. You faithful, let us cry out, possessing as our commander great Gabriel: "Maiden Full of Grace, rejoice thou, with thee is the Lord our God, Who abundantly granteth His Great Mercy to the world through thee."

Chorus: *From the morning watch until night, from the morning watch let Israel hope in the Lord.*

Reader: Who can tell thy mysteries, O pure one? Thou art known, O Lady, as the throne of the Most High, and thou hast removed from earth to Heaven on this day. Majestically and sublime, thy glory beameth with graces divinely bright. You virgins, be lifted up unto the height with the Mother of Christ the King. Maiden Full of Grace, rejoice thou, with thee is the Lord our God, Who abundantly granteth His Great Mercy to the world through thee.

Chorus: For with the Lord there is mercy, and with Him is plenteous redemption; and He shall redeem Israel out of all his iniquities.

Reader: Who can tell thy mysteries, O pure one? Thou art known, O Lady, as the throne of the Most High, and thou hast removed from earth to Heaven on this day. Majestically and sublime, thy glory beameth with graces divinely bright. You virgins, be lifted up unto the height with the Mother of Christ the King. Maiden Full of Grace, rejoice thou, with thee is the Lord our God, Who abundantly granteth His Great Mercy to the world through thee.

Sticheroi From Psalm 116

Chorus: O praise the Lord, all you nations; praise Him, all you peoples.

Reader: Thy Dormition is now glorified by dominions, powers, principalities and thrones, authorities, cherubim and the dread seraphim; the earth born are filled with joy, adorned with thy divine glory and majesty; and kings worship, falling down with all the angels and archangels, and they sing: "Maiden Full of Grace, rejoice thou, with thee is the Lord our God, Who abundantly granteth His Great Mercy to the world through thee."

Chorus: For He has made His mercy to prevail over us, and the truth of the Lord abides forever.

Reader: Thy Dormition is now glorified by dominions, powers, principalities and thrones, authorities, cherubim and the dread seraphim; the earth born are filled with joy, adorned with thy divine glory and majesty; and kings worship, falling down with all the angels and archangels, and they sing: "Maiden Full of Grace, rejoice thou, with thee is the Lord our God, Who abundantly granteth His Great Mercy to the world through thee."

Glory be to the Father and to the Son and to the Holy Spirit.
Both now and forever, and unto the ages of ages. Amen.

[Priest censes and processes whilst:]

DOXASTICON FOR THE DORMITION IN EIGHT TONES

Tone 1   Magnificent, happy and earthy.   *C, D, Eb, F, G, A, Bb, C.*

Verily, the God mantled Apostles were caught up on all sides, ascending the clouds by a divine sign.

Tone 5   Stimulating, dancing, and rhythmical.   *C, D, Eb, F, G, A, Bb, C.*

And they came up to thy most pure, life originating resting place to kiss it reverently.

Tone 2   Majesty, gentleness, hope, repentance and sadness.   *E, F, G, Ab, B, C.*

As for the most sublime heavenly powers, they came with their own chief.

Tone 6   Rich texture, funereal character, sorrowful tone.   *D, Eb, F##, G, A, Bb, C##, D.*

To escort, enwrapped in awe, thine all honoured, God receiving body, they went before in a super earthly manner, shouting invisibly to the heavenly ranks: "Behold the Queen of all, the divine Maiden, has come."

Tone 3   Arrogant, brave, and mature atmosphere.   *F, G, A, A#, C, D, E, F.*

Lift up the gates and receive super earthly wise the Mother of everlasting Light.

Tone 7   Manly character and strong melody.   *F, G, A, A#, C, D, E, F.*

For through her hath salvation come to the whole human race. And she is the one on whom it is impossible to gaze, and whom we never can honour sufficiently.

Tone 4   Festive, joyous and expressing deep piety.   *C, D, Eb, F, G, A, Bb, C.*

For the honour through which she became sublime transcendeth all understanding.

Tone 8   Humility, tranquillity, repose, suffering, pleading.   *C, D, Eb, F, G, A, Bb, C.*

Wherefore, O undefiled Theotokos, everlasting with thy life bearing Son, intercede with Him unceasingly that He may preserve and save thy new people from every hostile assault; for we have taken thee unto us as our helper.

Tone 1   Magnificent, happy and earthy.   *C, D, Eb, F, G, A, Bb, C.*

Therefore, do we magnify thee with voices of joy unto all ages.

[During the above:]

The Holy Entrance

Deacon: *(Soto voce)*   Let us pray to the Lord. Lord have mercy.

Priest: *(Soto voce)*   In the evening and in the morning and at noon we praise Thee, we bless Thee, we give thanks unto Thee, and we pray unto Thee, O Master of all, Lord Who lovest mankind; Direct our prayer as incense before Thee, and incline not our hearts unto words of thought of evil, but deliver us from all who seek after our souls. For unto Thee, O Lord, Lord are our eyes, and in Thee have we hoped. Put us not to shame, O our God. For unto Thee are due all glory, honour and worship, to the Father, the Son and the Holy Spirit, both now and forever, and to the ages of ages.

Deacon: Amen.

[Censing]

Deacon: *(Soto voce)* Master, bless the Holy Entrance.

Priest: *(Soto voce)* Blessed is the Entrance to Thy Holy place; both now and forever, and unto the ages of ages. Amen.

Deacon: *(Aloud)* Wisdom. Stand up.

O Gladsome Light

O Gladsome Light of the holy glory of the immortal Father; Heavenly holy, blessed Jesus Christ.

Now that we have come to the setting of the sun, and behold the Evening Light.

We praise God; Father, Son and Holy Spirit.

For meet it is at all time to worship Thee, with voices of praise;

O Son of God and Giver of Life. Therefore all the world doth glorify Thee.

Prokeimenon

Deacon: The Evening Prokeimenon.

[Sunday]

    Tone 8   *Humility, tranquillity, repose, suffering, pleading.*   *C, D, Eb, F, G, A, Bb, C.*

Reader: Behold now, bless the Lord, all you servants of the Lord.

People: Behold now, bless the Lord, all you servants of the Lord.

Reader: You who stand in the temple of the Lord, in the courts of the House of our God.

People: Behold now, bless the Lord, all you servants of the Lord.

Reader: Behold now, bless the Lord | all you servants of the Lord.

[Monday]

    Tone 4   *Festive, joyous and expressing deep piety.*   *C, D, Eb, F, G, A, Bb, C.*

Reader: The Lord shall hear me, when I cry unto Him.

People: The Lord shall hear me, when I cry unto Him.

Reader: When I called upon Thee, O God of my righteousness; Thou didst hearken unto me.

People: The Lord shall hear me, when I cry unto Him.

Reader: The Lord shall hear me | when I cry unto Him.

[Tuesday]

    Tone 1   *Magnificent, happy and earthy.*   *C, D, Eb, F, G, A, Bb, C.*

Reader: Thy mercy, O Lord, shall follow me all the days of my life.

People: Thy mercy, O Lord, shall follow me all the days of my life.

Reader: The Lord is my shepherd, I shall not want; He makes me to lie down in green pastures.

People: Thy mercy, O Lord, shall follow me all the days of my life.

Reader: Thy mercy, O Lord | shall follow me all the days of my life.

[Wednesday]

    Tone 5   *Stimulating, dancing, and rhythmical.*   *C, D, Eb, F, G, A, Bb, C.*

Reader: Save me, O God, by Thy Name, and judge me by Thy strength.

People: *Save me, O God, by Thy Name, and judge me by Thy strength.*

Reader: Verse. Hear my prayer, O God; give ear to the words of my mouth.

People: *Save me, O God, by Thy Name, and judge me by Thy strength.*

Reader: Save me, O God, by Thy Name | and judge me by Thy strength.

[Thursday]

    Tone 6   *Rich texture, funereal character, sorrowful tone.*   *D, Eb, F##, G, A, Bb, C##, D.*

Reader: My help cometh from the Lord, Who hath made heaven and earth.

People: *My help cometh from the Lord, Who hath made heaven and earth.*

Reader: Verse. I lift up my eyes to the hills, from where my help shall come.

People: *My help cometh from the Lord, Who hath made heaven and earth.*

Reader: My help cometh from the Lord | Who hath made heaven and earth.

[Friday]

    Tone 7   *Manly character and strong melody.*   *F, G, A, A#, C, D, E, F.*

Reader: Thou, O God, art my helper, and Thy mercy shall go before me.

People: *Thou, O God, art my helper, and Thy mercy shall go before me.*

Reader: Deliver me from my enemies, O God; and deliver me from those who rise up against me.

People: *Thou, O God, art my helper, and Thy mercy shall go before me.*

Reader: Thou, O God, art my helper | and Thy mercy shall go before me.

[If used as a Vesperal Liturgy change from here to the Liturgy *right to the* Epistle.*]*

THE OLD TESTAMENT READINGS

The First Passage

Deacon: Wisdom.

Reader: The reading is from Genesis (28:10-17).

Deacon: Let us attend.

Reader: Jacob went out from the well of the oath (Beersheba), and went toward Haran. And he came upon a certain place, and slept there, because the sun was set; and he took of the stones of that place, and put them for his pillows, and lay down in that place to sleep. And he dreamed, and behold, a ladder set up on the earth, and the top of it reached to Heaven, and behold, the Angels of God ascending and descending on it. And behold, the Lord stood above it and said: I am the God of Abraham thy father and the God of Isaac, fear not; the land whereon thou liest, to thee shall I give it, and to thy seed; and thy seed shall be as the sand of the earth, and it shall spread abroad to the sea, and to the south, and to the north, and to the east; and in thee and thy seed shall all the tribes of the earth be blessed. And behold, I am with thee, and I shall keep thee in all places whither thou goest, and shall bring thee again into this land; for I shall not forsake thee, until I have done all that which I have spoken to thee of. And Jacob awaked out of his sleep, and he said: The Lord is in this place, and I knew it not. And he was afraid and said: How dreadful is this place. This is none other but the house of God, and this is the gate of Heaven.

The Second Passage

Deacon: Wisdom.

Reader: The reading is from The Prophecy of Ezekiel the Prophet (43:27-44:4).

Deacon: Let us attend.

Reader: Upon the eighth day and so forward, the priests shall make your whole burnt offerings upon the altar, and your peace offerings, and I shall accept you, saith the Lord. Then He brought me back by the way of the outer gate of the sanctuary, which looketh toward the east; and it was shut. And the Lord said unto me: This gate shall be shut, it shall not be opened, and no man shall enter in by it; because the Lord, the God of Israel, shall enter in by it, and it shall be shut. For this Prince shall sit on it to eat bread before the Lord; He shall enter by the way of the porch of that gate, and shall come forth by the way of the same. And He brought me by the way of the north gate before the house, and I looked, and behold, the house of the Lord was full of glory.

The Third Passage

Deacon: Wisdom.

Reader: The reading is from Proverbs (9:1-11).

Deacon: Let us attend.

Reader: Wisdom hath builded herself a house, and hath established seven pillars. She hath killed her beasts; she hath mingled her wine; she hath also prepared her table. She hath sent forth her servants, making invitation to a feast with a loud proclamation, and saying: Whoso is foolish, let him turn aside to me; as for them that want understanding, she saith: Come, eat of my bread and drink of the wine which I have mingled for you. Forsake foolishness, and you shall live, and go in search of understanding that you may live, and achieve understanding in knowledge. He that reproveth evil men getteth to himself shame; and he that rebuketh an ungodly man shall himself be blamed, for rebukes unto the ungodly are as wounds to him. Reprove not evil men, lest they hate thee; rebuke a wise man, and he shall love thee. Give occasion to a wise man, and he shall become yet wiser; teach a just man, and he shall receive more learning. The fear of the Lord is the beginning of wisdom, and the counsel of Saints is understanding. For to know the Law is the property of a good mind, for in this wise thou shalt live long, and years of life shall be added to thee.

The Litany Of Fervent Supplication

Deacon: Let us all say with our whole soul, and with our whole mind let us say:

People: *Lord, have mercy.*

Deacon: Lord Almighty, God of our Fathers, we pray Thee, hearest and have mercy.

People: *Lord, have mercy.*

Deacon: Have mercy on us, O God, according to Thy great mercy, we pray Thee; hear us and have mercy.

People: *Lord, have mercy.* **(x3)**

Deacon: Also we pray for our Archbishop Nikitas.

People: *Lord, have mercy.* **(x3)**

Deacon: For our Sovereign Lady, Queen Elizabeth, the Royal family, our Welsh Assembly Government, and all in authority, let us pray to the Lord.

People: *Lord, have mercy.* **(x3)**

Deacon: Also we pray for mercy, life, peace, health, salvation, visitation, pardon and forgiveness of sins for the servants of God, all devout and Orthodox Christians, those who dwell in or visit this city or town and parish, the wardens and members of this church and their families and all who have asked for our prayers, unworthy though we are.

People: *Lord, have mercy.* **(x3)**

Deacon: Also we pray for the blessed and ever remembered founders of this holy church, and for all our brothers and sisters who have gone to their rest before us, and who lie here asleep in the true faith; and for the Orthodox everywhere *[and the servants of God N and N – (names given before the service)]* and that they may be pardoned all their offences, both voluntary and involuntary.

People: *Lord, have mercy.* **(x3)**

Deacon: Also we pray for those who bring offerings, those who care for the beauty of this holy and venerable house, for those who labour in its service, for those who sing, and for the people here present, who await Thy great and rich mercy.

People: *Lord, have mercy.* **(x3)**

Priest: For Thou, O God, art merciful and love mankind, and to Thee we givest glory, to the Father, the Son and the Holy Spirit, both now and forever, and unto the ages of ages.

People: *Amen.*

The Evening Prayer

Reader: Vouchsafe, O Lord, to keep us this evening without sin. Blessed art Thou, O Lord, the God of our fathers, and praised and glorified is Thy name unto the ages. Amen.

Let Thy mercy, O Lord, be upon us, according as we have hoped in Thee.

Blessed art Thou, O Lord, teach me Thy statutes.

Blessed art Thou, O Master, give me understanding of Thy statutes.

Blessed art Thou, O Holy One, enlighten me by Thy statutes.

O Lord, Thy mercy endures forever; disdain not the work of Thy hands. To Thee is due praise, to Thee is due song, to Thee is due glory, to the Father, and to the Son, and to the Holy Spirit; both now and forever, and unto the ages of ages. Amen.

The Litany Of Supplication

Deacon: Let us complete our evening prayer unto the Lord.

People: *Lord, have mercy.*

Deacon: Help us; save us; have mercy on us; and keep us, O God, by Thy grace.

People: *Lord, have mercy.*

Deacon: That the whole evening may be perfect, holy, peaceful and sinless, let us ask of the Lord.

People: *Grant this, O Lord.*

Deacon: An angel of peace, a faithful guide, a guardian of our souls and bodies, let us ask of the Lord.

People: *Grant this, O Lord.*

Deacon: Pardon and remission of our sins and transgressions, let us ask of the Lord.

People: *Grant this, O Lord.*

Deacon: All things good and profitable for our souls and peace for the world, let us ask of the Lord.

People: *Grant this, O Lord.*

Deacon: That we may complete the remaining time of our life in peace and repentance, let us ask of the Lord.

People: *Grant this, O Lord.*

Deacon: A Christian ending to our life, painless, blameless, peaceful, and a good defence before the fearful judgement seat of Christ, let us ask of the Lord.

People: *Grant this, O Lord.*

Deacon: Calling to remembrance our all holy, immaculate, most blessed and glorious Lady Theotokos and ever virgin Mary, with all the Saints: let us commend ourselves and one another, and all our life to Christ our God.

People: *To Thee, O Lord.*

Priest: For Thou art a good God and lovest mankind, and to Thee we ascribe glory: to the Father, and to the Son, and to the Holy Spirit; both now and forever, and to the ages of ages.

People: *Amen.*

The Peace

Priest: Peace be with you all.

People: *And with thy spirit.*

Deacon: Let us bow our heads unto the Lord.

People: *To Thee, O Lord.*

Priest: O Lord our God, Who did bow the heavens and come down for the salvation of mankind: Look upon Thy servants and Thine inheritance; for to Thee, the fearful Judge Who yet loves mankind, have Thine servants bowed their heads and submissively inclined their necks, awaiting not help from men but entreating Thy mercy and looking confidently for Thy salvation. Guard them at all times, both during this present evening and in the approaching night, from every foe, from all adverse powers of the devil, and from vain thoughts and from evil imaginations.

Blessed and glorified be the might of Thy kingdom: of the Father, and of the Son, and of the Holy Spirit; both now and forever, and unto the ages of ages.

People: Amen.

The Aposticha For The Dormition

Tone 4   Festive, joyous and expressing deep piety.   *C, D, Eb, F, G, A, Bb, C.*

Come you people, let us praise the all holy, undefiled Virgin, from whom did issue incarnate, in an ineffable manner, the Word of the Father, crying, and saying, Blessed art thou among women, and blessed is thy womb which did contain Christ. Placing thy soul between His holy hands, intercede thou with Him, O undefiled one, to save our souls.

Chorus: *Arise, O Lord, into Thy resting place: Thou and the ark which Thou hast sanctified.*

Reader: O most holy and undefiled Virgin, the multitudes of angels in heaven and men on earth do bless thine all honoured falling asleep; for thou didst become a Mother to Christ God, the Creator of all. Thee do we supplicate that thou mayest continue interceding with Him for our sakes, who place our hope, after God, on thee, O all praised, unwedded Theotokos.

Chorus: *The Lord hath sworn in truth unto David: He shall not turn from it.*

Reader: Let us, O peoples, sing to Christ God today with the song of David who saith, The virgins that follow her shall be brought before the king, with gladness and rejoicing; for she who is of the seed of David, through whom we have been deified, hath been translated at the hands of her Son and Master with surpassing glory. Wherefore, save us who do confess that thou art the Theotokos from every tribulation, and deliver our souls from danger.

Chorus: *Glory be to the Father, and to the Son, and to the Holy Spirit;*
        Both now and forever, and unto the ages of ages. Amen.

Doxasticon For The Dormition

Tone 4   Festive, joyous and expressing deep piety.   *C, D, Eb, F, G, A, Bb, C.*

When thou wast translated to Him Who was born of thee in an inexplicable way, O virgin Theotokos, there were present James, the brother of the Lord and first of the Chief Priests, and Peter, the honoured head and leader of theologians, with the rest of the divine rank of the Apostles, clearly uttering divine words, praising the amazing divine mystery, the mystery of the dispensation of Christ God, and with joy preparing thy body which was the God-receiving originator of life, O most glorified one, while the most holy and honoured angels looked from on high, struck with astonishment and surprise, and saying to one another: "Lift you your gates and receive you the mother of the Maker of heaven and earth. Let us laud with songs of praise her sanctified, noble body which contained the Lord, invisible to us. Therefore, we, too, celebrate thy memory, O all praised one, crying: 'Exalt the state of Christians and save our souls.'"

Hymn Of Simeon The God Receiver

Reader: Lord, now lettest Thou Thy servant depart in peace, according to Thy word, for mine eyes have seen Thy salvation, which Thou hast prepared before the face of all peoples; a light of revelation for the Gentiles, and the glory of Thy people Israel.

Trisagion Prayers

Holy God, Holy Mighty, Holy Immortal, have mercy on us. **(x3)**

Glory be to the Father, and to the Son, and to the Holy Spirit;
Both now and forever, and unto the ages of ages. Amen.

O Most Holy Trinity, have mercy on us.
O Lord, cleanse us from our sins.
O Master, pardon our iniquities.
O Holy One, visit and heal our infirmities, for Thy names sake.

Lord have mercy. **(x3)**

Glory be to the Father and to the Son and to the Holy Spirit;
Both now and forever, and unto the ages of ages. Amen.

People: *Our Father, Who art in Heaven, hallowed be Thy Name. Thy Kingdom come, Thy will be done, on earth as it is in Heaven. Give us this day our daily bread, and forgive us our trespasses, as we forgive those who trespass against us; and lead us not into temptation, but deliver us from the evil one. Amen.*
Priest: For Thine is the kingdom, the power, and the glory, of the Father, and the Son and the Holy Spirit, both now and ever, and to the ages of ages.
People: *Amen.*

Reader: O Lord, Jesus Christ, Son of God, have mercy on us.

Apolytikion Of The Dormition

Tone 1   Magnificent, happy and earthy.   *C, D, Eb, F, G, A, Bb, C.*

In thy birth giving, O Theotokos, thou didst keep and preserve virginity; and in thy falling asleep thou hast not forsaken the world; for thou wast translated into life, being the Mother of Life. Wherefore, by thine intercessions, deliver our souls from death. **(x3)**

The Dismissal

Deacon: Wisdom.

People: *Holy Father, bless.*

Priest: Christ our God, the Existing One, is blessed, always, now and forever, and unto the ages of ages.

People: *Amen.*

Reader: Preserve, O god, the holy Orthodox faith and all Orthodox Christians, unto the ages of ages.

People: *Amen.*

Priest: Most holy Theotokos, save us.

Reader: Greater in honour than the Cherubim and beyond compare more glorious than the Seraphim; without corruption thou gavest birth to God the Word, truly the Theotokos, we magnify thee.

Priest: Glory to Thee, O Christ, our God and our hope, glory to Thee.

Reader: *Glory be to the Father, and to the Son, and to the Holy Spirit;*

Both now and forever, and unto the ages of ages.

People: *Amen.*

Lord, have mercy. **(x3)**

Holy Father, bless.

Priest: May Christ our true God, through the intercessions of His all immaculate and all blameless holy Mother - whose Dormition and translation into the heavens we now celebrate - by the might of the Precious and Life giving Cross; by the protection of the honourable Bodiless Powers of Heaven; at the supplication of the honourable, glorious Prophet, Forerunner and Baptist John; of the holy, glorious and all laudable apostles; of the holy, glorious and right victorious Martyrs; of our venerable and God bearing Fathers; of *Saint N.,* the patron and protector of this holy community; of the holy and righteous ancestors of God, Joachim and Anna, and of all the saints: have mercy on us and save us, forasmuch as He is good and loveth mankind.

People: *Amen.*

Priest: Through the prayers of our holy Fathers; O Lord Jesus Christ our God; have mercy on us and save us.

People: *Amen.*

Great Vespers With The Lamentations For The Theotokos

Epitaphios (or festal icon) is decorated with fresh flowers.]

Trisagion Prayers

Priest: Blessed is our God, always, now and forever, and unto the ages of ages.

People: *Amen.*

Reader: Come, let us worship God, our King.

Come, let us worship and fall down before Christ, our King and our God.

Come, let us worship and fall down before Christ Himself, our King and our God.

Psalm 103

Of David. Concerning The Formation Of The World.

Bless the Lord, O my soul. O Lord my God, Thou hast been exceedingly magnified. Confession and majesty hast Thou put on, Who covered Thyself with light as with a garment, Who stretched out the heaven as it were a curtain; Who supports His chambers in the waters, Who appoints the clouds for His ascent, Who walks upon the wings of the winds, Who makes His angels spirits, and His ministers a flame of fire, Who establishes the earth in the sureness thereof; it shall not be turned back for ever and ever. The abyss like a garment is His mantle; upon the mountains shall the waters stand. At Thy rebuke they shall flee, at the voice of Thy thunder shall they be afraid.

The mountains rise up and the plains sink down to the place where Thou hast established them. Thou appointed a boundary that they shall not pass, neither return to cover the earth. He sends forth springs in the valleys; between the mountains shall the waters run. They shall give drink to all the beasts of the field; the wild asses shall wait to quench their thirst. Beside them shall the birds of the heaven lodge, from the midst of the rocks shall they give voice. He waters the mountains from His chambers; the earth shall be satisfied with the fruit of Thy works.

He causes the grass to grow for the cattle, and green herb for the service of men, To bring forth bread out of the earth; and wine makes glad the heart of man. To make his face cheerful with oil; and bread strengthens mans heart. The trees of the plain shall be satisfied, the cedars of Lebanon, which Thou hast planted. There shall the sparrows make their nests; the house of the heron is chief among them. The high mountains are a refuge for the harts, and so is the rock for the hares. He has made the moon for seasons; the sun knows his going down. Thou appointed the darkness, and there was the night, wherein all the beasts of the forest shall go abroad. Young lions roaring after their prey, and seeking their food from God. The sun arises, and they are gathered together, and they lay them down in their dens.

But man shall go forth unto his work, and to his labour until the evening. How magnified are Thy works, O Lord. In wisdom hast Thou made them all; the earth is filled with Thy creation. So is this great and spacious sea, therein are things creeping innumerable, small living creatures with the great. There go the ships; there this dragon, whom Thou hast made to play therein. All things wait on Thee, to give them their food in due season; when Thou gavest it to them, they shall gather it. When Thou opened Thy hand, all things shall be filled with goodness; when Thou turned away Thy face, they shall be troubled. Thou wilt take their spirit, and they shall cease; and to their dust shall they return. Thou wilt send forth Thy Spirit, and they shall be created; and Thou shalt renew the face of the earth.

Let the glory of the Lord be unto the ages; the Lord shall rejoice in His works. Who looks on the earth and makes it tremble, Who touches the mountains and they smoke. I shall sing unto the Lord throughout my life, I shall chant to my God for as long as I have my being. May my words be sweet unto Him, and I shall rejoice in the Lord. O that sinners would cease from the earth, and they that work iniquity, that they should be no more. Bless the Lord, O my soul. The sun knows his going down, Thou appointed the darkness, and there was the night. How magnified are Thy works, O Lord. In wisdom hast Thou made them all.

After The Psalm

Glory be to the Father and to the Son and to the Holy Spirit;
Both now and forever, and unto the ages of ages. Amen.

Alleluia, alleluia, alleluia. Glory to Thee, O God. **(x3)**

The Great Litany

Deacon: In peace, let us pray to the Lord.

People: *Lord, have mercy.*

Deacon: For the peace from above, and for the salvation of our souls, let us pray to the Lord.

People: *Lord, have mercy.*

Deacon: For the peace of the whole world, for the good estate of the holy churches of God, and for the union of all men, let us pray to the Lord.

People: *Lord, have mercy.*

Deacon: For this Holy House, and for those who with faith, reverence, and fear of God, enter therein, let us pray to the Lord.

People: *Lord, have mercy.*

Deacon: For our father and Archbishop Nikitas, for the venerable Priesthood, the Diaconate in Christ, for all the clergy and the people, let us pray to the Lord.

People: *Lord, have mercy.*

Deacon: For Her Majesty, the Queen, for the First Minister, for all civil authorities, and for our Armed Forces, let us pray to the Lord.

People: *Lord, have mercy.*

Deacon: That He shall aid them and grant them victory over every enemy and adversary, let us pray to the Lord.

People: *Lord, have mercy.*

Deacon: For this city, and for every city and land, and for the faithful who dwell therein, let us pray to the Lord.

People:	*Lord, have mercy.*
Deacon:	For healthful seasons, for abundance of the fruits of the earth, and for peaceful times, let us pray to the Lord.
People:	*Lord, have mercy.*
Deacon:	For travellers by sea, by land, and by air; for the sick and the suffering; for captives and their salvation, let us pray to the Lord.
People:	*Lord, have mercy.*
Deacon:	For our deliverance from all tribulation, wrath, danger, and necessity, let us pray to the Lord.
People:	*Lord, have mercy.*
Deacon:	Help us; save us; have mercy on us; and keep us, O God, by Thy grace.
People:	*Lord, have mercy.*
Deacon:	Calling to remembrance our all holy, immaculate, most blessed and glorious Lady Theotokos and Ever Virgin Mary, with all the Saints: let us commend ourselves and each other, and all our life unto Christ our God.
People:	*To Thee, O Lord.*
Priest:	For to Thou art due all glory, honour, and worship: to the Father, and to the Son, and to the Holy Spirit; Both now and forever and unto the ages of ages.
People:	*Amen.*

Psalm 140

Choir: Lord, I have cried to Thee: hear me. Hear me, O Lord.

Lord, I have cried to Thee: hear me. Receive the voice of my prayer.

When I call upon Thee, hear me, O Lord. Let my prayer arise as incense in Thy sight,

And let the lifting up of my hands be an evening sacrifice. Hear me, O Lord.

Kekragarion
Sticheroi From Psalm 140

• Set, O Lord, a watch before my mouth, and a door of enclosure round about my lips.

• Incline not my heart to words of evil, to make excuses for sins.

• Those that work iniquity; I shall not join with their number.

• The righteous man shall chasten me with mercy and reprove me; as for the oil of the sinner, let it not anoint my head.

• For yet more is my prayer in the presence of their pleasures; their judges have been swallowed up by the rock.

• They shall hear my words, for they be sweetened; as a clod of earth is broken upon the earth, so have their bones been scattered into hades.

• To Thee O Lord are mine eyes. In Thee have I hoped; take not my soul away.

• Keep me from the snare which they have laid for me, and from the stumbling blocks of them that work iniquity.

- The sinners shall fall into their own net; I am alone until I pass by.

Sticheroi From Psalm 141

- With my voice to the Lord have I cried, with my voice have I made supplication.
- I shall pour out before Him my supplications; my afflictions shall I declare before Him.
- When my spirit was fainting within me, then Thou knewest my paths.
- In this way wherein I have walked they hid for me a snare.
- I looked on my right hand, and beheld, and there was none that knew me.
- Flight has failed me, and there is none that watches out for my soul.
- I cried to Thee, O Lord; I said: Thou art my hope, my portion in the land of the living.
- Attend unto my supplication, for I am brought very low.
- Deliver me from them that persecute me, for they are stronger than I.
- Bring my soul out of prison. That I may confess Thy name.
- The righteous shall patiently wait for me until Thou shalt reward me.

Sticheroi From Psalm 129

- Out of the depths have I cried unto Thee, O Lord. O Lord, hear my voice.
- Let Thine ears be attentive to the voice of my supplication.
- If Thou should mark iniquities, O Lord; O Lord, who shall stand? For with Thee there is forgiveness.

O strange wonder, great and marvellous. For the fount of life is laid within a sepulchre; a ladder to Heaven's heights doth the small grave become. Be glad, O Gethsemane, the sanctuary of her that gave birth to God. You faithful, let us cry out, possessing as our commander great Gabriel: "Maiden Full of Grace, rejoice thou, with thee is the Lord our God, Who abundantly granteth His Great Mercy to the world through thee."

- 5. For Thy name's sake have I patiently waited for Thee, O Lord; my soul has patiently waited for Thy word, my soul has hoped in the Lord.

O strange wonder, great and marvellous. For the fount of life is laid within a sepulchre; a ladder to Heaven's heights doth the small grave become. Be glad, O Gethsemane, the sanctuary of her that gave birth to God. You faithful, let us cry out, possessing as our commander great Gabriel: "Maiden Full of Grace, rejoice thou, with thee is the Lord our God, Who abundantly granteth His Great Mercy to the world through thee."

- 4. From the morning watch until night, from the morning watch let Israel hope in the Lord.

Who can tell thy mysteries, O pure one? Thou art known, O Lady, as the throne of the Most High, and thou hast removed from earth to Heaven on this day. Majestically and sublime, thy glory beameth with graces divinely bright. You virgins, be lifted up unto the height with the Mother of Christ the King. Maiden Full of

Grace, rejoice thou, with thee is the Lord our God, Who abundantly granteth His Great Mercy to the world through thee.

• 3. For with the Lord there is mercy, and with Him is plenteous redemption; and He shall redeem Israel out of all his iniquities.

Who can tell thy mysteries, O pure one? Thou art known, O Lady, as the throne of the Most High, and thou hast removed from earth to Heaven on this day. Majestically and sublime, thy glory beameth with graces divinely bright. You virgins, be lifted up unto the height with the Mother of Christ the King. Maiden Full of Grace, rejoice thou, with thee is the Lord our God, Who abundantly granteth His Great Mercy to the world through thee.

Sticheroi From Psalm 116

• 2. O praise the Lord, all you nations; praise Him, all you peoples.

Thy Dormition is now glorified by dominions, powers, principalities and thrones, authorities, cherubim and the dread seraphim; the earth born are filled with joy, adorned with thy divine glory and majesty; and kings worship, falling down with all the angels and archangels, and they sing: "Maiden Full of Grace, rejoice thou, with thee is the Lord our God, Who abundantly granteth His Great Mercy to the world through thee."

• 1. For He has made His mercy to prevail over us, and the truth of the Lord abides forever.

Thy Dormition is now glorified by dominions, powers, principalities and thrones, authorities, cherubim and the dread seraphim; the earth born are filled with joy, adorned with thy divine glory and majesty; and kings worship, falling down with all the angels and archangels, and they sing: "Maiden Full of Grace, rejoice thou, with thee is the Lord our God, Who abundantly granteth His Great Mercy to the world through thee."

Glory be to the Father, and to the Son, and to the Holy Spirit;
Both now and forever, and unto the ages of ages. Amen.

Theotokion

Tone 8   Humility, tranquillity, repose, suffering, pleading.   C, D, Eb, F, G, A, Bb, C.

Verily, the King of Heaven, for His love to mankind, didst appear on earth; and with men did He deal; for He took unto Himself a body from the pure Virgin. And from her did He issue in the adopted body, He being one Son, dual in Nature, not dual in Person. Wherefore, do we confess, preaching the truth that Christ our God is perfect God and perfect Man. Therefore, O Mother who hast no groom, beseech Him to have mercy upon our souls.

[Whilst:]

The Holy Entrance

Deacon: *(Soto voce)* Let us pray to the Lord. Lord have mercy.

Priest: *(Soto voce)* In the evening and in the morning and at noon we praise Thee, we bless Thee, we give thanks unto Thee, and we pray unto Thee, O Master of all, Lord Who lovest mankind; Direct our prayer as incense before Thee, and incline not our hearts unto words of thought of evil, but deliver us from all who seek after our souls. For unto Thee, O Lord, Lord are our eyes, and in Thee have we hoped. Put us not to shame, O our God. For unto Thee are due all glory, honour and worship, to the Father, the Son and the Holy Spirit, both now and forever, and to the ages of ages.

Deacon: Amen.

[Censing]

Deacon: *(Soto voce)* Master, bless the Holy Entrance.

Priest: *(Soto voce)* Blessed is the Entrance to Thy Holy place; both now and forever, and unto the ages of ages. Amen.

Deacon: *(Aloud)* Wisdom. Stand up.

O Gladsome Light

O Gladsome Light of the holy glory of the immortal Father; Heavenly holy, blessed Jesus Christ.

Now that we have come to the setting of the sun, and behold the Evening Light.

We praise God; Father, Son and Holy Spirit.

For meet it is at all time to worship Thee, with voices of praise;

O Son of God and Giver of Life. Therefore all the world doth glorify Thee.

Prokeimenon

Priest: The Evening Prokeimenon.

[Saturday]   Tone 6 *Rich texture, funeral, sorrowful.*   *D, Eb, F##, G, A, Bb, C##, D.*

Reader: The Lord is clothed with strength and He has girded Himself.

People: *The Lord is King, He is clothed with majesty.*

Reader: For He established the world which shall not be shaken.

People: *The Lord is King, He is clothed with majesty.*

Reader: Holiness becomes Thine house, O Lord, to the length of days.

People: *The Lord is King, He is clothed with majesty.*

Reader: The Lord is King | *He is clothed with majesty.*

The Litany Of Fervent Supplication

Deacon: Let us all say with our whole soul, and with our whole mind let us say:

People: *Lord, have mercy.*

Deacon: Lord Almighty, God of our Fathers, we pray Thee, hearest and have mercy.

People: *Lord, have mercy.*

Deacon: Have mercy on us, O God, according to Thy great mercy, we pray Thee; hear us and have mercy.

People: *Lord, have mercy.* **(x3)**

Deacon: Also we pray for our Archbishop <u>Nikitas</u>.

People: *Lord, have mercy.* **(x3)**

Deacon: For our Sovereign Lady, Queen <u>Elizabeth</u>, the Royal family, our Welsh Assembly Government, and all in authority, let us pray to the Lord.

People: *Lord, have mercy.* **(x3)**

Deacon: Also we pray for mercy, life, peace, health, salvation, visitation, pardon and forgiveness of sins for the servants of God, all devout and Orthodox Christians, those who dwell in or visit this city or town and parish, the wardens and members of this church and their families and all who have asked for our prayers, unworthy though we are.

People: *Lord, have mercy.* **(x3)**

Deacon: Also we pray for the blessed and ever remembered founders of this holy church, and for all our brothers and sisters who have gone to their rest before us, and who lie here asleep in the true faith; and for the Orthodox everywhere *[and the servants of God N and N – (names given before the service)]* and that they may be pardoned all their offences, both voluntary and involuntary.

People: *Lord, have mercy.* **(x3)**

Deacon: Also we pray for those who bring offerings, those who care for the beauty of this holy and venerable house, for those who labour in its service, for those who sing, and for the people here present, who await Thy great and rich mercy.

People: *Lord, have mercy.* **(x3)**

Priest: For Thou, O God, art merciful and love mankind, and to Thee we givest glory, to the Father, the Son and the Holy Spirit, both now and forever, and unto the ages of ages.

People: *Amen.*

Reader: Vouchsafe, O Lord, to keep us this evening without sin. Blessed art Thou, O Lord, the God of our fathers, and praised and glorified is Thy name unto the ages. Amen.

Let Thy mercy, O Lord, be upon us, according as we have hoped in Thee.

Blessed art Thou, O Lord, teach me Thy statutes.

Blessed art Thou, O Master, give me understanding of Thy statutes.

Blessed art Thou, O Holy One, enlighten me by Thy statutes.

O Lord, Thy mercy endures forever; disdain not the work of Thy hands. To Thee is due praise, to Thee is due song, to Thee is due glory, to the Father, and to the Son, and to the Holy Spirit; both now and forever, and unto the ages of ages. Amen.

The Litany Of Supplication

Deacon: Let us complete our evening prayer unto the Lord.

People: *Lord, have mercy.*

Deacon: Help us; save us; have mercy on us; and keep us, O God, by Thy grace.

People: *Lord, have mercy.*

Deacon: That the whole evening may be perfect, holy, peaceful and sinless, let us ask of the Lord.

People: *Grant this, O Lord.*

Deacon: An angel of peace, a faithful guide, a guardian of our souls and bodies, let us ask of the Lord.

People: *Grant this, O Lord.*

Deacon: Pardon and remission of our sins and transgressions, let us ask of the Lord.

People: *Grant this, O Lord.*

Deacon: All things good and profitable for our souls and peace for the world, let us ask of the Lord.

People: *Grant this, O Lord.*

Deacon: That we may complete the remaining time of our life in peace and repentance, let us ask of the Lord.

People: *Grant this, O Lord.*

Deacon: A Christian ending to our life, painless, blameless, peaceful, and a good defence before the fearful judgement seat of Christ, let us ask of the Lord.

People: *Grant this, O Lord.*

Deacon: Calling to remembrance our all holy, immaculate, most blessed and glorious Lady Theotokos and Ever Virgin Mary, with all the Saints: let us commend ourselves and one another, and all our life to Christ our God.

People: *To Thee, O Lord.*

Priest: For Thou art a good God and lovest mankind, and to Thee we ascribe glory: to the Father, and to the Son, and to the Holy Spirit; both now and forever, and to the ages of ages.

People: *Amen.*

Priest: Peace be with you all.

People: *And with thy spirit.*

Deacon: Let us bow our heads unto the Lord.

People: *To Thee, O Lord.*

Priest: O Lord our God, Who did bow the heavens and come down for the salvation of mankind: Look upon Thy servants and Thine inheritance; for to Thee, the fearful Judge Who yet loves mankind, have Thine servants bowed their heads and submissively inclined their necks, awaiting not help from men but entreating Thy mercy and looking confidently for Thy salvation. Guard them at all times, both during this present evening and in the approaching night, from every foe, from all adverse powers of the devil, and from vain thoughts and from evil imaginations. Blessed and glorified be the might of Thy kingdom: of the Father, and of the Son, and of the Holy Spirit; both now and forever, and unto the ages of ages.

People: *Amen.*

The Aposticha From The Octoechos *(Triodion if Lent)* With The Following Stichoi

Stichos 1:

To Thee have I lifted up my eyes, to Thee that dwells in heaven. Behold, as the eyes of servants look at the hands of their masters, as the eyes of the handmaid look at the hands of her mistress, so do our eyes look to the Lord our God, until He take pity on us.

Stichos 2:

Have mercy on us, O Lord, have mercy on us, for greatly are we filled with abasement. Greatly has our soul been filled therewith; let reproach come upon them that prosper, and abasement on the proud.

Choir: *The Lord is King, He is clothed with majesty.*

Reader: Let us glorify Christ risen from the dead; for He did take unto Himself a soul and a body; and He separated one from the other in the Passion, when His pure soul went down to Hades that He led captive; and the holy body saw no corruption in the grave, the body of the Redeemer, Saviour of our souls.

Choir: *For He established the world which shall not be shaken.*

Reader: With psalms and songs of praise, O Christ, do we glorify Thy Resurrection from the dead, by which Thou didst deliver us from the rebellion of Hades. And since Thou art God, Thou didst grant us eternal life and the Great Mercy.

Choir: *Holiness becomes Thine house, O Lord, to the length of days.*

Reader: O Lord of all, O incomprehensible One; O Maker of heaven and earth, when Thou didst suffer in Thy Passion on the Cross, Thou didst pour out for me passionlessness; and when Thou didst submit to burial and didst rise in glory, Thou didst raise Adam with Thee by a mighty hand. Wherefore, glory to Thy third day Resurrection by which Thou didst grant us eternal life and forgiveness of sins; for Thou alone art compassionate.

Glory be to the Father, and to the Son, and to the Holy Spirit;
[Daily Doxasticon – if available]
Both now and forever, and unto the ages of ages. Amen.
[Seasonal Doxasticon – if available]

Hymn Of Simeon The God Receiver

Reader: Lord, now lettest Thou Thy servant depart in peace, according to Thy word, for mine eyes have seen Thy salvation, which Thou hast prepared before the face of all peoples; a light of revelation for the Gentiles, and the glory of Thy people Israel.

[Clergy come to stand before the epitaphios.]

First Stasis

Eirmos

[To the melodies of the Lamentations chanted at the epitaphios of Christ.]

Tone 5   Stimulating, dancing, and rhythmical.   *C, D, Eb, F, G, A, Bb, C.*

- In a grave they laid Thee, O my Life and my Christ, and now also the Mother of Life; a strange sight both to angels and men.
- We magnify thee O pure Theotokos; and we honour thy holy Dormition as we bow before thine honourable tomb.
- How, O Mary, canst thou die thou who art the life of faithful ones and how can the tomb contain thy body which contained the One Which cannot be contained?
- Queen who gavest birth to God the King of the heavens, thou art now royally translated, O pure one to the kingdom of the heavens.
- From the earth thou wast translated but thou didst not forsake the earth now All holy Theotokos liberate the whole world from mighty ones.
- Gabriel was sent from God to announce to thee the good news of thine imminent departure from this life O thou pure and spotless heavenly Lady.
- Receive, O Mother, from thy children, our love and these hymns and odes to bid thee farewell which we offer from the depth of our souls.
- Leave us not orphaned, O Mother as thou dost go from earth to heaven, where thou wilt be reunited with thy Son and thy God.
- Come with me, O Anna. Come and stand with us now. Lead us in the festive praises of Mary thine own daughter, the Mother of God.
- The God of glory thy Son, O pure one now admits thee as His Mother with glory and enthrones thee at His right hand.
- The holy Apostles, O pure Theotokos, when they saw thine all holy body fell before it weeping reverently.
- The gate enters the gate, and heaven enters heaven, O ineffable and wondrous mystery. Now the throne draws near to the throne of God.

Glory be to the Father and to the Son and to the Holy Spirit;

Triadicon

Word of God, we hymn Thee. God of all things art Thou; with Thy Father and Thy Spirit Most Holy praised and we glorify Thy nature divine.

Both now and forever, and unto the ages of ages. Amen.

Every generation blesses thee, O Theotokos, Ever Virgin and sovereign Lady, and we glorify thy Dormition.
[slow:]

Eirmos

In a grave they laid Thee, O my Life and my Christ, and now also the Mother of Life; a strange sight both to angels and men.

Second Stasis

Eirmos

> *Tone 5   Stimulating, dancing, and rhythmical.*   *C, D, Eb, F, G, A, Bb, C.*

• Right it is indeed, Life bestowing Lord, to magnify Thee who hast glorified Thy Mother at the time of her life bearing repose.

• Right it is indeed to magnify thee, Theotokos, for thy divine and blameless soul is entrusted to the hands of God.

• Shudder, O you heavens. and, O earth, give ear unto these words: God descended once before for our sake He descends again today for His Mother.

• Though heaven receives thine undefiled body, O Lady yet grace hath been poured out covering the whole face of the earth.

• Now Joachim rejoiceth seeing the great glory of his only child who indeed didst bear a divine Child truly inexplicable and inspired.

• Gethsemane is blessed for it gained thy virginal and blessed tomb it hath been greatly honoured as the royal bridal chamber.

• Angels reverently attend to thy most pure sepulchre, O pure one and a light from it doth shine forth a place lighted by the light of God.

• Thou didst leave thy pure belt and entrusted it to holy Thomas as a witness of thy translation from the earth unto God above.

• Mighty kings of the earth and the wealthy among all earths peoples pray to thee, O All holy Virgin as a daughter of the King of heaven.

• The glorious city of the Lord, about which they spoke so gloriously, was translated from earth to heaven and was led into the house of God.

• Mary, thou only high Queen of heaven above and of earth here below, lead into thy kingdom those who glorify thy holy Dormition.

• Holy and Ever Virgin Lady, Mary Theotokos, Queen and Mother, take now thy rest and sleep and rule unto ages of ages with God.

Glory be to the Father and to the Son and to the Holy Spirit;

O eternal God, Word co-unoriginate and Spirit, make firm the faith of the Orthodox against heresy and error, O good One.

Both now and forever, and unto the ages of ages. Amen.

Grant true life to the faithful O all blameless and pure holy Virgin, thou who gavest birth unto Life Itself and who hast now departed unto Life.

[slow:]
Eirmos

Right it is indeed, Life bestowing Lord, to magnify Thee who hast glorified Thy Mother at the time of her life bearing repose.

Third Stasis

Eirmos

Tone 3   *Arrogant, brave, and mature atmosphere.*   *F, G, A, A#, C, D, E, F.*

- Every generation to thy grave comes bringing its dirge of praises, O Virgin.
- All of creation to the grave comes bringing a farewell hymn to our Lady.
- Christs holy Disciples tend to the body of Mary, Mother of my God.
- Orders of Angels and Archangels, invisibly hymn her presence.
- Pious Women with the Apostles, now cry out their lamentations.
- She who was at Cana at the marriage hath been called with the Apostles.
- The Master descendeth to Gethsemane with countless hosts of heaven.
- The choir of the Disciples, seeing the Lord descend in glory greatly rejoiceth.
- Let the earth leap for joy as it beholdeth our God from heaven descending.
- Let us go out quickly meeting the Lord Jesus Who cometh once more among us.
- Let us be attentive, God now speaketh with His most pure Mother.
- Most sweet Mother, come and rejoice with thine own most sweet Child, Jesus.
- Behold now thy Son cometh to bring thee into His home in the heavens.
- Come, My most lovely one and enjoy the beauty of thine own Son thy Maker.
- Come indeed, My Mother. Come into divine joy and enter into the kingdom.
- "What shall I bring Thee O my Son, the God-Man" the Maiden cried to the Master.
- "What shall I bring Thee O my God in heaven, except my soul and body."
- The Father I glorify, to the Son I sing a hymn, the Holy Spirit I worship.
- Adam and Eve came out to behold the glory of their own Virgin offspring.
- Blessed be the parents Joachim and Anna who for the world bore a daughter.
- Grant to thy Church peace, to thy flock salvation, through thy most holy Dormition.

Glory be to the Father and to the Son and to the Holy Spirit;

Triadicon

O Thou Triune Godhead, Father, Son and Spirit, upon Thy world have mercy.

Both now and forever, and unto the ages of ages. Amen.

Make thy servants worthy, O most holy Virgin to see thy Son's kingdom.

[slow:]

Eirmos

Tone 3   Arrogant, brave, and mature atmosphere.   *F, G, A, A#, C, D, E, F.*

Every generation to thy grave comes bringing its dirge of praises, O Virgin.

Trisagion Prayers

Holy God, Holy Mighty, Holy Immortal, have mercy on us. **(x3)**

> *Glory be to the Father, and to the Son, and to the Holy Spirit;*
>
> *Both now and forever, and unto the ages of ages. Amen.*

O Most Holy Trinity, have mercy on us.

O Lord, cleanse us from our sins.

O Master, pardon our iniquities.

O Holy One, visit and heal our infirmities, for Thy names sake.

Lord have mercy. **(x3)**

> *Glory be to the Father and to the Son and to the Holy Spirit;*
>
> *Both now and forever, and unto the ages of ages. Amen.*

People: *Our Father, Who art in Heaven, hallowed be Thy Name. Thy Kingdom come, Thy will be done, on earth as it is in Heaven. Give us this day our daily bread, and forgive us our trespasses, as we forgive those who trespass against us; and lead us not into temptation, but deliver us from the evil one. Amen.*

Priest: For Thine is the kingdom, the power, and the glory, of the Father, and the Son and the Holy Spirit, both now and ever, and to the ages of ages.

People: *Amen.*

Resurrectional Apolytikion

Tone 8   Humility, tranquillity, repose, suffering, pleading.   *C, D, Eb, F, G, A, Bb, C.*

From the heights Thou didst descend, O compassionate One, and Thou didst submit to the three day burial, that Thou might deliver us from passion; Thou art our life and our Resurrection, O Lord, glory to Thee.

> *Glory be to the Father and to the Son and to the Holy Spirit;*
>
> *Both now and forever, and unto the ages of ages. Amen.*

[If a procession be made with the epitaphios, whilst this is repeated as many times as necessary:]

Resurrectional Theotokion

Tone 1   *Magnificent, happy, and earthy character.*   *C, D, Eb, F, G, A, Bb, C.*

As Gabriel cried aloud unto thee: "Rejoice, O Virgin," with that cry did the Lord of all become incarnate in thee, O holy ark, as spake the righteous David; and thou wast revealed, as more spacious than the heavens, in that thou bore thy Creator. Wherefore, glory to Him Who abided in thee; glory to Him Who came from thee; glory to Him, Who through thy birth giving hath set us free.

The Dismissal

Deacon: Wisdom.

People: *Holy Father, bless.*

Priest: Christ our God, the Existing One, is blessed, always, now and forever, and unto the ages of ages.

People: *Amen.*

Reader: Preserve, O God, the holy Orthodox faith and all Orthodox Christians, unto the ages of ages.

People: *Amen.*

Priest: Most holy Theotokos, save us.

Reader: Greater in honour than the Cherubim and beyond compare more glorious than the Seraphim; without corruption thou gavest birth to God the Word, truly the Theotokos, we magnify thee.

Priest: Glory to Thee, O Christ, our God and our hope, glory to Thee.

Reader: Glory be to the Father, and to to Son, and to the Holy Spirit, both now and for ever, both and to the ages of ages.

People: *Amen.*

     Lord, have mercy. **(x3)**

     Holy Father, bless.

Priest: May He who rose from the dead, Christ our true God, through the prayers of His most holy Mother, by the power of the precious and life giving Cross, through the protection of the honoured, Bodiless powers of Heaven, through the intercessions of the honoured, glorious prophet, forerunner and baptist John, of the holy, all praised and glorious Apostles, of the holy, glorious and triumphant Martyrs, of our venerable and God bearing Fathers and Mothers who have shone forth in the ascetic life, of the holy and righteous ancestors of God, Joachim and Anna, of *[patronal saint(s)]* to whom the church is dedicated, of *[Saint N]* whose memory we celebrate today, and of all the Saints, have mercy on us and save us, for He is good and loves mankind.

People: *Amen.*

Priest: Through the prayers of our holy Fathers; O Lord Jesus Christ our God; have mercy on us and save us.

People: *Amen.*

Great Parakleses For The Dormition Of The Theotokos

With The Great Supplicatory Canon To The Most Holy Theotokos As Sung During The Dormition Fast

[With a priest.]

The Parakleses Service is served during times of tribulation, but also on each evening of the Dormition Fast, August 1-13, inclusive. In the Dormition Fast, the Little and Great Parakleses canons can be chanted in alternating sequence from day to day, at the end of Vespers or in a standalone service. If a parish knows only the Little Parakleses, this alone can be chanted each time. We begin this sequence with the Little Parakleses, except when August 1 falls on Sunday. We do not chant the Parakleses on any Saturday evening and also not on the paramon of the Feast of Transfiguration (the evening on August 5). On Sunday evening and on the day of Transfiguration in the evening the Great Parakleses is chanted. Accordingly, the series of Parakleses unfolds for the intervening days. The table below shows the series of Parakleses.

Chart For Calculating Which Parakleses Canon To Use

L = Little Parakleses / G = Great Parakleses / – = no Parakleses service on this day

+ = celebrate Great Vespers for the Transfiguration on this day

[Remember to use Orthodox daybreak.]

Aug	1st	2nd	3rd	4th	5th	6th	7th	8th	9th	10th	11th	12th	13th
Monday	L	G	L	G	– +	–	G	L	G	L	G	L	–
Tuesday	L	G	L	G	– +	G	L	G	L	G	L	–	G
Wednesday	L	G	L	–	– +	G	L	G	L	G	–	G	L
Thursday	L	G	–	G	– +	G	L	G	L	–	G	L	G
Friday	L	–	G	L	– +	G	L	G	–	G	L	G	L
Saturday	–	G	L	G	– +	G	L	–	G	L	G	L	G
Sunday	G	L	G	L	– +	G	–	G	L	G	L	G	L

If Parakleses shall be offered with Vespers; it is chanted after "The Prayer of St Simeon" with the omission of the opening blessing of the Parakleses Service. Rather, at this point, the reader recites Psalm 142.

If the Parakleses Service is offered without Vespers as a standalone service; then as below.

We remember the names of the living during the three litanies. If it is a long list of names, then the priest can mention it in one, two or all of the litanies.

[An Icon of the Theotokos is placed on a stand in the centre of the Solea and the Holy Doors remains closed. The priest, being vested in exorasson and blue epitrachelion, standing on the Solea before the Icon of the Theotokos, makes three metanias and says out loud:]

Trisagion Prayers

Priest: Blessed is our God, always, both now and forever, and unto the ages of ages.

People: *Amen.*

Priest: Glory to Thee, our God, glory to Thee.

O Heavenly King, Comforter, Spirit of Truth, Who art everywhere present and fillest all things, Treasury of blessings and Giver of life: Come and abide in us and cleanse us from every impurity and save our souls, O Good One.

Reader: Holy God, Holy Mighty, Holy Immortal, have mercy on us. **(x3)**

Glory be to the Father, and to the Son, and to the Holy Spirit;
Both now and forever, and unto the ages of ages. Amen.

O Most Holy Trinity, have mercy on us.

O Lord, cleanse us from our sins.

O Master, pardon our iniquities.

O Holy One, visit and heal our infirmities, for Thy names sake.

Lord have mercy. **(x3)**

Glory be to the Father and to the Son and to the Holy Spirit;
Both now and forever, and unto the ages of ages. Amen.

People: *Our Father, Who art in Heaven, hallowed be Thy Name. Thy Kingdom come, Thy will be done, on earth as it is in Heaven. Give us this day our daily bread, and forgive us our trespasses, as we forgive those who trespass against us; and lead us not into temptation, but deliver us from the evil one.*

Priest: For Thine is the Kingdom, and the power, and the glory: of the Father, and of the Son, and of the Holy Spirit; both now and forever, and unto the ages of ages.

People: *Amen.*

Lord, have mercy. (x12)

Glory be to the Father and to the Son and to the Holy Spirit;
Both now and forever and unto the ages of ages. Amen.

Come, let us worship God, our King.

Come, let us worship and fall down before Christ, our King and our God.

Come, let us worship and fall down before Christ Himself, our King and our God.

Psalm 142

Hear my prayer, O Lord, give ear to my supplications. In Thy faithfulness answer me, and in Thy righteousness. Do not enter into judgement with Thy servant, for in Thy sight no one living is righteous. For the enemy has persecuted my soul; he has crushed my life to the ground; he has made me dwell in darkness, like those who have long been dead. Therefore my spirit is overwhelmed within me; my heart within me is distressed. I remember the days of old; I meditate on all Thy works; I muse on the work of Thine hands. I spread out my hands to Thee; my soul longs for Thee like a thirsty land. Answer me speedily, O Lord; my spirit fails. Do not hide Thy face from me, lest I be like those who go down into the pit. Cause me to hear Thy loving kindness in the morning, for in Thee do I trust; cause me to know the way in which I should walk, for I lift up my soul to Thee. Deliver me, O Lord, from mine enemies; in Thee I take shelter. Teach me to do Thy will, for Thou art my God; Thy Spirit is good. Lead me in the land of uprightness. Revive me, O Lord, for Thy names sake. For Thy righteousness' sake bring my soul out of trouble. In Thy mercy cut off mine enemies, and destroy all those who afflict my soul; for I am Thy servant.

God Is The Lord

People: *God is the Lord and has revealed Himself to us. Blessed is He who comes in the Name of the Lord.*

Reader: Give thanks to the Lord, for He is good; and His steadfast love endures forever.

People: *God is the Lord and has revealed Himself to us. Blessed is He who comes in the Name of the Lord.*

Reader: All nations surrounded me; in the Name of the Lord, I withstood them.

People: *God is the Lord and has revealed Himself to us. Blessed is He who comes in the Name of the Lord.*

Reader: This is the Lords doing and is marvellous in our eyes.

People: *God is the Lord and has revealed Himself to us. Blessed is He who comes in the Name of the Lord.*

Apolytikia And Theotokion

Tone 4   Festive, joyous and expressing deep piety.   *C, D, Eb, F, G, A, Bb, C.*

To the Theotokos let us run now most earnestly, we sinners all and wretched ones, and fall prostrate in repentance, calling from the depths of our souls: Lady, come unto our aid, have compassion upon us; hasten thou for we are lost in a throng of transgressions; turn not thy servants away with empty hands, for thee alone do we have as our only hope.

Glory be to the Father, and to the Son, and to the Holy Spirit;

[to your Patron Saint]. If yours is St Martin:

Troparion Of St Martin Of Tours

Tone 4   Festive, joyous and expressing deep piety.   *C, D, Eb, F, G, A, Bb, C.*

In signs and in miracles thou wert renowned throughout Gaul. By grace and adoption thou art a light for the world, O Martin, blessed of God. Alms deeds and compassion filled thy life with their splendours. Teaching and wise counsel were thy riches and treasures, which thou dispensest freely to those who honour thee.

Both now and forever, and unto the ages of ages. Amen.

Theotokion

Tone 4   Festive, joyous and expressing deep piety.   *C, D, Eb, F, G, A, Bb, C.*

O Theotokos, we shall not cease from speaking of all thy mighty acts, all we the unworthy ones; for if thou hadst not stood to intercede for us, who would have delivered us from such numerous dangers? Who would have preserved us all until now in true freedom? O Lady, we shall not turn away from thee; for thou dost always save thy servants from all manner of grief.

Psalm 50

Have mercy on me, O God, according to Thy great mercy; and according to the multitude of Thy compassions blot out my transgression. Wash me thoroughly from mine iniquity, and cleanse me from my sin. For I acknowledge mine iniquity, and my sin is ever before me. Against Thee, Thee only have I sinned, and done evil in Thy sight, that Thou mayest be found just when Thou speakest, and victorious when Thou art judged. For behold, I was conceived in iniquity, and in sin my mother bore me. For behold, Thou hast loved truth; Thou hast made known to me the hidden and secret things of Thy wisdom. Thou shalt sprinkle me with hyssop, and I shall be made clean; Thou shalt wash me, and I shall be whiter than snow. Make me to hear joy and gladness; that the humbled bones may rejoice. Turn Thy face away from my sins, and blot out all mine iniquities.

Create in me a clean heart, O God, and renew a steadfast spirit within me. Cast me not away from Thy presence, and take not Thy Holy Spirit from me. Restore to me the joy of Thy salvation, and establish me with Thy governing Spirit. I shall teach transgressors Thy ways, and the ungodly shall turn back to Thee. Deliver me from blood guiltiness, O God, the God of my salvation; my tongue shall joyfully declare Thy righteousness. Lord, open my lips, and my mouth shall declare Thy praise. For if Thou hadst desired sacrifice, I would give it; Thou dost not delight in burnt offerings. A sacrifice to God is a broken spirit; God shall not despise a broken and a humbled heart. Do good, O Lord, in Thy good pleasure to Zion, and let the walls of Jerusalem be builded. Then Thou shalt be pleased with a sacrifice of righteousness, with oblation and whole burned offerings. Then shall they offer bulls on Thine altar.

The Great Supplicatory Canon
Ode One

Most Holy Theotokos, save us.

Tone 8   Humility, tranquillity, repose, suffering, pleading.   *C, D, Eb, F, G, A, Bb, C.*

My humble soul is troubled by the rising tempests of afflictions and woes; and clouds of misfortunes overcome me, bringing darkness to my heart, O Bride of God. But since thou art the Mother of the Divine and Eternal Light, shine thy gladsome light and illumine me.

Most Holy Theotokos, save us.

From countless trials and afflictions, grievous woes, and from misfortunes of life have I been delivered by thy mighty strength, O spotless and immaculate Maid. I extol and I magnify thine immeasurable sympathy, and the loving care that thou hast for me.

Glory be to the Father, and to the Son, and to the Holy Spirit;

Having my hope now in thy mighty help, O Maid, I flee for refuge to thee; and unto thy shelter have I run wholeheartedly, O Lady, and I bow my knee; and I mourn and cry weeping: Do not disdain me, the wretched one, for thou art the refuge of Christian folk.

Both now and forever, and unto the ages of ages. Amen.

I shall not cease from making known most manifestly thy great deeds, Maid of God; for if thou wert not present to intercede in my behalf and importune thy Son and God, who would free and deliver me from such tempests and turbulence, and surmount the perils that trouble me?

Troparia After The First Ode

Tone 8   Humility, tranquillity, repose, suffering, pleading.   *C, D, Eb, F, G, A, Bb, C.*

Preserve and save, O Theotokos, thy servants from every danger. After God, do all of us for refuge flee unto thee; a firm rampart art thou and our protection. In thy goodwill, look thou on me, O all hymned Theotokos, and do thou behold my body's grievous infirmity, and heal thou the cause of my soul's sorrow.

Ode Three

Most Holy Theotokos, save us.

At a loss and despairing, I cry with pain unto thee: Hasten, O thou fervent protection; grant thou thy help to me, who am thy lowly slave and wretched servant, O Maiden; for with heartfelt fervour I come seeking for thine aid.

Most Holy Theotokos, save us.

Thou, O Lady, have truly been shown to be wondrous now in thy benefactions and mercies granted to me, O Maid; hence do I glorify and acclaim thee, whilst praising thy great loving care and thy boundless solicitude.

Glory be to the Father, and to the Son, and to the Holy Spirit;

Mighty storms of misfortunes, O Lady, pass over me; and the swelling waves of afflictions plunge me into the depths. Make haste, O Full of Grace; lend me thy helping hand quickly, for thou art my fervent protectress and sure support.

Both now and forever, and unto the ages of ages. Amen.

I profess thee, O Lady, as the true Mother of God: thee, who hast both banished and triumphed over the might of death; for as the source of Life, thou hast freed me from Hades' bonds, raising me to life, though to earth was I fallen down.

Troparia After The Third Ode

Tone 8   *Humility, tranquillity, repose, suffering, pleading.*   *C, D, Eb, F, G, A, Bb, C.*

Preserve and save, O Theotokos, thy servants from every danger. After God, do all of us for refuge flee unto thee; a firm rampart art thou and our protection. In thy goodwill, look thou on me, O all hymned Theotokos, and do thou behold my body's grievous infirmity, and heal thou the cause of my soul's sorrow.

Litany

[Censing the Icon of the Theotokos, whilst:]

Priest: Have mercy on us, O God, according to Thy Great Mercy, we pray Thee, hearken and have mercy.

People: *Lord, have mercy.* (**x3**)

Priest: Again we pray for all pious and Orthodox Christians.

People: *Lord, have mercy.* (**x3**)

Priest: Again we pray for our Archbishop <u>Nikitas</u>, and for all our brotherhood in Christ.

People: *Lord, have mercy.* (**x3**)

Priest: Again we pray for mercy, life, peace, health, salvation and visitation and pardon and remission of sins for the servants of God, all Orthodox Christians of true worship, who live and dwell in this community, the parishioners and benefactors of this holy temple, and all that serve, sing, labour and gather herein; and for the servants of God [Names], and for the suffering Christians of Syria, Lebanon, Palestine, Iraq, Egypt, all of the Middle East (add any other nations that may be appropriate) and for the forgiveness of their every transgression, both voluntary and involuntary.

People: *Lord, have mercy.* (**x3**)

Priest: For Thou art a merciful God Who lovest mankind, and unto Thee we ascribe glory: to the Father, and to the Son, and to the Holy Spirit; both now and forever, and unto the ages of ages.

People: Amen.

Kathisma

Tone 2   Majesty, gentleness, hope, repentance and sadness.   E, F, G, Ab, B, C.

O fervent advocate, invincible battlement, fountain of mercy, and sheltering retreat for the world, earnestly we cry to thee: Lady Mother of God, hasten thou, and save us from all imperilment, for thou alone art our speedy protectress.

The Great Supplicatory Canon (Continued)

Ode Four

Most Holy Theotokos, save us.

Tone 8   Humility, tranquillity, repose, suffering, pleading.   C, D, Eb, F, G, A, Bb, C.

Where else shall I find me another to be my help? To what refuge shall I hasten to be saved? Whose fervent aid shall I have in need? Alas, I am shaken by life's affliction and turbulence. In thee alone, O Maiden, do I hope, trust, and glory; and I run to thy shelter; do thou save me.

Most Holy Theotokos, save us.

I magnify and I proclaim, O thou all pure one, the sweet river of thy tender mercy and thy loving care; for with many gifts hath it greatly refreshed my tormented and truly lowly soul, afire in a furnace of misfortunes and sorrows; and I run to thy shelter; do thou save me.

Glory be to the Father, and to the Son, and to the Holy Spirit;

Thou, O pure Maid, all holy Virgin and spotless one, art mine only steadfast shelter and retreat, and mighty wall that cannot be breached, my weapon of salvation. Do not disdain me, the prodigal, O hope of the despairing and ally of the ailing, O thou gladness and help of afflicted ones.

Both now and forever, and unto the ages of ages. Amen.

How shall I laud, how shall I worthily sing the praise, of thy boundless mercies and compassions which have ever cooled and refreshed my soul, aflame and tormented, O Lady, and wounded grievously? Indeed thy benefactions and thy providence, Maiden, are bestowed upon me most abundantly.

Troparia After The Fourth Ode

Tone 8   Humility, tranquillity, repose, suffering, pleading.   *C, D, Eb, F, G, A, Bb, C.*

Preserve and save, O Theotokos, thy servants from every danger. After God, do all of us for refuge flee unto thee; a firm rampart art thou and our protection. In thy goodwill, look thou on me, O all hymned Theotokos, and do thou behold my body's grievous infirmity, and heal thou the cause of my soul's sorrow.

Ode Five

Most Holy Theotokos, save us.

As one grateful I cry out: Rejoice, O Virgin Mother; rejoice, O thou Bride of God; rejoice, O holy shelter; rejoice, O weapon and rampart invincible; rejoice, thou the protection and the assistance and salvation of all them that run to thee, O Maid of God.

Most Holy Theotokos, save us.

They that hate me without cause have made ready a dart and a sword and pit for me; and my hapless body do they seek to destroy and to rend in twain; and they seek to bring me into the depths of earth, O pure one; but be quick and come save me from them, O Maid.

Glory be to the Father, and to the Son, and to the Holy Spirit;

From all need and affliction and from all disease and harm do thou deliver me; and by thy power, in thy shelter preserve me unwounded, Maid; and from every peril and foes that hate and war against me do thou hasten to save me, O all hymned one.

Both now and forever, and unto the ages of ages. Amen.

What gift of thanksgiving shall I offer in gratefulness unto thee, O Maid, for thy boundless goodness and the favours and gifts that I have from thee? Hence, indeed I praise thee, and glorify and magnify thine inexpressible sympathy shown to me.

Troparia After The Fifth Ode

Tone 8   Humility, tranquillity, repose, suffering, pleading.   *C, D, Eb, F, G, A, Bb, C.*

Preserve and save, O Theotokos, thy servants from every danger. After God, do all of us for refuge flee unto thee; a firm rampart art thou and our protection. In thy goodwill, look thou on me, O all hymned Theotokos, and do thou behold my body's grievous infirmity, and heal thou the cause of my soul's sorrow.

Ode Six

Most Holy Theotokos, save us.

The storm clouds of grievous sorrows and distress shroud my hapless heart and soul in affliction, and with their gloom have they filled me, O Virgin. Yet, since thou barest the Light Unapproachable, be quick to drive them far from me with the breeze of your holy entreaties, Maid.

Most Holy Theotokos, save us.

A comfort art thou to me in my distress, and I have thee as a healer of all illness; of death art thou the most perfect destruction; thou art an unfailing fountain flowing with life, and speedy help and quick support of all them that are found in adversities.

Glory be to the Father, and to the Son, and to the Holy Spirit;

I shall not conceal the ever flowing spring of the sympathy thou hast for me, O Lady, nor the abyss of thine infinite mercy, nor yet the fountain of thy boundless miracles; but ceaselessly do I cry out and confess and declare and proclaim thy grace.

Both now and forever, and unto the ages of ages. Amen.

The turmoils of this life encircle me like unto bees about a honeycomb, O Virgin, and they have seized and now hold my heart captive, and I am pierced with the stings of afflictions, Maid; yet be thou, O all holy one, my defender and helper and rescuer.

Troparia After The Sixth Ode

Tone 8   Humility, tranquillity, repose, suffering, pleading.   *C, D, Eb, F, G, A, Bb, C.*

Preserve and save, O Theotokos, thy servants from every danger. After God, do all of us for refuge flee unto thee; a firm rampart art thou and our protection. In thy goodwill, look thou on me, O all hymned Theotokos, and do thou behold my body's grievous infirmity, and heal thou the cause of my soul's sorrow.

Litany

[Censing the Icon of the Theotokos, the Priest says:]

Priest: Have mercy on us, O God, according to Thy Great Mercy, we pray Thee, hearken and have mercy.

People: *Lord, have mercy.* **(x3)**

Priest: Again we pray for all pious and Orthodox Christians.

People: *Lord, have mercy.* **(x3)**

Priest: Again we pray for our Archbishop Nikitas, and for all our brotherhood in Christ.

People: *Lord, have mercy.* **(x3)**

Priest: Again we pray for mercy, life, peace, health, salvation and visitation and pardon and remission of sins for the servants of God, all Orthodox Christians of true worship, who live and dwell in this community, the parishioners and benefactors of this holy temple, and all that serve, sing, labour and gather herein; and for the servants of God [Names], and for the suffering Christians of Syria, Lebanon, Palestine, Iraq, Egypt, all of the Middle East *(and any other nations that may be appropriate)* and for the forgiveness of their every transgression, both voluntary and involuntary.

People: *Lord, have mercy.* **(x3)**

Priest: For Thou art a merciful God Who lovest mankind, and unto Thee we ascribe glory: to the Father, and to the Son, and to the Holy Spirit; both now and forever, and unto the ages of ages.

People: *Amen.*

[Priest enters the sanctuary through the south door and dons his phelonion.]

Kontakion For Ordinary Sundays

Tone 2   *Majesty, gentleness, hope, repentance and sadness.*   *E, F, G, Ab, B, C.*

O protection of Christians that cannot be put to shame, mediation unto the Creator most constant, O despise not the suppliant voices of those who have sinned; but be thou quick, O good one, to come unto our aid, who in faith cry unto thee: Hasten to intercession, and speed thou to make supplication, thou who dost ever protect, O Theotokos, them that honour thee.

Anavathmoi

Tone 4   *Festive, joyous and expressing deep piety.*   *C, D, Eb, F, G, A, Bb, C.*

From my youth up, many passions have warred against me. But do Thou help and save me, O my Saviour.

(x2)

You who hate Zion shall be put to confusion of the Lord; like grass in the fire shall you be withered up. **(x2)**

Glory be to the Father, and to the Son, and to the Holy Spirit;

Through the Holy Spirit is every soul quickened and exalted in purity, and made resplendent by the Triune Unity in mystic holiness.

Both now and forever, and unto the ages of ages. Amen.

Through the Holy Spirit the channels and streams of grace overflow showering all creation with invigorating Life.

[The priest opens the curtain and the Holy Doors.]

Prokeimenon

Priest: Wisdom. The prokeimenon.

Reader: I shall proclaim Thy Name from generation to generation.

People: *I shall proclaim Thy Name from generation to generation.*

Reader: Hearken, O daughter, and see, and incline thine ear; and forget thine own people;

And thy fathers house and the King shall greatly desire thy beauty.

People: *I shall proclaim Thy Name from generation to generation.*

Reader: I shall proclaim Thy Name | from generation to generation.

Gospel Reading

Deacon: Wisdom. Attend. Let us hear the Holy Gospel.

Priest: Peace be with you all.

People: *And with thy spirit.*

Priest: The reading is from the Holy Gospel according to Luke (10:38-42; 11:27-28).

People: *Glory to Thee, O Lord, glory to Thee.*

Deacon: Let us attend.

Priest: At that time, Jesus entered a certain village; and a woman named Martha received Him into her house. And she had a sister called Mary, who sat at the Lord's feet and listened to His teaching. But Martha was distracted with much serving; and she went to Him and said, "Lord, dost Thou not care that my sister has left me to serve alone? Tell her then to help me." But the Lord answered her, "Martha, Martha, you are anxious and troubled about many things; one thing is needful. Mary has chosen the good portion, which shall not be taken away from her." As He said this, a woman in the crowd raised her voice and said to Him, "Blessed is the womb that bore Thee, and the breasts that Thou didst suck." But He said, "Blessed rather are those who hear the word of God and keep it."

People: *Glory to Thee, O Lord, glory to Thee.*

Glory be to the Father, and to the Son, and to the Holy Spirit;

Troparia

Tone 2   *Majesty, gentleness, hope, repentance and sadness.*   *E, F, G, Ab, B, C.*

O Father, Word and Spirit, Trinity in unity: blot out the multitude of our transgressions.

Both now and forever, and unto the ages of ages. Amen.

Through the intercessions of the Theotokos, O Thou Who art merciful, blot out the multitude of our transgressions.

Troparion

Tone 6   Rich texture, funereal character, sorrowful tone.   *D, Eb, F##, G, A, Bb, C##, D.*

Chorus: *Have mercy upon me, O God, according to Thy loving kindness: according to the multitude of Thy tender mercies blot out my transgressions.*

Reader: O entrust me not, I pray, to any human protection, O our Lady, holy one, but do thou accept the prayer of thy supplicant. Sorrow hath fettered me, and I am unable to endure and bear the demons' darts; a shelter have I not, neither place to run, I, the wretched one; embattled from all sides am I, and no consolation have I but thee. Mistress of creation, protection and hope of faithful ones: turn not away when I pray to thee; do that which shall profit me.

Theotokia

Tone 2   Majesty, gentleness, hope, repentance and sadness.   *E, F, G, Ab, B, C.*

From thee is no one turned away ashamed and empty who doth run to thee for refuge, O pure Virgin Theotokos; but he asketh the favour and receiveth the gift from thee, unto the profit of his own request. The transformation of the afflicted and the relief of those in sickness art thou in truth, O Virgin Theotokos; save thy people and thy flock, thou who art the peace of the embattled, and who art the calm of the storm driven, the only protectress of those who believe.

The Intercession

Priest: O God, save Thy people, and bless Thine inheritance. Visit Thy world with mercies and compassions. Exalt the horn of Orthodox Christians, and send down upon us Thy rich mercies. Through the intercessions of our all immaculate Lady Theotokos and Ever Virgin Mary; by the might of the precious and life giving Cross; by the protection of Michael, Gabriel, Raphael and all the honourable Bodiless Powers of Heaven; at the supplications of the honourable, glorious Prophet, Forerunner and Baptist John, and his righteous parents Zachariah and Elizabeth; of the holy, glorious prophets: Moses and Aaron, Elijah and Elisha, David and Jesse, the Three Holy Children Shadrach, Meshach and Abednego, Daniel the "man of desires;" Simeon the God receiver and the Prophetess Anna; and of all the holy prophets; of the holy, glorious, all laudable Apostles Peter and Paul, the patrons and protectors of the Church, the Twelve, the Seventy, and of all the holy apostles and equals-to-the-apostles, especially Constantine and Helen; of our fathers among the Saints, great Hierarchs and Ecumenical Teachers: Basil the Great, Gregory the Theologian and John Chrysostom; Athanasius, Cyril and John the Merciful, patriarchs of Alexandria, Nicholas the wonder worker, Archbishop of Myra in Lycia, Spyridon, the wonder worker, Bishop of Trimythous, Sophronios, Patriarch of Jerusalem, Meletios, Archbishop of Antioch, Nektarios the wonder worker, Bishop of Pentapolis, Theodore, Bishop of Edessa; Innocent, metropolitan of Moscow and Jacob Netsvetov, Evangelizers of Alaska, and Tikhon, patriarch of Moscow, Enlighteners of North America; John, Wonder worker of Shanghai and San Francisco, and the holy, glorious and right victorious Great Martyrs: George the Trophy-Bearer, Demetrios the Myrrh streaming, Theodore the soldier, Theodore the General, Stephen the Archdeacon and First Martyr, James the Persian, and Menas the wonder worker; of the holy, glorious and right victorious Hieromartyrs:

Ignatius the God bearer of Antioch, Xaralampos of Magnesia, Eleutherios of Illyricum, Polycarp of Smyrna, Peter of Damascus, Cyprian of Antioch, the former magician, Milos of Babylon; Habib, Gurias and Samonas of Edessa; Juvenaly of Iliamna, Ananias of "the Seventy" of Damascus, Jacob of Hamatoura, and Joseph of Damascus; of the holy, glorious, and right victorious Martyrs: the Forty Holy Martyrs of Sebastia, Sergius and Amphian of Beirut, Trophimos, Savatios and Dorymedon of Antioch, Artemios of Antioch, Thomas of Antioch, Peter of Bosra, the children Asterios, Claudios, Neon, and Neonilla of Cilicia, Galaktion and Epistimia of Homs, Romanos of Antioch, Silvanos, Luke and Makios of Homs, Joseph the New Martyr of Aleppo, Cyril the Deacon of Baalbek, Julitta and her son Kyriakos of Iconium, Andrew the General of Syria; Antony of Damascus, Thomas of Damascus, Victor of Damascus; Sergios and Bacchos of Syria, and Peter the Aleut; of the holy, glorious, and right victorious women Martyrs: the Forty Holy Martyrs at Heraclea, Great Martyrs Thekla the First Martyr, Barbara of Baalbek, Anastasia of Rome, Katherine of Alexandria, Kyriaki of Nicomedia, Photeini the Samaritan Woman and her sisters Anatole, Photo, Photis, Paraskeve, and Kyriake; Marina of Antioch in Pisidia, Paraskeva of Rome, Anastasia of Rome the "deliverer from potions," Irene of Thessalonica, Irene of the Balkans; Sophia and Irene of Egypt; Paraskeva of Iconium, Tatiana of Rome, Fevronia of Mesopotamia, Evdokia the Penitent of Baalbek, Pelagia of Antioch, Pelagia of Tarsus, Vevaia of Edessa, Basilissa and Anastasia of Rome, disciples of Peter and Paul; Sophia and her daughters Faith, Hope and Love of Rome; Leonilla and her grandchildren and companions in Cappadocia; Domnina and her children Berina and Prosdoki of Edessa; Bassa of Edessa; Theodora of Tyre, Theodosia of Tyre, Christina of Tyre; Domnina of Anazarbus; Virgin-martyrs Lucy of Syracuse and Lucy of Campania; Lucy of Rome; Lucy, Cyprilla, and Aroa of Libya; Thomaïs of Alexandria; and Akylina of Byblos; of our venerable and God bearing Fathers who shone in the ascetic life: Anthony the Great, Euthymios the Great, Arsenios the Great, Savvas the Sanctified, Ephraim and Isaac the Syrians, Makarios, Pakhomios and Paisios the Greats of Egypt; Simeon the Stylite, Simeon of the Wondrous Mountain, Daniel the Stylite, Alexios the Man of God, Theodosios the head of monasteries, John of Damascus, Cosmas the Hymnographer of Maïuma, Andrew of Crete, Romanos the Melodist, Maximos the Confessor, Mark the Anchorite, John Cassian the Roman, Simeon the New Theologian; Onouphrios of Egypt; Peter, Athanasius, Paul and Paisios the New of Mount Athos, Maron of Cyrrhus in Syria, John of Edessa, Simeon of Homs (Emesa), the Fool-for-Christ, Thomas of Syria, the Fool-for-Christ; Seraphim of Sarov, and Herman of Alaska; of our venerable and God bearing Mothers Mary Magdalene; Mary, the wife of Cleopas; Joanna the wife of Chuza; Salome the mother of the sons of Zebedee; Susanna; and Mary and Martha, the sisters of Lazarus, and all the holy Myrrh bearing women; Right-believing Tamara, queen of Georgia; Olga, princess of Kiev and equal-to-the-apostles; of the Holy and Righteous Mothers of the Three Hierarchs: Emmelia (Basil the Great), Nona (Gregory the Theologian) and Anthousa (John Chrysostom); and Macrina, the sister of Basil the Great; of our venerable and God-bearing Mothers who shone in the ascetic life: Mary of Egypt, Pelagia the Penitent, Thaïs of Egypt, Kyra of Syria, Domnina of Syria, Marana of Veria, Publia the Confessor of Antioch, Anastasia the Patrician of Alexandria, Martha the mother of Simeon the Stylite; Xenia of Rome and Xenia of St Petersburg the Fool-for-Christ; Paraskeva the New of the Balkans; Thomaïs of Lesbos the wonder worker; and Pansemne of Antioch; of the holy Unmercenaries and Healers: Panteleimon the Great-Martyr, Hermolaos the Hieromartyr, Cosmos and Damian of Asia, Cosmos and Damian of Rome, Cyrus and John of Arabia, Julian of Homs, and Anthimos of Arabia; of (Saints Ns., other holy ones of local devotion), *[Patron Saint of the Temple e.g.* Saint Martin of Tours*]*, *[Patron Saint of the country e.g.* Saint David of Wales*]*; of the holy and righteous ancestors of God, Joachim and Anna; of Joseph the Betrothed and James the Brother of God; of *(Name(s) of the Saint(s) of the day)*, whose memory we celebrate today, and of all Thy Saints: we beseech Thee, O most merciful Lord, hearken unto the petitions of us sinners who make our supplications unto Thee, and have mercy upon us.

People: Lord, have mercy. **(x12)**

[Priest, with phelonion, comes out the north door and resumes his place in front of the icon.]

Priest: Through the mercies and compassions and love for mankind of Thine Only begotten Son, with Whom Thou art blessed, together with Thine All Holy, and good, and Life giving Spirit: now and ever, and unto ages of ages.

People: Amen.

The Great Supplicatory Canon (Continued)
Ode 7

Most Holy Theotokos, save us.

Tone 8   Humility, tranquillity, repose, suffering, pleading.   *C, D, Eb, F, G, A, Bb, C.*

Illumine my way, for I am darkened by the night of many sins, O Theotokos; thou hast brought forth the Light, and art in truth the blameless and undefiled vessel of light; hence with love do I praise thee.

Most Holy Theotokos, save us.

Be my shelter and protection and my help and boast, O Virgin Theotokos; of all manner of help have I now been stripped naked, O strength of those bereft of help, and thou hope of those without hope.

Glory be to the Father, and to the Son, and to the Holy Spirit;

With my whole soul and understanding and with all my heart and with my lips I praise thee, having truly enjoyed thy many benefactions; yet boundless are thy miracles, and thy goodness is unending.

Both now and forever, and unto the ages of ages. Amen.

Look thou with graciousness upon me, and dispel the evil plight that doth beset me; and from grievous distress and harm and temptations and perils do thou rescue me in thine infinite mercy.

Troparia After The Seventh Ode

Tone 8   Humility, tranquillity, repose, suffering, pleading.   C, D, Eb, F, G, A, Bb, C.

Preserve and save, O Theotokos, thy servants from every danger. After God, do all of us for refuge flee unto thee; a firm rampart art thou and our protection. In thy goodwill, look thou on me, O all hymned Theotokos, and do thou behold my body's grievous infirmity, and heal thou the cause of my soul's sorrow.

Ode 8

Most Holy Theotokos, save us.

Be thou moved to compassion, O Virgin, and disdain me not, for life's tempests overwhelm me. But be thou quick, O modest one, and lend me thy helping hand, O Maiden, for I perish drowning engulfed by life's misfortunes.

Most Holy Theotokos, save us.

Times of sorrows, necessity, and trouble, and misfortunes in life have found me, O pure Maiden; and from all sides temptations have encircled me; but be thou mine ally, and do thou protect me in thine almighty shelter.

Glory be to the Father, and to the Son, and to the Holy Spirit;

In distress I have thee, Maid, as my haven, and in sorrows and griefs thou art my joy and gladness; and in all illness, thou hast been my quick help, and rescuer in perils, and in all temptations my guardian and protectress.

Both now and forever, and unto the ages of ages. Amen.

Rejoice, fiery throne of the Lord God; rejoice, thou sacred vessel that art filled with manna; rejoice, thou golden lamp stand and unquenchable lamp; rejoice, O glory of virgins and the boast and adornment of mothers.

Troparia After The Eighth Ode

Tone 8   Humility, tranquillity, repose, suffering, pleading.   C, D, Eb, F, G, A, Bb, C.

Preserve and save, O Theotokos, thy servants from every danger. After God, do all of us for refuge flee unto thee; a firm rampart art thou and our protection. In thy goodwill, look thou on me, O all hymned Theotokos, and do thou behold my body's grievous infirmity, and heal thou the cause of my soul's sorrow.

Ode 9

Most Holy Theotokos, save us.

To whom else shall I flee, O thou Maid most pure, and to whom shall I run for help and be saved? Where shall I go, and where shall I find me a safe retreat? Whose warm protection shall I have? Who shall be a helper in my distress? In thee alone I hope, Maid; in thee alone I glory; and trusting in thee, I have fled to thee.

Most Holy Theotokos, save us.

To number thy great deeds and thy mighty acts is not possible for man, O Bride of God, nor yet can one tell of the unfathomable abyss of thine unending miracles that surpass all knowledge, and which are wrought for those that venerate thee and honour thee with longing as the true Mother of our Lord and God.

Glory be to the Father, and to the Son, and to the Holy Spirit;

With anthems of thanksgiving I glorify and chant praise to thine infinite mercy, and thy boundless might I confess unceasingly unto all; and with my soul and heart and mind and my lips I magnify and proclaim the many benefactions that thou hast poured upon me in thy compassion, O thou Bride of God.

Both now and forever, and unto the ages of ages. Amen.

Accept thou mine entreaty and my poor prayer, and disdain not my weeping and sighs, O Maid, nor my lament, but be quick to help me since thou art good. Do thou fulfil mine every plea; thou canst do this in that thou broughtest forth our mighty God and Master, if thou but look upon me and bow down to mine utter lowliness.

Troparia After The Ninth Ode

Tone 8   Humility, tranquillity, repose, suffering, pleading.   *C, D, Eb, F, G, A, Bb, C.*

Preserve and save, O Theotokos, thy servants from every danger. After God, do all of us for refuge flee unto thee; a firm rampart art thou and our protection. In thy goodwill, look thou on me, O all hymned Theotokos, and do thou behold my body's grievous infirmity, and heal thou the cause of my soul's sorrow.

[Priest censes the icon of the Theotokos at the centre of the church, whilst:]

Theotokion

Tone 8   Humility, tranquillity, repose, suffering, pleading.   *C, D, Eb, F, G, A, Bb, C.*

[Archangel Gabriel: It is truly right to call thee blessed, who gavest birth to God, ever-blessed and God-obedient the Mother of our God.] Greater in honour than the Cherubim and beyond compare more glorious than the Seraphim; without corruption thou gavest birth to God the Word, truly the Mother of God, we magnify thee.

[Priest does the great censing of the church, whilst:]

The Megalynaria

Tone 8   Humility, tranquillity, repose, suffering, pleading.   *C, D, Eb, F, G, A, Bb, C.*

Higher than the heavens above art thou, and thou art much purer than the radiance of the sun; for thou hast redeemed us out of the curse that held us. O Mistress of creation, with hymns we honour thee. From the great abundance of all my sins, ill am I in body, ailing also am I in soul. Thee have I as refuge. Do thou therefore help me, O hope of all the hopeless, for thou art full of grace. O Lady and Mother of Christ our God, receive supplication from us wretches, who beg of thee that thou make entreaty unto the One born from thee. O Mistress of creation, do thou intercede for us.

Now we chant with eagerness unto thee with this ode most joyful, O all hymned Mother of our God. Together with the Baptist and all the saintly Chorus', beseech, O Theotokos, that we find clemency. Speechless be the lips of the impious who refuse to reverence thy revered Icon which is known by the name Directress and which hath been depicted for us by the Apostle Luke, the Evangelist.

Megalynarion Of The Church Temple

O all you arrays of angelic hosts, with the Holy Baptist, the Apostles' twelve numbered band, all the Saints together, as well as God's birth giver, pray make you intercession for our deliverance.

Trisagion

Reader: Holy God, Holy Mighty, Holy Immortal, have mercy on us. **(x3)**

Glory be to the Father, and to the Son, and to the Holy Spirit;
Both now and forever, and unto the ages of ages. Amen.

O Most Holy Trinity, have mercy on us.

O Lord, cleanse us from our sins.

O Master, pardon our iniquities.

O Holy One, visit and heal our infirmities, for Thy names sake.

Lord have mercy. **(x3)**

Glory be to the Father and to the Son and to the Holy Spirit;
Both now and forever, and unto the ages of ages. Amen.

People: *Our Father, Who art in Heaven, hallowed be Thy Name. Thy Kingdom come, Thy will be done, on earth as it is in Heaven. Give us this day our daily bread, and forgive us our trespasses, as we forgive those who trespass against us; and lead us not into temptation, but deliver us from the evil one.*

Priest: For Thine is the Kingdom, and the power, and the glory: of the Father, and of the Son, and of the Holy Spirit; both now and forever, and unto the ages of ages.

People: *Amen.*

Apolytikion Of St Stephen The Archdeacon

Tone 4   Festive, joyous and expressing deep piety.   *C, D, Eb, F, G, A, Bb, C.*

The crown of the Kingdom hath adorned the brow of thy head because of the contests that thou hast endured for Christ God, thou first of the martyred Saints; for when thou hadst censured the Jews' madness, thou saw Christ thy Saviour standing at the right hand of the Father. O Stephen, ever pray Him for us, that He would save our souls.

Glory be to the Father and to the Son and to the Holy Spirit;
Both now and forever, and unto the ages of ages. Amen.

Theotokion

Tone 4   Festive, joyous and expressing deep piety.   *C, D, Eb, F, G, A, Bb, C.*

The Mystery which was hidden from everlasting and was unknown of the angels, O Theotokos, was revealed through thee, to those who dwell upon earth. In that God, having become incarnate - in unconfused union - of His own good shall accepted the Cross for our sake. Whereby He raised again the first created, and hath saved our souls from death.

Troparia Of Contrition

Tone 6   Rich texture, funereal character, sorrowful tone.   *D, Eb, F##, G, A, Bb, C##, D.*

Have mercy on us, O Lord, have mercy on us; for laying aside all defence we sinners offer unto Thee, as Master, this supplication: have mercy on us.

Glory be to the Father, and to the Son, and to the Holy Spirit;

O Lord, have mercy on us, for in Thee have we put our trust; be not exceedingly wroth with us, nor remember our iniquities, but look down upon us even now, as Thou art compassionate, and deliver us from our enemies; for Thou art our God, and we are Thy people; we are all the work of Thy hands, and we call upon Thy Name.

Both now and forever, and unto the ages of ages. Amen.

Open unto us the door of thy compassion, O blessed Theotokos. As we set our hope in thee, may we not be confounded; through thee may we be delivered from all adversities, for thou art the salvation of the race of Christians.

[If August 2 or 3 are Fridays:]

Apolytikia And Theotokion For The Martyrs And The Departed

Tone 2   Majesty, gentleness, hope, repentance and sadness.   *E, F, G, Ab, B, C.*

O apostles, martyrs, prophets, hierarchs, righteous, and just ones, who have finished your course well and have kept the Faith: seeing you have boldness with the Saviour, beseech Him for us, since He is good, that our souls be saved, we pray.

Glory be to the Father, and to the Son, and to the Holy Spirit;

Keep Thy servants in remembrance, O Lord, since Thou art good, and do Thou forgive their every sin in this life; for no man is without sin, except for Thee Who art able to grant rest even unto those that have departed hence.

Both now and forever, and unto the ages of ages. Amen.

O holy Mother of the Ineffable Light, with reverence we magnify thee, honouring thee with angelic hymns.

August 4

Apolytikion Of The Forefeast Of The Transfiguration

Tone 4   Festive, joyous and expressing deep piety.   *C, D, Eb, F, G, A, Bb, C.*

Come, let us all welcome the Transfiguration of Christ, and joyously celebrate the bright prefestival, O you faithful, and let us cry: Nigh at hand now is the day of God-given gladness, as the Sovereign Master goeth up on Mount Tabor to flash forth with the beautiful light of His Divinity.

August 6 - 12

Apolytikion Of The Transfiguration

Tone 7   Manly character and strong melody.   *F, G, A, A#, C, D, E, F.*

When, O Christ our God, Thou wast transfigured on the mountain, Thou didst reveal Thy glory to Thy Disciples in proportion as they could bear it. Let Thine everlasting light also enlighten us sinners, through the intercessions of the Theotokos. O Thou Bestower of light, glory to Thee.

Apolytikion Of The Forefeast Of The Dormition

Tone 4   Festive, joyous and expressing deep piety.   *C, D, Eb, F, G, A, Bb, C.*

In faith, O you people, leap for joy while clapping your hands; and gather in gladness on this day with longing and shout in radiant jubilation. For the Theotokos cometh nigh to departing from the earth unto the heights; and we glorify her with glory as the Mother of God in our unceasing hymns.

[continue all:]

Final Litany

[Censing the Icon of the Theotokos:]

Priest: Have mercy on us, O God, according to Thy Great Mercy, we pray Thee, hearken and have mercy.

People: *Lord, have mercy.* **(x3)**

Priest: Again we pray for all pious and Orthodox Christians.

People: *Lord, have mercy.* **(x3)**

Priest: Again we pray for our Archbishop Nikitas and for all our brotherhood in Christ.

People: *Lord, have mercy.* **(x3)**

Priest: Again we pray for mercy, life, peace, health, salvation and visitation and pardon and forgiveness of sins for the servants of God [Names], the parishioners, members of the parish council and organizations, donors and benefactors of this holy temple, and for the suffering Christians of Syria, Lebanon, Palestine, Iraq, Egypt, and all of the Middle East *(and any other nations that may be appropriate).*

People: *Lord, have mercy.* **(x3)**

Priest: Again we pray that He may keep this holy church and this city and every city and countryside from wrath, famine, plague, earthquake, flood, fire, the sword, foreign invasion, civil war and sudden death; that our good God, Who lovest mankind, shall be gracious, favourable and conciliatory and turn away and dispel all the wrath stirred up against us and all sickness, and may deliver us from His righteous chastisement which impendeth on us, and have mercy upon us.

People: *Lord, have mercy.* **(x40)**

Priest: Again we pray that the Lord our God may hearken unto the voice of the supplication of us sinners, and have mercy upon us.

People: *Lord, have mercy.* **(x3)**

Priest: Hear us, O God our Saviour, the Hope of all the ends of the earth and of those who are far off upon the sea; and be gracious, be gracious, O Master, upon our sins, and have mercy upon us. For Thou art a merciful God and lovest mankind, and unto Thee do we ascribe glory: to the Father, and to the Son, and to the Holy Spirit; both now and forever, and unto the ages of ages.

People: *Amen.*

The Dismissal

Deacon: Wisdom.

People: *Holy Father, bless.*

Priest: Christ our God, the Existing One, is blessed, always, both now and forever, and unto the ages of ages.

People: *Amen.*

Preserve, O God, the Holy Orthodox Faith and all Orthodox Christians, unto the ages of ages. Amen.

Priest: Most Holy Theotokos, save us.

People: *Greater in honour than the Cherubim and beyond compare more glorious than the Seraphim; Without corruption thou gavest birth to God the Word, truly the Theotokos, we magnify thee.*

Priest: Glory to Thee, O Christ our God and our hope, glory to Thee.

Chorus: *Glory be to the Father, and to the Son, and to the Holy Spirit; Both now and forever, and unto the ages of ages. Amen.*

Lord, have mercy. **(x3)**

Holy Father, bless.

Priest: May Christ our true God, through the intercessions of His all immaculate and all blameless Holy Mother; of Saint N., the patron and protector of this holy community; of the holy and righteous ancestors of God, Joachim and Anna; of (Name(s) of the Saint(s) of the day), whose memory we celebrate today, and of all the Saints: have mercy on us and save us, forasmuch as He is good and loveth mankind.

People: *Amen.*

[The clergy and faithful come forward and venerate the Icon of the Theotokos; whilst:]

Exaposteilaria

Tone 3   Arrogant, brave, and mature atmosphere.   *F, G, A, A#, C, D, E, F.*

O you Apostles from afar, being now gathered together here in the vale of Gethsemane, give burial to my body, and Thou, my Son and my God, receive Thou my spirit. Thou art the sweetness of Angels, the gladness of afflicted ones; and the protectress of Christians, O Virgin Mother of our Lord; be thou my helper, and save me from out of eternal torments.

I have thee as Mediatress with the man-befriending God; may He not censure my actions before the hosts of the Angels. I supplicate thee, O Virgin, come unto mine aid most quickly. Thou art a gold entwined tower and twelve wall encircled city, a throne besprinkled with sunbeams, a royal chair of the King. O inexplicable wonder that thou dost milk feed the Master.

Priest: Through the prayers of our Holy Fathers, Lord Jesus Christ our God, have mercy upon us and save us.

People: *Amen.*

Little Parakleses For The Dormition Of The Theotokos

With The Little Supplicatory Canon To The Most Holy Theotokos As Sung During The Dormition Fast

[With a priest.]

The Parakleses Service is served during times of tribulation, but also on each evening of the Dormition Fast, August 1-13, inclusive. In the Dormition Fast, the Little and Great Parakleses canons can be chanted in alternating sequence from day to day, at the end of Vespers or in a standalone service. If a parish knows only the Little Parakleses, this alone can be chanted each time. We begin this sequence with the Little Parakleses, except when August 1 falls on Sunday. We do not chant the Parakleses on any Saturday evening and also not on the paramon of the Feast of Transfiguration (the evening on August 5). On Sunday evening and on the day of Transfiguration in the evening the Great Parakleses is chanted. Accordingly, the series of Parakleses unfolds for the intervening days. The table below shows the series of Parakleses.

Chart For Calculating Which Parakleses Canon To Use

L = Little Parakleses / G = Great Parakleses / – = no Parakleses service on this day

+ = celebrate Great Vespers for the Transfiguration on this day

[Remember to use Orthodox daybreak.]

Aug	1st	2nd	3rd	4th	5th	6th	7th	8th	9th	10th	11th	12th	13th
Monday	L	G	L	G	– +	–	G	L	G	L	G	L	–
Tuesday	L	G	L	G	– +	G	L	G	L	G	L	–	G
Wednesday	L	G	L	–	– +	G	L	G	L	G	–	G	L
Thursday	L	G	–	G	– +	G	L	G	L	–	G	L	G
Friday	L	–	G	L	– +	G	L	G	–	G	L	G	L
Saturday	–	G	L	G	– +	G	L	–	G	L	G	L	G
Sunday	G	L	G	L	– +	G	–	G	L	G	L	G	L

If Parakleses shall be offered with Vespers; it is chanted after "The Prayer of St Simeon" with the omission of the opening blessing of the Parakleses Service. Rather, at this point, the reader recites Psalm 142.

If the Parakleses Service is offered without Vespers as a standalone service; then as below.

We remember the names of the living during the three litanies. If it is a long list of names, then the priest can mention it in one, two or all of the litanies.

[An Icon of the Theotokos is placed on a stand in the centre of the Solea and the Holy Doors remains closed. The priest, being vested in exorasson and blue epitrachelion, standing on the Solea before the Icon of the Theotokos, makes three metanias and says out loud:]

Trisagion Prayers

Priest: Blessed is our God, always, both now and forever, and unto the ages of ages.

People: *Amen.*

Priest: Glory to Thee, our God, glory to Thee.

O Heavenly King, Comforter, Spirit of Truth, Who art everywhere present and fillest all things, Treasury of blessings and Giver of life: Come and abide in us and cleanse us from every impurity and save our souls, O Good One.

Reader: Holy God, Holy Mighty, Holy Immortal, have mercy on us. **(x3)**

Glory be to the Father, and to the Son, and to the Holy Spirit;
Both now and forever, and unto the ages of ages. Amen.

O Most Holy Trinity, have mercy on us.

O Lord, cleanse us from our sins.

O Master, pardon our iniquities.

O Holy One, visit and heal our infirmities, for Thy names sake.

Lord have mercy. **(x3)**

Glory be to the Father and to the Son and to the Holy Spirit;
Both now and forever, and unto the ages of ages. Amen.

People: *Our Father, Who art in Heaven, hallowed be Thy Name. Thy Kingdom come, Thy will be done, on earth as it is in Heaven. Give us this day our daily bread, and forgive us our trespasses, as we forgive those who trespass against us; and lead us not into temptation, but deliver us from the evil one.*

Priest: For Thine is the Kingdom, and the power, and the glory: of the Father, and of the Son, and of the Holy Spirit; both now and forever, and unto the ages of ages.

People: *Amen.*

Lord, have mercy. (x12)

Glory be to the Father and to the Son and to the Holy Spirit;
Both now and forever and unto the ages of ages. Amen.

Come, let us worship God, our King.

Come, let us worship and fall down before Christ, our King and our God.

Come, let us worship and fall down before Christ Himself, our King and our God.

Psalm 142

Hear my prayer, O Lord, give ear to my supplications. In Thy faithfulness answer me, and in Thy righteousness. Do not enter into judgement with Thy servant, for in Thy sight no one living is righteous. For the enemy has persecuted my soul; he has crushed my life to the ground; he has made me dwell in darkness, like those who have long been dead. Therefore my spirit is overwhelmed within me; my heart within me is distressed. I remember the days of old; I meditate on all Thy works; I muse on the work of Thine hands. I spread out my hands to Thee; my soul longs for Thee like a thirsty land. Answer me speedily, O Lord; my spirit fails. Do not hide Thy face from me, lest I be like those who go down into the pit. Cause me to hear Thy loving kindness in the morning, for in Thee do I trust; cause me to know the way in which I should walk, for I lift up my soul to Thee. Deliver me, O Lord, from mine enemies; in Thee I take shelter. Teach me to do Thy will, for Thou art my God; Thy Spirit is good. Lead me in the land of uprightness. Revive me, O Lord, for Thy names sake. For Thy righteousness' sake bring my soul out of trouble. In Thy mercy cut off mine enemies, and destroy all those who afflict my soul; for I am Thy servant.

God Is The Lord

People: *God is the Lord and has revealed Himself to us. Blessed is He who comes in the Name of the Lord.*

Reader: Give thanks to the Lord, for He is good; and His steadfast love endures forever.

People: *God is the Lord and has revealed Himself to us. Blessed is He who comes in the Name of the Lord.*

Reader: All nations surrounded me; in the Name of the Lord, I withstood them.

People: *God is the Lord and has revealed Himself to us. Blessed is He who comes in the Name of the Lord.*

Reader: This is the Lords doing and is marvellous in our eyes.

People: *God is the Lord and has revealed Himself to us. Blessed is He who comes in the Name of the Lord.*

Apolytikia And Theotokion

Tone 4   Festive, joyous and expressing deep piety.   C, D, Eb, F, G, A, Bb, C.

To the Theotokos let us run now most earnestly, we sinners all and wretched ones, and fall prostrate in repentance, calling from the depths of our souls: Lady, come unto our aid, have compassion upon us; hasten thou for we are lost in a throng of transgressions; turn not thy servants away with empty hands, for thee alone do we have as our only hope.

Glory be to the Father, and to the Son, and to the Holy Spirit;

[to your Patron Saint]. If yours is St Martin:

Troparion Of St Martin Of Tours

Tone 4   Festive, joyous and expressing deep piety.   *C, D, Eb, F, G, A, Bb, C.*

In signs and in miracles thou wert renowned throughout Gaul. By grace and adoption thou art a light for the world, O Martin, blessed of God. Alms deeds and compassion filled thy life with their splendours. Teaching and wise counsel were thy riches and treasures, which thou dispensest freely to those who honour thee.

Both now and forever, and unto the ages of ages. Amen.

Theotokion

Tone 4   Festive, joyous and expressing deep piety.   *C, D, Eb, F, G, A, Bb, C.*

O Theotokos, we shall not cease from speaking of all thy mighty acts, all we the unworthy ones; for if thou hadst not stood to intercede for us, who would have delivered us from such numerous dangers? Who would have preserved us all until now in true freedom? O Lady, we shall not turn away from thee; for thou dost always save thy servants from all manner of grief.

Psalm 50

Have mercy on me, O God, according to Thy great mercy; and according to the multitude of Thy compassions blot out my transgression. Wash me thoroughly from mine iniquity, and cleanse me from my sin. For I acknowledge mine iniquity, and my sin is ever before me. Against Thee, Thee only have I sinned, and done evil in Thy sight, that Thou mayest be found just when Thou speakest, and victorious when Thou art judged. For behold, I was conceived in iniquity, and in sin my mother bore me. For behold, Thou hast loved truth; Thou hast made known to me the hidden and secret things of Thy wisdom. Thou shalt sprinkle me with hyssop, and I shall be made clean; Thou shalt wash me, and I shall be whiter than snow. Make me to hear joy and gladness; that the humbled bones may rejoice. Turn Thy face away from my sins, and blot out all mine iniquities.

Create in me a clean heart, O God, and renew a steadfast spirit within me. Cast me not away from Thy presence, and take not Thy Holy Spirit from me. Restore to me the joy of Thy salvation, and establish me with Thy governing Spirit. I shall teach transgressors Thy ways, and the ungodly shall turn back to Thee. Deliver me from blood guiltiness, O God, the God of my salvation; my tongue shall joyfully declare Thy righteousness. Lord, open my lips, and my mouth shall declare Thy praise. For if Thou hadst desired sacrifice, I would give it; Thou dost not delight in burnt offerings. A sacrifice to God is a broken spirit; God shall not despise a broken and a humbled heart. Do good, O Lord, in Thy good pleasure to Zion, and let the walls of Jerusalem be builded. Then Thou shalt be pleased with a sacrifice of righteousness, with oblation and whole burned offerings. Then shall they offer bulls on Thine altar.

The Little Supplicatory Canon
Ode One

Most Holy Theotokos, save us.

Tone 8   *Humility, tranquillity, repose, suffering, pleading.*   *C, D, Eb, F, G, A, Bb, C.*

By many temptations am I distressed; in search of salvation unto thee have I taken flight. O Mother of the Word and Ever Virgin, from all ordeals and afflictions deliver me.

Most Holy Theotokos, save us.

Attacks of the passions disquiet me; my soul to repletion has been filled with despondency. Be-still them, O Maiden, with the calmness of thine own Son and thy God, O All blameless One.

Glory be to the Father, and to the Son, and to the Holy Spirit;

To Christ God, the Saviour; thou gavest birth. I beg thee, O Virgin, from afflictions deliver me. For now unto thee I flee for refuge, bringing to thee both my soul and my reasoning.

Both now and forever, and unto the ages of ages. Amen.

Diseased is my body and my soul. Do thou make me worthy of divine guidance and thy care, O thou who alone art God's Mother, for thou art good, and the Birth giver of the Good.

Ode Three

Most Holy Theotokos, save us.

I have thee as the shelter and the defence of my life. Thee, the Theotokos and Virgin; pilot and govern me into thy sheltered port, for thou art author of good things and staff of the faithful, O thou only lauded one.

Most Holy Theotokos, save us.

I beseech thee, O Virgin, do thou dispel far from me all of the distress of despair and turbulence in my soul; for thou, O Bride of God, hast given birth to the Lord Christ, Who is Prince of Peace, O thou only all blameless one.

Glory be to the Father, and to the Son, and to the Holy Spirit;

Since thou gavest birth unto our Benefactor, the cause of good, from the wealth of thy loving kindness, do thou pour forth on all; for thou canst do all things, since thou didst bear Christ, the One Who is mighty in power; for blessed of God art thou.

Both now and forever, and unto the ages of ages. Amen.

With most grievous diseases and with corrupt passions, too, I am put to trial, O Virgin; come thou unto mine aid; for I know thee to be an inexhaustible treasure of unfailing healing, O only all blameless one.

Troparia After The Third Ode

Tone 8   Humility, tranquillity, repose, suffering, pleading.   *C, D, Eb, F, G, A, Bb, C.*

Preserve and save, O Theotokos, thy servants from every danger. After God, do all of us for refuge flee unto thee; a firm rampart art thou and our protection. In thy goodwill, look thou on me, O all hymned Theotokos, and do thou behold my body's grievous infirmity, and heal thou the cause of my soul's sorrow.

Litany

[Censing the Icon of the Theotokos, whilst:]

Priest: Have mercy on us, O God, according to Thy Great Mercy, we pray Thee, hearken and have mercy.

People: *Lord, have mercy.* **(x3)**

Priest: Again we pray for all pious and Orthodox Christians.

People: *Lord, have mercy.* **(x3)**

Priest: Again we pray for our Archbishop Nikitas, and for all our brotherhood in Christ.

People: *Lord, have mercy.* **(x3)**

Priest: Again we pray for mercy, life, peace, health, salvation and visitation and pardon and remission of sins for the servants of God, all Orthodox Christians of true worship, who live and dwell in this community, the parishioners and benefactors of this holy temple, and all that serve, sing, labour and gather herein; and for the servants of God *[Names]*, and for the suffering Christians of Syria, Lebanon, Palestine, Iraq, Egypt, all of the Middle East *(add any other nations that may be appropriate)* and for the forgiveness of their every transgression, both voluntary and involuntary.

People: *Lord, have mercy.* **(x3)**

Priest: For Thou art a merciful God Who lovest mankind, and unto Thee we ascribe glory: to the Father, and to the Son, and to the Holy Spirit; both now and forever, and unto the ages of ages.

People: *Amen.*

Kathisma

Tone 2   Majesty, gentleness, hope, repentance and sadness.   *E, F, G, Ab, B, C.*

O fervent advocate, invincible battlement, fountain of mercy, and sheltering retreat for the world, earnestly we cry to thee: Lady Mother of God, hasten thou, and save us from all imperilment, for thou alone art our speedy protectress.

The Little Supplicatory Canon (Continued)
Ode Four

Most Holy Theotokos, save us.

Tone 8   *Humility, tranquillity, repose, suffering, pleading.*   *C, D, Eb, F, G, A, Bb, C.*

Lull the tempest of all my sins, and bestill the raging of passions with thy calm; for progenitress art thou of Him Who is Lord and Helmsman, O thou Bride of God.

Most Holy Theotokos, save us.

O bestow out of the abyss of thy great compassion on me thy supplicant; for thou brought forth One compassionate Who is Saviour of all who sing hymns to thee.

Glory be to the Father, and to the Son, and to the Holy Spirit;

While delighting, O spotless one, in thy many favours, a hymn of thankfulness do we all raise up in song to thee, knowing thee to be the Mother of our God.

Both now and forever, and unto the ages of ages. Amen.

Having thee as our staff and hope, and as our salvation's unshaken battlement, from all manner of adversity are we then redeemed, O thou all lauded one.

Ode Five

Most Holy Theotokos, save us.

Pure one, fill my heart with rejoicing unto plenitude, and grant thine undefiled felicity, since thou didst give birth unto Him Who is the cause of joy.

Most Holy Theotokos, save us.

Come, deliver us out of dangers, O pure Mother of God, since thou art Mother of deliverance, and of the peace which doth surpass all human reasoning.

Glory be to the Father, and to the Son, and to the Holy Spirit;

Dissipate the gloom of my trespasses, O Bride of God, with the clear brightness of thy radiance, for thou didst bear the Light divine which was before all time.

Both now and forever, and unto the ages of ages. Amen.

Heal me, O pure one, of the sickness which the passions bring, and make me worthy of thy guardianship, and by thy prayers and intercessions grant thou health to me.

Ode Six

Most Holy Theotokos, save us.

My nature, held by corruption and by death, hath He saved from out of death and corruption, for unto death He, Himself, hath submitted. Wherefore, O Virgin, do thou intercede with Him Who is in truth thy Lord and Son to redeem me from enemies' wickedness.

Most Holy Theotokos, save us.

I know thee as the protection of my life and most safe fortification, O Virgin. Disperse the horde of my many temptations and put to silence demonic audacity. Unceasingly I pray to thee: From corruption of passions deliver me.

Glory be to the Father, and to the Son, and to the Holy Spirit;

A bulwark of safe retreat art thou to us, and of souls art thou the perfect salvation, and a relief in distresses, O Maiden; and in thy light do we ever exult with joy. O Lady, do thou also now from all passions and perils deliver us.

Both now and forever, and unto the ages of ages. Amen.

Bedridden, I lie supine with sickness now, and no healing for my flesh is existent except for thee, who didst bear the world's Saviour, our God, the Healer of every infirmity. I pray to thee, for thou art good: From corruption of illnesses raise me up.

Troparia After The Sixth Ode

Tone 8   Humility, tranquillity, repose, suffering, pleading.   C, D, Eb, F, G, A, Bb, C.

Preserve and save, O Theotokos, thy servants from every danger. After God, do all of us for refuge flee unto thee; a firm rampart art thou and our protection. O spotless one, who inexpressibly in the last days didst by a word bring forth the Word; do thou make request of Him, as one who hath motherly boldness.

Litany

[Censing the Icon of the Theotokos, the Priest says:]

Priest: Have mercy on us, O God, according to Thy Great Mercy, we pray Thee, hearken and have mercy.

People: *Lord, have mercy.* **(x3)**

Priest: Again we pray for all pious and Orthodox Christians.

People: *Lord, have mercy.* **(x3)**

Priest: Again we pray for our Archbishop <u>Nikitas</u>, and for all our brotherhood in Christ.

People: *Lord, have mercy.* **(x3)**

Priest: Again we pray for mercy, life, peace, health, salvation and visitation and pardon and remission of sins for the servants of God, all Orthodox Christians of true worship, who live and dwell in this community, the parishioners and benefactors of this holy temple, and all that serve, sing, labour and gather herein; and for the servants of God *[Names]*, and for the suffering Christians of Syria, Lebanon, Palestine, Iraq, Egypt, all of the Middle East *[and any other nations that may be appropriate]* and for the forgiveness of their every transgression, both voluntary and involuntary.

People: *Lord, have mercy.* **(x3)**

Priest: For Thou art a merciful God Who lovest mankind, and unto Thee we ascribe glory: to the Father, and to the Son, and to the Holy Spirit; both now and forever, and unto the ages of ages.

People: *Amen.*

[Priest enters the sanctuary through the south door and dons his phelonion.]

Kontakion For Ordinary Sundays

Tone 2   Majesty, gentleness, hope, repentance and sadness.   *E, F, G, Ab, B, C.*

O protection of Christians that cannot be put to shame, mediation unto the Creator most constant, O despise not the suppliant voices of those who have sinned; but be thou quick, O good one, to come unto our aid, who in faith cry unto thee: Hasten to intercession, and speed thou to make supplication, thou who dost ever protect, O Theotokos, them that honour thee.

Anavathmoi

Tone 4   Festive, joyous and expressing deep piety.   *C, D, Eb, F, G, A, Bb, C.*

From my youth up, many passions have warred against me. But do Thou help and save me, O my Saviour. **(x2)**

You who hate Zion shall be put to confusion of the Lord; like grass in the fire shall you be withered up. **(x2)**

Glory be to the Father, and to the Son, and to the Holy Spirit;

Through the Holy Spirit is every soul quickened and exalted in purity, and made resplendent by the Triune Unity in mystic holiness.

Both now and forever, and unto the ages of ages. Amen.

Through the Holy Spirit the channels and streams of grace overflow showering all creation with invigorating Life.

[The priest opens the curtain and the Holy Doors.]

Prokeimenon

Priest: Wisdom. The prokeimenon.

Reader: I shall proclaim Thy Name from generation to generation.

People: *I shall proclaim Thy Name from generation to generation.*

Reader: Hearken, O daughter, and see, and incline thine ear; and forget thine own people;

And thy fathers house and the King shall greatly desire thy beauty.

People: *I shall proclaim Thy Name from generation to generation.*

Reader: I shall proclaim Thy Name | from generation to generation.

Gospel Reading

Deacon: Wisdom. Attend. Let us hear the Holy Gospel.

Priest: Peace be with you all.

People: *And with thy spirit.*

Priest: The reading is from the Holy Gospel according to Luke (1:39-49, 56).

People: *Glory to Thee, O Lord, glory to Thee.*

Deacon: Let us attend.

Priest: In those days, Mary arose and went with haste into the hill country, to a city of Judah, and she entered the house of Zachariah and greeted Elizabeth. And when Elizabeth heard the greeting of Mary, the babe leaped in her womb; and Elizabeth was filled with the Holy Spirit and she exclaimed with a loud cry, "Blessed art thou among women, and blessed is the fruit of thy womb. And why is this granted me, that the mother of my Lord should come to me? For behold, when the voice of thy greeting came to my ears, the babe in my womb leaped for joy. And blessed is she who believed that there would be a fulfilment of what was spoken to her from the Lord." And Mary said, "My soul magnifies the Lord, and my spirit rejoices in God my Saviour, for He has regarded the low estate of his handmaiden. For behold, henceforth all generations shall call me blessed; for He Who is mighty has done great things for me, and holy is His Name." And Mary remained with her about three months, and returned to her home.

People: *Glory to Thee, O Lord, glory to Thee.*

Troparia

Glory be to the Father, and to the Son, and to the Holy Spirit;

Tone 2   Majesty, gentleness, hope, repentance and sadness.   *E, F, G, Ab, B, C.*

O Father, Word and Spirit, Trinity in unity: blot out the multitude of our transgressions.

Both now and forever, and unto the ages of ages. Amen.

Through the intercessions of the Theotokos, O Thou Who art merciful, blot out the multitude of our transgressions.

Troparion

Tone 6   Rich texture, funereal character, sorrowful tone.   *D, Eb, F##, G, A, Bb, C##, D.*

Chorus: *Have mercy upon me, O God, according to Thy loving kindness: according to the multitude of Thy tender mercies blot out my transgressions.*

Reader: O entrust me not, I pray, to any human protection, O our Lady, holy one, but do thou accept the prayer of thy supplicant. Sorrow hath fettered me, and I am unable to endure and bear the demons' darts; a shelter have I not, neither place to run, I, the wretched one; embattled from all sides am I, and no consolation have I but thee. Mistress of creation, protection and hope of faithful ones: turn not away when I pray to thee; do that which shall profit me.

Theotokia

Tone 2   Majesty, gentleness, hope, repentance and sadness.   *E, F, G, Ab, B, C.*

From thee is no one turned away ashamed and empty who doth run to thee for refuge, O pure Virgin Theotokos; but he asketh the favour and receiveth the gift from thee, unto the profit of his own request. The transformation of the afflicted and the relief of those in sickness art thou in truth, O Virgin Theotokos; save thy people and thy flock, thou who art the peace of the embattled, and who art the calm of the storm driven, the only protectress of those who believe.

The Intercession

Priest: O God, save Thy people, and bless Thine inheritance. Visit Thy world with mercies and compassions. Exalt the horn of Orthodox Christians, and send down upon us Thy rich mercies. Through the intercessions of our all immaculate Lady Theotokos and Ever Virgin Mary; by the might of the precious and life giving Cross; by the protection of Michael, Gabriel, Raphael and all the honourable Bodiless Powers of Heaven; at the supplications of the honourable, glorious Prophet, Forerunner and Baptist John, and his righteous parents Zachariah and Elizabeth; of the holy, glorious prophets: Moses and Aaron, Elijah and Elisha, David and Jesse, the Three Holy Children Shadrach, Meshach and Abednego, Daniel the "man of desires;" Simeon the God receiver and the Prophetess Anna; and of all the holy prophets; of the holy, glorious, all laudable Apostles Peter and Paul, the patrons and protectors of the Church, the Twelve, the Seventy, and of all the holy apostles and equals-to-the-apostles, especially Constantine and Helen; of our fathers among the Saints, great Hierarchs and Ecumenical Teachers: Basil the Great, Gregory the Theologian and John Chrysostom; Athanasius, Cyril and John the Merciful, patriarchs of Alexandria, Nicholas the wonder worker, Archbishop of Myra in Lycia, Spyridon, the wonder worker, Bishop of Trimythous, Sophronios, Patriarch of Jerusalem, Meletios, Archbishop of Antioch, Nektarios the wonder worker, Bishop of Pentapolis, Theodore,

Bishop of Edessa; Innocent, metropolitan of Moscow and Jacob Netsvetov, Evangelisers of Alaska, and Tikhon, patriarch of Moscow, Enlighteners of North America; John, Wonder worker of Shanghai and San Francisco, and the holy, glorious and right victorious Great Martyrs: George the Trophy-Bearer, Demetrios the Myrrh streaming, Theodore the soldier, Theodore the General, Stephen the Archdeacon and First Martyr, James the Persian, and Menas the wonder worker; of the holy, glorious and right victorious Hieromartyrs: Ignatius the God bearer of Antioch, Xaralampos of Magnesia, Eleutherios of Illyricum, Polycarp of Smyrna, Peter of Damascus, Cyprian of Antioch, the former magician, Milos of Babylon; Habib, Gurias and Samonas of Edessa; Juvenaly of Iliamna, Ananias of "the Seventy" of Damascus, Jacob of Hamatoura, and Joseph of Damascus; of the holy, glorious, and right victorious Martyrs: the Forty Holy Martyrs of Sebastia, Sergius and Amphian of Beirut, Trophimos, Savatios and Dorymedon of Antioch, Artemios of Antioch, Thomas of Antioch, Peter of Bosra, the children Asterios, Claudios, Neon, and Neonilla of Cilicia, Galaktion and Epistimia of Homs, Romanos of Antioch, Silvanos, Luke and Makios of Homs, Joseph the New Martyr of Aleppo, Cyril the Deacon of Baalbek, Julitta and her son Kyriakos of Iconium, Andrew the General of Syria; Antony of Damascus, Thomas of Damascus, Victor of Damascus; Sergios and Bacchos of Syria, and Peter the Aleut; of the holy, glorious, and right victorious women Martyrs: the Forty Holy Martyrs at Heraclea, Great Martyrs Thekla the First Martyr, Barbara of Baalbek, Anastasia of Rome, Katherine of Alexandria, Kyriaki of Nicomedia, Photeini the Samaritan Woman and her sisters Anatole, Photo, Photis, Paraskeve, and Kyriake; Marina of Antioch in Pisidia, Paraskeva of Rome, Anastasia of Rome the "deliverer from potions," Irene of Thessalonica, Irene of the Balkans; Sophia and Irene of Egypt; Paraskeva of Iconium, Tatiana of Rome, Fevronia of Mesopotamia, Evdokia the Penitent of Baalbek, Pelagia of Antioch, Pelagia of Tarsus, Vevaia of Edessa, Basilissa and Anastasia of Rome, disciples of Peter and Paul; Sophia and her daughters Faith, Hope and Love of Rome; Leonilla and her grandchildren and companions in Cappadocia; Domnina and her children Berina and Prosdoki of Edessa; Bassa of Edessa; Theodora of Tyre, Theodosia of Tyre, Christina of Tyre; Domnina of Anazarbus; Virgin-martyrs Lucy of Syracuse and Lucy of Campania; Lucy of Rome; Lucy, Cyprilla, and Aroa of Libya; Thomaïs of Alexandria; and Akylina of Byblos; of our venerable and God bearing Fathers who shone in the ascetic life: Anthony the Great, Euthymios the Great, Arsenios the Great, Savvas the Sanctified, Ephraim and Isaac the Syrians, Makarios, Pakhomios and Paisios the Greats of Egypt; Simeon the Stylite, Simeon of the Wondrous Mountain, Daniel the Stylite, Alexios the Man of God, Theodosios the head of monasteries, John of Damascus, Cosmas the Hymnographer of Maïuma, Andrew of Crete, Romanos the Melodist, Maximos the Confessor, Mark the Anchorite, John Cassian the Roman, Simeon the New Theologian; Onouphrios of Egypt; Peter, Athanasius, Paul and Paisios the New of Mount Athos, Maron of Cyrrhus in Syria, John of Edessa, Simeon of Homs (Emesa), the Fool-for-Christ, Thomas of Syria, the Fool-for-Christ; Seraphim of Sarov, and Herman of Alaska; of our venerable and God bearing Mothers Mary Magdalene; Mary, the wife of Cleopas; Joanna the wife of Chuza; Salome the mother of the sons of Zebedee; Susanna; and Mary and Martha, the sisters of Lazarus, and all the holy Myrrh bearing women; Right-believing Tamara, queen of Georgia; Olga, princess of Kiev and equal-to-the-apostles; of the Holy and Righteous Mothers of the Three Hierarchs: Emmelia (Basil the Great), Nona (Gregory the Theologian) and Anthousa (John Chrysostom); and Macrina, the sister of Basil the Great; of our venerable and God-bearing Mothers who shone in the ascetic life: Mary of Egypt, Pelagia the Penitent, Thaïs of Egypt, Kyra of Syria, Domnina of Syria, Marana of Veria, Publia the Confessor of Antioch, Anastasia the Patrician of Alexandria, Martha the mother of Simeon the Stylite; Xenia of Rome and Xenia of St Petersburg the Fool-for-Christ; Paraskeva the New of the Balkans; Thomaïs of Lesbos the wonder worker; and Pansemne of Antioch; of the holy Unmercenaries and Healers: Panteleimon the Great-Martyr, Hermolaos the Hieromartyr, Cosmos and Damian of Asia, Cosmos and Damian of Rome, Cyrus and John of Arabia, Julian of Homs, and Anthimos of Arabia; of *(Saints Ns., other holy ones of local devotion)*, *[Patron Saint of the Temple e.g.* Saint Martin of Tours*]*, *[Patron Saint of the country e.g.* Saint David of Wales*]*; of the holy and righteous ancestors of God, Joachim and Anna; of Joseph the Betrothed and James the Brother of God; of *(Name(s) of the Saint(s) of the day)*, whose memory we celebrate today, and of all Thy Saints: we beseech Thee, O most merciful Lord, hearken unto the petitions of us sinners who make our supplications unto Thee, and have mercy upon us.

People: *Lord, have mercy.* (**x12**)

[Priest, still with phelonion, comes out the north door and resumes his place in front of the icon.]

Priest: Through the mercies and compassions and love for mankind of Thine Only begotten Son, with Whom Thou art blessed, together with Thine All Holy, and good, and Life giving Spirit: now and ever, and unto ages of ages.

People: *Amen.*

The Little Supplicatory Canon (Continued)
Ode 7

Most Holy Theotokos, save us.

Tone 8   *Humility, tranquillity, repose, suffering, pleading.*   C, D, Eb, F, G, A, Bb, C.

Having willed thus, O Saviour, to dispense our salvation in Thine economy, Thou dweltest in the Maid's womb, and unto all creation as protectress didst show her forth. O God of our Fathers, blessed art Thou.

Most Holy Theotokos, save us.

Make request, O pure Mother, to thy Son Who hath willed to grant mercy unto us, to rescue from transgressions and from the soul's defilement those who cry out most faithfully: O God of our Fathers, blessed art Thou.

Glory be to the Father, and to the Son, and to the Holy Spirit;

A fount of incorruption and a tower of safety is she who gave Thee birth. A treasure of salvation and portal of repentance hast Thou provided her to them that shout: O God of our Fathers, blessed art Thou.

Both now and forever, and unto the ages of ages. Amen.

Deign to grant restoration from diseases of body and soul to those who run to thy divine protection with faith, O Theotokos, and thus grant them recovery; for Mother of Christ our Saviour art thou.

Ode 8

Most Holy Theotokos, save us.

Do not disdain those who seek the aid that thou dost grant, for, O Virgin Maiden, they do hymn thee, and they all exalt thee unto ages forever.

Most Holy Theotokos, save us.

On all who hymn thee with faith, O Virgin, and exalt thy truly ineffable Offspring, thou poured forth a great abundance of thy cures and healings.

Glory be to the Father, and to the Son, and to the Holy Spirit;

All the diseases that plague my soul dost thou make well, and the sufferings of the flesh thou healest also; wherefore, O thou Maiden full of grace, I glorify thee.

Both now and forever, and unto the ages of ages. Amen.

All the assaultings of the temptations dost thou quell, and the onslaughts of the passions dost thou banish; wherefore do we hymn thee to all ages, O Virgin.

Ode 9

Most Holy Theotokos, save us.

The torrent of my weeping spurn not with refusal, for thou didst give birth to Him Who doth take away all tears from every face, O thou Virgin, for He is Christ indeed.

Most Holy Theotokos, save us.

Do thou, O Virgin Maiden, fill my heart with gladness, for thou art she who received all the fullness of joy and made to vanish away all sorrow of sinfulness.

Most Holy Theotokos, save us.

A haven and protection, and a wall unshaken, and a rejoicing and shelter and place of retreat do thou become, O thou Virgin, for those who flee to thee.

Glory be to the Father, and to the Son, and to the Holy Spirit;

Illumine with the radiance of thy light, O Virgin, all those who piously call thee the Mother of God; and do thou banish away all darkness of ignorance.

Both now and forever, and unto the ages of ages. Amen.

Brought low am I, O Virgin, in a place of sickness and in a dwelling of anguish. Grant healing to me, transforming all of my illness into full healthfulness.

[Priest censes the icon of the Theotokos at the centre of the church, whilst:]

Theotokion

Tone 8   Humility, tranquillity, repose, suffering, pleading.   C, D, Eb, F, G, A, Bb, C.

[Archangel Gabriel: It is truly right to call thee blessed, who gavest birth to God, ever-blessed and God-obedient the Mother of our God.] Greater in honour than the Cherubim and beyond compare more glorious than the Seraphim; without corruption thou gavest birth to God the Word, truly the Mother of God, we magnify thee.

[Priest does the great censing of the church, whilst:]

The Megalynaria

Tone 8   Humility, tranquillity, repose, suffering, pleading.   C, D, Eb, F, G, A, Bb, C.

Higher than the heavens above art thou, and thou art much purer than the radiance of the sun; for thou hast redeemed us out of the curse that held us. O Mistress of creation, with hymns we honour thee. From the great abundance of all my sins, ill am I in body, ailing also am I in soul. Thee have I as refuge. Do thou therefore help me, O hope of all the hopeless, for thou art full of grace. O Lady and Mother of Christ our God, receive supplication from us wretches, who beg of thee that thou make entreaty unto the One born from thee. O Mistress of creation, do thou intercede for us.

Now we chant with eagerness unto thee with this ode most joyful, O all hymned Mother of our God. Together with the Baptist and all the saintly Chorus', beseech, O Theotokos, that we find clemency. Speechless be the lips of the impious who refuse to reverence thy revered Icon which is known by the name Directress and which hath been depicted for us by the Apostle Luke, the Evangelist.

Megalynarion Of The Church Temple

O all you arrays of angelic hosts, with the Holy Baptist, the Apostles' twelve numbered band, all the Saints together, as well as God's birth giver, pray make you intercession for our deliverance.

Trisagion Prayers

Reader: Holy God, Holy Mighty, Holy Immortal, have mercy on us. **(x3)**

Glory be to the Father, and to the Son, and to the Holy Spirit;
Both now and forever, and unto the ages of ages. Amen.

O Most Holy Trinity, have mercy on us.

O Lord, cleanse us from our sins.

O Master, pardon our iniquities.

O Holy One, visit and heal our infirmities, for Thy names sake.

Lord have mercy. **(x3)**

Glory be to the Father and to the Son and to the Holy Spirit;
Both now and forever, and unto the ages of ages. Amen.

People: *Our Father, Who art in Heaven, hallowed be Thy Name. Thy Kingdom come, Thy will be done, on earth as it is in Heaven. Give us this day our daily bread, and forgive us our trespasses, as we forgive those who trespass against us; and lead us not into temptation, but deliver us from the evil one.*

Priest: For Thine is the Kingdom, and the power, and the glory: of the Father, and of the Son, and of the Holy Spirit; both now and forever, and unto the ages of ages.

People: *Amen.*

August 1

Apolytikion Of St Stephen The Archdeacon

Tone 4   Festive, joyous and expressing deep piety.   *C, D, Eb, F, G, A, Bb, C.*

The crown of the Kingdom hath adorned the brow of thy head because of the contests that thou hast endured for Christ God, thou first of the martyred Saints; for when thou hadst censured the Jews' madness, thou saw Christ thy Saviour standing at the right hand of the Father. O Stephen, ever pray Him for us, that He would save our souls.

Glory be to the Father and to the Son and to the Holy Spirit;
Both now and forever, and unto the ages of ages. Amen.

Theotokion

Tone 4   Festive, joyous and expressing deep piety.   *C, D, Eb, F, G, A, Bb, C.*

The Mystery which was hidden from everlasting and was unknown of the angels, O Theotokos, was revealed through thee, to those who dwell upon earth. In that God, having become incarnate - in unconfused union - of

His own good will accepted the Cross for our sake. Whereby He raised again the first created, and hath saved our souls from death.

Troparia Of Contrition

Tone 6   Rich texture, funereal character, sorrowful tone.   *D, Eb, F##, G, A, Bb, C##, D.*

Have mercy on us, O Lord, have mercy on us; for laying aside all defence we sinners offer unto Thee, as Master, this supplication: have mercy on us.

Glory be to the Father, and to the Son, and to the Holy Spirit;

O Lord, have mercy on us, for in Thee have we put our trust; be not exceedingly wroth with us, nor remember our iniquities, but look down upon us even now, as Thou art compassionate, and deliver us from our enemies; for Thou art our God, and we are Thy people; we are all the work of Thy hands, and we call upon Thy Name.

Both now and forever, and unto the ages of ages. Amen.

Open unto us the door of thy compassion, O blessed Theotokos. As we set our hope in thee, may we not be confounded; through thee may we be delivered from all adversities, for thou art the salvation of the race of Christians.

[If August 2 or 3 are Fridays:]

Apolytikia And Theotokion For The Martyrs And The Departed

Tone 2   Majesty, gentleness, hope, repentance and sadness.   *E, F, G, Ab, B, C.*

O apostles, martyrs, prophets, hierarchs, righteous, and just ones, who have finished your course well and have kept the Faith: seeing you have boldness with the Saviour, beseech Him for us, since He is good, that our souls be saved, we pray.

Glory be to the Father, and to the Son, and to the Holy Spirit;

Keep Thy servants in remembrance, O Lord, since Thou art good, and do Thou forgive their every sin in this life; for no man is without sin, except for Thee Who art able to grant rest even unto those that have departed hence.

Both now and forever, and unto the ages of ages. Amen.

O holy Mother of the Ineffable Light, with reverence we magnify thee, honouring thee with angelic hymns.

August 4

Apolytikion Of The Forefeast Of The Transfiguration

Tone 4   Festive, joyous and expressing deep piety.   C, D, Eb, F, G, A, Bb, C.

Come, let us all welcome the Transfiguration of Christ, and joyously celebrate the bright prefestival, O you faithful, and let us cry: Nigh at hand now is the day of God-given gladness, as the Sovereign Master goeth up on Mount Tabor to flash forth with the beautiful light of His Divinity.

August 6 - 12

Apolytikion Of The Transfiguration

Tone 7   Manly character and strong melody.   F, G, A, A#, C, D, E, F.

When, O Christ our God, Thou wast transfigured on the mountain, Thou didst reveal Thy glory to Thy Disciples in proportion as they could bear it. Let Thine everlasting light also enlighten us sinners, through the intercessions of the Theotokos. O Thou Bestower of light, glory to Thee.

August 13

Apolytikion Of The Forefeast Of The Dormition

Tone 4   Festive, joyous and expressing deep piety.   C, D, Eb, F, G, A, Bb, C.

In faith, O you people, leap for joy while clapping your hands; and gather in gladness on this day with longing and shout in radiant jubilation. For the Theotokos cometh nigh to departing from the earth unto the heights; and we glorify her with glory as the Mother of God in our unceasing hymns.

[continue all:]

Final Litany

[Censing the Icon of the Theotokos:]

Priest: Have mercy on us, O God, according to Thy Great Mercy, we pray Thee, hearken and have mercy.

People: *Lord, have mercy.* **(x3)**

Priest: Again we pray for all pious and Orthodox Christians.

People: *Lord, have mercy.* **(x3)**

Priest: Again we pray for our Archbishop Nikitas and for all our brotherhood in Christ.

People: *Lord, have mercy.* **(x3)**

Priest: Again we pray for mercy, life, peace, health, salvation and visitation and pardon and forgiveness of sins for the servants of God [Names], the parishioners, members of the parish council and organizations, donors and benefactors of this holy temple, and for the suffering Christians of Syria, Lebanon, Palestine, Iraq, Egypt, and all of the Middle East *(and any other nations that may be appropriate).*

People: *Lord, have mercy.* **(x3)**

Priest: Again we pray that He may keep this holy church and this city and every city and countryside from wrath, famine, plague, earthquake, flood, fire, the sword, foreign invasion, civil war and sudden death; that our good God, Who lovest mankind, shall be gracious, favourable and conciliatory and turn away and dispel all the wrath stirred up against us and all sickness, and may deliver us from His righteous chastisement which impendeth on us, and have mercy upon us.

People: *Lord, have mercy.* **(x40)**

Priest: Again we pray that the Lord our God may hearken unto the voice of the supplication of us sinners, and have mercy upon us.

People: *Lord, have mercy.* **(x3)**

Priest: Hear us, O God our Saviour, the Hope of all the ends of the earth and of those who are far off upon the sea; and be gracious, be gracious, O Master, upon our sins, and have mercy upon us. For Thou art a merciful God and lovest mankind, and unto Thee do we ascribe glory: to the Father, and to the Son, and to the Holy Spirit; both now and forever, and unto the ages of ages.

People: *Amen.*

The Dismissal

Deacon: Wisdom.

People: *Holy Father, bless.*

Priest: Christ our God, the Existing One, is blessed, always, both now and forever, and unto the ages of ages.

People: *Amen.*

   Preserve, O God, the Holy Orthodox Faith and all Orthodox Christians, unto the ages of ages. Amen.

Priest: Most Holy Theotokos, save us.

People: *Greater in honour than the Cherubim and beyond compare more glorious than the Seraphim;*

   Without corruption thou gavest birth to God the Word, truly the Theotokos, we magnify thee.

Priest: Glory to Thee, O Christ our God and our hope, glory to Thee.

Chorus: *Glory be to the Father, and to the Son, and to the Holy Spirit;*

   Both now and forever, and unto the ages of ages. Amen.

People: *Lord, have mercy.* **(x3)**

Holy Father, bless.

Priest: May Christ our true God, through the intercessions of His all immaculate and all blameless Holy Mother; of Saint N., the patron and protector of this holy community; of the holy and righteous ancestors of God, Joachim and Anna; of (Name(s) of the Saint(s) of the day), whose memory we celebrate today, and of all the Saints: have mercy on us and save us, forasmuch as He is good and loveth mankind.

People: *Amen.*

[The clergy and faithful come forward and venerate the Icon of the Theotokos; whilst:]

Exaposteilaria

Tone 3   Arrogant, brave, and mature atmosphere.   *F, G, A, A#, C, D, E, F.*

O you Apostles from afar, being now gathered together here in the vale of Gethsemane, give burial to my body, and Thou, my Son and my God, receive Thou my spirit. Thou art the sweetness of Angels, the gladness of afflicted ones; and the protectress of Christians, O Virgin Mother of our Lord; be thou my helper, and save me from out of eternal torments.

I have thee as Mediatress with the man-befriending God; may He not censure my actions before the hosts of the Angels. I supplicate thee, O Virgin, come unto mine aid most quickly. Thou art a gold entwined tower and twelve wall encircled city, a throne besprinkled with sunbeams, a royal chair of the King. O inexplicable wonder that thou dost milk feed the Master.

Priest: Through the prayers of our Holy Fathers, Lord Jesus Christ our God, have mercy upon us and save us.

People: Amen.

The Theophany Of Our Lord And Saviour Jesus Christ. The Service For The Great Sanctification Of The Water. 6th January

Idiomela

Tone 8   Humility, tranquillity, repose, suffering, pleading.   *C, D, Eb, F, G, A, Bb, C.*

The voice of the Lord upon the waters cries, saying: Come all of ye, and take the Spirit of wisdom, the Spirit of understanding, the Spirit of the fear of God, by the appearance of Christ. Today the nature of water is sanctified, and the Jordan is cloven, and its waters shall be held from flowing, the Master being shown washed therein. Thou didst come to the river as a man, O Christ King. Thou hastenest, O good One, to receive baptism as a servant at the hands of the Forerunner, for the sake of our sins, O Lover of mankind.

Glory be to the Father, and to the Son, and to the Holy Spirit;
Both now and forever, and to the ages of ages. Amen.

Toward the voice in the wilderness: Prepare the way of the Lord. Thou didst come taking the likeness of a servant, seeking baptism, O Thou Who knowest no sin. The waters saw Thee and were afraid, and the Forerunner trembled and cried, saying: How shall the Light seek to be lit for the lamp? How shall the servant place His hand upon the Master? Wherefore, sanctify me and the waters, O Saviour, Who takes away the sin of the world.

The Old Testament Readings - The First Passage

Deacon: Wisdom.

Reader: The Reading from the prophecy of Isaiah (35:1-10).

Deacon: Let us attend.

Reader: These things says the Lord: the wilderness and the dry land shall be glad, the desert shall rejoice and blossom; like the lily. It shall blossom abundantly, and rejoice with joy and singing. The glory of Lebanon shall be given to it, the majesty of Carmel and Sharon. They shall see the glory of the Lord, the majesty of our God. Strengthen the weak hands, and make firm the feeble knees. Say to those who are of a fearful heart, "Be strong, and fear not. Behold, thy God shall come with vengeance, with the recompense of God. He shall come and save ye." Then the eyes of the blind shall be opened, and the ears of the deaf unstopped; then shall the lame man leap like a hart, and the tongue of the mute sing for joy. For waters shall break forth in the wilderness, and streams in the desert; the burning sand shall become a pool, and the thirsty ground springs of water; the haunt of jackals shall become a swamp, the grass shall become reeds and rushes. And a highway shall be there, and it shall be called the Holy Way; the unclean shall not pass over it, and fools shall not err therein. No lion shall be there, nor shall any ravenous beast come up on it; they shall not be found there, but the redeemed shall walk there. And the ransomed of the Lord shall return, and come to Zion with singing; everlasting joy shall be upon their heads; they shall obtain joy and gladness, and sorrow and sighing shall flee away.

The Second Passage

Deacon: Wisdom.

Reader: The Reading from the prophecy of Isaiah (55:1-13).

Deacon: Let us attend.

Reader: These things says the Lord: Every one who thirsts, come to the waters; and he who has no money, come, buy and eat. Come, buy wine and milk without money and without price. Why do you spend thy money for that which is not bread, and thy labour for that which does not satisfy? Hearken diligently to Me, and eat what is good, and delight thyselves in fatness. Incline thy ear, and come to Me; hear, that thy soul may live; and I shall make with you an everlasting covenant: my steadfast, sure love for David. Behold, I made him a witness to the people, a leader and commander for the people. Behold, you shall call nations that you know not, and nations that knew you not shall run to Thee, because of the Lord thy God, and of the Holy One of Israel, for He has glorified Thee. Seek the Lord while He may be found, call upon Him while He is near; let the wicked forsake His way, and the unrighteous man His thoughts; let him return to the Lord, that He may have mercy on him, and to our God, for He shall abundantly pardon. For My thoughts are not thy thoughts, neither are thy ways My ways, says the Lord. For as the heavens are higher than the earth, so are My ways higher than thy ways and My thoughts than thy thoughts. For as the rain and the snow come down from heaven, and return not thither but water the earth, making it bring forth and sprout, giving seed to the sower and bread to the eater, so shall My word be that goes forth from My mouth; it shall not return to Me empty, but it shall accomplish that which I purpose, and prosper in the thing for which I sent it. For you shall go out in joy, and be led forth in peace; the mountains and the hills before you shall break forth into singing, and all the trees of the field shall clap their hands. Instead of the thorn shall up come the cypress; instead of the brier shall up come the myrtle; and it shall be to the Lord for a memorial, for an everlasting sign which shall not be cut off.

The Third Passage

Deacon: Wisdom.

Reader: The Reading from the prophecy of Isaiah (12:3-6).

Deacon: Let us attend.

Reader: These things says the Lord: With joy you shall draw water from the wells of salvation. And you shall say in that day: Give thanks to the Lord, call upon His Name; make known His deeds among the nations, proclaim that His Name is exalted. Sing praises to the Lord, for He has done gloriously; let this be known in all the earth. Shout, and sing for joy, O inhabitant of Zion, for great in thy midst is the Holy One of Israel.

Prokeimenon

Deacon: Let us attend.

Reader: The Lord is my Light and My salvation: whom shall I fear?

People: *The Lord is my Light and My salvation: whom shall I fear?*

Reader: The Lord is the Protector of my life: of whom shall I be afraid?

People: *The Lord is my Light and My salvation: whom shall I fear?*

Reader: The Lord is my Light and My salvation | whom shall I fear?

The Fourth Passage

Deacon: Wisdom.

Reader: The Reading from the 1st letter of the Apostle Paul to the Corinthians 10:1-4.

Deacon: Let us attend.

Reader: Brethren, I would not have you ignorant, that all our ancestors were under the cloud, and all passed through the sea; and were all baptised to Moses in the cloud and in the sea; and all ate the same spiritual meat; and all drank from the same spiritual drink: for they drank of that spiritual Rock that followed them: and that Rock was Christ.

Priest: Peace be to thou who readest.

Reader: And with thy spirit.

Halleluiarion

People: *Halleluiah, Halleluiah, Halleluiah.*

Reader: The voice of the Lord upon the waters. The God of glory thunders. The Lord is on many waters.

People: *Halleluiah, Halleluiah, Halleluiah.*

Reader: What ails thee, O sea, that thou fleddest? And thee Jordan, that Thou didst turn back?

People: *Halleluiah, Halleluiah, Halleluiah.*

Gospel

Deacon: Wisdom. Attend. Let us hear the Holy Gospel.

Priest: Peace be with you all.

People: And with thy spirit.

Priest: The Reading Is From The Holy Gospel according to St Mark (1:9-11).

People: Glory to Thee, O Lord, glory to Thee.

Deacon: Let us attend.

Priest: In those days Jesus came from Nazareth of Galilee, and was baptised by John in the Jordan. And when He came up out of the water, immediately He saw the heavens opened and the Spirit descending upon Him like a dove; and a voice came from Heaven: Thou art My beloved Son; I am well pleased with Thee.

People: *Glory to Thee, O Lord, glory to Thee.*

The Augmented Great Litany

Deacon: In peace let us pray to the Lord.

People: *Lord, have mercy.*

Deacon: For the peace from above and the salvation of our souls, let us pray to the Lord.

People: *Lord, have mercy.*

Deacon: For peace in the whole world, the welfare of the holy churches of God, and the union of all men, let us pray to the Lord.

People: *Lord, have mercy.*

Deacon: For this holy Temple, and for those who enter it with faith, reverence and the fear of God, let us pray to the Lord.

People: *Lord, have mercy.*

Deacon: For the Most Holy Orthodox Patriarchs, for His Eminence Nikitas, for the honourable Priesthood, the Diaconate in Christ, and for all the clergy and the people, let us pray to the Lord.

People: *Lord, have mercy.*

Deacon: For our Country, our Sovereign Prince, our Government, and all in seats of authority, let us pray to the Lord.

People: *Lord, have mercy.*

Deacon: For this City, and for every city and land, and for those who live in them by faith, let us pray to the Lord.

People: *Lord, have mercy.*

Deacon: For seasonable weather, the abundance of the fruits of the earth and peaceful times, let us pray to the Lord.

People: *Lord, have mercy.*

Deacon: For those who are travelling by land, air and water, for the sick, the suffering, for prisoners and captives, and for their salvation, let us pray to the Lord.

People: *Lord, have mercy.*

For The Blessing Of The Waters.

Deacon: That this water be sanctified by the power, act and descent of the Holy Spirit, let us pray to the Lord.

People: *Lord, have mercy.*

Deacon: That in this water may be planted the action of purification that belongs to the Trinity transcendent in essence, let us pray to the Lord.

People: *Lord, have mercy.*

Deacon: That it may be granted the grace of redemption and the blessing of the Jordan, let us pray to the Lord.

People: *Lord, have mercy.*

Deacon: That we may be lit by the light of knowledge and true worship, by the descent of the Holy Spirit, let us pray to the Lord.

People: *Lord, have mercy.*

Deacon: That this water may become a gift for sanctification, redemption for sins, for the healing of soul and body, and for every meet benefit, let us pray to the Lord.

People: *Lord, have mercy.*

Deacon: That this water may be beneficial for eternal life, let us pray to the Lord.

People: *Lord, have mercy.*

Deacon: That it may drive away all the cunning devices of our enemies, visible and invisible, let us pray to the Lord.

People: *Lord, have mercy.*

Deacon: For those who drink there from and take home for the sanctification of their homes, let us pray to the Lord.

People: *Lord, have mercy.*

Deacon: That it may be for those who drink and receive there from in faith a purification for their souls and bodies, let us pray to the Lord.

People: *Lord, have mercy.*

Deacon: That we may be worthy to be filled with sanctification, as we receive of these waters, by the appearance of the Holy Spirit, in an invisible manner, let us pray to the Lord.

People: *Lord, have mercy.*

Deacon: That the Lord may answer the voice of our beseeching, even of us who are sinners, and have mercy upon us, let us pray to the Lord.

People: *Lord, have mercy.*

Deacon: For our deliverance from all tribulation, wrath, danger, and necessity, let us pray to the Lord.

People: *Lord, have mercy.*

Deacon: Help us; save us; have mercy on us; and keep us, O God, by Thy grace.

People: *Lord, have mercy.*

Deacon: Calling to remembrance our all holy, immaculate, most blessed and glorious Lady, Theotokos and ever virgin Mary, with all the Saints let us commend ourselves and each other, and all our life unto Christ our God.

People: *To Thee, O Lord.*

Priest: *[soto voce]* O Lord Jesus Christ, the only begotten Son, Who remains in the bosom of the Father, true God, Fountain of life and immortality, Light of Light, O Thou Who comest into the world to lighten it, lighten our minds by Thy Holy Spirit and accept us as we offer Thee magnification and gratitude for Thy great and wonderful works which are from eternity, and for Thy dispensation of salvation in these last days, in which Thou did put on our weak, poor creation, condescending, O King of all, even to become Man. And Thou didst consent also to be baptised at the hand of a servant, that by the sanctification of the nature of water, O sinless One, Thou mightest prepare for us a way for the renewal of birth by water and the Spirit, restoring to us our first freedom. Wherefore, as we celebrate the memory of this divine mystery, we beseech Thee, O Lover of mankind, to sprinkle us, Thine unworthy servants, according to Thy divine promise, with purifying water, and the gift of Thy compassion. May the prayers of us sinners over this water be wholly acceptable to Thy goodness, that Thou mayest grant through it Thy blessing to us and to all Thy believing people, to the glory of Thy holy, adored Name.

Priest: *[aloud]* For to Thee, together with Thine unoriginate Father and Thine all holy, good and life giving Spirit, belong all glory, honour and worship; now and ever, and to the ages of ages.

People: *Amen.*

The Great Prayer Of The Blessing Of The Water

Deacon: Let us pray to the Lord.

People: *Lord, have mercy.*

Priest: O Trinity, transcendent in essence, in goodness and in Divinity, the Almighty Who watches over all, invisible and incomprehensible, O Creator of intelligent essences, natures endowed with speech, the Goodness of utter and unapproachable Light, that lights everyone that comes into the world: lighten me also, Thine unworthy servant. Illuminate the eyes of my mind so that I may venture to praise Thy countless benevolences and Thy might. Let my prayer on behalf of this people be wholly acceptable, so that my sins may not prevent the descent here of Thy Holy Spirit; that I may be allowed to cry to Thee without condemnation, and say: We glorify Thee, O Master, Lover of mankind, the Almighty King before eternity. We glorify Thee, O Creator and Author of all. We glorify Thee, O only begotten Son, Who are without father on the side of Thy Mother, and without mother on the side of Thy Father; for in the preceding feast we have beheld Thee a babe, and in this present feast we behold Thee perfect man, O our perfect God, appearing from the Perfect; for today we have reached the time of the Feast, and the rank of saints gathers with us, and the angels celebrate with humans. Today the grace of the Holy Spirit has descended on the waters in the likeness of a dove. Today has shone the Sun that sets not, and the world is lit by the light of the Lord. Today the moon shines with the world in its radiating beams. Today the shining stars adorn the universe with the splendour of their radiance. Today the clouds from heaven moisten mankind with showers of justice. Today the Uncreated One accepts of His own will the laying on of hands by His own creation. Today the Prophet and Forerunner draws near to the Master, and halts in trembling when he witnesses the condescension of God towards us. Today the waters of the Jordan are changed into healing by the presence of the Lord. Today the whole universe is watered by mystical streams. Today the sins of mankind are blotted out by the waters of the Jordan. Today has paradise been opened to mankind, and the Sun of righteousness has shone for us. Today the bitter water is changed at the hands of Moses to sweetness by the presence of the Lord. Today are we delivered from the ancient mourning, and like a new Israel we have been saved. Today we have escaped from darkness and, by the light of the knowledge of God, we have been illuminated. Today the darkness of the world vanishes with the appearance of our God. Today the whole creation is lighted from on high. Today error is annulled, and the coming of the Lord prepares for us a way of salvation. Today the celestials celebrate with the terrestrials, and the terrestrials commune with the celestials. Today the assembly of noble and great voiced Orthodoxy rejoices. Today the Lord comes to baptism to elevate mankind above. Today the Unbowable bows to His servant to deliver us from slavery. Today we have bought the kingdom of heaven, for the kingdom of heaven has no end. Today the land and the sea have divided between them the joy of the world, and the world has been filled with rejoicing.

The waters saw Thee, O God, the waters saw Thee; they were afraid. Jordan turned back when it beheld the fire of the Godhead coming down and descending upon it in the flesh. Jordan turned back at beholding the Holy Spirit descending in the likeness of a dove and hovering over Thee. Jordan turned back when it saw the Invisible visible, the Creator incarnate, and the Master in the likeness of a servant. Jordan turned back and the mountains shouted with joy at beholding God in the flesh. And the clouds gave voice, wondering at Him Who cometh, Who is Light of Light, true God of true God, drowning in the Jordan the death of sin, the thorn of error, and bond of Hades, granting the world the baptism of salvation. So also am I, Thine unworthy and sinful servant, as I proclaim Thy great wonders, encompassed by fear, crying reverently to Thee, and saying:

[The following thrice.]

Priest: Great art Thou, O Lord, and wonderful are Thy works, and no word does justice to the praise of Thy wonders.

People: *Glory to Thee, O Lord, glory to Thee.*

Priest: For by Thy will Thou didst bring out all things out of non-existence into existence; and by Thy might Thou dost control creation, and by Thy providence Thou governest the world. It is Thou who didst organise creation from four elements, and crowned the cycle of the year with four seasons. Before Thee tremblest noetic powers; the sun praises Thee, the moon worships Thee; the stars submit to Thee, the light obeys Thee, the tempests tremble, the springs worship Thee. Thou didst spread out the heavens like a tent; Thou didst establish the earth upon the waters. Thou didst surround the sea with sand. Thou didst pour out the air for breathing. The angelic hosts serve Thee; the ranks of the archangels worship Thee, the many eyed cherubim and the six winged seraphim, as they stand in Thy presence and fly about Thee, hiding in fear from Thine unapproachable glory. While remaining a boundless God, beginning-less and ineffable, Thou didst come to earth, taking the likeness of a servant, and became man. By the feeling of Thy compassion, O Master, Thou couldest not bear to see mankind defeated by Satan, but did come and save us; for to Thee do we attribute grace, and preach mercy, and conceal not benevolence. The sons of our nature Thou didst free; the virginal womb by Thy Nativity Thou didst sanctify. Therefore, all creation has praised Thee in Thine appearance; for Thou our God did appear on earth, and among men Thou didst walk. The courses of the Jordan Thou did sanctify, having sent to it from heaven Thine all holy Spirit, and did crush the heads of the dragons nestling therein.

[The priest makes the sign of the Cross over the water THRICE, saying each time:]

Priest: Wherefore, Thou King and Lover of mankind, be present now by the descent of Thy Holy Spirit, and sanctify this water.

People: *Amen.*

Priest: And grant it the grace of redemption and the blessing of the Jordan. Make it a fount of incorruptibility, a gift for sanctification, a redemption for sins, an elixir for maladies, a destroyer of demons, unapproachable by the adverse powers and full of angelic powers; so that to all who drink there from and receive thereof it may be for the sanctification of their souls and bodies, for the healing of sufferings, for the sanctification of homes and for every befitting benefit. For Thou art our God who with water and the Spirit renewed our nature made old by sin. Thou art our God who did drown sin in the water at the time of Noah. Thou art our God Who in the sea did deliver the Hebrews from the bondage of Pharaoh at the hands of Moses. Thou art our God Who did cleave the rock in the wilderness, so that the waters gushed out and the valleys overflowed, thus satisfying Thy thirsty people. Thou art our God who with fire and water did deliver Israel from the error of Baal at the hands of Elisha.

[The following thrice.]

Priest: Wherefore, O Master, sanctify this water by Thy Holy Spirit.

People: *Amen.*

Priest: Grant to all who touch it and who are anointed by it and who receive thereof sanctification, blessing, cleansing and health. Save, O Lord, Thy servants, our faithful civil authorities. Keep them under Thy shadow in peace. Subdue under their feet every enemy and adversary. Grant to them the means of salvation and eternal life. Be mindful, O Lord, of our Father and Archbishop Nikitas, all the priesthood, the diaconate in Christ, every priestly order, and all Thy people here present, together with all our brethren who are absent for a just cause. Have mercy on them and on us according to Thy loving kindness.

People: *Amen.*

Priest: That Thine all holy Name may be glorified by the elements, by angels and by humans, by visible and invisible creatures, together with the Father and the Holy Spirit, now and ever, and unto the ages of ages.

People: *Amen.*

The Peace

Priest: Peace be with you all.

People: *And with thy spirit.*

Deacon: Let us bow down our heads unto the Lord.

People: *To Thee, O Lord.*

[All bow their heads as the priest says the following prayer:]

Priest: Incline Thine ear, O Lord, and hear us. O Thou who didst sanctify water when Thou didst consent to be baptised in the Jordan, bless us all, who by the bowing of our heads have signified our bondage; and make us worthy to be filled with Thy sanctification, by the receiving of this water and its sprinkling. Let it be to us, O Lord, for health of soul and body. For Thou art the sanctification of our souls and bodies, and to Thee we ascribe glory, thanks giving and worship, with the Father Who has no beginning and Thine all holy, good and Life giving Spirit, the God and Author of life, now and ever, and to the ages of ages.

People: *Amen.*

[The priest blesses the water in the form of a cross, and immerses the hand cross up and down, holding it straight, into the water.]

Apolytikion Of The Theophany Of Christ

Tone 1 *Magnificent, happy and earthy.*   C, D, Eb, F, G, A, Bb, C.

When Thou, O Lord, wert baptised in the Jordan, worship of the Trinity was made manifest; for the voice of the Father bore witness to Thee, calling Thee His beloved Son. And the Spirit in the form of a dove confirmed the truth of His word. O Christ our God, Who has appeared and enlightened the world, glory to Thee. **(x3)**

[As the priest sprinkles the Holy Water on all the people, the Chorus sings:]

Kontakion Of The Theophany Of Christ

Tone 4   Festive, joyous and expressing deep piety.   *C, D, Eb, F, G, A, Bb, C.*

Today Thou hast appeared to the universe, O Lord, and Thy light has been shed upon us, who praise Thee with knowledge, saying, Thou hast come and appeared, O unapproachable Light.

Idiomelon

Tone 6   Rich texture, funereal character, sorrowful tone.   *D, Eb, F##, G, A, Bb, C##, D.*

Let us praise, O believers, the great dispensation of God that works for us; for He Who alone is pure and spotless, having become man because of our fall, purifies us in the Jordan, sanctifying us and the waters and crushing the heads of the dragons in the water. Let us, therefore, O brethren, draw water with gladness, for those who draw it in faith shall be granted in an invisible manner the grace of the Spirit, by the presence of Christ God, the Saviour of our souls.

[Return to The Great Dismissal of the Divine Liturgy.
The Sanctified Water may be distributed amongst the clergy and faithful afterwards.]

The Order For The Lesser Sanctification Of The Water

[Priest places the Gospel; a wooden, silver bound Cross; a censer; a bowl of water; two candlesticks with their candles; a few branches of basil and a clean white towel on a small table.

Priest in rasson and epitrachelion.]

The Trisagion Prayers

Deacon: Holy Father, Bless.

Priest: Blessed is our God always, now and forever, and unto the ages of ages.

People: *Amen.*

Priest: O Heavenly King, Comforter, Spirit of Truth, Who art everywhere present and fillest all things, Treasury of blessings and Giver of life: Come and abide in us and cleanse us from every impurity and save our souls, O Good One.

Reader: Holy God, Holy Mighty, Holy Immortal, have mercy on us. **(x3)**

Glory be to the Father, and to the Son, and to the Holy Spirit;
Both now and forever, and unto the ages of ages. Amen.

O Most Holy Trinity, have mercy on us.

O Lord, cleanse us from our sins.

O Master, pardon our iniquities.

O Holy One, visit and heal our infirmities, for Thy names sake.

Lord have mercy. **(x3)**

Glory be to the Father and to the Son and to the Holy Spirit;
Both now and forever, and unto the ages of ages. Amen.

People: *Our Father, Who art in Heaven, hallowed be Thy Name. Thy Kingdom come, Thy will be done, on earth as it is in Heaven. Give us this day our daily bread, and forgive us our trespasses, as we forgive those who trespass against us; and lead us not into temptation, but deliver us from the evil one. Amen.*

Priest: For Thine is the Kingdom, and the power, and the glory; of the Father, and of the Son, and of the Holy Spirit, now and ever, and unto the ages of ages.

People: *Amen.*

Lord, have mercy. **(x12)**

Glory be to the Father and to the Son and to the Holy Spirit.
Both now and ever and to the ages of ages, Amen.

O come let us worship God our King.

O come let us worship and fall down before Christ our King and God.

O come let us worship and fall down before Christ Himself, our King and our God.

Psalm 142

Reader: Lord, hear my prayer; in Thy truth give ear to my supplications; in Thy righteousness hear me. Enter not into judgement with Thy servant, for no one living is justified in Thy sight. For the enemy has pursued my soul; he has crushed my life to the ground. He has made me to dwell in darkness, like those that have long been dead, and my spirit within me is overwhelmed; my heart within me is distressed. I remembered the days of old, I meditated on all Thy works, I pondered on the creations of Thine hands. I stretched forth my hands to Thee; my soul longs for Thee like a thirsty land. Lord, hear me quickly; my spirit fails. Turn not Thy face away from me, lest I be like those who go down into the pit. Let me hear Thy mercy in the morning; for in Thee have I put my trust. Lord, teach me to know the way wherein I should walk; for I lift up my soul to Thee. Rescue me, Lord, from mine enemies, to Thee have I fled for refuge. Teach me to do Thy will, for Thou art my God. Thy good Spirit shall lead me on a level path. Lord, for Thy names sake Thou shalt preserve my life. In Thy righteousness Thou shalt bring my soul out of trouble, and in Thy mercy Thou shalt utterly destroy my enemies. And Thou shalt destroy all those who afflict my soul, for I am Thy servant.

God Is The Lord

People: *God is the Lord and has revealed Himself to us.*

Blessed is He who comes in the Name of the Lord.

Reader: Give thanks to the Lord, for He is good; and His steadfast love endures forever.

People: *God is the Lord and has revealed Himself to us.*

Blessed is He who comes in the Name of the Lord.

Reader: All nations surrounded me; in the Name of the Lord, I withstood them.

People: *God is the Lord and has revealed Himself to us.*

Blessed is He who comes in the Name of the Lord.

Reader: This is the Lords doing and is marvellous in our eyes.

People: *God is the Lord and has revealed Himself to us.*

Blessed is He who comes in the Name of the Lord.

Troparia

Tone 4   Festive, joyous and expressing deep piety.   *C, D, Eb, F, G, A, Bb, C.*

To thee, O Theotokos, we sinners now flee. In repentance we bow down before thee, saying: "O Sovereign Lady, help us: have compassion on us, make haste to help, for we perish in the multitude of our sins Turn us not empty away, for we have thee as our only hope.

Glory be to the Father, and to the Son, and to the Holy Spirit;

Both now and forever, and unto the ages of ages. Amen.

Theotokion

Never, O Theotokos, shall we, unworthy, cease to proclaim thy powers: for if thou didst not hasten to our aid, making intercession, who would have delivered us from our manifold adversities? Who would have preserved us free to this day? We shall not forsake you, O Lady, for thou savest thy servants from all malicious foes.

Psalm 50

Have mercy on me, O God, according to Thy great mercy; and according to the multitude of Thy compassions blot out my transgression. Wash me thoroughly from mine iniquity, and cleanse me from my sin. For I acknowledge mine iniquity, and my sin is ever before me. Against Thee, Thee only have I sinned, and done evil in Thy sight, that Thou mayest be found just when Thou speakest, and victorious when Thou art judged. For behold, I was conceived in iniquity, and in sin my mother bore me. For behold, Thou hast loved truth; Thou hast made known to me the hidden and secret things of Thy wisdom. Thou shalt sprinkle me with hyssop, and I shall be made clean; Thou shalt wash me, and I shall be whiter than snow. Make me to hear joy and gladness; that the humbled bones may rejoice. Turn Thy face away from my sins, and blot out all mine iniquities.

Create in me a clean heart, O God, and renew a steadfast spirit within me. Cast me not away from Thy presence, and take not Thy Holy Spirit from me. Restore to me the joy of Thy salvation, and establish me with Thy governing Spirit. I shall teach transgressors Thy ways, and the ungodly shall turn back to Thee. Deliver me from blood guiltiness, O God, the God of my salvation; my tongue shall joyfully declare Thy righteousness. Lord, open my lips, and my mouth shall declare Thy praise. For if Thou hadst desired sacrifice, I would give it; Thou dost not delight in burnt offerings. A sacrifice to God is a broken spirit; God shall not despise a broken and a humbled heart. Do good, O Lord, in Thy good pleasure to Zion, and let the walls of Jerusalem be builded. Then Thou shalt be pleased with a sacrifice of righteousness, with oblation and whole burned offerings. Then shall they offer bulls on Thine altar.

Chorus: *All Holy Theotokos, guard, protect and keep thy servants.*

Troparia

Tone 6   Rich texture, funeral character, sorrowful tone.   *D, Eb, F##, G, A, Bb, C##, D.*

O Virgin who from the Angel received, hail. And gave birth to the Life giver Himself, thy Creator, save them that magnify you. **(x3)**

Refrain: *Most holy Theotokos, protect, guard and keep thy servants.*

We sing of thy Son, O Theotokos, and cry aloud: from all adversities save thy servants, O Immaculate One.

Refrain: *Most holy Theotokos, protect, guard and keep thy servants.*

The praise of Kings, Prophets, Apostles, and Martyrs are you, and Intercessor of the world, O All Immaculate One.

Refrain: *Most holy Theotokos, protect, guard and keep thy servants.*

Every Orthodox tongue praises, blesses, and glorifies thy immaculate Birth giving, O Mary, Bride of God.

Refrain: *Most holy Theotokos, protect, guard and keep thy servants.*

I beseech Thee, O my Christ, give to me also, though unworthy, remission of offences, I beseech Thee; through the intercessions of her that bore Thee, in that Thou art compassionate.

Refrain: *Most holy Theotokos, protect, guard and keep thy servants.*

In thee, O Theotokos, have I put my hope. Save me by thy prayers; grant for me remission of sins.

Refrain: *Most holy Theotokos, protect, guard and keep thy servants.*

Give me life, Thou that hast borne the Life giver and Saviour: save me through thy prayers, O blessed Hope of our souls.

Refrain: *Most holy Theotokos, protect, guard and keep thy servants.*

O Virgin immaculate, who did conceive in thy Womb the Creator of all people: through thy prayers save our souls.

Refrain: *Most holy Theotokos, protect, guard and keep thy servants.*

All praised Theotokos, who through the word of an Angel, in a manner beyond reason, gave birth to the Word, pray that He shall save our souls.

Refrain: *Most holy Theotokos, protect, guard and keep thy servants.*

Through thy intercessions, O Lady, make thy Son a merciful Judge unto me, who am a sinner above all people.

Refrain: *Most holy Theotokos, protect, guard and keep thy servants.*

With binding duty we cry to thee, Hail. O immaculate Theotokos Ever Virgin; through thine intercessions are saved those that pray to thee.

Refrain: *Most holy Theotokos, protect, guard and keep thy servants.*

Deliver me from the fire eternal, and the torments that await me, O all praised Lady, that I may be delivered from all tribulation.

Refrain: *Most holy Theotokos, protect, guard and keep thy servants.*

All praised Sovereign Lady, we pray thee: do not overlook the prayers of thy servants, so that we might be delivered from all tribulation.

Refrain: *Most holy Theotokos, protect, guard and keep thy servants.*

From every sickness and infirmity. Deliver us, who have recourse unto thee and thy holy Protection.

Refrain: *Most holy Theotokos, protect, guard and keep thy servants.*

Marvellous wonder shown to thee, O Theotokos: for our sake the Creator of All and our God was in our likeness born to thee.

Refrain: *Most holy Theotokos, protect, guard and keep thy servants.*

Thy Temple, O Theotokos, was shown forth as remedy without price of ills, the consolation of our wounded souls.

Refrain: *Most holy Theotokos, protect, guard and keep thy servants.*

O All Holy Theotokos, who hast borne the Saviour, save thy servants from adversity and from all other necessity.

Refrain: *Most holy Theotokos, protect, guard and keep thy servants.*

From every ban under which they labour deliver thy servants from every ailment of body and spirit, O thou most Holy.

Refrain: *Most holy Theotokos, protect, guard and keep thy servants.*

Through thy intercessions, O Virgin Theotokos, save all that have recourse unto you; deliver all from sorrow and necessity.

Refrain: *Most holy Theotokos, protect, guard and keep thy servants.*

Who, having recourse unto thy Temple, O Theotokos, does not receive speedy healing both of soul and body, O All immaculate?

Refrain: *Most holy Theotokos, protect, guard and keep thy servants.*

Entreated by the Saints and heavenly Hosts, O Merciful One, through her that bore Thee, do Thou cleanse me.

Refrain: *Most holy Theotokos, protect, guard and keep thy servants.*

Spare, O Saviour, the souls of our brethren, who died in the Hope of Life; loose, and remit their sins.

Refrain: *Most holy Theotokos, protect, guard and keep thy servants.*

Hail. O Virgin, Mercy Seat of the world; Hail. O Receptacle of the Manna and Candelabrum all golden of the light divine, O Bride of God unwedded.

Glory be to the Father, and to the Son, and to the Holy Spirit;

Triadikon
We sing unto Thee, O God in Three Persons, crying aloud the thrice Holy Hymn, entreating that we may receive salvation.

Both now and forever, and unto the ages of ages. Amen.

Theotokion
Refrain: *Most holy Theotokos, save us.*

O Virgin, who has borne the Saviour, the Sovereign of the world: pray unto Him that He shall save our souls.

Refrain: *Most holy Theotokos, save us.*

Hail. O Mount, Hail. O Bush that burned and yet was not consumed; Hail. O Gate, Hail. O Ladder and Altar Divine, Hail. Sovereign Lady, the Helper of all.

Refrain: *Most holy Theotokos, save us.*

Through the prayers of Thy Holy Mother, and of Thy Holy Saints, O Merciful God, to Thy people grant Thy great mercies.

Refrain: *Most holy Theotokos, save us.*

Through the prayers of the glorious Archangels, the Angels, and all the heavenly Hosts, mightily preserve Thy servants, O Saviour.

Refrain: *Most holy Theotokos, save us.*

Through the prayers of the glorious Prophet and Forerunner John the Baptist, and of all Thy Saints, mightily preserve Thy servants, O my Christ and Saviour.

Refrain: *Most holy Theotokos, save us.*

Through the prayers of the glorious Apostles, and the victorious Martyrs, and of all Thy Saints, grant Thy mercies to Thy servants.

Refrain: *Most holy Theotokos, save us.*

Through the prayers of the glorious Unmercenaries, O Theotokos, preserve thy servants, in that thou art Intercessor and Confirmer of the world.

> *Glory be to the Father, and to the Son, and to the Holy Spirit;*

Triadikon

The Father and the Son and the Holy Spirit we glorify saying: O Holy Trinity, save our souls.

> *Both now and forever, and unto the ages of ages. Amen.*

Theotokion

O Virgin who in mystery did conceive and bring forth in these latter days thy Creator: save us who magnify thee. Open for us the door of thy tender compassion, O blessed Theotokos; and as we set our hope in thee, let us never be confounded; through thee may we be delivered from all adversity; thou, who art the salvation of all good Christian folk.

Deacon: Let us pray to the Lord.

People: *Lord have mercy.*

Priest: For Holy art Thou, O God, and to Thee art due all glory, honour and adoration: to the Father and to the Son and to the Holy Spirit, both now and ever and to the ages of ages.

People: *Amen.*

Troparia

Tone 8   Humility, tranquillity, repose, suffering, pleading.   *C, D, Eb, F, G, A, Bb, C.*

• Now draws nigh the time that sanctifies all men, and a just Judge awaits us; turn then, O my soul, to repentance, like the Adulteress tearfully crying: have mercy on me, O Lord.

• O Christ, the Fountain, Who did sprinkle the waters of healing in the all holy Temple of the Virgin, Thou, today, through the sprinkling of blessing did expel the maladies of ailing, O Thou Physician of our souls and bodies.

• As a Virgin thou knewest not man, but gave birth; and as a Mother unwedded, a Virgin didst thou remain; entreat then, O Mary Theotokos, Christ our God that He shall save us.

• O All Holy Theotokos Virgin, guide aright the works of our hands, and entreat pardon for our transgressions, when we chant the angelic Hymn:

People: *Holy God, Holy Mighty, Holy Immortal: have mercy on us.* **(x3)**

Glory be to the Father, and to the Son, and to the Holy Spirit;
Both now and forever, and unto the ages of ages. Amen.

Holy Immortal: have mercy on us.

Deacon: With power.

People: *Holy God, Holy Mighty, Holy Immortal: have mercy on us.*

Deacon: Let us attend. The prokeimenon.

Prokeimenon

Reader: The Lord is my Light and my Saviour; whom then shall I fear?

People: *The Lord is my Light and my Saviour; whom then shall I fear?*

Reader: The Lord is the defender of my life; of whom then shall I be afraid?

People: *The Lord is my Light and my Saviour; whom then shall I fear?*

Reader: The Lord is my Light and my Saviour | whom then shall I fear?

Epistle

Priest: Wisdom.

Reader: The Reading is from the letter of the Blessed Apostle Paul to the Hebrews (2:11 18).

Priest: Let us attend.

Reader: Brethren, he who sanctifies and those who are sanctified have all one origin. That is why he is not ashamed to call them brethren, saying: "I shall proclaim Thy name to my brethren, in the midst of the congregation I shall praise Thee. And again: "I shall put my trust in Him." And again: "Here am I, and the children God has given me." Since therefore the children share in flesh and blood, he himself likewise partook of the same nature, that through death he might destroy him who has the power of death, that is, the devil, and deliver all those who through fear of death were subject to lifelong bondage. For surely it is not with angels that he is concerned but with the descendants of Abraham. Therefore he had to be made like his brethren in every respect, so that he might become a merciful and faithful high priest in the service of God, to make expiation for the sins of the people. For because he himself has suffered and been tempted, he is able to help those who are tempted.

Priest: Peace be to thee who readest.

Reader: And with thy spirit.

Chorus: *Halleluia, Halleluia, Halleluia.*

Reader: My heart hath poured forth a good word.

Chorus: *Halleluia, Halleluia, Halleluia.*

Reader: I speak of my works to the king.

Chorus: *Halleluia, Halleluia, Halleluia.*

The Gospel

Deacon: Wisdom. Stand up. Let us hear the Holy Gospel.

Priest: Peace be with you all.

People: *And with thy spirit.*

Deacon: The reading is from the Holy Gospel according to John (5:1-4).

People: *Glory to Thee, O God; Glory to Thee.*

Priest: Let us attend.

Deacon: At that time, there was a feast of the Jews, and Jesus went up to Jerusalem. Now there is in Jerusalem by the Sheep Gate a pool, in Hebrew called Bethesda, which has five porticoes. In these lay a multitude of invalids, blind, lame, paralyzed, waiting for the moving of the water. For an angel of the Lord went down at certain seasons into the pool and troubled the water. And whoever stepped in first after the troubling of the water was healed of whatever disease he had.

People: *Glory to Thee, O God; Glory to Thee.*

[Deacon lifts orarion and:]

The Ektenia Of Blessing

Deacon: In peace let us pray to the Lord.

People: *Lord have mercy.*

Deacon: For the peace from above; for the salvation of our souls; let us pray to the Lord.

People: *Lord have mercy.*

Deacon: For the peace of the whole world; for the stability of the holy Churches of God; and for the union of all; let us pray to the Lord.

People: *Lord have mercy.*

Deacon: For this holy House; and for them that with faith, reverence, and the fear of God enter therein; let us pray to the Lord.

People: *Lord have mercy.*

Deacon: For our Most Reverend Archbishop Nikitas, for all the Clergy, and the people, let us pray to the Lord.

People: *Lord have mercy.*

Deacon: For the First Minister, the Royal Family and for all civil authorities; let us pray to the Lord.

People: *Lord have mercy.*

Deacon: For this city, for every city and land, for the faithful that dwell in them, let us pray to the Lord.

People: *Lord have mercy.*

Deacon: For seasonable weather; for abundance of the fruits of the earth, and for peaceful seasons; let us pray to the Lord.

People: *Lord have mercy.*

Deacon: For all them that travel by land or sea, or in the air; for the sick, and the afflicted; for captives, and for their salvation; let us pray to the Lord.

People: *Lord have mercy.*

Deacon: That this water might be hallowed by the might, and operation, and descent of the Holy Spirit, let us pray to the Lord.

People: *Lord have mercy.*

Deacon: That there may descend upon these waters the cleansing operation of the super substantial Trinity; let us pray to the Lord.

People: *Lord have mercy.*

Deacon: That this water may be to the healing of souls and bodies, and to the banishment of every hostile power, let us pray to the Lord.

People: *Lord have mercy.*

Deacon: That there may be sent down upon it the Grace of Redemption, the blessing of the Jordan; let us pray to the Lord.

People: *Lord have mercy.*

Deacon: For all of them who need God to help and give protection, let us pray to the Lord.

People: *Lord have mercy.*

Deacon: That He shall illuminate us with the Light of understanding of the Consubstantial Trinity; let us pray to the Lord.

People: *Lord have mercy.*

Deacon: That the Lord our God shall show us forth as sons and daughters and heirs of His Kingdom through the partaking and sprinkling of these waters; let us pray to the Lord.

People: *Lord have mercy.*

Deacon: That He shall deliver us from all tribulation, wrath, danger, and necessity, let us pray to the Lord.

People: *Lord have mercy.*

Deacon: Help us; save us; have mercy on us; and keep us, O God, by Thy Grace.

People: *Lord have mercy.*

Deacon: Calling to remembrance our all Holy, pure, exceedingly blessed glorious Lady Theotokos and Ever Virgin Mary, with all the Saints, let us commend ourselves and one another and all our life to Christ our God.

People: *To Thee, O Lord.*

Deacon: For unto Thee do we send up all glory, honour, and worship: to the Father and to the Son and to the Holy Spirit, both now and ever, and to the ages of ages.

People: *Amen.*

Priest: Let us pray to the Lord.

People: *Lord have mercy.*

Prayer 1

Priest: O Lord our God, Who are mighty in counsel and wondrous in all Thy deeds: the Creator of all things: Who keep Thy Covenant and Thy mercy upon all those who love Thee and keep Thy commandments: Who receive the devout tears of all that are in distress: for this cause didst Thou come in the similitude of a servant, scorning not our image but giving true health to the body and saying, "Lo. Thou art healed, sin no more." And with clay did make mans eyes whole, and having commanded him to wash, made him by Thy word rejoice in the light, putting to confusion the floods of passions of enemies; and drying up the bitter sea of life of the same, subduing the waves of sensual desires heavy to be endured: do Thou, the same Lord and King Who lovest mankind, Who has granted to us to clothe ourselves in the garment of snowy whiteness, by water and by Spirit: send down on us Thy blessing, and through the partaking of this water, through sprinkling with it, wash away the defilement of passions.

Yea, we beseech Thee, visit our weaknesses, O Good One, and heal our infirmities both of spirit and of body through Thy mercy; through the prayers of the all pure, exceedingly blessed Lady Theotokos and Ever Virgin Mary; Through the intercessions of the precious and life creating Cross; through the protection of the glorious bodiless Powers of the Heavens; through the intercessions of the glorious Prophet and Forerunner John the Baptist; of the holy, glorious and all praiseworthy Apostles; of the holy and theophoric Fathers; of our Fathers among the Saints, the great Hierarchs and ecumenical Teachers, Basil the Great, Gregory the Theologian, and John Chrysostom; of our Fathers the Saints, Athanasios, Kyrillos, and John the Merciful, Patriarchs of Alexandria; of Nicholas Bishop of Myra in Lycia; of Spyridon the Wonderworker Of Trymitheus; of the holy, glorious Martyrs, George the Victorious, Demetrios the Exhaler of Myrrh, Theodore of Tyron and Theodore Stratilatis; and of the holy and glorious Hieromartyrs Charalambos and Eleutherios, and of all the righteous Martyrs; of the holy and righteous forefathers Joachim and Anna; of the holy wonder working Unmercenaries, Kosmas and Damian, Kyros and John, Panteleimon and Hermolaus; Samson and Diomedes, Mokios and Anekitas, Thallelaios and Tryphon; of Saint *[Saints of the Day]*, whose memory we commemorate; and of all Thy Saints.

[Each time in a louder voice:]

Priest: And guard, O Lord, thine Orthodox people.

Reader: Amen.

Priest: And guard, O Lord, thine Orthodox people.

Reader: Amen.

Priest: And guard, O Lord, thine Orthodox people.

Reader: Amen. **(x3)**

Priest: Preserve, Lord, the First Minister, the Royal Family, and all the other Civil Authorities enabled by the American people; save, O God, all Orthodox Bishops who rightly divide the word of Thy truth, granting unto them spiritual and bodily health; be merciful unto this Christian habitation which labours for Thee; have in remembrance, O God, every priestly and monastic order and their salvation; have in remembrance, O God, both those that hate us and those who love us, the brethren who serve with us; the people here present; and who for any cause are worthy of blessing and have gone forth having empowered us, unworthy though we are, to pray, for them; have in remembrance, O God, our brethren who are in captivity and affliction, and show mercy unto them according to Thy great Mercy, delivering them from every tribulation.

For Thou art the Fountain of healing, O Christ our God, and to Thee do we send up all glory, together with Thine Eternal Father and Thine All Holy, Good, and Life creating Spirit, both now and forever, and to the ages of ages.

People: Amen.

Priest: Peace be with you all.

People: *And with thy spirit.*

Prayer 2

Priest: O great and most high God, worshipped in Holy Trinity; pre-eternal Nature and super essential Grandeur; inscrutable Power and ineffable Authority; Source of wisdom and truly unsearchable Sea of goodness; thou, O Master who lovest mankind, art God who wrought wonders before the ages. No mind can comprehend thee, and no word is able to explain. We pray thee now, look down upon us thy humble and unworthy servants. And grant to our mind the spirit of wisdom and understanding, and to our tongue utterance worthy of reaching the hearing of thy goodness and of obtaining the mercy of thy grace; for man's power both to will and to act cometh from thee and from thy vivifying gift.

[Each time in a louder voice, and each time he blesses over the water with his hand:]

Priest: Therefore, O Master who lovest mankind, do thou thyself be present even now, through the descent of thy Holy Spirit, and sanctify this water.

People: Amen.

Priest: Therefore, O Master who lovest mankind, do thou thyself be present even now, through the descent of thy Holy Spirit, and sanctify this water.

People: *Amen.*

Priest: Therefore, O Master who lovest mankind, do thou thyself be present even now, through the descent of thy Holy Spirit, and sanctify this water.

People: *Amen.* **(x3)**

Priest: Thou hast given our race the laver of regeneration, that we might wash away the pollutions of sin and be rid of all the various illnesses that befall us. Do Thou also vouchsafe us, having been thus sprinkled, to keep our hearts free from an evil conscience; and, having bodily bathed in clean water, to bear fruit and to increase in every good work. And grant us always and with unflagging diligence to show sympathy towards the needy and to care for our suffering brethren; and to become worthy of thy compassion, and to obtain the relief from our souls infirmities and from physical pain. And send down to us, by means of this water, the healings that Thou bestowest in Thy love for mankind. And let this spiritual ministry which we are performing be not for physical pleasure but for the healing of soul. Yea, O Master, who by water and the Spirit hast given us a garment white as snow to wear, send down upon us Thy blessing for the wiping away of the defilement of the passions through partaking of this water and being sprinkled therewith; through the intercessions of our all immaculate Lady Theotokos and Ever Virgin Mary; by the might of the precious and life giving cross; by the protection of the honourable bodiless powers of heaven; at the supplications of the honourable, glorious Prophet, Forerunner and Baptist John; of the holy, glorious, all laudable apostles; of our fathers among the saints, great hierarchs and ecumenical teachers Basil the Great, Gregory the Theologian and John Chrysostom; Athanasios, Cyril and John the Merciful, patriarchs of Alexandria; Nicholas of Myra in Lycia, Spyridon of Trimythous, Nektarios of Pentapolis, the Wonder workers, and Raphael of Brooklyn; of the holy and glorious great martyrs, George the Trophy bearer, Demetrios the Myrrh streaming, Theodore the Soldier, Theodore the General and Menas the Wonder worker; of the hieromartyrs Ignatius the God bearer of Antioch, Polycarp, Charalambous, Eleftherios, Joseph of Damascus and Jacob of Hamatoura; of the holy great women martyrs Thekla, Barbara, Anastasia, Katherine, Kyriaki, Photeini, Marina, Paraskeva and Irene; of our venerable and God bearing fathers who shone in the ascetic life, Antony the Great, Efthymios, Païsios, Sabbas the Sanctified, Theodosios the head of monasteries, Onouphrios, Athanasios and Peter of Athos; of our venerable Mothers Mary of Egypt, Pelagia and Thaïs; of holy, glorious and wonder working unmercenary healers Cosmas and Damian, Cyros and John, Panteleimon and Hermolaos, Sampson and Diomedes, Mokios and Anikitos, Thallelaios, Tryphon and Julian of Emessa; of *[Patron saint of the temple];* of the holy and righteous ancestors of God, Joachim and Anna; and of all Thy saints.

[Priest faces east and with the Cross in his right hand makes the sign of the cross in the air:]

Priest: Through their intercessions, guard, O Lord, *(thy servants N nd N)* all pious and Orthodox Christians.

[Priest faces west:]

Priest: Guard, O Lord, thy servant our Father and Archbishop <u>Nikitas</u> and all in priestly and monastic orders.

[Priest faces south:]

Priest: Guard, O Lord, this holy house and all who abide herein.

[Priest faces north:]

Priest: Guard, O Lord, this city *(town / village / island / holy monastery)* and every city and town and the faithful who dwell therein.

[Priest faces east and lays aside the Cross:]

Priest: And grant them health of soul and body and all their petitions which are unto salvation and life eternal. Be mindful, O Lord, of those who bear fruit and do good works in thy holy churches and who remember the poor. Be mindful, O Lord, of every priestly and monastic order. Be mindful, O Lord, of all the people here present and those who are absent for a cause worthy of a blessing. Be mindful, O Lord, of our brethren in captivity; look down upon them all and heal them, and according to thy great mercy grant them all of their petitions which are unto salvation and life eternal. For it is thou who dost bless and sanctify all things, O our God, and unto thee do we ascribe glory, to the Father and to the Son and to Holy Spirit, now and ever, and unto the ages of ages.

People: *Amen.*

Priest: Peace be to you all.

People: *And with thy spirit.*

Deacon: Let us bow our heads unto the Lord.

People: *To thee, O Lord.*

Priest: *(soto voce)*   Bow down Thine ear and listen to us, O Lord, Who deigned to be baptised in the river Jordan, and there sanctified the water. Bless us all who by the bowing of our heads do show forth our apprehension that we are Thy servants. Grant that we may be filled with Thy sanctification through the partaking of this water, and let it be for us, O Lord, for the health of soul and body.

(Aloud)   For Thou art the sanctification of our souls and bodies, and to Thee do we send up all glory; to the Father, and to the Son, and to the Holy Spirit, both now and ever, and to the ages of ages.

People: *Amen.*

[Priest blesses the water, making in it the sign of the cross with the hand cross and basil. He then submerges the sanctification cross and basil in the water and raises it above his head, holding it with both hands.

Whilst:]

Troparion

Tone 1   Magnificent, happy and earthy.   *C, D, Eb, F, G, A, Bb, C.*

Priest: O Lord, save Thy people and bless Thine inheritance.

Grant victories to the Orthodox Christians over their adversaries.

And by virtue of Thy Cross, preserve Thy commonwealth.

Chorus: Soson Kyrie ton lao sou, Ke evlogison, tin klironomian sou, Nikas tis Vasilevsii;

Kata varvaron doroumen as Ke to son filaton dia ton stavron sou politev ma.

Chorus: O Lord, save Thy people and bless Thine inheritance.

Grant victories to the Orthodox Christians over their adversaries.

And by virtue of Thy Cross, preserve Thy commonwealth.

[Priest sprinkles the Holy Water in the form of the Cross; Whilst:]

Tone 2   Majesty, gentleness, hope, repentance and sadness.   *E, F, G, Ab, B, C.*

Chorus: Make us worthy of thy gifts, O Virgin Theotokos, overlooking our transgressions; give healing through faith to them that accept thy blessing, O Immaculate One.

[Priest kisses Cross.

People kiss the cross as the priest sprinkles them and the entire temple or house with the sanctified water. Whilst:]

Troparia

Tone 4   Festive, joyous and expressing deep piety.   *C, D, Eb, F, G, A, Bb, C.*

Reader: O holy Unmercenaries, who had a fountain of healing, give healing to all that ask; in that you have been given gifts most excellent from the everlasting Font of the Saviour. For the Lord has said to you: Lo. To you and your fellows has been given power over all unclean spirits, to drive them off with healing and free from every ill and wound; wherefore, abiding in that command, freely have you received, freely give healing of all our passions.

Chorus: Glory be to the Father, and to the Son, and to the Holy Spirit;

Reader: Regard the prayer of thy servants, O all immaculate One; allay the fierce risings against us, and assuage our every woe; for in thee have we a certain hope secured; so by thy intercessions, O Lady, put us not to shame when we cry to thee: listen when we plead: Hail. O Lady, Helper of men, the Joy and Protection of our souls.

Chorus: Both now and forever, and unto the ages of ages. Amen.

Chorus: Accept, O Lady, the prayers of thy servants, delivering us from every pain and sorrow.

[Deacon lifts orarion:]

Litany

Deacon: Have mercy on us, O God, according to Thy great Mercy we beseech Thee, hear us and have mercy.

People: *Lord have mercy.*

Deacon:: Again we pray for our Most Reverend Archbishop Nikitas and for all our brethren in Christ.

People: *Lord have mercy.*

Deacon: Again we pray for mercy, life, peace, health, salvation, protection, pardon and remission of the sins of the servants of God, all pious and Orthodox Christians who dwell in this city, and of the servants of God, the members, trustees, contributors, and benefactors of this Holy Church.

People: *Lord have mercy.*

Deacon: Furthermore, we pray that He shall save this our *[city / town / village / monastery]* and this Holy Temple, and every city and countryside from pestilence, famine, earthquake, flood, fire, and the sword; from invasion of enemies, and from civil war; and that our good God, Who loves mankind, shall be graciously favourable and easy to be entreated with, and shall turn away all wrath stirred up against us and deliver us from all His righteous chastisement which impends against us, and have mercy on us.

People: *Lord have mercy.* **(x40)**

Deacon: Again we pray that the Lord our God listens to the voice of the supplication of us sinners, and has mercy on us.

People: *Lord have mercy.* **(x3)**

Deacon: Hear us, O God our Saviour, the Hope of all the ends of the earth and of those far off at sea, or in the air: show mercy, show mercy O Master, upon our sins, and have mercy on us. For Thou art a merciful God and love mankind, and to Thee do we send up all Glory: to the Father, and to the Son, and to the Holy Spirit, both now and ever, and to the ages of ages.

People: *Amen.*

Priest: Peace be to you all.

People: *And with thy spirit.*

Priest: Grant us forgiveness of our trespasses.

People: *Amen.*

Priest: Shelter us under the shelter of thy wings.

People: *Amen.*

Priest: Drive away from us every enemy and adversary.

People: *Amen.*

Priest: Give peace to our life.

People: *Amen.*

Priest: O Lord, have mercy on us and on Thy world and save our souls, for Thou art a merciful God and lovest mankind.

People: *Amen.*

The Little Dismissal

Priest: Glory to thee, O Christ our God and our Hope, glory to thee.

Reader: *Glory be to the Father, and to the Son, and to the Holy Spirit;*

Both now and forever, and unto the ages of ages. Amen.

Lord, have mercy. **(x3)**

[For a Priest] Holy Father, bless.

[For a Bishop] Holy Master, bless.

Priest: May (*Sundays:* He who rose from the dead), Christ our true God, through the intercessions of his all immaculate and all blameless holy Mother; *[Saints of the day]*; of the holy, glorious and right victorious martyrs; of the holy and wonder working unmercenary healers; *[Patron saint of the temple]*; of the holy and righteous ancestors of God, Joachim and Anna; and of all the saints: have mercy upon us, and save us, forasmuch as he is good and loveth mankind.

People: *Amen.*

[If a bishop has served:]

Chorus: *Preserve, O Lord, our master and chief priest. And grant him many years. Many years to thee, master. Many years to thee, master. Many years, to thee, master.*

[If a bishop has only presided without serving:]

Chorus: *Many years, master.*

Priest: Through the prayers of our holy fathers, O Lord Jesus Christ our God, have mercy upon us, and save us.

People: *Amen.*

Theophany House Blessing

[After Theophany (January 6ᵗʰ), it is customary for the Priest to visit the homes of his parishioners, bringing with him the "Jordan Water" for the traditional Theophany House Blessing.

The First Great Sanctification of Water is performed at the end of the Divine Liturgy on the Paramon of Theophany (January 5ᵗʰ). While that water may be given to the faithful to drink on that day and throughout the coming year, it is only the water from the Second Great Sanctification, that is performed on Theophany, that is used for the Theophany House Blessing.

All who reside in the household should be present for the Blessing. In anticipation of the arrival of the Priest to the house, the lamps, hand censer and incense in the family icon corner should be prepared. (If there is no icon corner, a small table should be placed on the eastern wall of the main room of the dwelling; the table, covered with a white cloth, should be set with one or more icons standing upright, a candle in a candlestand, a hand censer and incense). A small bowl along with several sprigs of evergreen bound together with a ribbon should also be placed in the icon corner (or on the table), along with a clearly printed list of the Baptismal names of the members of the household.

Upon the arrival of the Priest, he is to be greeted by all of the family members, each of whom asks the Priests blessing and reverences his right hand. Then a family member lights the lamps (or candle) and hand censer and turns off all televisions, radios, etc. Lights should be turned on in all the rooms of the house that are to be blessed. Then the entire family gathers with the Priest before the icon corner (or table) to begin the Theophany House Blessing.

The Priest, vested in rasson, faces the icons, blesses and dons his epitrachelion saying the usual vesting prayer. He puts incense upon the lighted charcoal in the hand censer and blesses it saying the usual prayer. He puts his hand cross at the icon corner (or on the table) and, after pouring "Jordan Water" into the bowl provided by the family, he blesses himself whilst intoning:]

The Trisagion Prayers

Priest: Blessed is our God, always, now and ever, and unto the ages of ages.

People: Amen.

Priest: Glory to Thee, our God. Glory to Thee.

O Heavenly King, the Comforter, the Spirit of Truth; who art everywhere present and fillest all things; Treasury of blessings, and giver of life: come and abide in us, and cleanse us from every impurity, and save our souls, O Good One.

Reader: Holy God, Holy Mighty, Holy Immortal, have mercy on us. **(x3)**

Glory be to the Father, and to the Son, and to the Holy Spirit;

Both now and forever, and unto the ages of ages. Amen.

O Most Holy Trinity, have mercy on us.

O Lord, cleanse us from our sins.

O Master, pardon our iniquities.

O Holy One, visit and heal our infirmities, for Thy names sake.

Lord have mercy. **(x3)**

Glory be to the Father, and to the Son, and to the Holy Spirit;
Both now and forever, and unto the ages of ages. Amen.

People: *Our Father, who art in heaven, hallowed be Thy name. Thy Kingdom come. Thy will be done, on earth as it is in heaven. Give us this day our daily bread; and forgive us our trespasses, as we forgive those who trespass against us; and lead us not into temptation, but deliver us from the evil one.*

Priest: For Thine is the kingdom, the power, and the glory, of the Father, and the Son and the Holy Spirit, both now and forever, and to the ages of ages.

People: *Amen.*

Apolytikion Of Theophany

Tone 1   *Magnificent, happy and earthy.*   *C, D, Eb, F, G, A, Bb, C.*

Priest: When Thou, O Lord, wast baptised in the Jordan, worship of the Trinity was made manifest. For the voice of the Father bore witness to Thee, calling Thee His beloved Son. And the Spirit, in the likeness of a dove, confirmed the truth of His word. O Christ our God, who hast appeared and enlightened the world, glory to Thee.

Ektenia

Priest: Have mercy on us, O God, according to Thy great mercy, we pray Thee, hearken and have mercy.

People: *Lord, have mercy.* **(x3)**

Priest: Again we pray for all pious and Orthodox Christians.

People: *Lord, have mercy.* **(x3)**

Priest: Again we pray for our Archbishop Nikitas, and all our brotherhood in Christ.

People: *Lord, have mercy.* **(x3)**

Priest: Again we pray for mercy, life, peace, health, salvation, visitation and pardon and forgiveness of sins for the servants of God, *[name all those who dwell in the house that is to be blessed]* NN., and for all pious and Orthodox Christians who live and dwell in this community.

People: *Lord, have mercy.* **(x3)**

Priest: For Thou art a merciful God and lovest mankind, and unto Thee we ascribe glory to the Father and to the Son and to the Holy Spirit, both now and forever, and unto the ages of ages.

People: *Lord, have mercy.* **(x3)**

[Facing the people:]

Priest: Peace be with you all.

People: And with thy spirit.

Priest: Let us bow down our heads unto the Lord.

People: To Thee, O Lord.

[All bow their heads.

Priest faces the icon of Christ and prays:]

Priest: Let us pray to the Lord.

People: Lord, have mercy.

Priest: Our God our Saviour, the True Light, who wast baptised by John in the Jordan to renew all men by the water of regeneration, and who didst condescend to enter under the roof of Zacchaeus, and didst thereby bring salvation to him and all his household: Do Thou now also, the same Lord, keep safe from harm all those who dwell herein. Vouchsafe them sanctification, purification and health of body, and grant their petitions which are unto salvation and life everlasting: For blessed art Thou, O Christ our God, and unto Thee we ascribe glory together with Thine unoriginate Father and Thine all holy and good and life giving Spirit, both now and forever, and unto the ages of ages.

People: Amen.

[Head of the household takes up a lighted candle and leads through the house the Priest, who carries the bowl of "Jordan Water" and, using his hand cross together with the bound sprigs of evergreen, sprinkles each room with the "Jordan Water." It is customary that he sprinkle each doorway upon the lintel and at each side. Whilst:

Theophany season (January 6th to January 14th);]

Apolytikion Of The Theophany Of Christ

Tone 1 Magnificent, happy and earthy. C, D, Eb, F, G, A, Bb, C.

Priest: When Thou, O Lord, wert baptised in the Jordan, worship of the Trinity was made manifest; for the voice of the Father bore witness to Thee, calling Thee His beloved Son. And the Spirit in the form of a dove confirmed the truth of His word. O Christ our God, Who has appeared and enlightened the world, glory to Thee.

[After January 15th:]

Apolytikion Of The Exaltation Of The Holy Cross

Tone 1 Magnificent, happy and earthy. C, D, Eb, F, G, A, Bb, C.

Priest: (i, iii) O Lord, save Thy people and bless Thine inheritance.

Grant victories to the Orthodox Christians over their adversaries.

And by virtue of Thy Cross, preserve Thy commonwealth.

Priest: (ii) Soson Kyrie ton lao sou, Ke evlogison, tin klironomian sou, Nikas tis Vasilevsii;

Kata varvaron doroumen as Ke to son filaton dia ton stavron sou politev ma.

[The members of the household may walk behind the Priest, or they may remain at the icon corner (or table). The procession through the house ends at the icon corner (or table). The Priest replaces the bowl and sprigs of evergreen in the icon corner (or on the table), holds the hand cross and faces the people:]

The Dismissal

Priest: Glory to Thee, O Christ our God and our Hope. Glory to Thee.

Reader: *Glory be to the Father, and to the Son, and to the Holy Spirit;*

Both now and forever, and unto the ages of ages. Amen.

Lord, have mercy. (x3)

Holy Father, bless.

Priest: May He who deigned to be baptised by John in the Jordan for our salvation, Christ our true God, through the intercessions of His all immaculate and all blameless holy Mother, at the supplications of *[Saint of the Temple]*, of the holy and righteous ancestors of God Joachim and Anna, and of all the saints: have mercy on us, and save us, forasmuch as He is good and loveth mankind.

Priest: Through the prayers of our holy Fathers; O Lord Jesus Christ our God; have mercy on us and save us.

People: *Amen.*

Priest: O Lord Jesus Christ, Son of God, for the sake of the prayers of Thy most pure Mother, of our holy and God bearing fathers, of *[Saint of the Temple]*, of _____ *(saints of the day),* and of all the saints, have mercy on us and save us, for Thou art good and the Lover of mankind.

People: Amen.

[Facing the holy icons, the Priest holds the hand cross:]

Priest: Grant, O Lord, a peaceful life, health, salvation and furtherance in all good things to Thy servant(s), *[name all those who dwell in the house] NN.,* and preserve him / her / them for many years.

[Priest turns and blesses the people thrice with the hand-cross as all sing:]

God grant you many years.

God grant you many years.

God grant you many many many many years.

[Householders reverence the hand cross and the Priests hand, and are blessed with the "Jordan Water."

It is customary for the head of the household to discreetly present the Priest with an envelope containing an honorarium and a list of the Living and Departed for whom the family requests his prayers during the New Year.]

[After the Divine Liturgy, or on that evening.]

Priest: Blessed is our God, always, now and ever, and unto ages of ages.

People: *Amen.*

Reader: Come, let us worship God, our King.

Come, let us worship and fall down before Christ, our King and our God.

Come, let us worship and fall down before Christ Himself, our King and our God.

Psalm 103

Bless the Lord, O my soul. O Lord my God, Thou hast been exceedingly magnified. Confession and majesty hast Thou put on, Who covered Thyself with light as with a garment, Who stretched out the heaven as it were a curtain; Who supports His chambers in the waters, Who appoints the clouds for His ascent, Who walks upon the wings of the winds, Who makes His angels spirits, and His ministers a flame of fire, Who establishes the earth in the sureness thereof; it shall not be turned back for ever and ever. The abyss like a garment is His mantle; upon the mountains shall the waters stand. At Thy rebuke they shall flee, at the voice of Thy thunder shall they be afraid. The mountains rise up and the plains sink down to the place where Thou hast established them. Thou appointed a boundary that they shall not pass, neither return to cover the earth. He sends forth springs in the valleys; between the mountains shall the waters run. They shall give drink to all the beasts of the field; the wild asses shall wait to quench their thirst. Beside them shall the birds of the heaven lodge, from the midst of the rocks shall they give voice. He waters the mountains from His chambers; the earth shall be satisfied with the fruit of Thy works.

He causes the grass to grow for the cattle, and green herb for the service of men, To bring forth bread out of the earth; and wine makes glad the heart of man. To make his face cheerful with oil; and bread strengthens mans heart. The trees of the plain shall be satisfied, the cedars of Lebanon, which Thou hast planted. There shall the sparrows make their nests; the house of the heron is chief among them. The high mountains are a refuge for the harts, and so is the rock for the hares. He has made the moon for seasons; the sun knows his going down. Thou appointed the darkness, and there was the night, wherein all the beasts of the forest shall go abroad. Young lions roaring after their prey, and seeking their food from God. The sun arises, and they are gathered together, and they lay them down in their dens.

But man shall go forth unto his work, and to his labour until the evening. How magnified are Thy works, O Lord. In wisdom hast Thou made them all; the earth is filled with Thy creation. So is this great and spacious sea, therein are things creeping innumerable, small living creatures with the great. There go the ships; there this dragon, whom Thou hast made to play therein. All things wait on Thee, to give them their food in due season; when Thou gavest it to them, they shall gather it. When Thou opened Thy hand, all things shall be filled with goodness; when Thou turned away Thy face, they shall be troubled. Thou wilt take their spirit, and they shall cease; and to their dust shall they return. Thou wilt send forth Thy Spirit, and they shall be created; and Thou shalt renew the face of the earth. Let the glory of the Lord be unto the ages; the Lord shall rejoice in

His works. Who looks on the earth and makes it tremble, Who touches the mountains and they smoke. I shall sing unto the Lord throughout my life, I shall chant to my God for as long as I have my being. May my words be sweet unto Him, and I shall rejoice in the Lord. O that sinners would cease from the earth, and they that work iniquity, that they should be no more. Bless the Lord, O my soul. The sun knows his going down, Thou appointed the darkness, and there was the night. How magnified are Thy works, O Lord. In wisdom hast Thou made them all.

After The Psalm

Glory be to the Father and to the Son and to the Holy Spirit;

Both now and forever, and unto the ages of ages. Amen.

Halleluiah, Halleluiah, Halleluiah. Glory to Thee, O God. **(x3)**

O our God and our Hope, glory to Thee.

The Augmented Great Litany

Deacon: In peace, let us pray to the Lord.

People: *Lord, have mercy.*

Deacon: For the peace from above, and for the salvation of our souls, let us pray to the Lord.

People: *Lord, have mercy.*

Deacon: For the peace of the whole world, for the good estate of the holy churches of God, and for the union of all men, let us pray to the Lord.

People: *Lord, have mercy.*

Deacon: For this Holy House, and for those who with faith, reverence, and fear of God, enter therein, let us pray to the Lord.

People: *Lord, have mercy.*

Deacon: For our Archbishop Nikitas, for the venerable Priesthood, the Diaconate in Christ, for all the clergy and the people, let us pray to the Lord.

People: *Lord, have mercy.*

Deacon: For Her Majesty Elizabeth the Queen, for the First Minister of Wales, for all civil authorities, and for our Armed Forces everywhere, let us pray to the Lord.

People: *Lord, have mercy.*

Deacon: For this city, and for every city and land, and for the faithful who dwell therein, let us pray to the Lord.

People: *Lord, have mercy.*

Deacon: For healthful seasons, for abundance of the fruits of the earth, and for peaceful times, let us pray to the Lord.

People: *Lord, have mercy.*

Deacon: For travellers by sea, by land, and by air; for the sick and the suffering; for captives and their salvation, let us pray to the Lord.

People: *Lord, have mercy.*

Deacon: For the people here present who await the grace of the Holy Spirit, let us pray to the Lord.

People: *Lord, have mercy.*

Deacon: For those that bow their hearts and their knees before the Lord, let us pray to the Lord.

People: *Lord, have mercy.*

Deacon: That He may strengthen us so that we may bring to perfection those things that are well pleasing unto Him, let us pray to the Lord.

People: *Lord, have mercy.*

Deacon: That He may send down His rich mercies upon us, let us pray to the Lord.

People: *Lord, have mercy.*

Deacon: That He may accept the bending of our knees as incense before Him, let us pray to the Lord.

People: *Lord, have mercy.*

Deacon: For those that are in need of His help, let us pray to the Lord.

People: *Lord, have mercy.*

Deacon: For our deliverance from all tribulation, wrath, danger, and necessity, let us pray to the Lord.

People: *Lord, have mercy.*

Deacon: Help us; save us; have mercy on us; and keep us, O God, by Thy grace.

People: *Lord, have mercy.*

Deacon: Calling to remembrance our all holy, immaculate, most blessed and glorious Lady Theotokos and ever virgin Mary, with all the Saints: let us commend ourselves and each other, and all our life unto Christ our God.

People: *To Thee, O Lord.*

Priest: For unto Thee are due all glory, honour, and worship: to the Father, and to the

Son, and to the Holy Spirit; now and ever and unto ages of ages.

People: *Amen.*

Psalm 140

Chorus: Lord, I have cried to Thee: hear me. Hear me, O Lord.

Lord, I have cried to Thee: hear me. Receive the voice of my prayer.

When I call upon Thee, hear me, O Lord. Let my prayer arise as incense in Thy sight,

And let the lifting up of my hands be an evening sacrifice. Hear me, O Lord.

Kekragarion
Sticheroi From Psalm 140

• Set, O Lord, a watch before my mouth, and a door of enclosure round about my lips.

• Incline not my heart to words of evil, to make excuses for sins.

• Those that work iniquity; I shall not join with their number.

• The righteous man shall chasten me with mercy and reprove me; as for the oil of the sinner, let it not anoint my head.

• For yet more is my prayer in the presence of their pleasures; their judges have been swallowed up by the rock.

• They shall hear my words, for they be sweetened; as a clod of earth is broken upon the earth, so have their bones been scattered into hades.

• To Thee O Lord are mine eyes. In Thee have I hoped; take not my soul away.

• Keep me from the snare which they have laid for me, and from the stumbling blocks of them that work iniquity.

• The sinners shall fall into their own net; I am alone until I pass by.

Sticheroi From Psalm 141

• With my voice to the Lord have I cried, with my voice have I made supplication.

• I shall pour out before Him my supplications; my afflictions shall I declare before Him.

• When my spirit was fainting within me, then Thou knewest my paths.

• In this way wherein I have walked they hid for me a snare.

• I looked on my right hand, and beheld, and there was none that knew me.

• Flight has failed me, and there is none that watches out for my soul.

• I cried to Thee, O Lord; I said: Thou art my hope, my portion in the land of the living.

• Attend unto my supplication, for I am brought very low.

• Deliver me from them that persecute me, for they are stronger than I.

• Bring my soul out of prison.

• That I may confess Thy name.

• The righteous shall patiently wait for me until Thou shalt reward me.

Sticheroi From Psalm 129

• Out of the depths have I cried unto Thee, O Lord. O Lord, hear my voice.

• Let Thine ears be attentive to the voice of my supplication.

For Pentecost

Tone 4   *Festive, joyous and deep piety.*   *C, D, Eb, F, G, A, Bb, C.*

Chorus: *6) If Thou, O Lord, shouldest mark iniquities, O Lord, who shall stand? For with Thee there is forgiveness.*

Reader: Today all the nations in the city of David beheld wonders, when the Holy Spirit descended in fiery tongues, as the God inspired Luke spake; for he said: The Disciples of Christ being gathered together, there was a sound as of a mighty wind, and it filled the whole house where they were sitting. And they began to speak strange doctrines and strange teachings with diverse tongues, to the Holy Trinity.

Chorus: *5) Because of Thy Name have I waited for Thee, O Lord; my soul hath waited upon Thy word, my soul hath hoped in the Lord.*

Reader: Today all the nations in the city of David beheld wonders, when the Holy Spirit descended in fiery tongues, as the God inspired Luke spake; for he said: The Disciples of Christ being gathered together, there was a sound as of a mighty wind, and it filled the whole house where they were sitting. And they began to speak strange doctrines and strange teachings with diverse tongues, to the Holy Trinity.

Chorus: *4) From the morning watch until night, from the morning watch let Israel trust in the Lord.*

Reader: The Holy Spirit hath ever been, is and ever shall be; for He is wholly without beginning and without end. Yet He is in covenant with the Father and the Son, counted as Life and Life giver, Light and Light giver, good by nature and a Fountain of goodness, through whom the Father is known and the Son glorified. And by all it is understood that one power, one rank, one worship are of the Holy Trinity.

Chorus: *3) For with the Lord there is mercy and with Him is abundant redemption, and He shall deliver Israel from all his iniquities.*

Reader: The Holy Spirit hath ever been, is and ever shall be; for He is wholly without beginning and without end. Yet He is in covenant with the Father and the Son, counted as Life and Life giver, Light and Light giver, good by nature and a Fountain of goodness, through whom the Father is known and the Son glorified. And by all it is understood that one power, one rank, one worship are of the Holy Trinity.

Chorus: *2) Praise the Lord, all you nations; praise Him, all you people.*

Reader: Light, Life, and a living noetic Fountain is the Holy Spirit, good, upright, noetic Spirit of understanding, and purifying offences, God understanding, presiding, and purifying offences, God and deifying, Fire projecting from Fire, speaking, active, Distributor of gifts, through whom all the Prophets, the Apostles of God, and the Martyrs are crowned, a strange Report, a strange sight, a Fire divided for the distribution of gifts.

Chorus: *1) For His mercy is great toward us, and the truth of the Lord endureth forever.*

Reader: Light, Life, and a living noetic Fountain is the Holy Spirit, good, upright, noetic Spirit of understanding, and purifying offences, God understanding, presiding, and purifying offences, God and deifying, Fire projecting from Fire, speaking, active, Distributor of gifts, through whom all the Prophets, the Apostles of God, and the Martyrs are crowned, a strange Report, a strange sight, a Fire divided for the distribution of gifts.

> *Glory be to the Father, and to the Son, and to the Holy Spirit;*
> *Both now and forever, and unto ages of ages. Amen.*

[Clergy process with Gospel, (no censer) whilst:]

Doxasticon For Pentecost

Tone 6   Rich texture, funeral character, sorrowful tone.   *D, Eb, F##, G, A, Bb, C##, D.*

O Heavenly King, the Comforter, the Spirit of Truth; who art everywhere present and fillest all things; Treasury of blessings, and giver of life: come and abide in us, and cleanse us from every impurity, and save our souls, O Good One.

[During procession this dialogue, QUIET:]

The Holy Entrance

Deacon: Let us pray to the Lord.

People: *Lord, have mercy.*

Priest: In the evening and in the morning and at noonday we praise Thee, we bless Thee, we give thanks unto Thee, and we pray unto Thee, O Master of all, Lord Who lovest mankind: Direct our prayer as incense before Thee, and incline not our hearts unto words or thoughts of evil, but deliver us from all who seek after our souls. For unto Thee, O Lord, Lord, are our eyes, and in Thee have we hoped. Put us not to shame, O our God. For unto Thee are due all glory, honour, and worship: to the Father and to the Son and to the Holy Spirit, now and ever, and unto ages of ages.

Deacon: Amen.

[The clergy process to the centre of the solea and recite this next dialogue QUIET.]

Deacon: Bless, father, the Holy Entrance.

Priest: Blessed is the entrance to Thy Holy Place, always, now and ever, and unto ages of ages. Amen.

(After the Chorus has finished, the following is said ALOUD.)

Deacon: Wisdom. Let us attend.

O Gladsome Light

O Gladsome Light of the holy glory of the immortal Father. Heavenly holy, blessed Jesus Christ;

Now that we have come to the setting of the sun, and behold the Evening Light;

We praise God; Father, Son and Holy Spirit. For meet it is at all time to worship Thee, with voices of praise;

O Son of God and Giver of Life. Therefore all the world doth glorify Thee.

Deacon: The Evening Prokeimenon.

The Great Prokeimenon

Tone 7   Manly character and strong melody.   *F, G, A, A#, C, D, E, F.*

Chorus: *Who is so great a god as our God? Thou art the God Who worketh wonders.* **(x2)**

Reader: Thou hast made Thy power known among the peoples;

With Thine arm hast Thou redeemed Thy people.

Chorus: *Who is so great a god as our God? Thou art the God Who worketh wonders.*

Reader: And I said: Now have I made a beginning;

This change hath been wrought by the right hand of the Most High.

Chorus: *Who is so great a god as our God? Thou art the God Who worketh wonders.*

Reader: I remembered the works of the Lord; for I shall remember Thy wonders from the beginning.

Chorus: *Who is so great a god as our God? | Thou art the God Who worketh wonders.*

The First Kneeling Prayer

Deacon: Again and again, let us, on bended knees, pray to the Lord.

People: *Lord, have mercy.*

prostration

Priest: O pure and blameless Lord, Who art without beginning, invisible and incomprehensible, unsearchable, unchangeable, immeasurable, and unbounded, Who art without evil and alone immortal, who dwellest in the unapproachable light, Maker of Heaven and earth and the seas and all that was created therein, Who grantest to all their petitions before asking, to Thee we pray and of Thee we ask, O philanthropic Master, the Father of our Lord and God and Saviour Jesus Christ, Who for us men and for our salvation came down from Heaven and was incarnate of the Holy Spirit and of the ever virgin Mary, the noble Theotokos; Who first didst teach by word, and then gave testimony in deed while bearing the saving Passion, teaching us Thine unworthy, sinful, and miserable servants, to offer Thee our supplications with bent heads and knees, for our sins and human ignorance.

Wherefore, O most merciful and philanthropic Lord, hear us on whatever day we call upon Thee, and especially on this day of Pentecost, whereon, after our Lord Jesus Christ had ascended into Heaven and sat at Thy right hand, O God and Father, He sent down the Holy Spirit to his Disciples, the holy Apostles, Who alighted on each of them and filled them all with His inexhaustible and divine grace; and they did speak in strange tongues, prophesying Thy great deeds. Hear us who beseech Thee, and remember us, wretched and condemned. Deliver us from the sinful captivity of our souls by Thy loving intercession. Accept us, who kneel down before Thee and cry out: we have sinned, and we have cleaved unto Thee from our birth, even from our mother's womb. Thou art our God, but as our life passes in vanity, we have therefore been stripped of Thine aid, and have been deprived of every defence. Yet do we trust in Thy compassion and cry unto Thee: Remember not the sins of our youth and ignorance; cleanse us of our secret sins. Reject us not in our old age, and forsake us not when our strength fails. Before we return to the earth, prepare us to return to Thee, and attend to us in favour and grace. Measure our transgressions according to Thy compassion, and set the depth of Thy compassions against the multitude of our offences.

Look down from the height of Thy holiness upon Thy people who stand and await abundant mercy from Thee. Visit us with Thy goodness and deliver us from the possession of Satan and preserve our life with Thy holy and solemn laws. Commit Thy people unto a faithful guardian angel. Gather us all unto Thy kingdom. Grant forgiveness to those who put their trust in Thee, relinquish us and them from sin. Purify us by the operation of Thy Holy Spirit and remove from us the wiles of the adversary.

Blessed art Thou, O Lord, Almighty Master, Who hast illumined the day with the light of the sun and the night with the glow of fire, Who hast made us worthy to pass the course of the day and draw near to the onset of the night; hear our petitions and those of all Thy people. Forgive us all our sins, both voluntary and involuntary, and accept our evening supplications. Send down the multitude of Thy mercies and compassions upon Thine inheritance. Encompass us with Thy holy angels. Arm us with the weapons of Thy justice. Envelop us with Thy righteousness. Protect us by Thy power, and deliver us from every oppression and from every conspiracy of the adversary. Grant us that this evening and the approaching night and all the days of our life may be perfect, holy, peaceful, sinless, without doubt and vain imaginings, by the intercessions of the holy Theotokos and all the saints who have done Thy will from the beginning of time.

[All stand.]

Deacon: Help us; save us; have mercy on us; raise us up; and keep us, O God, by Thy grace.

People: *Lord, have mercy.*

Deacon: Calling to remembrance our all holy, immaculate, most blessed and glorious Lady Theotokos and Ever Virgin Mary, with all the Saints: let us commend ourselves and each other, and all our life unto Christ our God.

People: *To Thee, O Lord.*

Priest: For Thine it is to show mercy on us and to save us, O our God, and unto Thee we ascribe glory: to the Father, and to the Son, and to the Holy Spirit; now and ever and unto ages of ages.

People: *Amen.*

The Litany Of Fervent Supplication

Deacon: Let us say with our whole soul, and with our whole mind, let us say.

People: *Lord, have mercy.*

Deacon: O Lord Almighty, the God of our Fathers, we pray Thee, hearken and have mercy.

People: *Lord, have mercy.*

Deacon: Have mercy on us, O God, according to Thy great mercy, we pray Thee, hearken and have mercy.

People: *Lord, have mercy.* **(x3)**

Deacon: Again we pray for all pious and Orthodox Christians.

People: *Lord, have mercy.* **(x3)**

Deacon: Again we pray for our Archbishop Nikitas.

People: *Lord, have mercy.* **(x3)**

Deacon: Again we pray for our brethren: the priests, hieromonks, deacons, hierodeacons and monastics and all our brotherhood in Christ.

People: *Lord, have mercy.* **(x3)**

Deacon: Again we pray for mercy, life, peace, health, salvation and visitation and pardon and remission of sins for (the servants of God, *[Names]*, and all Orthodox Christians of true worship, who live and dwell in this community.

People: *Lord, have mercy.* **(x3)**

Deacon: Again we pray for the blessed and ever memorable founders of this holy church and for (the departed servants of God, *[Names]*, and) all our fathers and brethren, the Orthodox departed this life before us, who here and in all the world lie asleep in the Lord.

People: *Lord, have mercy.* **(x3)**

Deacon: Again we pray for those who bear fruit and do good works in this holy and all venerable temple, those who serve and those who sing, and for all the people here present, who await Thy great and rich mercy.

People: *Lord, have mercy.* **(x3)**

Priest: For Thou art a merciful God and lovest mankind, and unto Thee we ascribe glory: to the Father, and to the Son, and to the Holy Spirit; now and ever, and unto ages of ages.

People: *Amen.*

The Second Kneeling Prayer

Deacon: Again and again, let us, on bended knees, pray to the Lord.

People: *Lord, have mercy.*

prostration

Priest: O Lord Jesus Christ our God, Who hast given Thy peace to mankind and, being present still in this life, doth ever grant the gift of the All holy Spirit to the faithful, as an inheritance that can never be taken away, Thou hast sent down today in a manner most clear, this grace upon Thy holy Disciples and Apostles, and didst place into their mouths and on their lips the tongues of fire. Through them all mankind, through the hearing of the ear, hath received knowledge of God in their own languages. We have been enlightened by the light of the Spirit, being emancipated from delusion as from darkness, and through the distribution of the perceptible tongues of fire and the wondrous action of the same, we have been taught the faith that is in Thee, and we have been illumined so as to praise Thee with the Father and the Holy Spirit, in one Godhead, Power and Authority.

Wherefore, O Splendour of the Father, the Likeness of his Essence, His immutable and unchangeable Nature, Thou art the fountain of salvation and grace. Open my lips, sinner that I am, and teach me how and for what I must pray; for Thou dost know the multitude of my sins, but Thine unbounded compassion doth overcome the enormity thereof. Behold, I come and stand before Thee in fear and dismay, casting my soul's despair into the depth of Thy mercy. Govern my life, O Thou Who rulest the whole creation with Thy word and with the unutterable power of Thy wisdom. O tranquil Haven of the storm tossed, make known to me the way in which I should walk. Grant to my thoughts the spirit of Thy wisdom, and bestow upon mine ignorance the spirit of Thine understanding. Overshadow mine acts with the spirit of Thy fear; a right spirit renew Thou within me, and by Thy Sovereign Spirit strengthen Thou mine unstable mind, that I may be worthy each day to do Thy commandments, being guided by Thy righteous Spirit into that which is profitable, ever mindful of Thy glorified second Coming, which shall search out our life's deeds. Let me not be led astray by the corrupting pleasures of this world, but strengthen me to delight in the treasures to come. For Thou, O Master, didst say, "Whatever you ask in My Name you shall receive" from God the Father, co-eternal with Thee.

Therefore, I, a sinner, implore Thy goodness at the descent of Thy Holy Spirit: grant Thou my request for salvation. Yea, good Lord, Who grantest all riches and benevolence, Thou art He, the merciful and pitying, Who givest us more than we ask, Who hast become a Partaker with us in the flesh without sin. Thou art He Who, for His love for mankind, dost have compassion for those who bend the knee to Thee, having become an offering for our sins. Grant, O Lord, Thy compassion to Thy people, and incline Thine ear to us from Thy Holy Heaven; sanctify us by the saving might of Thy right hand. Cover us with the shelter of Thy wings and turn not away from the work of Thy hands. Against Thee only do we sin, yet Thee only do we worship. We know not how to bow to a strange god, nor to stretch forth our hands to a different god. Pardon our iniquities, O Master, and accepting our requests on bended knee, extend to us all a helping hand, and accept the prayers of all as fragrant incense acceptable to Thy most righteous Kingdom.

O Lord, Lord, Thou Who hast delivered us from every arrow that comes by day, save us from everything that walketh in darkness, and accept the lifting up of our hands as an evening sacrifice. Consider us worthy to pass the night blamelessly and experience no evil. Deliver us from Satan. Grant our souls contrition, and our thoughts concern over our accountability at Thy just and terrible judgement. Nail our flesh to the fear of Thee, and mortify our earthly members, that in the tranquillity of sleep we may be enlightened by the contemplation of Thy precepts. Drive from us every unseemly fantasy and injurious desire. Raise us up at the time of prayer confirmed in the faith and progressing in Thy commandments.

[All stand.]

Deacon: Help us; save us; have mercy on us; raise us up; and keep us, O God, by Thy grace.

People: *Lord, have mercy.*

Deacon: Calling to remembrance our all holy, immaculate, most blessed and glorious Lady Theotokos and ever virgin Mary, with all the Saints: let us commend ourselves and each other, and all our life unto Christ our God.

People: *To Thee, O Lord.*

Priest: Through the favour and grace of Thine only begotten Son, with Whom Thou art blessed, together with Thine All holy, Good and Life giving Spirit; now and ever and unto ages of ages.

People: *Amen.*

The Evening Prayer

Reader: Vouchsafe, O Lord, to keep us this evening without sin. Blessed art Thou, O Lord, the God of our fathers, and praised and glorified is Thy name unto the ages. Amen.

Let Thy mercy, O Lord, be upon us, according as we have hoped in Thee.

Blessed art Thou, O Lord, teach me Thy statutes.

Blessed art Thou, O Master, give me understanding of Thy statutes.

Blessed art Thou, O Holy One, enlighten me by Thy statutes.

O Lord, Thy mercy endures forever; disdain not the work of Thy hands. To Thee is due praise, to Thee is due song, to Thee is due glory, to the Father, and to the Son, and to the Holy Spirit; both now and forever, and unto the ages of ages. Amen.

The Third Kneeling Prayer

Deacon: Again and again, let us, on bended knees, pray to the Lord.

People: Lord, have mercy.

prostration

Priest: O Christ our God, the ever flowing Spring, life giving, illuminating, creative Power, co-eternal with the Father, Who hast most excellently fulfilled the whole dispensation of the salvation of mankind, and didst tear apart the indestructible bonds of death, break asunder the bolts of Hades, and tread down the multitude of evil spirits, offering Thyself as a blameless Sacrifice and offering us Thy pure, spotless and sinless body, Who, by this fearsome, inscrutable divine service didst grant us life everlasting; O Thou Who didst descend into Hades, and demolish the eternal bars, revealing an ascent to those who were in the lower abode; Who with the lure of divine wisdom didst entice the dragon, the head of subtle evil, and with Thy boundless power bound him in abysmal hell, in inextinguishable fire, and extreme darkness.

O Wisdom of the Father, Thou great of Name Who dost manifest Thyself a great Helper to those who are in distress; a luminous Light to those who sit in darkness and the shadow of death; Thou art the Lord of everlasting glory, the beloved Son of the Most High Father, eternal Light from eternal Light, Thou Sun of justice. Hear Thou us who beseech Thee, and give rest the souls of our parents, brethren, and the rest of our kinsmen in the flesh, and those who are of the fold of faith who have fallen asleep, and for whom we celebrate this memorial; for Thou hast power over all, and in Thy hands Thou holdest all the boundaries of the earth.

O Almighty Master, God of our fathers, Lord of mercy and Creator of all the races of mankind, the mortals and the immortals, and of all nature, animate and inanimate, of life and of the end of life, of sojourning here and translation there, Who dost measure the years of life and set the times of death, Who bringest down to Hades and raisest up, binding in infirmity and releasing unto power, dispensing present things according to need and ordering those to come as is expedient, quickening with the hope of Resurrection those that are smitten with the sting of death. Thyself, O Master of all, God our Saviour, the Hope of all the ends of the earth and of those who are far off upon the sea, Who, on this last and great and saving day of Pentecost, didst show forth to us the mystery of the Holy Trinity, consubstantial and co-eternal, undivided and unmingled, and didst pour out the descent and presence of Thy holy and life giving Spirit in the form of tongues of fire upon Thy holy Apostles, appointing them to be the evangelists of our pious faith and showing them to be confessors and preachers of the true theology; Who also, on this all perfect and saving feast, dost deign to receive oblations and supplications for those bound in Hades, and grantest unto us the great hope that rest and comfort shall be sent down from Thee to the departed from the grief that binds them.

Hear us, Thy humble and piteous ones who pray, and give rest to the souls of Thy servants who have fallen asleep before us, in a place of brightness, a place of verdure, a place of repose, whence all sickness, sorrow and sighing have fled away; and do thou place their souls in the tabernacles of the righteous;

and make them worthy of peace and repose. For the dead praise Thee not, O Lord, neither do those in Hades dare to offer Thee confession, but we, the living, bless Thee and supplicate Thee and offer favourable prayers and sacrifices for their souls.

O great and eternal God, holy and loving toward mankind, Who dost make us worthy to stand at this hour before Thine unapproachable glory, praising and glorifying Thy wonders: be gracious to us, Thine unworthy servants, and grant us grace that from a humble and contrite heart we may offer Thee the thrice holy glorification and gratitude for Thy great gifts which Thou didst grant and dost still grant unto us. Remember, O Lord, our weakness and destroy us not in our iniquities; but be merciful to our humility that, fleeing from the darkness of sin, we may walk in the day of righteousness and, clothed with the armour of light, may persevere unassailed from every attack of the evil one, so that with boldness we may glorify Thee in all things, the only true God and Lover of mankind.

For in truth, O Master and Creator of all, Thine is the great and original Mystery; the temporary death of Thy creatures, and their restoration thereafter unto eternal repose. In all things we confess Thy grace, at our entrance into this world and at our going out there from, O Thou Who by Thy unfailing promises didst hold out to us the hope of everlasting life, resurrection, and incorruptible life, which shall be ours hereafter at Thy Second Coming. For Thou art the Author of our resurrection, the impartial Judge of those that have lived, the Lover of mankind and the Master and Lord of recompense, Who didst partake with us, on equal terms, of flesh and blood, through Thine extreme condescension, and of our irreproachable passions, wherein Thou didst willingly submit to temptation, since Thou dost possess tenderness and compassion, and Thyself, having suffered temptation, art become for us, who are tempted, the Helper which Thou Thyself hadst promised to be; and therefore Thou hast led us to Thy passionlessness.

Wherefore, O Master, accept our prayers and supplications, and grant repose to our fathers, mothers, brothers, sisters, children, relatives, and kinsfolk, and all those who have gone to their final rest with the hope of resurrection and life everlasting. Set their names and souls in the Book of Life; in the bosoms of Abraham, Isaac and Jacob; in the land of the living, the Kingdom of Heaven, in the paradise of delight, leading all into Thy Holy dwelling place by Thy radiant angels, and raise our bodies with Thee on the day that Thou hast appointed, according to Thine unfailing promise. There is no death, O Lord, to Thy departing servants who cast off our bodies and come unto Thee, O God, but a transition from sorrowful things to things pleasant and sweet, to rest and joy. And though we have sinned against Thee, be Thou compassionate unto them and us; for there is none without stain before Thee, even though his life be but a day, except Thou alone, O Lord Jesus Christ our God, through Whom we all trust to attain mercy and the remission of sins.

Therefore, O God, through Thy grace and love of mankind, pardon, remit and forgive our sins and theirs, both voluntary and involuntary offences., which we have committed either wilfully or through ignorance, openly or in secret whether by word, deed, or thought and all our acts and movements. As for those who have preceded us, grant them emancipation and repose. To those of us who are here, bless us, and give us and all Thy people a blessed and peaceful end to life. At Thy fearsome and dreadful coming open to us Thy fathomless love of mankind, making us worthy of Thy Kingdom. O great and most exalted God, Who alone hast immortality and dwellest in the unapproachable light, Who in wisdom didst bring into being all creation, Who hast divided the light and the darkness, setting the sun to rule the day, and the moon and stars to rule the night, Who on this day didst vouchsafe unto us sinners as worthy through confession to present ourselves before Thy presence and to offer to Thee our evening praise: O philanthropic God, set our prayers like incense before Thee, and receive them as a sweet fragrance. Grant that this evening and the approaching night may be peaceful and serene for us. Clothe us with the armour of light, and deliver us from nightly terrors and from everything that walketh in darkness. Vouchsafe that the slumber which Thou didst grant us for rest from our weakness be also free from every satanic imagination. Yea, O Master, Bestower of all good things, may we, being moved to compunction upon our beds, call to remembrance Thy Name in the night that, enlightened by meditation on Thy commandments, we may rise up in joyfulness of soul to glorify Thy goodness, offering up prayers and supplications unto Thy tender love, for our sins and for those of all Thy people, whom do Thou visit in mercy, through the intercessions of the Holy Theotokos.

[All stand.]

Deacon: Help us; save us; have mercy on us; raise us up; and keep us, O God, by Thy grace.

People: *Lord, have mercy.*

Deacon: Calling to remembrance our all holy, immaculate, most blessed and glorious Lady Theotokos and ever virgin Mary, with all the Saints: let us commend ourselves and each other, and all our life unto Christ our God.

People: *To Thee, O Lord.*

Priest: For Thou art the Repose of our souls and bodies, and unto Thee we ascribe glory: to the Father, and to the Son, and to the Holy Spirit, now and ever, and unto ages of ages.

People: *Amen.*

The Litany Of Supplication

Deacon: Let us complete our evening prayer unto the Lord.

People: *Lord, have mercy.*

Deacon: Help us; save us; have mercy on us; and keep us, O God, by Thy grace.

People: *Lord, have mercy.*

Deacon: That the whole evening may be perfect, holy, peaceful and sinless, let us ask of the Lord.

People: *Grant this, O Lord.*

Deacon: An angel of peace, a faithful guide, a guardian of our souls and bodies, let us ask of the Lord.

People: *Grant this, O Lord.*

Deacon: Pardon and remission of our sins and transgressions, let us ask of the Lord.

People: *Grant this, O Lord.*

Deacon: All things good and profitable for our souls and peace for the world, let us ask of the Lord.

People: *Grant this, O Lord.*

Deacon: That we may complete the remaining time of our life in peace and repentance, let us ask of the Lord.

People: *Grant this, O Lord.*

Deacon: A Christian ending to our life, painless, blameless, peaceful, and a good defence before the fearful judgement. seat of Christ, let us ask of the Lord.

People: *Grant this, O Lord.*

Deacon: Calling to remembrance our all holy, immaculate, most blessed and glorious Lady Theotokos and ever virgin Mary, with all the Saints: let us commend ourselves and each other, and all our life unto Christ our God.

People: *To Thee, O Lord.*

Priest: For Thou art a good God and lovest mankind, and unto Thee we ascribe glory: to the Father, and to the Son, and to the Holy Spirit, now and ever, and unto ages of ages.

People: *Amen.*

The Peace

Priest: Peace be with you all.

People: *And to thy spirit.*

Deacon: Let us bow down our heads unto the Lord.

People: *To Thee, O Lord.*

[All bow their heads as the priest says the following prayer:]

Priest: O Lord our God, Who didst bow the heavens and come down for the salvation of mankind: Look upon Thy servants and Thine inheritance; for unto Thee, the fearful Judge Who yet lovest mankind, have Thy servants bowed their heads and submissively inclined their necks, awaiting not help from men but entreating Thy mercy and looking confidently for Thy salvation. Guard them at all times, both during this present evening and in the approaching night, from every foe, from all adverse powers of the devil, and from vain thoughts and from evil imaginations. Blessed and glorified be the might of Thy kingdom: of the Father, and of the Son, and of the Holy Spirit; now and ever, and unto ages of ages.

People: *Amen.*

The Aposticha For Holy Spirit Monday

    Tone 3   Arrogant, brave, and mature atmosphere.   *F, G, A, A#, C, D, E, F.*

Now, the tongues have become manifest wonders to all; for the Jews, of whom cometh Christ after the flesh, were divided by lack of faith. They fell from the divine grace and the divine light which we, the Gentiles, have attained, who are established by the sayings of the Disciples, giving utterance to the glory of God, the All beneficent, with whom we bend our hearts as well as our knees, and worship the Holy Spirit in faith, being strengthened by the Saviour of our souls.

Chorus: *Create in me a clean heart, O God, and renew a right spirit within me.*

Reader: Now, the comforting Spirit hath been poured on all flesh; for, starting with the rank of the Apostles, He extended grace through the communion of believers, certifying His effective presence by the distribution of tongues to the Disciples in fiery likeness for the praise and glory of God. Wherefore, being noetically illumined with them and confirmed in the steadfast Faith, we beseech the Holy Spirit to save our souls.

Chorus: *Cast me not away from Thy face, and take not Thy Holy Spirit from me.*

Reader: Now, the Apostles of Christ have put on might and power from above; for the Comforter hath renewed them, and in them renewed the knowledge of the new mysteries which they proclaimed to us in tones and resounding words, teaching us to worship the all bountiful God of the eternal, simple Nature of three Persons. Wherefore, being illumined by their teachings, let us worship the Father, Son and Holy Spirit, beseeching them to save our souls.

Chorus: *Glory be to the Father, and to the Son, and to the Holy Spirit;*
Both now and forever, and unto ages of ages. Amen.

Doxasticon For Pentecost

Tone 8   *Humility, tranquillity, repose, suffering, pleading.*   *C, D, Eb, F, G, A, Bb, C.*

Come you nations, let us worship the three personned Godhead, a Son in the Father, with a Holy Spirit; for the Father timelessly hath begotten the Son, equal to Him in eternity and the throne; and the Holy Spirit was in the Father, glorified with the Son, one Might, one Substance, one Godhead, which we all worship, saying, Holy God Who created everything through the Son with the help of the Holy Spirit; Holy Mighty, in Whom we knew the Father, and through Whom the Holy Spirit came to the world; Holy Immortal One, the comforting Spirit, proceeding from the Father and resting in the Son; O Holy Trinity, glory to Thee.

The Hymn Of St Simeon The God Receiver

Reader: Lord, now lettest Thou Thy servant depart in peace, according to Thy word, for mine eyes have seen Thy salvation, which Thou hast prepared before the face of all peoples; a light of revelation for the Gentiles, and the glory of Thy people Israel.

The Trisagion Prayers

People: Holy God, Holy Mighty, Holy Immortal: have mercy on us. **(x3)**

Chorus: *Glory be to the Father, and to the Son, and to the Holy Spirit;*
Both now and forever, and unto ages of ages. Amen.

O Most Holy Trinity, have mercy on us.

O Lord, cleanse us from our sins.

O Master, pardon our iniquities.

O Holy One, visit and heal our infirmities, for Thy names sake.

Lord have mercy. **(x3)**

Chorus: *Glory be to the Father and to the Son and to the Holy Spirit;*
Both now and forever, and unto the ages of ages. Amen.

People: *Our Father, Who art in Heaven, hallowed be Thy Name. Thy Kingdom come, Thy will be done, on earth as it is in Heaven. Give us this day our daily bread, and forgive us our trespasses, as we forgive those who trespass against us; and lead us not into temptation, but deliver us from the evil one.*

Priest: For Thine is the kingdom, and the power, and the glory: of the Father, and of the Son, and of the Holy Spirit; now and ever, and unto ages of ages.

People: *Amen.*

Apolytikion Of Pentecost

Tone 8   Humility, tranquillity, repose, suffering, pleading.   C, D, Eb, F, G, A, Bb, C.

Blessed art Thou, O Christ our God, Who hast revealed the fishermen as most wise, having sent upon them the Holy Spirit, and through them Thou hast fished the universe, O Lover of mankind, glory to Thee. **(x3)**

The Dismissal

Deacon: Wisdom.

People: *Holy Father, bless.*

Priest: Christ our God, the Existing One, is blessed, always, now and ever, and unto ages of ages.

People: *Amen.*

Reader: Preserve, O God, the holy Orthodox faith and all Orthodox Christians, unto ages of ages. Amen.

Priest: Most holy Theotokos, save us.

Reader: Greater in honour than the Cherubim and beyond compare more glorious than the Seraphim; without corruption thou gavest birth to God the Word, truly the Theotokos, we magnify thee.

Priest: Glory to Thee, O Christ our God and our hope, glory to Thee.

Chorus: *Glory be to the Father, and to the Son, and to the Holy Spirit;*
Both now and forever, and unto the ages of ages. Amen.

Lord have mercy. **(x3)**

Holy Father, bless.

Priest: May He Who emptied Himself from the divine bosom of the Father, and came down from Heaven to earth, and took upon Himself all of our nature, and deified it; and afterwards ascended again into Heaven and sat at the right hand of God the Father, and sent down upon His Holy Disciples and Apostles the Divine and Holy Spirit, one in essence, equal in power, equal in glory, and co-everlasting with Him, and through Him enlightened them, and through them the whole world, Christ our true God: through the intercessions of His all immaculate and all blameless holy Mother; of the holy, glorious, all laudable, God proclaiming and Spirit bearing apostles, and of all the saints: have mercy on us and save us, forasmuch as He is good and loveth mankind.

Priest: Through the prayers of our holy fathers, Lord Jesus Christ our God, have mercy upon us and save us.

People: *Amen.*

Readers Vespers For The Eve Of The Annunciation

[When a priest is not present.]

The Trisagion Prayers

Reader: Through the prayers of our holy Fathers, O Lord Jesus Christ our God; have mercy on us.

People: *Amen. Glory to Thee, our God, glory to Thee.*

Reader: O Heavenly King, Comforter, Spirit of Truth, Who art everywhere present and fillest all things, Treasury of blessings and Giver of life: Come and abide in us, and cleanse us from every impurity, and save our souls, O Good One.

Holy God, Holy Mighty, Holy Immortal, have mercy on us. **(x3)**

> *Glory be to the Father, and to the Son, and to the Holy Spirit;*
> *Both now and forever, and unto the ages of ages. Amen.*

O Most Holy Trinity, have mercy on us.

O Lord, cleanse us from our sins.

O Master, pardon our iniquities.

O Holy One, visit and heal our infirmities, for Thy names sake.

Lord have mercy. **(x3)**

> *Glory be to the Father and to the Son and to the Holy Spirit;*
> *Both now and forever, and unto the ages of ages. Amen.*

People: *Our Father, Who art in Heaven, hallowed be Thy Name. Thy Kingdom come, Thy will be done, on earth as it is in Heaven. Give us this day our daily bread, and forgive us our trespasses, as we forgive those who trespass against us; and lead us not into temptation, but deliver us from the evil one. Amen.*

Reader: O Lord, Jesus Christ, Son of God, have mercy on us. Amen.

Lord, have mercy. **(x12)**

> *Glory be to the Father and to the Son and to the Holy Spirit.*
> *Both now and forever and unto the ages of ages, Amen.*

Come let us worship God our King.

Come let us worship and fall down before Christ our King and our God.

Come let us worship and fall down before Christ Himself, our King and our God.

Psalm 103

Of David. Concerning the Formation of the World.

Bless the Lord, O my soul. O Lord my God, Thou hast been exceedingly magnified. Confession and majesty hast Thou put on, Who covered Thyself with light as with a garment, Who stretched out the heaven as it were a curtain; Who supports His chambers in the waters, Who appoints the clouds for His ascent, Who walks upon the wings of the winds, Who makes His angels spirits, and His ministers a flame of fire, Who establishes the earth in the sureness thereof; it shall not be turned back for ever and ever. The abyss like a garment is His mantle; upon the mountains shall the waters stand. At Thy rebuke they shall flee, at the voice of Thy thunder shall they be afraid.

The mountains rise up and the plains sink down to the place where Thou hast established them. Thou appointed a boundary that they shall not pass, neither return to cover the earth. He sends forth springs in the valleys; between the mountains shall the waters run. They shall give drink to all the beasts of the field; the wild asses shall wait to quench their thirst. Beside them shall the birds of the heaven lodge, from the midst of the rocks shall they give voice. He waters the mountains from His chambers; the earth shall be satisfied with the fruit of Thy works.

He causes the grass to grow for the cattle, and green herb for the service of men, To bring forth bread out of the earth; and wine makes glad the heart of man. To make his face cheerful with oil; and bread strengthens mans heart. The trees of the plain shall be satisfied, the cedars of Lebanon, which Thou hast planted. There shall the sparrows make their nests; the house of the heron is chief among them. The high mountains are a refuge for the harts, and so is the rock for the hares. He has made the moon for seasons; the sun knows his going down. Thou appointed the darkness, and there was the night, wherein all the beasts of the forest shall go abroad. Young lions roaring after their prey, and seeking their food from God. The sun arises, and they are gathered together, and they lay them down in their dens.

But man shall go forth unto his work, and to his labour until the evening. How magnified are Thy works, O Lord. In wisdom hast Thou made them all; the earth is filled with Thy creation. So is this great and spacious sea, therein are things creeping innumerable, small living creatures with the great. There go the ships; there this dragon, whom Thou hast made to play therein. All things wait on Thee, to give them their food in due season; when Thou gavest it to them, they shall gather it. When Thou opened Thy hand, all things shall be filled with goodness; when Thou turned away Thy face, they shall be troubled. Thou wilt take their spirit, and they shall cease; and to their dust shall they return. Thou wilt send forth Thy Spirit, and they shall be created; and Thou shalt renew the face of the earth.

Let the glory of the Lord be unto the ages; the Lord shall rejoice in His works. Who looks on the earth and makes it tremble, Who touches the mountains and they smoke. I shall sing unto the Lord throughout my life, I shall chant to my God for as long as I have my being. May my words be sweet unto Him, and I shall rejoice in the Lord. O that sinners would cease from the earth, and they that work iniquity, that they should be no more. Bless the Lord, O my soul. The sun knows his going down, Thou appointed the darkness, and there was the night. How magnified are Thy works, O Lord. In wisdom hast Thou made them all.

After The Psalm

Glory be to the Father and to the Son and to the Holy Spirit;
Both now and forever, and unto the ages of ages. Amen.

Halleluiah, Halleluiah, Halleluiah. Glory to Thee, O God. **(x3)**

Lord, have mercy. **(x3)**

Glory be to the Father and to the Son and to the Holy Spirit;
Both now and forever, and unto the ages of ages. Amen.

Lord, have mercy. **(x12)**

Psalm 64

To Thee is due praise, O God, in Zion; and unto Thee shall a vow be rendered in Jerusalem. Hearken unto my prayer, for unto Thee shall all flesh come. The words of lawless men have overpowered us, but to our ungodliness shalt Thou be merciful. Blessed is he whom Thou hast chosen and hast taken to Thyself; he shall dwell in Thy courts. We shall be filled with the good things of Thy house; holy is Thy temple, wonderful in righteousness. Hearken unto us, O God our Saviour, Thou hope of all the ends of the earth and of them that be far off at sea, Who settest fast the mountains by Thy strength, Who art girded round about with power, Who troublest the hollow of the sea; as for the roar of its waves, who shall withstand them? The heathen shall be troubled, and the dwellers of the farthest regions shall be afraid at Thy signs; Thou shalt make the outgoings of the morning and the evening to delight. Thou hast visited the earth and abundantly watered her; Thou hast multiplied the means of enriching her. The river of God is filled with waters; Thou hast prepared their food, for thus is the preparation thereof. Do Thou make her furrows drunk with water, multiply her fruits; in her showers shall she be glad when she sprouteth forth. Thou shalt bless the crown of the year with Thy goodness, and Thy plains shall be filled with fatness. Enriched shall be the mountains of the wilderness, and the hills shall be girded with rejoicing. The rams of the flock have clothed themselves with fleece, and the valleys shall abound with wheat; they shall cry aloud, yea, they shall chant hymns unto Thee.

Psalm 65
For the End. Of Resurrection.

Shout with jubilation unto the Lord all the earth; chant you unto His name, give glory in praise of Him. Say unto God: How awesome are Thy works. In the multitude of Thy power shall Thine enemies be proved false unto Thee. Let all the earth worship Thee and chant unto Thee; let them chant unto Thy name, O Most High. Come and see the works of the Lord, how awesome He is in His counsels, more than the sons of men. He turneth the sea into dry land; in the river shall they pass through on foot. There shall we rejoice in Him, in Him that is ruler in His sovereignty for ever. His eyes look upon the nations; let not them that embitter Him be exalted in themselves. O bless our God, you nations, and make the voice of His praise to be heard, Who hath established my soul in life, and permitteth not my feet to be shaken. For Thou hast proved us, O God, and by fire hast Thou tried us even as silver is tried by fire. Thou hast brought us into the snare, Thou hast laid afflictions upon our back, Thou madest men to mount upon our heads. We went through fire and water, and Thou didst bring us out into refreshment. I shall go into Thy house with a whole burnt offering; to Thee shall I pay my vows which my lips pronounced and which my mouth had spoken in mine affliction. Whole burnt offerings full of marrow shall I offer unto Thee, with incense and rams; oxen and goats shall I offer unto Thee. Come and hear, and I shall declare unto you, all you that fear God, what things He hath done for my soul. Unto Him with my mouth have I cried, and I exalted Him with my tongue. If in my heart I regarded unrighteousness, let the Lord not hear me. Wherefore God hath hearkened unto me, He hath been attentive to the voice of my supplication. Blessed is God Who hath not turned away my prayer, nor His mercy away from me.

Psalm 66

God be gracious unto us and bless us, and cause His face to shine upon us and have mercy on us, That we may know upon the earth Thy way, among all the nations Thy salvation. Let the peoples give Thee praise, O God, let all the peoples praise Thee. Let the nations be glad and rejoice, for Thou shalt judge peoples with uprightness; and nations shalt Thou guide upon the earth. Let the peoples give Thee praise, O God, let all the peoples praise Thee; the earth hath yielded her fruit. Let God, our God, bless us; let God bless us, and let all the ends of the earth fear Him.

After The Psalm

Glory be to the Father and to the Son and to the Holy Spirit;
Both now and forever, and unto the ages of ages. Amen.

Halleluiah, Halleluiah, Halleluiah. Glory to Thee, O God. **(x3)**

Lord, have mercy. **(x3)**

Glory be to the Father and to the Son and to the Holy Spirit;
Both now and forever, and unto the ages of ages. Amen.

Psalm 67

Let God arise and let His enemies be scattered, and let them that hate Him flee from before His face. As smoke vanisheth, so let them vanish; as wax melteth before the fire, so let sinners perish at the presence of God. And let the righteous be glad; let them rejoice in the presence of God, let them delight in gladness. Sing unto God, chant unto His name; prepare you the way for Him that rideth upon the setting of the sun. Lord is His name; yea, rejoice before Him. Let them be troubled at His presence, Who is a father of orphans and a judge to the widows. God is in His holy place, God settleth the solitary in a house, Mightily leading forth them that were shackled, and likewise them that embitter Him, them that dwell in tombs. O God, when Thou wentest forth before Thy people, when Thou didst traverse the wilderness, The earth was shaken and the heavens dropped dew, at the presence of the God of Sinai, at the presence of the God of Israel. A rain freely given shalt Thou ordain, O God, for Thine inheritance; yea, it became weak, but Thou shalt restore it. Thy living creatures shall dwell therein; Thou hast prepared it in Thy goodness for the poor man, O God. The Lord shall give speech with great power to them that bring good tidings. He that is the King of the hosts of His beloved one shall divide the spoils for the beauty of the house. Even if you sleep among the lots, you shall have the wings of a dove covered with silver, and her pinions of sparkling gold. When He that is in the heavens ordaineth kings over her, they shall be made snow white in Selmon. The mountain of God is a butter mountain, a curdled mountain, a butter mountain. Why suppose you that there be other curdled mountains? This is the mountain wherein God is pleased to dwell, yea, for the Lord shall dwell therein to the end. The chariot host of God is ten thousandfold, yea, thousands of them that abound in number; the Lord is among them at Sinai, in His holy place. Thou hast ascended on high, Thou leddest captivity captive, Thou didst receive gifts among men (yea, for they were disobedient) that Thou mightest dwell there. Blessed is the Lord God, blessed is the Lord day by day; the God of our salvation shall prosper us along the way. Our God is the God of salvation, and the pathways leading forth from death are those of the Lords Lord. But God shall crush the heads of His enemies, the hairy crown of them that continue in their trespasses. The Lord said: I shall return from Bashan. I shall return in the deeps of the sea, That thy foot may be dipped in blood, yea, the tongue of thy dogs in that of thine enemies. Thy processionals have been seen, O God, the processionals of my God, of my King Who is in His sanctuary. Princes went before, and after them the chanters, in the midst of timbrel playing maidens. In congregations bless you God, the Lord from the well springs of Israel. Yonder is Benjamin the younger in rapture, the princes of Judah their rulers, the princes of Zabulon, the princes of Nephthalim. Give Thou command, O God, unto Thy hosts; strengthen, O God, this which Thou hast wrought in us. Because of Thy temple in Jerusalem, kings shall bring gifts unto Thee. Rebuke the wild beasts of the reed, that congregation of bulls among the heifers of the peoples, lest they exclude them that have been proved like silver. Scatter the nations that desire wars; ambassadors shall come out of Egypt; Ethiopia shall hasten to stretch out her hand unto God. You kingdoms of the earth, sing unto God; chant you unto the Lord, unto Him that rideth the heaven of heaven towards the dayspring. Lo, He shall utter with His voice a voice of power. Give you glory unto God; His magnificence is over Israel and His power is in the clouds. Wondrous is God in His saints; the God of Israel, He shall give power and strength unto His people. Blessed is God.

After The Psalm

Glory be to the Father and to the Son and to the Holy Spirit;
Both now and forever, and unto the ages of ages. Amen.

Halleluiah, Halleluiah, Halleluiah. Glory to Thee, O God. **(x3)**

Lord, have mercy. **(x3)**

Glory be to the Father and to the Son and to the Holy Spirit;

Both now and forever, and unto the ages of ages. Amen.

Psalm 68

Save me, O God, for the waters are come in unto my soul. I am stuck fast in the mire of the deep, and there is no sure standing. I am come into the deeps of the sea, and a tempest hath overwhelmed me. I am grown weary with crying, my throat is become hoarse; from my hoping in my God, mine eyes have failed me. They that hate me without a cause are multiplied more than the hairs of my head. Mine enemies are grown strong, they that persecute me unjustly; then did I restore that which I took not away. O God, Thou knowest my foolishness, and my transgressions are not hid from Thee. Let not them that wait on Thee be ashamed for my sake, O Lord, Thou Lord of hosts. Nor let them that seek after Thee be confounded for my sake, O God of Israel. Because for Thy sake I have borne reproach, shame hath covered my face. I am become a stranger unto my brethren, and an alien unto the sons of my mother. For the zeal of Thy house hath eaten me up, and the reproaches of them that reproach Thee are fallen on me. Yea, with fasting I covered my soul, and it was turned into a reproach for me. And I made sackcloth my clothing, and I became a proverb to them. And they prated against me, they that sit in the gates; and they made a song about me, they that drink wine. But as for me, with my prayer I cry unto Thee, O Lord; it is time for Thy good pleasure. O God, in the multitude of Thy mercy hearken unto me, in the truth of Thy salvation. Save me from the mire, that I be not stuck therein; let me be delivered from them that hate me and from the deeps of the waters. Let not the tempest of water overwhelm me, nor let the deep swallow me up, nor let the pit shut its mouth upon me. Hearken unto me, O Lord, for Thy mercy is good; according to the multitude of Thy compassions, look upon me. Turn not Thy countenance away from Thy servant, for I am afflicted; quickly hearken unto me. Attend unto my soul and deliver it; because of mine enemies, rescue me. For Thou knowest my reproach, my shame and my humiliation. Before Thee are all that afflict me; my soul hath awaited reproach and misery. And I waited for one that would grieve with me, but there was no one; and for them that would comfort me, but I found none. And they gave me gall for my food, and for my thirst they gave me vinegar to drink. Let their table before them be for a snare, for a recompense and for a stumbling block. Let their eyes be darkened that they may not see, and their back do Thou continually bow down. Pour out upon them Thy wrath, and let the fury of Thy wrath take hold upon them. Let their habitation be made desolate, and in their tents let there be none to dwell. For they persecuted him whom Thou hast smitten, and to the pain of my wounds have they added. Add iniquity to their iniquity, and let them not enter into Thy righteousness. Let them be blotted out of the book of the living, and with the righteous let them not be written. Poor and in sorrow am I; may Thy salvation, O God, be quick to help me. I shall praise the name of my God with an ode, I shall magnify Him with praise. And this shall please God more than a young calf that hath horns and hooves. Let beggars behold it and be glad; seek after God, and your soul shall live. For the Lord hath hearkened unto the poor and hath not despised them that are fettered for His sake. Let the heavens and the earth praise Him, the sea and all the creeping things therein. For God shall save Zion, and the cities of Judea shall be builded; and they shall dwell therein and inherit it. And the seed of Thy servants shall possess it, and they that love Thy name shall dwell therein.

Psalm 69

O God, be attentive to help me; Lord, make haste to help me. Let them be ashamed and confounded who seek after my life. Let them be turned back and be ashamed who desire evil against me. Let them be turned back because of their shame who say to me: "Well done. Well done." Let all those who seek Thee rejoice and be glad in Thee, O God, and let those who love Thy salvation say continually: *"Let the Lord be magnified."* But as for me, I am poor and needy; O God help me. Thou art my help and my deliverer; Lord; do not delay.

After The Psalm

Glory be to the Father and to the Son and to the Holy Spirit;
Both now and forever, and unto the ages of ages. Amen.

Halleluiah, Halleluiah, Halleluiah. Glory to Thee, O God. **(x3)**
Lord, have mercy. **(x3)**

Glory be to the Father and to the Son and to the Holy Spirit;
Both now and forever, and unto the ages of ages. Amen.

Lord, have mercy. **(x3)**

Psalm 140

Lord, I have cried to Thee: hear me. Hear me, O Lord.

Lord, I have cried to Thee: hear me. Receive the voice of my prayer.

When I call upon Thee, hear me, O Lord. Let my prayer arise as incense in Thy sight,

And let the lifting up of my hands be an evening sacrifice. Hear me, O Lord.

Kekragarion
Sticheroi From Psalm 140

• Set, O Lord, a watch before my mouth, and a door of enclosure round about my lips.

• Incline not my heart to words of evil, to make excuses for sins.

• Those that work iniquity; I shall not join with their number.

• The righteous man shall chasten me with mercy and reprove me; as for the oil of the sinner, let it not anoint my head.

• For yet more is my prayer in the presence of their pleasures; their judges have been swallowed up by the rock.

• They shall hear my words, for they be sweetened; as a clod of earth is broken upon the earth, so have their bones been scattered into hades.

• To Thee O Lord are mine eyes. In Thee have I hoped; take not my soul away.

• Keep me from the snare which they have laid for me, and from the stumbling blocks of them that work iniquity.

• The sinners shall fall into their own net; I am alone until I pass by.

Psalm 141

- With my voice to the Lord have I cried, with my voice have I made supplication.
- I shall pour out before Him my supplications; my afflictions shall I declare before Him.
- When my spirit was fainting within me, then Thou knewest my paths.
- In this way wherein I have walked they hid for me a snare.
- I looked on my right hand, and beheld, and there was none that knew me.
- Flight has failed me, and there is none that watches out for my soul.
- I cried to Thee, O Lord; I said: Thou art my hope, my portion in the land of the living.
- Attend unto my supplication, for I am brought very low.
- Deliver me from them that persecute me, for they are stronger than I.
- Bring my soul out of prison.
- That I may confess Thy name.
- The righteous shall patiently wait for me until Thou shalt reward me.

Sticheroi From Psalm 129

- Out of the depths have I cried unto Thee, O Lord. O Lord, hear my voice.
- Let Thine ears be attentive to the voice of my supplication.
- If Thou should mark iniquities, O Lord; O Lord, who shall stand? For with Thee there is forgiveness.
- For Thy name's sake have I patiently waited for Thee, O Lord; my soul has patiently waited for Thy word, my soul has hoped in the Lord.
- From the morning watch until night, from the morning watch let Israel hope in the Lord.
- For with the Lord there is mercy, and with Him is plenteous redemption; and He shall redeem Israel out of all his iniquities.
-

Sticheroi From Psalm 116

- O praise the Lord, all you nations; praise Him, all you peoples.
- For He has made His mercy to prevail over us, and the truth of the Lord abides forever.

Glory be to the Father and to the Son and to the Holy Spirit;
Both now and forever, and unto the ages of ages. Amen.

O Gladsome Light

O Gladsome Light of the holy glory of the immortal Father;

Heavenly holy, blessed Jesus Christ;

Now that we have come to the setting of the sun, and behold the Evening Light;

We praise God; Father, Son and Holy Spirit.

For meet it is at all time to worship Thee, with voices of praise;

O Son of God and Giver of Life. Therefore all the world doth glorify Thee.

Prokeimenon

Reader: The Prokeimenon.

[Sunday]   *Tone 8*   *Humility, tranquillity, repose, suffering, pleading.*   *C, D, Eb, F, G, A, Bb, C.*

Reader: Behold now, bless the Lord, all you servants of the Lord.

People: *Behold now, bless the Lord, all you servants of the Lord.*

Reader: You that stand in the house of the Lord; in the courts of the house of our God.

People: *Behold now, bless the Lord, all you servants of the Lord.*

Reader: Behold now, bless the Lord | all you servants of the Lord.

[Monday]   *Tone 4*   *Festive, joyous and expressing deep piety.*   *C, D, Eb, F, G, A, Bb, C.*

Reader: The Lord shall hearken unto me when I cry unto Him.

People: *The Lord shall hearken unto me when I cry unto Him.*

Stichos: When I called upon Thee, O God of my righteousness; Thou didst hearken unto me.

People: *The Lord shall hearken unto me when I cry unto Him.*

Reader: The Lord shall hearken unto me | when I cry unto Him.

[Tuesday]   *Tone 1*   *Magnificent, happy and earthy.*   *C, D, Eb, F, G, A, Bb, C.*

Reader: Thy mercy, O Lord, shall pursue me all the days of my life.

People: *Thy mercy, O Lord, shall pursue me all the days of my life.*

Reader: The Lord is my shepherd, and I shall not want.

In a place of green pasture, there has He made me to dwell.

People: *Thy mercy, O Lord, shall pursue me all the days of my life.*

Reader: Thy mercy, O Lord | shall pursue me all the days of my life.

[Wednesday]   *Tone 5*   *Stimulating, dancing, and rhythmical.*   *C, D, Eb, F, G, A, Bb, C.*

Reader: O God, in Thy name save me, and in Thy strength Thou judgest me.

People: *O God, in Thy name save me, and in Thy strength Thou judgest me.*

Reader: O God, hearken to my prayer, give ear to the words of my mouth.

People: *O God, in Thy name save me, and in Thy strength Thou judgest me.*

Reader: O God, in Thy name save me | and in Thy strength Thou judgest me.

[Thursday]   *Tone 6*   *Rich texture, funereal character, sorrowful tone.*   *D, Eb, F##, G, A, Bb, C##, D.*

Reader: My help comes from the Lord, who has made the heaven and the earth.

People: *My help comes from the Lord, who has made the heaven and the earth.*

Stichos: I lifted up my eyes to the mountains from where comes my help.

People: *My help comes from the Lord, who has made the heaven and the earth.*

Reader: My help comes from the Lord | who has made the heaven and the earth.

| [Friday] | Tone 7 | *Manly character and strong melody.* | *F, G, A, A#, C, D, E, F.* |

Reader: O God, my helper art Thou, and Thy mercy shall go before me.

People: *O God, my helper art Thou, and Thy mercy shall go before me.*

Reader: Rescue me from mine enemies, O God. And from them that rise up against me redeem me.

People: *O God, my helper art Thou, and Thy mercy shall go before me.*

Reader: O God, my helper art Thou | and Thy mercy shall go before me.

| [Saturday] | Tone 6 | *Rich texture, funereal character, sorrowful tone.* | *D, Eb, F##, G, A, Bb, C##, D.* |

Stichos 1: The Lord is clothed with strength and He has girded Himself.

People: *The Lord is King, He is clothed with majesty.*

Stichos 2: For He established the world which shall not be shaken.

People: *The Lord is King, He is clothed with majesty.*

Stichos 3: Holiness becomes Thine house, O Lord, to the length of days.

Lord, have mercy. **(x3)**

Vouchsafe, O Lord, to keep us this evening without sin. Blessed art Thou, O Lord, the God of our fathers, and praised and glorified is Thy name unto the ages. Amen.

Let Thy mercy, O Lord, be upon us, according as we have hoped in Thee.

Blessed art Thou, O Lord, teach me Thy statutes.
Blessed art Thou, O Master, give me understanding of Thy statutes.
Blessed art Thou, O Holy One, enlighten me by Thy statutes.

O Lord, Thy mercy endures forever; disdain not the work of Thy hands. To Thee is due praise, to Thee is due song, to Thee is due glory, to the Father, and to the Son, and to the Holy Spirit; both now and forever, and unto the ages of ages. Amen.

Lord, have mercy. **(x3)**

Lord, now lettest Thou Thy servant depart in peace, according to Thy word, for mine eyes have seen Thy salvation, which Thou hast prepared before the face of all peoples; a light of revelation for the Gentiles, and the glory of Thy people Israel.

Holy God, Holy Mighty, Holy Immortal, have mercy on us. **(x3)**

Glory be to the Father and to the Son and to the Holy Spirit;
Both now and forever, and unto the ages of ages. Amen.

O Most Holy Trinity, have mercy on us.

O Lord, cleanse us from our sins.

O Master, pardon our iniquities.

O Holy One, visit and heal our infirmities, for Thy names sake.

Lord have mercy. **(x3)**

Glory be to the Father and to the Son and to the Holy Spirit;
Both now and forever, and unto the ages of ages. Amen.

People: *Our Father, Who art in Heaven, hallowed be Thy Name. Thy Kingdom come, Thy will be done, on earth as it is in Heaven. Give us this day our daily bread, and forgive us our trespasses, as we forgive those who trespass against us; and lead us not into temptation, but deliver us from the evil one. Amen.*

Reader: O Lord, Jesus Christ, Son of God, have mercy on us. Amen.

Through the prayers of our holy Fathers; O Lord Jesus Christ our God; have mercy on us and save us. Amen.

Dismissal Hymns Of The Day

Glory be to the Father and to the Son and to the Holy Spirit;

Troparion Of The Annunciation Of The Most Holy Mother Of God

Tone 4   Festive, joyous and expressing deep piety.   *C, D, Eb, F, G, A, Bb, C.*

Today is the beginning of our salvation and the manifestation of the mystery which is from eternity. The Son of God becomes the Son of the Virgin, and Gabriel announces grace. So with him let us also cry to the Mother of God: *"Rejoice, thou who art full of grace. The Lord is with thee."*

Tone 2   Majesty, gentleness, hope, repentance and sadness.   *E, F, G, Ab, B, C.*

The memory of the just is celebrated with hymns of praise, but the Lords testimony is sufficient for thee, O Forerunner; for thou hast proved to be truly even more venerable than the Prophets since thou wast granted to baptise in the running waters Him Whom they proclaimed. Wherefore, having contested for the truth, thou didst rejoice to announce the good tidings even to those in Hades: that God hath appeared in the flesh, taking away the sin of the world and granting us great mercy.

Both now and forever, and unto the ages of ages. Amen.

Lord, have mercy. **(x12)**

Amen.

The Lord God make steadfast the holy and blameless Faith of the pious and Orthodox Christians, with His holy Church and this *[city / town / village / monastery / island]*, unto the ages of ages. Amen.

Greater in honour than the Cherubim and beyond compare more glorious than the Seraphim; without corruption thou gavest birth to God the Word, truly the Theotokos, we magnify thee.

Glory be to the Father and to the Son and to the Holy Spirit;
Both now and forever, and unto the ages of ages. Amen.

Lord have mercy. **(x3)**

Through the prayers of our holy Fathers, O Lord Jesus Christ our God; have mercy on us and save us. Amen.

[At Great Vespers before the Aposticha.]

Glory be to the Father, and to the Son, and to the Holy Spirit;

Both now and forever, and unto the ages of ages. Amen.

The Doxasticon At The Litia Procession

Tone 2   Majesty, gentleness, hope, repentance and sadness.   *E, F, G, Ab, B, C.*

Today doth Gabriel make announcement to her who is full of grace, saying: Hail, O groomless and unwedded Maiden. Let not my strange appearance dazzle thee, nor be dismayed at me; for I am the archangel. Verily, the serpent did deceive Eve of old, and now I bring thee glad tidings of joy. Thou shalt remain without corruption, and shalt give birth to the Lord, O pure one.

[After the Litia hymn is chanted stichirarically (slowly), and the procession of clergy and altar servers has finished at the solea, the clergy now begin the Service of Litia & Artoklasia.]

The Litia

Deacon: Have mercy upon us, O God, according to Thy great goodness, we pray Thee, hearken and have mercy.

People: *Lord, have mercy.* **(x3)**

Deacon: Again we pray for all pious and Orthodox Christians.

People: *Lord, have mercy.* **(x3)**

Deacon: Again we pray for our father and Archbishop Nikitas and all our brotherhood in Christ.

People: *Lord, have mercy.* **(x3)**

Deacon: Again we pray for every Christian soul, afflicted and weary, in need of Gods mercies and help; for the protection of this holy house and those who sing therein and the people here present; for the peace and stability of the whole world; for the good estate of the holy churches of God; for the salvation and help of our fathers and brethren who with diligence and fear of God labour and serve; for those who are gone away and those who are abroad; for those who travel by sea, land and air; for the healing of those who lie in infirmity; for the deliverance of captives; for those imprisoned and in danger; for our brethren who are serving and who are remembered for their labour, and for all who await the mercies of God, let us say.

People: *Lord, have mercy.* **(x3)**

Deacon: Again we pray for mercy, life, peace, health, salvation and visitation and pardon and forgiveness of sins for the servants of God, the parishioners, members of the parish council and organizations, donors and benefactors of this holy temple and those here present who celebrate this holy feast.

People: *Lord, have mercy.* **(x3)**

Deacon: Again we pray that He may keep this holy church and this city and every city and countryside from wrath, famine, plague, earthquake, flood, fire, the sword, foreign invasion, civil war and sudden death; that our good God, Who lovest mankind, shall be gracious, favourable and conciliatory and turn away and dispel all the wrath stirred up against us and all sickness, and may deliver us from His righteous chastisement which impendeth on us, and have mercy upon us.

People: *Lord, have mercy.* **(x40)**

Deacon: Again we pray that the Lord our God may hearken unto the voice of the supplication of us sinners, and have mercy upon us.

People: *Lord, have mercy.* **(x3)**

Priest: Hear us, O God our Saviour, the Hope of all the ends of the earth and of those who are far off upon the sea; and be gracious, be gracious, O Master, upon our sins, and have mercy upon us. For Thou art a merciful God and lovest mankind, and unto Thee do we ascribe glory: to the Father, and to the Son, and to the Holy Spirit; both now and forever, and unto the ages of ages.

People: *Amen.*

The Peace

Priest: Peace be to all.

People: *And with thy spirit.*

Deacon: Let us bow our heads unto the Lord.

People: *To Thee, O Lord.*

The Intercession

Priest: O Master, great in mercy, Lord Jesus Christ our God, through the intercessions of our all immaculate Lady Theotokos and Ever Virgin Mary - whose Annunciation we now celebrate – by the might of the precious and life giving Cross; by the protection of the honourable bodiless Powers of heaven; at the supplication of the honorable, glorious prophet, forerunner and Baptist John; of the holy, glorious, all laudable apostles Peter and Paul, and of all the holy apostles; of our fathers among the saints, great hierarchs and ecumenical teachers, Basil the Great, Gregory the Theologian and John Chrysostom; Athanasius, Cyril and John the Merciful, patriarchs of Alexandria; Nicholas of Myra, Spyridon of Trimythous and Nektarios of Pentapolis, the Wonder workers; of our fathers among the saints Tikhon, patriarch of Moscow and Raphael, bishop of Brooklyn; of the holy, glorious, great martyrs, George the Trophy bearer, Demetrios the Myrrh streamer, Theodore the Soldier, Theodore the General, and Menas the Wonderworker; of the hieromartyrs Ignatius the God bearer of Antioch, Charalampos and Eleutherios; of the holy, glorious great women martyrs, Thekla, Barbara, Anastasia, Katherine, Kyriaki, Photeini, Marina, Paraskeva and Irene; of the holy, glorious, right victorious martyrs; of our venerable and God bearing fathers who shone in the ascetic life; of Saint *N.*, the patron and protector of this holy community; of the holy and righteous ancestors of God, Joachim and Anna, and of all Thy saints; make our prayer acceptable;

People: *Amen.*

Priest: Grant us forgiveness of our trespasses;

People: *Amen.*

Priest: Shelter us under the shelter of Thy wings;

People: *Amen.*

Priest: Drive away from us every enemy and adversary;

People: *Amen.*

Priest: Give peace to our life.

People: *Amen.*

Priest: O Lord, have mercy on us and on Thy world and save our souls, for Thou art a merciful God and lovest mankind.

People: *Amen.*

Theotokion

      Tone 5   *Stimulating, dancing, and rhythmical.*   *C, D, Eb, F, G, A, Bb, C.*

Clergy: Rejoice, O Virgin Theotokos, Mary full of grace, the Lord is with thee. Blessed art thou among women, and blessed is the fruit of thy womb;

The Artoklasia

Chorus: *For thou hast borne the Saviour of our souls.*

Deacon: Let us pray to the Lord.

People: *Lord, have mercy.*

Priest: O Lord Jesus Christ our God, Who didst bless the five loaves in the wilderness and didst satisfy the five thousand therewith, Thyself bless these loaves, this wheat, wine and oil, and multiply them in this city, in the houses of those who celebrate this feast and in all thy world, and sanctify the faithful who partake of them. For it is Thou Who dost bless and sanctify all things, O Christ our God, and unto Thee do we ascribe glory, together with Thine unoriginate Father and Thine all holy, good and life giving Spirit, now and ever, and unto ages of ages.

People: *Amen.*

*[**Clergy** sing this once, then **Chorus** sings it twice:]*

Troparion

      Tone 7   *Manly character and strong melody.*   *F, G, A, A#, C, D, E, F.*

Rich men have turned poor and gone hungry; but they that seek the Lord shall not be deprived of any good thing.

[Great Vespers resumes with the Aposticha.

This Dismissal is used at Great Vespers when the Litia and Artoklasia are served. The usual one is not said. This follows the Apolytikia.]

The Great Dismissal

Deacon: Let us pray to the Lord.

People: *Lord, have mercy.*

Priest: The blessing of the Lord and His mercy come upon you through His divine grace and love towards mankind, always, now and ever, and unto ages of ages.

People: *Amen.*

Priest: Glory to Thee, O Christ our God and our Hope, glory to Thee.

Chorus: *Glory be to the Father, and to the Son, and to the Holy Spirit;*

Both now and forever, and unto the ages of ages. Amen.

Lord, have mercy. **(x3)**

Holy Father, bless.

Priest: May He Who condescended to become incarnate of the Holy Spirit and the Virgin Mary for us men and for our salvation, and rose from the dead, Christ our true God, through the intercessions of His all immaculate and all blameless holy Mother, whose Annunciation we now celebrate; by the might of the Precious and Life giving Cross; by the protection of the honourable Bodiless Powers of Heaven; at the supplication of the honorable, glorious Prophet, Forerunner and Baptist John; of the holy, glorious and all laudable apostles; of the holy, glorious and right victorious Martyrs; of our venerable and God bearing Fathers; of Saint *N.*, the patron and protector of this holy community; of the holy and righteous ancestors of God, Joachim and Anna; and of all the saints: have mercy on us and save us, forasmuch as He is good and loveth mankind.

People: *Amen.*

Priest: Through the prayers of our Holy Fathers, Lord Jesus Christ our God, have mercy upon us and save us.

People: *Amen.*

Parakleses For Advent

[With a priest. Have Troparion ready.]

In Preparation For The Great Feast Of The Nativity-In-The-Flesh
Of Our Lord God And Saviour Jesus Christ.

- *Holy Doors and curtain remain closed as all takes place on the solea.*
- *Priest, vested in exorasson, epitrachelion and phelonion, stands in the centre of the solea before an analogion upon which has been placed an icon of the Most Holy Theotokos and the Divine Child.*
- *He makes three metanias and blesses himself.*

The Trisagion Prayers

Deacon: Holy Father, Bless.

Priest: Blessed is our God always, now and forever, and unto the ages of ages.

People: Amen.

Priest: O Heavenly King, Comforter, Spirit of Truth, Who art everywhere present and fillest all things, Treasury of blessings and Giver of life: Come and abide in us and cleanse us from every impurity and save our souls, O Good One.

Reader: Holy God, Holy Mighty, Holy Immortal, have mercy on us. **(x3)**

> *Glory be to the Father, and to the Son, and to the Holy Spirit;*
> *Both now and forever, and unto the ages of ages. Amen.*

O Most Holy Trinity, have mercy on us.

O Lord, cleanse us from our sins.

O Master, pardon our iniquities.

O Holy One, visit and heal our infirmities, for Thy names sake.

Lord have mercy. **(x3)**

> *Glory be to the Father and to the Son and to the Holy Spirit;*
> *Both now and forever, and unto the ages of ages. Amen.*

People: Our Father, Who art in Heaven, hallowed be Thy Name. Thy Kingdom come, Thy will be done, on earth as it is in Heaven. Give us this day our daily bread, and forgive us our trespasses, as we forgive those who trespass against us; and lead us not into temptation, but deliver us from the evil one.

Priest: For Thine is the kingdom, and the power and the glory of the Father and of the Son and of the Holy Spirit, now and forever and to the ages of ages.

People: Amen.

People: *Lord have mercy.* **(x12)**

Glory be to the Father and to the Son and to the Holy Spirit,
Both now and forever and unto the ages of ages. Amen.

Come, let us worship God, our King.

Come, let us worship and fall down before Christ, our King and our God.

Come, let us worship and fall down before Christ Himself, our King and our God.

[Priest goes to Readers stand whilst:]

Psalm 142

Reader: Hear my prayer, O Lord, give ear to my supplications. In Thy faithfulness answer me, and in Thy righteousness. Do not enter into judgement with Thy servant, for in Thy sight no one living is righteous. For the enemy has persecuted my soul; he has crushed my life to the ground; he has made me dwell in darkness, like those who have long been dead. Therefore my spirit is overwhelmed within me; my heart within me is distressed. I remember the days of old; I meditate on all Thy works; I muse on the work of Thine hands. I spread out my hands to Thee; my soul longs for Thee like a thirsty land. Answer me speedily, O Lord; my spirit fails. Do not hide Thy face from me, lest I be like those who go down into the pit. Cause me to hear Thy loving kindness in the morning, for in Thee do I trust; cause me to know the way in which I should walk, for I lift up my soul to Thee. Deliver me, O Lord, from mine enemies; in Thee I take shelter. Teach me to do Thy will, for Thou art my God; Thy Spirit is good. Lead me in the land of uprightness. Revive me, O Lord, for Thy names sake. For Thy righteousness' sake bring my soul out of trouble. In Thy mercy cut off mine enemies, and destroy all those who afflict my soul; for I am Thy servant.

God Is The Lord

People: *God is the Lord and has revealed Himself to us. Blessed is He who cometh in the Name of the Lord.*

Reader: Give thanks to the Lord, for He is good; and His steadfast love endures forever.

People: *God is the Lord and has revealed Himself to us. Blessed is He who cometh in the Name of the Lord.*

Reader: All nations surrounded me; in the Name of the Lord, I withstood them.

People: *God is the Lord and has revealed Himself to us. Blessed is He who cometh in the Name of the Lord.*

Reader: This is the Lords doing and is marvellous in our eyes.

People: *God is the Lord and has revealed Himself to us. Blessed is He who cometh in the Name of the Lord.*

Troparion

Tone 4   Festive, joyous and expressing deep piety.   C, D, Eb, F, G, A, Bb, C.

Make ready, O Bethlehem, for Eden hath been opened for all. Prepare, O Ephratha, for the Tree of Life hath blossomed forth in the cave from the Virgin. For her womb did appear as a super-sensual paradise in which is planted that holy Vine; if we should eat thereof we shall live and not die as Adam of old. Christ shall be born, raising the image that fell at the beginning. **(x3)**

Psalm 50

Have mercy on me, O God, according to Thy great mercy; and according to the multitude of Thy compassions blot out my transgression. Wash me thoroughly from mine iniquity, and cleanse me from my sin. For I acknowledge mine iniquity, and my sin is ever before me. Against Thee, Thee only have I sinned, and done evil in Thy sight, that Thou mayest be found just when Thou speakest, and victorious when Thou art judged. For behold, I was conceived in iniquity, and in sin my mother bore me. For behold, Thou hast loved truth; Thou hast made known to me the hidden and secret things of Thy wisdom. Thou shalt sprinkle me with hyssop, and I shall be made clean; Thou shalt wash me, and I shalt be whiter than snow. Make me to hear joy and gladness; that the humbled bones may rejoice. Turn Thy face away from my sins, and blot out all mine iniquities.

Create in me a clean heart, O God, and renew a steadfast spirit within me. Cast me not away from Thy presence, and take not Thy Holy Spirit from me. Restore to me the joy of Thy salvation, and establish me with Thy governing Spirit. I shall teach transgressors Thy ways, and the ungodly shall turn back to Thee. Deliver me from blood guiltiness, O God, the God of my salvation; my tongue shall joyfully declare Thy righteousness. Lord, open my lips, and my mouth shall declare Thy praise. For if Thou hadst desired sacrifice, I would give it; Thou dost not delight in burned offerings. A sacrifice to God is a broken spirit; God shall not despise a broken and a humbled heart. Do good, O Lord, in Thy good pleasure to Zion, and let the walls of Jerusalem be builded. Then Thou shalt be pleased with a sacrifice of righteousness, with oblation and whole burned offerings. Then shall they offer bulls on Thine altar.

The Canon

Ode 1

Reader: A triumphant force once laid low all the armed hosts of Pharoah in the deep: even so the glorious Lord, the Word made flesh, has blotted out malignant sin; for He has greatly been glorified.

Chorus: *Glory to Thee, our God, glory to Thee.*

Reader: O King of all, wishing man to be enrolled in the book of life, Thou hast enrolled Thyself according to the law of Caesar. As a stranger hast Thou come unto Thine own, calling back to heaven those who were unhappily estranged from paradise.

Chorus: *Glory be to the Father and to the Son and to the Holy Spirit;*

Reader: O Bethlehem, receive Christ; for, made flesh, he comes to dwell in thee, opening Eden to me. Make ready, O Cave, to behold most strangely contained in thee, Him Who cannot be contained, Who now is made poor in the wealth of His tender mercies.

Chorus: *Both now and forever, and unto the ages of ages. Amen.*

Reader: Christ comes to be born, granting in His goodness a strange rebirth to those sprung from Adam. Be glad, the whole nature of mortal man, Thou that art barren and bearest not: the Master has come to make thee a mother of many children.

Ode 3

Reader: The desert flowered as a lily at Thy coming, O Lord, even the Church of the Gentiles that was barren: and in that same coming is my heart established.

Chorus: Glory to Thee, our God, glory to Thee.

Reader: Redeeming me from the bands of evil, O Lord who lovest mankind, Thou comest to be wrapped as a babe in swaddling bands. I venerate Thy divine condescension.

Chorus: Glory be to the Father and to the Son and to the Holy Spirit;

Reader: The Virgin draws nigh to bear Thee, O Lord, Who, shining timelessly from the Father, hast now come to be in time, setting us loose from the temporal passions of our souls.

Chorus: Both now and forever, and unto the ages of ages. Amen.

Reader: Lord most merciful and full of pity, seeking me who had gone astray in transgression, Thou hast come to dwell in a cave as in heaven, thereby preparing the heavenly mansions for me.

Kathisma

Tone 1   Magnificent, happy and earthy.   *C, D, Eb, F, G, A, Bb, C.*

Rejoice exceedingly, O Zion: make ready, O Bethlehem. The upholder of all things, sending a star before Him, has made known His condescension without measure. He before whom the heavenly powers tremble, our only God, without suffering change is born in very truth from the Virgin.

Ektenia Of Supplication

Priest: Have mercy on us, O God, according to thy great mercy, we beseech thee; hearken and have mercy.

People: Lord have mercy. **(x3)**

Priest: We pray for our Archbishop Nikitas, the priests, hieromonks, deacons, hierodeacons and monastics and for all our brethren in Christ.

People: Lord have mercy. **(x3)**

Priest: Again we pray that as Thou didst deem a lowly cave to be a fit dwelling for the Lord Almighty, so Thou wouldst ever make our souls and bodies temples wirthy to contain the uncontainable God.

People: Lord have mercy. **(x3)**

Priest: Again we pray Thee, O Lord, that Thou wouldst make us worthy to praise and glorify Thee together with the angels and shepherds.

People: Lord have mercy. **(x3)**

Priest: We give thanks unto Thee, O Lord, that Thou hast chosen us from the the barren Church of the Gentiles and hast grafted us, a young olive shoot, upon the root and stock of righteous Abraham; and we pray Thee to open our ears that we might heed the Prophets warning and "prepare the way of the Lord".

People: Lord have mercy. **(x3)**

Priest: Again we pray for mercy, life, peace, health, salvation and visitation and pardon and forgiveness of sins for the servants of God, all Orthodox Christians of true worship, now gathered to prepare for the feast of Thy holy nativity.

People: Lord have mercy. **(x3)**

Priest: For Thou art a merciful God and lovest mankind, and unto Thee we ascribe glory to the Father and to the Son and to the Holy Spirit, both now and forever and unto the ages of ages.

People: Amen.

Ode 4

Reader: Thou hast come forth from a Virgin, neither angel nor ambassador, but the Lord Himself made flesh, and to me who am man Thou hast brought salvation. Therefore, I cry unto Thee: "Glory to Thy power, O Lord."

Chorus: Glory to Thee, our God, glory to Thee.

Reader: Let the creation now cast off all things old, beholding Thee the Creator made a child. For through Thy birth Thou dost shape all things afresh, making them new once more and leading them back again to their first beauty.

Chorus: Glory to Thee, our God, glory to Thee.

Reader: The magi who had been led on their way by a divine star, stood before Thee, in wonder at Thy marvellous birth; and bearing girfts, they see the Sun that rose from the Virgin cloud.

Chorus: Glory be to the Father and to the Son and to the Holy Spirit;

Reader: Behold the Virgin comes like a young heifer, bearing in her womb the fatted Calf that takes away the sins of the world. Let the creation, as it keeps fast, exceedingly rejoice.

Chorus: Both now and forever, and unto the ages of ages. Amen.

Reader: The preaching of the prophets, foretelling the manifestation of Christ, has today received its saving fulfillment: for He has come in the flesh to enlighten those in peril of darkness.

Ode 5

Reader: Thou are become mediator between God and man, O Christ our God; for through Thee, O Master, we have access from the darkness of ignorance to Thy Father, the Author of light.

Chorus: *Glory to Thee, our God, glory to Thee.*

Reader: Let the people that once sat in darkness see the Light shine forth that knows no evening: Him, Whom the star once made known to kings from Persia who worshipped fire.

Chorus: *Glory be to the Father and to the Son and to the Holy Spirit;*

Reader: The great King comes in haste to enter a small cave, that He may make me great who had grown small, and that, as transcendent God, by His poverty without measure He may enrich me who had grown poor.

Chorus: *Both now and forever, and unto the ages of ages. Amen.*

Reader: "Now is Christ born of Jacob," so Balaam said "and He shall rule over nations, and His kingdom shall be exalted in grace and shall perpetually remain."

Ode 6

Reader: Compassed about in an abyss of sun, in the unsearchable abyss of Thy tender mercies do I call: bring me out from corruption, O God.

Chorus: *Glory to Thee, our God, glory to Thee.*

Reader: Christ, in strange wise, comes to His own. Let us make ourselves strangers to sin, and let us receive Him Who dwells in the souls of the meek.

Chorus: *Glory be to the Father and to the Son and to the Holy Spirit;*

Reader: Thou, O Bethlehem, art not least among cities; for in thee is born the King and Lord Who shall tend as a shepherd the people that is His own.

Chorus: *Both now and forever, and unto the ages of ages. Amen.*

Reader: How shall a small cave receive Thee, for Whom the world cannot find room, O Thou Whom none can comprehend. O Thou, Who with the Father art without beginning, how shalt Thou appear as a small Child.

Kontakion

Tone 3   *Arrogant, brave, and mature atmosphere.*   *F, G, A, A#, C, D, E, F.*

Today the Virgin cometh to the cave to give birth in an ineffable manner to the pre-eternal Word. Rejoice, therefore, O universe, when Thou hearest, and glorify with the angels and shepherds Him who shall appear by His own will as a new Child, the pre-eternal God.

Ektenia Of Supplication

Priest: Have mercy on us, O God, according to thy great mercy, we beseech thee; hearken and have mercy.

People: *Lord have mercy.* (**x3**)

Priest: We pray for our Archbishop Nikitas, the priests, hieromonks, deacons, hierodeacons and monastics and for all our brethren in Christ.

People: *Lord have mercy.* (**x3**)

Priest: Again we pray that as Thou didst deem a lowly cave to be a fit dwelling for the Lord Almighty, so Thou wouldst ever make our souls and bodies temples wirthy to contain the uncontainable God.

People: *Lord have mercy.* (**x3**)

Priest: Again we pray Thee, O Lord, that Thou wouldst make us worthy to praise and glorify Thee together with the angels and shepherds.

People: *Lord have mercy.* (**x3**)

Priest: We give thanks unto Thee, O Lord, that Thou hast chosen us from the the barren Church of the Gentiles and hast grafted us, a young olive shoot, upon the root and stock of righteous Abraham; and we pray Thee to open our ears that we might heed the Prophets warning and "prepare the way of the Lord".

People: *Lord have mercy.* (**x3**)

Priest: Again we pray for mercy, life, peace, health, salvation and visitation and pardon and forgiveness of sins for the servants of God, all Orthodox Christians of true worship, now gathered to prepare for the feast of Thy holy nativity.

People: *Lord have mercy.* (**x3**)

Priest: For Thou art a merciful God and lovest mankind, and unto Thee we ascribe glory to the Father and to the Son and to the Holy Spirit, both now and forever and unto the ages of ages.

People: Amen.

First Antiphon Of The Anavathmoi

Tone 4   *Festive, joyous and expressing deep piety.*   *C, D, Eb, F, G, A, Bb, C.*

Reader: From the years of my youth, many passions combat me; but You, Who are my Saviour, assist me and save me. (**x2**)

Chorus: *You haters of Zion shall be put to shame by the Lord Almighty, for as grass in the fire, you shall all be withered.* (**x2**)

Chorus: *Glory be to the Father and to the Son and to the Holy Spirit;*

Reader: By the Holy Spirit, every soul is made living, is exalted, and made shining through purification, by the Threefold Oneness, in a hidden manner.

Chorus: *Both now and forever and unto the ages of ages. Amen.*

Reader: By the Holy Spirit, the streams of grace are flowing, watering, all of the creation, granting life upon.

Prokeimenon

Reader: I shall remember your Holy Name from generation to generation.

Chorus: *I shall remember your Holy Name from generation to generation.*

Reader: Listen, O Daughter, and see, and incline your ear;

And forget your people and your fathers house and the King shall desire your beauty.

Chorus: *I remember Your Holy Name from generation to generation.*

Reader: I shall remember your Holy Name | from generation to generation.

The Holy Gospel

Deacon: And that he shall vouchsafe to us to listen to the Holy Gospel; let us pray to the Lord God.

People: *Lord have mercy.* **(x3)**

Priest: Peace be with you all.

People: *And with thy spirit.*

Priest: The reading is from the Holy Gospel according to Luke.

People: *Glory to Thee O Lord, glory to Thee.*

Deacon: Let us attend.

In those days, Mary arose and went into the hill country with haste, into a city of Judah; and entered into the house of Zachariah and greeted Elizabeth. And it came to pass, that, when Elizabeth heard the salutation of Mary, the babe leaped in her womb; and Elizabeth was filled with the Holy Spirit and she spake out with a loud voice and said: "Blessed art thou amongst women, and blessed is the fruit of thy womb. And whence is this to me, that the mother of my Lord should come to me? For behold, when the voice of thy salutation come into mine ears, the babe leaped in my womb for joy. And blessed is she that believed: for there shall be a fulfilment of those things which bave been spoken to her from the Lord." And Mary said "My soul magnifies the Lord, and my spirit has rejoiced in God my Saviour. For He has regarded the lowly state of His maidservant; for behold, henceforth all generations shall call me blessed. For He who is mighty has done great things for me, and holy is His name." And Mary abided with her about three months, and returned to her own house.

People: *Glory to Thee O Lord, glory to Thee.*

Chorus: *Glory be to the Father and to the Son and to the Holy Spirit;*

Tone 2   Majesty, gentleness, hope, repentance and sadness.   E, F, G, Ab, B, C.

Reader: Through the intercessions of the prophets, O Merciful One, blot out the multitude of my transgressions.

Chorus: *Both now and forever, and unto the ages of ages. Amen.*

Reader: Through the intercessions of the prophets, O Merciful One, blot out the multitude of my transgressions.

Tone 6   Rich texture, funeral, sorrowful.   D, Eb, F##, G, A, Bb, C##, D.

Have mercy on me, O God, according to Thy great mercy, according to the multitude of Thy compassions blot out my transgressions.

The sayings of the prophets are now fulfilled, for our God shall be born of the Virgin Mary in fashion past words, and yet shall remain such as he was before His birth. The magi come together bearing gifts, the shepherds abide in the fields, and we also sing; "O Lord, born of a Virgin, glory to Thee."

The Intercession

Priest: O God, save Thy people and bless Thine inheritance. Visit Thy world with mercy and compassions. Exalt the horn or Orthodox Christians, and send down upon us Thy rich mercies. Through the intercessions of our All Immaculate Lady Theotokos and Ever Virgin Mary; by the might of the precious and Life Giving Cross; by the protection of the honourable bodiless powers of heaven; at the supplication of the honourable, glorious Prophet, Forerunner and Baptist John, and all of the holy prophets; of the glorious, all laudable Apostles; of our fathers among the saints, great hierarchs, and oecumenical teachers, Basil the Great, Gregory the Theologian, and John Chrysostom; Athanasios, Cyril, and John the Merciful, patriarchs of Alexandria; Nicholas of Myra in Lycia, Spyridon of Trimythous and Nektarois of Pentapolis, the wonder workers; of the holy and glorious great martyrs, George the Trophy Bearer, Demetrios the Myrrh Streaming, Theodore the Soldier, Theodore the General and Menas the Wonder Worker; of the hieromartyrs, Ignatios the God Bearer of Antioch, Xaralambous and Eleftherios; of the holy, glorious great martyrs: Thekla, Barbara, Anastasia, Katherine, Kyriaki, Photini, Marina, Paraskeva and Irene; of our venerable and God bearing fathers who shone in the ascetic life: Anthony the Great, Evthymios, Paisios, Sabbas the Sanctified, Theodosios the head of monasteries, Onouphrios, Athanasios and Peter af Athos; our holy mothers, Mary of Egypt, Macrina, Pelagia and Thais; of the holy, glorious and wonder working unmercenary healers, Cosmas and Damian, Cyros and John, Panteleimon and Hermolaos; of *[St N, patron of this parish]*; of the holy and righteous ancestors of God, Joachim and Anna; of *[Ss N & N of the day]* whose memory we celebrate and of all Thy saints, we beseech Thee, O only most merciful Lord, hearken unto the petitions of us sinners who make our supplications unto Thee, and have mercy on us.

People: *Lord have mercy.* **(x12)**

Priest: Through the mercy and compassions and love for mankind of Thine only begotten Son, with Whom Thou art blessed, together with Thine all holy and good and Life Giving Spirit; both now and forever and unto the ages of ages.

People: Amen.

[Priest goes to the Readers Stand whilst:]

Ode 7

Reader: The profane command of a lawless tyrant fanned the flame exceeding high; but Christ cast the dew of the Spirit over the Children who feared God: blessed is He and exalted above all.

Chorus: *Glory to Thee, our God, glory to Thee.*

Reader: Let clouds drop water from on high; He Who in glory makes the clouds His chariot, comes borne upon a cloud, that is the Virgin. The Light that knows no evening, He comes to shine on those who were in darkness and in peril.

Chorus: *Glory be to the Father and to the Son and to the Holy Spirit;*

Reader: O army of divine angles, make ready to sing the praises of the ineffable condescension of the Lord. O you magi, come with all speed; O shepherds, make haste. Christ is come, the predestined Expectation of the nations and their Deliverance.

Chorus: *Both now and forever, and unto the ages of ages. Amen.*

Reader: "What is this great and strange wonder? How do I uphold Thee who upholdest all the world by Thy word? O my Son Who art without beginning, Thy birth is beyond all speech." So spake the All Pure, fearfully holding Christ in her arms.

Ode 8

Reader: In Babylon of old, by the command of God, the fiery furnace worked in contrary ways: burning the Chaldeans, it refreshed the faithful as they sang: "O all you works of the Lord, bless you the Lord."

Chorus: *Glory to Thee, our God, glory to Thee.*

Reader: The blameless Lady was amazed at the height of the mystery, in truth past speech, that covered the heavens with knowledge, and she said: "The heavenly throne is consumed in flames as it holds Thee; how is it, then, that I carry Thee, my Son?"

Chorus: *Glory be to the Father and to the Son and to the Holy Spirit;*

Reader: "Thou didst bear the likeness of Thy Father, O my Son. How then hast Thou become poor and taken upon Thyself the likeness of a servant? How shall I lay Thee in a manger of beasts without reason, who dost deliver all men from unreason? I sing the praises of Thy compassion."

Chorus: *Both now and forever, and unto the ages of ages. Amen.*

Reader: Be joyful all the earth; behold, Christ draws nigh to be born in Bethlehem. Be glad, O sea; dance for joy, Thou congregation of prophets, seeing the fuulfilment of your words; rejoice, O all you righteous.

Ode 9

Reader: The Son of the Fahter without beginning has appeared to us, God the Lord made flesh of the Virgin, to give light to those in darkness, and to gather the dispersed. Therefore the far famed Theotokos do we magnify.

Chorus: *Glory to Thee, our God, glory to Thee.*

Reader: Let the kings of the whole earth sing rejoicing, and let the companies of the nations be in exceeding joy. Mountains and hills and hollows, rivers and seas, and the whole creation, magnify the Lord Who now is born.

Chorus: *Glory to Thee, our God, glory to Thee.*

Reader: As far as it was right, Thou wast seen by the prophets. Made man in the last times, Thou hast appeared to all in Bethlehem, city of Judah, and a star showed Thee to the star gazers. O Thou Who passest all interpretation.

Chorus: *Glory be to the Father and to the Son and to the Holy Spirit;*

Reader: Behold, the Most Holy Word comes unto His own in a holy body that is not His. By a strange birth He makes His own the world that was estranged. To Him let us sing in praise, Who became poor for us.

Chorus: *Both now and forever, and unto the ages of ages. Amen.*

Reader: "O sweetest Child, how shall I feed Thee Who givest food to all? How shall I hold Thee Who holdest all things in Thy power? How shall I wrap Thee in swaddling clothes, who dost wrap the whole earth in clouds?" So cried the all pure Lady whom in faith we magnify.

[Priest censes the icon on the analogion, whilst:]

Reader: *[Archangel Gabriel:* It is truly right to call thee blessed, who gavest birth to God, ever-blessed and God-obedient the Mother of our God.] Greater in honour than the Cherubim and beyond compare more glorious than the Seraphim; without corruption thou gavest birth to God the Word, truly the Mother of God, we magnify thee.

[Priest does the great censing, whilst:]

The Megalynaria

Tone 8   *Humility, tranquillity, repose, suffering, pleading.*   *C, D, Eb, F, G, A, Bb, C.*

Reader: Higher than the heavens above art Thou, and Thou art much purer than the radiance of the sun; for Thou hast redeemed us out of the curse that held us. O Mistress of creation, with hymns we honour thee.

Chorus: *From the great abundance of all my sins, ill am I in body, ailing also am I in soul. Thee have I as refuge; do Thou, therefore help me, O hope of all the hopeless, for Thou art full of grace.*

Reader: O Lady amd Mother of Christ our God, receive supplication from us sinners who beg of thee that thou make entreatry unto One born from thee; O Mistress of creation, pray thou to God for us.

Chorus: *Now that we chant with eagerness unto thee with this ode most joyful, O all hymned Mother of our God; together with the Baptist and all the saintly Chorus', beseech, O Theotokos, that we may find clemency.*

Reader: Let us purge our bodies and souls of sin, that with a pure conscience we may welcome in Bethlehem Christ the King of glory who cometh to be born of the Virgin pure and sinless. Come, let us worship Him.

Chorus: *Thou, O lowly manger, prepare thyself. Hasten, O you shepherds, for the birth of Christ is at hand. Hurry on, you magi, and gather, all you angels, and shout. "To Thee be glory Who for our sakes art born.*

Reader: "Glory be to God Who is born today of the Virgin Mother in the city of Bethlehem." Thus cry men and angels with voices joined in chorus in worship of the Saviours Holy Nativity.

Troparion To The Patron Saint Of The Parish

e.g. Troparion Of St Martin Of Tours

Tone 4   *Festive, joyous and expressing deep piety.*   *C, D, Eb, F, G, A, Bb, C.*

In signs and in miracles thou wert renowned throughout Gaul. By grace and adoption thou art a light for the world, O Martin, blessed of God. Alms deeds and compassion filled thy life with their splendours. Teaching and wise counsel were thy riches and treasures, which thou dispensest freely to those who honour thee.

[Priest stands befoe the analogion and censes the icon during this last Megalynarion:]

Chorus: *O all you array of angelic hosts, with the holy Baptist, the Apostles twelve numbered band, all the saints together, as well as Gods Birthgiver, pray make you intercession for our deliverance.*

Reader: Holy God, Holy Mighty, Holy Immortal, have mercy on us. **(x3)**

Glory be to the Father, and to the Son, and to the Holy Spirit;
Both now and forever, and unto the ages of ages. Amen.

O Most Holy Trinity, have mercy on us.
O Lord, cleanse us from our sins.
O Master, pardon our iniquities.
O Holy One, visit and heal our infirmities, for Thy names sake.

Lord have mercy. **(x3)**

Glory be to the Father and to the Son and to the Holy Spirit;
Both now and forever, and unto the ages of ages. Amen.

People: *Our Father, Who art in Heaven, hallowed be Thy Name. Thy Kingdom come, Thy will be done, on earth as it is in Heaven. Give us this day our daily bread, and forgive us our trespasses, as we forgive those who trespass against us; and lead us not into temptation, but deliver us from the evil one.*
Priest: For Thine is the kingdom, and the power and the glory of the Father and of the Son and of the Holy Spirit, now and forever and to the ages of ages.
People: *Amen.*

Troparion

Tone 4   *Festive, joyous and expressing deep piety.*   *C, D, Eb, F, G, A, Bb, C.*

Make ready, O Bethlehem, for Eden hath been opened for all. Prepare, O Ephratha, for the Tree of Life hath blossomed forth in the cave from the Virgin. For her womb did appear as a super-sensual paradise in which is planted that holy Vine; if we should eat thereof we shall live and not die as Adam of old. Christ shall be born, raising the image that fell at the beginning. **(x3)**

The Final Ektenia

Priest: Have mercy on us, O God, according to thy great mercy, we beseech thee; hearken and have mercy.
People: *Lord have mercy.* **(x3)**
Priest: Again we pray for all pious and Orthodox Christians.
People: *Lord have mercy.* **(x3)**

Priest: We pray for our Archbishop <u>Nikitas</u>, the priests, hieromonks, deacons, hierodeacons and monastics and for all our brethren in Christ.

People: *Lord have mercy.* **(x3)**

Priest: Again we pray for mercy, life, peace, health, salvation and visitation and pardon and forgiveness of sins for the servants of God, all pious and Orthodox Christians who live and dwell in this community.

People: *Lord have mercy.* **(x3)**

Priest: Again we pray that he shall keep this holy church and this city and every city and countryside from wrath, famine, pestilence, earthquake, flood, fire, the sword, foreign invasion, civil war and sudden death; that our good God, Who loveth mankind, shall be gracious, favourable and conciliatory and turn away and dispel all the wrath stirred up against us and all sickness, and may deliver us from His righteous chastisement which impendeth against us, and have mercy on us.

People: *Lord have mercy.* **(x3)**

Priest: Again we pray that the Lord our God shall hearken unto the voice of supplication of us sinners, and have mercy on us.

People: *Lord have mercy.* **(x3)**

Priest: Hear us, O God our Saviour, the Hope of all the ends of the earth and of those who are far off upon the sea, and be gracious, be gracious, O Master, upon our sins, and have mercy on us; for Thou art a merciful God and lovest mankind, and unto Thee we ascribe glory to the Father and to the Son and to the Holy Spirit, both now and forever, and unto the ages of ages.

People: Amen.

The Dismissal

Priest: Glory to Thee, O Christ God our hope, glory to Thee.

Reader: *Glory to the Father and to the Son, and to the Holy Spirit;*

Both now and forever and unto the ages of ages. Amen.

Lord have mercy. **(x3)**

Holy Father Bless.

Priest: May Christ our true God, through the intercessions of his all immaculate and all blameless holy Mother; by the might of the precious and life giving Cross; by the protection fo the honourabnle bodiless powers of heaven; at the supplication of the honourable, glorious Prophet, Forerunner and Baptist John and all the holy prophets; of the holy, glorious and all laudable Apostles; of the holy, glorious and right victorious martyrsl; of our venerable and God bearing Fathers; of *[Saint N - the patron saint of the church]*; of the holy and righteous ancestors of God, Joachim and Anna; of *[Ss N&N – the saints of the day]* whose memory we celebrate and of all the saints; have mercy on us and save us, forasmuch as He is good and loves mankind.

People: *Amen.*

Priest: Through the prayers of our holy fathers, Lord Jesus Christ our God, have mercy upon us and save us.

People: *Amen.*

Trisagion Prayers

Priest: Blessed is our God, always, now and forever, and unto the ages of ages.

People: *Amen.*

Reader: Come, let us worship God, our King.

Come, let us worship and fall down before Christ, our King and our God.

Come, let us worship and fall down before Christ Himself, our King and our God.

Psalm 103

Of David. Concerning The Formation Of The World.

Bless the Lord, O my soul. O Lord my God, Thou hast been exceedingly magnified. Confession and majesty hast Thou put on, Who covered Thyself with light as with a garment, Who stretched out the heaven as it were a curtain; Who supports His chambers in the waters, Who appoints the clouds for His ascent, Who walks upon the wings of the winds, Who makes His angels spirits, and His ministers a flame of fire, Who establishes the earth in the sureness thereof; it shall not be turned back for ever and ever. The abyss like a garment is His mantle; upon the mountains shall the waters stand. At Thy rebuke they shall flee, at the voice of Thy thunder shall they be afraid.

The mountains rise up and the plains sink down to the place where Thou hast established them. Thou appointed a boundary that they shall not pass, neither return to cover the earth. He sends forth springs in the valleys; between the mountains shall the waters run. They shall give drink to all the beasts of the field; the wild asses shall wait to quench their thirst. Beside them shall the birds of the heaven lodge, from the midst of the rocks shall they give voice. He waters the mountains from His chambers; the earth shall be satisfied with the fruit of Thy works.

He causes the grass to grow for the cattle, and green herb for the service of men, To bring forth bread out of the earth; and wine makes glad the heart of man. To make his face cheerful with oil; and bread strengthens mans heart. The trees of the plain shall be satisfied, the cedars of Lebanon, which Thou hast planted. There shall the sparrows make their nests; the house of the heron is chief among them. The high mountains are a refuge for the harts, and so is the rock for the hares. He has made the moon for seasons; the sun knows his going down. Thou appointed the darkness, and there was the night, wherein all the beasts of the forest shall go abroad. Young lions roaring after their prey, and seeking their food from God. The sun arises, and they are gathered together, and they lay them down in their dens.

But man shall go forth unto his work, and to his labour until the evening. How magnified are Thy works, O Lord. In wisdom hast Thou made them all; the earth is filled with Thy creation. So is this great and spacious sea, therein are things creeping innumerable, small living creatures with the great. There go the ships; there this dragon, whom Thou hast made to play therein. All things wait on Thee, to give them their food in due season; when Thou gavest it to them, they shall gather it. When Thou opened Thy hand, all things shall be filled with goodness; when Thou turned away Thy face, they shall be troubled. Thou wilt take their spirit, and they shall cease; and to their dust shall they return. Thou wilt send forth Thy Spirit, and they shall be created; and Thou shalt renew the face of the earth.

Let the glory of the Lord be unto the ages; the Lord shall rejoice in His works. Who looks on the earth and makes it tremble, Who touches the mountains and they smoke. I shall sing unto the Lord throughout my life, I shall chant to my God for as long as I have my being. May my words be sweet unto Him, and I shall rejoice in the Lord. O that sinners would cease from the earth, and they that work iniquity, that they should be no more. Bless the Lord, O my soul. The sun knows his going down, Thou appointed the darkness, and there was the night. How magnified are Thy works, O Lord. In wisdom hast Thou made them all.

After The Psalm

Glory be to the Father and to the Son and to the Holy Spirit;
Both now and forever, and unto the ages of ages. Amen.

Halleluiah, Halleluiah, Halleluiah. Glory to Thee, O God. **(x3)**

The Great Litany

Deacon: In peace, let us pray to the Lord.

People: *Lord, have mercy.*

Deacon: For the peace from above, and for the salvation of our souls, let us pray to the Lord.

People: *Lord, have mercy.*

Deacon: For the peace of the whole world, for the good estate of the holy churches of God, and for the union of all men, let us pray to the Lord.

People: *Lord, have mercy.*

Deacon: For this Holy House, and for those who with faith, reverence, and fear of God, enter therein, let us pray to the Lord.

People: *Lord, have mercy.*

Deacon: For our father and Archbishop Nikitas, for the venerable Priesthood, the Diaconate in Christ, for all the clergy and the people, let us pray to the Lord.

People: *Lord, have mercy.*

Deacon: For Her Majesty Elizabeth the Queen, for the First Minister, for all civil authorities, and for our Armed Forces, let us pray to the Lord.

People: *Lord, have mercy.*

Deacon: That He shall aid them and grant them victory over every enemy and adversary, let us pray to the Lord.

People: *Lord, have mercy.*

Deacon: For this city, and for every city and land, and for the faithful who dwell therein, let us pray to the Lord.

People: *Lord, have mercy.*

Deacon: For healthful seasons, for abundance of the fruits of the earth, and for peaceful times, let us pray to the Lord.

People: *Lord, have mercy.*

Deacon: For travellers by sea, by land, and by air; for the sick and the suffering; for captives and their salvation, let us pray to the Lord.

People: *Lord, have mercy.*

Deacon: For our deliverance from all tribulation, wrath, danger, and necessity, let us pray to the Lord.

People: *Lord, have mercy.*

Deacon: Help us; save us; have mercy on us; and keep us, O God, by Thy grace.

People: *Lord, have mercy.*

Deacon: Calling to remembrance our all holy, immaculate, most blessed and glorious Lady Theotokos and ever virgin Mary, with all the Saints: let us commend ourselves and each other, and all our life unto Christ our God.

People: *To Thee, O Lord.*

Priest: For to Thou art due all glory, honour, and worship: to the Father, and to the Son, and to the Holy Spirit; Both now and forever and unto the ages of ages.

People: *Amen.*

Psalm 140

Chorus: Lord, I have cried to Thee: hear me. Hear me, O Lord.

Lord, I have cried to Thee: hear me. Receive the voice of my prayer.

When I call upon Thee, hear me, O Lord. Let my prayer arise as incense in Thy sight,

And let the lifting up of my hands be an evening sacrifice. Hear me, O Lord.

Kekragarion

Sticheroi From Psalm 140

• Set, O Lord, a watch before my mouth, and a door of enclosure round about my lips.

• Incline not my heart to words of evil, to make excuses for sins.

• Those that work iniquity; I shall not join with their number.

• The righteous man shall chasten me with mercy and reprove me; as for the oil of the sinner, let it not anoint my head.

• For yet more is my prayer in the presence of their pleasures; their judges have been swallowed up by the rock.

• They shall hear my words, for they be sweetened; as a clod of earth is broken upon the earth, so have their bones been scattered into hades.

• To Thee O Lord are mine eyes. In Thee have I hoped; take not my soul away.

• Keep me from the snare which they have laid for me, and from the stumbling blocks of them that work iniquity.

• The sinners shall fall into their own net; I am alone until I pass by.

Sticheroi From Psalm 141

- With my voice to the Lord have I cried, with my voice have I made supplication.

- I shall pour out before Him my supplications; my afflictions shall I declare before Him.

- When my spirit was fainting within me, then Thou knewest my paths.

- In this way wherein I have walked they hid for me a snare.

- I looked on my right hand, and beheld, and there was none that knew me.

- Flight has failed me, and there is none that watches out for my soul.

- I cried to Thee, O Lord; I said: Thou art my hope, my portion in the land of the living.

- Attend unto my supplication, for I am brought very low.

- Deliver me from them that persecute me, for they are stronger than I.

- Bring my soul out of prison. That I may confess Thy name.

- The righteous shall patiently wait for me until Thou shalt reward me.

Sticheroi From Psalm 129

- Out of the depths have I cried unto Thee, O Lord. O Lord, hear my voice.

- Let Thine ears be attentive to the voice of my supplication.

- 6. **Chorus:** *If Thou should mark iniquities, O Lord; O Lord, who shall stand? For with Thee there is forgiveness.*

Reader: Come, let us rejoice in the Lord, proclaiming the present mystery; for He hath broken the middle wall of partition, and the flaming spear shall turn about, and the Cherubim shall admit all to the Tree of Life. As for me, I shall return to enjoy the bliss of Paradise from which I was driven away before, by reason of iniquity; for the likeness of the Father, and the Person of His eternity, which it is impossible to change, hath taken the likeness of a servant, coming from a Mother who hath not known wedlock; free from transubstantiation, since He remained as He was, true God, and took what had not been, having become Man for His love of mankind. Wherefore, let us lift our voices unto Him crying, O Thou Who wast born of the Virgin, O God, have mercy upon us.

- 5. **Chorus:** *For Thy name's sake have I patiently waited for Thee, O Lord; my soul has patiently waited for Thy word, my soul has hoped in the Lord.*

Reader: Come, let us rejoice in the Lord, proclaiming the present mystery; for He hath broken the middle wall of partition, and the flaming spear shall turn about, and the Cherubim shall admit all to the Tree of Life. As for me, I shall return to enjoy the bliss of Paradise from which I was driven away before, by reason of iniquity; for the likeness of the Father, and the Person of His eternity, which it is impossible to change, hath taken the likeness of a servant, coming from a Mother who hath not known wedlock; free from transubstantiation, since He remained as He was, true God, and took what had not been, having become Man for His love of mankind. Wherefore, let us lift our voices unto Him crying, O Thou Who wast born of the Virgin, O God, have mercy upon us.

• 4. *Chorus:* *From the morning watch until night, from the morning watch let Israel hope in the Lord.*

Reader: When the Lord Jesus was born of the holy Virgin, the whole creation was lighted, the shepherds keeping watch, the Magi worshipping, the angels praising, and Herod trembling; for the God and Saviour of our souls hath appeared in the flesh.

• 3. *Chorus:* *For with the Lord there is mercy, and with Him is plenteous redemption; and He shall redeem Israel out of all his iniquities.*

Reader: When the Lord Jesus was born of the holy Virgin, the whole creation was lighted, the shepherds keeping watch, the Magi worshipping, the angels praising, and Herod trembling; for the God and Saviour of our souls hath appeared in the flesh.

Sticheroi From Psalm 116

• 2. *Chorus:* *O praise the Lord, all you nations; praise Him, all you peoples.*

Reader: Thy kingdom, O Christ God, is a kingdom of all ages; and Thy rule is from generation to generation; for Thou Who wast incarnate of the Holy Spirit and became Man from Mary the ever Virgin, hast caused a light to shine on us by Thy presence, O Christ God; O Light of Light, O Radiance of the Father, Thou hast illuminated all creation; and every breath doth praise Thee, O Likeness of the glory of the Father. Wherefore, O everlasting God, Who art before eternity, Who didst shine forth from the Virgin, O God, have mercy upon us.

• 1. *Chorus:* *For He has made His mercy to prevail over us, and the truth of the Lord abides forever.*

Reader: What shall we render to Thee, O Christ, for that Thou didst appear on earth as a man for our sake? Verily, every individual of the creatures Thou didst create shall offer Thee thanksgiving. The angels shall tender Thee praise; the heavens, the star; the Magi, gifts; the shepherds, wonder; the earth, the cave; the wilderness, the manger; and we men, a virgin Mother. Wherefore, O God before the ages, have mercy upon us.

Chorus: *Glory be to the Father and to the Son and to the Holy Spirit.*

Doxasticon For The Nativity Of Christ

Tone 2   *Majesty, gentleness, hope, repentance and sadness.*   *E, F, G, Ab, B, C.*

Reader: When Augustus became supreme ruler of the earth, the multiplicity of rule among men ceased. And when Thou becamest human from the spotless one, the worship of many heathen gods also ceased. Then the cities came under one worldly rule; and the nations believed in one divine supremacy. The nations were enrolled by an order of Caesar; but we believers were enrolled in the name of Thy Divinity, O our incarnate God. Wherefore, great are Thy mercies, glory to Thee.

Chorus: *Both now and forever, and unto the ages of ages. Amen.*

[Whilst:]

The Holy Entrance

Deacon: *(Soto voce)* Let us pray to the Lord. Lord have mercy.

Priest: *(Soto voce)* In the evening and in the morning and at noon we praise Thee, we bless Thee, we give thanks unto Thee, and we pray unto Thee, O Master of all, Lord Who lovest mankind; Direct our prayer as incense before Thee, and incline not our hearts unto words of thought of evil, but deliver us from all who seek after our souls. For unto Thee, O Lord, Lord are our eyes, and in Thee have we hoped. Put us not to shame, O our God. For unto Thee are due all glory, honour and worship, to the Father, the Son and the Holy Spirit, both now and forever, and to the ages of ages.

Deacon: Amen.

[Censing]

Deacon: *(Soto voce)* Master, bless the Holy Entrance.

Priest: *(Soto voce)* Blessed is the Entrance to Thy Holy place; both now and forever, and unto the ages of ages. Amen.

Deacon: *(Aloud)* *Wisdom. Stand up.*

O Gladsome Light

O Gladsome Light of the holy glory of the immortal Father; Heavenly holy, blessed Jesus Christ.

Now that we have come to the setting of the sun, and behold the Evening Light.

We praise God; Father, Son and Holy Spirit.

For meet it is at all time to worship Thee, with voices of praise;

O Son of God and Giver of Life. Therefore all the world doth glorify Thee.

THE FIRST SERIES OF OLD TESTAMENT READINGS
The First Passage

Deacon: Wisdom.

Reader: The reading is from the book of Genesis. (1:1-13).

Deacon: Let us attend.

Reader: In the beginning, God created the heavens and the earth. The earth was without form and void, and darkness was upon the face of the deep; and the Spirit of God was moving over the face of the waters. And God said, "Let there be light"; and there was light. And God saw that the light was good; and God separated the light from the darkness. God called the light Day, and the darkness he called Night. And there was evening and there was morning, one day. And God said, "Let there be a firmament in the midst of the waters, and let it separate the waters from the waters." And God made the firmament and separated the waters which were under the firmament from the waters which were above the firmament. And it was so. And God called the firmament Heaven. And there was evening and there was morning, a second day. And God said, "Let the waters under the heavens be gathered together into one place, and let the dry land appear." And it was so. God called the dry land Earth, and the waters that were gathered together he called Seas. And God saw that it was good. And God said, "Let the earth put forth vegetation, plants yielding seed, and fruit trees bearing fruit in which is their seed, each according to its kind, upon the earth." And it was so. The earth brought forth vegetation, plants yielding seed according to their own kinds, and trees bearing fruit in which is their seed, each according to its kind. And God saw that it was good. And there was evening and there was morning, a third day.

The Second Passage

Deacon: Wisdom.

Reader: The reading is from the book of Numbers. (24:2-3, 5-9, 17-18).

Deacon: Let us attend.

Reader: The Spirit of God came upon Balaam, and he took up his discourse, and said, How fair are your tents, O Jacob, your encampments, O Israel. Like valleys that stretch afar, like gardens beside a river, like aloes that the Lord has planted, like cedar trees beside the waters. Water shall flow from his buckets, and his seed shall be in many waters, his king shall be higher than Agag, and his kingdom shall be exalted. God brings him out of Egypt; he has as it were the horns of the wild ox, he shall eat up the nations of his adversaries, and shall break their bones in pieces, and pierce them through with his arrows. He couched, he lay down like a lion, and like a lioness; who shall rouse him up? Blessed be everyone who blesses you, and cursed be everyone who curses you. I see him, but not now; I behold him, but not nigh: a star shall come forth out of Jacob, and a sceptre shall rise out of Israel; it shall crush the forehead of Moab, and break down all the sons of Sheth. Edom shall be dispossessed, Seir also, his enemies, shall be dispossessed, while Israel does valiantly.

The Third Passage

Deacon: Wisdom.

Reader: The reading from the Prophecy of Micah. (4:6-7, 5:2-4).

Deacon: Let us attend.

Reader: In that day, says the Lord, I shall assemble the lame and gather those who have been driven away, and those whom I have afflicted; and the lame I shall make the remnant; and those who were cast off, a strong nation; and the Lord shall reign over them in Mount Zion from this time forth and for evermore. But you, O Bethlehem Ephratha, who are little to be among the clans of Judah, from you shall come forth for Me one who is to be ruler in Israel, whose origin is from of old, from ancient days. Therefore, he shall give them up until the time when she who is in travail has brought forth; then the rest of his brethren shall return to the people of Israel. And he shall stand and feed his flock in the strength of the Lord, in the majesty of the name of the Lord his God. And they shall dwell secure, for now he shall be great to the ends of the earth.

Troparion Of The Nativity

Tone 6   Rich texture, funereal character, sorrowful tone.   *D, Eb, F##, G, A, Bb, C##, D.*

Chorus: *Disguised, O Saviour, Thou wast born in a cave;*

But Heaven proclaimed Thee to all, taking for its mouth a star.

Reader: And it offered Thee the Magi worshipping Thee in faith.

Wherefore, with them, have mercy upon us.

Stichoi From Psalm 86

Tone 6   Rich texture, funereal character, sorrowful tone.   D, Eb, F##, G, A, Bb, C##, D.

Chorus: *Whose foundation is in the holy mountains;*

The Lord loveth the gates of Zion more than all the dwellings of Jacob.

Reader: And it offered Thee the Magi worshipping Thee in faith. Wherefore, with them, have mercy upon us.

Chorus: *Glorious things are said of thee, O City of God. I shall be mindful of Rahab and Babylon knowing me.*

Reader: And it offered Thee the Magi worshipping Thee in faith. Wherefore, with them, have mercy upon us.

Chorus: *Behold, O strange nations, Philistia, Tyre and Ethiopia.*

Reader: And it offered Thee the Magi worshipping Thee in faith. Wherefore, with them, have mercy upon us.

Chorus: *Those were born there. And of the mother Zion it shall be said:*

"This man and that man is born in her, and the highest Himself hath founded her."

Reader: And it offered Thee the Magi worshipping Thee in faith. Wherefore, with them, have mercy upon us.

Chorus: *The Lord shall tell in His writing of peoples and of princes of them that have been in her;*

The dwelling in thee is as it were of all rejoicing.

Reader: And it offered Thee the Magi worshipping Thee in faith. Wherefore, with them, have mercy upon us.

Chorus: *Glory be to the Father and to the Son and to the Holy Spirit;*

Both now and forever, and unto the ages of ages. Amen.

Troparion Of The Nativity

Tone 6   Rich texture, funereal character, sorrowful tone.   D, Eb, F##, G, A, Bb, C##, D.

Chorus: *Disguised, O Saviour, Thou wast born in a cave;*

But Heaven proclaimed Thee to all, taking for its mouth a star.

Reader: And it offered Thee the Magi worshipping Thee in faith. Wherefore, with them, have mercy upon us.

THE SECOND SERIES OF OLD TESTAMENT READINGS
The First Passage

Deacon: Wisdom.

Reader: The reading from the Prophecy of Isaiah (11:1-10).

Deacon: Let us attend.

Reader: Thus saith the Lord: There shall come forth a shoot from the stump of Jesse, and a branch shall grow out of his roots. And the Spirit of the Lord shall rest upon him, the spirit of wisdom and understanding, the spirit of counsel and might, the spirit of knowledge and the fear of the Lord. And his delight shall be in the fear of the Lord. He shall not judge by what his eyes see, or decide by what his ears hear; but with righteousness he shall judge the poor, and decide with equity for the meek of the earth; and he shall smite the earth with the rod of his mouth, and with the breath of his lips he shall slay the wicked. Righteousness shall be the girdle of his waist, and faithfulness the girdle of his loins. The wolf shall dwell with the lamb, and the leopard shall lie down with the kid, and the calf and the lion and the fatling together, and a little child shall lead them. The cow and the bear shall feed; their young shall lie down together; and the lion shall eat straw like the ox. The sucking child shall play over the hole of the asp, and the weaned child shall put his hand on the adder's den. They shall not hurt or destroy in all of my holy mountain; for the earth shall be full of the knowledge of the Lord as the waters cover the sea. In that day the root of Jesse shall stand as an ensign to the peoples; him shall the nations seek, and his dwellings shall be glorious.

The Second Passage

Deacon: Wisdom.

Reader: The reading from the Prophecy of Jeremiah (Baruch 3:36-4:4).

Deacon: Let us attend.

Reader: This is our God; no other can be compared to Him. He found the whole way to knowledge, and gave it to Jacob His servant and to Israel whom He loved. Afterward He appeared upon earth and lived among men. This is the book of the commandments of God, and the law that endures forever. All who hold fast to it shall live, and those who forsake it shall die. Turn, O Jacob, and take hold of it; walk toward the way of its brightness. Do not give your glory to another or your advantages to an alien people. Happy are we, O Israel, for we know what is pleasing to God.

The Third Passage

Deacon: Wisdom.

Reader: The reading from the Prophecy of Daniel (2:31-36, 44-45).

Deacon: Let us attend.

Reader: Daniel said to Nebuchadnezzar, You saw, O king, and behold, a great image. This image, mighty and of exceeding brightness, stood before you, and its appearance was frightening. The head of this image was of fine gold, its breast and arms of silver, its belly and thighs of bronze, its legs of iron, its feet partly of iron and partly of clay. As you looked, a stone was cut out by no human hand, and it smote the image on its feet of iron and clay, and broke them in pieces; then the iron, the clay, the bronze, the silver, and the gold, all together were broken in pieces, and became like the chaff of the summer threshing floors; and the wind carried them away, so that not a trace of them could be found. But the stone that struck the image became a great mountain and filled the whole earth. This was the dream; now we shall tell the king its interpretation. And in the days of those kings, the God of Heaven shall set up a kingdom which shall never be destroyed, nor shall its sovereignty be left to another people. It shall break in pieces all these kingdoms and bring them to an end, and it shall stand forever; just as you saw that a stone was cut from a mountain by no human hand, and that it broke in pieces the iron, the bronze, the clay, the silver, and the gold. A great God has made known to the king what shall be hereafter. The dream is certain, and its interpretation sure.

Troparion Of The Nativity

Tone 6   Rich texture, funereal character, sorrowful tone.   *D, Eb, F##, G, A, Bb, C##, D.*

Chorus: *Thou hast shone forth from the Virgin, O Christ, noetic Sun of Justice.*

           And a star pointed to Thee, Thou uncontainable One, Who wast contained in a cave.

Reader: And the Magi were led to Thy worship.

           Wherefore, with them, we magnify Thee, O Thou Giver of Life; glory to Thee.

Stichoi From Psalm 92

Tone 6   Rich texture, funereal character, sorrowful tone.   *D, Eb, F##, G, A, Bb, C##, D.*

Chorus: *The Lord is King, He is clothed with majesty.*

           The Lord is clothed with strength and He has girded Himself.

Reader: And the Magi were led to Thy worship.

           Wherefore, with them, we magnify Thee, O Thou Giver of Life; glory to Thee.

Chorus: *For He hath established the world, which shall not be moved. Thy throne is prepared from old.*

Reader: And the Magi were led to Thy worship.

           Wherefore, with them, we magnify Thee, O Thou Giver of Life; glory to Thee.

Chorus: *The floods have lifted up, O Lord; the floods have lifted up their voice.*

           The floods have lifted up their waves, with the noise of many waters.

Reader: And the Magi were led to Thy worship.

           Wherefore, with them, we magnify Thee, O Thou Giver of Life; glory to Thee.

Chorus: *Wonderful are the surges of the sea. Wonderful is the Lord on high.*

           Thy testimonies are become exceedingly credible.

Reader: And the Magi were led to Thy worship.

           Wherefore, with them, we magnify Thee, O Thou Giver of Life; glory to Thee.

Chorus: *Holiness becometh Thy house, O Lord, for evermore.*

Reader: And the Magi were led to Thy worship.

           Wherefore, with them, we magnify Thee, O Thou Giver of Life; glory to Thee.

Chorus: *Glory be to the Father and to the Son and to the Holy Spirit;*

           Both now and forever, and unto the ages of ages. Amen.

Troparion Of The Nativity

Tone 6   Rich texture, funereal character, sorrowful tone.   *D, Eb, F##, G, A, Bb, C##, D.*

Chorus: *Thou hast shone forth from the Virgin, O Christ, noetic Sun of Justice.*

           And a star pointed to Thee, Thou uncontainable One, Who wast contained in a cave.

Reader: And the Magi were led to Thy worship.

           Wherefore, with them, we magnify Thee, O Thou Giver of Life; glory to Thee.

THE THIRD SERIES OF OLD TESTAMENT READINGS

The First Passage

Deacon: Wisdom.

Reader: The reading from the Prophecy of Isaiah (9:6-7).

Deacon: Let us attend.

Reader: For to us a child is born, to us a Son is given; and the government shall be upon His shoulders, and his name shall be called *"Wonderful Counsellor, Mighty God, Everlasting Father, Prince of Peace."* Of the increase of His government and of peace there shall be no end, upon the throne of David, and over His kingdom, to establish it, and to uphold it with justice and with righteousness from this time forth and for evermore. The zeal of the Lord of hosts shall do this.

The Second Passage

Deacon: Wisdom.

Reader: The reading from the Prophecy of Isaiah (7:10-16; 8:1-4, 9-10).

Deacon: Let us attend.

Reader: Again the Lord spoke to Ahaz, saying, *"Ask a sign of the Lord your God; let it be deep as Sheol or high as Heaven."* But Ahaz said, *"I shall not ask, and I shall not put the Lord to the test."* And he said, *"Hear then, O house of David. Is it too little for you to weary men, that you weary my God also? Therefore the Lord Himself shall give you a sign. Behold, a Virgin shall conceive and bear a son, and shall call his name Emmanuel. He shall eat curds and honey when he knows how to refuse the evil and choose the good. For before the child knows how to refuse the evil and choose the good, the land before whose two kings you are in dread shall be deserted."* Then the Lord said to me, *"Take a large tablet and write upon it in common characters, 'Belonging to Maher-shalal-hash-baz.'"* And I had reliable witnesses, Uriah the priest and Zachariah the son of Jeberechiah, to attest for me. And I went to the prophetess, and she conceived and bore a son. Then the Lord said to me, *"Call his name Maher-shalal-hash-baz; for before the child knows how to cry 'My father' or 'My mother,' the wealth of Damascus and the spoil of Samaria shall be carried away before the king of Assyria."* Be broken, you peoples, and be dismayed; give ear, all you far countries; gird yourselves and be dismayed; gird yourselves and be dismayed. Take counsel together, but it shall come to naught; speak a word, but it shall not stand, for God is with us.

The Prayer Of The Trisagion Hymn

Priest *[Quiet]*: O Holy God, Who restest in the Holy Place; Who art hymned by the Seraphim with thrice-Holy cry, and glorified by the Cherubim, and worshiped by every Heavenly Power; Who out of nothingness hast brought all things into being; Who hast created man according to Thine image and likeness and hast adorned him with Thine every gift; Who givest to him that askest wisdom and understanding; Who despisest not the sinner, but hast appointed repentance unto salvation; Who hast vouchsafed unto us, Thy humble and unworthy servants, even in this hour, to stand before the glory of Thy Holy Altar and to offer the worship and praise which are due unto Thee: Thyself, O Master, receive even from the mouth of us sinners the Thrice Holy

Hymn, and visit us in Thy goodness. Pardon us every transgression, both voluntary and involuntary; sanctify our souls and bodies; and grant us to serve Thee in holiness all the days of our life: through the intercessions of the Holy Theotokos and of all the Saints, who from the beginning of the world have been well pleasing unto Thee.

Deacon: Let us pray to the Lord.

People: *Lord, have mercy.*

Priest: For holy art Thou, O our God, and unto Thee do we ascribe glory:

To the Father, and to the Son, and to the Holy Spirit; now and ever...

Deacon: ...and unto the ages of ages.

People: Amen.

Prokeimenon

Deacon: Let us attend. The Prokeimenon.

Reader: The Lord hath said to me: Thou art my Son, this day have I begotten Thee.

People: *The Lord hath said to me: Thou art my Son, this day have I begotten Thee.*

Reader: Ask of Me, and I shall give Thee the Gentiles for Thine inheritance.

People: *The Lord hath said to me: Thou art my Son, this day have I begotten Thee.*

Reader: The Lord hath said to me: Thou art my Son | this day have I begotten Thee.

The Epistle

Deacon: Wisdom.

Reader: The reading from the Epistle of St. Paul to the Hebrews (1:1-12).

Deacon: Let us attend.

Reader: Brethren, in many and various ways, God spoke of old to our fathers by the prophets; but in these last days He has spoken to us by a Son, Whom He appointed the heir of all things, through Whom also He created the world. He reflects the glory of God and bears the very stamp of His nature, upholding the universe by His word of power. When He had made purification for sins, He sat down at the right hand of the Majesty on high, having become as much superior to angels, as the name He has obtained is more excellent than theirs. For to what angel did God ever say, "Thou art My Son, today I have begotten Thee"? Or again, "I shall be to Him a Father, and He shall be to Me a son"? And again, when He brings the First-born into the world, He says, "Let all God's angels worship Him." Of the angels He says, "Who makes His angels winds, and His servants flames of fire." But of the Son He says, "Thy throne, O God, is forever and ever, the righteous sceptre is the sceptre of Thy kingdom. Thou hast loved righteousness and hated lawlessness; therefore God, Thy God, has anointed Thee with the oil of gladness beyond Thy comrades." And, "Thou, O Lord, didst found the earth in the beginning, and the heavens are the work of Thy hands; they shall perish, but Thou remainest; they shall all grow old like a garment, like a mantle Thou wilt roll them up, and they shall be changed. But Thou art the same, and Thy years shall never end."

Priest: Peace be to thee that readest.

Reader: And with thy spirit.

The Halleluiarion

People: *Halleluiah, Halleluiah, Halleluiah.*

Reader: The Lord said unto my Lord: sit Thou at My right hand; Until I make Thine enemies Thy footstool.

People: *Halleluiah, Halleluiah, Halleluiah.*

Reader: The Lord shall send Thee a rod of strength out of Zion.

People: *Halleluiah, Halleluiah, Halleluiah.*

Reader: From the womb before the morning star have I begotten Thee.

People: *Halleluiah, Halleluiah, Halleluiah.*

The Gospel

Deacon: Wisdom. Attend. Let us hear the Holy Gospel.

Priest: Peace be with you.

People: *And with thy spirit.*

Priest: The reading from the Holy Gospel according to Luke (2:1-20).

People: *Glory to Thee, O Lord, glory to Thee.*

Deacon: Let us attend.

Priest: In those days a decree went out from Caesar Augustus that all the world should be enrolled. This was the first enrolment, when Quirinius was governor of Syria. And all went to be enrolled, each to his own city. And Joseph also went up from Galilee, from the city of Nazareth, to Judea, to the city of David, which is called Bethlehem, because he was of the house and lineage of David, to be enrolled with Mary, his betrothed, who was with child. And while they were there, the time came for her to be delivered. And she gave birth to her First-born Son and wrapped Him in swaddling cloths, and laid Him in a manger, because there was no place for them in the inn. And in that region there were shepherds out in the field, keeping watch over their flock by night. And an angel of the Lord appeared to them, and the glory of the Lord shone around them, and they were filled with fear. And the angel said to them, "Be not afraid; for behold, I bring you good news of a great joy which shall come to all the people; for to you is born this day in the city of David a Saviour, Who is Christ the Lord. And this shall be a sign for you: you shall find a babe wrapped in swaddling cloths and lying in a manger." And suddenly there was with the angel a multitude of the Heavenly host praising God and saying, "Glory to God in the highest, and on earth peace among men with whom He is pleased." When the angels went away from them into Heaven, the shepherds said to one another, "Let us go over to Bethlehem and see this thing that has happened, which the Lord has made known to us." And they went with haste, and found Mary and Joseph, and the babe lying in a manger. And when they saw it they made known the saying which had been told them concerning this child; and all who heard it wondered at what the shepherds told them. But Mary kept all these things, pondering them in her heart. And the shepherds returned, glorifying and praising God for all they had heard and seen, as it had been told them.

People: *Glory to Thee, O Lord, glory to Thee.*

The Litany Of Fervent Supplication

Deacon: Let us all say with our whole soul, and with our whole mind let us say:

People: *Lord, have mercy.*

Deacon: Lord Almighty, God of our Fathers, we pray Thee, hearest and have mercy.

People: *Lord, have mercy.*

Deacon: Have mercy on us, O God, according to Thy great mercy, we pray Thee; hear us and have mercy.

People: *Lord, have mercy.* **(x3)**

Deacon: Also we pray for our Archbishop Nikitas.

People: *Lord, have mercy.* **(x3)**

Deacon: For our Sovereign Lady, Queen Elizabeth, the Royal family, our Welsh Assembly Government, and all in authority, let us pray to the Lord.

People: *Lord, have mercy.* **(x3)**

Deacon: Also we pray for mercy, life, peace, health, salvation, visitation, pardon and forgiveness of sins for the servants of God, all devout and Orthodox Christians, those who dwell in or visit this city or town and parish, the wardens and members of this church and their families and all who have asked for our prayers, unworthy though we are.

People: *Lord, have mercy.* **(x3)**

Deacon: Also we pray for the blessed and ever remembered founders of this holy church, and for all our brothers and sisters who have gone to their rest before us, and who lie here asleep in the true faith; and for the Orthodox everywhere *[and the servants of God N and N – (names given before the service)]* and that they may be pardoned all their offences, both voluntary and involuntary.

People: *Lord, have mercy.* **(x3)**

Deacon: Also we pray for those who bring offerings, those who care for the beauty of this holy and venerable house, for those who labour in its service, for those who sing, and for the people here present, who await Thy great and rich mercy.

People: *Lord, have mercy.* **(x3)**

Priest: For Thou, O God, art merciful and love mankind, and to Thee we givest glory, to the Father, the Son and the Holy Spirit, both now and forever, and unto the ages of ages.

People: *Amen.*

The Evening Prayer

Reader: Vouchsafe, O Lord, to keep us this evening without sin. Blessed art Thou, O Lord, the God of our fathers, and praised and glorified is Thy name unto the ages. Amen.

Let Thy mercy, O Lord, be upon us, according as we have hoped in Thee.

Blessed art Thou, O Lord, teach me Thy statutes.
Blessed art Thou, O Master, give me understanding of Thy statutes.

Blessed art Thou, O Holy One, enlighten me by Thy statutes.

O Lord, Thy mercy endures forever; disdain not the work of Thy hands. To Thee is due praise, to Thee is due song, to Thee is due glory, to the Father, and to the Son, and to the Holy Spirit; both now and forever, and unto the ages of ages. Amen.

The Litany Of Supplication

Deacon: Let us complete our evening prayer unto the Lord.

People: *Lord, have mercy.*

Deacon: Help us; save us; have mercy on us; and keep us, O God, by Thy grace.

People: *Lord, have mercy.*

Deacon: That the whole evening may be perfect, holy, peaceful and sinless, let us ask of the Lord.

People: *Grant this, O Lord.*

Deacon: An angel of peace, a faithful guide, a guardian of our souls and bodies, let us ask of the Lord.

People: *Grant this, O Lord.*

Deacon: Pardon and remission of our sins and transgressions, let us ask of the Lord.

People: *Grant this, O Lord.*

Deacon: All things good and profitable for our souls and peace for the world, let us ask of the Lord.

People: *Grant this, O Lord.*

Deacon: That we may complete the remaining time of our life in peace and repentance, let us ask of the Lord.

People: *Grant this, O Lord.*

Deacon: A Christian ending to our life, painless, blameless, peaceful, and a good defence before the fearful judgement seat of Christ, let us ask of the Lord.

People: *Grant this, O Lord.*

Deacon: Calling to remembrance our all holy, immaculate, most blessed and glorious Lady Theotokos and ever virgin Mary, with all the Saints: let us commend ourselves and one another, and all our life to Christ our God.

People: *To Thee, O Lord.*

Priest: For Thou art a good God and lovest mankind, and to Thee we ascribe glory: to the Father, and to the Son, and to the Holy Spirit; both now and forever, and to the ages of ages.

People: *Amen.*

The Peace

Priest: Peace be with you.

People: *And with thy spirit.*

Deacon: Let us bow down our heads unto the Lord.

People: *To Thee, O Lord.*

Priest: O Lord our God, Who did bow the heavens and come down for the salvation of mankind: Look upon Thy servants and Thine inheritance; for to Thee, the fearful Judge Who yet loves mankind, have Thine servants bowed their heads and submissively inclined their necks, awaiting not help from men but entreating Thy mercy and looking confidently for Thy salvation. Guard them at all times, both during this present evening and in the approaching night, from every foe, from all adverse powers of the devil, and from vain thoughts and from evil imaginations. Blessed and glorified be the might of Thy kingdom: of the Father, and of the Son, and of the Holy Spirit; both now and forever, and unto the ages of ages.

People: Amen.

Aposticha

Reader: **1.** O people, let us celebrate the forefeast of the Nativity of Christ. Raising our minds on high, let us go to Bethlehem in spirit. With the eyes of the soul, let us gaze upon the Virgin as she hastens to the cave to give birth to our God, the Lord of all. When he beheld this wonder, Joseph thought he saw a mortal wrapped as a baby in swaddling clothes; but from all that came to pass, he understood that it was the true God, Who grants the world great mercy.

Chorus: *God comes from Teman; the Holy One from the mountain overshadowed by the forest.*

Reader: **2.** O people, let us celebrate the forefeast of the Nativity of Christ. Raising our minds on high, let us go to Bethlehem in spirit. With the eyes of the soul, let us gaze upon the Virgin as she hastens to the cave to give birth to our God, the Lord of all. When he beheld this wonder, Joseph thought he saw a mortal wrapped as a baby in swaddling clothes; but from all that came to pass, he understood that it was the true God, Who grants the world great mercy.

Chorus: *O Lord, I have heard Your renown and feared, O Lord, Your work.*

Reader: **3.** Hear, O heaven. Give ear, O earth. Behold the Son and Word of God the Father comes forth to be born of a Maiden who has not known man, by the good pleasure of the Father and the work of the Holy Spirit. Make ready, O Bethlehem. Throw open your gates, O Eden. For He Who exists forever comes to be that which He was not; and He Who formed all creation, now takes a form, granting the world great mercy.

Chorus: *Glory be to the Father, and to the Son, and to the Holy Spirit;*
Both now and forever, and unto the ages of ages. Amen.

Reader: **4.** Make ready, O cave, to receive the Mother who bears Christ within her womb. O manger, receive the Word who destroyed the sins of mankind. O shepherds, keep watch and then bear witness to the awesome wonder. O Magi, come from Persia and bring your gifts to the King. For the Lord has appeared from a Virgin Mother; yet she bowed to Him as a servant and spoke to Him within her heart saying, *"How were You conceived in me? How did you grow in me, O Jesus, my Saviour and my God?"*

Hymn Of Simeon The God Receiver

Reader: Lord, now lettest Thou Thy servant depart in peace, according to Thy word, for mine eyes have seen Thy salvation, which Thou hast prepared before the face of all peoples; a light of revelation for the Gentiles, and the glory of Thy people Israel.

Trisagion Prayers

Holy God, Holy Mighty, Holy Immortal, have mercy on us. **(x3)**

Glory be to the Father, and to the Son, and to the Holy Spirit;
Both now and forever, and unto the ages of ages. Amen.

O Most Holy Trinity, have mercy on us.

O Lord, cleanse us from our sins.

O Master, pardon our iniquities.

O Holy One, visit and heal our infirmities, for Thy names sake.

Lord have mercy. **(x3)**

Glory be to the Father and to the Son and to the Holy Spirit;
Both now and forever, and unto the ages of ages. Amen.

People: *Our Father, Who art in Heaven, hallowed be Thy Name. Thy Kingdom come, Thy will be done, on earth as it is in Heaven. Give us this day our daily bread, and forgive us our trespasses, as we forgive those who trespass against us; and lead us not into temptation, but deliver us from the evil one.*

Priest: For Thine is the kingdom, the power, and the glory, of the Father, and the Son and the Holy Spirit, both now and ever, and to the ages of ages.

People: *Amen.*

Troparion Of Paramony

Reader: At that time, since Mary was of the house of David, she registered with the Venerable Joseph in Bethlehem. She was with child, having conceived virginally. Her time was come and they could find no room in the inn, but the cave seemed a joyful palace for the Queen. Christ is born to renew the likeness that been lost of old.

The Dismissal

Deacon: Wisdom.

People: *Holy Father, bless.*

Priest: Christ our God, the Existing One, is blessed, always, now and forever, and unto the ages of ages.

People: *Amen.*

Reader: Preserve, O god, the holy Orthodox faith and all Orthodox Christians, unto the ages of ages.

People: *Amen.*

Priest: Most holy Theotokos, save us.

Reader: Greater in honour than the Cherubim and beyond compare more glorious than the Seraphim; without corruption thou gavest birth to God the Word, truly the Theotokos, we magnify thee.

Priest: Glory to Thee, O Christ, our God and our hope, glory to Thee.

Reader: *Glory be to the Father, and to the Son, and to the Holy Spirit;*

Both now and forever, and unto the ages of ages. Amen.

People: *Amen.*

Lord, have mercy. **(x3)**

Holy Father, bless.

Priest: May He who rose from the dead, Christ our true God, through the prayers of His most holy Mother, by the power of the precious and life giving Cross, through the protection of the honoured, Bodiless powers of Heaven, through the intercessions of the honoured, glorious prophet, forerunner and baptist John, of the holy, all praised and glorious Apostles, of the holy, glorious and triumphant Martyrs, of our venerable and God bearing Fathers and Mothers who have shone forth in the ascetic life, of the holy and righteous ancestors of God, Joachim and Anna, of *[patronal saint(s)]* to whom the church is dedicated, of *[Saint N]* whose memory we celebrate today, and of all the Saints, have mercy on us and save us, for He is good and loves mankind.

People: *Amen.*

Priest: Through the prayers of our holy Fathers; O Lord Jesus Christ our God; have mercy on us and save us.

People: *Amen.*

An akathist is a service to honour God, Mary, any saint, the patron of your parish, angels including your guardian angel, and so many more. Each akathist is a long poem to the person in particular and include much detail. Hence it is not really possible to substitute one saints name into the akathist for another, the whole akathist must be found. As there are thousands of saints it is not possible to include an akathist for all of them. This section includes just a handful of akathists that shall inevitably used in the course of a year and so give some advance in seeking out and recognising an akathist for your own need.

An akathist may also be termed a canon. This is a piece of music that has calls and responses. In this way an akathist has sung parts and an oft repeated refrain to whomsoever the akathist is named.

An akathist may comprise either of two forms: a set of eight odes or a less chaptered, more list like variety. The sharp eyed shall notice that each of the second type of akathist comprises nine odes (or songs), but ode 2 is always missing. Ode 2 only appears in the Akathist of St Andrew of Crete. It is a reminder that the subject matter of that ode 2 is so deep that other akathists should not infringe upon the gravity of it.

The word "akathist" is from the Greek "kathisma" meaning "sitting" and "a" meaning "without"; so "without sitting". "Kathisma" also refers to the seat or throne of a bishop, hence "cathedra" and also the church building wherein the bishop resides "cathedral".

Traditionally an Orthodox church has seats or benches around the outer walls; these are for the use of the elderly, infirm, pregnant ladies etc. The congregation is normally expected to stand in the presence of our King and Lord – just as one is expected to do in the presence of human royalty. There are certain sections during where anyone may sit down, such as the "Kathisma". These are groups of Psalms. Hence one can see that during an akathist we are instructed to stand. During the oft repeated refrains we cross ourselves and bow, this is difficult if you are not standing.

It is not necessary to learn Ancient Greek to fulfil the role of Reader. However, if possible it would be of benefit to learn the translations of the individual Greek words used herein (mostly for variables), as this shall help to understand the function that they serve.

Akathist To Our Sweetest Lord Jesus Christ

Kontakion 1

Warrior Chieftain and Lord, Vanquisher of hell, I Thy creature and servant offer Thee songs of praise, for Thou hast delivered me from eternal death. But as Thou hast unutterable loving kindness, free me from every danger, as I cry: Jesus, Son of God, have mercy on me.

Oikos 1

Creator of Angels and Lord of Hosts. As of old Thou didst open ear and tongue to the deaf and dumb, likewise open now my perplexed mind and tongue to the praise of Thy Most Holy Name, that I may cry to Thee:

Jesus All Wonderful, Angels' Astonishment.

Jesus All Powerful, Forefathers' Deliverance.

Jesus All Sweetest, Patriarchs' Exaltation.

Jesus All Glorious, Kings' Stronghold.

Jesus All Beloved, Prophets' Fulfilment.

Jesus All Marvellous, Martyrs' Strength.

Jesus All Peaceful, Monks' Joy.

Jesus All Gracious, Presbyters' Sweetness.

Jesus All Merciful, Fasters' Abstinence.

Jesus All Tenderest, Saints' Rejoicing.

Jesus All Honourable, Virgins' Chastity.

Jesus everlasting, Sinners' Salvation.

People: *Jesus, Son of God, have mercy on me.*

Kontakion 2

As when seeing the widow weeping bitterly, O Lord, Thou wast moved with pity, and didst raise her son from the dead as he was being carried to burial, likewise have pity on me, O Lover of men, and raise my soul, deadened by sins, as I cry, Halleluiah.

People: *Halleluiah.*

Oikos 2

Seeking to know what passes knowledge, Philip asked: "Lord, show us the Father"; and Thou didst answer him: "Have I been so long with you and yet hast thou not known that I am in the Father and the Father in Me?" Likewise, O Inconceivable One, with fear I cry to Thee:

Jesus, Eternal God.

Jesus, All Powerful King.

Jesus, Long suffering Master.

Jesus, All Merciful Saviour.

Jesus, my gracious Guardian.

Jesus, cleanse my sins.

Jesus, take away my iniquities.

Jesus, pardon my unrighteousness.

Jesus, my Hope, forsake me not.

Jesus, my Helper, reject me not.

Jesus, my Creator, forget me not.

Jesus, my Shepherd, lose me not.

People: *Jesus, Son of God, have mercy on me.*

Kontakion 3

Thou Who didst endue with power from on high Thy Apostles who tarried in Jerusalem, O Jesus, clothe also me, stripped bare of all good work, with the warmth of Thy Holy Spirit, and grant that with love I may sing to Thee: Halleluiah.

People: *Halleluiah.*

Oikos 3

In the abundance of Thy mercy, O Jesus, Thou hast called publicans and sinners and infidels. Now despise me not who am like them, but as precious myrrh accept this song:

Jesus, Invincible Power.

Jesus, Infinite Mercy.

Jesus, Radiant Beauty.

Jesus, Unspeakable Love.

Jesus, Son of the Living God.

Jesus, have mercy on me, a sinner.

Jesus, hear me who was conceived in iniquity.

Jesus, cleanse me who was born in sin.

Jesus, teach me who am worthless.

Jesus, enlighten my darkness.

Jesus, purify me who am unclean.

Jesus, restore me, a prodigal.

People: *Jesus, Son of God, have mercy on me.*

Kontakion 4

Having an interior storm of doubting thoughts, Peter was sinking. But beholding Thee, O Jesus, in the flesh walking on the waters, he confessed Thee to be the true God; and receiving the hand of salvation, he cried: Halleluiah.

People: *Halleluiah.*

Oikos 4

When the blind man heard Thee, O Lord, passing by on the way, he cried: Jesus, Son of David, have mercy on me. And Thou didst call him and open his eyes. Likewise enlighten the spiritual eyes of my heart with Thy love as I cry to Thee and say:

Jesus, Creator of those on high.

Jesus, Redeemer of those below.

Jesus, Vanquisher of the powers of hell.

Jesus, Adorner of every creature.

Jesus, Comforter of my soul.

Jesus, Enlightener of my mind.

Jesus, Gladness of my heart.

Jesus, Health of my body.

Jesus, my Saviour, save me.

Jesus, my Light, enlighten me.

Jesus, deliver me from all torments.

Jesus, save me despite my unworthiness.

People: *Jesus, Son of God, have mercy on me.*

Kontakion 5

As of old Thou didst redeem us from the curse of the law by Thy Divinely shed Blood, O Jesus, likewise rescue me from the snares in which the serpent has entangled us through the passions of the flesh, through lustful suggestions and evil despondency, as we cry to Thee: Halleluiah.

People: *Halleluiah.*

Oikos 5

Seeing the Creator in human form and knowing Him to be their Lord, the Hebrew children sought to please Him with branches, crying: Hosanna. But we offer Thee a song, saying:

Jesus, True God.

Jesus, Son of David.

Jesus, Glorious King.

Jesus, Innocent Lamb.

Jesus, Wonderful Shepherd.

Jesus, Guardian of my infancy.

Jesus, Nourisher of my youth.

Jesus, Praise of my old age.

Jesus, my Hope at death.

Jesus, my Life after death.

Jesus, my Comfort at Thy Judgement.

Jesus, my Desire, let me not then be ashamed.

People: *Jesus, Son of God, have mercy on me.*

Kontakion 6

In fulfilment of the words and message of the inspired Prophets, O Jesus, Thou didst appear on earth, and Thou Who art uncontainable didst dwell with men. Thenceforth, being healed through Thy wounds, we learned to sing: Halleluiah.

People: *Halleluiah.*

Oikos 6

When the light of Thy truth dawned on the world, devilish delusion was driven away; for the idols, O our Saviour, have fallen, unable to endure Thy strength. But we who have received salvation, cry to Thee:

Jesus, the Truth, dispelling falsehood.

Jesus, the Light above all lights.

Jesus, the King, surpassing all in strength.

Jesus, God, constant in mercy.

Jesus, Bread of Life, fill me who am hungry.

Jesus, Source of Knowledge, refresh me who am thirsty.

Jesus, Garment of Gladness, clothe my nakedness.

Jesus, Veil of Joy, cover my unworthiness.

Jesus, Giver to those who ask, give me sorrow for my sins.

Jesus, Finder of those who seek, find my soul.

Jesus, Opener to those who knock, open my wretched heart.

Jesus, Redeemer of sinners, wash away my sins.

People: *Jesus, Son of God, have mercy on me.*

Kontakion 7

Desiring to unveil the mystery hidden from all ages, Thou wast led as a sheep to the slaughter, O Jesus, and as a lamb before its shearer. But as God Thou didst rise from the dead and didst ascend with glory to Heaven, and along with Thyself Thou didst raise us who cry: Halleluiah.

People: *Halleluiah.*

Oikos 7

The Creator has shown us a marvellous Creature, Who took flesh without seed from a Virgin, rose from the tomb without breaking the seal, and entered bodily the Apostles' room when the doors were shut. Therefore, marvelling at this we sing:

Jesus, Uncontainable Word.

Jesus, Inscrutable Intelligence.

Jesus, Incomprehensible Power.

Jesus, Inconceivable Wisdom.

Jesus, Undepictable Deity.

Jesus, Boundless Dominion.

Jesus, Invincible Kingdom.

Jesus, Unending Sovereignty.

Jesus, Supreme Strength.

Jesus, Eternal Power.

Jesus, my Creator, have compassion on me.

Jesus, my Saviour, save me.

People: *Jesus, Son of God, have mercy on me.*

Kontakion 8

Seeing God wondrously incarnate, let us shun the vain world and set our mind on things divine; for God descended to earth to raise to Heaven us who cry to Him: Halleluiah.

People: *Halleluiah.*

Oikos 8

Being both below and above, Thou didst never falter, O Thou immeasurable One, when Thou didst voluntarily suffer for us, and by Thy death our death didst put to death, and by Thy Resurrection didst grant life to those who sing:

Jesus, Sweetness of the heart.

Jesus, Strength of the body.

Jesus, Purity of the soul.

Jesus, Brightness of the mind.

Jesus, Gladness of the conscience.

Jesus, Sure Hope.

Jesus, Memory Eternal.

Jesus, High Praise.

Jesus, my most exalted Glory.

Jesus, my Desire, reject me not.

Jesus, my Shepherd, recover me.

Jesus, my Saviour, save me.

People: *Jesus, Son of God, have mercy on me.*

Kontakion 9

The Angelic Hosts in Heaven glorify unceasingly Thy most holy Name, O Jesus, crying: Holy, Holy, Holy. But we sinners on earth, with our frail voices cry: Halleluiah.

People: *Halleluiah.*

Oikos 9

We see most eloquent orators voiceless as fish when they must speak of Thee, O Jesus our Saviour. For it is beyond their power to tell how Thou art both perfect man and immutable God at the same time. But we, marvelling at this Mystery, cry faithfully:

Jesus, Eternal God.

Jesus, King of Kings.

Jesus, Lord of Lords.

Jesus, Judge of the living and the dead.

Jesus, Hope of the hopeless.

Jesus, Comforter of the mournful.

Jesus, Glory of the poor.

Jesus, condemn me not according to my deeds.

Jesus, cleanse me according to Thy mercy.

Jesus, take from me despondency.

Jesus, enlighten the thoughts of my heart.

Jesus, make me ever mindful of death.

People: *Jesus, Son of God, have mercy on me.*

Kontakion 10

Wishing to save the world, O Sunrise of the East, Thou didst come to the dark Occident of our nature, and didst humble Thyself even to the point of death. Therefore Thy Name is exalted above every name, and from all the tribes of earth and heaven, Thou dost hear: Halleluiah.

People: *Halleluiah.*

Oikos 10

King Eternal, Comforter, true Christ. Cleanse us from every stain as Thou didst cleanse the Ten Lepers, and heal us as Thou didst heal the greedy soul of Zacchaeus the publican, that we may cry to Thee with compunction and say:

Jesus, Treasurer Incorruptible.

Jesus, Unfailing Wealth.

Jesus, Strong Food.

Jesus, Inexhaustible Drink.

Jesus, Garment of the poor.

Jesus, Defender of widows.

Jesus, Protector of orphans.

Jesus, Helper of toilers.

Jesus, Guide of pilgrims.

Jesus, Pilot of voyagers.

Jesus, Calmer of tempests.

Jesus, raise me who am fallen.

People: *Jesus, Son of God, have mercy on me.*

Kontakion 11

Tenderest songs I, though unworthy, offer to Thee, and like the woman of Canaan, I cry to Thee: O Jesus, have mercy on me. For it is not my daughter, but my flesh violently possessed with passions and burning with fury. So grant healing to me, who cry to Thee: Halleluiah.

People: *Halleluiah.*

Oikos 11

Having previously persecuted Thee Who art the Light that enlightens those who are in the darkness of ignorance, Paul experienced the power of the voice of divine enlightenment, and understood the swiftness of the souls conversion to God. Likewise, enlighten the dark eye of my soul, as I cry:

Jesus, my All powerful King.

Jesus, my Almighty God.

Jesus, my Immortal Lord.

Jesus, my most glorious Creator.

Jesus, my most kind Teacher and Guide.

Jesus, my most compassionate Shepherd.

Jesus, my most gracious Master.

Jesus, my most merciful Saviour.

Jesus, enlighten my senses darkened by passions.

Jesus, heal my body scabbed with sins.

Jesus, cleanse my mind from vain thoughts.

Jesus, keep my heart from evil desires.

People: *Jesus, Son of God, have mercy on me.*

Kontakion 12

Grant me Thy grace, O Jesus, Absolver of all debts, and receive me who repent, as Thou didst receive Peter who denied Thee, and call me who am downcast, as of old Thou didst call Paul who persecuted Thee, and hear me crying to Thee: Halleluiah.

People: *Halleluiah.*

Oikos 12

Praising Thy Incarnation, we all glorify Thee and, with Thomas, we believe that Thou art our Lord and God, sitting with the Father and coming to judge the living and the dead. Grant that then I may stand on Thy right hand, who now cry:

Jesus, Eternal King, have mercy on me.

Jesus, sweet scented Flower, make me fragrant.

Jesus, beloved Warmth, make me warm.

Jesus, Eternal Temple, shelter me.

Jesus, Garment of Light, adorn me.

Jesus, Pearl of great price, beam on me.

Jesus, precious Stone, illumine me.

Jesus, Sun of Righteousness, shine on me.

Jesus, holy Light, make me radiant.

Jesus, deliver me from sickness of soul and body.

Jesus, rescue me from the hands of the adversary.

Jesus, save me from the unquenchable fire and from the other eternal torments.

People: *Jesus, Son of God, have mercy on me.*

Kontakion 13

O most sweet and most generous Jesus. Receive this our humble prayer, as Thou didst receive the widows mite and keep Thy faithful people from all enemies, visible and invisible, from foreign invasion, from disease and hunger, from all tribulations and mortal wounds, and deliver from future torments all who cry to Thee: Halleluiah.

People: *Halleluiah.*

Oikos 1

Creator of Angels and Lord of Hosts. As of old Thou didst open ear and tongue to the deaf and dumb, likewise open now my perplexed mind and tongue to the praise of Thy Most Holy Name, that I may cry to Thee:

Jesus All Wonderful, Angels' Astonishment.

Jesus All Powerful, Forefathers' Deliverance.

Jesus All Sweetest, Patriarchs' Exaltation.

Jesus All Glorious, Kings' Stronghold.

Jesus All Beloved, Prophets' Fulfilment.

Jesus All Marvellous, Martyrs' Strength.

Jesus All Peaceful, Monks' Joy.

Jesus All Gracious, Presbyters' Sweetness.

Jesus All Merciful, Fasters' Abstinence.

Jesus All Tenderest, Saints' Rejoicing.

Jesus All Honourable, Virgins' Chastity.

Jesus everlasting, Sinners' Salvation.

People: *Jesus, Son of God, have mercy on me.*

Kontakion 1

Warrior Chieftain and Lord, Vanquisher of hell, I Thy creature and servant offer Thee songs of praise, for Thou hast delivered me from eternal death. But as Thou hast unutterable loving kindness, free me from every danger, as I cry: Jesus, Son of God, have mercy on me.

Prayers To Our Lord Jesus Christ

O All wise and All gracious Lord, Our Saviour, Who didst enlighten all the ends of the world by the radiance of Thy Coming, and Who didst call us into Thy Holy Church through the promise of the inheritance of incorruptible and eternal good. Graciously look down on us, Thy worthless servants, and remember not our iniquities, but according to Thy infinite mercies forgive all our sins. For though we transgress Thy holy will, we do not deny Thee, Our God and Saviour. Against Thee alone do we sin, yet Thee alone do we serve, in Thee alone do we believe, to Thee alone do we come, and Thy servants only do we wish to be. Remember the infirmity of our nature and the temptations of the adversary and the worldly enticements and seducements which surround us on all sides, and against which, according to Thy word, we can do nothing without Thy help. Cleanse us and save us. Enlighten our minds that we may firmly believe in Thee, our only Saviour and Redeemer. Inspire our hearts that we may wholly love Thee, our only God and Creator. Direct our steps that we may unstumblingly walk in the light of Thy commandments. Yea, our Lord and Creator, show us Thy great and abundant kindness, and make us live all the days of our life in holiness and truth, that at the time of Thy glorious Second Coming, we may be worthy to hear Thy gracious call into Thy Heavenly Kingdom. Grant us, Thy sinful and unprofitable servants, to receive Thy Kingdom, and that in the enjoyment of its ineffable beauty, we may ever glorify Thee, together with Thy Eternal Father and Thy Ever living Divine Spirit to the ages of ages. Amen.

Sweetest Lord Jesus, strong Son of God, Who didst shed Thy precious Blood and die for love of my love, I am ready to die for love of Thy love. Sweetest Jesus, my Life and my All, I love and adore Thee. Thee only do I wish for my Spouse, as Thou dost wish me for Thy bride. I give myself to Thee. I surrender myself to Thee. O Jesus, Thou Whose heart is ever turned to me, heal my heart, that I may feel the sweetness of Thy love, that I may taste no sweetness but Thee, seek no love but Thee, love no beauty but Thee. I have no desire but to please Thee and to do Thy will. Teach me to repent, and to take up the Cross daily and follow Thee with joy. Teach me to pray with faith and love. Thyself pray in me, that with Thee I may love my enemies and pray for them. Jesus, Thou art life in my death, strength in my weakness, light in my darkness, joy in my sorrow, courage in my faint heartedness, peace in my agitation, obedience in my prayer, glory in my dishonour, and deliverance from my dishonour. Glory and thanks to Thee Jesus my Saviour and Healer. Amen.

Akathist To Our Most Holy Lady Mother Of God

Kontakion 1

To Thee the Champion Leader, we, thy servants dedicate a feast of victory and of thanksgiving as ones rescued out of sufferings, O Theotokos; but as thou art one with might which is invincible, from all dangers that can be do thou deliver us, that we may cry to thee: Rejoice, thou Bride unwedded.

Oikos 1

An Archangel was sent from Heaven to say to the Mother of God: Rejoice. And seeing Thee, O Lord, taking bodily form, he was amazed and with his bodiless voice he stood crying to her such things as these:

Rejoice, thou through whom joy shall flash forth.

Rejoice, thou through whom the curse shall cease.

Rejoice, revival of fallen Adam.

Rejoice, redemption of the tears of Eve.

Rejoice, height hard to climb for human thoughts.

Rejoice, depth hard to contemplate even for the eyes of Angels.

Rejoice, thou who art the Kings throne.

Rejoice, thou who bearest Him Who bears all.

Rejoice, star that causest the Sun to appear.

Rejoice, womb of the divine incarnation.

Rejoice, thou through whom creation becomes new.

Rejoice, thou through whom the Creator becomes a babe.

All: *Rejoice, O Bride unwedded.*

Kontakion 2

Aware that she was living in chastity, the holy Virgin said boldly to Gabriel: "Thy strange message is hard for my soul to accept. How is it thou speakest of the birth from a seedless conception?" And she cried: *Halleluiah.*

All: *Halleluiah.*

Oikos 2

Seeking to know what passes knowledge, the Virgin cried to the ministering spirit: "Tell me, how can a son be born from a chaste womb?" Then he spoke to her in fear, only crying aloud thus:

Rejoice, initiate of Gods ineffable will.

Rejoice, assurance of those who pray in silence.

Rejoice, prelude of Christs' miracles.

Rejoice, crown of His dogmas.

Rejoice, heavenly ladder by which God came down.

Rejoice, bridge that conveys us from earth to heaven.

Rejoice, wonder of angels blazed abroad.

Rejoice, wound of demons bewailed afar.

Rejoice, thou who ineffably gavest birth to the Light.

Rejoice, thou who didst reveal thy secret to none.

Rejoice, thou who surpassest the knowledge of the wise.

Rejoice, thou who givest light to the minds of the faithful.

All: Rejoice, O Bride unwedded.

Kontakion 3

The power of the Most High then overshadowed the Virgin for conception, and showed her fruitful womb as a sweet meadow to all who wish to reap salvation, as they sing: *Halleluiah.*

All: Halleluiah.

Oikos 3

Pregnant with the Divine indwelling the Virgin ran to Elizabeth whose unborn babe at once recognized her embrace, rejoiced, and with leaps of joy as songs, cried to the Mother of God:

Rejoice, scion of an undying Shoot.

Rejoice, field of untainted fruit.

Rejoice, thou who labourest for Him Whose labour is love.

Rejoice, thou who givest birth to the Father of our life.

Rejoice, corn land yielding a rich crop of mercies.

Rejoice, table bearing a wealth of forgiveness.

Rejoice, thou who revivest the garden of delight.

Rejoice, thou who preparest a haven for souls.

Rejoice, acceptable incense of intercession.

Rejoice, purification of all the world.

Rejoice, favour of God to mortals.

Rejoice, access of mortals to God.

All: Rejoice, O Bride unwedded.

Kontakion 4

Sustaining from within a storm of doubtful thoughts, the chaste Joseph was troubled. For knowing thee to have no husband, he suspected a secret union, O Immaculate One. But when he learned that thy conception was of the Holy Spirit, he exclaimed: *Halleluiah.*

All: Halleluiah.

Oikos 4

The shepherds heard Angels carolling Christs' incarnate Presence, and running like sheep to their shepherd, they beheld him as an innocent Lamb fed at Marys breast, and they sang to her and said:

Rejoice, mother of the Lamb and the Shepherd.

Rejoice, fold of spiritual sheep.

Rejoice, defence against invisible enemies.

Rejoice, key to the gates of Paradise.

Rejoice, for the things of Heaven rejoice with the earth.

Rejoice, for the things of earth join chorus with the Heavens.

Rejoice, never-silent voice of the Apostles.

Rejoice, invincible courage of the martyrs.

Rejoice, firm support of faith.

Rejoice, radiant blaze of grace.

Rejoice, thou through whom hell was stripped bare.

Rejoice, thou through whom we are clothed with glory.

All: *Rejoice, O Bride unwedded.*

Kontakion 5

Having sighted the divinely moving star, the Wise Men followed its light and held it as a lamp by which they sought a powerful King. And as they approached the Unapproachable, they rejoiced and shouted to Him: *Halleluiah.*

All: *Halleluiah.*

Oikos 5

The sons of the Chaldees saw in the hands of the Virgin Him Who with His hand made man. And knowing Him to be the Lord although He had taken the form of a servant, they hastened to worship Him with their gifts and cried to her who is blessed:

Rejoice, mother of the never-setting Star.

Rejoice, dawn of the mystic Day.

Rejoice, thou who didst extinguish the furnace of error.

Rejoice, thou who didst enlighten the initiates of the Trinity.

Rejoice, thou who didst banish from power the inhuman tyrant.

Rejoice, thou who hast shown us Christ as the Lord and Lover of men.

Rejoice, thou who redeemest from pagan worship.

Rejoice, thou who dost drag from the mire of works.

Rejoice, thou who hast stopped the worship of fire.

Rejoice, thou who hast quenched the flame of the passions.

Rejoice, guide of the faithful to chastity.

Rejoice, joy of all generations.

All: *Rejoice, O Bride unwedded.*

Kontakion 6

Turned God-bearing heralds, the Wise Men returned to Babylon. They fulfilled Thy prophecy and to all preached Thee as the Christ, and they left Herod as a trifler, who could not sing: *Halleluiah.*

All: *Halleluiah.*

Oikos 6

By shining in Egypt the light of truth, Thou didst dispel the darkness of falsehood, O Saviour. For, unable to endure Thy strength, its idols fell; and those who were freed from their spell cried to the Mother of God:

Rejoice, uplifting of men.

Rejoice, downfall of demons.

Rejoice, thou who hast trampled on the delusion of error.

Rejoice, thou who hast exposed the fraud of idols.

Rejoice, sea that has drowned the spiritual Pharaoh.

Rejoice, rock that has refreshed those thirsting for Life.

Rejoice, pillar of fire guiding those in darkness.

Rejoice, shelter of the world broader than a cloud.

Rejoice, sustenance-replacing Manna.

Rejoice, minister of holy delight.

Rejoice, land of promise.

Rejoice, thou from whom flows milk and honey.

All: *Rejoice, O Bride unwedded.*

Kontakion 7

When Simeon was about to depart this life of delusion, Thou wast brought as a Babe to him. But he recognized Thee as also perfect God, and marvelling at Thy ineffable wisdom, he cried: *Halleluiah.*

All: *Halleluiah.*

Oikos 7

The Creator showed us a new creation when He appeared to us who came from Him. For He sprang from an unsown womb and kept it chaste as it was, that seeing the miracle we might sing to her and say:

Rejoice, flower of incorruption.

Rejoice, crown of continence.

Rejoice, flashing symbol of the resurrection.

Rejoice, mirror of the life of the Angels.

Rejoice, tree of glorious fruit by which the faithful are nourished.

Rejoice, bush of shady leaves by which many are sheltered.

Rejoice, thou who bearest the Guide of those astray.

Rejoice, thou who givest birth to the Redeemer of captives.

Rejoice, pleader before the Just Judge.

Rejoice, forgiveness of many sinners.

Rejoice, robe of freedom for the naked.

Rejoice, love that vanquishes all desire.

All: *Rejoice, O Bride unwedded.*

Kontakion 8

Seeing the Child Exile, let us be exiles from the world and transport our minds to Heaven. For the Most High God appeared on earth as lowly man, because He wished to draw to the heights those who cry to Him: *Halleluiah.*

All: *Halleluiah.*

Oikos 8

Wholly present was the infinite Word among those here below, yet in no way absent from those on high; for this was a divine condescension and not a change of place. And His birth was from a God-possessed Virgin who heard words like these:

Rejoice, container of the uncontainable God.

Rejoice, door of solemn mystery.

Rejoice, doubtful report of unbelievers.

Rejoice, undoubted boast of the faithful.

Rejoice, all-holy chariot of Him Who rides on the Cherubim.

Rejoice, all-glorious temple of Him Who is above the Seraphim.

Rejoice, thou who hast united opposites.

Rejoice, thou who hast joined virginity and motherhood.

Rejoice, thou through whom sin has been absolved.

Rejoice, thou through whom Paradise is opened.

Rejoice, key to the Kingdom of Christ.

Rejoice, hope of eternal blessings.

All: *Rejoice, O Bride unwedded.*

Kontakion 9

All angel kind was amazed at the great act of Thy incarnation; for they saw the inaccessible God as a man accessible to all, dwelling with us and hearing from all: *Halleluiah.*

All: *Halleluiah.*

Oikos 9

We see most eloquent orators dumb as fish before thee, O Mother of God. For they dare not ask: How canst thou bear a Child and yet remain a Virgin? But we marvel at the mystery, and cry with faith:

Rejoice, receptacle of the Wisdom of God.

Rejoice, treasury of His Providence.

Rejoice, thou who showest philosophers to be fools.

Rejoice, thou who constrainest the learned to silence.

Rejoice, for the clever critics have made fools of themselves.

Rejoice, for the writers of myths have died out.

Rejoice, thou who didst break the webs of the Athenians.

Rejoice, thou who didst fill the nets of the fishermen.

Rejoice, thou who drawest us from the depths of ignorance.

Rejoice, thou who enlightenest many with knowledge.

Rejoice, ship of those who wish to be saved.

Rejoice, haven for sailors on the sea of life.

All: *Rejoice, O Bride unwedded.*

Kontakion 10

Wishing to save the world, the Ruler of all came to it spontaneously. And though as God He is our Shepherd, for us He appeared to us as a Man; and having called mankind to salvation by His own Perfect Manhood, as God He hears: *Halleluiah.*

All: *Halleluiah.*

Oikos 10

Thou art a wall to virgins and to all who run to thee, O Virgin Mother of God. For the Maker of heaven and earth prepared thee, O Immaculate One, and dwelt in thy womb, and taught all to call to thee:

Rejoice, pillar of virginity.

Rejoice, gate of salvation.

Rejoice, founder of spiritual reformation.

Rejoice, leader of divine goodness.

Rejoice, for thou didst regenerate those conceived in shame.

Rejoice, for thou gavest understanding to those robbed of their senses.

Rejoice, thou who didst foil the corrupter of minds.

Rejoice, thou who gavest birth to the Sower of chastity.

Rejoice, bride chamber of a virgin marriage.

Rejoice, thou who dost wed the faithful to the Lord.

Rejoice, fair mother and nurse of virgins.

Rejoice, betrother of holy souls.

All: *Rejoice, O Bride unwedded.*

Kontakion 11

Every hymn falls short that aspires to embrace the multitude of Thy many mercies. For if we should offer to Thee, O Holy King, songs numberless as the sand, we should still have done nothing worthy of what Thou hast given to us who shout to Thee: *Halleluiah.*

All: *Halleluiah.*

Oikos 11

We see the Holy Virgin as a flaming torch appearing to those in darkness. For having kindled the Immaterial Light, she leads all to divine knowledge; she illumines our minds with radiance and is honoured by our shouting these praises:

Rejoice, ray of the spiritual Sun.

Rejoice, flash of unfading splendour.

Rejoice, lightning that lights up our souls.

Rejoice, thunder that stuns our enemies.

Rejoice, for thou didst cause the refulgent Light to dawn.

Rejoice, for thou didst cause the river of many-streams to gush forth.

Rejoice, living image of the font.

Rejoice, remover of the stain of sin.

Rejoice, laver that washes the conscience clean.

Rejoice, bowl for mixing the wine of joy.

Rejoice, aroma of the fragrance of Christ.

Rejoice, life of mystical festivity.

All: *Rejoice, O Bride unwedded.*

Kontakion 12

When He Who forgives all men their past debts wished to restore us to favour, of His own will He came to dwell among those who had fallen from His grace; and having torn up the record of their sins, He hears from all: *Halleluiah.*

All: *Halleluiah.*

Oikos 12

While singing to thy Child, we all praise thee as a living temple, O Mother of God. For the Lord Who holds all things in His hand dwelt in thy womb, and He sanctified and glorified thee, and taught all to cry to thee:

Rejoice, tabernacle of God the Word.

Rejoice, saint greater than the saints.

Rejoice, ark made golden by the Spirit.

Rejoice, inexhaustible treasury of Life.

Rejoice, precious diadem of pious kings.

Rejoice, adorable boast of devoted priests.

Rejoice, unshaken tower of the Church.

Rejoice, impregnable wall of the Kingdom.

Rejoice, thou through whom we obtain our victories.

Rejoice, thou before whom our foes fall prostrate.

Rejoice, healing of my body. Rejoice, salvation of my soul.

All: *Rejoice, O Bride unwedded.*

Kontakion 13

O all-praised Mother who didst bear the Word holiest of all the Saints, accept this our offering, and deliver us from all offence, and redeem from future torment those who cry in unison to thee: *Halleluiah, Halleluiah, Halleluiah.*

All: *Halleluiah, Halleluiah, Halleluiah.*

Kontakion 1

To Thee the Champion Leader, we, thy servants dedicate a feast of victory and of thanksgiving as ones rescued out of sufferings, O Theotokos: but as thou art one with might which is invincible, from all dangers that can be do thou deliver us, that we may cry to thee: Rejoice, thou Bride unwedded.

Oikos 1

An Archangel was sent from Heaven to say to the Mother of God: Rejoice. And seeing Thee, O Lord, taking bodily form, he was amazed and with his bodiless voice he stood crying to her such things as these:

Rejoice, thou through whom joy shall flash forth.

Rejoice, thou through whom the curse shall cease.

Rejoice, revival of fallen Adam.

Rejoice, redemption of the tears of Eve.

Rejoice, height hard to climb for human thoughts.

Rejoice, depth hard to contemplate even for the eyes of Angels.

Rejoice, thou who art the Kings throne.

Rejoice, thou who bearest Him Who bears all.

Rejoice, star that causest the Sun to appear.

Rejoice, womb of the divine incarnation.

Rejoice, thou through whom creation becomes new.

Rejoice, thou through whom the Creator becomes a babe.

All: *Rejoice, O Bride unwedded.*

Theotokion

My most gracious Queen, my hope, Mother of God, shelter of orphans, and intercessor of travellers, strangers and pilgrims, joy of those in sorrow, protectress of the wronged, see my distress, see my affliction. Help me, for I am helpless. Feed me, for I am a stranger and pilgrim. You know my offence; forgive and resolve it as thou wilt. For I know no other help but thee, no other intercessor, no gracious consoler but thee, O Mother of God, to guard and protect me throughout the ages.

All: *Amen.*

Akathist To The Mother Of Gods Icon "Joy Of All Who Sorrow"

July 23rd <u>With Coins.</u>

The origin of the ancient "Joy Of All Who Sorrow" icon is undocumented. The first recorded miracle related to this icon happened in 1688. At the time, the Russian Orthodox Church was ruled by Patriarch Joachim. His sister, the lady Euphemia, was sick and had suffered for a long time with an abdominal abscess, which was an open sore. It seems that it was so serious that Euphemia's internal organs could be seen and there were very real fears for her life. Her ardent prayer to the Mother of God was answered in that she understood that she must have a molieben (service of intercession) sung before the "Joy Of All Who Sorrow" icon that was kept in the Transfiguration Church in Ordynka. The priest was summoned. He brought the icon, served the molieben, with the great blessing of water, and blessed the ailing woman with the holy water. Euphemia's life was spared and she recovered from her malady. Giving thanks to the Mother of God, Euphemia made public the news of her miraculous healing and so this icon came to prominence. The Church established a commemorative festival, on 24 October, in honour of the miracle.

October 24th <u>Without Coins.</u>

In the icon the Mother of God is shown in glory in the centre surrounded by supplicants, the sick, the suffering, the poor, the bereaved and people who are in need or sorrow. On either side of the Mother of God are angels who are directing the petitions to her. The petitions are represented by small scrolls. The original icon (the Moscow one), shows the Holy Virgin holding the Christ Child but there is a second "Joy Of All Who Sorrow" icon, in St Petersburg. This one is known as the icon "with coins".

This copy of the "Joy Of All Who Sorrow" icon, showing the Mother of God not holding the Christ Child, was found washed up on the bank of the Neva River and was kept in a chapel in the village of Klochka. It was dark and obscure. In 1888, in a violent thunderstorm, the building was struck by lightning causing considerable damage. The walls were charred and the alms box was broken scattering the contents on the floor. When the people inspected the damage, they found the icon face down on the floor. When it was lifted, not only had it become bright and clear, but the coins were adhering to the surface. The renewal of this icon was seen as a sign from heaven and it is commemorated annually on 23 July.

Kontakion 1

To Thee, the Champion Leader, we Thy servants dedicate a feast of victory and of thanksgiving as ones rescued from eternal death by the grace of Christ our God, Who was born of thee, and by thy maternal mediation before Him. As thou dost have invincible might, free us from all sorrow and misfortune who cry aloud:

All: *Rejoice, O Virgin Theotokos, full of Grace, joy of all who sorrow.*

Oikos 1

The Archangel Gabriel was sent from Heaven to declare unto thee: *"Rejoice"*, and to announce the Divine Incarnation of Christ, Who desired to be born of thee, the joy of the whole world that was languishing in sorrow. Wherefore, heavy laden with sins, but having obtained the hope of salvation in thee, we cry out to thee with compunction:

Rejoice, goodwill of God toward sinners.

Rejoice, strong help for those who repent before the Lord God.

Rejoice, restoration of fallen Adam.

Rejoice, redemption of the tears of Eve.

Rejoice, thou who dost remove the stain of sin.

Rejoice, laver in which the conscience is washed clean.

Rejoice, thou who didst bear the Redeemer who freely cleanses us of our transgressions.

Rejoice, wondrous reconciliation of all mankind with God.

Rejoice, bridge that truly leads us from death to life.

Rejoice, thou who saves the world from the flood of sin.

Rejoice, heavenly ladder by which the Lord descended for us.

Rejoice, cause of sanctification for all.

All: *Rejoice, O Virgin Theotokos, full of Grace, joy of all who sorrow.*

Kontakion 2

Beholding the streams of wonders that pour forth from thy holy icon, O most blessed Mother of God, good helper of those who pray, support of the oppressed, hope of the hopeless, consolation of those who grieve, nourishment for the hungry, garment for the naked, chastity of virgins, guide for strangers, assistance of those who labour, restorer of sight to the blind, hearing to the deaf and healing to the sick, through thee do we thankfully chant unto God: *Halleluiah.*

All: *Halleluiah.*

Oikos 2

Seeking to understand the incomprehensible reasons for the bitter sorrows that assail us, and in need of consolation, we flee to thee O Mother and Virgin. In that thou art good, teach us to see in them the merciful providence of thy good Son for the salvation of our souls and the cleansing of our many transgressions, that we may joyfully cry to thee:

Rejoice, calm haven of the tempest tossed.

Rejoice, sure confirmation of those in doubt.

Rejoice, gracious mother of loving kindness.

Rejoice, ready helper of all in misfortunes and temptations.

Rejoice, thou who doth soothe away the sorrows of our sins.

Rejoice, thou who doth heal the grief of our spiritual infirmity.

Rejoice, thou who doth teach us to disdain the vain pleasures of this world.

Rejoice, thou who doth lead our minds from this world to the one which transcends it.

Rejoice, thou who doth draw us from the desire for earthly things to the heavenly love of God.

Rejoice, thou who grantest us consolation and a life of Grace amidst our very sorrows.

Rejoice, pledge of eternal blessings.

Rejoice, promise of everlasting joy.

All: *Rejoice, O Virgin Theotokos, full of Grace, joy of all who sorrow.*

Kontakion 3

With power from on high strengthen us, afflicted as we are, in body and soul, O good Lady, and vouchsafe unto us thy visitation and motherly care, dispelling the gloom of despondency that entraps us, so that being held in thine embrace, we may unceasingly cry out to God: *Halleluiah.*

All: *Halleluiah.*

Oikos 3

O thou who hast an ineffable wealth of loving kindness, stretch forth the hand of thine assistance unto all who sorrow, curing infirmities and healing the passions, and disdain not even me, O Blessed Lady, as I lie upon the bed of mine affliction and cry unto thee:

Rejoice, priceless treasury of mercy.

Rejoice, hope of all who are in despair.

Rejoice, healer of my body.

Rejoice, salvation of my soul.

Rejoice, unfailing strengthener of the infirm.

Rejoice, aid and support of the disabled.

Rejoice, thou who speedily quenches the wrath of God by thy supplication.

Rejoice, thou who tamest our passions by the power of thy prayers.

Rejoice, sight for the blind and hearing for the deaf.

Rejoice, feet for the lame, speech for the dumb.

Rejoice, visitation of good cheer for the sick.

Rejoice, for through thee Grace filled healings are granted to all according to the measure of their faith.

All: *Rejoice, O Virgin Theotokos, full of Grace, joy of all who sorrow.*

Kontakion 4

A tempest of misfortunes and temptations besets me, and no longer can I endure its raging. But as thou art the merciful mother of my Saviour and God, lift up thy hands to thy Son, beseeching Him to regard the bitter sorrow of my heart and to raise me up from the abyss of despair, who cry to Him: *Halleluiah.*

All: *Halleluiah.*

Oikos 4

O most holy Virgin and Mother, hearing the prophecy of the righteous Simeon: *"A sword shall pierce through thine own soul"*, thou didst keep all these sayings in thy heart, understanding that the joy of a mothers heart over her children can be accompanied with much grief in this world. Wherefore, as one tried and tested in everything and able to commiserate with a mothers sorrows, we cry to thee:

Rejoice, thou who didst bear the Christ Child, the Saviour of the world.

Rejoice, thou who deliverest the world from sorrows.

Rejoice, thou who didst endure hearing the blasphemies and slanders hurled at thy Son.

Rejoice, thou who didst suffer together with Him through His passion.

Rejoice, consolation of the sorrows of mothers.

Rejoice, gracious protector of their children.

Rejoice, speedy helper amid misfortunes.

Rejoice, corrector of those who go stray.

Rejoice, nurse of infants.

Rejoice, teacher of the young.

Rejoice, mother of the orphaned.

Rejoice, help of widows.

All: *Rejoice, O Virgin Theotokos, full of Grace, joy of all who sorrow.*

Kontakion 5

Beholding the Divinely flowing Blood of thy Son poured forth upon the Cross of our salvation, as the handmaiden of the Lord, thou didst humbly subject thyself to the will of our Father in heaven, giving us an example of endurance and patience, that amid the raging of temptations and misfortunes we may cry aloud to God: *Halleluiah.*

All: *Halleluiah.*

Oikos 5

Seeing thee crucified with Him in thy heart, and standing with His beloved disciple by the Cross, thy Son and God uttered: *"Woman, behold thy son"*, and to His disciple: *"Behold thy mother"*, thereby giving thee as sons all who believe in Him. Thus having in thee a good mother and placing all our hope in thee, despite grieving as partakers of the sorrows and sufferings of thy Son, we cry to thee:

Rejoice, mother of the Christian race.

Rejoice, thou who didst adopt us at the Cross of thy Son.

Rejoice, thou who didst unite God with mankind.

Rejoice, thou who didst join the faithful to the Lord.

Rejoice, mother who didst bear the Lamb who takes away the sin of the world.

Rejoice, cup that draws joy for us from the Fountain of Immortality.

Rejoice, surety of the salvation of sinners.

Rejoice, search for the perishing.

Rejoice, unexpected joy of sinners.

Rejoice, raising up of all the fallen.

Rejoice, healer of all infirmities.

Rejoice, alleviation of every sorrow.

All: *Rejoice, O Virgin Theotokos, full of Grace, joy of all who sorrow.*

Kontakion 6

O Mother of God, all the ends of the earth proclaim thy mercies, for by thy sacred protection thou dost shelter the whole Christian race for whom thou dost supplicate Christ our Saviour and doth deliver from all misfortune thy pious and God fearing servants who faithfully cry out to God: *Halleluiah.*

All: *Halleluiah.*

Oikos 6

Beholding the radiant grace that shines forth from thy most wondrous icon, O Mother of God, and falling down before it with tears, we beseech thee; disperse the clouds of temptations that have come upon us, so that we may cry out to thee with joy:

Rejoice, thou who dost carry the supplications of the faithful unto thy Son and God.

Rejoice, thou who dost pray for us all at the throne of thy Son.

Rejoice, intercessor before God, who dost save the world from calamities.

Rejoice, help of the Christian race, given to us by God.

Rejoice, tree of goodly shade, whereby many are sheltered.

Rejoice, tree bearing heavenly fruit, whereby the faithful are nourished.

Rejoice, shelter of the world, more spacious than a cloud.

Rejoice, land of promise, from whence flows milk and honey.

Rejoice, celestial radiance, unceasingly illuminating the faithful.

Rejoice, pillar of fire, guiding the elect to their heavenly inheritance.

Rejoice, field yielding an abundance of compassion.

Rejoice, bestower of every blessing.

All: Rejoice, O Virgin Theotokos, full of Grace, joy of all who sorrow.

Kontakion 7

Thou, O Lady Theotokos, didst command the ailing Euphemia to have a molieben served before thy most sacred image, the Joy of All Who Sorrow, and having received healing, she was commanded to proclaim, to all, the mercies bestowed through this wondrous icon, so that the source of gracious healings be not hidden from those in need. Wherefore O Lady, we hide not thy good deeds, and thankfully glorifying God, we cry to Him: *Halleluiah.*

All: Halleluiah.

Oikos 7

Thy temple, in which we bow down before thy wonder working icon, is shown to be a new pool of Siloam, surpassing the one of old, O Most Pure Theotokos; for health of body is given not once a year and only to the first come, but thou dost always heal every ailment and every disease of soul and body of those who hasten to thee with faith and love. Wherefore we cry to thee:

Rejoice, spring wherein our sorrows are washed away.

Rejoice, cup whereby we partake of joy and salvation.

Rejoice, rock giving drink to those who thirst for life.

Rejoice, nectar sweetening the salty waters of the sea of life.

Rejoice, inexhaustible fountain of life giving waters.

Rejoice, vessel for washing away the stain of sin.

Rejoice, release of our burdens.

Rejoice, relief of our weariness and pain.

Rejoice, healing of our afflictions.

Rejoice, deliverance from disasters.

Rejoice, trampling down of demons.

Rejoice, humiliation of enemies.

All: Rejoice, O Virgin Theotokos, full of Grace, joy of all who sorrow.

Kontakion 8

Strangers and pilgrims are we upon this earth, according to the words of the Apostle: enduring perils at the hands of enemies, perils at the hands of relatives, perils at the hands of false brethren, and in much want and sorrow. And in that thou art our teacher, guide and guardian O Lady, do thou bring us to the calm haven and pray that thy Son shall grant us remission of our transgressions before the end, that we may unceasingly cry to God: *Halleluiah.*

All: *Halleluiah.*

Oikos 8

Our whole life on earth is painful and filled with grief because of false accusations, reproaches, insults, and various other misfortunes and temptations, for the flesh is weak and our spirit is failing. Therefore, to thee do we flee, O Mother of God, falling down before thine all pure icon. Fill our sorrowful hearts with joy and gladness, that we may cry to thee:

Rejoice, guide directing us to our heavenly homeland.

Rejoice, Queen of Heaven, who dost open for us the gates of Paradise.

Rejoice, loving one who hast mercy upon us.

Rejoice, thou who dost order our life well.

Rejoice, fleece bedewed, that Gideon foresaw.

Rejoice, blessed womb that contained the uncontainable God of all.

Rejoice, bush that burned and yet remained unconsumed.

Rejoice, unassailable wall.

Rejoice, life giving fountain.

Rejoice, never fading bloom.

Rejoice, softening of the hearts of the wicked.

Rejoice, conscience of believers.

All: *Rejoice, O Virgin Theotokos, full of Grace, joy of all who sorrow.*

Kontakion 9

Every manifestation of life in this world partakes of sorrow: glory does not endure, wealth and power crumble, beauty and health fade away, and friends and neighbours leave us or are taken away by death. Wherefore we implore thee, sweeten our sorrows, thou channel of blessings, bestowing incorruptible joy upon us who cry out to God: *Halleluiah.*

All: *Halleluiah.*

Oikos 9

The most eloquent orators are lost for words to console the sorrowful; but through thy love and mercy, O Lady Theotokos, speak consolation to our hearts, dispersing the clouds of our sorrows and the gloom of our despair with the radiance of thy glory, that we may cry out to thee:

Rejoice, thou who hast made glad all the Christians who have confidence in thee.

Rejoice, joy and tranquillity of the world.

Rejoice, channel of divine goodness.

Rejoice, hope of eternal blessings.

Rejoice, rescuer of those who seek salvation.

Rejoice, harbour for the voyages of life.

Rejoice, faithful preserver of those who, after God, put their trust in thee.

Rejoice, vesture for all who are stripped of pride and arrogance.

Rejoice, preserver and confirmation for all.

Rejoice, fortification and sacred refuge of all the faithful.

Rejoice, help of those who faithfully pray to thee.

Rejoice, radiant knowledge of Grace.

All: *Rejoice, O Virgin Theotokos, full of Grace, joy of all who sorrow.*

Kontakion 10

Desiring to save the human race from eternal torment and unending sorrow, the Lord God Who loves mankind dwelt in thine Ever Virgin womb, and appointed thee, His own mother, to be the helper, protector, and defender of all who are in danger of perishing, so that thou mightest be the consolation of the grieving, the joy of the sorrowful and the hope of the despairing, releasing them from eternal torment by the power of thine intercession, and leading to heavenly glory all who faithfully cry to thy Son and our God: *Halleluiah.*

All: *Halleluiah.*

Oikos 10

Thou art the bulwark of virgins, O Lady Theotokos, and of all who flee to thy protection. Wherefore we beseech thee: help, protect, and preserve from temptations, afflictions, and misfortunes all of us, orphans and helpless ones, who cry out to thee with faith and love:

Rejoice, pillar of virginity.

Rejoice, chosen vessel of purity and chastity.

Rejoice, crown of those who, by chastity, make war upon the flesh.

Rejoice, bestower of eternal rejoicing upon those who labour profitably in the monastic life.

Rejoice, thou who dost quench the flame of the passions.

Rejoice, thou who dost dispel the darkness of temptations.

Rejoice, guide to chastity.

Rejoice, rampart of purity.

Rejoice, reformation of mankind.

Rejoice, thou by whom we are raised up from the fall.

Rejoice, steadfast affirmation of the Faith.

Rejoice, pleasing incense of prayer.

All: *Rejoice, O Virgin Theotokos, full of Grace, joy of all who sorrow.*

Kontakion 11

We, thy servants, offer to thee a hymn of contrition, O Lady Theotokos, for thou art the all powerful helper of our race. Soothe the pains of those who flee to thee; appease the wrath of God that has been justly aroused against us because of our sins; deliver us from every bitter pain and sorrow, who cry to God, through thee: *Halleluiah.*

All: Halleluiah.

Oikos 11

O Lady Theotokos, thy most honoured icon, a light bearing lamp lit by the ember of the grace of God, has appeared unto us for our sanctification and consolation. Now, honouring this sacred image with our hymns and, with faith, bowing down in veneration following the example of our holy father and hierarch John, we cry out to thee:

Rejoice, thou who by thy mighty assistance doth deliver us from all calamities.

Rejoice, thou who dost protect us from power of earthquakes and floods.

Rejoice, thou who doth provide for us against hunger of body and soul.

Rejoice, thou who dost quench the fire of passions by the dew of thy prayers.

Rejoice, thou who dost save us from the ravages of pestilence.

Rejoice, mighty helper in battles.

Rejoice, defender from the invasions of enemies.

Rejoice, thou who dost preserve us from civil strife.

Rejoice, easy passage of all who sail upon the sea.

Rejoice, good guide of those who travel.

Rejoice, liberation of captives.

Rejoice, speedy deliverer from the righteous wrath of God that threatens us.

All: Rejoice, O Virgin Theotokos, full of Grace, joy of all who sorrow.

Kontakion 12

Wishing to give a pledge of grace to mankind, thou didst reveal thy healing icon to us, O Mother of God, from whom streams of wonders are poured forth for those who approach with faith and whose infirmities and sorrows are healed. Therefore we joyfully cry through thee to God: *Halleluiah.*

All: Halleluiah.

Oikos 12

Lauding thy mercies and wonders, O Theotokos, we all praise thee as our steadfast intercessor, and bowing down with compunction before thee who doth pray for us, we implore thee to lift up thy hands to thy Son, that always in this life, and after our death, His mercy may continually be upon us who cry out to thee:

Rejoice, our unashamed hope in life and after our repose.

Rejoice, thou who doth grant a peaceful end of this life to those who honour thee.

Rejoice, our hope and defence on the Day of Judgement.

Rejoice, supplication of the just Judge.

Rejoice, deliverance from everlasting torment.

Rejoice, hope of eternal salvation.

Rejoice, key to the Kingdom of Christ.

Rejoice, portal of Paradise.

Rejoice, bridge leading to the heavens.

Rejoice, refuge and good intercessor for all repentant sinners.

Rejoice, joy of the angels.

Rejoice, glory and consolation of all the righteous.

All: *Rejoice, O Virgin Theotokos, full of Grace, joy of all who sorrow.*

Kontakion 13

O all hymned, divinely favoured Mother, thou who didst bear Christ the King, our Lord and God, to the joy of heaven and earth: hearken unto the voice of thy sorrowing servants and having received this our small supplication, deliver us from every affliction, sorrow, and temptation; heal our infirmities, destroy vicious slanders, drive far from us every evil and enemy, and deliver from future torment those who, in faith, cry to thee: *Halleluiah.* **(x3)**

Oikos 1 (repeated)

The Archangel Gabriel was sent from Heaven to declare unto thee: *"Rejoice"*, and to announce the divine Incarnation of Christ, Who desired to be born of thee, the joy of the whole world that was languishing in sorrow. Wherefore, heavy laden with sins, but having obtained the hope of salvation in thee, we cry out to thee with compunction:

Rejoice, goodwill of God toward sinners.

Rejoice, strong help for those who repent before the Lord God.

Rejoice, restoration of fallen Adam.

Rejoice, redemption of the tears of Eve.

Rejoice, thou who dost remove the stain of sin.

Rejoice, laver in which the conscience is washed clean.

Rejoice, thou who didst bear the Redeemer, Who freely cleanses us of our transgressions.

Rejoice, wondrous reconciliation of all mankind with God.

Rejoice, bridge that truly leads us from death to life.

Rejoice, thou who saves the world from the flood of sin.

Rejoice, heavenly ladder by which the Lord descended to us.

Rejoice, cause of sanctification for all.

All: *Rejoice, O Virgin Theotokos, full of Grace, joy of all who sorrow.*

Kontakion 1 (repeated)

To Thee, the Champion Leader, we Thy servants dedicate a feast of victory and of thanksgiving as ones rescued from eternal death by the grace of Christ our God, Who was born of thee, and by thy maternal mediation before Him. As thou dost have invincible might, free us from all sorrow and misfortune who cry aloud:

All: *Rejoice, O Virgin Theotokos, full of Grace, joy of all who sorrow.*

First Prayer

O Lady Most Holy and Theotokos, thou art more honourable than the Cherubim and more glorious beyond compare than the Seraphim, O divinely chosen maiden, joy of all who sorrow; grant consolation even unto us who are sunk in sorrow, for apart from thee, we have no refuge or assistance. Thou alone art the mediatress of our joy and, in that thou art the Mother of God and Mother of mercy, standing at the throne of the All Holy Trinity, thou art able to help us, for no one who flees to thee departs ashamed. Therefore, hearken now, in the day of our sorrow, unto us who bow down before thine icon and implore thee with tears: drive away from us the sorrows and grief that assail us in this temporal life, and by thy powerful intercession may we not be deprived of eternal joy in the Kingdom of thy Son and our God.

All: *Amen.*

Second Prayer

Most Blessed Queen, O Theotokos my hope, guardian of orphans and intercessor for strangers, joy of the sorrowful, protectress of the oppressed; beholding my misfortune, thou dost see my sorrow. Help me, for I am infirm; feed me, for I am a stranger. Thou knowest mine offences: do thou loose them, as thou dost will, for I have none other help but thee, nor any other intercessor save thee, O Mother of God. Do thou preserve and protect me unto the ages of ages.

All: *Amen.*

Third Prayer

O Most Holy Virgin, Mother of the Lord of the hosts on high, Queen of heaven and earth, almighty intercessor of our country: receive this hymn of praise and thanksgiving from us, thine unworthy servants, and carry our prayers to the throne of Christ our God, thy Son, that He may be merciful towards our unrighteousness and extend His grace to those who honour thine all honourable name and bow down before thy wonder working icon with faith and love. For we are not worthy to be pitied by Him. Therefore we beg thee as our undoubted and speedy intercessor: hearken thou unto us thy supplicants. Overshadow us with thine almighty protection, and request of God thy Son: zeal and vigilance, concerning souls, for our pastors; wisdom and strength for civil authorities; justice and equity for judges; knowledge and humility for those who teach; love and concord between husbands and wives; obedience for children; patience for the oppressed; fear of God for the oppressors; strength of spirit for the sorrowful; restraint for the wayward; and for all of us, the spirit of understanding and piety, the spirit of mercy and meekness, the spirit of purity and righteousness. Yea, O Most Holy Lady, take pity on thine afflicted people: gather the dispersed, guide to the right path those who have gone astray, support the aged, teach the young sobriety, nourish the infants, and look down with the gaze of thy merciful assistance upon us all. Raise us up from the abyss of sin and open the eyes of our hearts to the vision of salvation. Take pity on us here and now, both in the land of our earthly sojourn and at the dread judgement of thy Son. Cause our fathers and brethren who have passed from this life in faith and repentance to abide in eternal life with the angels and all the saints, for thou, O Lady, art the glory of all in heaven and the hope of us upon the earth. After God, thou art our hope and the helper of all who turn to thee with faith. Therefore, to thee do we pray, and as to an all powerful helper, to thee do we entrust ourselves and *(here can be inserted the names of our family, our friends and anyone who has asked us to pray for them)* and all our life, now and ever, and unto the ages of ages.

All: *Amen.*

Theotokion (from the Sixth Hour)

Seeing that we have no boldness on account of our many sins, do thou beseech Him that was born of thee, O Virgin Theotokos for the supplication of a mother availeth much to win the Masters favour. Disdain not the prayers of sinners, O all pure one, for merciful and mighty to save is He Who deigned also to suffer for our sake.

Akathist To Saints Peter And Paul

Kontakion I

The Lord Who said of Himself: I am the good Shepherd, said unto thee, O first-enthroned Peter: If thou lovest Me, feed My sheep. And He Who said: I am Jesus, said of thee, O pre-eminent Apostle Paul: He is a chosen vessel unto Me, to bear My name before the gentiles. And likewise to all your colleagues, His apostles, He said: As My Father hath sent Me, even so send I you; go ye, and teach all nations. And ye, receiving such grace from your good Chief Shepherd, as the foremost shepherds and teachers of all the world, from all misfortunes preserve you us on the pasture of salvation, that we may cry out to you: Rejoice, O holy first enthroned Peter and Paul, with all the holy apostles.

Ikos I

Blessed art thou, Simon, son of Jonas. said Christ, the Son of the living God, unto thee, O right glorious Apostle Peter. How then can we worthily call thee blessed who hast been called blessed by God Himself? Yet drawn faithfully, by a debt of love alone, we cry out to thee thus:

Rejoice, first among the apostles, foundation of the holy Church;

Rejoice, mighty pillar and ground of the Orthodox Faith.

Rejoice, ardent lover of the teaching of Christ;

Rejoice, first seated among the council of the apostles.

Rejoice, good gate keeper of the kingdom of heaven;

Rejoice, renowned physician for them that repent of their sins.

Rejoice, thou who spurned the vanity of the world and loved the spiritual life;

Rejoice, thou who didst forsake corruptible nets and didst fish the whole world with incorruptible ones.

Rejoice with Peter, O Paul, for you both shone forth like two great beacons;

Rejoice, O you who like a pair of steeds were harnessed by God to His chariot of noetic light.

Rejoice, all you holy apostles, beholders of God, for you are the light of all the world;

Rejoice, for through you the Faith which saveth us hath shone forth from Christ in every place.

Rejoice, O holy first enthroned Peter and Paul, with all the holy apostles.

Kontakion II

O teacher of the gentiles, who received thy title wondrously from on high, thou didst believe when Jesus said unto thee: Saul, why persecutest thou Me Who cannot be touched by unbelief? Yet believe thou henceforth; for, lo. contrary audacity darkeneth thee, but I have chosen thee to be a witness to My judgements before the rulers, the nations and the children of Israel. And thou, O Apostle Paul, called such things by God, didst cry out: Halleluiah.

Ikos II

Hearing a voice from heaven, O Saul, thou wast thereafter unable to see; for thou hadst adversely persecuted the Inaccessible One and didst receive blindness of thine eyes in return for thy zeal for the law; but, guided to the font, thou didst attain unto divine baptism, where, having been immersed with faith, the sight of thy bodily and spiritual eyes was restored. Wherefore, mindful of thy miraculous calling, we cry out to thee:

Rejoice, O apostles called by God, sent forth to preach to all the nations;

Rejoice, chosen vessel which pourest forth the sweetness of the Faith of Christ upon all men.

Rejoice, beholder of the divine Light which illumineth from on high;

Rejoice, thou who more than others wast enlightened by grace after the shadow of the Old Covenant.

Rejoice, thou who on earth didst converse with the Lord Jesus Who appeared to thee;

Rejoice, thou who with His strength didst dare to denounce them that were adamant in their unbelief.

Rejoice, thou who hast enlightened the whole world with thy divinely wise writings;

Rejoice, thou who, following Christ, didst labour more than others for the salvation of man.

Rejoice with Paul, O Peter, for you overshadow the holy Church as the two cherubim did the ark;

Rejoice, you who stand before the throne of the Most High like two seraphim.

Rejoice, all you holy apostles, for you are like the heavens which proclaim the glory of God;

Rejoice, for you are the stars which crown the Church, the Bride of Christ.

Rejoice, O holy first enthroned Peter and Paul, with all the holy apostles.

Kontakion III

Thou wast struck with horror, O holy Apostle Peter, beholding the sheet descending from on high, filled with all manner of living creatures, moreover with unclean beasts, wherein was set forth a parable of Gods love for man, signifying that it is not fitting to reject them that from all the nations desire to believe in Christ Jesus. And understanding this mystery, thou didst cry out to God: Halleluiah.

Ikos III

Naught that is vile or unclean hath ever passed my lips. thou didst say, O most blessed Apostle Peter. But divine Providence answered thee with a voice from heaven, saying: What God hath cleansed, that do thou not revile, calling it unclean; for the Saviour cameth not to call the righteous, but sinners, to repentance. And we, knowing what was revealed to thee, cry out:

Rejoice, O apostle, who mercifully openest the kingdom of heaven;

Rejoice, thou who not only watchest over men, but over the affairs of all the nations.

Rejoice, thou who with thy love coverest the multitude of our sins;

Rejoice, thou who perfectest our meagre repentance with thy mercy.

Rejoice, speedy helper for them that call upon thee amid spiritual tribulations;

Rejoice, thou who by thy supplication raisest up those dead of body and soul.

Rejoice, thou who strengthenest with the Holy Spirit the faithful who hearken unto thy word;

Rejoice, thou who woundest the unbelieving with thy words, as with darts.

Rejoice with Peter, O Paul, in that you are as the two eyes of the Church, endued with divine sight;

Rejoice, ever vigilant guides watching over the new Israel.

Rejoice, all you holy apostles, for you are as a guard upon the walls of Jerusalem;

Rejoice, O our instructors, who keep watch over the souls of Christians.

Rejoice, O holy first enthroned Peter and Paul, with all the holy apostles.

Kontakion IV

To the Jews living in Damascus didst thou begin to preach, O apostle Paul, enlightened of God, that they might believe in Christ Jesus the Son of God; and they were astonished at how one who before had persecuted them that believed in the name of Christ had - O, the wonder. - himself been transformed into a believer. Wherefore, they took counsel together to slay thee; but knowing their intent and the hardness of their hearts, thou didst leave them in the blindness of their unbelief and, let down over the wall in a basket by the faithful, thou didst cry out to God: Halleluiah.

Ikos IV

With great zeal, O holy Paul, thou didst preach to turn away from the prescriptions of the old law and circumcision and to make haste to the font of divine baptism, proclaiming this not only to the Jews, but also to the gentiles whose most loving teacher thou wast. Wherefore, we exclaim unto thee thus:

Rejoice, preacher sent by God to announce repentance unto sinners;

Rejoice, teacher of piety with thunderous voice, denouncer of ungodliness.

Rejoice, merciful inviter of them among the gentiles that are astray, yet hasten to the Faith of Christ;

Rejoice, true guide to the straight path.

Rejoice, ship which keepest the faithful from drowning in sin;

Rejoice, helmsman who guidest us to the haven of the pleasing of God.

Rejoice, quickly interceding comforter of the sorrowful;

Rejoice, healer who acceptest no recompense for curing ailments of body and soul.

Rejoice with Paul, O Peter, for you are like two wings furnished unto the Church by Christ, the great Eagle;

Rejoice, for you are like two wings given to her, the dove, by the Holy Spirit.

Rejoice, all you holy apostles, who are whole as doves and through hope have been furnished with wings like eagles;

Rejoice, for where Christ was in the body, there were you gathered together.

Rejoice, O holy first enthroned Peter and Paul, with all the holy apostles.

Kontakion V

Sweating from thine earthly labours and providing for thyself by fishing, O holy Apostle Peter, thou wast called to be an apostle and didst believe in Christ Who nurtureth abundantly, Who fed a thousand people with five loaves; and thou didst follow Him, labouring for food which perisheth not, but abideth unto everlasting life; and thou didst cry out to Him as God: Halleluiah.

Ikos V

Forbidden by the chief priests and elders of the Jews to teach the name of the Lord Jesus, O blessed Apostle Peter, arming thyself with steadfast faith, thou didst answer: We ought to obey God rather than man. And having endured imprisonment and stripes for this, thou didst depart from the presence of the council, rejoicing that they were counted worthy to suffer shame for the name of the Lord. Wherefore, we also offer to thee exclamations of joy, saying:

Rejoice, thou who didst put the council of the Jews to shame by the writings of the prophets concerning Christ;

Rejoice, thou who didst rend asunder the false threats of the Pharisees and Sadducees like a spiders web.

Rejoice, thou who didst work many miracles through the grace of the Holy Spirit;

Rejoice, thou who grantest sight to the blind and the ability to walk to the lame.

Rejoice, thou who by thy shadow didst raise the sick from their beds of pain;

Rejoice, thou who didst heal them that suffered from many unclean spirits.

Rejoice, thou who summonest fishermen to a wondrous catch;

Rejoice, thou who drawest the unbelieving to faith as if they were voiceless fish.

Rejoice with Peter, O Paul, for you are like two breasts of the Church, the Bride of Christ, our Mother;

Rejoice, for you are like two grapes of the voice, which nourish us and make us glad.

Rejoice, all you holy apostles, for you are branches of Christ, the true Vine;

Rejoice, for you are good husbandmen of the vineyard of Christ.

Rejoice, O holy first enthroned Peter and Paul, with all the holy apostles.

Kontakion VI

An Israelite of the tribe of Benjamin, a Pharisee according to the law, a persecutor of the Church of God in thy zeal, didst thou call thyself, O holy Apostle Paul, not hiding thy former hot temper against them that believed in Christ Jesus; but as thou didst greatly persecute the Church of God and didst strive to destroy it, so now, gloriously adorned by thee, and made steadfast in might by thy mellifluous teachings, it crieth unto God: Halleluiah.

Ikos VI

Who shall separate us from the love of God? Shall tribulation, or distress, or persecution, or like things? thou didst say, O Apostle Paul, preacher of the Word beloved of God, bringing all to the love of Christ Who sincerely believe in Him, that with boldness and thanksgiving we may endure tribulation for Gods sake. Wherefore, we lovingly exclaim to thee these things:

Rejoice, thou who wast a zealot for the law named Saul;

Rejoice, lover of Christ, named Paul, perfected in grace.

Rejoice, light of divine knowledge, illumining them that are in the darkness of unbelief;

Rejoice, star guiding them that languish in the depths of iniquity.

Rejoice, thou who betrothest the souls of the faithful to Christ and summonest them to the heavenly bridal chamber;

Rejoice, thou who didst endure many tribulations and hast made others also steadfast to endure them.

Rejoice, thou into whose hands God placed mighty powers;

Rejoice, thou whose sweat soaked kerchief healed the sick.

Rejoice with Paul, O Peter, for you are like the two pillars which uphold the Church of the heavenly Solomon;

Rejoice, you who, like two lilies on its pillars, adorn the sanctuary of God.

Rejoice, all you holy apostles, for like flowers do you impart fragrance to all the world;

Rejoice, you who through your fragrance dispel the stench of all iniquity.

Rejoice, O holy first enthroned Peter and Paul, with all the holy apostles.

Kontakion VII

On thine arrival in Lydda, O blessed Apostle Peter, thou didst amaze the people living there when by the name of Jesus Christ thou didst raise up Æneas, who had lain abed, sick of the palsy, for eight years, and didst cause him to walk; in Joppa thou didst likewise, by thy supplication, return to life the dead Tabitha; and, summoned to Caesaria, thou didst enlighten with divine baptism Cornelius the centurion with all in his household. Wherefore, we all straightway cry aloud to God in unity of soul: Halleluiah.

Ikos VII

Simon Magus thought to acquire the grace of the Holy Spirit with silver; but thou, O blessed Apostle Peter, didst condemn him to inherit damnation with his silver and didst sternly forbid both the avaricious practice of simony and the theft of sacred things. Wherefore, we exclaim unto thee thus:

Rejoice, thou who enriched the Church of Christ with the grace of the Spirit;

Rejoice, thou who didst forbid the reception of recompense for holy things in the Church.

Rejoice, thou by whom avarice was cut off, as the root of all evils, through the grace of the Spirit;

Rejoice, thou by whom covetousness is cast away by sanctity as a type of idolatry.

Rejoice, thou who didst lead a hard life for the sake of Christ;

Rejoice, thou who didst fulfil well the commandment of Christ: you cannot serve God and Mammon.

Rejoice, thou who didst sternly punish the sacrilege of Ananias with death;

Rejoice, thou who didst likewise commit Sapphira, who was guilty of that sin, to the same punishment.

Rejoice with Peter, O Paul, for you are like two olive trees which pour forth mercy;

Rejoice, for you are like two lamps radiating wisdom.

Rejoice, all you holy apostles, as tender olive shoots;

Rejoice, for because of you is all like a fruitful olive tree in the house of God.

Rejoice, O holy first enthroned Peter and Paul, with all the holy apostles.

Kontakion VIII

Having attained unto the third heaven because of thy sanctity of body and soul and been enriched with ineffable benefactions, thou didst descend from thence, O divinely blessed Apostle Paul, and didst astonish all, filling those of the Jews and of the gentiles who believed in Christ with thy teachings of the knowledge of God. And together with them, all we, the faithful, who have a share of thine heavenly teaching, cry out to God: Halleluiah.

Ikos VIII

A model for the faithful, thou didst joyfully endure many stripes, beatings and stonings of thy body for the sake of sweet Jesus, O Apostle Paul, called by God, manifestly indicating that it is the part of them that believe in Christ Jesus to undergo all manner of tribulations thankfully, for His sake. Wherefore, we also cry out to thee, using such exclamations as these:

Rejoice, thou who didst joyfully bear the wounds of the Lord on thy body;

Rejoice, adamant firm of body and soul, who mightily endured all manner of tribulation.

Rejoice, insuperable confessor of Christ before the nations and their rulers;

Rejoice, teacher invincible in the face of the Israelite teachers of the law.

Rejoice, luminous star which shone forth from the third heaven;

Rejoice, greatly fruitful branch which buddest forth from paradise, full of spiritual food.

Rejoice, thou who by thy teaching hast illumined all the earth as with an unwaning light;

Rejoice, thou who hast fed the faithful throughout the world with the produce of thy works as with most comely fruits.

Rejoice with Paul, O Peter, for you are as two trees in the midst of the garden of the Church;

Rejoice, you who put forth the fruit of life and good understanding.

Rejoice, all you holy apostles, who are like noetic palm trees and cedars;

Rejoice, you who have been transplanted to heaven as the garden of the heavenly Father.

Rejoice, O holy first enthroned Peter and Paul, with all the holy apostles.

Kontakion IX

Thou wast possessed of an all embracing concern for all who came to the Faith of Christ, O blessed Apostle Peter, that their heart and soul become one. Wherefore, thou didst appoint for their needs a minister, the chaste Stephen, and six other deacons; and thou thyself, together with the rest of the apostles, didst dedicate thyself to prayer and the preaching of the Word, instructing all the faithful, who cried out with oneness of mind to God: Halleluiah.

Ikos IX

Aflame with zeal for thy Lord, thou didst cut off the ear of Malchus, for he seemed to thee as one disinclined to heed the writings of the prophets concerning Jesus Christ. But, reproved for such audacity by thy Teacher, O blessed Apostle Peter, thou didst thankfully bear His reproach and all its contrary results. Wherefore, mindful of thy zeal, we cry aloud to thee thus:

Rejoice, thou who didst surpass the rest of the disciples in thy zeal for Christ;

Rejoice, manful sword bearer of Christ in the garden.

Rejoice, thou who didst follow Christ, Who was being led to His suffering, even to the house of Caiaphas;

Rejoice, thou who wast prepared for prison and death for the sake of thy Lord.

Rejoice, thou who with bitter lamentation didst heal thy weakness in denying thy Master;

Rejoice, thou who after the Lords resurrection wast summoned to thy former dignity.

Rejoice, thou who hast provided a model of repentance for the rest of us sinners;

Rejoice, thou who didst vow to forgive the weakness of the penitent many times over.

Rejoice with Peter, O Paul, for you are like the tables of the law of the Lord;

Rejoice, teachers of love for God and neighbour.

Rejoice, all you holy apostles, who perfectly kept all the commandments of the Lord;

Rejoice, you who left all and followed after Christ, and found all in Him.

Rejoice, O holy first enthroned Peter and Paul, with all the holy apostles.

Kontakion X

Great testimony didst thou produce from the sayings of the prophets concerning Christ in the face of the leaders of the Jews, and before the Procurator Festus and King Agrippa, O Apostle Paul, who wast called of God, and all were utterly set at naught; for many of the Jews quoted books to thee in their frenzy, and thou wast answered by both Festus and Agrippa falsely, and wast condemned to be sent to Rome. But, enduring everything with thanksgiving, thou didst cry out with the faithful to God: Halleluiah.

Ikos X

O Apostle Paul, who wast led to proclaim the life creating Trinity in the third heaven, most elect vessel of the great mysteries of God: declaring the good news before the gentiles, the judges and rulers, thou didst promise salvation unto them that desire to believe in Christ Jesus and receive holy baptism in the name of the Trinity. Wherefore, all we the faithful, being of good hope concerning that salvation, cry out to thee thus:

Rejoice, mystagogue of great understanding of the revelation of the Lord;

Rejoice, confessor of the one God in three Persons.

Rejoice, thou who didst proclaim Christ to be the one Foundation of the faithful;

Rejoice, thou who hast made all the pious steadfast in that confession.

Rejoice, thou who didst endure raging reproaches from the unbelieving Festus;

Rejoice, thou who didst utter words of truth and chastity in his presence.

Rejoice, thou who didst most clearly recount thine heavenly vision to King Agrippa;

Rejoice, thou who didst manifestly denounce his error which is not consonant with the Faith of Christ.

Rejoice, O Paul, with Peter, for you are like two silver trumpets of Moses;

Rejoice, you who call those of earth and beneath the earth to battle against evil.

Rejoice, all you holy apostles, who have suffered cruelly as valiant warriors of Christ;

Rejoice, you who have vanquished the kingdoms of the earth by faith and have received heavenly things.

Rejoice, O holy first enthroned Peter and Paul, with all the holy apostles.

Kontakion XI

Having slain Iakovos, the brother of John, Herod went on to seize thee as well, O divinely blessed Apostle Peter; and he placed thee under heavy guard in prison to await execution. Yet while fervent prayer was being offered up by the Church for thy deliverance, the angel of the Lord loosed thy bonds and led thee through the gates, which opened of themselves, and thou didst think that thou wast beholding a dream. But when the angel departed, thou didst come to thy senses and didst truly realize that thou hadst been freed; and thou didst cry out to God in thanksgiving: Halleluiah.

Ikos XI

That which had been asked by Philip: Lord, show us the Father. didst thou come to know, O blessed Apostle Peter, on Mount Tabor, whereon, beholding the all glorious transformation of the countenance of the transfigured Lord, thou didst hear the voice of God the Father say of Him from heaven: This is My beloved Son, in Whom I am well pleased; hear you Him. And we cry out to thee who wast counted worthy of such a revelation:

Rejoice, reliable witness of the transfiguration of Christ;

Rejoice, renowned one who heard the divine voice of the Father from heaven.

Rejoice, thou who didst behold the countenance of the Son of God illumined like the sun;

Rejoice, thou who didst most splendidly receive the overshadowing of the Holy Spirit in the cloud.

Rejoice, thou to whom the most exalted mystery was disclosed upon the mountain;

Rejoice, thou to whom the majestic glory of the all holy Trinity was made manifest.

Rejoice, thou who heardest that the departure of Christ was to take place in Jerusalem;

Rejoice, thou who, following Christ, didst accomplish thy departure on a cross in Rome.

Rejoice with Peter, O Paul, for you are two noetic mountains like Tabor and Hermon;

Rejoice, you who from the east and the west revealed the promised land in heaven.

Rejoice, all you holy apostles, like the mountains of Sion;

Rejoice, you who let the sweetness of salvation fall upon us.

Rejoice, you holy first enthroned Peter and Paul, with all the holy apostles.

Kontakion XII

We hymn thee who standest on equal footing with the cherubim, O most blessed Apostle Paul, who wast enlightened by divine wisdom in the third heaven; for, hearing ineffable words there which it is not lawful for a man to utter, thou didst travel the whole world therewith, teaching all to believe in the crucified Christ, the Son of God, and to chant unceasingly unto Him as the true God: Halleluiah.

Ikos XII

Full of the great revelation of divine mysteries, O chosen vessel of Jesus, all wise Apostle Paul, thou didst diligently bear forth the name of God Who hath appeared in the flesh and saveth them that believe in Him; and having converted many of the gentiles and fought the good fight, in the city of Rome thou didst finish thy course most gloriously for the name of thy Lord, and didst then receive therein a crown of righteousness. Wherefore, we cry out to thee thus:

Rejoice, great lover of the name of Jesus, who suffered greatly for Him;

Rejoice, thou who bore witness before those of heaven of earth and beneath the earth concerning His name.

Rejoice, for thou didst bear witness well concerning the Lord in Jerusalem;

Rejoice, thou who thus wast commanded by Him to bear witness also in Rome.

Rejoice, thou who denounced the Emperor Nero and converted his consort to the Christian Faith;

Rejoice, thou who in the same Rome didst bow thine head beneath the sword, executed with Peter, who was crucified head downward.

Rejoice, for at the severing of thine honoured head milk flowed forth;

Rejoice, for this great wonder drew many soldiers to the Faith.

Rejoice with Paul, O Peter, for you are like two rivers of living water gushing forth from the wellspring of the Holy Spirit;

Rejoice, you who were shown forth by the confluence of the two rivers named Jor and Dan.

Rejoice, all you holy apostles, like torrents of rivers which gladden the city of the Church of God;

Rejoice, for you are like streams of sweetness which give all the faithful to drink from the cup of salvation.

Rejoice, O holy first enthroned Peter and Paul, with all the holy apostles.

Kontakion XIII

O most glorious and laudable disciples of Christ, Peter and Paul, first enthroned and equally enthroned holy Apostles, who have enlightened all the universe with the holy Faith and shall come with Christ to judge the whole world. Your proper dignity is not on earth, but is the glory and praise rendered in heaven. Accepting now our unworthy entreaty, by your worthy supplications preserve us from all misfortunes, and beseech Christ, the just Judge, to be merciful to us at the last judgement, that, saved by your mediation, we may chant unto God our Saviour: Halleluiah, Halleluiah, Halleluiah. **(x3)**

Ikos I

Blessed art thou, Simon, son of Jonas. said Christ, the Son of the living God, unto thee, O right glorious Apostle Peter. How then can we worthily call thee blessed who hast been called blessed by God Himself? Yet drawn faithfully, by a debt of love alone, we cry out to thee thus:

Rejoice, first among the apostles, foundation of the holy Church;

Rejoice, mighty pillar and ground of the Orthodox Faith.

Rejoice, ardent lover of the teaching of Christ;

Rejoice, first seated among the council of the apostles.

Rejoice, good gate keeper of the kingdom of heaven;

Rejoice, renowned physician for them that repent of their sins.

Rejoice, thou who spurned the vanity of the world and loved the spiritual life;

Rejoice, thou who didst forsake corruptible nets and didst fish the whole world with incorruptible ones.

Rejoice with Peter, O Paul, for you both shone forth like two great beacons;

Rejoice, O you who like a pair of steeds were harnessed by God to His chariot of noetic light.

Rejoice, all you holy apostles, beholders of God, for you are the light of all the world;

Rejoice, for through you the Faith which saveth us hath shone forth from Christ in every place.

Rejoice, O holy first enthroned Peter and Paul, with all the holy apostles.

Kontakion I

The Lord Who said of Himself: I am the good Shepherd, said unto thee, O first enthroned Peter: If thou lovest Me, feed My sheep. And He Who said: I am Jesus, said of thee, O pre-eminent Apostle Paul: He is a chosen vessel unto Me, to bear My name before the gentiles. And likewise to all your colleagues, His apostles, He said: As My Father hath sent Me, even so send I you; go ye, and teach all nations. And ye, receiving such grace from your good Chief Shepherd, as the foremost shepherds and teachers of all the world, from all misfortunes preserve you us on the pasture of salvation, that we may cry out to you: Rejoice, O holy first enthroned Peter and Paul, with all the holy apostles.

Prayers To The Holy Pre-Eminent Apostles Peter & Paul

I

O most glorious Apostles Peter and Paul, who laid down your lives for Christ and beautified His pasture with your blood. Hearken unto the prayers and sighs of your children which are now offered up with contrite heart. For, lo. we have darkened ourselves with iniquities, and for this cause have we been covered with misfortunes as with showers; and we have become exceeding poor in the oil of a good life, and we cannot fend off the ravening wolves which boldly strive to lay hands on the inheritance of God. O you mighty ones. bear you our infirmities and separate yourselves not from us in spirit, that we not depart utterly from the love of God; but with your mighty assistance defend us, that the Lord have mercy on us all for the sake of your prayers, that He rend asunder the handwriting of our countless sins, and that He vouchsafe us with all the saints the blessed kingdom and the wedding feast of His Lamb, to Whom be honour and glory, thanksgiving and worship, unto the ages of ages. Amen.

II

O holy Peter, chief of the apostles, rock of faith fixed firmly upon Christ, the chief Cornerstone, through thy confession. Pray thou that, unmoved by the imaginations of my mind and carnal lusts, I, too, may through faith be fixed firmly upon this same Christ, the Rock living, chosen and precious; that through love I may be made perfect as a temple of the Spirit, wherein I may offer up spiritual sacrifices unto Jesus Christ our God. O holy Paul, chief of the apostles, chosen vessel of Christ, overflowing with grace and the glory of God. Entreat thou the Creator, Who hath authority over creation, that He make of me, who am now a vessel of perdition, a vessel of honour for Himself, sanctified and fitting, ready for every good work, unto the ages of ages. Amen.

III

O you foremost of the apostles: Peter, steadfast exponent of the Faith of Christ, and Paul, melodious swallow of the teaching of the Lord. We perceive you to be a much flowing river recounting the words of Christ, gushing forth from the breast of the Lord, disclosing to us the depths of the well of divinely revealed truths. We see you to be lamps which make things clear for us with streams of the fervour of divine love from heaven. We bless you, for you endured tribulation and pain to sow the seed of divine teaching, and with your footsteps went round all the ends of the earth. With compunction we entreat you, O holy Apostles: cause us, in our sinful foolishness, to fall prostrate before the Lord, our Teacher; cause you that the head of our pride be cut off, and haste you to raise us up by your unceasing supplications, that there, with the Chorus of the angels and the apostles, we may glorify the Father of all, Who is wondrous in His saints, Who sent our Lord Jesus Christ into the world, and the Holy Spirit, Who is one in essence with Them, unto the ages of ages. Amen.

IV

O holy Peter, chief of the apostles, rock of faith steadfast in thy confession, foundation of the Church immovable in Christ, pastor of the rational flock of Christ, keeper of the keys to the kingdom of heaven, fisherman most wise who from the depths of unbelief dost draw forth men. Thee do I humbly entreat, that the net of thy divine draught encompass me and draw me forth from the abyss of perdition. I know that thou hast received from God the authority to loose and to bind; release me who am bound fast with bonds of sin, show forth thy mercy on me, wretch that I am, and give life to my soul which hath been slain by sins, as before thou didst raise up Tabitha from the dead; restore me to the good path, as before thou didst restore the lame man at the Beautiful Gates, who had been lame from his mothers womb; and as thou didst heal all the infirm by thy shadow, may the grace given thee by God overshadow me, healing my ailments of body and soul. For thou canst do all things, O holy one, through the power of Christ, for Whose sake thou didst forsake all to follow in His steps. Wherefore, pray thou to Him in my behalf, wretch that I am, that by thy supplications He may deliver me from all evil and teach me with a pure heart to send up glory to the Father, and to the Son, and to the Holy Spirit, now and ever, and unto the ages of ages. Amen.

V

O holy Paul, eminent among the apostles, chosen vessel of Christ, recounter of heavenly mysteries, teacher of all the nations, clarion of the Church, renowned orator, who didst endure many misfortunes for the name of Christ, who didst traverse the sea and didst go about the land, and didst convert us from the deception of idolatry. Thee do I entreat and to thee do I cry: disdain me not, defiled as I am, but raise me up who have fallen through sinful sloth, as in Lystra thou didst raise up the man who had been lame from his mothers womb; and as thou didst give life unto Euthyches who lay dead, so also raise me up from my dead works; and as at thine entreaty the foundation of the prison once quaked and thou didst loose the bonds of the prisoners, so draw me out of the snare of the enemy, and strengthen me to do the will of God. For thou canst do all things by the authority given thee by God, to Whom is due all glory, honour and worship, with His unoriginate Father and His all holy, good and life creating Spirit, now and ever, and unto ages of ages. Amen.

Trisagion Prayers

Reader: In the Name of the Father and of the Son and of the Holy Spirit.

People: *Amen. Glory to Thee, our God, glory to Thee.*

Reader: O Heavenly King, Comforter, Spirit of Truth, Who art everywhere present and fillest all things, Treasury of blessings and Giver of life: Come and abide in us and cleanse us from every impurity and save our souls, O Good One.

Holy God, Holy Mighty, Holy Immortal, have mercy on us. **(x3)**

Glory be to the Father, and to the Son, and to the Holy Spirit;
Both now and forever, and unto the ages of ages. Amen.

O Most Holy Trinity, have mercy on us.

O Lord, cleanse us from our sins.

O Master, pardon our iniquities.

O Holy One, visit and heal our infirmities, for Thy names sake.

Lord have mercy. **(x3)**

Glory be to the Father and to the Son and to the Holy Spirit;
Both now and forever, and unto the ages of ages. Amen.

People: Our Father, Who art in Heaven, hallowed be Thy Name. Thy Kingdom come, Thy will be done, on earth as it is in Heaven. Give us this day our daily bread, and forgive us our trespasses, as we forgive those who trespass against us; and lead us not into temptation, but deliver us from the evil one. Amen.

Lord, have mercy. **(x3)**

Glory be to the Father and to the Son and to the Holy Spirit;
Both now and forever and unto the ages of ages. Amen.

Come, let us worship God, our King.

Come, let us worship and fall down before Christ, our King and our God.

Come, let us worship and fall down before Christ Himself, our King and our God.

Kontakion 1

To the holy and righteous Joachim and Anna, forebears of Christ and elect among the human race, who gave birth to the holy Maiden of whom the Son of God was born in the flesh. Since you have great boldness before Christ our God and stand before His heavenly Throne, earnestly entreat Him that we may be delivered from all misfortune and thus may unceasingly cry aloud to you:

Rejoice, holy and righteous Joachim and Anna, Ancestors of God.

Oikos 1

An angelic messenger was sent to you by God, O holy and righteous Ancestors of God, when you both expressed your sorrow - you Joachim in the wilderness, and you Anna in the garden - offering up supplication to God. Thus, the incorporeal one brought the joyful tidings that you would give birth to an all blessed daughter in whom the whole human race would be blessed, and with the angel we also offer you joyful praise:

Rejoice, branches of the vine of life who blossomed forth holiness from the root of David.

Rejoice, for you gave birth to a daughter more blessed than all generations of men.

Rejoice, most honoured forbears of the Incarnate Son of God.

Rejoice, most excellent disclosers of the mystery hidden from before time began.

Rejoice, closest relatives in the flesh to the Consolation of Israel.

Rejoice, blood relatives of the Redeemer Who was promised to the world.

Rejoice, holy and righteous Joachim and Anna, Ancestors of God.

Kontakion 2

Seeing himself belittled by the high priest in the Temple of Jerusalem because of his lack of children, the holy Joachim was sorely distressed. In bitterness of soul he withdrew to his flocks in the wilderness. There he offered fervent supplication with tears, that the Lord would grant him to be called "father" by a child of his own. He therefore added fasting to prayer, and in the contrition of his heart cried aloud to God Almighty: Halleluiah.

Oikos 2

Knowing the extent of her husband's grief, the holy Anna wept bitterly in her house and prayed that the Lord would remove from her the reproach of barrenness. Rightfully remembering the patience of the righteous ones, we humbly cry out thus:

Rejoice, divinely chosen pair who gave birth to the one who would become the Mother of One of the Trinity.

Rejoice, for you brought forth an immaculate Mother for your Creator.

Rejoice, blessed pair who raised a daughter who is most blessed among women.

Rejoice, for God heard your petitions amid your barrenness.

Rejoice, for your tearful entreaties passed up to Heaven and reached the ear of the God of Israel.

Rejoice, for your temporal reproach has been transformed into eternal glory in Heaven and on earth.

Rejoice, holy and righteous Joachim and Anna, Ancestors of God.

Kontakion 3

Filled with the power of God, the angel of the Lord appeared to the holy Joachim in the wilderness and spoke to him. "God has heard your prayer and has been pleased to grant you His grace. Behold, Anna your wife shall conceive and bear you a daughter who shall be the joy of the whole world." Having said these things, the incorporeal one commanded Joachim to return to the Temple of Jerusalem. There he would find his spouse praying, that with her he might also chant the hymn of praise to the God of Israel: Halleluiah.

Oikos 3

Having great sorrow in your heart, O holy Anna, you entered the garden of your home where your eye saw little chicks lying in a bird's nest in a tree. You immediately added supplications to your prayers, that the Lord might permit you to become the mother of a child. And, lo, the angel of the Lord appeared and spoke to you. "Your prayer has been heard, your sighs have passed beyond the clouds and your tears have come before God. Behold, you shall conceive and bear an all blessed daughter in whom all the peoples of the earth shall be blessed, and through whom salvation shall be given to all the world. Her name shall be Mary." Mindful of these most angelic tidings, let us chant these things to the Ancestors of God:

Rejoice, for you were chosen for ineffable glory.

Rejoice, for you walked blamelessly in all the Commandments of the Lord.

Rejoice, for you received eternal consolation amid your fleeting sorrow.

Rejoice, for you were exalted beyond expectation by the Right Hand of God.

Rejoice, for you showed humility in your tribulation, and the Lord God remembered you.

Rejoice, for you were chosen to become the forbearers of the Son of God.

Rejoice, holy and righteous Joachim and Anna, Ancestors of God.

Kontakion 4

Beset by a storm of doubt and perplexed by the angel's tidings to him, the righteous Joachim immediately set out for the city of Jerusalem. There he found before the gates of the Temple the holy Anna, greatly glorifying the Lord. She declared to Joachim the joy of the angelic appearance and the prediction of childbirth. After Joachim had told his spouse of his own vision, he then cried with her to the Lord: Halleluiah.

Oikos 4

When Anna's relatives and friends heard of her all glorious conceiving, they glorified the God of Israel. The divinely wise Anna promised the fruit of her womb to the service of God, and offered up fervent thanks to the Lord. In the same manner, earnestly singing the most glorious conception of the holy Maiden Mary, we say to her blessed parents:

Rejoice, joyous heralds announcing the Redeemer Who is come into the world.

Rejoice, grandparents of God Who in His mercy assumed our form.

Rejoice, through your blessed daughter, you provided flesh for the Word of God.

Rejoice, for you called the Incarnate God your grandson.

Rejoice, worthy servants of the great mystery of piety.

Rejoice, most excellent means of God's condescension to men.

Rejoice, holy and righteous Joachim and Anna, Ancestors of God.

Kontakion 5

You were chosen to give birth in the flesh to the all holy Birth giver of God, the divinely radiant star who showed forth Christ God, the Sun of Righteousness. O most blessed Joachim and Anna, you have thereby received the enviable title of Ancestors of God. Upon her holy birth, Heaven and earth rejoiced and the entire human race was sanctified, crying to the God of Israel Who is wondrous in His saints: Halleluiah.

Oikos 5

As parents, O righteous Joachim and Anna, you gazed tenderly at the Mother of the Creator, the holy Maiden Mary who was born of you, and you reverently ministered to her as the ark of God. We therefore beseech you not to turn away from us who fall down before you in prayer, but also attend to us who say:

Rejoice, for you were filled with radiant jubilation at the birth of the holy Maiden Mary.

Rejoice, for you were filled with delight at the sight of your most blessed daughter.

Rejoice, for you were moved to compunction at the sound of her voice.

Rejoice, for after these things, you were blessed by the high priest of God.

Rejoice, for you nurtured the unblemished ewe lamb in your pious home.

Rejoice, for you received the Mother of the Lamb and Shepherd as your daughter.

Rejoice, holy and righteous Joachim and Anna, Ancestors of God.

Kontakion 6

You were shown to be proclaimers of the wonders of God, O Saints, when you fulfilled your vow to God and with glory brought the three year old holy Maiden Mary to the Temple of God, so that she might abide in the Holy of Holies. Because of these things, you hastened with joy to chant to the God of your fathers this glorification: Halleluiah.

Oikos 6

The divine Maiden shone forth like the full moon at her honoured entry into the Temple of the Lord, and the angels marvelled at her beauty. Taking her from your hands, O holy Joachim and Anna, the high priest Zachariah led her into the Holy of Holies with honour, for she was truly the living ark of God, and he blessed you as is proper with such praises as these:

Rejoice, for you have given birth to the universal joy of the human race.

Rejoice, for you have nurtured the cause of the restoration of mankind.

Rejoice, for you brought the living ark of God to the Temple of the Lord.

Rejoice, for you gave your holy daughter to dwell in the Holy of Holies.

Rejoice, for you are revealed as the relatives of God Who shall become incarnate.

Rejoice, for you conversed with the angels.

Rejoice, holy and righteous Joachim and Anna, Ancestors of God.

Kontakion 7

Having fulfilled the desire of your soul and given your promise to God, O all blessed Joachim, you departed this earthly life in holiness and righteousness, passing on to the Lord. We therefore ask you to petition Him that we also may be counted worthy to receive a peaceful and unashamed end, crying to Him: Halleluiah.

Oikos 7

You led a new and God pleasing life in your widowhood, O holy Anna, abiding in the Temple of God and ministering to your all blessed daughter. For this reason, we praise you as a true and God pleasing widow and the grandmother of Christ. With love we fervently honour you and your husband, Joachim the grandfather of God, and offer you such hymns as these:

Rejoice, just ones whose righteousness shines like the sun forever.

Rejoice, friends of the angels, who truly dwell with the saints in the presence of God.

Rejoice, for you stand near the Throne of Heaven.

Rejoice, for you have great boldness before Christ God.

Rejoice, adornment of the Church Triumphant in Heaven.

Rejoice, good support of the Church militant on earth.

Rejoice, holy and righteous Joachim and Anna, Ancestors of God.

Kontakion 8

Holy and righteous Anna, having reached the end of your earthly journey in the arms of your holy daughter, the Birth giver of God Mary, you slept the sleep of death and were transported to God with hope. Glorifying your holy dormition, we entreat you, O most honoured grandmother of God: When we also begin to fall into the sleep of death, beseech Christ the Saviour that our soul may part gently from our body and escape the power of the demons, that we may be granted eternal salvation and may cry to Him in the joy of the saints: Halleluiah.

Oikos 8

The whole Christian world blesses you as is proper, O holy and righteous Ancestors of God, Joachim and Anna, and in prayer glorifies your honoured names. The Church of Christ celebrates your memory with splendour and offers hymns of praise to you.

Rejoice, beacons who graciously illumine the darkness of our soul.

Rejoice, for you mercifully look down upon mortals from the heavenly heights of your glory.

Rejoice, for you ever pray with Mary the Birth giver of God.

Rejoice, for you thereby move Christ God to great mercy.

Rejoice, for you save from all misfortune those who cherish the Faith and who love one another because of you.

Rejoice, for you deliver those who call on your help in prayer from a violent and sudden death.

Rejoice, holy and righteous Joachim and Anna, Ancestors of God.

Kontakion 9

All the angels of God and the Chorus' of the saints of God in Heaven greet you, O holy and righteous Ancestors of God, Joachim and Anna, and on earth the generations of men praise you with prayerful hymns and cry to God in thanksgiving for your intercession: Halleluiah.

Oikos 9

Our eloquence does not suffice to praise you fittingly, O holy forbears of Christ. Yet, knowing that you are merciful, we trust that you shall not reject our inadequate praises. Rather, be fervent intercessors and advocates for us before the Lord, fulfilling the deficiency of our soul with your holy supplication, that we may cry to you this hymn of thanksgiving:

Rejoice, mediators who win for us the joy and eternal glory we desire.

Rejoice, fervent advocates before the Lord who acquire temporal and eternal blessings for us.

Rejoice, by your intercession, you preserve the faithful from deadly pestilence.

Rejoice, by your supplication, you dispel deadly plagues.

Rejoice, by your mediation, you cause earthquakes and violent storms to cease and you restore calm.

Rejoice, for amid all tribulation and misfortune, you hasten to our aid.

Rejoice, holy and righteous Joachim and Anna, Ancestors of God.

Kontakion 10

Holy and righteous Ancestors of God, Joachim and Anna, you have shown yourselves to be beneficial helpers of those who desire salvation of soul and diligently strive for this. O holy forebears, you are the guardians of monks and nuns, and you likewise offer supplication to God for all the faithful. For this cause, in thanksgiving to Christ the King of Glory, Who has glorified you throughout the world, all people may cry out: Halleluiah.

Oikos 10

With the bulwark of your prayers, O holy and righteous Ancestors of God, Joachim and Anna, preserve and protect us from the temptations of the diabolical one that seeks the destruction of our soul. We know that your petition before the face of Christ our God, your Grandson according to the flesh, is able to accomplish much. Never cease to make supplication to Him in behalf of all who lovingly honour you and cry aloud:

Rejoice, fruitful olive trees pouring forth the oil of the mercy of God upon us in abundance.

Rejoice, cypress trees of excellent foliage who turn the burning heat of our passions into the stillness of dispassion.

Rejoice, purple and fine linen of which the tabernacle of God's dwelling place was wrought.

Rejoice, turtle doves mated for life, who brought forth the immaculate dove.

Rejoice, for you reign eternally with your daughter, the Queen of all.

Rejoice, for you celebrate with her in splendour in her heavenly mansion in Zion on high.

Rejoice, holy and righteous Joachim and Anna, Ancestors of God.

Kontakion 11

Mercifully accept our hymns of praise and do not deprive us of your compassion, O holy Joachim and Anna, Ancestors of God. We are unworthy of your holy intercession because of our sins. Knowing that you are good and full of pity, however, we implore you to grant us mediation and to help us cleanse ourselves from defilement of sin through repentance. Thus, in purity of heart we may chant to our Creator the hymn of praise: Halleluiah.

Oikos 11

Brethren, let us recognize the holy Ancestors of God, Joachim and Anna, as two radiant candles which lit the universal lamp. Mercifully illumined with the brightness of their heavenly glory, let us endeavour to become worthy by singing to them such words as these:

Rejoice, for you were counted worthy to raise her who is beyond compare more glorious than the seraphim.

Rejoice, for you were resplendent with heavenly brightness.

Rejoice, for you were filled with the sweet fragrance of the Spirit.

Rejoice, for you bear to God the incense of your prayers for the whole Christian world.

Rejoice, for you ever stand before the Throne of Christ with Mary the God bearer and John the Baptist.

Rejoice, for we fall before you and honour the power of God in you.

Rejoice, holy and righteous Joachim and Anna, Ancestors of God.

Kontakion 12

Holy Ancestors of God, Joachim and Anna, ask the Lord to grant us divine grace and mercy, forgiveness of sins and correction of life. Never cease to entreat the countenance of Almighty God in our behalf, for you have acquired great boldness before Him. Falling down before you with fervour for this purpose, we beseech you as our true intercessors and helpers, and with real compunction we cry to the Creator of all: Halleluiah.

Oikos 12

Singing of the great might of your intercession before God, O righteous Joachim and Anna, we sing also the praises of His all immaculate Mother who was born of you. In our zeal we offer you these right fitting praises:

Rejoice, for you are glorified from the East even to the West.

Rejoice, our protectors whose vigilance in intercession is never waning.

Rejoice, for you grant your gracious help to every Christian soul.

Rejoice, most excellent healers who attend to those in pain and sorrow.

Rejoice, for you fulfil the entreaties and petitions of the pious.

Rejoice, most diligent and pleasing mediators who obtain for us temporal and eternal good things.

Rejoice, holy and righteous Joachim and Anna, Ancestors of God.

Kontakion 13

Holy and righteous Ancestors of God, Joachim and Anna, we entreat you with zeal and love, falling down before the footstool of your feet. We ask that you beseech the Lord God to deliver us from the everlasting damnation prepared for sinners. Saved therefore by the loving kindness of our God and aided by your holy prayers, we may sing in thanksgiving to Him the angelic hymn: Halleluiah. Halleluiah. Halleluiah. **(x3)**

Kontakion 1 (repeated)

To the holy and righteous Joachim and Anna, forbears of Christ and elect among the human race, who gave birth to the holy Maiden of whom the Son of God was born in the flesh. Since you have great boldness before Christ our God and stand before His heavenly Throne, earnestly entreat Him that we may be delivered from all misfortune and thus may unceasingly cry aloud to you:

Rejoice, O holy and righteous Joachim and Anna, Ancestors of God.

Oikos 1 (repeated)

An angelic messenger was sent to you by God, O holy and righteous Ancestors of God, when you both expressed your sorrow - you Joachim in the wilderness, and you Anna in the garden - offering up supplication to God. Thus, the incorporeal one brought the joyful tidings that you would give birth to an all blessed daughter in whom the whole human race would be blessed, and with the angel we also offer you joyful praise:

Rejoice, branches of the vine of life who blossomed forth holiness from the root of David.

Rejoice, for you gave birth to a daughter more blessed than all generations of men.

Rejoice, most honoured forbears of the Incarnate Son of God.

Rejoice, most excellent disclosers of the mystery hidden from before time began.

Rejoice, closest relatives in the flesh to the Consolation of Israel.

Rejoice, blood relatives of the Redeemer Who was promised to the world.

Rejoice, holy and righteous Joachim and Anna, Ancestors of God.

A Prayer

Ancestors of God, Joachim and Anna, your distress and reproach were overcome by the Almighty God, and thereby the Saviour of the world came into the world through your holy daughter, Mary. Your prayers were abundantly answered by our merciful God Who rewards patience, humility and compunction. We praise you for your faith and for your commitment to prayer, and we implore your compassion upon our lack of fruitfulness in the Christian virtues. Holy and righteous Joachim and Anna, teach us to be living temples of the grace of God, so that we also may devote ourselves to holiness and bring forth treasures which are pleasing to Him. Growing older with each passing day, we ask your guidance that we might reach a peaceful end on this earth and thereby be united with you forever in the Kingdom of Heaven. Amen.

Akathist To St Nicholas The Wonder Worker

For Those Seeking a Husband or Wife

If the parent, together with the son or daughter who is seeking a spouse, read the akathist to St Nicholas for forty days, they shall find that, as patron saint of families, St Nicholas shall send them someone. If the parent is not Orthodox or has departed this life, then their place can be taken by another close relative (brother/sister, Godfather / Godmother, for example) or a close friend.

Kontakion 1

O champion Wonder Worker and exceeding pleaser of Christ, who pourest out for the whole world the most precious myrrh of mercy and an inexhaustible sea of miracles, I praise thee with love, O Hierarch Nicholas; and as thou hast boldness towards the Lord, deliver me from all misfortunes that I may cry to thee: Rejoice, O Nicholas, great Wonder Worker.

Ikos 1

The Creator revealed thee to be an angel in form though earthly by nature; for, foreseeing the fruitful goodness of thy soul, O most blessed Nicholas, He taught all to cry to thee thus:

Rejoice, thou who wast purified from thy mothers womb.

Rejoice, thou who wast hallowed even to the end.

Rejoice, thou who didst amaze thy parents by thy birth.

Rejoice, thou who didst show power of soul straightway after birth.

Rejoice, garden of the promised land.

Rejoice, flower of divine planting.

Rejoice, virtuous vine of the vineyard of Christ.

Rejoice, wonder working tree of the paradise of Jesus.

Rejoice, lily blossoming in paradise.

Rejoice, myrrh of the fragrance of Christ.

Rejoice, for through thee weeping is banished.

Rejoice, for through thee rejoicing is brought into being.

People: *Rejoice, Nicholas, O great Wonder Worker.*

Kontakion 2

Seeing the effusion of thy myrrh, O divinely wise one, we are enlightened in soul and body, understanding thee to be a wonderful life giving source of myrrh, O Nicholas; for with miracles poured out like waters by the grace of God, thou waterest them that faithfully cry to God: Halleluiah.

People: *Halleluiah.*

Ikos 2

Giving the reason knowledge of the Holy Trinity beyond reason, with the holy fathers in Nicea thou wast a champion of the confession of the Orthodox Faith; for thou didst confess the Son equal to the Father, everlasting and enthroned together with Him, and thou didst expose the foolish Arius. Therefore the faithful have learned to sing to thee:

Rejoice, great pillar of piety.

Rejoice, city of refuge for the faithful.

Rejoice, firm stronghold of Orthodoxy.

Rejoice, venerable vessel and praise of the Holy Trinity.

Rejoice, thou who didst preach the Son equal in honour to the Father.

Rejoice, thou who didst expel the demonic Arius from the Council of the saints.

Rejoice, O father, glorious beauty of the fathers.

Rejoice, most wise goodness of all the divinely wise.

Rejoice, thou who utterest words of fire.

Rejoice, thou who guidest so well thy flock.

Rejoice, for through thee faith is affirmed.

Rejoice, for through thee heresy is overthrown.

People: *Rejoice, Nicholas, O great Wonder Worker.*

Kontakion 3

Through power given thee from on high thou didst wipe every tear from the face of those who cruelly suffer, O father Nicholas the bearer of God; for thou wast shown to be a feeder of the hungry, an exceeding good pilot of those on the high seas, a healer of the ailing and thou hast proved to be a helper to all that cry to God: Halleluiah.

People: *Halleluiah.*

Ikos 3

Truly, father Nicholas, a song should be sung to thee from heaven, and not from earth; for how can any man proclaim the greatness of thy holiness? But conquered by thy love, we cry to thee thus:

Rejoice, example for lambs and shepherds.

Rejoice, holy purification of morals.

Rejoice, container of great virtues.

Rejoice, pure and honourable abided of holiness.

Rejoice, all shining lamp, beloved by all.

Rejoice, golden rayed and blameless light.

Rejoice, worthy converser with angels.

Rejoice, good guide of men.

Rejoice, pious rule of faith.

Rejoice, model of spiritual meekness.

Rejoice, for through thee we are delivered from bodily passions.

Rejoice, for through thee we are filled with spiritual delights.

People: *Rejoice, Nicholas, O great Wonder Worker.*

Kontakion 4

A storm of bewilderment confuses our minds: How can we worthily hymn thy wonders, O blessed Nicholas? For no man can count them, even though he had many tongues and willed to tell of them; but we make bold to sing to God Who is wonderfully glorified in thee: Halleluiah.

People: *Halleluiah.*

Ikos 4

People far and near heard of the greatness of thy miracles, O divinely wise Nicholas, for through the air with the light wings of grace thou art accustomed to forestalling those in misfortunes, swiftly delivering all who cry to thee thus:

Rejoice, deliverance from sorrow.

Rejoice, giving of grace.

Rejoice, dispeller of unexpected evils.

Rejoice, planter of good desires.

Rejoice, swift comforter of those in misfortune.

Rejoice, dread punisher of wrongdoers.

Rejoice, abyss of miracles poured out by God.

Rejoice, tablets of the law of Christ written by God.

Rejoice, strong uplifting of the fallen.

Rejoice, affirmation of them that stand aright.

Rejoice, for through thee all deception is laid bare.

Rejoice, for through thee all truth is realised.

People: *Rejoice, Nicholas, O great Wonder Worker.*

Kontakion 5

Thou didst appear as a divinely moving star, guiding those who sail upon the cruel sea who once were threatened with immediate death, if thou hadst not come to the help of those who called on thee, O Wonder Worker saint Nicholas; for, having forbidden the flying demons who shamelessly wanted to sink the ship, thou didst drive them away and teach the faithful whom God saves through thee to cry: Halleluiah.

People: *Halleluiah.*

Ikos 5

The maidens, prepared for a dishonourable marriage because of their poverty, saw thy great compassion to the poor, O most blessed father Nicholas, when by night thou secretly gavest their aged father three bags of gold, thereby saving him and his daughters from falling into sin. Wherefore, thou hearest this from people:

Rejoice, treasury of greatest mercy.

Rejoice, container of providence for people.

Rejoice, food and consolation of those that flee to thee.

Rejoice, inexhaustible bread of the hungry.

Rejoice, God given wealth of those living in poverty on earth.

Rejoice, swift uplifting of the poor.

Rejoice, speedy hearing of the needy.

Rejoice, pleasant care of the sorrowful.

Rejoice, blameless provider for the three maidens.

Rejoice, fervent guardian of purity.

Rejoice, hope of the hopeless.

Rejoice, delight of all the world.

People: *Rejoice, Nicholas, O great Wonder Worker.*

Kontakion 6

The whole world proclaims thee, O most blessed Nicholas, to be a swift intercessor in misfortunes; for, oftentimes going before those that travel by land and sea, thou helpest them in a single moment, at the same time keeping from evils all that cry to God: Halleluiah.

People: *Halleluiah.*

Ikos 6

Thou didst shine as a living light, bringing deliverance to the commanders who received sentence to an unjust death, who called on thee, O good shepherd Nicholas, when thou didst at once appear in a dream to the Emperor, terrifying him and ordering him to set them free unharmed. Therefore, together with them we too gratefully cry to thee:

Rejoice, thou who helpest them that fervently call on thee.

Rejoice, thou who deliverest from unjust death.

Rejoice, thou who preservest from false slander.

Rejoice, thou who destroyest the counsels of the unrighteous.

Rejoice, thou who tearest lies to shreds like cobwebs.

Rejoice, thou who gloriously exaltest truth.

Rejoice, freeing of the innocent from their shackles.

Rejoice, quickening of the dead.

Rejoice, revealer of righteousness.

Rejoice, exposer of unrighteousness.

Rejoice, for through thee the innocent were saved from the sword.

Rejoice, for through thee they took pleasure in the light.

People: *Rejoice, Nicholas, O great Wonder Worker.*

Kontakion 7

Wishing to drive out the blasphemous stench of heresy, thou didst appear as a truly fragrant, mystical myrrh, O Nicholas; by shepherding the people of Myra, thou hast filled the whole world with thy gracious myrrh. And so, drive away from us the stench of abominable sin that we may acceptably cry to God. Halleluiah.

People: *Halleluiah.*

Ikos 7

We understand thee to be a new Noah, a guide of the ark of salvation, O holy father Nicholas, who drivest away the storm of all evils by thy direction, and bringest Divine calm to those that cry thus:

Rejoice, calm haven of the storm tossed.

Rejoice, sure preservation of those that are drowning.

Rejoice, good pilot of those that sail upon the deeps.

Rejoice, thou who rulest the raging of the sea.

Rejoice, guiding of those in whirlwinds.

Rejoice, warming of those in frosts.

Rejoice, radiance that drivest away the gloom of sorrow.

Rejoice, beacon that lightest all the ends of the earth.

Rejoice, thou who deliverest people from the abyss of sin.

Rejoice, thou who castest satan into the abyss of hell.

Rejoice, for through thee we boldly call on the abyss of Divine mercy.

Rejoice, for, delivered through thee from the flood of wrath, we find peace with God.

People: *Rejoice, Nicholas, O great Wonder Worker.*

Kontakion 8

Thy sacred church is shown to be a strange wonder to those that run to thee, O blessed Nicholas; for, by offering in it even a small supplication, we receive healing from great illnesses, if only, after God, we place our hope in thee, faithfully crying aloud: Halleluiah.

People: *Halleluiah.*

Ikos 8

Thou art truly a helper to all, O bearer of God Nicholas, and thou hast gathered together all that flee to thee, for thou art a deliverer, a nourisher and a swift healer to all on earth, moving all to cry out in praise to thee thus:

Rejoice, source of all manner of healing.

Rejoice, helper of those that suffer cruelly.

Rejoice, dawn shining for prodigals in the night of sin.

Rejoice, heaven sent dew for those in the heat of labours.

Rejoice, thou who givest prosperity to those that need it.

Rejoice, thou who preparest an abundance for those that ask.

Rejoice, thou who often forestallest supplications.

Rejoice, thou who renewest the strength of the aged and grey haired.

Rejoice, exposer of many who have strayed from the true path.

Rejoice, faithful servant of Divine mysteries.

Rejoice, for through thee we trample down envy.

Rejoice, for through thee we come to lead a moral life.

People: *Rejoice, Nicholas, O great Wonder Worker.*

Kontakion 9

Assuage all our pains, O Nicholas our great intercessor, dispensing gracious healings, delighting our souls and gladdening the hearts of all that fervently run to thee for help and cry to God: Halleluiah.

People: *Halleluiah.*

Ikos 9

We see how the orators of the ungodly with their vain wisdom were put to shame by thee, O divinely wise father Nicholas; for thou didst confute Arius the blasphemer who divided the Godhead, and Sabellius who confused the Persons of the Holy Trinity, but thou hast strengthened us in Orthodoxy. Therefore we cry to thee thus:

Rejoice, shield that defendest piety.

Rejoice, sword that cuttest down impiety.

Rejoice, teacher of the Divine commandments.

Rejoice, destroyer of impious teachings.

Rejoice, ladder raised up by God, by which we climb to heaven.

Rejoice, God given protection, by which many are protected.

Rejoice, thou who makest wise the unwise by thy words.

Rejoice, thou who movest the slothful by thine examples.

Rejoice, inextinguishable brightness of the commandments of God.

Rejoice, brightest ray of the statutes of the Lord.

Rejoice, for through thy teaching the heads of heretics are broken.

Rejoice, for through thee the faithful are counted worthy of glory.

People: *Rejoice, Nicholas, O great Wonder Worker.*

Kontakion 10

Wishing to save thy soul, thou didst truly subject thy flesh to the spirit, O our father Nicholas; for first by silence and struggling with thoughts, thou didst add contemplation to action, and by contemplation thou didst acquire perfect knowledge, with which thou didst boldly converse with God and Angels, ever crying: Halleluiah.

People: *Halleluiah.*

Ikos 10

Thou art a rampart, O most blessed one, to those that praise thy miracles and to all that flee to thine intercession; wherefore, free us too who are poor in virtue, from poverty, temptation, sickness and diverse needs, as we cry to thee with love thus:

Rejoice, thou who deliverest from eternal wretchedness.

Rejoice, thou who bestowest incorruptible riches.

Rejoice, imperishable food for those that hunger after righteousness.

Rejoice, inexhaustible drink for those that thirst for life.

Rejoice, thou who preservest from revolt and war.

Rejoice, thou who freest us from bonds and captivity.

Rejoice, most glorious intercessor in misfortunes.

Rejoice, greatest defender in misfortunes.

Rejoice, thou who hast snatched many from destruction.

Rejoice, thou who hast kept countless numbers unharmed.

Rejoice, for through thee sinners escape a frightful death.

Rejoice, for through thee those that repent obtain Eternal Life.

People: *Rejoice, Nicholas, O great Wonder Worker.*

Kontakion 11

Thou didst bring a song to the Most Holy Trinity, surpassing others in thought, word, and deed, O most blessed Nicholas; for with much searching thou didst explain the precepts of the true Faith, guiding us to sing with faith, hope and love to the One God in Trinity: Halleluiah.

People: *Halleluiah.*

Ikos 11

We see thee as a radiant and inextinguishable ray of light for those in the darkness of this life, O Divinely chosen father Nicholas; for thou dost converse with the immaterial angelic lights on the uncreated light of the Trinity and thou enlightenest the souls of the faithful who cry to thee thus:

Rejoice, radiance of the Threefold sun of light.

Rejoice, daystar of the unsetting Sun.

Rejoice, lamp kindled by the Divine Flame.

Rejoice, for thou hast quenched the demonic flame of impiety.

Rejoice, bright preaching of the true faith.

Rejoice, shining radiance of the light of the Gospel.

Rejoice, lightning that consumest heresies.

Rejoice, thunder that terrifiest tempters.

Rejoice, teacher of true knowledge.

Rejoice, revealer of the mystery of perception.

Rejoice, for through thee the worship of creation has been trampled down.

Rejoice, for through thee we have learned to worship the Creator in the Trinity.

People: *Rejoice, Nicholas, O great Wonder Worker.*

Kontakion 12

Knowing the grace that has been given thee by God, joyfully we celebrate thy memory as is due, O most glorious father Nicholas, and with all our souls we run to thy miraculous intercession; unable to count thy most glorious deeds, which are like unto the sand of the sea and the multitude of the stars, at a loss to understand, we cry to God: Halleluiah.

People: *Halleluiah.*

Ikos 12

Singing of thy miracles, we praise thee, O all praised Nicholas; for in thee God Who is glorified in the Trinity is wondrously glorified. But even if we were to offer thee a multitude of psalms and hymns composed from the soul, O holy Wonder Worker, we would do nothing to equal the gift of thy miracles, and amazed by them we cry to thee thus:

Rejoice, servant of the King of kings and the Lord of lords.

Rejoice, dweller together with His heavenly servants.

Rejoice, aid of faithful kings.

Rejoice, exaltation of the race of Christians.

Rejoice, namesake of victory.

Rejoice, eminent victor.

Rejoice, mirror of all the virtues.

Rejoice, strong buttress of all who run to thee.

Rejoice, after God and the Birth giver of God, all our hope.

Rejoice, health of our bodies and salvation of our souls.

Rejoice, for through thee we are freed from eternal death.

Rejoice, for through thee we are counted worthy of life unending.

People: *Rejoice, Nicholas, O great Wonder Worker.*

Kontakion 13

O most holy and most wonderful father Nicholas, consolation of all that sorrow, accept our present offering, and entreat the Lord that we may be delivered from Gehenna through thy intercession that is pleasing to God, that with thee we may sing: Halleluiah.

People: *Halleluiah.*

Ikos 1

The Creator revealed thee to be an angel in form though earthly by nature; for, foreseeing the fruitful goodness of thy soul, O most blessed Nicholas, He taught all to cry to thee thus:

Rejoice, thou who wast purified from thy mothers womb.

Rejoice, thou who wast hallowed even to the end.

Rejoice, thou who didst amaze thy parents by thy birth.

Rejoice, thou who didst show power of soul straightway after birth.

Rejoice, garden of the promised land.

Rejoice, flower of divine planting.

Rejoice, virtuous vine of the vineyard of Christ.

Rejoice, wonder working tree of the paradise of Jesus.

Rejoice, lily blossoming in paradise.

Rejoice, myrrh of the fragrance of Christ.

Rejoice, for through thee weeping is banished.

Rejoice, for through thee rejoicing is brought into being.

People: *Rejoice, Nicholas, O great Wonder Worker.*

Kontakion 1

O champion Wonder Worker and exceeding pleaser of Christ, who pourest out for the whole world the most precious myrrh of mercy and an inexhaustible sea of miracles, I praise thee with love, O Hierarch Nicholas; and as thou hast boldness towards the Lord, deliver me from all misfortunes that I may cry to thee:

People: *Rejoice, Nicholas, O great Wonder Worker.*

Trisagion Prayers

Reader: In the Name of the Father and of the Son and of the Holy Spirit.

People: *Amen. Glory to Thee, our God, glory to Thee.*

Reader: O Heavenly King, Comforter, Spirit of Truth, Who art everywhere present and fillest all things, Treasury of blessings and Giver of life: Come and abide in us and cleanse us from every impurity and save our souls, O Good One.

Holy God, Holy Mighty, Holy Immortal, have mercy on us. **(x3)**

Glory be to the Father, and to the Son, and to the Holy Spirit;
Both now and forever, and unto the ages of ages. Amen.

O Most Holy Trinity, have mercy on us.

O Lord, cleanse us from our sins.

O Master, pardon our iniquities.

O Holy One, visit and heal our infirmities, for Thy names sake.

Lord have mercy. **(x3)**

Glory be to the Father and to the Son and to the Holy Spirit;
Both now and forever, and unto the ages of ages. Amen.

People: Our Father, Who art in Heaven, hallowed be Thy Name. Thy Kingdom come, Thy will be done, on earth as it is in Heaven. Give us this day our daily bread, and forgive us our trespasses, as we forgive those who trespass against us; and lead us not into temptation, but deliver us from the evil one. Amen.

Lord, have mercy. **(x3)**

Glory be to the Father and to the Son and to the Holy Spirit;
Both now and forever and unto the ages of ages. Amen.

Come, let us worship God, our King.

Come, let us worship and fall down before Christ, our King and our God.

Come, let us worship and fall down before Christ Himself, our King and our God.

Oikos 1

Refrain: *Saints of Britain, pray to God for us.*

The sea became dry land for the Hosts of Israel, who passed over singing the song of salvation: And in the midst of these northern waters the numberless saints of these islands join in the hymn of victory and triumph.

Refrain: First Apostles and Saints of Britain, pray to God for us.

He who revealed the Philip the Way, the Truth and the Life sent forth His Apostles into the uttermost lands that even in their day their life giving teachings might call the Isles of Britain to give praise to Christ.

Refrain: Saints of Britain, pray to God for us.

Even from the womb, O God, Thou callest each by name. Thou alone canst number the Saints of this land. Grant then the aid of their mighty intercession to us who feebly echo their hymn of victory.

Glory be to the Father, and to the Son, and to the Holy Spirit;
Both now and forever, and unto the ages of ages. Amen.

Set in Avalon, a church of wattles made by holy hands the Son of God and of the Virgin Himself did dedicate to the Mother of God, that in these northern lands the first of churches should honour her who is the first among men and Angels.

Oikos 3

Refrain: Protomartyrs and Saints of Britain, pray to God for us.

Among the first let us praise the martyrs Alban the first killed, with Julius and Aaron and all those who by their blood baptised our land for Christ the Immovable Rock of our confession.

Refrain: Saint Pádraig and all Saints of Britain, pray to God for us.

In thy youth, O Pádraig, seized from the house of thy parents, through the prayer of misery and exile thou didst find God who, delivering thee out of slavery, called thee to be the ransoming of thy captors.

Refrain: Saint Pádraig and all Saints of Britain, pray to God for us.

Nothing of this world or of its pleasures delighted thee but to be bishop and apostle of the land of thy bondage and to accomplish in the span of thine own life the conversion of Ireland to worship the Trinity.

Glory be to the Father, and to the Son, and to the Holy Spirit;
Both now and forever, and unto the ages of ages. Amen.

The Virgin, consenting to the words of the Archangel, became the Mother of her own Creator. The land of Ireland, in an image of this mystery, became the Teacher of those who first taught her the way of Salvation. Instead of thy fathers, sons are born unto thee.

Oikos 4

Refrain: Saints of Britain, pray to God for us.

Sufferings unnumbered beset Thy British Saints, O Lord, and barbarous hordes arose to slaughter Thy baptised children. But Thou didst not suffer the darkness to overcome the light of the Gospel that Pádraig had kindled.

Refrain: Saint Columcille and all Saints of Britain, pray to God for us.

Of exile, the headstrong prince made an Apostolate and was called Columcille - the dove of good tidings, winning by love an army of souls for salvation and lighting on Iona a lamp to lighten the Scots.

Refrain: Saint Columcille and all Saints of Britain, pray to God for us.

Four and thirty years, O Columcille, didst thou labour in sowing but who can count the years of reaping? The unnumbered saints who took light from thy lamp, winning kings and kingdoms to the light of Christ.

> *Glory be to the Father, and to the Son, and to the Holy Spirit;*
> *Both now and forever, and unto the ages of ages. Amen.*

Blessed art thou in all generations, O Mother and Virgin, thou mountain overshadowed by the grace of God who didst bear for us Christ, the Light of the Gentiles. Save us by thine intercessions.

Oikos 5

Refrain: Saint David, Saint Nonna and all Saints of Britain, pray to God for us.

Right early let us rise to seek after God and to honour David, a dove among men, born of a saintly mother, who in Jerusalem was made a bishop that he might gather the Welsh to the flock of Christ.

Refrain: Saint Ninian and all Saints of Britain, pray to God for us.

If all were to be numbered by name and by achievements a hundred songs would not suffice for their praise. Ninian and Petroc, Paulinus and Sampson and countless others whose names are written in heaven.

Refrain: Holy Virgins and all Saints of Britain, pray to God for us.

The Virgins who follow Thee, let us praise them also, Ebba and Ursula, Winefrede and Bega with the holy abbess Hilda of Whitby and White and Awdrey, whose holy relics still protect us.

Glory be to the Father, and to the Son, and to the Holy Spirit;
Both now and forever, and unto the ages of ages. Amen.

At Thy right hand is set the Queen in a vesture of gold. O Virgin of virgins, alone mother and virgin, Strengthen us by thy mighty intercession Who with the hosts of the saints of Britain call thee blessed.

Oikos 6

Refrain: Saints of Britain, pray to God for us.

In the belly of the sea monster, the prophet Jonah cried out unto the Lord, and was delivered. In tribulation, the church of Thy Saints, calling upon Thee, likewise found salvation out of captivity.

Refrain: Saint Gregory and all Saints of Britain, pray to God for us.

Not as Angles, but as Angels in their beauty, the captives appeared to blessed Gregory in the slave market, and, mourning that they should be in ignorance of the Gospel, He resolved that they should be delivered from the wrath of God and taught to sing 'Halleluiah'.

Refrain: Saint Augustine and all Saints of Britain, pray to God for us.

Proclaiming the song, 'Halleluiah,' Augustine and his disciples carried Thy pure Icon and Thy precious Cross before the king. And he, edified both by their lives and their teaching was baptised into the Name of the Trinity.

Glory be to the Father, and to the Son, and to the Holy Spirit;
Both now and forever, and unto the ages of ages. Amen.

Rejoicing sevenfold in Augustine and his successors let us praise among them that new apostle from Tarsus, the blessed Theodore, who, by his endeavours, united this land to bless the Mother of God.

Oikos 7

Refrain: Saint Aidan and all Saints of Britain, pray to God for us.

Aidan the blessed, by his preaching of the Gospel, made holy the island of Lindisfarne; by his bishopric made of the Northumbrian nation a Christian people and won two kings to the ranks of the martyrs so that kings, priests and people might bless God for ever.

Refrain: King and Martyr Oswald and all Saints of Britain, pray to God for us.

In the sight of the heathen, Oswald, the holy king and Martyr, set up Thy Cross, O Christ, for an emblem of victory, beseeching Thy mercy against an arrogant and savage enemy, and trusting to Thee the just cause of his nation so that kings, priests and people might bless God for ever.

Refrain: Saint Cuthbert and all Saints of Britain, pray to God for us.

Seeking solitude, O Cuthbert, to crown thy monastic labour, choosing the sea for thy desert and Christ alone for thy consolation; at whose call, taking up thy cross, thou becamest a bishop, so that kings, priests and people might bless God for ever.

> *Glory be to the Father, and to the Son, and to the Holy Spirit;*
> *Both now and forever, and unto the ages of ages. Amen.*

Even death could not diminish thy light, O Cuthbert, for thine incorrupt relics, set on a hill in Durham, shone like a lamp for a people thou hadst not forsaken, proclaiming to them the incorruptible victory of Christ our God, whom magnifying we call the Virgin blessed.

Oikos 8

Refrain: Saints of Britain, pray to God for us.

To Him who saved the three children in the midst of the furnace, come, raise with us a hymn, O Birinus, Paulinus and all you coequal of the Apostles, who to every kingdom of the British sounded the voice of your preaching. Come also, you godly kings who nurtured the increase of their teaching; Cross exalting Oswald among their number, and Edmund, disciple of the Crucified who, as a lamb for the slaughter, offered his life for his people: Come, bless, praise and exalt God above all for ever.

Refrain: Saint George and all Saints of Britain, pray to God for us.

Holiness upon the head, like Aaron, true high priests have you appeared, O holy bishops, shepherds of the sheep of Christ in these lands; Swithin and Chad, Melitus, good John of Beverley and all you bishops, you wonder workers also, hermits, holy abbots and you who shone in the monastic life; come, join with all the martyrs of these lands, who sing with George the triumphant, our Patron, and with all the saints, blessing, praising and high exalting God for ever.

Refrain: Saint Andrew and all Saints of Britain, pray to God for us.

Even as wise stewards receiving the Talents of the Gospel, you missionary saints, like merchants, have traded your treasure and in other lands have brought forth fruits of your labours: Come then, you late apostles, and with Andrew the first called, who sanctified this land by his relics, and with all who blessed these islands in an age of faith: Aid us by your prayers, who in these latter days sing, bless, praise and exalt God above all for ever.

Glory be to the Father, and to the Son, and to the Holy Spirit;
Both now and forever, and unto the ages of ages. Amen.

Even the Angels dare not contemplate the mystery of thy maternity, O Theotokos, which the burning furnace prefigured of old; for in thy womb God and human nature were united, suffering neither confusion nor division: and we also, the inheritors of this mystery, emboldened by the protection of thy prayers, bless, praise and exalt God above all for ever.

Refrain: We praise, bless and worship the Lord, singing praises and exalting Him for ever.

Oikos 9

Refrain: Most holy Theotokos, save us.

To thee, the Bride who knewest not the embrace of a husband, the Virgin and Mother who gave birth to God, these islands raise a song of thanksgiving. By thy prayers save thine own people, O Theotokos.

Refrain: Most holy Theotokos, save us.

As a vesture of pure gold, O Theotokos, accept the beauty of these islands, and as an adornment of divers jewels the saints who therein have glorified thy Son.

Refrain: Most holy Theotokos, save us.

O Theotokos, the boldness of the apostles who in diverse ages preached in this our land, succour in our confession us, the inheritors of their teaching, for we are made strong, O Virgin, by thy prayers.

Glory be to the Father, and to the Son, and to the Holy Spirit;
Both now and forever, and unto the ages of ages. Amen.

O joy of our martyred kings, aid of our wonder workers, shepherd of our bishops, succour of all our saints: Grant that to their number we also may be gathered by thy mighty intercession, O Theotokos.

Troparion

Reader: O Angel of God, my holy Guardian, keep my life in the fear of Christ God, strengthen my mind in the true way and wound my soul with heavenly love, so that guided by Thee, I may obtain the great mercy of Christ God.

Chorus: *Glory be to the Father and to the Son and to the Holy Spirit.*

Both now and forever and unto the ages of ages. Amen.

Theotokion

O holy Lady, Mother of our God, thou didst amazingly bear the Creator of People: with my Guardian Angel always pray His kindness to save my soul inhibited and bound by passions, and grant me remission of sins.

Ode 1

Eirmos

Tone 8   Humility, tranquillity, repose, suffering, pleading.   *C, D, Eb, F, G, A, Bb, C.*

Let us sing to the Lord Who led His people through the Red Sea, for He alone has gloriously triumphed.

People: *Jesus, Son of God, have mercy on us.*

Troparia

Grant me, Thy servant, O Saviour, worthily to sing a song and to praise the fleshless Angel, my Guide and Guardian.

People: *Holy Angel, my Guardian, pray for me.*

I lay alone in folly and idleness, O my Guide and Guardian; forsake not me who am perishing.

Chorus: *Glory be to the Father and to the Son and to the Holy Spirit.*

Guide my mind by thy prayer to fulfil the commandments of God, and to receive from God remission of sins, and teach me to hate all wickedness, I pray thee.

Chorus: *Both now and forever and unto the ages of ages. Amen.*

Theotokion

With my Guardian Angel, O Virgin, pray for me thy servant to the Bountiful One, and teach me to fulfil the commandments of thy Son and my Creator.

Ode 3

Eirmos

Thou art the strengthening of all who come to Thee, O Lord, Thou art the Light of those in darkness, and my spirit sings of Thee.

People: Holy Angel, my Guardian, pray for me.

Troparia

All my thoughts and my soul I have committed to thee, O my Guardian; deliver me from all attacks of the enemy.

People: Holy Angel, my Guardian, pray for me.

The enemy troubles and tramples on me, and teaches me to follow my own desires; but, O my Guide, forsake not the dying.

Chorus: Glory be to the Father and to the Son and to the Holy Spirit.

Grant me to sing with thanksgiving and fervour to my Creator and God, and to thee my good Angel Guardian: O my deliverer, rescue me from foes that trouble me.

Chorus: Both now and forever and unto the ages of ages. Amen.

Theotokion

Heal, O immaculate one, the most painful wounds of my soul, and drive away the enemies ever fighting against me.

People: Lord, have mercy. **(x3)**

Chorus: Glory be to the Father and to the Son and to the Holy Spirit.
Both now and forever and unto the ages of ages. Amen.

Sedalion

From the love of my soul I cry to thee, O Guardian of my soul, my most holy Angel. Protect and guard me always from the hunting of the evil one, and guide me to the heavenly life; teach me and enlighten me and strengthen me.

Chorus: Glory be to the Father and to the Son and to the Holy Spirit.
Both now and forever and unto the ages of ages. Amen.

Theotokion

Immaculate Virgin, Mother of God, who gavest birth without seed to the Lord of all, pray Him with my Guardian Angel to deliver me from all doubt, and to give to my soul feeling and light, and to cleanse me from sin, for thou alone art a quick defender.

Ode 4

Eirmos

I have heard, O Lord, the mystery of Thy plan. I contemplate Thy works, and glorify Thy divine nature.

People: *Holy Angel, my Guardian, pray for me.*

Troparia

Pray to God the Lover of men, and leave me not, O my Guardian, but ever keep my life in peace, and grant me the invincible salvation.

People: *Holy Angel, my Guardian, pray for me.*

As the defender and guardian of my life I received thee from God; O Angel. I pray thee, O holy one, free me from all harm.

Chorus: *Glory be to the Father and to the Son and to the Holy Spirit.*

Cleanse my foulness by thy holiness, O my Guardian, and may I be drawn from the left side by thy prayers, and become a partaker of glory.

Chorus: *Both now and forever and unto the ages of ages. Amen.*

Theotokion

Perplexity confronts me through the evil surrounding me, O immaculate one, but deliver me from it speedily, for I run only to thee.

Ode 5

Eirmos

Rising early we cry to Thee, O Lord; save us, for Thou art our God, and other than Thee we know none.

People: *Holy Angel, my Guardian, pray for me.*

Troparia

As thou hast boldness towards God, my holy Guardian, pray Him to deliver me from the evils which offend me.

People: *Holy Angel, my Guardian, pray for me.*

O radiant light, make radiant my soul, my Guide and Guardian Angel, given to me by God.

Chorus: *Glory be to the Father and to the Son and to the Holy Spirit.*

Keep me awake who sleep from the burden of my sins, O Angel of God, and by thy prayers raise me up to glorify Him.

Chorus: *Both now and forever and unto the ages of ages. Amen.*

Theotokion

O Lady Mary, Virgin Mother of God, O hope of the faithful, subdue the attacks of the enemy, and to those who sing to thee give joy.

Ode 6

Eirmos

Grant me a garment of Light, O Thou Who wrappest Thyself in Light for a garment, most merciful Christ our God.

People: *Holy Angel, my Guardian, pray for me.*

Troparia

Deliver me from every misfortune and accident and save me from sorrow, I pray, O holy Angel, given to me as my good Guardian by God.

People: *Holy Angel, my Guardian, pray for me.*

Enlighten my mind, O good one, and illumine me, I pray thee, O holy Angel, and teach me to think always positively and profitably.

Chorus: *Glory be to the Father and to the Son and to the Holy Spirit.*

Calm my heart from present disturbance, and strengthen me to be awake to the good, my Guardian, and miraculously guide me in quietness of life

Chorus: *Both now and forever and unto the ages of ages. Amen.*

Theotokion

The Word of God dwelt in thee, O Mother of God, and showed thee to men as the heavenly ladder. For by thee the Most High descended to us.

Chorus: *Lord, have mercy.* **(x3)**

> *Glory be to the Father and to the Son and to the Holy Spirit.*
> *Both now and forever and unto the ages of ages. Amen.*

Kontakion

Have compassion on me, O holy Angel of the Lord, my Guardian, and leave me not, impure as I am, but irradiate me with the Divine Light, and make me worthy of the Heavenly Kingdom.

Oikos

Grant my soul, humiliated by many temptations, the ineffable Heavenly Glory, O holy intercessor and singer with the Chorus' of fleshless Powers of God. Have mercy and keep me, and illumine my soul with good thoughts, that I may be enriched by thy glory, O my Angel; subdue my foes who wish me evil, and make me worthy of the Heavenly Kingdom.

Ode 7

Eirmos

Having arrived in Babylon from Judea, the children of old by their faith in the Trinity trod down the flame of the furnace singing: O God of our fathers, blessed art Thou.

People: *Holy Angel, my Guardian, pray for me.*

Troparia

Have mercy and pray for me, Angel of the Lord, for I have thee as my defender for the whole of my life, the Guide and Guardian, given me by God forever.

People: *Holy Angel, my Guardian, pray for me.*

Let not my sinful pilgrim soul, given thee chaste by God, be murdered by robbers, O Holy Angel, but lead it to the way of repentance.

Chorus: *Glory be to the Father and to the Son and to the Holy Spirit.*

My whole soul is disgraced by evil thoughts and acts, but make haste, O my Guide, and grant me healing with good thoughts, that I may always follow the right way.

Chorus: *Both now and forever and unto the ages of ages. Amen.*

To Jesus

Fill with wisdom and divine strength all who cry with faith, through the Mother of God, to Thee, O Personal Wisdom of the Highest: O God of our fathers, blessed art Thou.

Ode 8

Eirmos

The King of Heaven, Whom Hosts of Angels praise, let us praise and exalt throughout all ages.

People: *Holy Angel, my Guardian, pray for me.*

Troparia

Strengthen the life of thy servant and never leave me, O gracious Angel, sent by God.

People: *Holy Angel, my Guardian, pray for me.*

I ever hymn thee, O Good Angel, Guide and Guardian of my soul, most blessed spirit.

Chorus: *Glory be to the Father and to the Son and to the Holy Spirit.*

Be my Veil and Visor in the Judgement Day of all men, when all deeds, good and evil, shall be tried by fire.

Chorus: *Both now and forever and unto the ages of ages. Amen.*

Theotokion

Be the help and peace of thy servant, O Ever Virgin Mother of God, and leave me not bereft of thy protection.

Ode 9

Eirmos

Saved by thee, O pure Virgin, we confess thee to be supremely the Mother of God, and with Fleshless Chorus we magnify thee.

People: *O Jesus, Son of God, have mercy on us.*

Troparia

Have mercy on me, O my only Saviour, for Thou art merciful and kind hearted, and make me a member of the Chorus' of the Righteous.

People: *Holy Angel, my Guardian, pray for me.*

Grant me ever to think and do only what is useful, O Angel of the Lord, that I may be undefiled and strong in infirmity.

Chorus: *Glory be to the Father and to the Son and to the Holy Spirit.*

Having boldness towards the Heavenly King, pray Him, with the other Angels, to have mercy on me, wretched as I am.

Chorus: *Both now and forever and unto the ages of ages. Amen.*

Theotokion

O Virgin, who hast great boldness towards Him Who took flesh of thee, deliver me from attachments and grant me forgiveness and salvation by thy prayers.

Prayer To The Holy Guardian Angel

Holy Angel of Christ, I fall down and pray to thee, my holy Guardian, given me from holy Baptism for the protection of my sinful body and soul. By my laziness and bad habits, I have angered thy most pure light, and have driven thee away from me by all my shameful deeds, lies, slanders, envy, condemnation, scorn, disobedience, brotherly-hatred, grudges, love of money, adultery, anger, meanness, greed, excess, talkativeness, negative and evil thoughts, proud ways, dissolute madness, having self-will in all the desires of the flesh. O my evil will, which even the dumb animals do not follow. How canst thou look at me or approach me who am like a stinking dog? With what eyes, O Angel of Christ, wilt thou look at me so badly snared in evil deeds? How can I ask forgiveness for my bitter, evil and wicked deeds, into which I fall every day and night, and every hour? But I fall down and pray, O my holy Guardian: pity me, thy sinful and unworthy servant (Name). Be my helper and protector against my wicked enemy, by thy holy prayers, and make me a partaker of the Kingdom of God with all the Saints, always, now and ever, and to the ages of ages. Amen.

Akathist For The Repose Of Those Who Have Fallen Asleep

Kontakion 1

O Thou Who by Thy inscrutable Providence didst prepare the world for eternal beatitude and Who appointest times and seasons and the manner of our end: Forgive, O Lord, those who have died in past ages all their sins, receive them into the realms of light and joy, hasten to open Thy Fatherly arms to them, and hear us who celebrate their memory and sing:

All: O Lord of unutterable Love, remember Thy servant[s] ... who have fallen asleep *[in the service of their country]*.

Ikos 1

O Thou Who savest Adam and the whole human race from eternal perdition, Thou didst send Thy Son into the world, O Good God, and by His Cross and Resurrection Thou hast granted us also eternal life. Trusting to Thy infinite mercy, we look for the deathless Kingdom of Thy Glory, we implore Thee to grant it to those who have fallen asleep, and we pray:

Gladden, O Lord, souls wearied by the storms of life, that earth's sorrows and signings may not bury them in oblivion. Hear them, O Lord, in Thy bosom, as a mother responds to her children, and say to them: Your sins are forgiven you. Receive them, O Lord, into Thy calm and blessed haven that they may rejoice in Thy divine glory.

All: O Lord of unutterable Love, remember Thy servant[s] ... who have fallen asleep *[in the service of their country]*.

Kontakion 2

Enlightened by the illumination of the Most High, Saint Macarius heard a voice from a pagan skull: "When you pray for those suffering in Hell, there is relief for the heathen." O wonderful power of Christian prayer, by which even the infernal regions are illumined. Both believers and unbelievers receive comfort when we cry for the whole world: Halleluiah.
All: Halleluiah.

Ikos 2

Saint Isaac the Syrian once said: "A merciful heart is one that burns with love for men and animals and for the whole of creation, and at all times offers prayers with tears that they may be purified and kept." Likewise we all boldly ask the Lord for help for all the dead from the beginning of time and cry: Send down to us, O Lord, the gift of fervent prayer for the dead. Remember, O Lord, all who have charged us, unworthy as we are, to pray for them, and pardon the sins they have forgotten.

Remember, O Lord, all who have been buried without prayer. Receive, O Lord, into Thy dwellings all who have died of sorrow or joy by a sudden or untimely death.

All: O Lord of unutterable Love, remember Thy servant[s] ... who have fallen asleep *[in the service of their country]*.

Kontakion 3

We are to blame for the calamities in the world, for the sufferings of dumb creatures, and for the diseases and torments of innocent children, for through the fall of man the beatitude and beauty of all creation has been marred. O Christ our God, greatest of innocent Sufferers. Thou alone canst forgive all. Forgive, then, all and everything, and grant to the world its primordial prosperity, that the living and the dead may rejoice and cry: Halleluiah.

All: Halleluiah.

Ikos 3

O Glad Light, Redeemer of the world, embracing the whole universe with Thy love: behold, Thy cry from the Cross for Thy enemies is heard: "Father, forgive them." In the name of Thy all forgiving love we make bold to pray to our Heavenly Father for the eternal repose of Thy enemies and ours. Forgive, O Lord, those who have shed innocent blood, those who have sown our path of life with sorrows, those who have waded to prosperity through the tears of their neighbours. Condemn not, O Lord, those who persecute us with slander and malice. Repay with mercy those whom we have wronged or offended through ignorance, and grant that our prayer for them may be holy through the sacrament of reconciliation.

All: O Lord of unutterable Love, remember Thy servant[s] ... who have fallen asleep *[in the service of their country]*.

Kontakion 4

Save, O Lord, those who have died in grievous sufferings, those who were murdered, those buried alive, those who were drowned or burned, those who were torn by wild beasts, those who died of hunger or cold, from exposure in storms, or by falling from heights, and grant them all eternal joy for the sorrow of their death. May the time of their suffering be blessed as a day of redemption, for which they sing: Halleluiah.

All: Halleluiah.

Ikos 4

Recompense with the compassion of Thy infinite love, O Lord, all who have died in the full flush of their youth, who received on earth the thorny crown of suffering, who never experienced earthly joy.

Grant recompense to those who died from overwork, through exploitation or sweated labour. Receive, O Lord, into the bridal halls of Paradise boys and girls, and grant them joy at the marriage supper of Thy Son.

Comfort and console the grief of parents over their dead children. Give rest, O Lord, to all who have no one to offer prayer for them to Thee, their Creator, that their sins may vanish in the dazzling light of Thy forgiveness.

All: O Lord of unutterable Love, remember Thy servant[s] ... who have fallen asleep *[in the service of their country]*.

Kontakion 5

Thou hast given us death as a last prodigy to bring us to our senses and to repentance, O Lord. In its threatening light, earthly vanity is exposed, carnal passions and sufferings become subdued, in submissive reason is humbled. Eternal justice and righteousness opens to our gaze, and then the godless and those burdened with sins confess on their deathbed Thy real and eternal existence and cry to Thy mercy: Halleluiah.
All: Halleluiah.

Ikos 5

O Father of all consolation and comfort, Thou brightenest with the sun, delightest with fruits, and gladdenest with the beauty of the world both Thy friends and enemies. And we believe that even beyond the grave Thy loving kindness, which is merciful even to all rejected sinners, does not fail. We grieve for hardened and wicked blasphemers of Thy Holiness. May Thy saving and gracious will be over them.

Forgive, O Lord, those who have died without repentance. Save those who have committed suicide in the darkness of their mind, that the flame of their sinfulness may be extinguished in the ocean of Thy grace.

All: O Lord of unutterable Love, remember Thy servant[s] ... who have fallen asleep *[in the service of their country]*.

Kontakion 6

Terrible is the darkness of a soul separated from God, the torments of conscience, the gnashing of teeth, the unquenchable fire and the undying worm. I tremble at the thought of such a fate, and I pray for those suffering in Hell as for myself. May our song descend upon them as refreshing dew as we sing: Halleluiah.
All: Halleluiah.

Ikos 6

Thy light, O Christ our God, has shone upon those sitting in the darkness and shadow of death and those in Hell who cannot cry to Thee. Descend into the infernal regions of the earth, O Lord, and bring out into the joy of grace Thy children who have been separated from Thee by sin but who have not rejected Thee.

For they suffer cruelly. Have mercy on them. For they sinned against Heaven and before Thee, and their sins are infinitely grievous, and Thy mercy is infinite. Visit the bitter misery of souls separated from Thee. Have mercy, O Lord, on those who hated the truth out of ignorance. May Thy love be to them not a consuming fire but the coolness of Paradise:

All: O Lord of unutterable Love, remember Thy servant[s] ... who have fallen asleep *[in the service of their country]*.

Kontakion 7

Endeavouring to give help by Thy might power to Thy servants who have fallen asleep, Thou hast appeared to their loved ones, O Lord, in mysterious visions clearly inspiring them to pray, that they may remember the departed, and do good works and labours of faith and love for them, crying: Halleluiah.

All: Halleluiah.

Ikos 7

The universal Church of Christ unceasingly offers prayers every hour for the departed throughout the world, for the sins of the world are washed away by the most pure Blood of Thy divine crown, and the souls of those who have fallen asleep are translated from death to life and from earth to Heaven by the power of the prayers offered for them at God's altars. May the intercession of the Church for the dead, O Lord, be a ladder to Heaven. Have mercy on them, O Lord, through the intercession of the most holy Mother of God and all the Saints.

Forgive them their sins for the sake of Thy faithful who cry day and night to Thee. For the sake of innocent children, O Lord, have mercy on their parents, and by the tears of their mothers, forgive the sins of their children. For the sake of the prayers of innocent sufferers and the blood of martyrs, spare and have mercy on sinners. Receive, O Lord, our prayers and alms as a memorial of their virtues.

All: O Lord of unutterable Love, remember Thy servant[s] ... who have fallen asleep *[in the service of their country]*.

Kontakion 8

The whole world is a sacred and common graveyard, for in every place is the dust of our fathers and brothers. O Christ our God, Who alone unchangeably lovest us, forgive all who have died form the beginning till now, that they may sing with infinite love: Halleluiah.

All: Halleluiah.

Ikos 8

The day is coming, as a burning furnace, the great and terrible day of the Last Judgement, when the secrets of men shall be revealed and the books of conscience shall be torn apart. "Be reconciled with God." cries the Apostle Paul. "Be reconciled before that terrible day." Help us, O Lord, to fill up with the tears of the living what was lacking in the dead. May the sound of the Angel's trumpet, O Lord, be to them the glad announcement of their salvation and the joyful manumission of their freedom at the hour of Thy judgement. Crown with glory those who have suffered for Thee, O Lord, and cover the sins of the weak with Thy goodness. O Lord, Who knowest all by name, remember those who have sought salvation in the monastic life. Remember the blessed pastors with their spiritual children.

All: O Lord of unutterable Love, remember Thy servant[s] ... who have fallen asleep *[in the service of their country]*.

Kontakion 9

Bless swiftly passing time. For every hour, every moment brings eternity nearer. A new sorrow, a new gray hair are heralds of the coming world, witnesses of earthly corruption, for they say that all is passing and the Eternal kingdom draws near, where there is no sorrow, no sighing, no tears, but joyful singing: Halleluiah.
All: Halleluiah.

Ikos 9

Just as a tree loses its leaves after a time, so our days after a certain number of years come to an end. The festival of youth fades, the lamp of joy goes out, the alienation and dispossession of old age approaches. Friends and relations die. Where are you, young merrymakers? Their tombs are silent, but their souls are in Thy hand. Let us think how they watch us form the spiritual world.

O Lord, Who art the brightest Sun, illumine and warm the abodes of those who have fallen asleep. May the time of our bitter separation pass for ever. Grant us a joyful meeting in Heaven. Grant that all may be one with Thee, O Lord. Restore to the departed, O Lord, the purity of childhood and the genial spirit of youth, and may eternal life be to them a Paschal Festival.

All: O Lord of unutterable Love, remember Thy servant[s] ... who have fallen asleep *[in the service of their country]*.

Kontakion 10

Shedding silent tears at the graves of our relatives, we pray with hope, and cry expectantly: Tell us, O Lord, that their sins are forgiven. Give our spirit a secret assurance of it, that we may sing: Halleluiah.
All: Halleluiah.

Ikos 10

Looking back, I see the whole of our past life. What a vast multitude of people have departed from the first day until now. And many of them have done me good. In gratitude for what I owe them, with love I cry to Thee: Grant heavenly glory, O Lord, to my parents and those near and dear to me who watched over my cradle in childhood, and reared and educated me.

Glorify, O Lord, in the presence of the Holy Angels all who have told me the glad tidings of salvation and have taught me what is right and good, just and true by the holy example of their lives. Fill with delight, O Lord, those who fed me on hidden manna in the days of my sorrow and affliction. Recompense and save all benefactors and all who have helped others personally and by prayer.

All: O Lord of unutterable Love, remember Thy servant[s] ... who have fallen asleep *[in the service of their country]*.

Kontakion 11

O death, where is thy sting? Where is the gloom and terror that held sway in the past? From now on thou art the longed for means of inseparable union with God. Oh, the great peace of the mystical Sabbath. We long to die and to be with Christ, cries the Apostle. Therefore, we too look upon death as the gateway to eternal life, and cry: Halleluiah.

All: *Halleluiah.*

Ikos 11

The dead shall rise and those who are in the graves shall stand up, and those who are alive on earth shall exult when they stand with their spiritual bodies, radiantly glorious and incorrupt.

Dry bones, hear the word of the Lord: "I shall bring upon you a spirit of life, and shall lay sinews upon you; and I shall bring flesh upon you, and cover you with skin." Rise out of the ancient past, you who are redeemed by the Blood of the Son of God, restored to life by His death, for the light of the Resurrection has dawned upon you. Open to them now, O Lord, the whole abyss of Thy perfections. Thou hast shone upon them with the light of the sun and moon, that they may see the glory of the radiant Chorus' of Angels, Thou hast delighted them with the magnificence of the heavenly lights of East and West, that they may also see the never setting light of Thy Divinity.

All: O Lord of unutterable Love, remember Thy servant[s] ... who have fallen asleep *[in the service of their country]*.

Kontakion 12

Flesh and blood shall not inherit the Kingdom of God. While we live in the flesh, we are separated from Christ. And if we die, we live for eternity. For our corruptible body must put on incorruption, and this mortal nature must shine with immortality, that in the light of the eternal day we may sing: Halleluiah.

All: *Halleluiah.*

Ikos 12

We expect to meet the Lord, we expect the clear dawn of the Resurrection, we expect the rousing from their tombs of our dead relatives and acquaintances and their restoration to the most holy beauty of life. And we rejoice in the coming transfiguration of all creation, and cry to our Creator: O Lord, Who didst create the world for the triumph of joy and goodness, Who hast restored us to holiness from the depths of sin, grant that the dead may reign in the new creation, and may shine as heavenly lights in the day of their glory. May the Divine Lamb be their perpetual light.

Grant, O Lord, that we too may celebrate with them a deathless Passover. Unite the dead and the living in unending joy.

All: O Lord of unutterable Love, remember Thy servant[s] ... who have fallen asleep *[in the service of their country]*.

Kontakion 13

O most merciful and eternal Father, Whose will it is that all should be saved, Who didst send Thy Son to the lost and didst pour out Thy Life giving Spirit: Have mercy on our relatives and those who are near and dear to us who have fallen asleep, and on all who have died throughout the ages; forgive and save them, and by their intercession visit us, that with them we may shout to Thee, our God and Saviour, the song of victory: Halleluiah. Halleluiah. Halleluiah.

All: Halleluiah, Halleluiah, Halleluiah.

Kontakion 1

O Thou Who by Thy inscrutable Providence didst prepare the world for eternal beatitude and Who appointest times and seasons and the manner of our end: Forgive, O Lord, those who have died in past ages all their sins, receive them into the realms of light and joy, hasten to open Thy Fatherly arms to them, and hear us who celebrate their memory and sing:

All: O Lord of unutterable Love, remember Thy servant[s] ... who have fallen asleep *[in the service of their country]*.

Ikos 1

O Thou Who savest Adam and the whole human race from eternal perdition, Thou didst send Thy Son into the world, O Good God, and by His Cross and Resurrection Thou hast granted us also eternal life. Trusting to Thy infinite mercy, we look for the deathless Kingdom of Thy Glory, we implore Thee to grant it to those who have fallen asleep, and we pray: Gladden, O Lord, souls wearied by the storms of life, that earth's sorrows and signings may not bury them in oblivion. Hear them, O Lord, in Thy bosom, as a mother responds to her children, and say to them: Your sins are forgiven you. Receive them, O Lord, into Thy calm and blessed haven that they may rejoice in Thy divine glory.

All: O Lord of unutterable Love, remember Thy servant[s] ... who have fallen asleep *[in the service of their country]*.

Prayer For Those Who Have Fallen Asleep

O God of spirits and all flesh, Who hast trampled down death, overthrown the devil, and given life to Thy world: Give rest, O Lord, to the souls of Thy servants who have fallen asleep, Patriarchs, Metropolitans, Archbishops, Bishops, Priests and Deacons, Monks and Nuns, and all who have served Thee in Thy Church; the founders of all Churches and Monasteries, and all Orthodox forefathers, fathers, brothers and sisters who lie here and everywhere; officers and men of the armies and navies who have laid down their lives for their

Faith and country, all the faithful killed in civil wars, all who were drowned, burned, frozen to death, torn by wild beasts, all who died suddenly without repentance and had no time to be reconciled with the Church and with their enemies; all who took their own lives in a moment of mental unbalance; all who have asked us to pray for them, and those who have no one to pray for them, and all who died without a Christian burial, in a place of light, in a place of refreshment, in a place of repose, whence all suffering, sorrow, and sighing have fled away. Forgive every sin committed by them in thought, word and deed, for Thou art the good God and Lover of men. For there is no one who lives without sinning. Thou alone art without sin, and Thy righteousness in eternal righteousness, and Thy Word is Truth.

For Thou art the Resurrection, the Life, and the Repose of Thy servants who have fallen asleep *[names of the dead]*, O Christ our God, and to Thee we send up glory, with Thy Eternal Father, and Thy Holy and Good and Life giving Spirit, both now and forever and to the ages of ages. Amen.

A General Service of Prayer For Any Saint
Parakleses or Molieben

[With a priest.]

[Have Troparion ready.]

[This service has example variables for St Martin of Tours and St David of Wales.]

The Trisagion Prayers

Deacon: Holy Father, Bless.

Priest: Blessed is our God always, now and forever, and unto the ages of ages.

People: Amen.

Priest: O Heavenly King, Comforter, Spirit of Truth, Who art everywhere present and fillest all things, Treasury of blessings and Giver of life: Come and abide in us and cleanse us from every impurity and save our souls, O Good One.

Reader: Holy God, Holy Mighty, Holy Immortal, have mercy on us. **(x3)**

Glory be to the Father, and to the Son, and to the Holy Spirit;
Both now and forever, and unto the ages of ages. Amen.

O Most Holy Trinity, have mercy on us.

O Lord, cleanse us from our sins.

O Master, pardon our iniquities.

O Holy One, visit and heal our infirmities, for Thy names sake.

Lord have mercy. **(x3)**

Glory be to the Father and to the Son and to the Holy Spirit;
Both now and forever, and unto the ages of ages. Amen.

People: Our Father, Who art in Heaven, hallowed be Thy Name. Thy Kingdom come, Thy will be done, on earth as it is in Heaven. Give us this day our daily bread, and forgive us our trespasses, as we forgive those who trespass against us; and lead us not into temptation, but deliver us from the evil one.

Priest: For Thine is the kingdom, and the power and the glory of the Father and of the Son and of the Holy Spirit, now and forever and to the ages of ages.

People: Amen.

People: Lord have mercy. **(x12)**

Glory be to the Father and to the Son and to the Holy Spirit,
Both now and forever and unto the ages of ages. Amen.

Come, let us worship God, our King.

Come, let us worship and fall down before Christ, our King and our God.

Come, let us worship and fall down before Christ Himself, our King and our God.

Psalm 142

Hear my prayer, O Lord, give ear to my supplications. In Thy faithfulness answer me, and in Thy righteousness. Do not enter into judgement with Thy servant, for in Thy sight no one living is righteous. For the enemy has persecuted my soul; he has crushed my life to the ground; he has made me dwell in darkness, like those who have long been dead. Therefore my spirit is overwhelmed within me; my heart within me is distressed. I remember the days of old; I meditate on all Thy works; I muse on the work of Thine hands. I spread out my hands to Thee; my soul longs for Thee like a thirsty land. Answer me speedily, O Lord; my spirit fails. Do not hide Thy face from me, lest I be like those who go down into the pit. Cause me to hear Thy loving kindness in the morning, for in Thee do I trust; cause me to know the way in which I should walk, for I lift up my soul to Thee. Deliver me, O Lord, from mine enemies; in Thee I take shelter. Teach me to do Thy will, for Thou art my God; Thy Spirit is good. Lead me in the land of uprightness. Revive me, O Lord, for Thy names sake. For Thy righteousness' sake bring my soul out of trouble. In Thy mercy cut off mine enemies, and destroy all those who afflict my soul; for I am Thy servant.

After The Psalm

Glory be to the Father and to the Son and to the Holy Spirit,
Both now and forever and unto the ages of ages. Amen.

Halleluiah, Halleluiah, Halleluiah. Glory to Thee, O God. **(x3)**

Lord, have mercy. **(x3)**

God Is The Lord

People: *God is the Lord and has revealed Himself to us. Blessed is He who cometh in the Name of the Lord.*

Reader: Give thanks to the Lord, for He is good; and His steadfast love endures forever.

People: *God is the Lord and has revealed Himself to us. Blessed is He who cometh in the Name of the Lord.*

Reader: All nations surrounded me; in the Name of the Lord, I withstood them.

People: *God is the Lord and has revealed Himself to us. Blessed is He who cometh in the Name of the Lord.*

Reader: I shall not die, but live, and recount the deeds of the Lord.

People: *God is the Lord and has revealed Himself to us. Blessed is He who cometh in the Name of the Lord.*

Reader: The stone that the builders rejected has become the chief cornerstone.

   This is the Lords doing and is marvellous in our eyes.

People: *God is the Lord and has revealed Himself to us. Blessed is He who cometh in the Name of the Lord.*

*[If this service is to the **Saviour** then:]*

We do homage to Thy pure image, O Good One, entreating forgiveness of our transgressions, O Christ our God; for of Thine own good will Thou wert graciously pleased to ascend the cross in the flesh, that Thou mightest deliver from bondage to the enemy those whom Thou hadst fashioned. For that cause we cry aloud to Thee with thanksgiving. With joy Thou hast filled all things, O our Saviour, in that Thou didst come to save the world.

*[If this service is to the **Theotokos** then:]*

To the birth giver of God let us sinners and humble ones now diligently have recourse, and let us fall down in penitence exclaiming, from the bottom of our souls: "O Sovereign Lady, help us, have compassion on us. Show zeal, for we perish with the multitude of our sins; turn not thine servants empty away; for we have thee as our only hope."

*[If this service is to a Saint then insert their **Troparion** here:]*

Examples:

Troparion Of Saint Nicholas

   Tone 4   Festive, joyous and expressing deep piety.   *C, D, Eb, F, G, A, Bb, C.*

The truth of things revealed thee to thy flock as a rule of faith, a model of meekness and a teacher of temperance. Therefore thou hast won the heights of humility, riches by poverty. Holy Father Nicholas, intercede with Christ our God that our souls may be saved.

Troparion Of Saint David

   Tone 1   Magnificent, happy and earthy.   *C, D, Eb, F, G, A, Bb, C.*

Having worked miracles in thy youth, founded monasteries and converted the pagans who had sought to destroy thee, O Father David, Christ our God blessed thee to receive the episcopate at the place of His resurrection. Intercede for us, that our lives may be blessed and our souls may be saved.

Troparion Of St Martin Of Tours

   Tone 4   Festive, joyous and expressing deep piety.   *C, D, Eb, F, G, A, Bb, C.*

In signs and in miracles thou wert renowned throughout Gaul. By grace and adoption thou art a light for the world, O Martin, blessed of God. Alms deeds and compassion filled thy life with their splendours. Teaching and wise counsel were thy riches and treasures, which thou dispensest freely to those who honour thee.

   Glory be to the Father and to the Son and to the Holy Spirit,

*[If this service is to the **Saviour** then:]*

Priest: Glory to Thee our God glory to Thee.

   Deliver Thy servants from distress, O greatly merciful One.

   For we have diligent recourse to Thee; The merciful Deliverer of all men;

   O Lord Jesus Christ.

*[If this service is to the **Theotokos** then:]*

Priest: O most holy Theotokos, save us. Deliver thy servants from distress.

O Theotokos; for unto thee in God we have recourse;

As to a wall impregnable, and to thine intercession.

Look with benignity, O all hymned Theotokos;

Upon my dire bodily suffering, and heal the sickness of my soul.

*[If this service is to a **Saint** then:]*

Priest: Pray to God for us, O holy *N*, for we diligently have recourse to thee;

Who is a speedy help and intercessor for our souls.

Both now and forever and unto the ages of ages. Amen.

Psalm 50

Have mercy on me, O God, according to Thy great mercy; and according to the multitude of Thy compassions blot out my transgression. Wash me thoroughly from mine iniquity, and cleanse me from my sin. For I acknowledge mine iniquity, and my sin is ever before me. Against Thee, Thee only have I sinned, and done evil in Thy sight, that Thou mayest be found just when Thou speakest, and victorious when Thou art judged. For behold, I was conceived in iniquity, and in sin my mother bore me. For behold, Thou hast loved truth; Thou hast made known to me the hidden and secret things of Thy wisdom. Thou shalt sprinkle me with hyssop, and I shall be made clean; Thou shalt wash me, and I shalt be whiter than snow. Make me to hear joy and gladness; that the humbled bones may rejoice. Turn Thy face away from my sins, and blot out all mine iniquities.

Create in me a clean heart, O God, and renew a steadfast spirit within me. Cast me not away from Thy presence, and take not Thy Holy Spirit from me. Restore to me the joy of Thy salvation, and establish me with Thy governing Spirit. I shall teach transgressors Thy ways, and the ungodly shall turn back to Thee. Deliver me from blood guiltiness, O God, the God of my salvation; my tongue shall joyfully declare Thy righteousness. Lord, open my lips, and my mouth shall declare Thy praise. For if Thou hadst desired sacrifice, I would give it; Thou dost not delight in burned offerings. A sacrifice to God is a broken spirit; God shall not despise a broken and a humbled heart. Do good, O Lord, in Thy good pleasure to Zion, and let the walls of Jerusalem be builded. Then Thou shalt be pleased with a sacrifice of righteousness, with oblation and whole burned offerings. Then shall they offer bulls on Thine altar.

After The Psalm

Glory be to the Father and to the Son and to the Holy Spirit;

Both now and forever and unto the ages of ages. Amen.

Halleluiah, Halleluiah, Halleluiah. Glory to Thee, O God. **(x3)**

Lord, have mercy. **(x3)**

---

*If this service is to the **Saviour** then use* <u>Akathist To Christ</u> *above.*

---

*If this service is to the **Theotokos** then use* <u>Paraklesis To The Theotokos-Little</u> *above.*

---

*If this service is to a **Saint** then use that akathist.*

Akathist for St David

[The acrostic whereof is *"David droppeth miracles like holy dew."*]

Ode I

Eirmos

Tone 6   Rich texture, funereal character, sorrowful tone.   D, Eb, F##, G, A, Bb, C##, D.

With an upraised arm Christ drowned the chariots of Pharaoh and his power, and saved Israel, who sent up the hymn: Let us sing unto our wondrous God.

Refrain: *Holy Father David, pray to God for us.*

Deign Thou to fill my mouth with eloquence, O Christ, that I may praise the wondrous David, who enjoineth us, saying: Let us sing unto our wondrous God. A youth comely and full of divine grace, thou didst undertake to study well the Scriptures, O holy David, that thou mightest sing unto our wondrous God.

Verily did thy fellows behold a dove with beak of gold playing at thy holy lips, O glorious David, teaching thee to sing the praises of our wondrous God.

Refrain: *O most holy Theotokos, save us.*

Theotokion

In voices of exultation let us hymn the all pure and immaculate Theotokos, that, saved by her supplications, we may sing unto our wondrous God.

Ode III

Eirmos

All the heavens, which were established by Thee, O Word and Power of God, confess Thine ineffable glory and the creation of Thine all accomplishing hands; for there is none holy save Thee, O Lord.

Refrain: *Holy Father David, pray to God for us.*

Despising the vanity of the world, O sacred one, thou didst flee to the venerable Paulinus, great among ascetics, and he taught thee to cry out to the Master of all: There is none holy save Thee, O Lord. Destroying his bodily eyes by constant weeping, the elder Paulinus fell blind; but, full of the power of the Word of God, the holy David healed him, crying out: There is none holy save Thee, O Lord. Replete with the grace of God, David most great set it as his holy task to build many churches and to establish many monasteries, wherein the pious might sing: There is none holy save Thee, O Lord.

Refrain: *O most holy Theotokos, save us.*

Theotokion

O the heavenly glory of thine ineffable birth giving, O holy Virgin and Mother For in manner beyond the comprehension of man thou gavest birth to thine own Creator, the Word and Power of God.

Sessional Hymn

Tone 1   Magnificent, happy and earthy.   *C, D, Eb, F, G, A, Bb, C.*

Withdrawing from the tumults of the world, O holy David, thou didst willingly bend thy neck beneath the yoke of Christ, submitting in obedience to the holy Paulinus, who trained thee to contend with skill against the adversary of our race. Glory to the Judge of thy contest. Glory to Him Who gave thee the victory over Satan. Glory to Him Who hath awarded thee the wreath of victory.

Glory be to the Father, and to the Son, and to the Holy Spirit;
Both now and forever, and to the ages of ages. Amen.

Theotokion

Stretching forth thy divine hands wherewith thou didst bear the Creator Who in His goodness became incarnate, O all holy Virgin, beg thou that He deliver from temptations, sorrows and tribulations us who praise thee with love and cry out: Glory to Him Who dwelt within thee. Glory to Him Who came forth from thee. Glory to Him Who hath delivered us by thy birth giving.

Stavrotheotokion

In awe at Thy great and awesome forbearance, O Saviour, the all pure one lamented bitterly and cried out to Thee Who wast crucified on the Cross by the iniquitous and Whose side was pierced with a spear by the soldiers: Glory to Thy love for man. Glory to Thy goodness. Glory to Thee Who by Thy death hast rendered man immortal.

Ode IV

Eirmos

Thy virtue hath covered the heavens, O Christ, and all things have been filled with Thy praise, O Lord.

Refrain: *Holy Father David, pray to God for us.*

Pious men offered up praise to Christ at Glastonbury when the holy David restored the monastery there. Poisonous had the waters at Bath become, but by the power of Christ, David made them fit for use again. Enlightening all the Britons, everywhere the holy one went he built churches, wherein to praise the Lord.

Refrain: *O most holy Theotokos, save us.*

Theotokion

The Theotokos was full of the beauty of all the virtues; wherefore, the heavens resound with her praises.

Ode V

Eirmos

Enlighten me who rise at dawn out of the night, I pray, O Thou Who lovest mankind, and guide me in Thy precepts; and teach me to do Thy will, O Saviour.

Refrain: *Holy Father David, pray to God for us.*

Having filled the land with monastic habitations, the pious David made his abided in Menevia, where he taught the Saviours sacred precepts unto all. Mortifying all carnal mindedness, O God bearer, rising at dawn out of the night thou didst show thyself to be a worthy model of all the Christian virtues. Imitating the austerities of the ascetics of the Thebaïd, thy monks, bending their will to thine, O saint, committed themselves to fasting and constant prayer.

Refrain: *O most holy Theotokos, save us.*

Theotokion

Rising at dawn out of the night, I beg the merciful Mother of God with tears and sighs, that by her intercession I may learn to do the will of her Son.

Ode VI

Eirmos

With all my heart I cried out to the compassionate God, and He heard my cry from the uttermost depths of hades, and hath led my life up from corruption.

Refrain: *Holy Father David, pray to God for us.*

Abstaining from all but bread and pulse, and slaking their thirst with water alone, led by thee thy monks attained deliverance from corruption. Constant was thy mental prayer, O saint, for thou didst follow the injunction of the Apostle to pray without ceasing; and God led thee up from hades. Leading the sheep of thy flock like a good shepherd, O wondrous pastor, thou didst drive from them the demonic wolves, delivering their souls.

Refrain: *O most holy Theotokos, save us.*

Theotokion

Every true Christian crieth out in anguish to the compassionate Bride of God; and, hearkening to our pleas, she entreateth her Son to lead up their life from corruption.

Kontakion

Tone 4   Festive, joyous and expressing deep piety.   *C, D, Eb, F, G, A, Bb, C.*

O thou who didst willing take up thy cross and follow Christ the Lord, and didst fill thy land with new communities dedicated to Him, send down from heaven the grace of God, O great and wondrous David, that we Christians may prevail over all heresies, having thee as an invincible ally amid our struggle for piety.

Oikos

Let us now fittingly praise David, the bishop of Christ, for he was called by God from his mothers womb to sanctify the people of Wales, and by them was chosen to be their chief bishop; and conducting his ministry in a God pleasing manner, he brought multitudes to salvation by the gifts of the Spirit which abided in him; wherefore, he is the great boast of all the Welsh, and an invincible ally amid our struggle for piety.

Ode VII

Eirmos

We have sinned, we have committed iniquity, we have dealt unjustly before Thee. We have neither done nor acted as Thou hast commanded us. But forsake us not utterly, O God of our fathers.

Refrain: Holy Father David, pray to God for us.

Sinful and iniquitous is the accursed heresy of Pelagius, who belittled the power of divine grace and exalted the feeble efforts of mans will; but David set his blasphemy utterly at nought. Like mute fish did the defenders of Pelagius become, being utterly silenced when the holy one made clear the doctrines of piety by the grace and power wherewith Christ filled his godly mouth. Inspiring the faithful of Wales to turn from heresy and embrace the Truth, David was acclaimed as a champion of piety, who would in nowise forsake the true worship of the God of our fathers.

Refrain: O most holy Theotokos, save us.

Theotokion

Knowing the magnitude of our sinfulness and the multitude of our iniquities, we would despair of all mercy; but forsake us not utterly in thy supplications, O all immaculate and merciful Lady.

Ode VIII

Eirmos

In the flame the youths gave the command to hymn God the Father and Creator, the consubstantial Son and the Spirit of God: Let all creation bless the Lord and exalt Him supremely for all ages.

Refrain: Holy Father David, pray to God for us.

Ever did the holy David exhort his flock to worship the All holy Trinity the unoriginate Father, His only begotten Son, and the all holy Spirit in Orthodox manner exalting Him supremely for all ages. Having taken up the saving yoke of Christ with single mind, bear it to the end, the holy David cried out to his brethren, and whatsoever you have seen with me and heard, keep it and fulfil. O the love of the saint for the sheep which Christ, the Chief Shepherd, had given into his care. For, dying, he earnestly besought them to bless the Lord and exalt Him supremely for all ages.

Refrain: O most holy Theotokos, save us.

Theotokion

Lambent is the light of thy grace, and though the furnace of our fiery passions rageth mightily, rescue us from its flames, O Mother of our God Who is exalted supremely for all ages.

Ode IX

Eirmos

Finding everlasting deliverance from the dread sentence brought upon our race by our first father Adam, with the bodiless ones we glorify thine Offspring Who was begotten from on high, magnifying thee, the Theotokos, with hymns of praise.

Refrain: *Holy Father David, pray to God for us.*

You saints of Wales, like bees returning with all speed to the hive at the approach of a storm were ye, forewarned by God that thy father and bishop David would soon depart to his Master and Creator; wherefore, you magnified him with hymns. Dying in body, O holy bishop, thy pure soul took wing, and the venerable Kentigern beheld it, soaring aloft, upborne to the heights of heaven by the hands of angelic beings; wherefore, we praise and glorify thy holy memory with hymns of joy. Empty now lieth thy holy tomb, O protector of Wales, and over the ages thy precious relics have been dispersed near and far; yet in spirit thou abidest with all the saints of the Most High, ever sending heavenly aid to us who magnify thee with hymns.

Refrain: *O most holy Theotokos, save us.*

Theotokion

When we must needs stand before the dread tribunal of thy Son and give answer for our countless crimes, O daughter of Adam and Mother of Christ, stand thou with us, and plead for us who magnify thee, the all holy Theotokos, with hymns of praise.

The Little Litany

Deacon: Again and again in peace let us pray to the Lord.

People: *Lord have mercy.*

Deacon: Help us, save us, have mercy upon us and keep us O God, by thy grace.

People: *Lord have mercy.*

Deacon: Calling to remembrance our most holy, all undefiled, most blessed and glorious Lady, the Theotokos and ever virgin Mary, with all the Saints, let us commend ourselves and each other and all our life unto Christ our God.

People: *To Thee, O Lord.*

Priest: For blessed be Thy Name, and glorified be Thy Kingdom; Of the Father and of the Son and of the Holy Spirit. Both now and forever and to the ages of ages.

People: *Amen.*

Deacon: Let us attend.

Priest: Peace be with you all.

People: *And with thy spirit.*

Deacon: Wisdom. The Prokeimenon.

Prokeimenon

*[If this service is to the **Saviour** then:]*

Reader: Lord, we shall walk in the light of Thy countenance; and rejoice in Thy Name for evermore.

People: *Lord, we shall walk in the light of Thy countenance; and rejoice in Thy Name for evermore.*

Reader: Rejoice in the Lord, O you righteous. Praise befits the upright.

People: *Lord, we shall walk in the light of Thy countenance; and rejoice in Thy Name for evermore.*

Reader: Lord, we shall walk in the light of Thy countenance | and rejoice in Thy Name for evermore.

---

*[If this service is to the **Theotokos** then:]*

Reader: I shall call upon thy name from generation to generation.

People: *I shall call upon thy name from generation to generation.*

Reader: Rejoice in the Lord, O you righteous. Praise befits the upright.

People: *I shall call upon thy name from generation to generation.*

Reader: I shall call upon thy name | from generation to generation.

---

*[If this service is to a **Saint** then:]*

Reader: Right dear in the sight of the Lord is the death of His saints.

People: *Right dear in the sight of the Lord is the death of His saints.*

Reader: Rejoice in the Lord, O you righteous. Praise befits the upright.

People: *Right dear in the sight of the Lord is the death of His saints.*

Reader: Right dear in the sight of the Lord | is the death of His saints.

First Antiphon of the Anavathmoi

Tone 4   Festive, joyous and expressing deep piety.   *C, D, Eb, F, G, A, Bb, C.*

Reader: From the years of my youth, many passions combat me; but You, Who are my Saviour, assist me and save me. **(x2)**

Chorus: *You haters of Zion shall be put to shame by the Lord Almighty, for as grass in the fire, you shall all be withered.* **(x2)**

Chorus: *Glory be to the Father and to the Son and to the Holy Spirit;*

Reader: By the Holy Spirit, every soul is made living, is exalted, and made shining through purification, by the Threefold Oneness, in a hidden manner.

Chorus: *Both now and forever and unto the ages of ages. Amen.*

Reader: By the Holy Spirit, the streams of grace are flowing, watering, all of the creation, granting life upon.

Chorus: *I shall remember your Holy Name from generation to generation.*

Reader: Listen, O Daughter, and see, and incline your ear, and forget your people and your fathers house and the King shall desire your beauty.

Chorus: *I remember Your Holy Name from generation to generation.*

Little Litany

Deacon: Let us pray to the Lord.

People: *Lord have mercy.*

Priest: For Thou art holy, O our God and rest in the Saints, and to Thee do we ascribe glory to the Father and to the Son and to the Holy Spirit, both now and forever and to the ages of ages.

People: *Amen.*

Deacon: Let everything that has breath praise the Lord.

Reader: Praise the Lord from heaven, praise Him in the heights. **(x3)**

Deacon: And that he shall vouchsafe to us to listen to the Holy Gospel; let us pray to the Lord God.

People: *Lord have mercy.* **(x3)**

Priest: Peace be with you all.

People: *And with thy spirit.*

Priest: The reading is from the Holy Gospel according to *N.*

People: *Glory to Thee O Lord, glory to Thee.*

Deacon: Let us attend.

*[If this service is to the **Saviour** then:]*   Matthew 12. 27-30.

Priest or Deacon: And if I by Beelzebub cast out devils, by whom do your children cast them out? Therefore they shall be your judges. But if I cast out devils by the Spirit of God, then the kingdom of God is come into you. Or else how can one enter into a strong man's house, and spoil his goods, except he first bind the strong man? And then he shall spoil his house. He that is not with me is against me; and he that gathers not with me, scatters abroad.

*[If this service is to the **Theotokos** then:]* <u>Luke 1. 39-49, 56.</u>

Priest or Deacon: And Mary arose in those days, and went into the hill country in haste, into a city of Judea; And entered into the house of Zacharias, and saluted Elizabeth. And it came to pass, that, when Elizabeth heard the salutation of Mary, the babe leaped in her womb; and Elizabeth was filled with the Holy Ghost: And she spoke out with a loud voice, and said, Blessed art thou among women, and blessed is the fruit of thy womb. And how is this come to me, that the mother of my Lord should come to me? For, lo, as soon as the voice of thy salutation sounded in my ears, the babe leaped in my womb for joy. And blessed is she that believed: for there shall be a performance of those things which were told her from the Lord. And Mary said, My soul does magnify the Lord, and my spirit has rejoiced in God my Saviour. For he has regarded the low estate of his handmaiden: for, behold, from henceforth; all generations shall call me blessed. For he that is mighty has done to me great things; and holy is his name. And Mary abided with her about three months, and returned to her own house.

*[If this service is to a **Saint** then:]*   <u>Matthew 7. 8-11.</u>

Priest or Deacon: For every one that asks receives; and he that seeks finds; and to him that knocks it shall be opened. Or what man is there of you, whom if his son ask bread, shall give him a stone? Or if he ask a fish, shall he give him a serpent? If you then, being evil, know how to give good gifts to your children, how much more shall your Father, who is in heaven, give good things to them that ask him?

People: *Glory to Thee O Lord, glory to Thee.*

Little Litany

Deacon: Have mercy on us, O God, according to thy great mercy, we beseech thee; hearken and have mercy.

People: *Lord have mercy.* **(x3)**

Deacon: We pray for our Archbishop <u>Nikitas</u> and for all our brethren in Christ.

People: *Lord have mercy.* **(x3)**

Deacon: We pray for the mercy, life, peace, health and salvation of the servants of God (*N and N - insert names as requested here*) and for the persons who are here present.

People: *Lord have mercy.* **(x3)**

Deacon: We pray for all brethren and for all Christian people.

People: *Lord have mercy.* **(x3)**

Priest: For Thou art a merciful God who lovest mankind, and to Thee do we ascribe glory to the Father and to the Son and to the Holy Spirit, both now and forever and to the ages of ages.

People: *Amen.*

Priest: Hear us, O God our Saviour, the hope of all the ends of the earth and of those who are far off upon the sea, and show mercy, show mercy, O Master, upon us sinners, and be merciful unto us. For Thou art a merciful God who loves mankind, and to Thee we ascribe glory to the Father and to the Son and to the Holy Spirit. Both now and forever and ever and to the ages of ages.

People: *Amen.*

Deacon: Wisdom.

Priest: O most holy Theotokos, save us.

Reader: *[Archangel Gabriel:* It is truly right to call thee blessed, who gavest birth to God, ever-blessed and God-obedient the Mother of our God.] Greater in honour than the Cherubim and beyond compare more glorious than the Seraphim; without corruption thou gavest birth to God the Word, truly the Mother of God, we magnify thee.

Priest: Glory to Thee, O Christ God our hope, glory to Thee.

Reader: *Glory to the Father and to the Son, and to the Holy Spirit;*

   Both now and forever and unto the ages of ages. Amen.

Lord have mercy. **(x3)**

Holy Father Bless.

Priest: May Christ our true God, through the prayers of his most pure Mother, of Saint *N [the patron saint of the church]*; of Saint *N [for whom is this Parakleses]* and of all the saints, have mercy on us and save us, forasmuch as He is good and loves mankind.

People: *Amen.*

Akathist For Saint David Of Wales

[The acrostic whereof is *"David droppeth miracles like holy dew."*]

Ode I

Eirmos

Tone 6   Rich texture, funereal character, sorrowful tone.   *D, Eb, F##, G, A, Bb, C##, D.*

With an upraised arm Christ drowned the chariots of Pharaoh and his power, and saved Israel, who sent up the hymn: Let us sing unto our wondrous God.

Deign Thou to fill my mouth with eloquence, O Christ, that I may praise the wondrous David, who enjoineth us, saying: Let us sing unto our wondrous God. A youth comely and full of divine grace, thou didst undertake to study well the Scriptures, O holy David, that thou mightest sing unto our wondrous God.

Verily did thy fellows behold a dove with beak of gold playing at thy holy lips, O glorious David, teaching thee to sing the praises of our wondrous God.

Theotokion

In voices of exultation let us hymn the all pure and immaculate Theotokos, that, saved by her supplications, we may sing unto our wondrous God.

Ode III

Eirmos

All the heavens, which were established by Thee, O Word and Power of God, confess Thine ineffable glory and the creation of Thine all accomplishing hands; for there is none holy save Thee, O Lord.

Despising the vanity of the world, O sacred one, thou didst flee to the venerable Paulinus, great among ascetics, and he taught thee to cry out to the Master of all: There is none holy save Thee, O Lord. Destroying his bodily eyes by constant weeping, the elder Paulinus fell blind; but, full of the power of the Word of God, the holy David healed him, crying out: There is none holy save Thee, O Lord. Replete with the grace of God, David most great set it as his holy task to build many churches and to establish many monasteries, wherein the pious might sing: There is none holy save Thee, O Lord.

Theotokion

O the heavenly glory of thine ineffable birth giving, O holy Virgin and Mother For in manner beyond the comprehension of man thou gavest birth to thine own Creator, the Word and Power of God.

Sessional Hymn

Tone 1   Magnificent, happy and earthy.   *C, D, Eb, F, G, A, Bb, C.*

Withdrawing from the tumults of the world, O holy David, thou didst willingly bend thy neck beneath the yoke of Christ, submitting in obedience to the holy Paulinus, who trained thee to contend with skill against the adversary of our race. Glory to the Judge of thy contest. Glory to Him Who gave thee the victory over Satan. Glory to Him Who hath awarded thee the wreath of victory.

Glory be to the Father, and to the Son, and to the Holy Spirit;
Both now and forever, and to the ages of ages. Amen.

Theotokion

Stretching forth thy divine hands wherewith thou didst bear the Creator Who in His goodness became incarnate, O all holy Virgin, beg thou that He deliver from temptations, sorrows and tribulations us who praise thee with love and cry out: Glory to Him Who dwelt within thee. Glory to Him Who came forth from thee. Glory to Him Who hath delivered us by thy birthgiving.

Stavrotheotokion

In awe at Thy great and awesome forbearance, O Saviour, the all pure one lamented bitterly and cried out to Thee Who wast crucified on the Cross by the iniquitous and Whose side was pierced with a spear by the soldiers: Glory to Thy love for man. Glory to Thy goodness. Glory to Thee Who by Thy death hast rendered man immortal.

Ode IV

Eirmos

Thy virtue hath covered the heavens, O Christ, and all things have been filled with Thy praise, O Lord.

Pious men offered up praise to Christ at Glastonbury when the holy David restored the monastery there. Poisonous had the waters at Bath become, but by the power of Christ, David made them fit for use again. Enlightening all the Britons, everywhere the holy one went he built churches, wherein to praise the Lord.

Theotokion

The Theotokos was full of the beauty of all the virtues; wherefore, the heavens resound with her praises.

Ode V

Eirmos

Enlighten me who rise at dawn out of the night, I pray, O Thou Who lovest mankind, and guide me in Thy precepts; and teach me to do Thy will, O Saviour.

Having filled the land with monastic habitations, the pious David made his abided in Menevia, where he taught the Saviours sacred precepts unto all. Mortifying all carnal mindedness, O God bearer, rising at dawn out of the night thou didst show thyself to be a worthy model of all the Christian virtues. Imitating the austerities of the ascetics of the Thebaïd, thy monks, bending their will to thine, O saint, committed themselves to fasting and constant prayer.

Theotokion

Rising at dawn out of the night, I beg the merciful Mother of God with tears and sighs, that by her intercession I may learn to do the will of her Son.

Ode VI

Eirmos

With all my heart I cried out to the compassionate God, and He heard my cry from the uttermost depths of hades, and hath led my life up from corruption.

Abstaining from all but bread and pulse, and slaking their thirst with water alone, led by thee thy monks attained deliverance from corruption. Constant was thy mental prayer, O saint, for thou didst follow the injunction of the Apostle to pray without ceasing; and God led thee up from hades. Leading the sheep of thy flock like a good shepherd, O wondrous pastor, thou didst drive from them the demonic wolves, delivering their souls.

Theotokion

Every true Christian crieth out in anguish to the compassionate Bride of God; and, hearkening to our pleas, she entreateth her Son to lead up their life from corruption.

Kontakion

Tone 4   Festive, joyous and expressing deep piety.   *C, D, Eb, F, G, A, Bb, C.*

O thou who didst willing take up thy cross and follow Christ the Lord, and didst fill thy land with new communities dedicated to Him, send down from heaven the grace of God, O great and wondrous David, that we Christians may prevail over all heresies, having thee as an invincible ally amid our struggle for piety.

Oikos

Let us now fittingly praise David, the bishop of Christ, for he was called by God from his mothers womb to sanctify the people of Wales, and by them was chosen to be their chief bishop; and conducting his ministry in a God pleasing manner, he brought multitudes to salvation by the gifts of the Spirit which abided in him; wherefore, he is the great boast of all the Welsh, and an invincible ally amid our struggle for piety.

Ode VII

Eirmos

We have sinned, we have committed iniquity, we have dealt unjustly before Thee. We have neither done nor acted as Thou hast commanded us. But forsake us not utterly, O God of our fathers.

Sinful and iniquitous is the accursed heresy of Pelagius, who belittled the power of divine grace and exalted the feeble efforts of mans will; but David set his blasphemy utterly at nought. Like mute fish did the defenders of Pelagius become, being utterly silenced when the holy one made clear the doctrines of piety by the grace and power wherewith Christ filled his godly mouth. Inspiring the faithful of Wales to turn from heresy and embrace the Truth, David was acclaimed as a champion of piety, who would in nowise forsake the true worship of the God of our fathers.

Theotokion

Knowing the magnitude of our sinfulness and the multitude of our iniquities, we would despair of all mercy; but forsake us not utterly in thy supplications, O all immaculate and merciful Lady.

Ode VIII

Eirmos

In the flame the youths gave the command to hymn God the Father and Creator, the consubstantial Son and the Spirit of God: Let all creation bless the Lord and exalt Him supremely for all ages.

Ever did the holy David exhort his flock to worship the All holy Trinity the unoriginate Father, His only begotten Son, and the all holy Spirit in Orthodox manner exalting Him supremely for all ages. Having taken up the saving yoke of Christ with single mind, bear it to the end, the holy David cried out to his brethren, and whatsoever you have seen with me and heard, keep it and fulfil. O the love of the saint for the sheep which Christ, the Chief Shepherd, had given into his care. For, dying, he earnestly besought them to bless the Lord and exalt Him supremely for all ages.

Theotokion

Lambent is the light of thy grace, and though the furnace of our fiery passions rageth mightily, rescue us from its flames, O Mother of our God Who is exalted supremely for all ages.

Ode IX

Eirmos

Finding everlasting deliverance from the dread sentence brought upon our race by our first father Adam, with the bodiless ones we glorify thine Offspring Who was begotten from on high, magnifying thee, the Theotokos, with hymns.

You saints of Wales, like bees returning with all speed to the hive at the approach of a storm were ye, forewarned by God that thy father and bishop David would soon depart to his Master and Creator; wherefore, you magnified him with hymns. Dying in body, O holy bishop, thy pure soul took wing, and the venerable Kentigern beheld it, soaring aloft, upborne to the heights of heaven by the hands of angelic beings; wherefore, we praise and glorify thy holy memory with hymns of joy. Empty now lieth thy holy tomb, O protector of Wales, and over the ages thy precious relics have been dispersed near and far; yet in spirit thou abidest with all the saints of the Most High, ever sending heavenly aid to us who magnify thee with hymns.

Theotokion

When we must needs stand before the dread tribunal of thy Son and give answer for our countless crimes, O daughter of Adam and Mother of Christ, stand thou with us, and plead for us who magnify thee, the all holy Theotokos, with hymns.

Variables For St David, Bishop of Menevia - Enlightener of Wales

[Composed by Reader Isaac Lambertson]

Vespers

At "Lord, I have cried" Kekragarion, these stichera:

Tone 8   Humility, tranquillity, repose, suffering, pleading.   C, D, Eb, F, G, A, Bb, C.

O all glorious wonder. From childhood thou didst adorn thy life with virtue, and having been made a priest of Christ wast truly shown to be a luminary for His flock. Wherefore, having vanquished the demons by thy tireless spiritual warfare, in soul thou hast ascended on high, where thou beholdest thy Lord and Master face to face in the splendour of His glory.

O all glorious wonder that human flesh could be so mortified. For, following the ascetics of the desert thou didst lay waste thy body, resisting all the temptations of the flesh and putting away from thee all carnal thoughts, O David blessed of God; wherefore, arrayed in garments of purity as for a wedding feast, thou hast entered, rejoicing, into the joy of thy Lord.

O all glorious wonder, the grace of God which doth sanctify and deify filled thy humble soul, O David, and thou didst preach with eloquence against the accursed Pelagius, refuting his vile heresy, watchfully fending off from the faithful from its pernicious harm, and leading them in gladness into the splendid courts of Christ, to the mansions of the righteous.

Glory be to the Father, and to the Son, and to the Holy Spirit;

Idiomelon Of The Holy Bishop

Tone 3   Arrogant, brave, and mature atmosphere.   F, G, A, A#, C, D, E, F.

Come, O you assembly of the faithful, and with reverent voices let us praise the holy bishop David, who as a good shepherd guided his flock to the Faith with the word of Truth, by his virtues teaching them to tread the straight and narrow path which leadeth to paradise. Truly, for his obedience the Almighty hath bestowed upon him manifold spiritual gifts, which he freely imparteth to those who bless his holy memory, entreating Christ to have pity on us and grant us remission of sins.

Both now and forever, and to the ages of ages. Amen.

Theotokion, or this Stavrotheotokion:

Troparion Of Saint David

Tone 3   *Arrogant, brave, and mature atmosphere.*   *F, G, A, A#, C, D, E, F.*

Let the Christians of Wales join in gladsome chorus, uplifting their voices in joyous jubilation, as we celebrate the feast of the wondrous David, their holy father and enlightener, who now dwelleth with the saints on high, and doth ever earnestly intercede for us sinners.

The Trisagion Prayers

Deacon: Holy Father, Bless.

Priest: Blessed is our God always, now and forever, and unto the ages of ages.

People: *Amen.*

Priest: O Heavenly King, Comforter, Spirit of Truth, Who art everywhere present and fillest all things, Treasury of blessings and Giver of life: Come and abide in us and cleanse us from every impurity and save our souls, O Good One.

Reader: Holy God, Holy Mighty, Holy Immortal, have mercy on us. **(x3)**

Glory be to the Father, and to the Son, and to the Holy Spirit;
Both now and forever, and unto the ages of ages. Amen.

O Most Holy Trinity, have mercy on us.

O Lord, cleanse us from our sins.

O Master, pardon our iniquities.

O Holy One, visit and heal our infirmities, for Thy names sake.

Lord have mercy. **(x3)**

Glory be to the Father and to the Son and to the Holy Spirit;
Both now and forever, and unto the ages of ages. Amen.

People: *Our Father, Who art in Heaven, hallowed be Thy Name. Thy Kingdom come, Thy will be done, on earth as it is in Heaven. Give us this day our daily bread, and forgive us our trespasses, as we forgive those who trespass against us; and lead us not into temptation, but deliver us from the evil one.*

Priest: For Thine is the kingdom, and the power and the glory of the Father and of the Son and of the Holy Spirit, now and forever and to the ages of ages.

People: *Amen.*

People: *Lord, have mercy.* (**x12**)

Glory be to the Father and to the Son and to the Holy Spirit,
Both now and forever and unto the ages of ages. Amen.

O come let us worship God our King.

O come let us worship and fall down before Christ, our King and God.

O come let us worship and fall down before Christ Himself, our King and our God.

Psalm 142

Hear my prayer, O Lord, give ear to my supplications. In Thy faithfulness answer me, and in Thy righteousness. Do not enter into judgement with Thy servant, for in Thy sight no one living is righteous. For the enemy has persecuted my soul; he has crushed my life to the ground; he has made me dwell in darkness, like those who have long been dead. Therefore my spirit is overwhelmed within me; my heart within me is distressed. I remember the days of old; I meditate on all Thy works; I muse on the work of Thine hands. I spread out my hands to Thee; my soul longs for Thee like a thirsty land. Answer me speedily, O Lord; my spirit fails. Do not hide Thy face from me, lest I be like those who go down into the pit. Cause me to hear Thy loving kindness in the morning, for in Thee do I trust; cause me to know the way in which I should walk, for I lift up my soul to Thee. Deliver me, O Lord, from mine enemies; in Thee I take shelter. Teach me to do Thy will, for Thou art my God; Thy Spirit is good. Lead me in the land of uprightness. Revive me, O Lord, for Thy names sake. For Thy righteousness' sake bring my soul out of trouble. In Thy mercy cut off mine enemies, and destroy all those who afflict my soul; for I am Thy servant.

After The Psalm

Glory be to the Father and to the Son and to the Holy Spirit,
Both now and forever and unto the ages of ages. Amen.

Alleluia, Alleluia, Alleluia. Glory to Thee, O God. (**x3**)

Lord, have mercy. (**x3**)

Glory be to the Father and to the Son and to the Holy Spirit,

Both now and forever and unto the ages of ages. Amen.

Theotokion

My thoughts are unclean, my lips flattering, and my deeds are all defiled. What then can I do? How can I meet the Judge? O Sovereign Lady Virgin, supplicate unto thy Son and Maker and the Lord that He may receive my spirit in contrition, as the only Compassionate One.

Refrain: O most holy Theotokos, save us.

The Stavro-Theotokion

The undefiled youthful Maiden seeing the Youth voluntarily nailed on the tree, piteously bewailing, called out unto Him: Woe unto me, O my most beloved Child. What hath the graceless assembly of the Hebrews rendered unto Thee? They are bent on depriving me of Thee, O All beloved One.

Glory be to the Father and to the Son and to the Holy Spirit,

Both now and forever and unto the ages of ages. Amen.

Stavro-Theotokion

Seeing Thee crucified, O Christ, she who hath given Thee birth, cried: What a strange mystery do I see now, my Son? How, being hung in the flesh, dost Thou die on the tree, O Giver of life?

Theotokion Of The Resurrection

O pure virgin, gate of the Word, Mother of our God, supplicate that we may be saved.

Glory be to the Father and to the Son and to the Holy Spirit,

Both now and forever and unto the ages of ages. Amen.

Theotokion Of The Resurrection

O pure virgin, gate of the Word, Mother of our God, supplicate that we may be saved.

Refrain: O most holy Theotokos, save us.

Stavro-Theotokion

I cannot endure, O my Child, the sight of Thee dying on the tree, whereas Thou grantest vigour unto all, O that Thou mayest vouchsafe the divine and saving vigour unto those also who, through the fruit of the ancient transgression, have already fallen into the sleep of perdition, spake in tears the Virgin, whom we magnify.

Refrain: *O most holy Theotokos, save us.*

Theotokion

Thou, O pure one, hast renewed, with thy divine bringing forth, the mortal nature of the earth born ruined by passions, and hast raised all from death unto the life of incorruption; wherefore we all dutifully bless thee, O most glorious Virgin, as thou hast foretold.

Glory be to the Father and to the Son and to the Holy Spirit,
Both now and forever and unto the ages of ages. Amen.

Theotokion

The awful miracle of conception and unspeakable manner of giving birth that became known in thee, O pure Ever Virgin, frighten my mind and excite wonder in my thoughts; thy glory, O Theotokos, hath reached everywhere unto the salvation of our souls.

Refrain: We bless thee, O religious Father Teilo, and honour thy holy memory, O preceptor of monks and associate of angels.

Through mortification of the flesh thou, O sacred father, hast buried all the risings of passions, and after thy decease thou hast obtained unending life; wherefore the church of Christ doth celebrate today thy wonder worthy memory, the ornament of the ascetics. **(x2)**

Glory be to the Father and to the Son and to the Holy Spirit,
Both now and forever and unto the ages of ages. Amen.

Theotokion

Do set in the way of repentance us, who constantly deviate into the evil libertarianism, and anger the Most kind Lord, O most blessed Mary, that hadst no marital experience and art the refuge of despairing men and Gods dwelling place.

The Canon
Ode 1

Eirmos

Tone 8   Humility, tranquillity, repose, suffering, pleading.   *C, D, Eb, F, G, A, Bb, C.*

Having crossed the water as if it were dry land, and having escaped the evils of Egypt, the Israelites cried out: Let us sing unto our Deliverer and our God.

Refrain: Holy Father Teilo, pray to God for us.

Adorned with good moral qualities, from thine youth thou didst cleave unto Christ, and passions of thy flesh mortified with abstemiousness and art gone over unto the Life, O holy one.

Refrain: Holy Father Teilo, pray to God for us.

Having been the performer of the divine sayings and laws, thou hast become, O most wise father, filled with divine gifts and miracles, and hast unto all richly emitted thy rays.

Refrain: Holy Father Teilo, pray to God for us.

Helped by the strength of Christ, thou hast, O father, put down the power and might of the enemy, and honours for thy victory hast thou, O holy one, received in the brilliancy of miracles.

Refrain: Holy Father Teilo, pray to God for us.

Thou didst possess a good conscience, and the eye of thy heart was directed to God; wherefore, in answer to thy prayer, O most wise one, He counted thee with the just.

Refrain: O most holy Theotokos, save us.

Theotokion

The passions of my flesh and evil insinuations of my mind do appease, I implore thee, O most pure Virgin, and set me with my strayed mind into the right path.

Ode 3

Eirmos

Thou art the establishing of those that flee unto Thee, O Lord ; Thou art the light unto those in darkness and my spirit hymneth Thee.

Refrain: Holy Father Teilo, pray to God for us.

Being entirely devoted unto the Almighty, thou hast, O most wise holy father, escaped all the malice of the demons. Adorned with the height of humility, thou hast, with thine excellent works, hurled down to the ground the great boaster.

Refrain: *Holy Father Teilo, pray to God for us.*

Whilst still in the flesh, thou hast, O most wise father, humbled the high borne neck of the wicked one with the humility of thy words.

Refrain: *Holy Father Teilo, pray to God for us.*

Having as thy help Gods power, thou dost, O most wise and wonderful one, shed miracles and drivest away diseases.

Refrain: *O most holy Theotokos, save us.*

Theotokion
In becoming incarnate, the Maker hath found abided in thy womb, O all spotless one, unto the benefit of those who in faith hymn thee.

Kathisma
Tone 4   Festive, joyous and expressing deep piety.   *C, D, Eb, F, G, A, Bb, C.*

Thou hast vanquished the fleshly subtlety of passions, and having subdued the worst unto the best, thou didst, O most glorious father Teilo, by fasting destroy the wily scheming of the demons, and shonest forth in the world as a ray of the sun in the brilliant lustre of thy virtues; wherefore we hymn thee.

Glory be to the Father and to the Son and to the Holy Spirit,
Both now and forever and unto the ages of ages. Amen.

Theotokion
An unassailable wall unto us Christians art thou, O Theotokos Virgin, for fleeing unto thee for shelter we remain unhurt, and when we sin afresh, we possess in thee a supplicant; wherefore, in giving thanks, we cry unto thee: Hail thou, full of grace, the Lord is with thee.

Refrain: *O most holy Theotokos, save us.*

Stavro-Theotokion
O all spotless Virgin, Mother of Christ the God, a sword hath pierced thy most holy soul when thou beheldest thy Son and God voluntarily crucified; Him do not cease to supplicate, O most blessed one, to grant us the remission of our transgressions.

Ode 4

Eirmos

I have hearkened, O Lord, onto the mystery of Thine economy, comprehended Thy works and glorified Thy Godhead.

Refrain: *Holy Father Teilo, pray to God for us.*

Having made thy soul into a temple of the Holy Spirit, thou didst become, together with the highest hosts, heir of the Kingdom on high.

Refrain: *Holy Father Teilo, pray to God for us.*

Thou ever dost relieve from sufferings through manifold diseases those that have recourse unto thee; for thou, O holy one, hast obtained from the Lord the grace to work wonders and miracles.

Refrain: *Holy Father Teilo, pray to God for us.*

In the house of God hast thou, O Father Teilo, sprouted up as the best crop, being adorned with virtues and filled with the sweet smell of a wonderful fruit.

Refrain: *O most holy Theotokos, save us.*

Theotokion

A spiritual field art thou, O Ever Virgin, since out of a furrow thou hast brought forth an ear that feedeth the whole creation the God of all.

Ode 5

Eirmos

Watching early we cry out unto Thee: O Lord, save us, for Thou art our God, beside Thee we know none other.

Refrain: *Holy Father Teilo, pray to God for us.*

With thy purified mind, O all glorious one, dost thou behold the ineffable goodness of Christ, the God of all.

Refrain: *Holy Father Teilo, pray to God for us.*

Like unto Elijah in the chariot, thou, O father, hast ascended into heaven on thy virtues, being helped by the Spirit.

Refrain: *Holy Father Teilo, pray to God for us.*

Having contracted thy body with abstemiousness and purity, unto the breadth of the upper habitations hast thou reached, O father.

Refrain: *O most holy Theotokos, save us.*

Theotokion

Heal the blindness of my diseased mind, having given birth unto the Physician, even Christ, O all spotless Sovereign Lady.

Ode 6

Eirmos

Unto the Lord shall I pour my prayer and to Him shall I make known my sorrows, for my soul is become full of afflictions and my life hath come nigh unto the hades, and I shall pray as Jonah: O God, raise me up from corruption.

Refrain: *Holy Father Teilo, pray to God for us.*

With thy sacred prayers, O God blissful one, is slain the cunning serpent and therewith is destroyed the malice of those who demanded of thee a sign, for thou art Gods favourite, beaming with light, proved in thy faithfulness.

Refrain: *Holy Father Teilo, pray to God for us.*

With assiduous ploughing having renewed thy soul, thou hast, O sacred Father Teilo, most wisely thrown therein multi-fruitful seeds of virtues, and hast gathered in rich ears of multifarious healings.

Refrain: *Holy Father Teilo, pray to God for us.*

Helped by the strength of the Spirit, thou hast, O Father Teilo, put down the power and might of the enemy, and honours for thy victory hast thou, O holy one, received in the brilliancy of miracles.

Refrain: *O most holy Theotokos, save us.*

Theotokion

The Lord is with thee, O most pure one. As it hath pleased Him, He was with thee, O Maiden, and through thine intercession hath delivered us all from the dominion of the deceitful one; wherefore now we dutifully from generation to generation call thee blessed.

Kontakion From The Typikon

Tone 2   Majesty, gentleness, hope, repentance and sadness.   *E, F, G, Ab, B, C.*

Having divinely armed thyself with the purity of thy soul and unceasing prayers firmly grasping as a spear, thou, our Father Teilo, hast pierced the armies of the demon; supplicate unceasingly for us all.

Oikos

Having conceived a loving attachment to the divine commandments of Christ, and a hatred for the delights of this world, thou hast with diligence achieved thine end and wast a lamp that did enlighten the ends with the spiritual lustre. Wherefore falling down before thee I implore thee: Enlighten my spiritual eyes to hymn thine exploits of fasting, watchfulness, shedding tears, labours and maceration of the body, for the sake of the blissful future life, of which thou art now in the enjoyment; Supplicate unceasingly for us.

Ode 7

Eirmos

From Judea coming the youths did once in Babylon tread down the flame of the furnace by their faith in the Trinity, singing: O God of our fathers, blessed art. Thou.

Refrain: *Holy Father Teilo, pray to God for us.*

Having strong mindedly gone through thine exploits of fasting, thou hast, O Father Teilo, humbled the proudest mind with the divine humility, singing: Blessed art Thou, O God of our fathers.

Refrain: *Holy Father Teilo, pray to God for us.*

In the house of God hast thou, O Father Teilo, sprouted up as the best crop, being adorned with virtues and filled with the sweet smell of a wonderful fruit.

Refrain: *Holy Father Teilo, pray to God for us.*

Having enlightened thy heart, thou, O Father Teilo, wast the superior of the sacred assembly, giving directions, teaching and bringing all under the will of God, singing: O God of our fathers, blessed art Thou.

Refrain: *O most holy Theotokos, save us.*

Theotokion

Having given birth unto a new Youth, the Unoriginate Word, thou, O Virgin, hast renewed us grown old through sin, and made us strong to sing: O God of our fathers, blessed art Thou.

Ode 8

Eirmos

The God spoken youths, whilst treading down in the furnace the flame with the fire, sung: Bless the Lord, you the works of the Lord.

Refrain: *Holy Father Teilo, pray to God for us.*

The heir of the divine habitations, thou didst, O Father Teilo, live as an angel; wherefore with the angels doth thy spirit rejoice. Having undeviatingly proceeded, O most wise and marvellous Father Teilo, along the divine paths leading to heaven, thou hast unto the end avoided those that lead to evil.

Refrain: *Holy Father Teilo, pray to God for us.*

Through the grace which hath found abided in thy soul, O Father Teilo, are driven away the unclean spirits that cunningly find their abided in men.

Refrain: *O most holy Theotokos, save us.*

Theotokion

Thou art, O Virgin, an inexhaustible source of water, drinking of which all become filled with the grace, being cleansed both in soul and body.

Ode 9

Eirmos

Every one became terrified at hearing of the ineffable Gods condescension, that the Most High did voluntarily come down even unto the flesh itself, having become man in the Virgins womb; wherefore we the faithful magnify the most pure Theotokos.

Refrain: *Holy Father Teilo, pray to God for us.*

Thy honoured shrine by the Holy Spirit richly sheddeth healings, cureth long standing diseases of those that have recourse unto thee, O Father Teilo; it driveth away the cunning, ferocious spirits and raiseth up the faithful to the praising of thine illustrious deeds.

Refrain: *Holy Father Teilo, pray to God for us.*

As a great sun that hast shone forth unto us in the greatness of thy deeds, O most wise one; thou hast enlightened the ends of the earth, and in thy death thou art gone from alight unto a brilliant light; wherefore we cry unto thee : Enlighten our thoughts, O holy Father Teilo.

Refrain: *Holy Father Teilo, pray to God for us.*

Thine enduring body bound with chains, O blessed one, doth heal by a touch incurable diseases, since God and Saviour hath greatly glorified thee, O most wise and wonder worthy Father Teilo; for thou hast made thyself famous with thy good works, O holy one.

Refrain: *Holy Father Teilo, pray to God for us.*

In the dales of fasting hast thou, O most praised Father Teilo, blossomed as a wild sweet smelling rose, and as a lily hast thou filled the consciences of the faithful with perfume of thy virtues and miracles; wherefore, O holy one, drive away from us the malodorous passions.

Refrain: *O most holy Theotokos, save us.*

Theotokion

Enlighten, O pure Virgin, my heart ever grieving for transgressions and on account of manifold worldly resorts, do not leave me a joy unto mine enemies, that I may glorify and lovingly hymn thee, O most hymned one.

Photagogicon

Thou hast flourished as Davids palm, O Father Teilo, and hast appeared an abided of the Holy Spirit, Who hath made thee famous in the universe, do unceasingly pray for us that in faith honour thy most honoured memory, O holy Teilo.

Refrain: *O most holy Theotokos, save us.*

Theotokion

We bless in unceasing odes thee, O Virgin, for unto One of the Trinity hast thou, O Theotokos, given birth and dost bear in thy divine arms the most abundant Word, unchangeable and immutable.

Idiomelic Stichera

Tone 6   Rich texture, funeral, sorrowful.   *D, Eb, F##, G, A, Bb, C##, D.*

O God bearer, most blessed Teilo; all the subtleties of thy flesh hast thou subjugated unto thy spirit, having strengthened thyself with the pains of fasting, and assayed as gold in the forge, hast thou appeared shining and wast a receptacle of the Most Holy Spirit. Having gathered multitudes of monks, thou hast with thine instructions, as with a ladder leading into heaven, brought them up unto the height of virtues. Remember us, honouring thy sacred memory, and supplicate that our souls may be saved. **(x2)**

Refrain: *Holy Father Teilo, pray to God for us.*

Today doth shine forth thy most illustrious and all festive memory, O most glorious Teilo, calling together multitudinous assemblies of the fasting and choirs of the religious, both truly angels and men, unto the praise of Christ, our God adored in the Trinity. Wherefore, coming up unto the sacred shrine of thy relics, we abundantly receive the gifts of healing and glorify Christ, the Saviour of our souls, Who hath crowned thee.

Refrain: *Holy Father Teilo, pray to God for us.*

O God bearer, most blessed Father Teilo; as the prophet of old, hast thou covered the earth with thy tears and never gave sleep unto thine eyes nor allowed dozing unto thine eyelids in manifesting the yearning of thy heart after Christ, Whom thou didst love; wherefore, wast thou a model unto monks and hast improved the manifestation of every virtue; wherefore, we also bless thee, magnifying Him Who hath glorified thee.

Glory be to the Father and to the Son and to the Holy Spirit,

O holy Father Teilo; having from childhood assiduously studied virtue, thou wast an organ of the Holy Spirit, and having obtained from Him the working of miracles, thou hast admonished the people to shun the sweets of life. Being now most clearly illumined with the divine light, enlighten also our thoughts, O our Father Teilo.

Both now and forever and unto the ages of ages. Amen.

Refrain: *O most holy Theotokos, save us.*

Theotokion
All my trust I place in thee, O Mother of God, do preserve me under thy shelter.

Refrain: *O most holy Theotokos, save us.*

Stavro-Theotokion
Many humiliations hast thou endured; seeing the Maker of all things lifted up on the cross, thou, O most pure one, with moaning didst say: O Most Holy Lord, my Son and my God. How is it that when Thou desirest to honour Thy creation, O Master, Thou dost suffer dishonour in the flesh? Glory unto Thy great mercy and Thy condescension, O Lover of man.

Glory be to the Father and to the Son and to the Holy Spirit,

Doxastikon

Tone 5 Stimulating, dancing, and rhythmical.   C, D, Eb, F, G, A, Bb, C.

Today is thy fullness of time. Today thou didst finish thy course and keep thy faith. Therefore Christ thy God honoured thee with martyrdom, as thou didst fly from roof to roof over houses like a beam of Divine Light. And when thou didst enter into thy tomb, which is thy Church of the Theotokos, thou didst strengthen the faith of the Lord's sheep, saying unto them, "Behold, the completed mystical sacrifice is escorted in to take and receive us as participants in the Blood. Therefore, let us with faith and longing draw near and become partakers in the Crucifixion, the Death of martyrdom and the Resurrection."

Both now and forever and unto the ages of ages. Amen.

Theotokíon

Tone 5 Stimulating, dancing, and rhythmical.   C, D, Eb, F, G, A, Bb, C.

The sign of the Virgin Bride who knew not wedlock was at one time revealed in the Red Sea; for there Moses did cleave the waters, and there Gabriel was the minister of a miracle. At that time Israel crossed the deep and their feet were not wet, and now the Virgin hath given birth to Christ without seed. The sea remained uncrossed after the passing of Israel, and the blameless one remained incorruptible after giving birth to Immanuel. Therefore, O eternal God, who wast before eternity, and who didst appear as man, have mercy upon us.

Glory be to the Father and to the Son and to the Holy Spirit,
Both now and forever and unto the ages of ages. Amen.

Theotokíon Of The Litiya

Tone 5 Stimulating, dancing, and rhythmical.   C, D, Eb, F, G, A, Bb, C.

We bless thee, O Virgin Theotokos, and we faithful rightly glorify thee, O thou unshakeable tower, impregnable house of defence, invincible help and shield, and refuge of our souls.

Stichera From The Kekragion

Tone 8 Humility, tranquillity, repose, suffering, pleading.   C, D, Eb, F, G, A, Bb, C.

A divine and light bearing lamp that is holy and precious, never remaineth hidden under the bushel of the thick covering of life, but the Lover of man placeth him on the summit of high miracles; through his intercessions grant, O Christ, unto Thy people great mercy.

Chorus: *Precious in the sight of the Lord is the death of His Saints. (Psalm 115:6)*

Stichos

    Tone 8   Humility, tranquillity, repose, suffering, pleading.   *C, D, Eb, F, G, A, Bb, C.*

Thou, all honoured one, hast set thyself to the plough with the work of thy hands, and ever working the things divine, thou didst not turn to look back, but wast directed into the Kingdom of Christ, the Incarnate God, unto the salvation of our souls.

Chorus: *Wondrous is God in His Saints; the God of Israel. (Psalm 67:35)*

    Tone 5   Stimulating, dancing, and rhythmical.   *C, D, Eb, F, G, A, Bb, C.*

Carried in a light boat of the body by the gentle breezes of thy gentle spirit, thou, O wise one, hast easily passed across the abyss of life, and having disposed of thy possessions for the priceless Pearl and obtained it, thou hast kept It unto thyself, finding thy bliss in the divine virtues thereof.

Refrain: *Holy Father Teilo, pray to God for us.*

Having preserved unhurt that which is in the image, and having through fasting made thy mind master over the perilous passions, thou hast ascended as far as possible unto that which is in the likeness; for, having manfully constrained thy nature, thou hast taken pains to subdue the inferior unto the higher, and to make the flesh a slave unto the spirit, wherefore thou, O hermit, hast appeared an instructor of the monks, teacher of good life, most certain rule of virtue. And now, in the heavens, when mirrors do no longer intervene, thou, our Father Teilo, dost clearly see the Holy Trinity and supplicate immediately for those that in faith and love honour thee.

Refrain: *Holy Father Teilo, pray to God for us.*

Thy festival, O God bearer, brighter than the sun hath come; it illumineth those that in faith have recourse unto thee, filleth with the sweet smell of immortality and sheddeth healings unto the souls, O holy father, intercessor for our souls.

Refrain: *Holy Father Teilo, pray to God for us.*

Through the furrows of abstinence having obtained victory over the sensual passions of the body, and having shewn on earth the zeal of the bodiless, thou hast subdued unto the spirit all desires of the flesh, O wonder worker, Father Teilo; wherefore, dwelling now in the heavenly habitations, do supplicate for our souls.

Refrain: *Holy Father Teilo, pray to God for us.*

O blissful Father Teilo; having laid the foundation of virtue, thou didst put off the ancient man with his hosts, and hast truly put on Christ; wherefore hast thou, O holy one, put to shame many armies of the enemy and wast instructor of the monks. Supplicate that our souls may be saved.

Refrain: *Holy Father Teilo, pray to God for us.*

We honour in thee, O Teilo our father, the teacher of the multitude of monks, for we have truly learned to walk straight in thy path. Blessed art thou that hast laboured for Christ and hast laid bare the might of the enemy; O friend of angels and companion of the holy and just ones, with them do supplicate unto the Lord that our souls may be saved.

Refrain: *Holy Father Teilo, pray to God for us.*

Stichos

Tone 6   Rich texture, funeral, sorrowful.   D, Eb, F##, G, A, Bb, C##, D.

O holy father, through all the earth is gone forth the sound of thine exertions, wherefore hast thou found in heaven the reward of thy labours; thou hast destroyed the armies of demons and hast reached the orders of angels, whom thou hast irreproachably emulated in thy life. Possessing boldness before Christ the God, do obtain peace for our souls.

Glory be to the Father and to the Son and to the Holy Spirit,
Both now and forever and unto the ages of ages. Amen.

Theotokíon

Tone 4   Festive, joyous and expressing deep piety.   C, D, Eb, F, G, A, Bb, C.

O most reverend Virgin, O thou by means of whom my Saviour Christ the Lord did appear to those lying in darkness, He being the Sun of justice, wishing to enlighten those whom He had made with His own hands after His likeness: thou art the temple, the gate, the palace and the throne of the King. Wherefore, O all praised one, thou hast attained with Him maternal privilege. Intercede ceaselessly for the salvation of our souls.

Refrain: *Holy Father Teilo, pray to God for us.*

Troparion From The Typikon

Tone 8   Humility, tranquillity, repose, suffering, pleading.   C, D, Eb, F, G, A, Bb, C.

In thee, O father, was manifestly preserved what is in the image of God, for having taken up thy cross, thou didst follow Christ, and by thine own example hast taught that the flesh is to be despised as transient, but that particular care should be bestowed on the soul, as a thing immortal; wherefore, together with the angels, rejoiceth also thine, O holy Teilo.

Refrain: *O most holy Theotokos, save us.*

Theotokíon

Tone 5   Stimulating, dancing, and rhythmical.   *C, D, Eb, F, G, A, Bb, C.*

Rejoice, O uncrossed gate. Rejoice, O wall and protection of those who hasten unto thee. Rejoice, O quiet haven who hast not known wedlock. O thou who hast given birth in the flesh to thy Creator and God, thou shalt continue to interceded for the sake of those who praise and worship thy birth giving.

Refrain: *O most holy Theotokos, save us.*

Theotokíon

Rejoice, O holy mountain whom the Lord crossed in passing.

Rejoice, O burning bush yet unconsumed.

Rejoice, O thou who alone art a bridge for the world towards God, translating the dead to eternal life.

Rejoice, O pure one, free of corruption, who didst give birth without wedlock to the Saviour of the World.

Refrain: *O most holy Theotokos, save us.*

Theotokíon

Thee, who art the mediatress for the salvation of our race, we praise, O Virgin Theotokos; for in the flesh assumed from thee, after that He had suffered the Passion of the Cross, thy Son and our God delivered us from corruption, because He is the Lover of mankind.

Refrain: *O most holy Theotokos, save us.*

Theotokíon

O all blameless one, thou hast been shown to be a brightly shining bridal chamber and golden tabernacle containing God the Word Who, for our salvation, took flesh from thee and destroyed the power of death.

Glory be to the Father and to the Son and to the Holy Spirit,
Both now and forever and unto the ages of ages. Amen.

Prokeimenon

Priest: Let us attend. The Prokeimenon.

Reader: Precious in the sight of the Lord is the death of His saints.

Chorus: *Precious in the sight of the Lord is the death of His saints.*

Reader: What shall I render unto the Lord for all His benefits towards me?

Chorus: *Precious in the sight of the Lord is the death of His saints.*

Reader: Precious in the sight of the Lord | is the death of His saints.

Let Every Breath Praise The Lord

Let every breath praise the Lord. Praise God in His sanctuary.

Praise Him in His mighty firmament. Let every breath praise the Lord.

The Gospel

Priest: Wisdom, stand up. Let us listen to the Holy Gospel. Peace be with you all.

People: *And with thy spirit.*

Priest: The Reading is From The Holy Gospel According To Matthew (11:27-30).

People: *Glory to Thee, O Lord, glory to Thee.*

Priest: All things are delivered unto me of my Father: and no man knoweth the Son, but the Father; neither knoweth any man the Father, save the Son, and he to whomsoever the Son shall reveal him. Come unto me, all you that labour and are heavy laden, and I shall give you rest. Take my yoke upon you, and learn of me; for I am meek and lowly in heart: and you shall find rest unto your souls. For my yoke is easy, and my burden is light.

People: *Glory to Thee, O Lord, glory to Thee.*

Psalm 50

Have mercy on me, O God, according to Thy great mercy; and according to the multitude of Thy compassions blot out my transgression. Wash me thoroughly from mine iniquity, and cleanse me from my sin. For I acknowledge mine iniquity, and my sin is ever before me. Against Thee, Thee only have I sinned, and done evil in Thy sight, that Thou mayest be found just when Thou speakest, and victorious when Thou art judged. For behold, I was conceived in iniquity, and in sin my mother bore me. For behold, Thou hast loved truth; Thou hast made known to me the hidden and secret things of Thy wisdom. Thou shalt sprinkle me with hyssop, and I shall be made clean; Thou shalt wash me, and I shalt be whiter than snow. Make me to hear joy and gladness; that the humbled bones may rejoice. Turn Thy face away from my sins, and blot out all mine iniquities.

Create in me a clean heart, O God, and renew a steadfast spirit within me. Cast me not away from Thy presence, and take not Thy Holy Spirit from me. Restore to me the joy of Thy salvation, and establish me with Thy governing Spirit. I shall teach transgressors Thy ways, and the ungodly shall turn back to Thee. Deliver me from blood guiltiness, O God, the God of my salvation; my tongue shall joyfully declare Thy righteousness. Lord, open my lips, and my mouth shall declare Thy praise. For if Thou hadst desired sacrifice, I would give it; Thou dost not delight in burned offerings. A sacrifice to God is a broken spirit; God shall not despise a broken and a humbled heart. Do good, O Lord, in Thy good pleasure to Zion, and let the walls of Jerusalem be builded. Then Thou shalt be pleased with a sacrifice of righteousness, with oblation and whole burned offerings. Then shall they offer bulls on Thine altar.

Glory be to the Father and to the Son and to the Holy Spirit,
By the intercessions of the prizewinners, O Merciful One, blot out the multitude of mine offences.

Both now and forever and unto the ages of ages. Amen.

Theotokion

By the intercessions of the Theotokos, O Merciful One, blot out the multitude of mine offences.

Reader: Have mercy on me, O God, according to Thy great mercy; and according to the multitude of Thy compassions blot out my transgression.

Stichera For The Saints

Tone 5   Stimulating, dancing, and rhythmical.   *C, D, Eb, F, G, A, Bb, C.*

Today we enter the Promised Land, for the blood of our Martyrs paved our way, the supplications of our Fathers assisted us, and God, regarding the lowly state of His Church, sowed in the womb of its land the seeds of holy martyrdom. Rejoice, all you who have crossed the threshold into heavenly glory, and intercede with the Compassionate God for the salvation of our souls. **(x2)**

Glory be to the Father and to the Son and to the Holy Spirit,

Doxastikon

Tone 5   Stimulating, dancing, and rhythmical.   *C, D, Eb, F, G, A, Bb, C.*

Unto the call of thy Lord hast thou, O all blessed Teilo, followed, when thou hadst forsaken the world and everything there is beautiful in the world, with fervour didst thou endure the hardships of the eremitical life and manfully repulsed the armies of the demons; wherefore in faith we also constantly praise in hymns thy memory. **(x2)**

Both now and forever and unto the ages of ages. Amen.

Theotokion

Tone 5   Stimulating, dancing, and rhythmical.   *C, D, Eb, F, G, A, Bb, C.*

Beneath thy compassion we take refuge, O Theotokos. Despise not our prayers in our necessity, but deliver us from harm, O only pure, only blessed one.

Lauds - The Praises
Psalm 148

Praise the Lord. Praise the Lord from the heavens; praise Him in the heights. Praise Him, all His angels; praise Him, all His hosts. Praise Him, sun and moon; praise Him, all you stars of light. Praise Him, you heavens of heavens, and you waters above the heavens. Let them praise the name of the Lord, for He commanded and they were created. He has also established them forever and ever; He has made a decree that shall not pass away. Praise the Lord from the earth, you great sea creatures and all the depths; Fire and hail, snow and clouds; stormy wind, fulfilling His word; Mountains and all hills; fruitful trees and all cedars; Beasts and all cattle; creeping things and flying fowl; Kings of the earth and all peoples; princes and all judges of the earth;

Both young men and maidens; old men and children. Let them praise the name of the Lord, for His name alone is exalted; His glory is above the earth and heaven. And He has exalted the horn of His people, the praise of all His saints - of the children of Israel, a people near to Him. Praise the Lord.

Psalm 149

Praise the Lord. Sing to the Lord a new song, and His praise in the congregation of saints. Let Israel rejoice in their Maker; let the children of Zion be joyful in their King. Let them praise His name with the dance; let them sing praises to Him with the timbrel and harp. For the Lord takes pleasure in His people; He shall beautify the humble with salvation. Let the saints be joyful in glory; let them sing aloud on their beds. Let the high praises of God be in their mouth, and a two edged sword in their hand, To execute vengeance on the nations, and punishments on the peoples; To bind their kings with chains, and their nobles with fetters of iron; To execute on them the written judgement; this honour have all His saints. Praise the Lord.

Psalm 150

Praise the Lord. Praise God in His sanctuary; praise Him in His mighty firmament. Praise Him for His mighty acts; praise Him according to His excellent greatness. Praise Him with the sound of the trumpet; praise Him with the lute and harp. Praise Him with the timbrel and dance; praise Him with stringed instruments and flutes. Praise Him with loud cymbals; praise Him with high sounding cymbals. Let everything that has breath praise the Lord. Praise the Lord.

After The Psalm

Glory be to the Father and to the Son and to the Holy Spirit;
Both now and forever and unto the ages of ages. Amen.

Alleluia, Alleluia, Alleluia. Glory to Thee, O God. **(x3)**

Great Doxology

Glory to God, Who has shown us the Light. Glory to God in the highest, and on earth, peace, good will toward men. We praise Thee. We bless Thee. We worship Thee. We glorify Thee and give thanks to Thee for Thy great glory. O Lord God, Heavenly King, God the Father Almighty. O Lord, the Only Begotten Son, Jesus Christ, and the Holy Spirit. \

O Lord God, Lamb of God, Son of the Father, Who takes away the sins of the world, have mercy on us. Thou, Who takes away the sins of the world, receive our prayer. Thou, Who sittest at the right hand of God the Father, have mercy on us. /

For Thou alone art holy, and Thou alone art Lord. Thou alone, O Lord Jesus Christ, are most high in the glory of God the Father. Amen. I shall give thanks to Thee every day and praise Thy Name forever and ever, Lord. Every day shall I bless Thee and praise Thy name forever, and to the ages of ages. Amen. \

Vouchsafe, O Lord, to keep us this day without sin. Blessed art Thou, O Lord, the God of our fathers, and praised and glorified is Thy Name forever. Amen. Let Thy mercy be upon us, O Lord, even as we have set our hope on Thee.

Blessed art Thou, O Master; teach me Thy statutes.

Blessed art Thou, O Lord; enlighten me with Thy commandments.

Blessed art Thou, O Holy One; make me to understand Thy precepts.

Lord, Thou hast been our refuge from generation to generation. I said, *"Lord, have mercy on me. Heal my soul, for I have sinned against Thee."* \

Lord, I flee to Thee for refuge. Teach me to do Thy will, for Thou art my God. For with Thee is the fountain of Life, and in Thy light we shall see light. Continue Thy loving kindness to those who know Thee.

Holy God, Holy Strong, Holy Immortal, have mercy on us.

Holy God, Holy Strong, Holy Immortal, have mercy on us.

Holy God, Holy Strong, Holy Immortal, have mercy on us.

Glory be to the Father, and to the Son, and to the Holy Spirit;

Both now and forever, and unto the ages of ages. Amen.

Holy Immortal, have mercy on us.

Holy God, Holy Strong, Holy Immortal, have mercy on us.

Today salvation has come into the world. Let us sing to Him who rose from the tomb, the Author of our life. For, destroying death by death, he has given us the victory and His great mercy. \

Apolytikion

Tone 5   Stimulating, dancing, and rhythmical.   *C, D, Eb, F, G, A, Bb, C.*

Let us honour with hymns the ascetic of the Lord as one that, by true abstemiousness and enduring patience, hath exterminated all the assaults of passions, and hath put to great shame the opposing enemy with all his pride, and is now supplicating the Lord that our souls may be saved. **(x2)**

Glory be to the Father and to the Son and to the Holy Spirit,

Both now and forever and unto the ages of ages. Amen.

Little Litany

Deacon: Have mercy on us, O God, according to thy great mercy, we beseech thee; hearken and have mercy.

People: *Lord have mercy.* **(x3)**

Deacon: We pray for our Archbishop Nikitas and for all our brethren in Christ.

People: *Lord have mercy.* **(x3)**

Deacon: We pray for the mercy, life, peace, health and salvation of the servants of God (*N and N - insert names as requested here)* and for the persons who are here present.

People: *Lord have mercy.* **(x3)**

Deacon: We pray for all brethren and for all Christian people.

People: *Lord have mercy.* **(x3)**

Priest: For Thou art a merciful God who lovest mankind, and to Thee do we ascribe glory to the Father and to the Son and to the Holy Spirit, both now and forever and to the ages of ages.

People: *Amen.*

Priest: Hear us, O God our Saviour, the hope of all the ends of the earth and of those who are far off upon the sea, and show mercy, show mercy, O Master, upon us sinners, and be merciful unto us. For Thou art a merciful God who loves mankind, and to Thee we ascribe glory to the Father and to the Son and to the Holy Spirit. Both now and forever and ever and to the ages of ages.

People: *Amen.*

Deacon: Wisdom.

Priest: O most holy Theotokos, save us.

Reader: *[Archangel Gabriel:* It is truly right to call thee blessed, who gavest birth to God, ever-blessed and God-obedient the Mother of our God.] Greater in honour than the Cherubim and beyond compare more glorious than the Seraphim; without corruption thou gavest birth to God the Word, truly the Mother of God, we magnify thee.

Priest: Glory to Thee, O Christ God our hope, glory to Thee.

Reader: *Glory to the Father and to the Son, and to the Holy Spirit;*
Both now and forever and unto the ages of ages. Amen.

Lord have mercy. **(x3)**
Holy Father, bless.

Priest: May Christ our true God, through the prayers of his most pure Mother, of Saint *N [the patron saint of the church]*; of Saint Teilo of Wales, and of all the saints, have mercy on us and save us, forasmuch as He is good and loves mankind.

People: *Amen.*

Priest: Through the prayers of our holy fathers, Lord Jesus Christ, our God, have mercy on us and save us.

People: *Amen.*

Parakleses For The Holy Hieromartyr Joseph of Damascus and his Companions (+ 10 July 1860)

[With a priest.]

[By Nun Mariam (Zaka), Abbess of the Holy Monastery of St John the Baptist, Douma El-Batroun, Lebanon Original Arabic Text 1993 – English Translation 2008.]

• *Allusions to the work of a weaver of cloth are directly related to St Josephs occupation as a weaver prior to his ordination.*

• *Allusions to the work of a blacksmith are directly related to St Josephs family name – al-Haddad الحدّاد – that, in Arabic, means "the blacksmith."*

The Trisagion Prayers

Deacon: Holy Father, Bless.

Priest: Blessed is our God always, now and forever, and unto the ages of ages.

People: Amen.

Priest: O Heavenly King, Comforter, Spirit of Truth, Who art everywhere present and fillest all things, Treasury of blessings and Giver of life: Come and abide in us and cleanse us from every impurity and save our souls, O Good One.

Reader: Holy God, Holy Mighty, Holy Immortal, have mercy on us. **(x3)**

Glory be to the Father, and to the Son, and to the Holy Spirit;
Both now and forever, and unto the ages of ages. Amen.

O Most Holy Trinity, have mercy on us.

O Lord, cleanse us from our sins.

O Master, pardon our iniquities.

O Holy One, visit and heal our infirmities, for Thy names sake.

Lord have mercy. (x3)

Glory be to the Father and to the Son and to the Holy Spirit;
Both now and forever, and unto the ages of ages. Amen.

People: Our Father, Who art in Heaven, hallowed be Thy Name. Thy Kingdom come, Thy will be done, on earth as it is in Heaven. Give us this day our daily bread, and forgive us our trespasses, as we forgive those who trespass against us; and lead us not into temptation, but deliver us from the evil one.

Priest: For Thine is the kingdom, and the power and the glory of the Father and of the Son and of the Holy Spirit, now and forever and to the ages of ages.

People: *Amen.*

People: *Lord, have mercy.* (x12)

Glory be to the Father and to the Son and to the Holy Spirit,
Both now and forever and unto the ages of ages. Amen.

O come let us worship God our King.

O come let us worship and fall down before Christ, our King and God.

O come let us worship and fall down before Christ Himself, our King and our God.

Psalm 142

Hear my prayer, O Lord, give ear to my supplications. In Thy faithfulness answer me, and in Thy righteousness. Do not enter into judgement with Thy servant, for in Thy sight no one living is righteous. For the enemy has persecuted my soul; he has crushed my life to the ground; he has made me dwell in darkness, like those who have long been dead. Therefore my spirit is overwhelmed within me; my heart within me is distressed. I remember the days of old; I meditate on all Thy works; I muse on the work of Thine hands. I spread out my hands to Thee; my soul longs for Thee like a thirsty land. Answer me speedily, O Lord; my spirit fails. Do not hide Thy face from me, lest I be like those who go down into the pit. Cause me to hear Thy loving kindness in the morning, for in Thee do I trust; cause me to know the way in which I should walk, for I lift up my soul to Thee. Deliver me, O Lord, from mine enemies; in Thee I take shelter. Teach me to do Thy will, for Thou art my God; Thy Spirit is good. Lead me in the land of uprightness. Revive me, O Lord, for Thy names sake. For Thy righteousness' sake bring my soul out of trouble. In Thy mercy cut off mine enemies, and destroy all those who afflict my soul; for I am Thy servant.

After The Psalm

Glory be to the Father and to the Son and to the Holy Spirit,
Both now and forever and unto the ages of ages. Amen.

Alleluia, Alleluia, Alleluia. Glory to Thee, O God. (x3)

Lord, have mercy. (x3)

Glory be to the Father and to the Son and to the Holy Spirit,

Doxastikon

Tone 5   Stimulating, dancing, and rhythmical.   *C, D, Eb, F, G, A, Bb, C.*

Today is thy fullness of time. Today thou didst finish thy course and keep thy faith. Therefore Christ thy God honoured thee with martyrdom, as thou didst fly from roof to roof over houses like a beam of Divine Light. And when thou didst enter into thy tomb, which is thy Church of the Theotokos, thou didst strengthen the faith of the Lord's sheep, saying unto them, "Behold, the completed mystical sacrifice is escorted in to take and receive us as participants in the Blood. Therefore, let us with faith and longing draw near and become partakers in the Crucifixion, the Death of martyrdom and the Resurrection."

Both now and forever and unto the ages of ages. Amen.

Theotokion

Tone 5   Stimulating, dancing, and rhythmical.   *C, D, Eb, F, G, A, Bb, C.*

The sign of the Virgin Bride who knew not wedlock was at one time revealed in the Red Sea; for there Moses did cleave the waters, and there Gabriel was the minister of a miracle. At that time Israel crossed the deep and their feet were not wet, and now the Virgin hath given birth to Christ without seed. The sea remained uncrossed after the passing of Israel, and the blameless one remained incorruptible after giving birth to Immanuel. Therefore, O eternal God, who wast before eternity, and who didst appear as man, have mercy upon us.

The Litiya Troparia

Tone 5   Stimulating, dancing, and rhythmical.   *C, D, Eb, F, G, A, Bb, C.*

O Chaste Joseph, thou didst refuse vain glory and the riches of this world, wherefore the Lord accounted thee worthy to share His Life. He forged thee upon the anvil, fashioned thee with the hammer, moulded thee as a new vessel and temple for the Holy Spirit, honouring thee for thy poverty and thy love for the Word and showed thee forth as a martyr for His Word and a witness to His great power.

O Priest Joseph, thou, like the chaste Joseph who fled from the riches and fame of Egypt, didst realize salvation by thy poverty and by undertaking to heal the wounds of thy Church, for thou didst love her poor, teach her ignorant, and bore her infirmities. Thou didst never take pleasure in the delights of mammon, but rather offered up thine own body as bread of life for those who love Christ thy Master, thy God and thy Teacher, for by all thine actions thou didst teach His Word and keep His Commandments.

Strike, O Joseph thou blacksmith, strike the face of falsehood with the word of truth. Dispel, O our Father, dispel the words of the heretics and the foreign sects by the holy Gospel. Having broken thy body as bread for those who hunger, and shed thy blood for those who thirst, thou didst hear the voice of thy Christ, O blessed

Father, having pleased Him by accomplishing His will. Therefore, intercede with Christ God that He would grant unto us His love for thee.

O Joseph thou Priest of the Lord, thou didst stand as a firm rock in the face of infirmities and as a instructor in ordeals, revealing the presence of God for those who knew Him not. You defended the sacraments and doctrines of the Church, breathing into thy students the Spirit of peace and the power of God the Indivisible Trinity.

Glory be to the Father and to the Son and to the Holy Spirit,

Doxastikon Of The Litiya

Tone 5   Stimulating, dancing, and rhythmical.   *C, D, Eb, F, G, A, Bb, C.*

Rejoice, O Joseph, thou Priest of the Most High and martyr for Christ. When thy slayers approached, thou didst remove from upon thy breast the Divine Sacrament and didst consume it, becoming thyself the broken Body of Christ. They spilled thy blood with that of thy companions, slashed thee, beat thee, spat upon thee, and dragged thee through the streets, thus making thee worthy of the love of thy Master. Having become like thy Lord in His Passion, intercede with Christ God to circumcise our minds, our souls and our hearts, thus making us, like thee, martyrs for His Word and for His Love.

Both now and forever and unto the ages of ages. Amen.

Theotokíon Of The Litiya

Tone 5   Stimulating, dancing, and rhythmical.   *C, D, Eb, F, G, A, Bb, C.*

We bless thee, O Virgin Theotokos, and we faithful rightly glorify thee, O thou unshakeable tower, impregnable house of defence, invincible help and shield, and refuge of our souls.

The Aposticha

Tone 8   Humility, tranquillity, repose, suffering, pleading.   *C, D, Eb, F, G, A, Bb, C.*

O Joseph Priest of the Most High, thou didst preach and teach, and didst copy a great number of manuscripts to instruct by the written word what thou didst proclaim by word, leaving as an inheritance for those who love the word and the Word of God, faithfully preserved and gathered in thy library the thousands of books that were incinerated upon thy martyrdom. Grant us who praise thee to learn from the unburned Vessel of the Word.

Chorus: *Precious in the sight of the Lord is the death of His Saints. (Psalm 115:6)*

Stichos

Reader: O Hieromartyr Joseph, when thou wast known as a preacher of the word and a teacher of logic and sciences, thy Lord chose thee to serve Him and called thee, saying, " O lamb of Christ, come. O Priest of the

Most High, approach." Thus thou didst draw near to Him as a poor youth full of love, endurance, knowledge, and evangelical steadfastness Since thou didst receive the gift of Christ, intercede with the compassionate God to accept us also.

Chorus: *Wondrous is God in His Saints; the God of Israel. (Psalm 67:35)*

Tone 5   Stimulating, dancing, and rhythmical.   *C, D, Eb, F, G, A, Bb, C.*

Rejoice, thou who didst blossom in the desert of the Lord from an Arabic Ghassanid root. For Christ our God made thee a shepherd of His sheep in the Church of Antioch, and today, on thy memorial, we bear witness that thou becamest an example for Priests and all believers. Therefore, O Lord, by the intercessions of Thy Martyr Joseph have mercy upon us and save us.

Yearning for knowledge from thy youth, thou overcamest poverty by weaving cloth by day and thine own soul by sciences at night, beseeching thy Lord to weave for thee a vestment to clothe thy temple, O His Spirit bearer. Thou standest witnessing in thy Church that the Lord, One of the Three Hypostases, became man for our salvation.

Poverty encouraged thee in thy youth, O Joseph, to study Arabic language, logic and sciences, and with thy soul thou didst eagerly study the Torah, the Psalms, and the Gospels Word. And so thou didst teach and proclaimed, crying out: "Come, you blessed of my Father, inherit in your poverty the kingdom prepared for you, and be enriched by the kingdom of the King of the heavens."

O Priest Joseph, showing a diligence befitting thy calling, thou didst honor thyself by preserving thy soul like Mary who conceived in her womb by the Holy Spirit. Thou didst labour and teach for the sake of Divine Love, and worthily delivered thy soul and those of thy companions unto thy Creator as a gift of love. Through their intercessions, O God, have mercy upon us and save us.

O Priest of the Most High, thou didst weave the vestment of thy salvation on the night of the night of thy marriage, when thou didst read of thy love for God the Word to thy spouse Mariam, and remained in thy poverty seeking the face of thy Lord. Thy children nourished thee with bread as thou didst nourish the world with bread of everlasting life, feeding their souls and teaching them to wait peacefully upon the Lord in all of their afflictions.

O Priest Joseph, today we praise thee on the feast of thy martyrdom, because thou wast fervent in faith, patient with great patience, meek, compassionate, humble, kind, zealous, calm, shrewd, strong, having no pride other than Christ thy God. Through thine intercessions make worthy of these Divine Gifts all of us who celebrate thy memory with faith.

Stichos

Reader: O Martyr Joseph, thou didst establish a new kind of martyrdom for divine love when thou didst found a school to teach theology as love of God, that those yearning for the word may become shepherds and Priests leading with the staff of Christ His rational sheep.

Glory be to the Father and to the Son and to the Holy Spirit,

Doxastikon

Tone 8   Humility, tranquillity, repose, suffering, pleading.   *C, D, Eb, F, G, A, Bb, C.*

Thou didst excel in preaching, O Joseph, for thy Lord granted thee the gift of proclaiming His Word, wherefore thou wast called the second John Chrysostom. To purify thee of vanity, Christ permitted the enemies of truth to confront thee so that thou couldst conquer them by the Name of thy Lord Who created thee and knew thee from the womb and guided thee and thy flock to salvation.

Both now and forever and unto the ages of ages. Amen.

Theotokíon

Tone 4   Festive, joyous and expressing deep piety.   *C, D, Eb, F, G, A, Bb, C.*

O most reverend Virgin, O thou by means of whom my Saviour Christ the Lord did appear to those lying in darkness, He being the Sun of justice, wishing to enlighten those whom He had made with His own hands after His likeness: thou art the temple, the gate, the palace and the throne of the King. Wherefore, O all praised one, thou hast attained with Him maternal privilege. Intercede ceaselessly for the salvation of our souls.

Apolytikion

Tone 5   Stimulating, dancing, and rhythmical.   *C, D, Eb, F, G, A, Bb, C.*

Come, you faithful, let us honour the martyr of Christ, a Priest of the Church of Antioch who by the word of the Word and by his blood and the blood of his companions baptised the land of Damascus, its Church and its people. Being immersed in the light of the Gospel from his youth, he worked and taught and defended the Church of Christ and her flock. O holy Joseph of Damascus, be for us an example, defending us and interceding for us fervently before the Saviour.

Theotokíon

Tone 5   Stimulating, dancing, and rhythmical.   *C, D, Eb, F, G, A, Bb, C.*

Rejoice, O uncrossed gate. Rejoice, O wall and protection of those who hasten unto thee. Rejoice, O quiet haven who hast not known wedlock. O thou who hast given birth in the flesh to thy Creator and God, thou shalt continue to interceded for the sake of those who praise and worship thy birth giving.

First Poetic Kathisma

Tone 5   Stimulating, dancing, and rhythmical.   *C, D, Eb, F, G, A, Bb, C.*

Today we praise with hymns the Hieromartyr Joseph and his companions who, in the flesh of sin and death, conquered death by death for Christ's sake, wherefore He elevated them to His Light and eternal life.

Glory be to the Father and to the Son and to the Holy Spirit,

O our righteous Father Joseph, thou didst love Christ and desire His Passion, wherefore thou didst offer thy body and thy companions to be devoured by the ignorant lions of this world, thus making thee an exquisite bread for the Saviour.

Both now and forever and unto the ages of ages. Amen.

Theotokíon

Rejoice, O holy mountain whom the Lord crossed in passing.

Rejoice, O burning bush yet unconsumed.

Rejoice, O thou who alone art a bridge for the world towards God, translating the dead to eternal life.

Rejoice, O pure one, free of corruption, who didst give birth without wedlock to the Saviour of the World.

Second Poetic Kathisma

Tone 3   Arrogant, brave, and mature atmosphere.   *F, G, A, A#, C, D, E, F.*

Rejoice, O Joseph thou boast of Antiochian ascetics, for thou didst inherit the spirit of thy predecessor, John of Damascus, joining him in preaching the theology of the Word. Thou wast slain together with thy companions for the love of the Triune God: Father, Son and Holy Spirit, Who breathed upon thee the spirit of martyrdom.

Glory be to the Father and to the Son and to the Holy Spirit,

Glory be to Thee, who hast breathed Thy Holy Spirit upon Thy chosen Joseph, whereby he became Thy son by following in the footsteps of Thy Son the Word. He enlightened Thy Church by his knowledge, fed her with Thy Body and Blood, and accepted martyrdom, offering up his body and blood as life for those who cry out: Glory to Thy supreme love for us, O Lord, since Thou hast accepted a Martyr from Antioch. Glory to thee.

Both now and forever and unto the ages of ages. Amen.

Theotokíon

Thee, who art the mediatress for the salvation of our race, we praise, O Virgin Theotokos; for in the flesh assumed from thee, after that He had suffered the Passion of the Cross, thy Son and our God delivered us from corruption, because He is the Lover of mankind.

Third Poetic Kathisma

Tone 5   Stimulating, dancing, and rhythmical.   *C, D, Eb, F, G, A, Bb, C.*

O you faithful, let us eagerly praise Joseph the Martyr of Christ and Priest of Antioch; for, in his youth, he offered himself at the altar of the Lord, learning of the divine mystery that he would become, like his Master, a sacrifice upon the holy table of the worlds temple in order to water the land of Antioch with his blood, wherefrom we drink the water of eternal life.

Glory be to the Father and to the Son and to the Holy Spirit,

In thy childhood, O Joseph, thou didst acquire knowledge, and, when faced with poverty, thou wast obliged to work to earn thy bread. But the Son and Word of the Father dwelt within thee and nourished thee with the bread of His commandments, and chose thee to carry His Word and teach it to His sheep. Today we praise thee, for thou hast been glorified by the Lord with martyrdom; wherefore, intercede with Christ God for the salvation of our souls.

Both now and forever and unto the ages of ages. Amen.

Theotokíon

O all blameless one, thou hast been shown to be a brightly shining bridal chamber and golden tabernacle containing God the Word Who, for our salvation, took flesh from thee and destroyed the power of death.

Prokeimenon

Reader: Wondrous is God in His saints.

Chorus: *Wondrous is God in His saints.*

Reader: In the saints that are in His earth hath the Lord been wondrous.

Chorus: *Wondrous is God in His saints.*

Reader: Wondrous is God | in His saints.

Let Every Breath Praise The Lord

Let every breath praise the Lord. Praise God in His sanctuary.

Praise Him in His mighty firmament. Let every breath praise the Lord.

The Gospel

Priest: The Reading is From The Holy Gospel According To Luke (12:8-12).

People: *Glory to Thee, O Lord, glory to Thee.*

Priest: Also I say unto you, Whosoever shall confess me before men, him shall the Son of man also confess before the angels of God: But he that denieth me before men shall be denied before the angels of

God. And whosoever shall speak a word against the Son of man, it shall be forgiven him: but unto him that blasphemeth against the Holy Ghost it shall not be forgiven. And when they bring you unto the synagogues, and unto magistrates, and powers, take no thought how or what thing you shall answer, or what you shall say: For the Holy Ghost shall teach you in the same hour what you ought to say.

People: *Glory to Thee, O Lord, glory to Thee.*

Psalm 50

Have mercy on me, O God, according to Thy great mercy; and according to the multitude of Thy compassions blot out my transgression. Wash me thoroughly from mine iniquity, and cleanse me from my sin. For I acknowledge mine iniquity, and my sin is ever before me. Against Thee, Thee only have I sinned, and done evil in Thy sight, that Thou mayest be found just when Thou speakest, and victorious when Thou art judged. For behold, I was conceived in iniquity, and in sin my mother bore me. For behold, Thou hast loved truth; Thou hast made known to me the hidden and secret things of Thy wisdom. Thou shalt sprinkle me with hyssop, and I shall be made clean; Thou shalt wash me, and I shalt be whiter than snow. Make me to hear joy and gladness; that the humbled bones may rejoice. Turn Thy face away from my sins, and blot out all mine iniquities.

Create in me a clean heart, O God, and renew a steadfast spirit within me. Cast me not away from Thy presence, and take not Thy Holy Spirit from me. Restore to me the joy of Thy salvation, and establish me with Thy governing Spirit. I shall teach transgressors Thy ways, and the ungodly shall turn back to Thee. Deliver me from blood guiltiness, O God, the God of my salvation; my tongue shall joyfully declare Thy righteousness. Lord, open my lips, and my mouth shall declare Thy praise. For if Thou hadst desired sacrifice, I would give it; Thou dost not delight in burned offerings. A sacrifice to God is a broken spirit; God shall not despise a broken and a humbled heart. Do good, O Lord, in Thy good pleasure to Zion, and let the walls of Jerusalem be builded. Then Thou shalt be pleased with a sacrifice of righteousness, with oblation and whole burned offerings. Then shall they offer bulls on Thine altar.

Glory be to the Father and to the Son and to the Holy Spirit,

By the intercessions of the prizewinners, O Merciful One, blot out the multitude of mine offences.

Both now and forever and unto the ages of ages. Amen.

Theotokion

Chorus: *By the intercessions of the Theotokos, O Merciful One, blot out the multitude of mine offences.*

Reader: Have mercy on me, O God, according to Thy great mercy; and according to the multitude of Thy compassions blot out my transgression.

The Post Gospel Idiomelon

Tone 6   Rich texture, funeral, sorrowful.   *D, Eb, F##, G, A, Bb, C##, D.*

When thou, O Priest, wast building temples of the human soul by the evangelical word, thou didst also erect holy temples to shelter the flock of Christ that crieth out His Name. Thou didst establish churches, inscribe and seal them with the Name of the All holy Trinity that they might be witnesses of our Holy Faith.

Ode I

Tone 5   Stimulating, dancing, and rhythmical.   *C, D, Eb, F, G, A, Bb, C.*

Refrain: *O Holy Martyrs of Christ, intercede on our behalf.*

Reader: O Joseph, in thy youth thou didst traverse the sea of thine earthly marriage by thy love for the Word. The world could not distract thee from this love, and, when thou didst hasten unto it as unto a refuge, Thy Lord elevated thee to know Him by His Word.

Chorus: *Glory to Thee, our God, glory to Thee.*

Reader: O Joseph, thou overcamest bodily delights by holding fast to the Word, the anchor of thy salvation, thus preparing thyself for what was to come, and while yet living on earth thou didst long for the life on high. Therefore thy Lord honoured thee by making thee a clarion of His Word.

Chorus: *Glory to Thee, our God, glory to Thee.*

Reader: Sing we all a triumphal hymn unto God the Word, Who sanctified thee by martyrdom, O Saint, because thou didst love Him more than thyself, wherefore He received thee at the end of thy struggle.

Refrain: *O Holy Martyrs of Christ, intercede on our behalf.*

Theotokíon

Reader: In peace we cry unto thee, O pure Lady who gavest birth for our joy: Enlighten our minds and souls, O all praised one, and lead us along the path of knowledge, beseeching thy Son and God to grant us all remission of sins.

Refrain: *O Holy Martyrs of Christ, intercede on our behalf.*

Ode III

Refrain: *O Holy Martyrs of Christ, intercede on our behalf.*

Reader: O Joseph the Priest, thou daily overcamest the disturbances of human nature by thine obedience to the Gospel of thy Master. By thy gentleness thou didst console His wretched ones and wipe away the tears of the sorrowful, and, in thine own poverty, thou didst feed His poor ones. Account us worthy of the same.

Chorus: *Glory to Thee, our God, glory to Thee.*

Reader: When thou foundest the Word of God to be thine own calm harbor, thou didst fill thyself with divine love, whereby thou leddest thy people and flock. Therefore the Lord preserved thee for them as a helpful father in their lives. Glory to our God in thee.

Chorus: *Glory to Thee, our God, glory to Thee.*

Theotokíon

Reader: When the multitude of women martyrs beheld thee, O Ever Virgin Mother who art blessed amongst women, they strove all the harder and offered themselves unto thy Son.

Refrain: *O Holy Martyrs of Christ, intercede on our behalf.*

Ode IV

Tone 5   *Stimulating, dancing, and rhythmical.*   *C, D, Eb, F, G, A, Bb, C.*

Refrain: *O Holy Martyrs of Christ, intercede on our behalf.*

Reader: 'Thou, O Lord, hast chosen me and known me from the womb.' Therefore, O our Father Joseph, thou didst devote thyself to learn the Word, whereby thou didst conquer thine ignorance and transmit the word to thy flock. Glory to the One who taught thee.

Chorus: *Glory to Thee, our God, glory to Thee.*

Reader: O our Father Joseph, thou becamest a clarion of theology and thereby defeated the deceivers who came to scatter the sheep of thy flock, for thou didst repel them by the staff of the Word of God and preserved Christ's lambs by the power of His Word.

Chorus: *Glory to Thee, our God, glory to Thee.*

Reader: O great athlete Joseph, by the sweet love of Christ and His Power which dwelt within thee, thou didst destroy the snares of the enemy which surrounded thee. And when thy Lord came unto thee, thou didst hasten unto Him, thus glorifying Him by thy love, thy struggles and thy martyrdom.

Refrain: *O Holy Martyrs of Christ, intercede on our behalf.*

Theotokíon

Reader: Beseech, O Virgin, the Timeless One who entered time through thee, to deliver my soul from the multitude of its persistent sins.

Refrain: *O Holy Martyrs of Christ, intercede on our behalf.*

Ode V

Tone 5   *Stimulating, dancing, and rhythmical.*   *C, D, Eb, F, G, A, Bb, C.*
Refrain: *O Holy Martyrs of Christ, intercede on our behalf.*

Reader: O our Father Joseph, when thou wast wed in thy youth thou overcamest the devices of thy nature by taking the Book of thy Lord from its shelf and thereby calmed thy bodily passions.

Chorus: *Glory to Thee, our God, glory to Thee.*

Reader: O our Father Joseph, thou didst manifest great love for thy Lord when thou wast led to bodily slaughter upon the altar of worldly concerns. Thou didst offer up thy life in martyrdom as a service to the Lord and His Church and as instruction for His people in theology, demonstrating that thou dost love thy Lord more than thine own self.

Chorus: *Glory to Thee, our God, glory to Thee.*

Reader: Thou didst defeat the darkness of thy soul by the Light of the Gospel through thine obedience to thy Master. And thus struggling against the passions of love for money and power, thou didst remain a loyal servant of thy Lord, proving to be a good steward of thy poverty and of the flock entrusted to thy care, building a temple for Him in thy heart until the noëtic Sun Himself enlightened thee with His Light, making of thee a ray to illumine His Church with thy light.

Refrain: *O Holy Martyrs of Christ, intercede on our behalf.*

Theotokíon
Reader: We praise Thee, O Virgin, for through thee God became man and wast revealed upon earth. Rejoice, O Good Land which brought forth the Grain of Wheat which feedeth every thing that hath breath.

Refrain: *O Holy Martyrs of Christ, intercede on our behalf.*

Ode VI

Tone 5   *Stimulating, dancing, and rhythmical.*   *C, D, Eb, F, G, A, Bb, C.*
Refrain: *O Holy Martyrs of Christ, intercede on our behalf.*

Reader: Thou didst spend thy days in weeping, O Joseph, and struggling against thy nature in order to be delivered from the monster of self will and, by obedience, to enter into the bosom of God thy Saviour.

Chorus: *Glory to Thee, our God, glory to Thee.*

Reader: When, with the Light of Christ, thou didst enlighten the life of thy family, all purified themselves for the sake of the Gospel, each according to his talent, and thus assisted thee in thy struggle and laboured to feed thee and thy flock, O poor one of Christ.

Chorus: *Glory to Thee, our God, glory to Thee.*

Reader: O Hieromartyr Joseph, thou wast asked to abandon thy flock by the temptation of money. But thou didst say, 'I have been ordained to serve this flock, and He who chose me sufficeth me.'

Refrain: *O Holy Martyrs of Christ, intercede on our behalf.*

Theotokion

Reader: Entering the womb of the Virgin, O Lord, Thou didst take upon Thee the form of a servant and thereby renewed my nature, O Master of all Who in the beginning formed Eve.

Refrain: *O Holy Martyrs of Christ, intercede on our behalf.*

Kontakion

Let us praise the all zealous Martyr of Christ, Joseph the Priest of the Most High, who from his childhood chose the Lord's good part and bore the word of the powerful staff of the Spirit, instructed, struggled, erected holy temples and offered his body and those of his companions for the sake of the Gospel. Therefore, let us cry out, saying, 'Rejoice, O Holy New Martyrs of Antioch.'

Oikos

Made strong with the might of God, O godly minded Joseph, thou wast shown by divine deeds to be worthy of thy calling as a Priest of the Most High. Thy blood, mingled with that of the multitude of thy companions, like the blood of the righteous Priest Zacharias and the fourteen thousand Holy Innocents, crieth out to God and beareth witness to thy martyric slaughter. Since thou now dost stand in company with them before the divine throne of the Creator, we cry out, saying: 'Rejoice, O Holy New Martyrs of Antioch.'

Synaxarion

[Speaking voice]

On the tenth of this month we commemorate the Holy Hieromartyr Yousef ibn Jirjis Mousa ibn Mouhana al-Haddad and his Companions. A married man, St Joseph of Damascus, as he is popularly known, was at first a weaver and then was ordained to the holy priesthood at the age of twenty-four in 1817, and assigned Great Economos of the Patriarchal Cathedral of the Dormition of the Most Holy Theotokos (al-Mariamiyeh) in the heart of the Old City of Damascus. On Monday, July 9th 1860 the brutal massacre of Christians, which began in the mountains of the Lebanon, spread to Damascus. Some Damascenes (including Michael Hawaweeny and his young wife Mariam who was bearing in her womb a son, the future St Raphael of Brooklyn) fled the Damascus for the port city of Beirut. The majority, however, took refuge in al-Mariamiyeh. Many had previously fled to Damascus from their mountain villages, while others came to the Cathedral from the Christian Quarter of Damascus and the villages that surrounded the city. St Joseph took up his communion kit containing the Reserved Sacrament, left his home and began to make his way to the Cathedral by jumping from rooftop to rooftop across the narrow streets of the Old City. As he went, he stopped to confess and commune the aged and infirm who could not flee their homes, encouraging them with stories from the Lives of the Great Martyrs. On Tuesday morning, July 10th, the Cathedral was surrounded, pillaged and burned by a fanatical crowd. Those inside the holy temple perished in the flames; of those who escaped and fled into the streets, most were shot or caught and forced back into the burning building, while only a few, including St Joseph, survived. As he roamed the narrow streets searching for survivors who needed, confessed and communed, St Joseph was surrounded by the enemies of Christ. Seeing that his end was near, St Joseph took out his communion kit and consumed what remained of the Body and Blood of Christ. Recognizing him as the "leader of the Christians," the persecutors savagely attacked him with axes. Then, binding his legs with ropes, they dragged his mutilated body through the streets to be mocked and spat upon by jeering onlookers. St Josephs sacred relics were then unceremoniously pitched into the city dump along with those of the other New Martyrs (numbering two thousand five hundred men plus women and children). St Joseph and his Companions were glorified by the Holy Synod of the Patriarchate of the Great City-of-God Antioch and all the East in the year of our salvation 1993.

Priest: Through their intercessions, O Christ our, have mercy upon us.
People: Amen.

Ode VII

Tone 5   *Stimulating, dancing, and rhythmical.*   *C, D, Eb, F, G, A, Bb, C.*
Refrain: O Holy Martyrs of Christ, intercede on our behalf.

Reader: O Joseph the contender, Priest of the Most High, as thou didst feed the poor, shouldered the sick, preached the Gospel and expelled the strange teachings of the heretics, thine enemies were burnt with rage, preparing their axes to strike thee down like a showbread for thy Christ.

Chorus: Glory to Thee, our God, glory to Thee.

Reader: O Hieromartyr Joseph, thou didst spend thy life instructing the Lords sheep of His evangelical love for their salvation, preparing them for the day of their slaughter upon the altar of His Church, to abundantly water the land of Damascus athirst for Divine martyrdom.

Chorus: Glory to Thee, our God, glory to Thee.

Reader: You mortified your flesh with poverty, O Martyrs, and animated your souls with the evangelical word. Therefore you deserved the wreaths of the Kingdom prepared for your martyrdom. Through their intercessions, O God, have mercy upon us and save us.

Refrain: *O Holy Martyrs of Christ, intercede on our behalf.*

Theotokíon
Reader: Through thine intercessions, O Lady, we who rightly believe that thou art the Theotokos, hope to be delivered from eternal fire, from darkness and from unseen and frightful enemies.

Refrain: *O Holy Martyrs of Christ, intercede on our behalf.*

Ode VIII

Tone 5   *Stimulating, dancing, and rhythmical.*   C, D, Eb, F, G, A, Bb, C.

Refrain: *O Holy Martyrs of Christ, intercede on our behalf.*

Reader: We venerate you, O strivers, for bearing the crucifixion of Christ in your bodies and watering His Church with your blood, whereby you entered eternal life and everlasting Light. Wherefore beseech Christ God for the salvation of all who believe in Him.

Chorus: *Glory to Thee, our God, glory to Thee.*

Reader: O Martyrs, we behold the Chorus' of angels surrounding you and holding the crowns of glory prepared for you. For when the Lord called out to you through the voice of your Priest, you bravely responded, saying as you offered up your spirits in martyrdom as a gift of love, "Now let us enter the Divine Mystery. Now let us enter into the Bridal Chamber of Light."

Chorus: *Glory to Thee, our God, glory to Thee.*

Reader: Rejoice, O women martyrs now clothed with the glory of Christ, for you accepted your poverty and raised your children in obedience to the Gospel. Therefore you became worthy to be mothers and witnesses for the Divine Love.

Refrain: *O Holy Martyrs of Christ, intercede on our behalf.*

Theotokíon
Reader: Let us praise the Virgin full of grace, since she is the Gate of Divine Entry, the Good Ladder for ascent to God, and the Directress for those who are saved.

Refrain: O Holy Martyrs of Christ, intercede on our behalf.

Deacon: The Theotokos and Mother of the Light.

Reader: [*Archangel Gabriel:*   It is truly right to call thee blessed, who gavest birth to God, ever-blessed and God-obedient the Mother of our God.] Greater in honour than the Cherubim and beyond compare more glorious than the Seraphim; without corruption thou gavest birth to God the Word, truly the Mother of God, we magnify thee.

Ode IX

Tone 5   *Stimulating, dancing, and rhythmical.*   *C, D, Eb, F, G, A, Bb, C.*

Refrain: O Holy Martyrs of Christ, intercede on our behalf.

Reader: Today we praise those who, in the flesh, overcame the weakness of their bodies and elevated their souls in evangelical struggle, loving their God more than themselves. Therefore the Lord honoured them with martyrdom and accepted them in the Heavenly Bridal Chamber as a sacrifice of love for the Trinity.

Chorus: Glory to Thee, our God, glory to Thee.

Reader: Joseph the Priest of the Most High and his companions preceded us to Thee, O Lord. Through their intercessions look upon us who struggle each day to do Thy Will, and if Thou shouldest accept us, permit us to dwell beneath Your feet in Thy glory.

Chorus: Glory to Thee, our God, glory to Thee.

Reader: O Theotokos, Mother of the One Who Is, Mary the Ever-Virgin, receive the souls of our holy and righteous Martyrs, and present them to the Lord God as a gift of faith and love from our Church.

Refrain: O Holy Martyrs of Christ, intercede on our behalf.

Theotokion

Reader: With the beauty of purity, O Virgin Mother, thou becamest a beautiful house of splendor; therefore we praise and exalt thee unto all ages.

Refrain: O Holy Martyrs of Christ, intercede on our behalf.

Exaposteilarion

Tone 3   *Arrogant, brave, and mature atmosphere.*   *F, G, A, A#, C, D, E, F.*

O assembly of the faithful, being now gathered together, let us celebrate the feast of the Martyrs of our Church and extol those who overcame with patience and steadfastness the wiles of the demons: Father Joseph of

Damascus and his Companions, who now hear from the heavenly chambers our supplications and who implore our God to have mercy upon us and save us. **(x3)**

Theotokíon

Tone 3   Arrogant, brave, and mature atmosphere.   *F, G, A, A#, C, D, E, F.*

When Jacob saw the ladder, which was a foreshadowing of thee, O Theotokos – thou glory of Martyrs, boast of the Righteous, magnificence of Angels, and Mediatress for the salvation of Prophets and of believers – he cried out, saying, "How dreadful is this place. This is none other than the house of God and the gate of heaven."

Stichera For The Saints

Tone 5   Stimulating, dancing, and rhythmical.   *C, D, Eb, F, G, A, Bb, C.*

Today we enter the Promised Land, for the blood of our Martyrs paved our way, the supplications of our Fathers assisted us, and God, regarding the lowly state of His Church, sowed in the womb of its land the seeds of holy martyrdom. Rejoice, all you who have crossed the threshold into heavenly glory, and intercede with the Compassionate God for the salvation of our souls. **(x2)**

The sheep of Thy flock were slaughtered for The Name's sake, O Lord. Accept today once more our prayers as a holocaust of thanksgiving offered upon the altar of Thy Divine Glory, and make us, together with Thy Martyrs, worthy to see Thy Light and to abide in it rather than in the darkness which envelops us.

Today we offer up supplication to the All holy Trinity and ask the intercessions of Mary the Most Holy Theotokos, and of the Forerunner of Christ, the Angels of God, the Righteous ones, the Martyrs and all the Saints, as we present our Martyrs Joseph and his Companions to the Lord God, beseeching Him to restore to the Church of Antioch her dignity through the blood of her Martyrs. Therefore, O Thou Who alone art able to blot out transgressions, accept us sinners and save our souls.

Glory be to the Father and to the Son and to the Holy Spirit,

Doxastikon

Tone 5   Stimulating, dancing, and rhythmical.   *C, D, Eb, F, G, A, Bb, C.*

O Joseph thou first man of the renaissance. In thy time thou alone didst bear the Cross of Antioch, having suffered schism in thy flock, faced the machinations of foreign missionaries, and shed copious tears for the infirmity, loss and ignorance of the people and shepherds of thy Church, beseeching the Lord God to release them from captivity. Thus we rejoice and exult in the Spirit of the Lord Who dwelleth in us as a result of thy martyrdom and that of thy companions. Now celebrating thine annual memorial we glorify Christ our Lord who, through thine intercessions, granteth us great mercy.

Both now and forever and unto the ages of ages. Amen.

Theotokion

Tone 5   Stimulating, dancing, and rhythmical.   *C, D, Eb, F, G, A, Bb, C.*

Beneath thy compassion we take refuge, O Theotokos. Despise not our prayers in our necessity, but deliver us from harm, O only pure, only blessed one.

<h3 style="text-align:center">Great Doxology</h3>

Glory to God, Who has shown us the Light. Glory to God in the highest, and on earth, peace, good will toward men. We praise Thee. We bless Thee. We worship Thee. We glorify Thee and give thanks to Thee for Thy great glory. O Lord God, Heavenly King, God the Father Almighty. O Lord, the Only Begotten Son, Jesus Christ, and the Holy Spirit. \

O Lord God, Lamb of God, Son of the Father, Who takes away the sins of the world, have mercy on us. Thou, Who takes away the sins of the world, receive our prayer. Thou, Who sittest at the right hand of God the Father, have mercy on us. /

For Thou alone art holy, and Thou alone art Lord. Thou alone, O Lord Jesus Christ, are most high in the glory of God the Father. Amen. I shall give thanks to Thee every day and praise Thy Name forever and ever, Lord. Every day shall I bless Thee and praise Thy name forever, and to the ages of ages. Amen. \

Vouchsafe, O Lord, to keep us this day without sin. Blessed art Thou, O Lord, the God of our fathers, and praised and glorified is Thy Name forever. Amen. Let Thy mercy be upon us, O Lord, even as we have set our hope on Thee.

Blessed art Thou, O Master; teach me Thy statutes.

Blessed art Thou, O Lord; enlighten me with Thy commandments.

Blessed art Thou, O Holy One; make me to understand Thy precepts.

Lord, Thou hast been our refuge from generation to generation. I said, *"Lord, have mercy on me. Heal my soul, for I have sinned against Thee."* \

Lord, I flee to Thee for refuge. Teach me to do Thy will, for Thou art my God. For with Thee is the fountain of Life, and in Thy light we shall see light. Continue Thy loving kindness to those who know Thee.

Holy God, Holy Strong, Holy Immortal, have mercy on us.

Holy God, Holy Strong, Holy Immortal, have mercy on us.

Holy God, Holy Strong, Holy Immortal, have mercy on us.

Glory be to the Father, and to the Son, and to the Holy Spirit;

Both now and forever, and unto the ages of ages. Amen.

Holy Immortal, have mercy on us.

Holy God, Holy Strong, Holy Immortal, have mercy on us.

Today salvation has come into the world. Let us sing to Him who rose from the tomb, the Author of our life. For, destroying death by death, he has given us the victory and His great mercy. \

Apolytikion

Tone 5   Stimulating, dancing, and rhythmical.   *C, D, Eb, F, G, A, Bb, C.*

Come, you faithful, let us honour the martyr of Christ, a Priest of the Church of Antioch who by the word of the

Word and by his blood and the blood of his companions baptised the land of Damascus, its Church and its people. Being immersed in the light of the Gospel from his youth, he worked and taught and defended the Church of Christ and her flock. O holy Joseph of Damascus, be for us an example, defending us and interceding for us fervently before the Saviour.

Glory be to the Father and to the Son and to the Holy Spirit,
Both now and forever and unto the ages of ages. Amen.

Little Litany

Deacon: Have mercy on us, O God, according to thy great mercy, we beseech thee; hearken and have mercy.

People: *Lord have mercy.* (**x3**)

Deacon: We pray for our Archbishop Nikitas and for all our brethren in Christ.

People: *Lord have mercy.* (**x3**)

Deacon: We pray for the mercy, life, peace, health and salvation of the servants of God (*N and N - insert names as requested here)* and for the persons who are here present.

People: *Lord have mercy.* (**x3**)

Deacon: We pray for all brethren and for all Christian people.

People: *Lord have mercy.* (**x3**)

Priest: For Thou art a merciful God who lovest mankind, and to Thee do we ascribe glory to the Father and to the Son and to the Holy Spirit, both now and forever and to the ages of ages.

People: *Amen.*

Priest: Hear us, O God our Saviour, the hope of all the ends of the earth and of those who are far off upon the sea, and show mercy, show mercy, O Master, upon us sinners, and be merciful unto us. For Thou art a merciful God who loves mankind, and to Thee we ascribe glory to the Father and to the Son and to the Holy Spirit. Both now and forever and ever and to the ages of ages.

People: *Amen.*

Deacon: Wisdom.

Priest: O most holy Theotokos, save us.

Reader: *[Archangel Gabriel:* It is truly right to call thee blessed, who gavest birth to God, ever-blessed and God-obedient the Mother of our God.] Greater in honour than the Cherubim and beyond compare more glorious than the Seraphim; without corruption thou gavest birth to God the Word, truly the Mother of God, we magnify thee.

Priest: Glory to Thee, O Christ God our hope, glory to Thee.

Reader: *Glory to the Father and to the Son, and to the Holy Spirit;*
Both now and forever and unto the ages of ages. Amen.

Lord have mercy. **(x3)**

Holy Father Bless.

Priest: May Christ our true God, through the prayers of his most pure Mother, of Saint *N [the patron saint of the church]*; of Saint Joseph of Damascus and of all the saints, have mercy on us and save us, forasmuch as He is good and loves mankind.

People: *Amen.*

[With a priest.]

The Trisagion Prayers

Deacon: Holy Father, Bless.

Priest: Blessed is our God always, now and forever, and unto the ages of ages.

People: *Amen.*

Priest: O Heavenly King, Comforter, Spirit of Truth, Who art everywhere present and fillest all things, Treasury of blessings and Giver of life: Come and abide in us and cleanse us from every impurity and save our souls, O Good One.

Reader: Holy God, Holy Mighty, Holy Immortal, have mercy on us. **(x3)**

Glory be to the Father, and to the Son, and to the Holy Spirit;
Both now and forever, and unto the ages of ages. Amen.

O Most Holy Trinity, have mercy on us.

O Lord, cleanse us from our sins.

O Master, pardon our iniquities.

O Holy One, visit and heal our infirmities, for Thy names sake.

Lord have mercy. **(x3)**

Glory be to the Father and to the Son and to the Holy Spirit;
Both now and forever, and unto the ages of ages. Amen.

People: *Our Father, Who art in Heaven, hallowed be Thy Name. Thy Kingdom come, Thy will be done, on earth as it is in Heaven. Give us this day our daily bread, and forgive us our trespasses, as we forgive those who trespass against us; and lead us not into temptation, but deliver us from the evil one.*

Priest: For Thine is the kingdom, and the power and the glory of the Father and of the Son and of the Holy Spirit, now and forever and to the ages of ages.

People: *Amen.*

Lord, have mercy. **(x12)**

Glory be to the Father and to the Son and to the Holy Spirit,
Both now and forever and unto the ages of ages. Amen.

O come let us worship God our King.
O come let us worship and fall down before Christ, our King and God.
O come let us worship and fall down before Christ Himself, our King and our God.

Psalm 142

Hear my prayer, O Lord, give ear to my supplications. In Thy faithfulness answer me, and in Thy righteousness. Do not enter into judgement with Thy servant, for in Thy sight no one living is righteous. For the enemy has persecuted my soul; he has crushed my life to the ground; he has made me dwell in darkness, like those who have long been dead. Therefore my spirit is overwhelmed within me; my heart within me is distressed. I remember the days of old; I meditate on all Thy works; I muse on the work of Thine hands. I spread out my hands to Thee; my soul longs for Thee like a thirsty land. Answer me speedily, O Lord; my spirit fails. Do not hide Thy face from me, lest I be like those who go down into the pit. Cause me to hear Thy loving kindness in the morning, for in Thee do I trust; cause me to know the way in which I should walk, for I lift up my soul to Thee. Deliver me, O Lord, from mine enemies; in Thee I take shelter. Teach me to do Thy will, for Thou art my God; Thy Spirit is good. Lead me in the land of uprightness. Revive me, O Lord, for Thy names sake. For Thy righteousness' sake bring my soul out of trouble. In Thy mercy cut off mine enemies, and destroy all those who afflict my soul; for I am Thy servant.

After The Psalm

Glory be to the Father and to the Son and to the Holy Spirit,
Both now and forever and unto the ages of ages. Amen.

Alleluia, Alleluia, Alleluia. Glory to Thee, O God. **(x3)**
Lord, have mercy. **(x3)**

Glory be to the Father and to the Son and to the Holy Spirit,

Both now and forever and unto the ages of ages. Amen.

Theotokion

Tone 5   Stimulating, dancing, and rhythmical.   *C, D, Eb, F, G, A, Bb, C.*

The sign of the Virgin Bride who knew not wedlock was at one time revealed in the Red Sea; for there Moses did cleave the waters, and there Gabriel was the minister of a miracle. At that time Israel crossed the deep and their feet were not wet, and now the Virgin hath given birth to Christ without seed. The sea remained uncrossed after the passing of Israel, and the blameless one remained incorruptible after giving birth to Immanuel. Therefore, O eternal God, who wast before eternity, and who didst appear as man, have mercy upon us.

Sticheroi From The Kekragarion

The Litiya Troparia

Tone 5   Stimulating, dancing, and rhythmical.   *C, D, Eb, F, G, A, Bb, C.*

Rejoice, radiant assembly of monks; sanctified fathers, hasten to honour him who hath preceded you in the way of virtue, Silouan the Athonite, given by God as a model of perseverance, a light for all those who follow Christ, that they may obtain His great mercy.

Chorus: Glory be to the Father and to the Son and to the Holy Spirit,

Rejoice, peoples of the earth, for a luminary hath risen in these latter times, by whom God illumineth all those among you who have been immersed in despondency and in the shadow of death. It is our Father Silouan crying to all: "In the darkness of hell do not despair, but come to the light, to Christ Who granteth His great mercy to all men."

Chorus: Both now and forever and unto the ages of ages. Amen.

Rejoice, all you powers of Heaven, and welcome him who now chanteth with you the praise and glory of God: Silouan, this simple monk of the Holy Mountain, who, sanctified by the Holy Spirit, was given to our time as an apostle and prophet teaching all men by his life and writings, that they may follow Christ Who giveth us His great mercy.

Refrain: O most holy Theotokos, save us.

Theotokion Of The Litiya

Tone 5   Stimulating, dancing, and rhythmical.   *C, D, Eb, F, G, A, Bb, C.*

We bless thee, O Virgin Theotokos, and we faithful rightly glorify thee, O thou unshakeable tower, impregnable house of defence, invincible help and shield, and refuge of our souls.

Chorus: *Glory be to the Father and to the Son and to the Holy Spirit,*

Aposticha

    Tone 8   Humility, tranquillity, repose, suffering, pleading.   *C, D, Eb, F, G, A, Bb, C.*

Holy Father Silouan, the fragrant odour of thy virtues is poured forth in the Church honouring thee this day; and the angels exult in Heaven, because thy love for God caused thee to shed abundant tears, which irrigate today the desert of human hearts burnt by despair. Thou hast followed Christ and treasured as a precious pearl His holy Name in thy heart; and the Holy Spirit, Who testified to the truth of thy salvation, enabled thee to love all men and wish that they be saved. With thee we honour and bless the Most Holy Trinity, and pray with fervour that we and all peoples of the earth may be given to recognize and honour our God and Lord through the Holy Spirit.

Chorus: *Both now and forever and unto the ages of ages. Amen.*

Theotokíon

Who shall not beautify thee, O Most Holy Virgin, who shall not hymn thy most pure giving of birth; the Only begotten Son, Who hath shone forth from the Father before the ages, hath come also from thee, O Pure One, unutterably incarnate, being in nature God, and having become in nature man for our sake, not divided in two persons, but made known in two Natures without fusion, to Him pray, O Pure and All blessed one, that there may be mercy on our souls.

Aposticha

    Tone 5   Stimulating, dancing, and rhythmical.   *C, D, Eb, F, G, A, Bb, C.*

Come, all you peoples of the earth and let us honour in our hymns this son of Russia, Silouan the Athonite, who undertook ascetic warfare in the fervour of the Spirit; he who felt roaring around him the flames of hell; he to whom was revealed the love of the Living Christ, because of which he prayed for you all that you would be given by the Holy Spirit to know your Lord and Creator, your Father and God, Who granteth the world His peace and great mercy.

Chorus: *Precious in the sight of the Lord is the death of His Saints. (Psalm 115:6)*

Luminous column of virtue, fighter of the desert, companion of holy monks, protector of all those assaulted by despair, upholder of all those fighting against demons, strong support of those who fall and their recovery: strengthen by thy pleasing prayers to Christ our God those who honour with love the Holy Name above all names.

Chorus: *Blessed is the man who feareth the Lord, who delighteth greatly in His commandments.*

Rejoice, venerable Father, who sojourneth amidst the Chorus' of angels in Heaven, since on earth thou hast truly been their companion, being judged worthy of the intercession of the Mother of God. Thou didst contemplate through thy fleshly eyes the Living Christ; then, being inflamed with divine love, thou didst submit thyself to the radiant grace of the Holy Spirit, which led thee above the snares and gloomy abysses in the way of blessed felicity; and before tasting death thou didst contemplate the glory of God.

Chorus: *Glory be to the Father and to the Son and to the Holy Spirit,*

We venerate thee, Silouan our holy Father, for thou hast taught a multitude of monks, and we have learned to walk in thy straight path. Blessed art thou in thy labours for Christ and in thy victory over the enemy; O friend of angels and companion of the saints on high, with them pray to Christ our God that our souls may be saved.

Chorus: *Both now and forever and unto the ages of ages. Amen.*

Theotokion

O Virgin unwedded, O Mother of God on high, thou hast ineffably conceived God in the flesh, and being beyond reproach, thou hast granted all purification of our transgression. Accept the supplications of thy servants, and do thou who now receivest our entreaties, pray for us all to be saved.

Apolytikion

Tone 4   *Festive, joyous and expressing deep piety.*   *C, D, Eb, F, G, A, Bb, C.*

By prayer thou didst receive Christ for thy Teacher in the way of humility, and the Spirit bare witness to salvation in thy heart; wherefore all peoples called unto hope rejoice in this day of thy memorial, O sacred father Silouan. Pray unto Christ our God for the salvation of our souls.

Chorus: *Glory be to the Father and to the Son and to the Holy Spirit,*

Theotokion

Thee, who art the mediatress for the salvation of our race, we praise, O Virgin Theotokos; for in the flesh assumed from thee, after that He had suffered the Passion of the Cross, thy Son and our God delivered us from corruption, because He is the Lover of mankind.

Chorus: *Both now and forever and unto the ages of ages. Amen.*

Theotokion

Tone 4   *Festive, joyous and expressing deep piety.*   *C, D, Eb, F, G, A, Bb, C.*

O most reverend Virgin, O thou by means of whom my Saviour Christ the Lord did appear to those lying in darkness, He being the Sun of justice, wishing to enlighten those whom He had made with His own hands after His likeness: thou art the temple, the gate, the palace and the throne of the King. Wherefore, O all praised one, thou hast attained with Him maternal privilege. Intercede ceaselessly for the salvation of our souls.

Refrain: *O most holy Theotokos, save us.*

Theotokion

Tone 5   Stimulating, dancing, and rhythmical.   *C, D, Eb, F, G, A, Bb, C.*

Rejoice, O uncrossed gate. Rejoice, O wall and protection of those who hasten unto thee. Rejoice, O quiet haven who hast not known wedlock. O thou who hast given birth in the flesh to thy Creator and God, thou shalt continue to interceded for the sake of those who praise and worship thy birth giving.

Refrain: *O most holy Theotokos, save us.*

Theotokion

Rejoice, O holy mountain whom the Lord crossed in passing.

Rejoice, O burning bush yet unconsumed.

Rejoice, O thou who alone art a bridge for the world towards God, translating the dead to eternal life.

Rejoice, O pure one, free of corruption, who didst give birth without wedlock to the Saviour of the World.

Glory be to the Father and to the Son and to the Holy Spirit,
Both now and forever and unto the ages of ages. Amen.

Theotokion

O all blameless one, thou hast been shown to be a brightly shining bridal chamber and golden tabernacle containing God the Word Who, for our salvation, took flesh from thee and destroyed the power of death.

Prokeimenon

Reader: Wondrous is God in His saints.

Chorus: *Wondrous is God in His saints.*

Reader: In the saints that are in His earth hath the Lord been wondrous.

Chorus: *Wondrous is God in His saints.*

Reader: Wondrous is God | in His saints.

Let Every Breath Praise The Lord

Let every breath praise the Lord. Praise God in His sanctuary.

Praise Him in His mighty firmament. Let every breath praise the Lord.

The Gospel

Reader: The Reading is From The Holy Gospel According To Luke (12:8-12).

People: *Glory to Thee, O Lord, glory to Thee.*

Reader: Also I say unto you, Whosoever shall confess me before men, him shall the Son of man also confess before the angels of God: But he that denieth me before men shall be denied before the angels of God. And whosoever shall speak a word against the Son of man, it shall be forgiven him: but unto him that blasphemeth against the Holy Ghost it shall not be forgiven. And when they bring you unto the synagogues, and unto magistrates, and powers, take no thought how or what thing you shall answer, or what you shall say: For the Holy Ghost shall teach you in the same hour what you ought to say.

People: *Glory to Thee, O Lord, glory to Thee.*

Psalm 50

Have mercy on me, O God, according to Thy great mercy; and according to the multitude of Thy compassions blot out my transgression. Wash me thoroughly from mine iniquity, and cleanse me from my sin. For I acknowledge mine iniquity, and my sin is ever before me. Against Thee, Thee only have I sinned, and done evil in Thy sight, that Thou mayest be found just when Thou speakest, and victorious when Thou art judged. For behold, I was conceived in iniquity, and in sin my mother bore me. For behold, Thou hast loved truth; Thou hast made known to me the hidden and secret things of Thy wisdom. Thou shalt sprinkle me with hyssop, and I shall be made clean; Thou shalt wash me, and I shalt be whiter than snow. Make me to hear joy and gladness; that the humbled bones may rejoice. Turn Thy face away from my sins, and blot out all mine iniquities.

Create in me a clean heart, O God, and renew a steadfast spirit within me. Cast me not away from Thy presence, and take not Thy Holy Spirit from me. Restore to me the joy of Thy salvation, and establish me with Thy governing Spirit. I shall teach transgressors Thy ways, and the ungodly shall turn back to Thee. Deliver me from blood guiltiness, O God, the God of my salvation; my tongue shall joyfully declare Thy righteousness. Lord, open my lips, and my mouth shall declare Thy praise. For if Thou hadst desired sacrifice, I would give it; Thou dost not delight in burned offerings. A sacrifice to God is a broken spirit; God shall not despise a broken and a humbled heart. Do good, O Lord, in Thy good pleasure to Zion, and let the walls of Jerusalem be builded. Then Thou shalt be pleased with a sacrifice of righteousness, with oblation and whole burned offerings. Then shall they offer bulls on Thine altar.

Chorus: *Glory be to the Father and to the Son and to the Holy Spirit,*

By the intercessions of the prizewinners, O Merciful One, blot out the multitude of mine offences.

Chorus: *Both now and forever and unto the ages of ages. Amen.*

Theotokíon

By the intercessions of the Theotokos, O Merciful One, blot out the multitude of mine offences.

Reader: Have mercy on me, O God, according to Thy great mercy; and according to the multitude of Thy compassions blot out my transgression.

Ode I

Eirmos

Tone 5   *Stimulating, dancing, and rhythmical.*   *C, D, Eb, F, G, A, Bb, C.*

Let us sing to the Lord who led His people through the red sea, for He alone is gloriously glorified.

Refrain: *O Holy Martyrs of Christ, intercede on our behalf.*

Without help and tears, how can I sing to thee holy Father Silouan, with unclean lips my song of admiration?

Refrain: *Holy Father Silouan, pray to God for us.*

With love thou didst follow thy Lord and sail upon the sea to come to the Holy Mountain, to exercise thyself in ascetic labours.

Refrain: *Holy Father Silouan, pray to God for us.*

There, thou didst confess all thy sins and abandon thyself to the joy of being forgiven, but immediately the enemy assaulted thee.

Refrain: *O most holy Theotokos, save us.*

Theotokíon

Out of His mercy to save me the Word of God hath willed in His goodness to become incarnate, O Virgin Mother, in thy womb.

Ode III

Eirmos

Thou art the strength of those who flee to Thee, O Lord, Thou art the light of those in darkness, and my spirit sings of Thee.

Refrain: *Holy Father Silouan, pray to God for us.*

Removing from thy flesh the arrows of demons, thou didst victoriously resist their assaults, acting according to the movement of the Spirit.

Refrain: *Holy Father Silouan, pray to God for us.*

None has ever fought like thee, surrounded as thou wast by dark despair, but the Christ of light enveloped thee.

Refrain: *Holy Father Silouan, pray to God for us.*

Under the rain of thy tears, thou didst put out the burning flame of passions, and thou didst become a river overflowing with the grace of the Spirit.

Refrain: *O most holy Theotokos, save us.*

Theotokíon

Under thy protection I do not fear, pure Virgin, the assault of the enemies. Being strong through thy help, I put to flight their legions.

Ode IV

Eirmos

I have heard, O Lord, the mystery of Thy plan. I contemplate Thy works, and glorify Thy divine nature.

Refrain: *Holy Father Silouan, pray to God for us.*

Illuminated by a burst of contemplation and action, blessed Father, thy heart hath become a pure dwelling of the Spirit.

Refrain: *Holy Father Silouan, pray to God for us.*

Love of thy brethren invadeth thy soul, O holy Father, and thy compassion hath spread unto all creation.

Refrain: *Holy Father Silouan, pray to God for us.*

Forgetting this earth thou hast elevated thy spirit towards Heaven and endured, venerable Father, the burns of asceticism as divine dew.

Refrain: *O most holy Theotokos, save us.*

Theotokíon

A Virgin hath given birth to one of the Holy Trinity, and this mystery hath been revealed to the pure hearted and to little ones.

Ode V

Eirmos

Rising early, we cry to Thee, O Lord: save us, for Thou art our God, and we know no other than Thee.

Refrain: *Holy Father Silouan, pray to God for us.*

Star among monks, thou hast reached the zenith of temperance. Venerable Father, thou hast appeared pouring on our souls the brilliance of thy purity.

Refrain: *Holy Father Silouan, pray to God for us.*

We call thee blessed, venerable Silouan, for, having ascended on the chariot of virtue, thou hast attained unto the farthest reaches of Heaven.

Refrain: *Holy Father Silouan, pray to God for us.*

Inflamed by the burning coal of thine impassible heart in ashes, blessed Father, thou hast transformed the dry wood of passions.

Refrain: *O most holy Theotokos, save us.*

Theotokíon

We sing to thee, Holy Mother of God, Virgin even after giving birth. On behalf of the world thou truly gavest birth in the flesh to the Divine Word.

Ode VI

Eirmos

I shall pour out my prayer to the Lord, and to Him I shall confess my grief; for my soul is full of evil and my life has drawn near to hell, and like Jonah I shall pray: raise me up from corruption, O God.

Refrain: *Holy Father Silouan, pray to God for us.*

O Father, guide me towards the haven of salvation. The drabness of pleasures and the darkness of sin have encircled me. In the light of the Spirit, pour forth thy brightness on my whole being.

Refrain: *Holy Father Silouan, pray to God for us.*

Thy prayer was confident: immediately the storm did stop, the hostile sea grew still, anguish departed from human hearts, and men gave thanks to God for what He granteth unto sinners.

Refrain: *Holy Father Silouan, pray to God for us.*

Fill the hearts of those singing to thee, through the stream of thine unceasing prayer, which thou thyself didst receive by unutterable grace from the Mother of God, having become her faithful servant.

Refrain: *O most holy Theotokos, save us.*

Theotokíon

Chosen from all eternity, thee we acknowledge as the Ark of holiness, the mercy seat that none has ever touched, the golden candle stand, the living table that hath carried, O Virgin, the bread of our life.

Kontakion

Tone 8 Humility, tranquillity, repose, suffering, pleading. C, D, Eb, F, G, A, Bb, C.

In thine earthly life thou didst serve Christ, following in His steps; and now in heaven thou seest Him Whom thou didst love and abidest with Him according to the promise; wherefore O Father Silouan, teach us the path wherein thou didst walk.

Oikos

Thou wast contemplating the icon; and, O marvel, the Living Christ was standing before thee, while thy whole being was covered by the grace of the Spirit. In Him thou didst recognise thy Lord and Saviour, and henceforth thou didst strive to walk in His footsteps. Having followed Him thou becamest for all peoples an apostle and prophet, teaching hope and salvation in Christ to all those who follow the path wherein thou didst walk.

Synaxarion

[Speaking voice] On this day we celebrate the memory of our venerable Father Silouan the Athonite.

Commemorative Verse

Having followed Christ Whom he kept in his heart, Silouan the Athonite carried the victory. He was raised on the twenty fourth to celestial heights, By Him Who preserves all men from despair.

Ode VII

Eirmos

In the furnace, the young men trampled on the flames with ardour, and the fire was changed into a refreshing dew as they cried out, *"O Lord our God, blessed art Thou throughout the ages."*

Refrain: *Holy Father Silouan, pray to God for us.*

Purified from the stain of passions, shimmering in the brightness of the Spirit, to the immaterial Light thou hast truly gone, blessed Father, in the Chorus' of ascetics throughout the ages.

Refrain: *Holy Father Silouan, pray to God for us.*

Surrounded by the flames of hell roaring against thee, thou didst look to the Lord, Who heard thy voice, O venerable Father, crying: *"O Lord our God, blessed art Thou."*

Refrain: *Holy Father Silouan, pray to God for us.*

Radiating light, Christ appeared to thee and showed thee the way of eternal blessedness, and in contrition thou didst cry out: *"O Lord our God, blessed art thou."*

Refrain: *O most holy Theotokos, save us.*

Theotokíon

She is the Virgin who Isaiah, the great prophet, hath indicated in the Spirit and, behold, in her flesh she hath conceived and given birth to God, to Whom we sing: *"O Lord our God, blessed art Thou."*

Ode VIII

Eirmos

In his wrath against the servants of God, the tyrant of the Chaldeans had his furnace stoked seven times. But seeing them saved by a better power he cried: "O you children bless your Creator and Redeemer, you priests praise Him, you peoples exalt Him throughout all ages."

Refrain: *Holy Father Silouan, pray to God for us.*

Bless the Lord, all you works of the Lord. On this day is exalted Silouan the faithful servant, who loved all creation and cried out: "Come, you peoples, to the knowledge of your Lord, love Him and serve Him; you peoples exalt Him throughout all ages."

Refrain: *Holy Father Silouan, pray to God for us.*

Having kept thy mind in hell without despairing, thou hast received the unction of the Spirit as fresh dew. To all men thou dost cry out: "Come, recognize Christ your Saviour, your Benefactor; you priests praise Him, you peoples exalt Him throughout all ages."

Refrain: *Holy Father Silouan, pray to God for us.*

No one has ever known God without having loved His enemies, thou didst say, O blessed Father, calling thy brothers to observe the commandments of Christ Who forgave His enemies on the Cross: therefore, O you priests praise Him, you peoples exalt Him throughout all ages.

Refrain: *O most holy Theotokos, save us.*

Theotokíon

Enlighten my darkened mind, O thou who hast conceived and given birth to the Creator of the human race, Who hath become man without being separated from the Father, the sinless Sovereign. For Him the entire creation crieth out: "O you children bless, you priests praise, you peoples exalt Christ throughout all ages."

Deacon: The Theotokos and Mother of the Light.

Reader: *[Archangel Gabriel:*   It is truly right to call thee blessed, who gavest birth to God, ever-blessed and God-obedient the Mother of our God.] Greater in honour than the Cherubim and beyond compare more glorious than the Seraphim; without corruption thou gavest birth to God the Word, truly the Mother of God, we magnify thee.

Ode IX

Eirmos

Every ear was astonished at the ineffable condescension of God; for the Most High willed to come down unto a body and became man in a virginal womb. All we the faithful magnify thee, O pure Mother of God.

Refrain: *Holy Father Silouan, pray to God for us.*

Magnify, O my soul, Silouan who hath found the source of all good and the accomplishment of His desire, wherein resounds praise and festivity, delighting in the heavenly habitations.

Refrain: *Holy Father Silouan, pray to God for us.*

By the sweat of thy brow, by thy sorrows, thou hast procured for us the sweetness of thy help; and thou hast driven away the bitterness of our passions. Thy relics burst forth with healings for us, purifying our souls of the gangrene of evil.

Refrain: *Holy Father Silouan, pray to God for us.*

Royally Christ hath crowned thee, for thou hast conquered the prince of this world and his armies. In the Chorus of holy monks thou art counted: with them intercede before Christ that He deliver from trials those who honour thee, O holy Father.

Refrain: *O most holy Theotokos, save us.*

Theotokion

As the dawn drives away the darkness, thou hast put an end, O divine Bride, to the ancestral curse, having given birth to the Infinite within the limits of the flesh; thou hast renewed nature and its laws and reunited by a marvellous mediation that which of old had been separated.

Exaposteilarion

Tone 3   Arrogant, brave, and mature atmosphere.   *F, G, A, A#, C, D, E, F.*

Desiring to live an angelic life, thou didst withdraw on the Holy Mountain; and thou didst serve thy brothers and wast watchful in prayer, having subdued the passions of the flesh; therefore, thou didst become, O Father, like the angels.

Chorus: *Glory be to the Father and to the Son and to the Holy Spirit,*

Desiring to live an angelic life, thou didst withdraw on the Holy Mountain; and thou didst serve thy brothers and wast watchful in prayer, having subdued the passions of the flesh; therefore, thou didst become, O Father, like the angels.

Chorus: *Both now and forever and unto the ages of ages. Amen.*

Desiring to live an angelic life, thou didst withdraw on the Holy Mountain; and thou didst serve thy brothers and wast watchful in prayer, having subdued the passions of the flesh; therefore, thou didst become, O Father, like the angels.

Lauds - The Praises

Stichera 1

Chorus: *Silouan, venerable Father, having taken on thy shoulders the yoke of Christ, thou didst follow Him on the Holy Mountain, exhausting thy body by ascetic labours and keeping prayer deep in thine heart. O boast of the ascetics and joy of all the monks, we sing to thee and honour thee in faith.*

Psalm 148

Praise the Lord. Praise the Lord from the heavens; praise Him in the heights. Praise Him, all His angels; praise Him, all His hosts. Praise Him, sun and moon; praise Him, all you stars of light. Praise Him, you heavens of heavens, and you waters above the heavens. Let them praise the name of the Lord, for He commanded and they were created. He has also established them forever and ever; He has made a decree that shall not pass away. Praise the Lord from the earth, you great sea creatures and all the depths; Fire and hail, snow and clouds; stormy wind, fulfilling His word; Mountains and all hills; fruitful trees and all cedars; Beasts and all cattle; creeping things and flying fowl; Kings of the earth and all peoples; princes and all judges of the earth; Both young men and maidens; old men and children. Let them praise the name of the Lord, for His name alone is exalted; His glory is above the earth and heaven. And He has exalted the horn of His people, the praise of all His saints - of the children of Israel, a people near to Him. Praise the Lord.

Stichera 2

Chorus: *Silouan, venerable Father, thou wast like a marvellous plant in the Garden of the Mother of God, the Most Pure One Who deigned to impart in thy heart unceasing Prayer as a rich sap that vivifies all lovers of the Holy Name of Jesus. In irrigating by thy tears the earth dried up by passions, in nurturing in thyself all the virtues in humility, and in not fearing the impetuous storms of demons, thou hast flourished beneath the Sun of Righteousness, Christ, and thou wast not shaken by the enlivening breath of the Spirit. Thou hast produced fruits in abundance: therefore we celebrate thee with love.*

Psalm 149

Praise the Lord. Sing to the Lord a new song, and His praise in the congregation of saints. Let Israel rejoice in their Maker; let the children of Zion be joyful in their King. Let them praise His name with the dance; let them sing praises to Him with the timbrel and harp. For the Lord takes pleasure in His people; He shall beautify the humble with salvation. Let the saints be joyful in glory; let them sing aloud on their beds. Let the high praises of God be in their mouth, and a two edged sword in their hand, To execute vengeance on the nations, and punishments on the peoples; To bind their kings with chains, and their nobles with fetters of iron; To execute on them the written judgement; this honour have all His saints. Praise the Lord.

Stichera 3

Chorus: *Assembled in faith we honour thee, Silouan, as an ascetic of Christ; and we believe that in truth He appeared to thee as thou wast standing before His holy Icon, smitten by despondency which drove thee to say: "God is inexorable." But He showed thee in the Holy Spirit His mercy and an assurance of thy salvation. Pray, O blessed one, Him Whom thou didst recognize then as thy Saviour and Lord, to grant salvation to those who sing thy name.*

Psalm 150

Praise the Lord. Praise God in His sanctuary; praise Him in His mighty firmament. Praise Him for His mighty acts; praise Him according to His excellent greatness. Praise Him with the sound of the trumpet; praise Him with the lute and harp. Praise Him with the timbrel and dance; praise Him with stringed instruments and flutes. Praise Him with loud cymbals; praise Him with high sounding cymbals. Let everything that has breath praise the Lord. Praise the Lord.

Stichera 4

Chorus: *O holy Father Silouan, thou hast been a tree growing in the vast sylvan abodes of all the monks of the Holy Mountain, and thou hast bowed under the breath of the Holy Spirit which filled thy life with knowledge and love of Christ our God. Intercede before Him that He may grant to our souls the radiant grace of His Spirit, and that He may have mercy on those who sing to thee.*

After The Psalm

Glory be to the Father and to the Son and to the Holy Spirit;
Both now and forever and unto the ages of ages. Amen.

Alleluia, Alleluia, Alleluia. Glory to Thee, O God. **(x3)**

Glory be to the Father and to the Son and to the Holy Spirit;

Apolytikion

Tone 6   Rich texture, funeral character, sorrowful tone.   *D, Eb, F##, G, A, Bb, C##, D.*

Venerable Father, thou hast prayed for all the people of the earth, who on this day have heard the renown of thy righteous deeds, through which thou hast found in Heaven the reward of thy labours. Thou hast endured the assaults of the demons, taking pity on them; and now thou hast joined the Chorus' of the angels, having imitated their pure life. In the boldness thou now hast before Christ our God, ask of Him peace for our souls.

Both now and forever and unto the ages of ages. Amen.

Theotokíon

Rejoice, radiant candlestick, more brilliant than the rays of the sun; rejoice, pure Sovereign Lady, who hath delivered us from the ancient curse. Thou art the hope of the hopeless, summoning to God the human race. Rejoice, brilliant palace of the Great King, fertile mountain from which came the Redeemer; rejoice divine and beautiful lamp of the Word of God; rejoice, all luminous lantern and throne of fire.

Great Doxology

Glory to God, Who has shown us the Light. Glory to God in the highest, and on earth, peace, good will toward men. We praise Thee. We bless Thee. We worship Thee. We glorify Thee and give thanks to Thee for Thy great glory. O Lord God, Heavenly King, God the Father Almighty. O Lord, the Only Begotten Son, Jesus Christ, and the Holy Spirit. \

O Lord God, Lamb of God, Son of the Father, Who takes away the sins of the world, have mercy on us. Thou, Who takes away the sins of the world, receive our prayer. Thou, Who sittest at the right hand of God the Father, have mercy on us. /

For Thou alone art holy, and Thou alone art Lord. Thou alone, O Lord Jesus Christ, are most high in the glory of God the Father. Amen. I shall give thanks to Thee every day and praise Thy Name forever and ever, Lord. Every day shall I bless Thee and praise Thy name forever, and to the ages of ages. Amen. \

Vouchsafe, O Lord, to keep us this day without sin. Blessed art Thou, O Lord, the God of our fathers, and praised and glorified is Thy Name forever. Amen. Let Thy mercy be upon us, O Lord, even as we have set our hope on Thee.

Blessed art Thou, O Master; teach me Thy statutes.

Blessed art Thou, O Lord; enlighten me with Thy commandments.

Blessed art Thou, O Holy One; make me to understand Thy precepts.

Lord, Thou hast been our refuge from generation to generation. I said, *"Lord, have mercy on me. Heal my soul, for I have sinned against Thee."* \

Lord, I flee to Thee for refuge. Teach me to do Thy will, for Thou art my God. For with Thee is the fountain of Life, and in Thy light we shall see light. Continue Thy loving kindness to those who know Thee.

Holy God, Holy Strong, Holy Immortal, have mercy on us.

Holy God, Holy Strong, Holy Immortal, have mercy on us.

Holy God, Holy Strong, Holy Immortal, have mercy on us.

Glory be to the Father, and to the Son, and to the Holy Spirit;

Both now and forever, and unto the ages of ages. Amen.

Holy Immortal, have mercy on us.

Holy God, Holy Strong, Holy Immortal, have mercy on us.

Today salvation has come into the world. Let us sing to Him who rose from the tomb, the Author of our life. For, destroying death by death, he has given us the victory and His great mercy. \

Little Litany

Deacon: Have mercy on us, O God, according to thy great mercy, we beseech thee; hearken and have mercy.

People: *Lord have mercy.* **(x3)**

Deacon: We pray for our Archbishop Nikitas and for all our brethren in Christ.

People: *Lord have mercy.* **(x3)**

Deacon: We pray for the mercy, life, peace, health and salvation of the servants of God (*N and N - insert names as requested here)* and for the persons who are here present.

People: *Lord have mercy.* **(x3)**

Deacon: We pray for all brethren and for all Christian people.

People: *Lord have mercy.* **(x3)**

Priest: For Thou art a merciful God who lovest mankind, and to Thee do we ascribe glory to the Father and to the Son and to the Holy Spirit, both now and forever and to the ages of ages.

People: *Amen.*

Priest: Hear us, O God our Saviour, the hope of all the ends of the earth and of those who are far off upon the sea, and show mercy, show mercy, O Master, upon us sinners, and be merciful unto us. For Thou art a merciful God who loves mankind, and to Thee we ascribe glory to the Father and to the Son and to the Holy Spirit. Both now and forever and ever and to the ages of ages.

People: *Amen.*

Deacon: Wisdom.

Priest: O most holy Theotokos, save us.

Reader: *[Archangel Gabriel:* It is truly right to call thee blessed, who gavest birth to God, ever-blessed and God-obedient the Mother of our God.] Greater in honour than the Cherubim and beyond compare more glorious than the Seraphim; without corruption thou gavest birth to God the Word, truly the Mother of God, we magnify thee.

Priest: Glory to Thee, O Christ God our hope, glory to Thee.

Reader: *Glory to the Father and to the Son, and to the Holy Spirit;*
Both now and forever and unto the ages of ages. Amen.

Lord have mercy. **(x3)**

Holy Father Bless.

Priest: May Christ our true God, through the prayers of his most pure Mother, of Saint *N [the patron saint of the church]*; of Saint Silouan of Athos and of all the saints, have mercy on us and save us, forasmuch as He is good and loveth mankind.

People: *Amen.*

Prayers

The daily prayers below are for those who have jobs, families and other reasons why they cannot lead a daily church life. These are the majority and further the Orthodox people by example and procreation.

At home, prepare an icon corner, such as this one. As well as Christ and the Theotokos in this arrangement, the other icons can be of the saints of the family.

If saying prayers with children show them which is their saint and show them how to cross themselves and bow to that icon. They will appreciate having their own special bit to do. Choose a regular sentence that is theirs that they can say. As they grow older they can take on more. Children love routine and doing the short Evening Prayers each day shall become important to them. They are sure to soon learn the Lords Prayer. See if they can pick up the Creed for use in Church.

The Trisagion Prayers

In the Name of the Father, and of the Son, and of the Holy Spirit. Amen.

Glory to Thee, our God, glory to Thee.

O Heavenly King, the Comforter, the Spirit of Truth; who art everywhere present and fillest all things; Treasury of blessings, and giver of life: come and abide in us, and cleanse us from every impurity, and save our souls, O Good One.

Holy God, Holy Mighty, Holy Immortal, have mercy on us. **(x3)**

Glory be to the Father, and to the Son, and to the Holy Spirit;
Both now and forever, and unto the ages of ages. Amen.

O Most Holy Trinity, have mercy on us.

O Lord, cleanse us from our sins.

O Master, pardon our iniquities.

O Holy One, visit and heal our infirmities, for Thy names sake.

Lord have mercy. **(x3)**

Glory be to the Father, and to the Son, and to the Holy Spirit;
Both now and forever, and unto the ages of ages. Amen.

Our Father, who art in heaven, hallowed be Thy name. Thy Kingdom come. Thy will be done, on earth as it is in heaven. Give us this day our daily bread; and forgive us our trespasses, as we forgive those who trespass against us; and lead us not into temptation, but deliver us from the evil one. Amen.

Troparia To The Holy Trinity

Having arisen from sleep, we fall down before Thee, O blessed One, and sing to Thee, O Mighty One, the angelic hymn: Holy. Holy. Holy. art Thou O God; through the Theotokos, have mercy on us.

Glory be to the Father, and to the Son, and to the Holy Spirit;

Having raised me from my bed and from sleep, O Lord, enlighten my mind and heart, and open my lips that I might praise Thee, O Holy Trinity: Holy. Holy. Holy. art Thou O God; through the Theotokos, have mercy on us.

Both now and forever and unto the ages of ages. Amen.

The Judge shall come suddenly and the acts of every man shall be revealed; but in the middle of the night we cry in fear: Holy. Holy. Holy. art Thou O God; through the Theotokos, have mercy on us.

Lord have mercy. **(x12)**

A Prayer To The Holy Trinity

Having arisen from sleep, I thank Thee, the Holy Trinity. In the abundance of Thy kindness and long patience, Thou hast not been angry with me for my laziness and sinfulness, nor hast Thou destroyed me in my lawlessness. Instead, in Thy usual love for mankind, Thou hast raised me as I lay in despair, that I might rise early and glorify Thy Reign. Enlighten now the eyes of my mind and open my lips, that I might learn of Thy words, understand Thy commandments, accomplish Thy will, hymn Thee in heart felt confession and praise Thine all holy name, of the Father and of the Son, and of the Holy Spirit, both now and forever and to the ages of ages. Amen.

The Symbol Of Faith

I believe in one God, Father, Almighty, Maker of heaven and earth, and of all things visible and invisible.

And in one Lord Jesus Christ, the only begotten Son of God, begotten from the Father before all ages; Light from Light, true God from true God; begotten not made; consubstantial with the Father, through Him all things were made. For our sake and for our salvation He came down from Heaven, and was incarnate from the Holy Spirit and the Virgin Mary and became man. He was crucified for us under Pontius Pilate, and suffered and was buried. He rose again on the third day in accordance with the Scriptures, and ascended into Heaven, and is seated at the right hand of the Father. He is coming again in glory to judge the living and the dead. And His kingdom shall have no end.

And in the Holy Spirit, the Lord, the Giver of life; Who proceeds from the Father; Who together with the Father and the Son is worshipped and glorified; Who spoke through the prophets. In One, Holy, Catholic, and Apostolic Church. I confess one baptism for the forgiveness of sins. I await the resurrection of the dead, And the life of the age to come. Amen.

A Prayer Of St Basil The Great

We bless Thee, most high God and Lord of mercies, Who ever doest great and unfathomable things for us - glorious and awesome things without number. Thou gavest us sleep for the repose of our frailty, relieving the labours of our over burdened flesh. We thank Thee for not destroying us in our lawlessness. Instead, Thou hast shown Thy usual love for mankind, and raised us, as we lay in despair, to glorify Thy Reign. Therefore, we implore Thy boundless goodness: enlighten our thoughts and eyes, and awaken our minds from the heavy sleep of laziness. Open our lips and fill them with Thy praise, that we may always hymn and confess Thee, the God glorified in all and by all, Father without beginning, with Thine only begotten Son and Thine all holy and life creating Spirit, both now and forever and unto the ages of ages. Amen.

Rejoice, O Virgin

Rejoice, O Virgin Theotokos. Mary full of grace, the Lord is with Thee. Blessed art Thou among women, and blessed is the fruit of Thy womb; For Thou hast borne the Saviour of our souls.

Morning Prayer Of The Last Elders Of Optina

O Lord, grant that I may meet all that this coming day brings to me with spiritual tranquillity. Grant that I may fully surrender myself to Thy holy Will. At every hour of this day, direct and support me in all things. Whatsoever news may reach me in the course of the day, teach me to accept it with a calm soul and firm conviction that all is subject to Thy holy Will. Direct my thoughts and feelings in all my words and actions. In all unexpected occurrences, do not let me forget that all is sent down from Thee. Grant that I may deal straightforwardly and wisely with every member of my family, neither embarrassing nor saddening anyone. O Lord, grant me the strength to endure the fatigue of the coming day and all the events that take place during it. Direct my will and teach me to pray, to believe, to hope, to be patient, to forgive, and to love. Amen.

[Private Prayers here]

Through the prayers of our holy Fathers, Lord Jesus Christ our God, have mercy upon us and save us. Amen.

The Trisagion Prayers

In the Name of the Father, and of the Son, and of the Holy Spirit. Amen.

Glory to Thee, our God, glory to Thee.

O Heavenly King, the Comforter, the Spirit of Truth; who art everywhere present and fillest all things; Treasury of blessings, and giver of life: come and abide in us, and cleanse us from every impurity, and save our souls, O Good One.

Holy God, Holy Mighty, Holy Immortal, have mercy on us. **(x3)**

Glory be to the Father, and to the Son, and to the Holy Spirit;
Both now and forever, and unto the ages of ages. Amen.

O Most Holy Trinity, have mercy on us.

O Lord, cleanse us from our sins.

O Master, pardon our iniquities.

O Holy One, visit and heal our infirmities, for Thy names sake.

Lord have mercy. **(x3)**

Glory be to the Father, and to the Son, and to the Holy Spirit;
Both now and forever, and unto the ages of ages. Amen.

Our Father, who art in heaven, hallowed be Thy name. Thy Kingdom come. Thy will be done, on earth as it is in heaven. Give us this day our daily bread; and forgive us our trespasses, as we forgive those who trespass against us; and lead us not into temptation, but deliver us from the evil one. Amen.

[Monday]   **Psalm 3. Of David, When He Fled From Absalom, His Son.**

Lord, how are they increased that trouble me. Many are they that rise up against me. Many there be which say of my soul; There is no help for him in God. But thou, O Lord, art a shield for me; my glory, and the lifter up of mine head. I cried unto the Lord with my voice, and he heard me out of his holy hill. I laid me down and slept; I awakened; for the Lord sustained me. I shall not be afraid of ten thousands of people, that have set themselves against me round about. Arise, O Lord; save me, O my God: for thou hast smitten all mine enemies upon the cheek bone; thou hast broken the teeth of the ungodly. Salvation belongeth unto the Lord: thy blessing is upon thy people.

Psalm 38. Of David. To The Chief Musician Jeduthun.

I said, I shall guard my ways, that I may not sin with my tongue. I set a watch to my mouth, while the wicked organised against me. I became dumb and was humbled, I held my peace for good; and my suffering was renewed. My heart was hot within me, while I was musing the fire burned. Then I spoke with my tongue: Lord, make known to me my end, and the number of my days, what it is; that I may know how frail I am. Behold, thou hast made my days as an hand breadth; and mine age is as nothing before thee. Verily every man alive is altogether vanity. Surely every man passes through as a shadow. Surely they are for nothing in turmoil. He heapeth up riches, and knoweth not who shall gather them. And now, Lord, for what do I wait? It is for thee. Even my existence is from thee. Deliver me from all my transgressions: make me not the reproach of the foolish. I was dumb, I opened not my mouth; because it is thee who did it. Remove thy scourge from me: I fainted due to the force of thine hand. When thou with rebukes dost correct man for iniquity, thou melts his soul like a spiders web: surely every man is vain for nothing. Hear my prayer, O Lord, and give ear unto my cry; hold not thy peace at my tears: for I am a stranger with thee, and a sojourner, as all my fathers were. O spare me, that I may recover strength, before I go hence, and be no more.

[Wednesday]   **Psalm 63. Of David. To The Chief Musician.**

Hear my voice, O God, in my prayer: preserve my life from fear of the enemy. Hide me from the secret counsel of the wicked; from the insurrection of the workers of iniquity: Who whet their tongue like a sword, and bend their bows to shoot their arrows, even bitter words: That they may shoot in secret at the perfect: suddenly do they shoot at him, and fear not. They encourage themselves in an evil matter: they commune of laying snares privily; they say, Who shall see them? They search out iniquities; they accomplish a diligent search: both the inward thought of every one of them, and the heart, is deep. But God shall shoot at them with an arrow; suddenly shall they be wounded. So they shall make their own tongue to fall upon themselves: all that see them shall flee away. And all men shall fear, and shall declare the work of God; for they shall wisely consider of his doing. The righteous shall be glad in the Lord, and shall trust in him; and all the upright in heart shall glory.

[Thursday]   **Psalm 88. Maschil Of Ethan The Ezrahite.**

I shall sing of the mercies of the Lord for ever: with my mouth shall I make known thy faithfulness to all generations. For I have said, Mercy shall be built up for ever: thy faithfulness shalt thou establish in the very heavens. I have made a covenant with my chosen, I have sworn unto David my servant, Thy seed shall I establish for ever, and build up thy throne to all generations. And the heavens shall praise thy wonders, O Lord: thy faithfulness also in the congregation of the saints. For who in the heaven can be compared unto the Lord? who among the sons of the mighty can be likened unto the Lord? God is greatly to be feared in the assembly of the saints, and to be had in reverence of all them that are about him. O Lord God of hosts, who is a strong Lord like unto thee? Or to thy faithfulness round about thee? Thou rulest the raging of the sea: when the waves thereof arise, thou stillest them. Thou hast broken Rahab in pieces, as one that is slain; thou hast scattered thine enemies with thy strong arm. The heavens are thine, the earth also is thine: as for the world and the fullness thereof, thou hast founded them. The north and the south thou hast created them: Tabor and Hermon shall rejoice in thy name. Thou hast a mighty arm: strong is thy hand, and high is thy right hand.

Justice and judgement are the habitation of thy throne: mercy and truth shall go before thy face. Blessed is the people that know the joyful sound: they shall walk, O Lord, in the light of thy countenance. In thy name shall they rejoice all the day: and in thy righteousness shall they be exalted. For thou art the glory of their strength: and in thy favour our horn shall be exalted. For the Lord is our defence; and the Holy One of Israel is our king. Then thou spake in vision to thy holy one, and said, I have laid help upon one that is mighty; I have exalted one chosen out of the people. I have found David my servant; with my holy oil have I anointed him: With whom my hand shall be established: mine arm also shall strengthen him. The enemy shall not exact upon him; nor the son of wickedness afflict him. And I shall beat down his foes before his face, and plague them that hate him. But my faithfulness and my mercy shall be with him: and in my name shall his horn be exalted. I shall set his hand also in the sea, and his right hand in the rivers. He shall cry unto me, Thou art my father, my God, and the rock of my salvation. Also I shall make him my first born, higher than the kings of the earth. My mercy shall I keep for him for evermore, and my covenant shall stand fast with him. His seed also shall I make to endure for ever, and his throne as the days of heaven. If his children forsake my law, and walk not in my judgements; If they break my statutes, and keep not my commandments; Then shall I visit their transgression with the rod, and their iniquity with stripes.

Nevertheless my loving kindness shall I not utterly take from him, nor suffer my faithfulness to fail. My covenant shall I not break, nor alter the thing that is gone out of my lips. Once have I sworn by my holiness that I shall not lie unto David. His seed shall endure for ever, and his throne as the sun before me. It shall be established for ever as the moon, and as a faithful witness in heaven. But thou hast cast off and abhorred, thou hast been wroth with thine anointed. Thou hast made void the covenant of thy servant: thou hast profaned his crown by casting it to the ground. Thou hast broken down all his hedges; thou hast brought his strong holds to ruin. All that pass by the way spoil him: he is a reproach to his neighbours.

Thou hast set up the right hand of his adversaries; thou hast made all his enemies to rejoice. Thou hast also turned the edge of his sword, and hast not made him to stand in the battle. Thou hast made his glory to cease, and cast his throne down to the ground. The days of his youth hast thou shortened: thou hast covered him with shame. How long, Lord? Wilt thou hide thyself for ever? shall thy wrath burn like fire? Remember how short my time is: wherefore hast thou made all men in vain? What man is he that liveth, and shall not see death? shall he deliver his soul from the hand of the grave? Lord, where are thy former loving kindnesses, which thou swarest unto David in thy truth? Remember, Lord, the reproach of thy servants; how I do bear in my bosom the reproach of all the mighty people; Wherewith thine enemies have reproached, O Lord; wherewith they have reproached the footsteps of thine anointed. Blessed be the Lord for evermore. Amen, and Amen.

[Friday:]   **Psalm 143**

Blessed be the Lord my strength, which teacheth my hands to war, and my fingers to fight: My goodness, and my fortress; my high tower, and my deliverer; my shield, and he in whom I trust; who subdueth my people under me. Lord, what is man, that thou takest knowledge of him. Or the son of man, that thou makest account of him. Man is like to vanity: his days are as a shadow that passeth away. Bow thy heavens, O Lord, and come down: touch the mountains, and they shall smoke. Cast forth lightning, and scatter them: shoot out thine arrows, and destroy them. Send thine hand from above; rid me, and deliver me out of great waters, from the hand of strange children; Whose mouth speaketh vanity, and their right hand is a right hand of falsehood. I shall sing a new song unto thee, O God: upon a psaltery and an instrument of ten strings shall I sing praises unto thee. It is he that giveth salvation unto kings: who delivereth David his servant from the hurtful sword. Rid me, and deliver me from the hand of strange children, whose mouth speaketh vanity, and their right hand is a right hand of falsehood: That our sons may be as plants grown up in their youth; that our daughters may be as corner stones, polished after the similitude of a palace: That our garners may be full, affording all manner of store: that our sheep may bring forth thousands and ten thousands in our streets: That our oxen may be strong to labour; that there be no breaking in, nor going out; that there be no complaining in our streets. Happy is that people, that is in such a case: yea, happy is that people, whose God is the Lord.

Commemorate The Living

Lord have mercy on: the leaders of the church, this nation, spiritual fathers and mothers, our parents and relatives, the old and the young, the needy, orphans, widows, those in sickness or sorrow, those in captivity or confinement. Remember, strengthen and comfort them and grant them speedy relief and freedom and deliverance.

[Private Prayers here.]

Commemorate The Departed

Remember Your servants who have fallen asleep: our grandparents, parents and family members and friends. Forgive them all their sins committed knowingly or unknowingly and grant them Your Kingdom, a portion of Your eternal blessing and the enjoyment of Your unending life.

[List the names of the departed.]

Troparion To The Holy Trinity

Having arisen from sleep, we fall down before Thee, O blessed One, and sing to Thee, O Mighty One, the angelic hymn: Holy. Holy. Holy. art Thou O God; through the Theotokos, have mercy on us.

Glory be to the Father, and to the Son, and to the Holy Spirit;

Having raised me from my bed and from sleep, O Lord, enlighten my mind and heart, and open my lips that I might praise Thee, O Holy Trinity: Holy. Holy. Holy. art Thou O God; through the Theotokos, have mercy on us.

Both now and forever and to the ages of ages. Amen.

The Judge shall come suddenly and the acts of every man shall be revealed; but in the middle of the night we cry in fear: Holy. Holy. Holy. art Thou O God; through the Theotokos, have mercy on us.

Lord have mercy. **(x12)**

Psalm 50

Have mercy on me, O God, according to Thy great mercy; and according to the multitude of Thy compassions blot out my transgression. Wash me thoroughly from mine iniquity, and cleanse me from my sin. For I acknowledge mine iniquity, and my sin is ever before me.

[Pause and remember your sinfulness.]

Against Thee, Thee only have I sinned, and done evil in Thy sight, that Thou mayest be found just when Thou speakest, and victorious when Thou art judged. For behold, I was conceived in iniquity, and in sin my mother bore me. For behold, Thou hast loved truth; Thou hast made known to me the hidden and secret things of Thy wisdom. Thou shalt sprinkle me with hyssop, and I shall be made clean; Thou shalt wash me, and I shall be whiter than snow. Make me to hear joy and gladness; that the humbled bones may rejoice. Turn Thy face away from my sins, and blot out all my iniquities.

Create in me a clean heart, O God, and renew a steadfast spirit within me. Cast me not away from Thy presence, and take not Thy Holy Spirit from me. Restore to me the joy of Thy salvation, and establish me with Thy governing Spirit. I shall teach transgressors Thy ways, and the ungodly shall turn back to Thee. Deliver me from blood guiltiness, O God, the God of my salvation; my tongue shall joyfully declare Thy righteousness. Lord, open my lips, and my mouth shall declare Thy praise. For if Thou hadst desired sacrifice, I would give it; Thou dost not delight in burnt offerings. A sacrifice to God is a broken spirit; God shall not despise a broken and a humbled heart. Do good, O Lord, in Thy good pleasure to Zion, and let the walls of Jerusalem be builded. Then Thou shalt be pleased with a sacrifice of righteousness, with oblation and whole burned offerings. Then shall they offer bulls on Thine altar.

A Prayer To The Holy Trinity

Having arisen from sleep, I thank Thee, the Holy Trinity. In the abundance of Thy kindness and long patience, Thou hast not been angry with me for my laziness and sinfulness, nor hast Thou destroyed me in my lawlessness. Instead, in Thy usual love for mankind, Thou hast raised me as I lay in despair, that I might rise early and glorify Thy Reign. Enlighten now the eyes of my mind and open my lips, that I might learn of Thy words, understand Thy commandments, accomplish Thy will, hymn Thee in heart felt confession and praise Thine all holy name, of the Father and of the Son, and of the Holy Spirit, now and forever and to the ages of ages. Amen.

The Symbol Of Faith

I believe in one God, Father, Almighty, Maker of heaven and earth, and of all things visible and invisible.

And in one Lord Jesus Christ, the only begotten Son of God, begotten from the Father before all ages; Light from Light, true God from true God; begotten not made; consubstantial with the Father, through Him all things were made. For our sake and for our salvation He came down from Heaven, and was incarnate from the Holy Spirit and the Virgin Mary and became man. He was crucified for us under Pontius Pilate, and suffered and was buried. He rose again on the third day in accordance with the Scriptures, and ascended into Heaven, and is seated at the right hand of the Father. He is coming again in glory to judge the living and the dead. And His kingdom shall have no end.

And in the Holy Spirit, the Lord, the Giver of life; Who proceeds from the Father; Who together with the Father and the Son is worshipped and glorified; Who spoke through the prophets. In One, Holy, Catholic, and Apostolic Church. I confess one baptism for the forgiveness of sins. I await the resurrection of the dead, And the life of the age to come. Amen.

Lesser Doxology

Glory to God, Who has shown us the Light. Glory to God in the highest, and on earth, peace, good will toward men. We praise Thee. We bless Thee. We worship Thee. We glorify Thee and give thanks to Thee for Thy great glory. O Lord God, Heavenly King, God the Father Almighty. O Lord, the Only Begotten Son, Jesus Christ, and the Holy Spirit. \ O Lord God, Lamb of God, Son of the Father, Who takes away the sins of the world, have mercy on us. Thou, Who takes away the sins of the world, receive our prayer. Thou, Who sittest at the right hand of God the Father, have mercy on us. / For Thou alone art holy, and Thou alone art Lord. Thou alone, O Lord Jesus Christ, are most high in the glory of God the Father. Amen. I shall give thanks to Thee every day and praise Thy Name forever and ever. Lord, Thou hast been our refuge from generation to generation. I said, *"Lord, have mercy on me. Heal my soul, for I have sinned against Thee."* \ Lord, I flee to Thee. Teach me to do Thy will, for Thou art my God. For with Thee is the fountain of Life, and in Thy light shall we see light. Continue Thy loving kindness to those who know Thee. Vouchsafe, O Lord, to keep us this day without sin. Blessed art Thou, O Lord, the God of our fathers, and praised and glorified is Thy Name forever. Amen. Let Thy mercy be upon us, O Lord, even as we have set our hope on Thee.

Blessed art Thou, O Master; teach me Thy statutes.

Blessed art Thou, O Lord; enlighten me with Thy commandments.

Blessed art Thou, O Holy One; make me to understand Thy precepts.

Thy mercy endures forever, O Lord. Do not despise the works of Thy hands. To Thee belongs worship, to Thee belongs praise, to Thee belongs glory: to the Father and to the Son and to the Holy Spirit, both now and forever and unto the ages of ages. Amen. \

A Prayer Of St Basil The Great

We bless Thee, most high God and Lord of mercies, Who ever doest great and unfathomable things for us glorious and awesome things without number. Thou gavest us sleep for the repose of our frailty, relieving the labours of our over burdened flesh. We thank Thee for not destroying us in our lawlessness. Instead, Thou hast shown Thy usual love for mankind, and raised us, as we lay in despair, to glorify Thy Reign. Therefore, we implore Thy boundless goodness: enlighten our thoughts and eyes, and awaken our minds from the heavy sleep of laziness. Open our lips and fill them with Thy praise, that we may always hymn and confess Thee, the God glorified in all and by all, Father without beginning, with Thine only begotten Son and Thine all holy and life giving Spirit, now and forever and to the ages of ages. Amen.

Rejoice, O Virgin

Rejoice, O Virgin Theotokos. Mary full of grace, the Lord is with thee. Blessed art thou among women, and blessed is the fruit of thy womb; for thou hast borne the Saviour of our souls.

Morning Prayer Of The Last Elders Of Optina

O Lord, grant that I may meet all that this coming day brings to me with spiritual tranquillity. Grant that I may fully surrender myself to Thy holy Will. At every hour of this day, direct and support me in all things. Whatsoever news may reach me in the course of the day, teach me to accept it with a calm soul and firm conviction that all is subject to Thy holy will. Direct my thoughts and feelings in all my words and actions. In all unexpected occurrences, do not let me forget that all is sent down from Thee. Grant that I may straightforwardly and wisely behave with every member of my family, neither embarrassing nor saddening anyone. O Lord, grant me the strength to endure the fatigue of the coming day and all the events that take place during it. Direct my will and teach me to pray, to believe, to hope, to be patient, to forgive, and to love. Amen.

Glory be to the Father and to the Son and to the Holy Spirit;
Both now and forever and unto the ages of ages. Amen.

Dismissal

Through the prayers of our holy Fathers, Lord Jesus Christ our God, have mercy upon us and save us. Amen.

Jesus Prayer

Lord Jesus Christ, Son of God, Have mercy on me a sinner.

Reflection

[Reflect on today's tasks and prepare yourself for the difficulties that you might face. Ask God for help.]

The Trisagion Prayers

In the Name of the Father, and of the Son, and of the Holy Spirit. Amen.

Glory to Thee, our God, glory to Thee.

O Heavenly King, the Comforter, the Spirit of Truth; who art everywhere present and fillest all things; Treasury of blessings, and giver of life: come and abide in us, and cleanse us from every impurity, and save our souls, O Good One.

Holy God, Holy Mighty, Holy Immortal, have mercy on us. **(x3)**

Glory be to the Father, and to the Son, and to the Holy Spirit;
Both now and forever, and unto the ages of ages. Amen.

O Most Holy Trinity, have mercy on us.

O Lord, cleanse us from our sins.

O Master, blot out our iniquities.

O Holy One, visit and heal our infirmities, for Thy names sake.

Lord have mercy. **(x3)**

Glory be to the Father, and to the Son, and to the Holy Spirit;
Both now and forever, and unto the ages of ages. Amen.

Our Father, who art in heaven, hallowed be Thy name. Thy Kingdom come. Thy will be done, on earth as it is in heaven. Give us this day our daily bread; and forgive us our trespasses, as we forgive those who trespass against us; and lead us not into temptation, but deliver us from the evil one. Amen.

O Gladsome Light

O Gladsome Light of the holy glory of the immortal Father. Heavenly holy, blessed Jesus Christ.

Now that we have come, to the setting of the sun, and behold the Evening Light;

We praise God; Father, Son and Holy Spirit.

For meet it is at all time to worship Thee, with voices of praise;

O Son of God and Giver of Life. Therefore all the world doth glorify Thee.

A Prayer for Forgiveness

O Lord our God, forgive all the sins I have committed this day in word, deed and thought, for Thou art good and lovest mankind. Grant me a peaceful sleep, free of restlessness. Send Thy Guardian Angel to protect and keep me from all harm. For Thou art the Guardian of our souls and bodies, and to Thee we ascribe glory; to the Father, and to the Son, and to the Holy Spirit. Both now and forever and unto the ages of ages. Amen.

The Symbol Of Faith

I believe in one God, Father, Almighty, Maker of heaven and earth, and of all things visible and invisible.

And in one Lord Jesus Christ, the only begotten Son of God, begotten from the Father before all ages; Light from Light, true God from true God; begotten not made; consubstantial with the Father, through Him all things were made. For our sake and for our salvation He came down from Heaven, and was incarnate from the Holy Spirit and the Virgin Mary and became man. He was crucified for us under Pontius Pilate, and suffered and was buried. He rose again on the third day in accordance with the Scriptures, and ascended into Heaven, and is seated at the right hand of the Father. He is coming again in glory to judge the living and the dead. And His kingdom shall have no end.

And in the Holy Spirit, the Lord, the Giver of life; Who proceeds from the Father; Who together with the Father and the Son is worshipped and together glorified; Who spoke through the prophets. In One, Holy, Catholic, and Apostolic Church. I confess one baptism for the forgiveness of sins. I await the resurrection of the dead, And the life of the age to come. Amen.

The Prayer Of The Hours

At all times and in every hour, Thou art worshipped and glorified in heaven and on earth, Christ our God. Long in patience, great in mercy and compassion, Thou lovest the righteous and showest mercy to sinners. Thou callest all to salvation through the promise of good things to come. Lord, receive our prayers at the present time. Direct our lives according to Thy commandments. Sanctify our souls. Purify our bodies. Set our minds aright. Cleanse our thoughts, and deliver us from all sorrow, evil and distress. Surround us with Thy holy angels, that, guarded and guided by their host, we may arrive at the unity of the faith and the understanding of Thine ineffable glory. For Thou art blessed to the ages of ages. Amen.

Prayer To Mother Mary

Beneath thy compassion we take refuge, Virgin Theotokos. Despise not our prayers in our necessities, but deliver us from harm, O only pure, only blessed One.

[Private Prayers here]

Through the prayers of our holy Fathers, Lord Jesus Christ our God, have mercy upon us and save us. Amen.

Prayer For The Acceptance Of Gods Will

O Lord, I know not what to ask of Thee. Thou alone knowest what are my true needs. Thou lovest me more than I myself know how to love. Help me to see my real needs which are concealed from me. I dare not ask for either a cross or consolation. I can only wait on Thee. My heart is open to Thee. Visit and help me for Thy great mercy's sake. Strike me and heal me. Cast me down and raise me up. I worship in silence Thy holy will and Thine inscrutable ways. I offer myself as a sacrifice to Thee. I put all my trust in Thee. I have no other desire than to fulfil Thy will. Teach me how to pray. Pray Thou Thyself in me. Amen.

Prayer By Agreement

Lord Jesus Christ, Son of God, Thou didst say with Thy most pure lips "Verily I say unto you, that if two of you shall agree on earth as touching anything that they shall ask, it shall be done for them of my Father who art in heaven." For where two or three are gathered together in my name, there am I in the midst of them."

Thy words are inviolable, O Lord, Thy mercy is unequalled, and Thy love for mankind has no end. Therefore we pray to Thee: Give us, Thy servants:

[Those who are praying.]

Who have agreed to ask of Thee health of soul and body for:

[Those for whom we are praying.]

And for all members of our families for the fulfilment of our request. But let it not be as we desire, but as Thou desirest O Lord; may Thy will be done unto the ages of ages. Amen.

Orthodox Prayers To Heal Sickness

Prayers For Yourself In Sickness

O Holy Father, heavenly Physician of the body and soul, Who hast sent Thine Only begotten Son, out Lord Jesus Christ, to heal ailments and deliver us from death; do Thou heal me, Thy servant, of all suffering, and restore me to health by the grace of Thy Divine Son, through the intercessions of our Most Holy Queen Ever Virgin Mary, the Mother of God, and all the saint. For Thou art the Fountain of all cure, O Lord, and we give thank to Thee: the Father, the Son, and the Holy Spirit, now and forever and unto the ages of ages. Amen.

O Lord Jesus Christ our Saviour, the Physician of our souls and bodies, Who didst become Man and suffer death on the Cross for our salvation, and through Thy tender love and compassion didst heal all manner of sickness and affliction: do Thou, O Lord, visit me in my suffering, and grant me grace and strength to bear this sickness with which I am afflicted, with Christian patience and submission to Thy will, trusting in Thy loving kindness and tender mercy. Bless, I pray Thee, the means used for my recovery, and those who administer them. I know, O Lord, that I justly deserve any punishment Thou mayest inflict upon me, for I have so often offended Thee and sinned against Thee in thought, word, and deed. Therefore, I humbly pray to Thee, look upon my weakness, and deal not with me according to my sins, but according to the multitude of Thy mercies. Have compassion on me, and let mercy and justice meet and deliver me from the sickness and suffering that I am undergoing. Grant that my sickness may be the means of my true repentance and amendment of my life according to Thy will, that I may spend the rest of my days in Thy love and fear; that my soul, being helped by Thy grace and sanctified by thy holy mysteries, may be prepared for its transition to the eternal life and there, in the company of Thy blessed saints, may praise and glorify Thee with Thy Eternal Father and Life creating Spirit. Amen.

Prayers For Someone Else Who Is Sickness

O Lord our God, the Physician of our souls and bodies, look down upon Thy servant *[Name]* and cure him of all infirmities of the flesh, in the Name our Lord and Saviour Jesus Christ, with Whom Thou art blessed, together with Thy Most Holy, Gracious, and Life creating Spirit, always, now and forever, and unto the ages of ages. Amen.

O Merciful Lord, visit and heal Thy sick servant *[Name]*, now lying on the bed of sickness and sorely afflicted, as Thou, O Saviour, didst once raise Peters wifes mother and the man sick of the palsy who was carried on his bed: for Thou alone hast borne the sickness and afflictions of our race, and with Thee nothing is impossible, for Thou art All Merciful.

Prayers For All Sick People

O Lord Almighty, healer of our souls and bodies, Who putteth down and raiseth up, Who chastiseth and healeth also; now, in Thy great mercy, visit our brothers and sisters who are sick. Stretch forth Thine hand that is full of healing and health, and raise them up, and cure them of their illness. Put away from them the spirit of disease and of every malady, pain and fever to which they are bound. And if they have sins and transgressions, grant to them remission of forgiveness, for Thou lovest humankind. Yea, O Lord my God, have pity on Thy creation, through the compassions of Thine only begotten Son, together with Thine all Holy, good and Life creating Spirit, with whom Thou art blessed; both now and forever, and unto the ages of ages. Amen.

Again we pray Thee, O Lord our God, that Thou wouldst hearken unto the voice of our supplication and prayer, and have mercy on Thy servant*(s) N.,* ....

Through Thy grace and compassions, and fulfil all *[his / her / their]* petitions, and pardon *[him / her / them]* all transgressions voluntary and involuntary; let *[his / her / their]* prayers and alms be acceptable before the throne of Thy dominion, and protect *[him / her / them]* from enemies visible and invisible, from every temptation, harm and sorrow, and deliver *[him / her / them]* from ailments, and grant *[him / her / them]* health and length of days: let us all say, O Lord, hearken and have mercy.

People: *Lord, have mercy.* **(x3)**

Look down, O Master, Lover of mankind, with Thy merciful eye, upon Thy servant*(s) N.* .... and hearken unto our supplication which is offered With faith, for Thou Thyself hast said: "All things whatsoever you shall ask in prayer, believe that you shall receive, and it shall be done unto you; and again: "Ask, and it shall be given you." Therefore we, though we be unworthy, yet hoping in Thy mercy, ask: Bestow Thy kindness upon Thy servant*(s) N,* .... and fulfil *[his / her / their]* good desires, preserve *[him / her / them]* all *[his / her / their]* days peacefully and calmly in health and length of days: let us all say, quickly hearken and graciously have mercy.

Again we pray for the people here present that await of Thee great and abundant mercy, for all the brethren, and for all Christians.

Ektenia For The Ailing

O Physician of souls and bodies, with compunction and contrite hearts we fall down before Thee, and groaning we cry unto Thee: Heal the sicknesses, heal the passions of the soul and body of Thy servant *N. (or the souls and bodies of Thy servants N....* and pardon *[him / her / them],* for Thou art kind hearted, all transgressions, voluntary and involuntary, and quickly raise *[him / her / them]* up from *[his / her / their]* bed of sickness, we pray Thee, hearken and have mercy.

People: *Lord, have mercy.* **(x3)**

O Thou Who desirest not the death of sinners, but rather that they should return to Thee and live: Spare and have mercy on Thy servant*(s) N.......* O Merciful One; banish sickness, drive away all passion, and all ailments, assuage chill and fever, and stretch forth Thy mighty arm, and as Thou didst raise up Jairus' daughter from her bed of sickness, restore *[him / her / them]* to health, we pray Thee, hearken and have mercy.

O Thou Who by Thy touch didst heal Peters mother-in-law who was sick with fever, do Thou now, in Thy loving kindness, heal Thy terribly suffering servant(s) of *[his / her / their]* malady, quickly granting *[him / her / them]* health, we diligently pray Thee, O Fount of healing, hearken and have mercy.

Again we pray to the Lord our God, that He may hearken unto the voice of the supplication of us sinners, and have mercy on His servant*(s), N...................* and protect *[him / her / them]* from all tribulation, harm, wrath and necessity, and from every sickness of soul and body, granting *[him / her / them]* health with length of days: let us all say, quickly hearken and have mercy.

For Those Who Journey

O Lord, Who dost guide the footsteps of mankind, graciously look upon Thy servant*(s) N....* and pardoning *[him / her / them]* every transgression, both voluntary and involuntary, bless the good intention of *[his / her / their]* counsel, and guide *[his / her / their]* goings out and comings in on the journey, we earnestly pray Thee, hearken and have mercy.

People: *Lord, have mercy.* **(x3)**

O Lord, Who didst most gloriously deliver Joseph from the animosity of his brethren, and didst lead him to Egypt, and through the blessing of Thy goodness didst make him to prosper in all things: Bless also *this (these)* Thy servant(s) who desireth (desire) to travel, and cause *[his / her / their]* journey to be safe and tranquil, we pray Thee, hearken and have mercy.

Thanksgiving For Petitions Granted

Giving thanks with fear and trembling, as unprofitable servants, unto Thy loving kindness, O Lord our Saviour and Master, for Thy benefits which Thou hast poured out abundantly on Thy servants, we fall down in worship and offer a doxology unto Thee as God, and fervently cry aloud to Thee: Deliver Thou Thy servants from all misfortune, and, as Thou art merciful, always fulfil the desires of us all unto good, we diligently pray Thee, hearken and have mercy.

People: *Lord, have mercy.* **(x3)**

In that Thou now hast mercifully hearkened unto the prayers of Thy servants, O Lord, and hast manifested upon us the tender compassion of Thy love for mankind, so also, in time to come, disdaining us not, do Thou fulfil, unto Thy glory, all good desires of Thy faithful, and show unto all of us Thine abundant mercy, disregarding all our iniquities, we pray the, hearken and have mercy.

People: *Lord, have mercy.* **(x3)**

These services often make reference to variables from other works. Some of these books are enormous and clearly cannot be contained herein. However just a couple are small enough to be quoted so that they are to hand and one may have practise in finding and inserting them.

The Katavasiae For The Seasons Of The Year

Katavasia Of The Cross

Ode 1

Tone 8   Humility, tranquillity, repose, suffering, pleading.   *C, D, Eb, F, G, A, Bb, C.*

Inscribing the invincible weapon of the Cross upon the waters, Moses marked a straight line before him with his staff and divided the Red Sea, opening a path for Israel who went over dry shod. Then he marked a second line across the waters and united them in one, overwhelming the chariots of Pharaoh. Therefore let us sing to Christ our God, for He hath been glorified.

Ode 3

The rod of Aaron is an image of this mystery, for when it budded it showed who should be priest. So in the Church, that once was barren, the wood of the Cross hath now put forth flower, filling her with strength and steadfastness.

Ode 4

O Lord, I have heard the mystery of Thy dispensation: I have considered Thy works, and I have glorified Thy Godhead.

Ode 5

O thrice blessed Tree, on which Christ the king and Lord was stretched. Through thee the beguiler fell, who tempted mankind with the tree. He was caught in the trap set by God, who was crucified upon thee in the flesh, granting peace unto our souls.

Ode 6

Jonah stretched out his hands in the form of a cross within the belly of the sea monster, plainly prefiguring the redeeming Passion. Cast out from thence after three days, he foreshadowed the marvellous Resurrection of Christ our God, who was crucified in the flesh and enlightened the world by His Rising on the third day.

Ode 7

The senseless decree of the wicked tyrant, breathing forth threats and blasphemy hateful to God, confused the people. Yet neither the fury of the wild beast nor the roaring of the fire could frighten the three Children: but standing together in the flame, fanned by the wind that brought refreshment as the dew, they sang: *"Blessed art Thou and praised above all, O our God and the God of our fathers."*

Chorus: *We praise, we bless, we worship the Lord, praising and supremely exalting Him unto all ages.*

Ode 8

O you Children, equal in number to the Trinity, bless you God the Father and creator; sing you the praises of the Word who descended and changed the fire to dew; and exalt you above all for ever the most Holy Spirit, who giveth life unto all.

The Magnificat (Luke 1:46-55).

My soul magnifies the Lord, and my spirit has rejoiced in God my Saviour. For He has regarded the lowly state of His maidservant; for behold, henceforth all generations shall call me blessed. For He who is mighty has done great things for me, and holy is His name. And His mercy is on those who fear Him from generation to generation. He has shown strength with His arm; he has scattered the proud in the imagination of their hearts. He has put down the mighty from their thrones, and exalted the lowly. He has filled the hungry with good things, and the rich He has sent empty away. He has helped His servant Israel, in remembrance of His mercy, as He spoke to our fathers, to Abraham and to his seed forever.

Ode 9

O Theotokos, thou art a mystical Paradise, who untilled hast brought forth Christ. He hath planted upon the earth the life-giving Tree of the Cross: therefore at its exaltation on this day, we worship Him and thee do we magnify.

Tone 4   *Festive, joyous and expressing deep piety.*   *C, D, Eb, F, G, A, Bb, C.*

Ode 1

I shall open my mouth, and the Spirit shall inspire it, and I shall utter the words of my song to the Queen and Mother: I shall be seen radiantly keeping feast and joyfully praising her wonders.

Ode 3

O Mother of God, thou living and plentiful fount, give strength to those united in spiritual fellowship, who sing hymns of praise to thee: and in thy divine glory vouchsafe unto them crowns of glory.

Ode 4

He who sitteth in glory upon the throne of the Godhead, Jesus the true God, is come in a swift cloud and with His sinless hands he hath saved those who cry: Glory to Thy power, O Christ.

Ode 5

The whole world was amazed at thy divine glory: for thou, O Virgin who hast not known wedlock, hast held in thy womb the God of all and hast given birth to an eternal Son, who rewards with salvation all who sing thy praises.

Ode 6

As we celebrate this sacred and solemn feast of the Mother of God, let us come, clapping our hands, O people of the Lord, and give glory to God who was born of her.

Ode 7

The holy children bravely trampled upon the threatening fire, refusing to worship created things in place of the Creator, and they sang in joy: *"Blessed art Thou and praised above all, O Lord God of our Fathers."*

Chorus: *We praise, we bless, we worship the Lord, praising and supremely exalting Him unto all ages.*

Ode 8

The Offspring of the Theotokos saved the holy children in the furnace. He who was then prefigured hath since been born on earth, and he gathers all the creation to sing: O all you works of the Lord, praise you the Lord and exalt Him above all for ever.

The Magnificat (Luke 1:46-55).

My soul magnifies the Lord, and my spirit has rejoiced in God my Saviour. For He has regarded the lowly state of His maidservant; for behold, henceforth all generations shall call me blessed. For He who is mighty has done great things for me, and holy is His name. And His mercy is on those who fear Him from generation to generation. He has shown strength with His arm; he has scattered the proud in the imagination of their hearts. He has put down the mighty from their thrones, and exalted the lowly. He has filled the hungry with good things, and the rich He has sent empty away. He has helped His servant Israel, in remembrance of His mercy, as He spoke to our fathers, to Abraham and to his seed forever.

Ode 9

Let every mortal born on earth, radiant with light, in spirit leap for joy; and let the host of the angelic powers celebrate and honour the holy feast of the Mother of God, and let them cry: Rejoice. Pure and blessed Ever Virgin, who gavest birth to God.

Tone 4   Festive, joyous and expressing deep piety.   C, D, Eb, F, G, A, Bb, C.

Ode 1

I shall open my mouth, and the Spirit shall inspire it, and I shall utter the words of my song to the Queen and Mother: I shall be seen radiantly keeping feast and joyfully praising her wonders.

Ode 3

O Mother of God, thou living and plentiful fount, give strength to those united in spiritual fellowship, who sing hymns of praise to thee: and in thy divine glory vouchsafe unto them crowns of glory.

Ode 4

Perceiving the unsearchable purpose of God concerning Thine incarnation from a Virgin, O Most High, the prophet Habakkuk cried: Glory to Thy power, O Lord.

Ode 5

The whole world was amazed at thy divine glory: for thou, O Virgin who hast not known wedlock, hast held in thy womb the God of all and hast given birth to an eternal Son, who rewards with salvation all who sing thy praises.

Ode 6

As we celebrate this sacred and solemn feast of the Mother of God, let us come, clapping our hands, O people of the Lord, and give glory to God who was born of her.

Ode 7

The holy children bravely trampled upon the threatening fire, refusing to worship created things in place of the Creator, and they sang in joy: *"Blessed art Thou and praised above all, O Lord God of our Fathers."*

Chorus: *We praise, we bless, we worship the Lord, praising and supremely exalting Him unto all ages.*

Ode 8

The Offspring of the Theotokos saved the holy children in the furnace. He who was then prefigured hath since been born on earth, and he gathers all the creation to sing: O all you works of the Lord, praise you the Lord and exalt Him above all for ever.

The Magnificat (Luke 1:46-55).

My soul magnifies the Lord, and my spirit has rejoiced in God my Saviour. For He has regarded the lowly state of His maidservant; for behold, henceforth all generations shall call me blessed. For He who is mighty has done great things for me, and holy is His name. And His mercy is on those who fear Him from generation to generation. He has shown strength with His arm; he has scattered the proud in the imagination of their hearts. He has put down the mighty from their thrones, and exalted the lowly. He has filled the hungry with good things, and the rich He has sent empty away. He has helped His servant Israel, in remembrance of His mercy, as He spoke to our fathers, to Abraham and to his seed forever.

Ode 9

Let every mortal born on earth, radiant with light, in spirit leap for joy; and let the host of the angelic powers celebrate and honour the holy feast of the Mother of God, and let them cry: Rejoice. Pure and blessed Ever Virgin, who gavest birth to God.

The Irmoi Of The Entry Of The Theotokos

Tone 4   Festive, joyous and expressing deep piety.   C, D, Eb, F, G, A, Bb, C.

Ode 1

I shall open my mouth, and the Spirit shall inspire it, and I shall utter the words of my song to the Queen and Mother: I shall be seen radiantly keeping feast and joyfully praising her entry.

Ode 3

O Mother of God, thou living and plentiful fount, give strength to those united in spiritual fellowship, who sing hymns of praise to thee: and on the day of thy venerable entry vouchsafe unto them crowns of glory.

Ode 4

Perceiving the unsearchable purpose of God concerning Thine incarnation from a Virgin, O Most High, the prophet Habakkuk cried: Glory to Thy power, O Lord.

Ode 5

The whole world was amazed at thy venerable entry: for thou, O Virgin who hast not known wedlock, thyself a Temple most pure, hast gone within the Temple of God, bestowing peace upon all who sing thy praises.

Ode 6

As we celebrate this sacred and solemn feast of the Mother of God, let us come, clapping our hands, O people of the Lord, and give glory to God who was born of her.

Ode 7

The holy children bravely trampled upon the threatening fire, refusing to worship created things in place of the Creator, and they sang in joy: *"Blessed art Thou and praised above all, O Lord God of our Fathers."*

Chorus: *We praise, we bless, we worship the Lord, praising and supremely exalting Him unto all ages.*

Ode 8

Hearken, O pure Virgin Maid: let Gabriel tell thee the counsel of the Most High that is ancient and true. Make ready to receive God: for through thee the Incomprehensible comes to dwell with mortal men. Therefore I cry rejoicing: O all you works of the Lord, bless you the Lord.

The Magnificat (Luke 1:46-55).

My soul magnifies the Lord, and my spirit has rejoiced in God my Saviour. For He has regarded the lowly state of His maidservant; for behold, henceforth all generations shall call me blessed. For He who is mighty has done great things for me, and holy is His name. And His mercy is on those who fear Him from generation to generation. He has shown strength with His arm; he has scattered the proud in the imagination of their hearts. He has put down the mighty from their thrones, and exalted the lowly. He has filled the hungry with good things, and the rich He has sent empty away. He has helped His servant Israel, in remembrance of His mercy, as He spoke to our fathers, to Abraham and to his seed forever.

Ode 9

Let no profane hand touch the living Ark of God, but let the lips of the faithful, chanting unceasingly the words of the angel to the Theotokos, cry out with joy: Truly art thou high above all, O pure Virgin.

Tone 1   Magnificent, happy and earthy.   *C, D, Eb, F, G, A, Bb, C.*

Ode 1

Christ is born, give you glory. Christ cometh from heaven, meet you Him. Christ is on earth, be you exalted. O all the earth, sing unto the Lord, and sing praises in gladness, O you people, for He hath been glorified.

Ode 3

To the Son who was begotten of the Father without change before all ages, and in the last times was without seed made flesh of the Virgin, to Christ our God let us cry aloud: Thou hast raised up our horn, holy art Thou, O Lord.

Ode 4

Rod of the root of Jesse, and flower that blossomed from his stem, O Christ, Thou hast sprung from the Virgin. From the Mountain overshadowed by the forest Thou hast come, made flesh from her that knew not wedlock, O God who art not formed from matter. Glory to Thy power, O Lord.

Ode 5

As Thou art God of peace and Father of mercies, Thou hast sent unto us Thine Angel of great counsel, granting us peace. So are we guided towards the light of the knowledge of God, and watching by night we glorify Thee, O Lover of mankind.

Ode 6

The sea monster spat forth Jonah as it had received him, like a babe from the womb: while the Word, having dwelt in the Virgin and taken flesh, came forth from her yet kept her uncorrupt. For being Himself not subject to decay, He preserved His Mother free from harm.

Ode 7

Scorning the impious decree, the Children brought up together in godliness feared not the threat of fire, but standing in the midst of the flames, they sang: O God of our fathers, blessed art Thou.

Chorus: *We praise, we bless, we worship the Lord, praising and supremely exalting Him unto all ages.*

Ode 8

The furnace moist with dew was the image and figure of a wonder past nature. For it burnt not the Children whom it had received, even as the fire of the Godhead consumed not the Virgin's womb into which it had descended. Therefore in praise let us sing: Let the whole creation bless the Lord and exalt Him above all for ever.

The Magnificat (Luke 1:46-55).

My soul magnifies the Lord, and my spirit has rejoiced in God my Saviour. For He has regarded the lowly state of His maidservant; for behold, henceforth all generations shall call me blessed. For He who is mighty has done great things for me, and holy is His name. And His mercy is on those who fear Him from generation to generation. He has shown strength with His arm; he has scattered the proud in the imagination of their hearts. He has put down the mighty from their thrones, and exalted the lowly. He has filled the hungry with good things, and the rich He has sent empty away. He has helped His servant Israel, in remembrance of His mercy, as He spoke to our fathers, to Abraham and to his seed forever.

Ode 9

A strange and most wonderful mystery do I see: the cave is heaven; the Virgin the throne of the cherubim; the manger a room, in which Christ, the God whom nothing can contain, is laid. Him do we praise and magnify.

Katavasia Of The Theophany Of Our Lord

Tone 2   Majesty, gentleness, hope, repentance and sadness.   *E, F, G, Ab, B, C.*

Ode 1

The Lord mighty in battle uncovered the foundation of the deep and led His servants on dry ground; but He covered their adversaries with the waters, for He hath been glorified.

Ode 3

The Lord who granteth strength unto our kings, and exalteth the horn of His anointed, is born of a Virgin and cometh unto baptism. Therefore let us, the faithful, cry aloud: None is holy as our God and none is righteous save Thee, O Lord.

Ode 4

He whom Thou hast called, O Lord, 'The voice of one crying in the wilderness,' heard Thy voice when Thou hast thundered upon many waters, bearing witness to Thy Son. Wholly filled with the Spirit that had come, he cried aloud: 'Thou art Christ, the wisdom and the power of God.'

Ode 5

Jesus, the Prince of Life, hath come to set loose from condemnation Adam the first formed man; and though as God He needeth no cleansing, yet for the sake of fallen man He is cleansed in the Jordan. In its streams He slew the enmity and bestoweth the peace that passeth all understanding.

Ode 6

The Voice of the Word, the Candlestick of the Light, the Morning Star and Forerunner of the Sun, cried in the wilderness to all the peoples: 'Repent and be cleansed while there is yet time. For lo, Christ is at hand, Who delivereth the world from corruption.

Ode 7

The breath of the wind heavy with dew and the descent of the angel of God preserved the Holy Children from all harm, as they walked in the fiery furnace. Refreshed with dew in the flames, they sang in thanksgiving: 'Blessed art Thou and praised above all, O Lord God of our fathers.'

Chorus: *We praise, we bless, we worship the Lord, praising and supremely exalting Him unto all ages.*

Ode 8

The Babylonian furnace, as it poured forth dew, foreshadowed a marvellous mystery: how the Jordan should receive in its streams the immaterial fire, and should encompass the Creator, when He was baptised in the flesh. Him do you peoples bless and exalt above all for ever.

The Magnificat (Luke 1:46-55).

My soul magnifies the Lord, and my spirit has rejoiced in God my Saviour. For He has regarded the lowly state of His maidservant; for behold, henceforth all generations shall call me blessed. For He who is mighty has done great things for me, and holy is His name. And His mercy is on those who fear Him from generation to generation. He has shown strength with His arm; he has scattered the proud in the imagination of their hearts. He has put down the mighty from their thrones, and exalted the lowly. He has filled the hungry with good things, and the rich He has sent empty away. He has helped His servant Israel, in remembrance of His mercy, as He spoke to our fathers, to Abraham and to his seed forever.

Ode 9

Every tongue is at a loss to praise thee as is due: even a spirit from the world above is filled with dizziness, when it seeketh to sing thy praises, O Theotokos. But since thou art good, accept our faith: Thou knowest well our love inspired by God, for thou art the Protector of Christians and we magnify thee.

Tone 2   Majesty, gentleness, hope, repentance and sadness.   *E, F, G, Ab, B, C.*

Ode 1

The Lord mighty in battle uncovered the foundation of the deep and led His servants on dry ground; but He covered their adversaries with the waters, for He hath been glorified.

Israel passed through the storm-tossed deep of the sea that God had turned into dry land; but the dark waters completely covered the chief captains of Egypt in a watery grave through the mighty strength of the right hand of the master.

Ode 3

The Lord who granteth strength unto our kings, and exalteth the horn of His anointed, is born of a Virgin and cometh unto baptism. Therefore let us, the faithful, cry aloud: None is holy as our God and none is righteous save Thee, O Lord.

From the ancient snares have we all been set loose, and the jaws of the devouring lions have been broken: Let us, then rejoice exceedingly and open wide our mouths, weaving with words a melody to the Word Whose delight it is to bestow gifts upon us.

Ode 4

He whom Thou hast called, O Lord, 'The voice of one crying in the wilderness,' heard Thy voice when Thou hast thundered upon many waters, bearing witness to Thy Son. Wholly filled with the Spirit that had come, he cried aloud: 'Thou art Christ, the wisdom and the power of God.'

Cleansed by the fire of a mystic vision the Prophet sang the praises of the renewal of mortal man. Filled with the inspiration of the Spirit, he raised his voice, telling of the incarnation of the ineffable word, Who hath shattered the dominion of the mighty.

Ode 5

Jesus, the Prince of Life, hath come to set loose from condemnation Adam the first formed man; and though as God He needeth no cleansing, yet for the sake of fallen man He is cleansed in the Jordan. In its streams He slew the enmity and bestoweth the peace that passeth all understanding.

By the cleansing of the Spirit have we been washed from the poison of the dark and unclean enemy, and we have set out upon a new path free from error, that leads to gladness of heart past all attainment, which only they attain whom God hath reconciled unto Himself.

Ode 6

The Voice of the Word, the Candlestick of the Light, the Morning Star and Forerunner of the Sun, cried in the wilderness to all the peoples: 'Repent and be cleansed while there is yet time. For lo, Christ is at hand, Who delivereth the world from corruption.

The Father in a voice full of joy made manifest His Beloved Whom He had begotten from the womb. 'Verily,' said He, 'this is My offspring, of the same nature as Myself: bearing light, He hath come forth from mankind, My living Word, in the divine providence made a mortal man.'

Ode 7

The breath of the wind heavy with dew and the descent of the angel of God preserved the Holy Children from all harm, as they walked in the fiery furnace. Refreshed with dew in the flames, they sang in thanksgiving: 'Blessed art Thou and praised above all, O Lord God of our fathers.'

He who stilled the heat of the flame of the furnace that mounted high in the air and encircled the godly Children, burnt the heads of the dragons in the streams of the Jordan: and He doth wash away with the dew of the Spirit all the stubborn gloom that sinning doth engender.

Ode 8

The Babylonian furnace, as it poured forth dew, foreshadowed a marvellous mystery: how the Jordan should receive in its streams the immaterial fire, and should encompass the Creator, when He was baptised in the flesh. Him do you peoples bless and exalt above all for ever.

The creation finds itself set free, and those in darkness are now made sons of the light: alone the prince of darkness groaneth. Let all the inheritance of the nations, that was before in misery, now bless with eagerness Him Who hath wrought this change.

Ode 9

Every tongue is at a loss to praise thee as is due: even a spirit from the world above is filled with dizziness, when it seeketh to sing thy praises, O Theotokos. But since thou art good, accept our faith: Thou knowest well our love inspired by God, for thou art the Protector of Christians and we magnify thee.

O most pure Bride, O blessed Mother, the wonders of Thy birth giving pass all understanding. Through thee we have obtained salvation in all things, and, as it is right and meet, we rejoice before thee our Benefactor, bearing as gift a song of thanksgiving.

Tone 3   *Arrogant, brave, and mature atmosphere.*   *F, G, A, A#, C, D, E, F.*

Ode 1

The Sun once shone with its rays upon dry land in the midst of the deep. For the water on both sides became firm as a wall while the people crossed the sea on foot, offering this song acceptable to God: Let us sing to the Lord; for gloriously is he glorified.

Ode 3

O Lord, the firm foundation of those that put their trust in Thee, do Thou confirm the Church, which Thou hast purchased with thy precious blood.

Ode 4

Thy virtue, O Christ, hath covered the heavens, for proceeding forth from the Ark of Thy sanctification, from Thine undefiled Mother, Thou hast appeared in the temple of Thy glory as an infant in arms, and the whole world hath been filled with Thy praise.

Ode 5

In a figure Isaiah saw God upon a throne, lifted up on high and borne in triumph by angels of glory; and he cried: 'Woe is me. For I have seen beforehand God made flesh, Lord of the light that knows no evening and King of peace.'

Ode 6

The Elder, having seen with his eyes the salvation that was to come to the peoples, cried aloud unto Thee: 'O Christ that comest from God, Thou art my God.'

Ode 7

O Word of God who in the midst of the fire hast dropped dew upon the children as they discoursed on things divine, and Who hast taken up Thy dwelling in the pure Virgin: Thee do we praise as with piety we sing: O God of our fathers, blessed art Thou.

Chorus: *We praise, we bless, we worship the Lord, praising and supremely exalting Him unto all ages.*

Ode 8

Standing together in the unbearable fire, yet not harmed by the flame, the children, champions of godliness, sang a divine hymn: O all you works of the Lord, bless you the Lord and exalt Him above all for ever.

The Magnificat (Luke 1:46-55).

My soul magnifies the Lord, and my spirit has rejoiced in God my Saviour. For He has regarded the lowly state of His maidservant; for behold, henceforth all generations shall call me blessed. For He who is mighty has done great things for me, and holy is His name. And His mercy is on those who fear Him from generation to generation. He has shown strength with His arm; he has scattered the proud in the imagination of their hearts. He has put down the mighty from their thrones, and exalted the lowly. He has filled the hungry with good things, and the rich He has sent empty away. He has helped His servant Israel, in remembrance of His mercy, as He spoke to our fathers, to Abraham and to his seed forever.

Ode 9

In the shadow and the letter of the Law, let us, the faithful, discern a figure: every male child that opens the womb shall be sanctified to God. Therefore do we magnify the first born Word and Son of the Father without beginning, the first born Child of a Mother who hath not known a man.

Katavasia Of The Great Canon

Tone 6   Rich texture, funereal character, sorrowful tone.   D, Eb, F##, G, A, Bb, C##, D.

Ode 1

He is for me unto salvation Helper and Protector. He is my God and I glorify Him, God of my fathers is He and I exalt Him, for He is greatly glorified.

Ode 3

O Lord, upon the rock of Thy commandments make firm my wavering heart, for Thou alone art Holy and Lord.

Ode 4

The Prophet heard of Thy coming, O Lord, and he was afraid: how thou wast to be born of a Virgin and revealed to men, and he said: "I have heard the report of Thee and I was afraid." Glory to Thy power, O Lord.

Ode 5

From the night I seek Thee early, O Lover of mankind: give me light, I pray Thee, and guide me in Thy commandments, and teach me, O Saviour, to do Thy will.

Ode 6

With my whole heart I cried to the all compassionate God: and He heard from the lowest depths of hell, and brought my life out of corruption.

Ode 7

We have sinned, we have transgressed, we have done evil in Thy sight; we have not kept or followed Thy commandments. But reject us not utterly, O God of our fathers.

Chorus: *We praise, we bless, we worship the Lord, praising and supremely exalting Him unto all ages.*

Ode 8

The hosts of heaven give Him glory; before Him tremble cherubim and seraphim; let everything that hath breath and all creation praise Him, bless Him, and exalt Him above all for ever.

The Magnificat (Luke 1:46-55).

My soul magnifies the Lord, and my spirit has rejoiced in God my Saviour. For He has regarded the lowly state of His maidservant; for behold, henceforth all generations shall call me blessed. For He who is mighty has done great things for me, and holy is His name. And His mercy is on those who fear Him from generation to generation. He has shown strength with His arm; he has scattered the proud in the imagination of their hearts. He has put down the mighty from their thrones, and exalted the lowly. He has filled the hungry with good things, and the rich He has sent empty away. He has helped His servant Israel, in remembrance of His mercy, as He spoke to our fathers, to Abraham and to his seed forever.

Ode 9

Conception without seed; nativity past understanding, from a Mother who never knew a man; childbearing undefiled. For the birth of God makes both natures new. Therefore, as the Mother of our God, with true worship all generations magnify thee.

Katavasia Of The Sunday Of Orthodoxy

Tone 4   Festive, joyous and expressing deep piety.   *C, D, Eb, F, G, A, Bb, C.*

Ode 1

Having traversed the depths of the Red Sea with dry shod feet, Israel of old vanquished the might of Amalek in the wilderness by Moses' arms stretched out in the form of the Cross.

Ode 3

Thy Church rejoiceth in Thee, O Christ, crying aloud: Thou art my strength, O Lord, my refuge and my consolation.

Ode 4

Beholding Thee lifted up upon the Cross, O Sun of righteousness, the Church stood rooted in place, crying out as is meet: Glory to Thy power, O Lord.

Ode 5

Thou hast come, O my Lord, as a light into the world: a holy light turning from the darkness of ignorance those who hymn Thee with faith.

Ode 6

I shall sacrifice to Thee with a voice of praise, O Lord, the Church crieth unto Thee, cleansed of the blood of demons by the blood which, for mercy's sake, flowed from Thy side.

Ode 7

The children of Abraham in the Persian furnace, afire with love of piety more than with the flame, cried out: Blessed art Thou in the temple of Thy glory, O Lord.

Chorus: *We praise, we bless, we worship the Lord, praising and supremely exalting Him unto all ages.*

Ode 8

Stretching forth his hands, Daniel shut the lions' mouths in the pit; and the young lovers of piety, girded about with virtue, quenched the power of the fire, crying out: Bless the Lord, all you works of the Lord.

The Magnificat (Luke 1:46-55).

My soul magnifies the Lord, and my spirit has rejoiced in God my Saviour. For He has regarded the lowly state of His maidservant; for behold, henceforth all generations shall call me blessed. For He who is mighty has done great things for me, and holy is His name. And His mercy is on those who fear Him from generation to generation. He has shown strength with His arm; he has scattered the proud in the imagination of their hearts. He has put down the mighty from their thrones, and exalted the lowly. He has filled the hungry with good things, and the rich He has sent empty away. He has helped His servant Israel, in remembrance of His mercy, as He spoke to our fathers, to Abraham and to his seed forever.

Ode 9

Christ, the Chief Cornerstone uncut by human hands, Who united the two disparate natures, was cut from thee, the unquarried mountain, O Virgin. Wherefore, in gladness we magnify thee, O Theotokos.

Katavasia Of The Sunday Of The Cross

Tone 1   Magnificent, happy and earthy.   *C, D, Eb, F, G, A, Bb, C.*

Ode 1

Moses the servant of God prefigured Thy Cross in days of old, when he divided the Red Sea with his rod and led Israel across on dry land; and he sang a song of deliverance unto Thee, O Christ our God.

Ode 3

Through Thy Cross, O Christ my Master, set me firmly on the rock of the faith: let not my mind be shaken by the assaults of the malicious enemy; for Thou alone art holy.

Ode 4

Seeing Thee, O mighty Lord, upon the Cross, the sun was seized with fear and hid its rays, with dread the whole creation glorified Thy long suffering, and the earth was filled with Thy praise.

Ode 5

Rising early in the morning we sing Thy praises, O Saviour of the world, for we have found peace through Thy Cross. By it Thou hast renewed mankind, and led us to the light that knows no evening.

Ode 6

Jonah in the belly of the whale foreshadowed with his outstretched hands the figure of the Cross; and he leapt out from the monster, saved by Thy power, O Word.

Ode 7

The Lord who delivered the Children from the flames took flesh and came upon the earth: nailed to the Cross, He has granted us salvation, the God of our fathers, who alone is blessed and greatly glorified

Chorus: *We praise, we bless, we worship the Lord, praising and supremely exalting Him unto all ages.*

Ode 8

Daniel, great among the prophets, was cast into the lions' den; but, stretching out his hands in the form of the Cross, he was delivered from their mouths and kept unharmed, blessing Christ our God forever.

The Magnificat (Luke 1:46-55).

My soul magnifies the Lord, and my spirit has rejoiced in God my Saviour. For He has regarded the lowly state of His maidservant; for behold, henceforth all generations shall call me blessed. For He who is mighty has done great things for me, and holy is His name. And His mercy is on those who fear Him from generation to generation. He has shown strength with His arm; he has scattered the proud in the imagination of their hearts. He has put down the mighty from their thrones, and exalted the lowly. He has filled the hungry with good things, and the rich He has sent empty away. He has helped His servant Israel, in remembrance of His mercy, as He spoke to our fathers, to Abraham and to his seed forever.

Ode 9

O Virgin Mother and true Theotokos, without seed thou hast borne Christ our God, who was lifted in the flesh upon the Cross. We and all the faithful, as is right, magnify thee with thy Son.

Katavasia Of The Annunciation Of The Theotokos

Ode 1

I shall open my mouth, and the Spirit shall inspire it, and I shall utter the words of my song to the Queen and Mother: I shall be seen radiantly keeping feast and joyfully praising her wonders.

Ode 3

O Mother of God, thou living and plentiful fount, give strength to those united in spiritual fellowship, who sing hymns of praise to thee: and in thy divine glory vouchsafe unto them crowns of glory.

Ode 4

He who sitteth in glory upon the throne of the Godhead, Jesus the true God, is come in a swift cloud and with His sinless hands he hath saved those who cry: Glory to Thy power, O Christ.

Ode 5

The whole world was amazed at thy divine glory: for thou, O Virgin who hast not known wedlock, hast held in thy womb the God of all and hast given birth to an eternal Son, who rewards with salvation all who sing thy praises.

Ode 6

Prefiguring Thy three day burial, the prophet Jonah cried out in the belly of the whale: 'Deliver me from corruption, O Jesus, King and Lord of hosts.'

Ode 7

The holy children bravely trampled upon the threatening fire, refusing to worship created things in place of the Creator, and they sang in joy: 'Blessed art Thou and praised above all, O Lord God of our Fathers.'

Chorus: *We praise, we bless, we worship the Lord, praising and supremely exalting Him unto all ages.*

Ode 8

Hearken, O pure Virgin Maid: Let Gabriel tell thee the counsel of the Most High that is ancient and true. Make ready to receive God: for through thee the Incomprehensible comes to dwell with mortal men. Therefore I cry rejoicing: O all you works of the Lord, bless you the Lord.

Ode 9

Let no profane hand touch the living Ark of God, but let the lips of the faithful, chanting unceasingly the words of the angel to the Theotokos, with joy cry out: Rejoice, thou who art full of grace, the Lord is with thee.

Ode 1

It is the Day of Resurrection, let us be radiant, O you people; Pascha, the Lords Pascha: for from death to life, and from earth to heaven, Christ God hath brought us, as we sing the song of victory.

Ode 3

Come, let us drink a new drink, not one miraculously brought forth from a barren rock but the Fountain of Incorruption, springing forth from the tomb of Christ, in Whom we are strengthened.

Ode 4

On divine watch let the God inspired Habakkuk stand with us, and show forth the light-bearing angel clearly saying: Today salvation is come to the world, for Christ is risen as Almighty.

Ode 5

Let us awake in the deep dawn, and instead of myrrh, offer a hymn to the Master, and we shall see Christ, the Sun of Righteousness, Who causeth life to dawn for all.

Ode 6

Thou didst descend into the nethermost parts of the earth, and didst shatter the eternal bars that held the fettered, O Christ, and on the third day, like Jonah from the whale, Thou didst arise from the tomb.

Ode 7

He Who delivered the Children from the furnace, became man, suffereth as a mortal, and through His Passion doth clothe mortality with the beauty of incorruption, He is the only blessed and most glorious God of our fathers.

Chorus: *We praise, we bless, we worship the Lord, praising and supremely exalting Him unto all ages.*

Ode 8

This chosen and holy day is the first of the Sabbaths, the queen and lady, the feast of feasts, and the festival of festivals, wherein we bless Christ unto the ages.

Ode 9

Shine, shine you new Jerusalem, for the glory of the Lord is dawning upon ye. Exult and be glad O Zion, and O Virgin Theotokos, be radiant in the rising of thy son.

Tone 5   Stimulating, dancing, and rhythmical.   *C, D, Eb, F, G, A, Bb, C.*

Ode 1

Let us sing unto the only Saviour and God, Who guided the people dry shod in the sea, and drowned Pharaoh with all his forces; for He is glorified.

Ode 3

By the power of Thy Cross, O Christ, do Thou make steadfast mine understanding, that I may hymn and glorify Thy saving Ascension.

Ode 4

I have heard the report of the mighty deed of Thy Cross, O Lord, how Paradise was opened thereby, and I cried: Glory to Thy power, O Lord.

Ode 5

Waking at dawn, we cry unto Thee, O Lord: Save us, for Thou art our God; besides Thee we know none other.

Ode 6

The abyss hath encompassed me, the sea monster is become my grave; but I cried unto Thee, the Lover of mankind, and Thy right hand saved me, O Lord.

Ode 7

O Thou Who didst save the Children who praised Thee in the furnace of fire, blessed art Thou, O God of our Fathers.

Chorus: *We praise, we bless, we worship the Lord, praising and supremely exalting Him unto all ages.*

Ode 8

Unto God the Son, Who was begotten of the Father before the ages and was incarnate of a Virgin Mother in these last times, give praise, O you priests, and supremely exalt Him, O you people, unto all the ages.

Ode 9

O thou who art God's Mother transcending mind and word, who ineffably in time gavest birth unto the Timeless One, thee do we the faithful magnify with one accord.

Tone 4   Festive, joyous and expressing deep piety.   *C, D, Eb, F, G, A, Bb, C.*

Ode 1

Covered by the divine cloud, he that was slow of tongue proclaimed the Law written by God; for having shaken off the impurity from the eye of his mind, He beholdeth Him That is, and he is initiated into the knowledge of the Spirit, While giving praise with God inspired songs.

Ode 3

Only the prayer of the Prophetess Anna, who of old brought a broken spirit unto the Mighty One and God of knowledge, loosed the fetters of a childless womb and the unruly rebuke of her with children.

Ode 4

O King of kings, even Thou Who art from the Only One, O Word, Who comest forth from the only uncaused Father, Thou, as our Benefactor, didst unfailingly send Thy Spirit, Equal in might, unto the Apostles, who sing: Glory to Thy power, O Lord.

Ode 5

O you children of the Church, whose likeness is like unto light, receive you the fire breathing dew of the Spirit, which is a redeeming purification of offences; for now hath the Law gone forth from Zion, even the Spirit's grace, in the form of tongues of fire.

Ode 6

Thou hast shown forth from the Virgin as forgiveness and salvation for us, O Christ Master; that, like as Jonah was reft from the belly of the sea monster, Thou mightest snatch from corruption all the fallen race of Adam.

Ode 7

The unison of instrumental music declared that all should worship the lifeless image wrought of gold; but the light-bearing grace of the Comforter doth teach us to cry out in reverence: O only Trinity, Equal in power and beginningless, blessed art Thou.

Chorus: *We praise, we bless, we worship the Lord, praising and supremely exalting Him unto all ages.*

Ode 8

The type of the Godhead prefigured in the resplendent three loosed the bonds and moistened the flames with dew. The Children praise, and all creation that was made doth bless, the only Saviour and Creator of all, as their Benefactor.

Ode 9

Rejoice, O Queen boast of virgins and mothers; for every eloquent and capable mouth is unable to extol thee worthily, and every mind is confounded in seeking to comprehend thy childbirth. Wherefore, with one accord do we glorify thee.

Tone 4   Festive, joyous and expressing deep piety.   C, D, Eb, F, G, A, Bb, C.

Ode 1

The Chorus' of Israel passed dry-shod across the Red Sea and the watery deep; and beholding the riders and captains of the enemy swallowed by the waters, they cried out for joy: 'Let us sing unto our God, for He hath been glorified.'

Ode 3

The bow of the mighty hath waxed feeble and the weak have girded themselves with strength: therefore is my heart established in the Lord.

Ode 4

I have heard of Thy glorious Dispensation, O Christ our God: how Thou wast born of the Virgin, that so Thou mightest deliver from error those who cry aloud to Thee: Glory to Thy power, O Lord.

Ode 5

Thou hast parted the light from the original chaos, that Thy works might celebrate Thee in light, O Christ, as their Creator: do Thou direct our paths in Thy light.

Ode 6

In mine affliction I cried unto the Lord, the God of my salvation, and He hearkened unto me.

Ode 7

Of old the Abrahamite Children in Babylon trampled down the flame of the furnace, whilst crying out with hymns: O God of our Fathers, blessed art Thou.

Chorus: We praise, we bless, we worship the Lord, praising and supremely exalting Him unto all ages.

Ode 8

In Babylon the Children, burning with zeal for God bravely trampled upon the threat of the tyrant and the fire; thrown into the midst of the flames but refreshed with dew they sang: 'O all you works of the Lord, bless you the Lord.'

The Magnificat (Luke 1:46-55).

My soul magnifies the Lord, and my spirit has rejoiced in God my Saviour. For He has regarded the lowly state of His maidservant; for behold, henceforth all generations shall call me blessed. For He who is mighty has done great things for me, and holy is His name. And His mercy is on those who fear Him from generation to generation. He has shown strength with His arm; he has scattered the proud in the imagination of their hearts. He has put down the mighty from their thrones, and exalted the lowly. He has filled the hungry with good things, and the rich He has sent empty away. He has helped His servant Israel, in remembrance of His mercy, as He spoke to our fathers, to Abraham and to his seed forever.

Ode 9

Thy birth giving was undefiled: God came forth from thy womb, and He appeared upon earth wearing flesh and made His dwelling among men; therefore we all magnify thee, O Theotokos.

Katavasia Of The Dormition Of The Theotokos

Ode 1

Tone 1   *Magnificent, happy and earthy.*   *C, D, Eb, F, G, A, Bb, C.*

Thy sacred and renowned memorial, O Virgin, is clothed in the embroidered raiment of divine glory. It hath brought all the faithful together in joy, and led by Miriam, with dances and timbrels, they sing the praises of thine Only-begotten Son: For He hath been greatly glorified.

Ode 3

O Christ, the Wisdom and the Power of God, who dost create and uphold all, establish the Church unshaken and unwavering: for only Thou art holy, who hast Thy resting place among the saints.

Ode 4

The dark sayings and riddles of the prophets foreshadowed Thine incarnation from a Virgin, O Christ, even the lightening of Thy brightness which was to come as light to lighten the gentiles; and the deep utters its voice to Thee in joy: 'Glory to Thy power, O Thou who lovest mankind.'

Ode 5

I shall declare the divine and ineffable beauty of Thine excellencies, O Christ. For Thou hast shone forth in Thine own Person as the co-eternal brightness from the eternal glory, and taking flesh from a virgin's womb, Thou hast arisen as the sun, giving light to those that were in darkness and shadow.

Ode 6

The fire within the whale, the monster dwelling in the salt waters of the sea, was a prefiguring of Thy three days' burial, and Jonah acted as interpreter. For, saved and unharmed, as though he had never been swallowed, he cried aloud: 'I shall sacrifice unto Thee with the voice of praise, O Lord.'

Ode 7

Divine Love, fighting against cruel wrath and fire, quenched the fire with dew and laughed the wrath to scorn, making the three stringed harp of the saints inspired by God sing in the midst of the flames in answer to the instruments of music: 'Blessed art Thou, O most glorious God, our God and the God of our fathers.'

Chorus: *We praise, we bless, we worship the Lord, praising and supremely exalting Him unto all ages.*

Ode 8

The all powerful Angel of God revealed to the Children a flame, that brought refreshment to the holy while it consumed the ungodly. And He made the Theotokos into a life giving fount, gushing forth to the destruction of death and to the life of those that sing: 'We who have been delivered praise the one and only Creator and exalt Him above all forever.'

The Magnificat (Luke 1:46-55).

My soul magnifies the Lord, and my spirit has rejoiced in God my Saviour. For He has regarded the lowly state of His maidservant; for behold, henceforth all generations shall call me blessed. For He who is mighty has done great things for me, and holy is His name. And His mercy is on those who fear Him from generation to generation. He has shown strength with His arm; he has scattered the proud in the imagination of their hearts. He has put down the mighty from their thrones, and exalted the lowly. He has filled the hungry with good things, and the rich He has sent empty away. He has helped His servant Israel, in remembrance of His mercy, as He spoke to our fathers, to Abraham and to his seed forever.

Ode 9

In thee, O Virgin without spot, the bounds of nature are overcome: for childbirth remains virgin and death is betrothed to life. O Theotokos, Virgin after bearing child and alive after death, do thou ever save thine inheritance.

Liturgical Colours For Vestments And Hangings

1) Gold

Feasts of our Lord Jesus Christ.
Feasts of Prophets.
Feasts of Apostles.
Feasts of the Holy Hierarchs.
When no colour is specified.

2) Light Blue

Feasts of the Theotokos.
Presentation of the Lord.
Annunciation.
Feasts of Bodiless Powers.
Feasts of Virgins.
Fifth Friday in Lent.
Dormition Fast until the Elevation of the Cross.

3) Purple of Dark Red

Cross of Our Lord.
Great and Holy Thursday.
Weekends of Lent.

4) Red

Feasts of Martyrs.
Feast of Saints Peter and Paul.
Advent.
Feasts of Angels.
Elevation of the Cross.

5) Green

Palm Sunday.
Pentecost until Saints Peter and Paul.
Holy Spirit Day.
Feasts of Monastic Saints.
Feasts of Ascetics.
Feasts of Fools for Christ.
Feasts of Prophets.
Feasts of Angels.

6) Black

Weekdays of Lent.
Great Week, but not Great Thursday.
Weekday funerals, memorials, and liturgies.

7) White

Epiphany.
Transfiguration.
Paschal season.
Funerals.
Theophany.
Christmas Day.

8) Orange or Rust

Saints Peter and Paul fast.
Feast of Saints Peter and Paul until Transfiguration.

Services With A Bishop – Notes

Orthros

1. After first verse of Psalm 148 *"Praise the Lord from the heavens; praise Him in the heights"*, bishop descends from the throne for Kairon, whilst:

    Chorus: *(slow)   Preserve, O Lord, our master and chief priest.*

2. *"Many years, master / Eis polla eti, dhespota"* coincides with the moment at the end of Kairon when the bishop turns and blesses the congregation. A cue that the bishop will soon turn is that he replaces upon his head the epanokalymmavkhon (the black clerical hat with monastic veil) that he removed for a prayer near the end of Kairon.

    Psalms continue with *"Praise you him all His angels"*. The bishop may say Kairon and enter the sanctuary to vest without this. You must check with him ahead of time to see how and when he will say Kairon.

    Psalms chanted slow (or repeated) to give the bishop time to vest. Do not proceed to *Glory* until the bishop and clergy are ready to exit the holy place. A cue that they are ready is that the curtain and / or holy doors shall be opened.

3.   **After The Lauds**

IF the bishop exits the sanctuary before *Glory*, there is no split between *Glory ...* and *Both now ...* **ELSE:**

    Chorus: *Glory be to the Father, and to the Son, and to the Holy Spirit;*   **then halt.**

    Bishop exits sanctuary through Holy Doors and blesses the congregation, whilst:

    Chorus: *Many years, master. / Eis polla eti, dhespota.* **(x1)**

    When bishop in place at the throne or the center of the solea, he shall bless the singers, then:

    Chorus: *Both now and forever, and unto the ages of ages. Amen.*

Divine Liturgy

BB.4   During the Litany of Peace the bishop is commemorated by name, so:

    Chorus: *(quick and soft) Many years, master / Eis polla eti, dhespota.* **(x1)** On same note as "Lord, Have Mercy"). Then *"Lord, have mercy"* as usual.

BB.11   During singing of the Eisodikon by the bishop and clergy; when the bishop begins to bless with the dikirion and trikirion:

    Chorus: *Many years, master / Eis polla eti, dhespota.* **(x1)** On same note as the Eisodikon.

Bishop enters sanctuary and sings the first apolytikion.

    Chorus: *Save us, O Son of God, risen from the dead. Save us who sing to Thee: Halleluiah.*

    Chorus: *[all the remaining apolytikia].*   It is usual for the bishop and clergy to sing the kontakion.

BB.13 Ephemes

Kyrie soson tous efsevis **(x2)**

Kyrie soson tous Basilis kai epakouson ymon.

Bartholomeou tou Panagio tatou kai Oikoumenikou Patriarchou Poll ta eti.

Grigoriou tou Sevasmio tou kai Theoprovlitou Archi-episkopou tis Agiotatis Archi-episkopis Thyatiron kai Megalis Bretanias ipertimou kai eksarhou Ditikis Evropis, kai Irlandis ymon the Patros kai pimenarthou polla ta eti.

BB.16 After the Gospel: *"Glory to thee, O Lord, glory to thee"* followed by *"Many years, master / Eis polla eti, dhespota"* as the bishop blesses.

BB.22 After Cherubic Hymn, whilst the bishop blesses the congregation:

> ***Chorus:*** *Many years, master / Eis polla eti, dhespota.* **(x1)**   On same note as the Cherubicon,

BB.29 Deacon: Let us love one another that with one mind we may confess:

> Instead of *"Father, Son and Holy Spirit ..."*

> ***Chorus:*** *I shall love thee, O Lord, my strength.* (For any concelebrated or Hierarchical Liturgy.)

BB.30 Bishop: Among the first.

> ***Chorus:*** *Amen.*

> **Priest:**   Among the first.

> ***Chorus:*** *And of all mankind.*

If a deacon is serving, Chorus responds *Amen* to both the bishop and the priests.

> **Deacon:**   And for those who offer these precious and holy gifts ... and of all mankind.

> ***Chorus:*** *And of all mankind.*

BB.51 Bishop concludes the dismissal:

> ***Chorus:*** *(slow and soft) Preserve, O Lord, our master and chief priest. /*
>
> > *Ton dhespotin kai archierea imon.*

Volumes in this series may be purchased as below.

A Compendium Of Orthodox Services – Volume 1.
www.amazon.co.uk/dp/1976973724

A Compendium Of Orthodox Services – Volume 2.
www.amazon.co.uk/dp/1977049265

The Divine Liturgy Of St John Chrysostom In Ancient Greek, English and Welsh.
www.amazon.co.uk/dp/1973516462

The Relationship Between Jewish And Christian Understandings Of "The Word Of God".
www.amazon.co.uk/dp/1549794280

The Time Travelling Saints Of Wales.
www.amazon.co.uk/dp/

END